Deep Mukherjee
Editor

Applied Econometric Analysis Using Cross Section and Panel Data

Springer

Editor
Deep Mukherjee
Department of Economic Sciences
Indian Institute of Technology Kanpur
Kanpur, Uttar Pradesh, India

ISSN 1431-1933 ISSN 2197-7178 (electronic)
Contributions to Economics
ISBN 978-981-99-4901-4 ISBN 978-981-99-4902-1 (eBook)
https://doi.org/10.1007/978-981-99-4902-1

This Springer imprint is published by the registered company Springer Nature Singapore Pte Ltd.
The registered company address is: 152 Beach Road, #21-01/04 Gateway East, Singapore 189721, Singapore

Paper in this product is recyclable.

In loving memory of Riddhiman Mukherjee

Preface

Economic data collecting has increased dramatically during the last three decades. However, economic data frequently have special traits. So, in the same time frame, econometricians have created a variety of methods for processing vast amounts of data and enhancing empirical economic research. This reference volume is a collection of 20 chapters on chosen advanced topics from cross-section and panel data econometrics. With the motto "keeping things simple," this book explores both theoretical and practical aspects of selected cutting-edge econometric techniques which are gaining popularity among applied economics. Each chapter, written by experienced applied researchers, in the book, combines a brief review of a particular econometric method with fresh application and practical aspects of empirical model estimation.

Why Another Book?

There are already some high-quality general textbooks and advanced textbooks on special topics "teaching" econometric theory. Also, there are a number of excellent reference books for graduate students and practitioners interested in continuing education in econometrics. From my experience of teaching econometrics courses and as an applied researcher, I have observed three facts.

First, the field of econometrics is evolving very fast and leading general textbooks are trying to cover some of the recent developments in revised editions. There are not many books, which can offer the reader an opportunity of learning the state of the art in econometrics in a simple manner, not just the theoretical one, but from the point of view of practitioners. However, if an instructor is looking for one book, which offers a basic introduction to state-of-the-art techniques and software guide with interesting detailed applications from various developing and developed countries, such a reference material is hard to find.

Second, although there are empirical illustrations in popular and leading textbooks, those model demonstrations are short and without any background behind the empirical model presented. These books are designed more around theoretical results by following theorem-proof style. In an applied econometrics course, if the instructor wishes to talk about application of a cutting-edge model or method, he/she has to refer to a journal article. My experience says that graduate students and applied researchers in general prefer reference books with a simple introduction to an advanced method or model with no theorems but with a longer discussion on empirical application, including software use.

Third, if the instructor relies on journal articles to teach advanced topics, even the smartest student in the class sometimes finds it difficult to assimilate analytically rich concepts, which are not explained well in student-friendly language. Moreover, a journal article often does not come with relevant software codes to reinforce the learning. So, journal articles also have their own limitations from the perspective of teaching.

Hence, in my humble assessment, there is still a vacuum for a reference book for one semester-long applied econometrics course for second year Ph.D. students and practitioners of econometrics. Ideally, that book shall cover various state-of-the-art methods and/or models in sync with the current research trends but still not discussed in typical graduate-level textbooks. I am editing this volume to fill such a void.

Plan and Organization of the Book

This reference book is designed to bridge the gap between advanced textbooks on theoretical developments in econometrics and the journal articles presenting applied econometric research. However, this volume does not aim at providing a comprehensive coverage of state-of-the-art econometric methods. The 20 chapters in this edited book give only a sample of the important topics in modern econometrics. There are 14 chapters in the category of Microeconometrics. Rest are in the area of Macroeconometrics.

This book is divided into two parts: the first segment is devoted to methods and models based on cross-sectional data, and the second one is dedicated to methods and models involving panel data. Each part consists of 10 chapters. All chapters are written to be as self-contained as possible. Each chapter is structured to begin with a discussion on theory. Authors introduce a cutting-edge model or method in the simplest possible manner and provide a little bit more details and explanation of what is found in typical journal articles using those techniques. More or less standard notations are used in all chapters. Each chapter provides a brief literature review on the empirical topic at hand and presents a fresh application in detail. Authors also show how to estimate the empirical models using various software. For most chapters, data and code files are available on the companion website.

Many chapters make student-friendly presentations of advanced theoretical models that are not presented in leading textbooks. Real-life applications cover many sub-fields like agricultural economics, development economics, environmental economics, and program evaluation. In addition, these empirical cases come from more than a dozen countries spread over all continents. Given these aspects, I hope that this volume's scope and contents ought to be appealing to a broad audience.

Possible Use of the Book

The book is relatively advanced in places. Therefore, the volume assumes prior training in statistics and econometrics. The main target group of this reference book is Ph.D. students of Economics, Public policy, and Management. Those who want to continue learning advanced econometrics, after completing at least one course on econometric theory or planning to apply advanced econometric models for research, may find this volume useful. Although the book includes only selected topics and will not serve as a textbook for an econometric theory course, it can be used as an easy-to-read reference for a semester-long "Applied Econometrics" or "Microeconometrics" course. The extensive coverage of this volume provides an instructor a lot of flexibility in choosing 10–12 chapters from this book for such a one-semester course. The most salient feature of the volume is that, for most of the chapters, data, and codes are available to get hands-on experience with econometric modeling. This book can also be used as a complementary reference along with other advanced-level econometrics textbooks.

Acknowledgements

Last but not the least, I would like to thank the authors of the volume for the excellent chapters they produced. This book would not have been possible without the kind contribution from these scholars. I greatly appreciate their patience in dealing with the requests and comments of the editor.

Kanpur, India Deep Mukherjee

Contents

About the Editor

Deep Mukherjee is Associate Professor at the Department of Economic Sciences of the Indian Institute of Technology (IIT) Kanpur. He obtained Ph.D. in Agricultural & Resource Economics from the University of Connecticut and MS in Quantitative Economics from the Indian Statistical Institute (ISI). His research and teaching interests lie in applied microeconomics and quantitative policy analysis. He has conducted significant fieldwork as part of research in the form of extension visits, focus group discussions, and household surveys in various parts of India. Prior to joining Ph.D. program, he worked for GE Capital International Services (now, Genpact) as Business Analyst.

Part I
Cross Section Analysis

Chapter 1
Count Data Regression: Modeling Diversification in Sports Participation in Spain

Jaume García, Cristina Muñiz, and María José Suárez

Abstract Count data models are specifically designed to deal with those cases where the dependent variable is an integer non-negative variable, taking a small number of (low) values, which is the usual situation when the variable to be explained represents the number of times a particular event occurs. This chapter presents an overview of the specific features of the count data models most commonly used in the economic literature, paying special attention to how the zeros are generated. An empirical illustration from the sports economics literature is also provided. Using data from the *Spanish Survey of Sporting Habits (2020)*, individual diversification of sports activity, measured by the number of sports practiced during a year, is studied. The empirical analysis has been implemented using *Stata* software. It takes into account the specific features of the dependent variable by estimating different count data models, starting with the standard versions used in the microeconometric literature (Poisson and Negative Binomial models) and extending these basic models by considering different specifications in terms of how the zeros are generated. Finally, specific attention is devoted to the interpretation of the estimated coefficients and the calculation of the marginal effects.

Keywords Overdispersion · Count variables · Excess of zeros · Zero-inflated models · Hurdle models

---

J. García (✉)
Universitat Pompeu Fabra, Barcelona, Spain
e-mail: jaume.garcia@upf.edu

C. Muñiz · M. J. Suárez
Universidad de Oviedo, Oviedo, Spain
e-mail: cmuniza@uniovi.es

M. J. Suárez
e-mail: msuarezf@uniovi.es

D. Mukherjee (ed.), *Applied Econometric Analysis Using Cross Section and Panel Data*, Contributions to Economics, https://doi.org/10.1007/978-981-99-4902-1_1

1.1 Introduction

Count data models are a type of discrete choice models characterized by the fact that the dependent variable is the count of the number of events that have occurred in a given interval. Examples of count variables are the number of visits to a doctor (Pohlmeier and Ulrich 1995), the number of inpatient stays in a hospital (Geil 1997), the number of goals scored in a football game (Inan 2021), the number of cultural events attended (Muñiz et al. 2014), the number of trips (Jang 2005), the number of patents applied for by a firm (Hausman et al. 1984), or the number of mergers and acquisitions made (Agrawal and Sensarma 2007) in a certain period. In all cases, the outcome only takes integer and non-negative values. Moreover, it usually takes a small number of values, including zero, and its distribution is right-skewed.

The statistical analysis of count variables goes back a long way in time. Cameron and Trivedi (2014) point out that the Poisson distribution, which is the simplest distribution that takes into account the specific characteristics of the count variables, was first proposed in 1837 by Siméon Denis Poisson, but there is an open debate about whether it was Abraham de Moivre who first referred to that distribution. Some applications were already made in the nineteenth century, while the negative binomial distribution was derived in the 1920s. However, the development of more advanced specifications and the generalization of the use of these models in econometrics occurred mainly in the second half of the twentieth century.

Several surveys, chapters, and books about count data models have been published in recent decades (e.g., Cameron and Trivedi 1986, 2014; Winkelmann 2008; Hilbe 2014; Dupuy 2018; Tang et al. 2023). The objective of this chapter is to present the main specifications applied in economic analysis when using cross-section data,[1] focusing on how the zeros are modeled, given that in most economic studies the outcome takes the value zero for a significant proportion of the sample. Depending on the reasons for observing a zero, some models may be more suitable than others.

In particular, this review starts with the simplest specifications, the Poisson and the Negative Binomial distributions. These specifications do not deal with the excess of zeros problem, so the zero-inflated versions of the Poisson and the Negative Binomial are explained. Then, an alternative specification that has also been applied in the literature is introduced, the hurdle model, highlighting the main differences in the specification of zeros between this model and the zero-inflated version. Finally, ordered models—intended for ordered qualitative outcomes—are proposed as an option that could also be used for count variables.

Additionally, the implementation of the models is illustrated with an empirical example from sports economics. Specifically, individual sports participation is studied, measured by the number of sports the individual has practiced during the previous year. This variable can be related to one of the four dimensions of the FITT principles (frequency, intensity, time, and type) defined by Rhodes et al. (2017): the type dimension. In previous studies, this dimension has been analyzed in terms of

[1] A discussion of the issues associated with the estimation of panel data models for count data can be found in Cameron and Trivedi (2005, 2022) and Sun and Zhao (2013).

the type of sport practiced (García et al. 2016), but in this chapter, a quantitative element (the number of sports) is taken into account. This dependent variable has the features of a count variable (integer, non-negative, and with a narrow range of variation). In the empirical application, the basic versions of count data models used in the microeconometric literature (Poisson and Negative Binomial models) are estimated, as well as the different specifications proposed for dealing with the excess of zeros problem, which is a controversial topic in the sports economics literature. The empirical results are discussed emphasizing the differences between the models, the interpretation of the coefficients, and the relevance of making use of the calculation of the marginal effects in these non-linear models. The database used in the empirical analysis is the 2020 *Spanish Survey of Sporting Habits*, which is the most important source of information about the sports habits of the Spanish population.

The rest of the chapter is organized as follows. In the next section, the different types of count data models are presented, paying special attention to the features of overdispersion and excess zeros. Section 1.3 presents an overview of the economic literature on sports participation with a specific reference to the analysis of diversification. In the fourth section, the data set and the definition of the variables used in the empirical application are described. In Sect. 1.5, the empirical results of the estimation of different models of the number of sports practiced are reported, discussing both the selection of the most appropriate model and the interpretation of the effects of the different explanatory variables. Section 1.6 concludes.

1.2 Econometric Analysis of Count Data Models

As mentioned above, the specific features of a count variable can be summarized by indicating that it is a non-negative discrete (integer) variable and it usually takes a small number of low values including zero. The simplest distribution which accounts for these specific features is the Poisson distribution, whose probability mass function is given by:

$$\Pr(y_i = Y_i) = P_{Y_i} = \frac{e^{-\mu_i}\mu_i^{Y_i}}{Y_i!}, \qquad \mu_i > 0 \tag{1.1}$$

where the subindex i refers to the ith individual and μ is the only parameter associated with this distribution and it represents both the expected value and the variance. Consequently, the only way to introduce explanatory variables (X) in this count data model is to make μ dependent on these variables. The usual parameterization is:

$$\mu_i = exp(X_i^{'}\beta) \tag{1.2}$$

This model is estimated by maximum likelihood and the log of the likelihood function (*ln L*) in the case of using a random sample (*N* observations) is:

$$ln\,L(\beta) = \sum_{i=1}^{N} \left[Y_i\, X_i^{'}\beta - exp(X_i^{'}\beta) - ln(Y_i!) \right] \tag{1.3}$$

As happens when using these parametric approximations, the Poisson distribution imposes a specific pattern for the corresponding probability mass function. In particular, the ratio between the probabilities of occurrence of two consecutive values is given by:

$$\frac{P_{Y_i}}{P_{Y_i-1}} = \frac{\mu_i}{Y_i} \tag{1.4}$$

Notice that the value of μ determines the mode of the distribution. For instance, for μ between 0 and 1, the pattern is decreasing and the mode is zero. In general, for μ between K and $K+1$, the mode will be K and the pattern of the probabilities is first increasing with y, up to K, and then tending to zero at a fast rate.

The most relevant feature of the Poisson distribution is the equality of the expected value and the variance, known as the equidispersion property. In principle, this is a very restrictive property from an econometric point of view and it is not usually representative of the features of the count variables in most of the empirical applications. One way of dealing with the limitation of the Poisson model of not being appropriate for situations where there is overdispersion (i.e., the variance is greater than the expected value) in the count variable, a common feature of count data variables in economic models,[2] is to look for a more flexible distribution in terms of the number of parameters that characterize it. The most used candidate is the Negative Binomial distribution, which can be defined straightforwardly or which can be motivated as a kind of extension of the Poisson distribution, highlighting the connection between the two models.

Suppose the parameter μ (now called μ^* to use the same notations as in the econometric computer package *Stata*) in the Poisson model is now dependent on observed heterogeneity (X) but also on unobserved heterogeneity by means of a random variable (v) such that:

$$\mu_i^* = \mu_i v_i = \exp(X_i^{'}\beta)\, v_i, \qquad v_i > 0 \tag{1.5}$$

Assuming that v has a Gamma distribution[3] with parameters $1/\gamma$ and γ, which means that $E(v) = 1$ and $\text{var}(v) = \gamma$, the marginal density of y is obtained by integrating out the random variable v:

---

[2] Underdispersion is not as usual, although some examples can be found in the empirical literature, e.g., Lord et al. (2010). Hilbe (2014) presents the generalized Poisson model, which is an extension of the basic version that includes a dispersion or scale parameter allowing for underdispersion.

[3] Some other distributions, like the log-normal or the inverse-Gaussian distribution, can be used as an alternative to the Gamma distribution, but simulated maximum likelihood methods are required.

$$h(y_i|\mu_i,\gamma) = \frac{\Gamma(\gamma^{-1}+y_i)}{\Gamma(\gamma^{-1})\Gamma(y_i+1)}\left(\frac{\gamma^{-1}}{\gamma^{-1}+\mu_i}\right)^{\gamma^{-1}}\left(\frac{\mu_i}{\mu_i+\gamma^{-1}}\right)^{y_i} \tag{1.6}$$

which corresponds to the Negative Binomial distribution, whose expected value and variance are:

$$\begin{aligned} E(y_i) &= \mu_i, \qquad \mu_i > 0 \\ \mathrm{var}(y_i) &= \mu_i\left[1+\gamma\,\mu_i\right], \qquad \gamma > 0 \end{aligned} \tag{1.7}$$

Notice that the equidispersion property of the Poisson model does not hold insofar as γ is different from zero and the Poisson model is a particular case of the Negative Binomial model ($\gamma = 0$).

Depending on whether the parameter γ is assumed to be constant (α using *Stata* notation) or the variance is assumed to be proportional to the expected value, i.e., $\gamma = \delta/\mu_i$, which means $var(y_i) = \mu_i(1+\delta)$, two alternative versions of the Negative Binomial model are considered in the empirical literature: type 2 (NB2) and type 1 (NB1), respectively. The most used model is the NB2, also known as the mean dispersion model, whereas the NB1 model is also referred to as the constant dispersion model. Testing for equidispersion (the Poisson model) reduces to testing whether α or δ are equal to zero depending on the type of Negative Binomial model you are using. This is done in *Stata* using a likelihood ratio test.

This model is estimated by maximum likelihood and the log likelihood function of the NB2 model in the case of using a random sample is:

$$ln\ L(\beta,\gamma) = \sum_{i=1}^{N}\left[\begin{array}{l} ln\left(\dfrac{\Gamma(\gamma^{-1}+Y_i)}{\Gamma(\gamma^{-1})\Gamma(Y_i+1)}\right) + \gamma^{-1}\ ln\left(\dfrac{\gamma^{-1}}{\gamma^{-1}+exp(X_i'\beta)}\right) \\ +Y_i\ ln\left(\dfrac{exp(X_i'\beta)}{exp(X_i'\beta)+\gamma^{-1}}\right) \end{array}\right] \tag{1.8}$$

These Poisson and Negative Binomial models are the count data counterparts of the Tobit model in the context of the limited dependent variable models. They deal with modeling a non-negative variable that takes the value zero for a significant proportion of observations by using the same model to explain whether the dependent variable is zero or not, and the positive values. They only differ in the kind of distribution of the dependent variable because of the integer values associated with a count variable.

In fact, one of the empirical issues associated with count variables is that the proportion of observations with a zero value for the dependent variable is greater than that which can be modeled assuming a Poisson or a Negative Binomial distribution, according to the structure of the probabilities implied by the corresponding probability mass functions. This is usually known in the literature as an excess of zeros problem. The usual way of dealing with this problem in the count data literature is to use the zero-inflated versions of the standard Poisson and Negative Binomial models. These are models that allow for the possibility of the zeros being generated by two processes: one generating zeros corresponding to potential non-participants and the second one allowing for some zeros being associated with optimal solutions (corner solutions in the Tobit terminology). Consequently, not only the excess of zeros, but also the limitation of the standard models, which use just one model to deal with the explanation of the zeros and the positive values of y, are taken into account.

The zero-inflated models include two equations. The first one is a binary discrete choice model fitting the probability of not being a potential participant ($D_i = 1$), in which the dependent variable (D) is not observed, usually called the *inflate* equation. The second equation fits the number of times a particular event occurs for those who are potential participants, including the possibility of zero occurrences, by using a standard count data model. The two equations are assumed to be independent. This specification replicates the double-hurdle model with independent errors used in the limited dependent variable literature.

Consequently, the probability of observing a zero is equal to the probability of not being a potential participant (P_i) plus the probability of observing a zero ($F(0)$) when being a potential participant:

$$\Pr(y_i = 0) = P_i + (1 - P_i)F(0) \tag{1.9}$$

where the probability of not being a potential participant P_i is:

$$P_i = \Pr(D_i = 1) = 1 - F^*(-Z_i^{'}\delta) = F^*(Z_i^{'}\delta) \tag{1.10}$$

where F^* is the cumulative distribution function of a logistic (Logit model) or a standardized normal distribution (Probit model), Z is the vector of explanatory variables of the potential non-participation equation, and δ is the vector of parameters. Notice that D is defined in the same way as in *Stata* in order to facilitate the interpretation of the results of the *inflate* equation.

The probability of observing a positive value of y is given by the probability of being a potential participant times the probability of y taking the positive value which is observed (Y_i), according to the probability mass function F of the corresponding standard model (Poisson or Negative Binomial) of the second equation, i.e.:

$$\Pr(y_i = Y_i) = (1 - P_i)F(Y_i) \qquad \text{if} Y_i > 0 \tag{1.11}$$

where the explanatory variables (X) of the second equation are introduced in the standard count data model through the parameter μ.

Consequently, the log of the likelihood function for these zero-inflated models is:

$$ln\ L(\beta, \delta, \gamma) = \sum_{Y_i=0} ln[P_i + (1 - P_i)\ F(0)] + \sum_{Y_i>0} [ln\ (1 - P_i) + ln\ F(Y_i)] \tag{1.12}$$

where $\gamma = 0$ in the zero-inflated Poisson model.

Notice that each of the standard count data models is a particular case of the corresponding zero-inflated version, when the probability of being a potential participant is one for all the individuals. The comparison between the standard and the zero-inflated versions can be made using any of the usual information criteria (Akaike, Bayesian) but, according to Wilson (2015), the use of Vuong's test for non-nested models is not appropriate in this case.

In terms of how the zeros are generated, an alternative specification is the so-called hurdle model, which considers that all of them can be associated with being a non-potential participant, but not as an optimal zero. This model can be interpreted as the count data version of the two-part model. Two equations are considered for this particular model. The first one corresponds to a binary discrete choice model for explaining whether the count variable is positive or zero, which is observed. The second equation corresponds to a count data model where the distribution of the count variable is truncated at zero because it only applies to individuals for whom the number of times of occurrence of the particular event is positive.[4]

Consequently, the probability of observing a zero, i.e., not being a participant, is given by:

$$Pr(y_i = 0) = Pr(D_i^* = 0) = 1 - Pr(D_i^* = 1) = 1 - P_i = F^*(-Z_i^{'}\delta) \quad (1.13)$$

where F^* is the cumulative distribution function of a logistic (Logit model) or a standardized normal distribution (Probit model), D^* is a dummy variable equal to 1 if the individual participates ($y_i > 0$) and Z is the vector of explanatory variables of the participation equation.

And the probability of observing a certain positive value of y is:

$$\Pr(y_i = Y_i) = P_i \frac{F(Y_i)}{1 - F(0)} if\ Y_i > 0 \quad (1.14)$$

where the standard distribution F is truncated at zero and the explanatory variables (X) of the second equation are introduced in the standard count data model through the parameter μ.

The log likelihood function of this hurdle version is:

$$ln\ L(\beta, \delta, \gamma) = \sum_{Y_i=0} ln\ (1 - P_i) + \sum_{Y_i>0} [ln\ (P_i) + ln\ F(Y_i) - ln\ (1 - F(0)] \quad (1.15)$$

where $\gamma = 0$ in the hurdle Poisson model.

Notice that this likelihood function can be maximized by estimating separately the discrete choice model for D^* and the truncated count data model for the observations with a positive value of the dependent variable (y). Additionally, it is worth

[4] See Feng (2021) and Green (2021) for a comparison of zero-inflated and hurdle models.

mentioning that the hurdle model is not a particular case of the corresponding zero-inflated version because a truncated model, and not a standard version, is estimated for those observations with a positive value for the number of times of occurrence of a particular event.

As an alternative to the usual count data models, ordered models (McCullagh 1980) could also be considered. Although they are intended for situations in which the dependent variable is a qualitative variable whose categories can be ordered according to the characteristic that is measured, they could be used for count variables where, to some extent, the interest is in explaining the probability of occurrence of a particular event and the values of the count variable can be considered as ordered.

The basic idea behind this model is that there is a latent variable (y^*), which is not observed by the econometrician, which measures the intensity of the occurrence of a particular event. What is observed is a discrete indicator, which approximates the level of this intensity, i.e., the number of times a particular event occurs—the observed (count) variable.

The structure of the ordered model is as follows:

$$\begin{aligned} & y_i^* = X_i^{'}\beta + \varepsilon_i \\ & y_i = j \quad \text{if } \kappa_j < y_i^* \leq \kappa_{j+1} \; j = 0, \ldots., J \\ & \kappa_0 = -\infty \quad \kappa_{J+1} = \infty \end{aligned} \tag{1.16}$$

where ε_i is the error term, whose distribution determines whether a Logit (logistic) or a Probit (standardized normal) is considered and κ_j are the cut points defining the intervals associated with the different values of the dependent variable (y) and are parameters to be estimated.

The probability of y taking a particular value j is:

$$\Pr(y_i = j) = \Pr\left(\kappa_j < y_i^* \leq \kappa_{j+1}\right) = F\left(\kappa_{j+1} - X_i^{'}\beta\right) - F\left(\kappa_j - X_i^{'}\beta\right) \tag{1.17}$$

where F is the cumulative distribution function corresponding to the error term. This is the contribution to the likelihood function of each observation in the sample.

The ordered model has the advantage of being more flexible in fitting these probabilities than the models mentioned previously, since there is no specific pattern for them, as happens in the case of the standard count data models. As with the previous specifications, the ordered model can be estimated through a single equation, treating zero as an additional category, but there is also a hurdle version, which separates the decisions to participate and the number of events to happen, and a zero-inflated version as in the case of count data models (Harris and Zhao 2007).

1.3 Sports Participation and Its Diversification

There is plenty of scientific evidence about the beneficial effects of regular physical activity on health (Rhodes et al. 2017). However, sedentary lifestyles have become a major problem in developed countries, to the extent that the World Health Organization has developed the *Global Action Plan on Physical Activity 2018–2030*, which sets the goal of reducing physical inactivity by 10% by 2025 and 15% by 2030. This plan connects with the 2030 Sustainable Development Goals (SDGs), an initiative promoted by the United Nations to boost economic growth taking into account environmental, economic, and social sustainability.

There is an extensive economics literature on the determinants of individual sports practice. A survey of the main theoretical approaches, the correlates of sports participation and its effect on health, well-being, social capital, and labor market outcomes has been done by Cabane and Lechner (2015). The literature review reveals that there is considerable heterogeneity in the definition of the variable under study. In fact, as Rhodes et al. (2017) indicate, physical activity has multiple dimensions: frequency, intensity, time, and type (FITT principles). Most economic studies about the correlates of physical activity analyze participation, time, and/or frequency of practice. The intensity of practice has been less studied in the literature and, regarding type, many researchers add any type of sport or physical activity whereas others examine specific sports, groups of sports with common characteristics, or physical activity done in different domains of daily life (leisure, work, commuting, etc.).

One of the characteristics of the variables that measure sports practice is that a high percentage of people do not play sports, so it becomes necessary to model the zeros in the dependent variable. The lack of participation may be due to different reasons: preferences, time or monetary constraints, or infrequency of practice, i.e., when the period of time considered in the survey is not long enough to capture sports practice. The reasons for observing zeros may determine the econometric specification.

This chapter focuses on the type dimension of sports, measured by the number of sports the individual has practiced in the previous year. The correlates of individual diversification of the sports activity are studied by estimating count data models to take into account the specific features of the dependent variable (integer, non-negative, and with a narrow range of variation).

The individual diversification of sports activity -also called multipractice or omnivorousness- has hardly been analyzed in the sports economics literature, but it has received more attention in the sociology and sport science fields. In some cases, diversification is studied to contribute to the debate about which is the best way to attain elite sport performance: either to specialize in one sport at early ages or to sample different sports as a child and specialize a little later (Bridge and Toms 2013). Other researchers analyze differences in diversification between countries (Lefèvre et al. 2021) or between social classes (Lefèvre and Ohl 2012). Although globalization could lead to the homogenization of tastes and behaviors, diversification in sports may vary between different countries with a different sociocultural environment or it may be a way to differentiate oneself from others in lower social positions. In this regard, the question is whether higher social classes have a more omnivorous behavior in their sporting activities than lower classes have, as some authors have found in the study of cultural demand. In particular, Lefèvre and Ohl (2012), using French data, obtain that, although it is frequent for people to practice more than one sport, higher social groups tend to be more omnivorous than the rest. Regarding differences between countries, on the one hand, Lefèvre et al. (2021) find that the Japanese are less likely to do sports than the French and those who participate are more likely to be single-sport practitioners. On the other hand, Lefèvre et al. (2020) compare France and Spain, and conclude that there are similarities in the factors associated with the number of sports practiced: males, younger people, more educated people, and those with sporty fathers tend to have a greater portfolio size.

Regarding the econometric methodology, count data models have already been applied in the literature on sports participation.[5] This is the case of Dawson and Downward (2011), who estimate different count data specifications for the UK (Poisson, Negative Binomial—NB-, Zero-inflated Poisson—ZIP,- and Zero-Inflated Negative Binomial—ZINB-) to study the number of hours and the number of days of sports participation. According to their results, the ZINB specification is the most suitable model for their data. Muñiz et al. (2014) and García et al. (2016) also estimate ZINB models to analyze the number of times that Spanish individuals play different types of sports. Anokye et al. (2012) opt for the Negative Binomial to model the number of days of sports practice in the previous four weeks by participants at a British university. Oliveira-Brochado et al. (2017) specify a two-part model—specifically a Negative Binomial hurdle model—to study participation and frequency (number of days per week) of the sport by Portuguese people and, more recently, García and Suárez (2021, 2023) also estimated two-part models for the number of days per week allocated to sports by Mexicans, where the frequency of practice by participants is modeled through truncated Poisson and Negative Binomial models.[6] Previous papers, by Slymen et al. (2006) and Lee et al. (2016), used zero-inflated models for the number of days per week practising physical activity by Hispanic females in San Diego (USA) and by patients with Parkinson's disease in South Korea, respectively. In a similar context of analysis of diversification, Lefèvre et al. (2020) apply a Negative Binomial hurdle model to analyze the number of sports practised by French and Spanish individuals.

[5] See Downward and Muñiz (2019) for a brief review of the econometric approaches used in the analysis of sports participation, where count data models are included.

[6] In García and Suárez (2020), a model for the number of days per week of sports practice is estimated using a version of the ordered model where the cut-points are known and a lognormal distribution is specified because their model is a kind of two-part model.

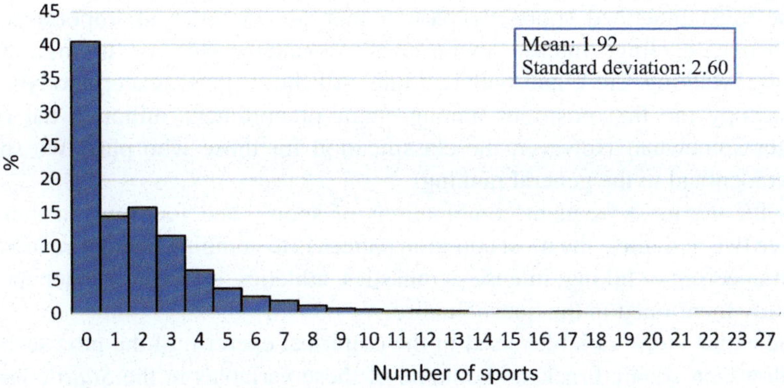

Fig. 1.1 Histogram of the number of sports practiced
Note: The values have been calculated using the corresponding weight factors

1.4 Data

The empirical analysis uses the 2020 edition of the *Spanish Survey of Sporting Habits*. This survey is conducted every five years and the last edition has been carried out by the Spanish Ministry of Culture and Sports together with the Higher Sports Council. The information was collected between September 2020 and January 2021. At that time, the lockdown due to the COVID-19 pandemic had already ended a few months earlier.

The survey is aimed at people aged 15 or over and gathers information about the sporting habits of the Spanish population, not only about their sports practice but also about attendance at sports events, sports equipment available at home, interest in sports information, relationship with sports organizations, etc.

According to the data provided by the survey, around 60% of Spaniards has played sports in the previous year and, among those who did sports, the vast majority (92%) practiced it at least once a week. Regarding the number of sports done by participants (variable *ndep* in the *Stata* commands reported in the next section), and focusing on the sample selected for the empirical analysis (where those respondents who are incapacitated for work or who state that they have practiced more than 30 sports in the previous year are dropped),[7] Fig. 1.1 shows that most of them do one or two activities. In fact, it is more frequent to practice two activities (26% of participants) than one (24%). The same occurs in France but not in Japan, where single practitioners predominate (Lefèvre et al. 2021). Moreover, less than 15% of the individuals who play sports do more than five activities. Thus, the distribution of the dependent variable is right-skewed and it is concentrated in a small range of values.

[7] Firstly, people who are incapacitated for work may not be able to play sports. Secondly, it is quite implausible to have played more than 30 sports. These restrictions reduce the sample size by around 1.6%.

The most practiced sports by participants are, in order of importance: light gymnastics, cycling, intense gymnastics, mountaineering or hiking, athletics (running, walking, etc.), and bodybuilding. All these sports, except bodybuilding, also occupy the first positions among single-practitioners, although the ranking changes somewhat. However, the classification for those who play two sports is almost identical to the general ranking.

As for the most frequent combinations of sports, and focusing on those who practice two activities, the most common pattern is to combine light gymnastics with mountaineering or hiking, intense gymnastics, athletics, cycling, or other sports not explicitly mentioned in the questionnaire.

The explanatory variables used in the empirical exercise of the next section are as follows (in square brackets the name of these variables in the *Stata* commands reported in the next section):

- *Gender*: male, female [*sexo*]
- *Age*: five age groups (younger than 25, 25–34, 35–44, 45–54, older than 54) [*g_edad*]
- *Education*: less than primary school, primary school, secondary school level 1, secondary school level 2, university degree [*estud_new*]
- *Employment status*: worker, unemployed, retired, student, housework, other situation [*sitlab*]
- *Marital status*: single, married, other situation [*sitpers_new*]
- *Health status*: very good, good, fair, bad, very bad [*estfis*]
- *Parents practicing sport*: yes, no [*pract_padres*]
- *Nationality*: Spanish, double nationality, foreigner [*nac*]
- *Municipality*: provincial capital, more than 50,000 inhabitants, fewer than 50,000 inhabitants [*tram_munic*]

Table 1.1 shows some descriptive statistics of these variables. Males, young people, and persons with secondary or university education are more likely to do sports. The same can be said of students, single persons, people in very good health, and those whose parents have played sports. Finally, it is interesting to note that the diversity of practice differs between sporty people depending on their sociodemographic characteristics. This information is included in Table 1.1. The figures show that the average number of activities is higher among males, young people, individuals with higher education level, students, single, and people in very good health.

1.5 Results

The estimates of the different models discussed in the methodology section, applied to the number of sports practiced by people in Spain, are reported in Tables 1.3 and 1.4. First, the fit and the appropriateness of the different specifications are discussed,

Table 1.1 Descriptive statistics

Variables	%	Sports participants (%)	Average number of sports by participant
Gender			
Male	48.49	65.52	3.450
Female	51.51	54.01	2.969
Age			
<25	11.96	79.78	4.392
25–34	13.18	75.44	3.678
35–44	17.77	70.71	3.324
45–54	18.88	62.62	3.065
>54	38.22	41.13	2.273
Education			
Less than primary school	2.35	19.15	2.019
Primary school	12.63	31.84	2.233
Secondary school level 1	23.76	52.55	3.064
Secondary school level 2	28.02	64.77	3.433
University degree	33.25	73.65	3.339
Employment status			
Worker	48.84	68.42	3.356
Unemployed	11.73	57.77	2.883
Retired	23.56	36.95	2.062
Student	9.55	81.01	4.454
Housework	4.58	39.16	2.224
Other employment situation	1.75	66.48	3.547
Marital status			
Single	36.81	64.51	3.518
Married	58.69	56.98	2.995
Other	4.50	53.33	3.537
Health status			
Very good	24.86	75.51	3.563
Good	51.59	62.04	3.125
Fair	18.12	39.39	2.965
Bad	4.16	31.93	2.667
Very bad	1.28	27.43	1.757
Parents practicing sport			
No	70.65	54.29	2.808
Yes	29.35	72.34	3.980

(continued)

Table 1.1 (continued)

Variables	%	Sports participants (%)	Average number of sports by participant
Nationality			
Spanish	91.00	59.63	3.203
Double nationality	3.27	59.90	3.707
Foreigner	5.72	58.82	3.309
Municipality			
Provincial capital	32.83	58.52	3.323
>50,000 inhabitants	20.92	60.08	3.057
<50.000 inhabitants	46.25	60.12	3.234

Note The values have been calculated using the corresponding weights

and then the comments on the interpretation of the coefficients and the calculation of the marginal effects of the explanatory variables on the dependent variable follow.

The empirical analysis has been done using *Stata* software. Table 1.2 shows the commands and the syntax used to estimate each of the models. More details about how to use *Stata* to estimate and analyze the different count data models discussed in this chapter can be found in Cameron and Trivedi (2022). The estimation of these models is also possible using other major statistical software packages. Friendly and Meyer (2015) provide procedures to estimate different count data models in *R*, whereas Hilbe (2014) shows the codes for running these models in *R*, *SAS*, and *Stata*. Other software packages such as *SPSS* or *LIMDEP* include procedures to estimate count data models too.

1.5.1 Comparison of the Different Models

The descriptive analysis of the dependent variable provides relevant information about the appropriateness of the standard models. As indicated in Fig. 1.1, the sample mean of the number of sports (1.92) is clearly smaller than the sample variance (6.76), which means that this variable has overdispersion and, consequently, the fit of the standard Poisson model should be worse than that of the Negative Binomial model.[8] In fact, the values of the log likelihood function reported in Table 1.3 confirm that the fit of the Negative Binomial Type 2 model (henceforth Negative Binomial) is much better. This evidence is corroborated by the fact that the estimate of the overdispersion parameter (α) is significantly different from zero, rejecting the Poisson specification.

[8] Results for the Negative Binomial Type 1 model are not reported here since it is hardly used in the empirical economic literature and the results point in the same direction as those of the Type 2 version.

Table 1.2 *Stata* commands

Poisson
poisson ndep i.sexo i.g_edad i.estud_new i.sitlab i.sitpers_new i.estfis i.pract_padres_new /// i.nac i.tram_munic
Negative Binomial
nbreg ndep i.sexo i.g_edad i.estud_new i.sitlab i.sitpers_new i.estfis i.pract_padres_new i.nac /// i.tram_munic
Zero-Inflated Poisson
zip ndep i.sexo i.g_edad i.estud_new i.sitlab i.sitpers_new i.pract_padres_new i.nac /// i.tram_munic, inflate(i.sexo i.g_edad i.estud_new i.sitlab i.sitpers_new i.estfis /// i.pract_padres_new i.nac i.tram_munic
Zero-Inflated Negative Binomial
zinb ndep i.sexo i.g_edad i.estud_new i.sitlab i.sitpers_new i.pract_padres_new i.nac /// i.tram_munic, inflate(i.sexo i.g_edad i.estud_new i.sitlab i.sitpers_new i.estfis /// i.pract_padres_new i.nac i.tram_munic
Poisson hurdle model
logit practica i.sexo i.g_edad i.estud_new i.sitlab i.sitpers_new i.estfis i.pract_padres_new /// i.nac i.tram_munic tpoisson ndep i.sexo i.g_edad i.estud_new i.sitlab i.sitpers_new i.pract_padres_new i.nac /// i.tram_munic tnbreg ndep i.sexo i.g_edad i.estud_new i.sitlab i.sitpers_new i.pract_padres_new i.nac /// i.tram_munic
Negative-Binomial hurdle model
logit practica i.sexo i.g_edad i.estud_new i.sitlab i.sitpers_new i.estfis i.pract_padres_new /// i.nac i.tram_munic tnbreg ndep i.sexo i.g_edad i.estud_new i.sitlab i.sitpers_new i.pract_padres_new /// i.nac i.tram_munic
Ordered logit
ologit ndep_o i.sexo i.g_edad i.estud_new i.sitlab i.sitpers_new i.estfis i.pract_padres_new /// i.nac i.tram_munic
Hurdle version of the ordered logit
logit practica i.sexo i.g_edad i.estud_new i.sitlab i.sitpers_new i.estfis i.pract_padres_new /// i.nac i.tram_munic ologit ndep_o i.sexo i.g_edad i.estud_new i.sitlab i.sitpers_new i.pract_padres_new /// i.nac i.tram_munic if ndep > 0

Note: The variable *practica* in the logit and in the Zero-Inflated models is a dummy variable equal to one when $ndep > 0$ and equal to zero when $ndep = 0$

In order to highlight the differences between models, it is useful to look at the adjusted probabilities for each value of the number of sports variable across models. The mean values of these adjusted probabilities and the corresponding relative frequencies in the sample are reported in Table 1.5. It is evident that the standard Poisson model is not able to reproduce the proportion of observations corresponding to individuals not practicing sports (22.58% versus 38.85% in the sample), whereas the Negative Binomial model captures this proportion better. In the case of the Poisson

Table 1.3 Standard models

	Poisson	NegBin	Ordered logit[1]
Gender (Ref.: Male)			
Female	−0.277***	−0.294***	−0.414***
Age (Ref.: <25)			
25–34	−0.088**	−0.116	−0.124
35–44	−0.219***	−0.249***	−0.269*
45–54	−0.343***	−0.381***	−0.545***
>54	−0.631***	−0.673***	−0.915***
Education (Ref.: Less than primary)			
Primary school	0.355**	0.328*	0.311
Secondary school level 1	0.660***	0.642***	0.609**
Secondary school level 2	0.875***	0.892***	0.989***
University degree	1.046***	1.083***	1.395***
Employment status (Ref.: Worker)			
Unemployed	−0.162***	−0.147***	−0.239***
Retired	−0.342***	−0.315***	−0.405***
Student	0.172***	0.188**	0.443***
Housework	−0.322***	−0.290***	−0.336**
Other employment situation	0.162**	0.200*	0.201
Marital status (Ref.: Single)			
Married	−0.008	0.006	−0.000
Other	−0.103**	−0.136	−0.217
Health status (Ref.: Very good)			
Good	−0.074***	−0.091**	−0.217***
Fair	−0.248***	−0.314***	−0.642***
Bad	−0.528***	−0.601***	−0.927***
Very bad	−0.834***	−0.774***	−0.995***
Parents practicing sport (Ref.: No)			
Yes	0.343***	0.344***	0.597***
Nationality (Ref.: Spanish)			
Double nationality	−0.020	0.036	−0.180
Foreigner	−0.067	−0.084	−0.237**

(continued)

Table 1.3 (continued)

	Poisson	NegBin	Ordered logit[1]
Municipality (Ref.: Provincial capital)			
>50,000 inhabitants	−0.043	−0.020	−0.021
<50.000 inhabitants	0.046**	0.072*	0.152***
Constant	0.299*	0.312	
α		0.766***	
Observations	5,151	5,151	5,151
log L	−10,449	−9,152	−8,981

Notes:
[1]The cut point estimates of the ordered Logit model are not reported
[2]*** p < 0.01, ** p < 0.05, * p < 0.10

model, the average probability of practicing one sport is higher than that of not practicing sports, and then it follows a decreasing pattern as the number increases. This is an expected result since the sample mean of the number of sports, which is an estimate of μ—the parameter of the Poisson distribution—is below 2 and, according to the result in expression (1.3), the mode should be 1, as happens in the adjusted probabilities of the Poisson model. Notice also that the Negative Binomial model is not able to replicate the observed pattern of the relative frequency (higher for $y = 2$ than for $y = 1$ and $y = 3$) because of the particular features of this distribution.

The zero-inflated versions of the standard models are designed to capture the potential problem of excess of zeros and/or the fact that the reason behind observing a zero could be either being a non-potential participant or an optimal choice by a potential participant. In Table 1.4, the estimated zero-inflated versions of the Poisson and the Negative Binomial models are reported. There is a substantial improvement in the value of the log likelihood model in the case of the zero-inflated Poisson model when compared to the standard version, as a consequence of the bad performance of the latter in estimating the probability of not practicing sport. The zero-inflated version of the Negative Binomial model also has a higher value of the log likelihood compared to its standard version, and it is also preferred to the zero-inflated Poisson version because the overdispersion parameter α is significantly different from zero.

As mentioned in the methodology section, strictly speaking, Vuong's test cannot be used to check the appropriateness of the standard versions versus the zero-inflated versions, but the change in the log likelihood values for both the Poisson and the Negative Binomial versions is so important that the zero-inflated versions are clearly preferred in terms of any of the usual information criteria. In fact, as it can be seen in Table 1.4, the second equation of the zero-inflated models (number of sports) does not include health status as an explanatory factor. This is because, when using the same set of variables in both equations, there were some problems with the estimation of the parameters, and their standard errors, of the health status variables and this kind of exclusion restriction was used to obtain convergence.

Table 1.4 Zero-inflated and hurdle (two-part) models

	Zero-inflated				Hurdle (two-part)			
	Poisson		NegBin		Tr. Poisson	Tr. NegBin	Ordered[1]	Logit[2]
	Number	Inflate	Number	Inflate	Number	Number	Number	1st hurdle
Gender (Ref.: Male)								
Female	−0.160***	0.435***	−0.219***	0.378***	−0.158***	−0.187***	−0.207***	−0.472***
Age (Ref.: <25)								
25–34	−0.048	0.196	−0.055	0.330	−0.047	−0.059	−0.062	−0.199
35–44	−0.161***	0.295	−0.188**	0.336	−0.159***	−0.187**	−0.197	−0.347*
45–54	−0.233***	0.513**	−0.257***	0.748*	−0.232***	−0.273***	−0.434**	−0.569***
>54	−0.442***	0.738***	−0.499***	0.970**	−0.441***	−0.516***	−0.797***	−0.886***
Education (Ref.: Less than primary)								
Primary school	0.128	−0.288	0.180	−0.204	0.128	0.119	−0.076	0.340
Secondary school level 1	0.293	−0.535	0.356	−0.453	0.289	0.292	0.110	0.653**
Secondary school level 2	0.389*	−0.915***	0.485*	−0.934*	0.385*	0.423	0.378	1.033***
University degree	0.448**	−1.448***	0.571**	−1.711***	0.442**	0.491*	0.561	1.530***
Employment status (Ref.: Worker)								
Unemployed	−0.128***	0.139	−0.127**	0.200	−0.128***	-0.133**	−0.224**	−0.188*
Retired	−0.242***	0.189	−0.227***	0.265	−0.257***	-0.272***	−0.468***	−0.291***
Student	0.153***	−0.144	0.164**	−0.185	0.153***	0.175**	0.478***	0.192
Housework	−0.211**	0.118	−0.230*	0.110	−0.208**	−0.225*	−0.394*	−0.227
Other employment situation	0.141**	−0.028	0.137	−0.117	0.142**	0.183	0.237	0.089

(continued)

Table 1.4 (continued)

	Zero-inflated				Hurdle (two-part)			
	Poisson		NegBin		Tr. Poisson	Tr. NegBin	Ordered[1]	Logit[2]
	Number	Inflate	Number	Inflate	Number	Number	Number	1st hurdle
Marital status (Ref.: Single)								
Married	−0.007	0.001	−0.020	−0.073	−0.008	−0.006	0.017	−0.004
Other	−0.073	0.249	−0.070	0.404	−0.068	−0.078	−0.081	−0.269*
Health status (Ref.: Very good)								
Good		0.411***		0.779***				−0.346***
Fair		1.037***		1.634***				−0.908***
Bad		1.296***		1.964***				−1.141***
Very bad		1.208***		1.671***				−1.055***
Parents practicing sport (Ref.: No)								
Yes	0.237***	−0.446***	0.282***	−0.426***	0.236***	0.263***	0.491***	0.521***
Nationality (Ref.: Spanish)								
Double nationality	0.093	0.348*	0.157	0.675**	0.087	0.141	0.153	−0.253
Foreigner	0.040	0.376**	0.029	0.601**	0.035	0.025	−0.029	−0.305**
Municipality (Ref.: Provincial capital)								
>50,000 inhabitants	−0.088***	−0.189*	−0.105**	−0.428**	−0.085***	−0.090*	−0.196**	0.105
<50,000 inhabitants	−0.011	−0.252***	−0.003	−0.383***	−0.011	−0.009	0.053	0.213***

(continued)

Table 1.4 (continued)

	Zero-inflated				Hurdle (two-part)			
	Poisson		NegBin		Tr. Poisson	Tr. NegBin	Ordered[1]	Logit[2]
	Number	Inflate	Number	Inflate	Number	Number	Number	1st hurdle
Constant	0.946***	−0.857**	0.751***	−1.901***	0.950***	0.814***		0.571*
α			0.416***			0,422***		
Observations	5,151	5,151	5,151	5,151	3,150	3,150	3,150	5,151
log L[3]	−9,494		−9,020		−9,493	−9,019	−8,947	

Notes:
[1]The cut point estimates of the ordered Logit model are not reported
[2]The Logit model of the first hurdle is the same for all the different versions of the hurdle model
[3]The log likelihood of the Logit model in the two-part hurdle models is included in the value, which appears in the second equation *** $p < 0.01$, ** $p < 0.05$, * $p < 0.10$

Table 1.5 Average of the adjusted probabilities for different values of y and the adjusted expected value of y

Prob.	Sample	Poisson	NegBin	Ordered Logit	Zero-infl Poisson	Zero-infl. NegBin	Hurdle Poisson	Hurdle NegBin	Hurdle ord. Logit
0	0.3885	0.2258	0.3593	0.3859	0.3886	0.3890	0.3885	0.3885	0.3885
1	0.1452	0.2562	0.2258	0.1437	0.1129	0.1686	0.1136	0.1696	0.1436
2	0.1633	0.2007	0.1388	0.1628	0.1388	0.1363	0.1388	0.1363	0.1611
3	0.1167	0.1356	0.0879	0.1179	0.1266	0.0989	0.1263	0.0986	0.1172
4	0.0660	0.0835	0.0573	0.0674	0.0954	0.0684	0.0952	0.0682	0.0673
5	0.0379	0.0479	0.0384	0.0387	0.0626	0.0462	0.0626	0.0461	0.0388
6	0.0239	0.0258	0.0262	0.0243	0.0370	0.0309	0.0370	0.0309	0.0244
7	0.0184	0.0131	0.0182	0.0187	0.0200	0.0205	0.0200	0.0206	0.0188
8	0.0109	0.0064	0.0129	0.0110	0.0100	0.0137	0.0100	0.0137	0.0110
9	0.0080	0.0029	0.0092	0.0080	0.0047	0.0091	0.0047	0.0091	0.0080
10	0.0052	0.0013	0.0066	0.0053	0.0020	0.0061	0.0021	0.0061	0.0053
11	0.0037	0.0005	0.0048	0.0037	0.0008	0.0040	0.0009	0.0041	0.0037
12	0.0035	0.0002	0.0036	0.0035	0.0003	0.0027	0.0003	0.0027	0.0035
13	0.0021	0.0001	0.0026	0.0021	0.0001	0.0018	0.0001	0.0018	0.0021
14	0.0012	0.0000	0.0020	0.0012	0.0000	0.0012	0.0000	0.0012	0.0012
15	0.0014	0.0000	0.0015	0.0014	0.0000	0.0008	0.0000	0.0008	0.0014
16	0.0016	0.0000	0.0011	0.0016	0.0000	0.0006	0.0000	0.0006	0.0016
17	0.0008	0.0000	0.0008	0.0008	0.0000	0.0004	0.0000	0.0004	0.0008
18	0.0002	0.0000	0.0006	0.0002	0.0000	0.0003	0.0000	0.0003	0.0002
19	0.0004	0.0000	0.0005	0.0004	0.0000	0.0002	0.0000	0.0002	0.0004
20	0.0002	0.0000	0.0004	0.0014	0.0000	0.0001	0.0000	0.0001	0.0014
E(y)	1.9851	1.9851	2.0003	2.0010	1.9847	1.9860	1.9842	1.9855	2.0010

The adjusted probabilities reported in Table 1.5 show that the zero-inflated versions are able to replicate the proportion of individuals who do not play sports. Moreover, the zero-inflated Poisson model reproduces the pattern of the relative frequencies associated with practicing one, two, and three sports better than the Negative Binomial model does, but it clearly underestimates the frequencies for one and two, and overestimates those corresponding to values between three and six, and then the estimated probabilities tend to zero more rapidly than the observed frequencies. In the case of the zero-inflated Negative Binomial model, the adjusted probabilities decrease with the number of sports practiced from the start, not capturing the pattern of the relative frequencies in the sample for values one, two, and three, but fitting quite well frequencies above three and the proportion of individuals practicing one, two or three sports (42.52% in the sample and 40.38% estimated by the Negative Binomial model, compared to the 37.83% estimated by the Poisson model).

As discussed in the methodology section, an alternative specification is the hurdle count data model, a two-part model in which all zeros come from potential non-participants and the second equation (number of sports) is estimated by using a truncated (at zero) distribution for the count variable. The estimates of the hurdle versions of the Poisson and the Negative Binomial model are reported in Table 1.4 using the same specification as for the zero-inflated versions, i.e., excluding health status in the second equation. Comparing the results shown in Table 1.4, the estimated coefficients differ between the hurdle and the zero-inflated models. This is because the first hurdle has a different definition depending on whether the zero-inflated or the hurdle version is considered, i.e., depending on how the zeros are generated. But the overall value of the log likelihood function is almost exactly the same for both versions of either the Poisson (−9,493) or the Negative Binomial model (−9,020), although it is marginally better for the hurdle models. This happens for this particular empirical exercise, but it cannot be generalized. In fact, when simplifying the specification by reducing the explanatory variables of the second equation, the difference between the two log likelihood values is more significant in favor of the hurdle model.

The main point about the above result is that, although the two models seem to have similar explanatory power, they provide a different interpretation about how the zeros are generated and, consequently, the decision about which model to choose has to be based on whether the characteristics of the data set (the period of reference associated with the question about the number of sports practiced) can be related to one or two potential sources of zeros. In this particular case, the question refers to the number of sports practiced during a year and zeros should be better associated with potential non-participants than with optimal choices made by people who are willing to practice sports. Notice that the similar performance of the zero-inflated and the hurdle models translates into almost exactly the same estimates for the probabilities of practicing a given number of sports, according to the values reported in Table 1.5.

It is also relevant to remember that the hurdle model is not nested into the corresponding zero-inflated version. This is because the second equation requires a distribution of a positive random variable for the dependent variable, the truncated (at zero) Poisson or Negative Binomial, whereas being nested would require assuming the unrestricted standard versions of these distributions. In the case in which this "nested" model is estimated, the log likelihood of the hurdle Negative Binomial model is −9,442, smaller than that of the zero-inflated model.

Finally, as mentioned above, the estimation of a count data model can be performed by using ordered discrete choice models. They have the advantage over the previous count data models that they do not impose any restriction on the adjusted probabilities associated with the values of the dependent variable. As is reported in Table 1.3, the standard ordered Logit model has a significantly better fit than the standard Poisson and Negative Binomial models. This is also the case when considering the estimates of the hurdle version of the ordered model, whose estimates are shown in the last column of Table 1.4. It should be mentioned that the dependent variable has been redefined in the case of those observations for which the number of sports is greater than 20 (four of them) (variable *ndep_o* in the Stata commands for the ordered models). The last category of the dependent variable in the ordered models corresponds to the case in which the number of sports is equal to or greater than 20. If this redefinition is not applied, the log likelihood increases to −8,958, still greater than that of the count data models. This flexibility of the ordered model becomes evident when looking at the adjusted probabilities in Table 1.5. In the case of the ordered hurdle model, they reproduce almost exactly the relative frequencies in the sample and, in particular, the specific profile of the probabilities associated with practicing one, two, and three sports.

1.5.2 Interpretation of the Coefficients and the Marginal Effects

Table 1.3 reports the coefficients of the explanatory variables for the standard models, corresponding to the elements of vector β in (1.2) or (1.5). According to the parameterization for the count data models, a positive coefficient implies a positive effect of the corresponding variable on the expected value of the number of sports, as in the case of the ordered model in terms of the latent variable y^* in (1.16).

In this regard, females have a lower expected value of the number of practiced sports compared to males because of the negative sign of the coefficient of this dummy. In the case of age, an interpretation of each individual coefficient can be made, concluding, for instance, that those who are in the age group 35–44 play a lower expected number of sports than those younger than 25 (the reference category). But an overall interpretation of the pattern of the age coefficients can be made, since the categories are ordered. Thus, age has a negative effect on the expected number of sports, not because the coefficients are negative but because the pattern they follow is decreasing. This also applies to the health status variable, whose categories are also ordered: the worse the health status the lower the expected value of the number of sports. Regarding other variables, education has a positive effect on the expected value of the dependent variable, as happens for those who live in small municipalities and those whose parents practice sport. Those who are not single are expected to practice fewer sports, as it is the case of those who are not Spanish. Finally, people who are either unemployed, retired, or doing housework have a lower expected number of sports compared to those who are working—the reference category—, whereas those who are students or are in the default category have a higher expected value.

We can also make an interpretation of the size of the effect of a unit change in each explanatory variable because, given expressions (1.2) and (1.5) for the count data models, increasing the k-th explanatory variable by one unit will multiply the expected number of sports by $\exp(\beta_k)$, which, for "small" values of β_k, means that the expected number of sports will increase by $(\beta_k \times 100)\%$.[9] This means that in the Poisson model, females have an expected value of the number of sports $\exp(-0.277)$

[9] Notice that by taking logs in (1.2) and (1.5), we end up with an expression similar to the log-linear version of the regression model and the interpretation is the same as mentioned above.

times that of males with the same characteristics (or exp(−0.294) for the Negative Binomial model), i.e., the expected value is 24.2% lower for females than for males. In the case of age, the coefficient for the group 25–34 implies that the expected value for the number of sports is 8.8% lower than that of people younger than 25 (this is a "good" approximation insofar as exp(−0.088) is 0.916).

Notice that the marginal effects, interpreted as the absolute change in the expected value of the dependent variable, are different for each individual because of the non-linearity of expressions (1.2) or (1.5), as becomes evident from the following expression, which corresponds to the effect of a continuous variable.[10]

$$\frac{\partial E(y_i|X_i)}{\partial X_i^k} = \beta_k \exp(X_i^{'}\beta) \tag{1.18}$$

In the case of qualitative variables, such as all those used in this exercise, the marginal effects are calculated as the change in the expected value of y when the dummy defined for each specific category changes from 0 to 1, i.e., when there is a change from the reference category to that associated with the dummy. In the first rows of Table 1.6, the average of the marginal effects of gender and health status on the expected value of the number of sports for all individuals in the sample are reported.[11] They look relatively similar for both the Poisson and the Negative Binomial model, despite having different explanatory power, but the difference is more significant in the case of fair health status because of the greater difference in the size of the coefficients in the two models. In the case of the ordered Logit model, the marginal effects are calculated by using the adjusted value of the expected number of sports obtained as the sum of the products of the adjusted probabilities times the different values of the number of sports.

But, as mentioned in the methodology section, the analysis of the effects of the covariates on the probabilities associated with the different values of y is as important as, or even more important, than studying the marginal effects on the expected value of y. In fact, this is the aspect where differences between models are more evident. Table 1.6 offers information on the marginal effects of gender and health status on the probabilities of practicing zero to four sports. Differences between the Poisson and the Negative Binomial model can be clearly appreciated, as well as differences with respect to the ordered Logit model.

Turning now to the zero-inflated and hurdle models, whose estimates are reported in Table 1.4, it is worth remembering that both are two-equation models but they differ in the role of the first equation: to explain whether or not the individual is a potential sports practitioner (zero-inflated model) or just whether the individual practices sport or not (hurdle model). This feature has to be taken into account

[10] There are several ways of reporting marginal effects. They can also be expressed as elasticities or semi-elasticities depending on the features of the explanatory variable. *Stata* allows for the possibility of choosing how the marginal effects are calculated.

[11] In some papers marginal effects are evaluated at the mean values of the explanatory variables. Consequently, when writing up the results of empirical research, it is important to make clear how the marginal effects are calculated.

Table 1.6 Marginal effects[1] of gender and health status (fair vs very good) on the probability of *n* and the expected value

	Poisson	NegBin	Ordered Logit	Zero infl Poisson	Zero infl. NegBin	Hurdle Poisson	Hurdle NegBin	Truncated Ord. Logit
Gender: female versus male								
Pr(0)	0.0715	0.0666	0.0804	0.0916	0.0768	0.0925	0.0925	0.0925
Pr(1)	0.0406	0.0153	0.0041	0.0089	0.0092	0.0084	−0.0010	−0.0063
Pr(2)	0.0010	−0.0043	−0.0102	−0.0028	−0.0046	−0.0032	−0.0104	−0.0184
Pr(3)	−0.0209	−0.0103	−0.0185	−0.0152	−0.0115	−0.0154	−0.0141	−0.0202
Pr(4)	−0.0268	−0.0112	−0.0156	−0.0212	−0.0134	−0.0212	−0.0141	−0.0145
E(y)	−0.5462	−0.5829	−0.4472	−0.5259	−0.5408	−0.5258	−0.5386	−0.4149
Health status: fair versus very good								
Pr(0)	0.0658	0.0725	0.1289	0.1836	0.1792	0.1857	0.1857	0.1857
Pr(1)	0.0366	0.0161	0.0049	−0.0433	−0.0604	−0.0447	−0.0607	−0.0540
Pr(2)	−0.0017	−0.0058	−0.0193	−0.0468	−0.0435	−0.0478	−0.0445	−0.0517
Pr(3)	−0.0213	−0.0121	−0.0309	−0.0377	−0.0283	−0.0381	−0.0295	−0.0330
Pr(4)	−0.0251	−0.0127	−0.0246	−0.0253	−0.0177	−0.0253	−0.0188	−0.0175
E(y)	−0.4735	−0.5950	−0.6795	−0.5321	−0.4996	−0.5319	−0.5312	−0.5408

Note: [1]Average marginal effects for all the individuals in the sample

when interpreting the results of the Logit models corresponding to this first stage. Additionally, the estimates of the first equation in the double-hurdle model (*Inflate*) correspond to defining the depending variable of the binary discrete choice model as equal to 1 if the individual is a potential non-participant and zero otherwise, as is done in the output produced by *Stata*. Regarding the interpretation of the estimated coefficients in the second equation, it must be done in terms of the effect of the corresponding variable on the expected number of sports for potential practitioners in the zero-inflated models, and conditional on being a practitioner in the hurdle model, proceeding as it was done when discussing the effects for the standard models.

Although this is not necessarily the case in all the empirical applications, in this particular exercise the coefficients of each explanatory variable have the same sign in both equations of all the versions of the zero-inflated and hurdle models, i.e., a variable, which has a positive effect (positive coefficient) on the expected number of sports also has a positive effect on the probability of being a potential practitioner in the zero-inflated model (negative coefficient of the *inflate* equation) and on the probability of practicing sport in the hurdle model. But the significance of those effects differs. For instance, the coefficients capturing the effect of the individual employment status are in most cases significant in the second equation (number of sports) of the zero-inflated model but not in the *inflate* equation, which is also the case to some extent for the hurdle equation. By contrast, the effect of education on the unconditional expectation of the number of sports works mainly through the probability of being a sports practitioner in the different versions of the hurdle model. The existence of different patterns depending on the equation considered is relevant in terms of the policies to be implemented to promote sports participation, depending on whether the aim is just to increase the number of sports practitioners or the diversification of this participation, measured in this example by the number of sports practiced. Notice that this differentiated pattern cannot be captured by the standard versions of the different models.

Table 1.6 reports the average of the marginal effects of gender and health status for these two-equation models on the unconditional probabilities and the unconditional expected number of sports for all the individuals in the sample. In the case of the zero-inflated count data models, the unconditional expectation of y is:

$$\begin{aligned} E(y_i|X_i, Z_i) &= exp(X_i^{'}\beta)\ Pr(D_i = 0) = exp(X_i^{'}\beta)\ (1 - P_i) \\ &= exp(X_i^{'}\beta)\ F^{*}(-Z_i^{'}\delta) \end{aligned} \tag{1.19}$$

where P_i is defined as in (1.10).

Similar to expression (1.18), the marginal effects on the unconditional expectation of the dependent variable for the zero-inflated count data models of the vectors X_i and Z_i are given by the following expressions:

$$\frac{\partial E(y_i|X_i, Z_i)}{\partial X_i^k} = \beta_k\, exp(X_i^{'}\beta)\ F^{*}(-Z_i^{'}\delta) \tag{1.20}$$

$$\frac{\partial E(y_i|X_i, Z_i)}{\partial Z_i^k} = -\ \delta_k\, exp(X_i^{'}\beta)\ \frac{\partial F^{*}(-Z_i^{'}\delta)}{\partial Z_i^k} \tag{1.21}$$

where $F*$ is defined in (1.10). When a variable is included in both X_i and Z_i, its marginal effect is the sum of the expressions (1.20) and (1.21).

In the case of the hurdle count data models, the unconditional expectation of y is:

$$\begin{aligned} E(y_i|X_i, Z_i) &= exp(X_i^{'}\beta)\ Pr(D_i^{*} = 1) = exp(X_i^{'}\beta) \\ P_i &= exp(X_i^{'}\beta)\ (1 \text{ - } F^{*}(-Z_i^{'}\delta)) \end{aligned} \tag{1.22}$$

where P_i is defined as in (1.13).

The marginal effects on the unconditional expectation of the dependent variable for the hurdle count data models of the vectors X_i and Z_i are given by the following expressions:

$$\frac{\partial E(y_i|X_i, Z_i)}{\partial X_i^k} = \beta_k\, exp(X_i^{'}\beta)(1 - F^{*}(-Z_i^{'}\delta)) \tag{1.23}$$

$$\frac{\partial E(y_i|X_i, Z_i)}{\partial Z_i^k} = \delta_k\, exp(X_i^{'}\beta)\ \frac{\partial F^{*}(-Z_i^{'}\delta)}{\partial Z_i^k} \tag{1.24}$$

Notice that the marginal effect of those variables included in both X_i and Z_i is the sum of the expressions (1.23) and (1.24).

It is worth pointing out that, although the marginal effects on the expected value of y are very similar across models, a substantial difference is observed between the standard and the two-equation versions when considering the marginal effect on the unconditional probabilities, in particular, on the probability of not being a sports practitioner ($y = 0$). For instance, having a fair health status increases this probability by approximately 18 percentage points compared to having a very good health status in the two-equation models, and by around 7 percentage points in the standard count data models. Focusing on the two-equation models, there are some differences between the Poisson versions and the rest when looking at the probabilities of practicing one sport or more than two sports, as a consequence of the equidispersion restriction associated with this model.

Finally, notice that the hurdle version of the ordered model, which has the best fit because of its flexibility, produces marginal effects that are quite similar to those of the Negative Binomial version of the hurdle model, which is the preferred specification among the typical count data models. In addition, although the fit is almost the same, the marginal effects of the Negative Binomial version of the hurdle model differ with respect to those of the zero-inflated model, probably as a consequence of the different assumptions about how the zeros are generated.

1.6 Concluding Remarks

In this chapter a review of the most commonly used count data models when using cross-section data is presented. The dependent variable is characterized as an integer non-negative variable, which takes a small number of (low) values, usually with a variance greater than the expected value (overdispersion) and with a relatively large proportion of zeros (excess of zeros). Particular attention is devoted to the specification of the different models used in the empirical literature in terms of how the zeros, which are observed, have been generated. In this regard, the zero-inflated versions of the standard models are discussed, and the ordered models are presented as an alternative way of estimating these models in which the dependent variable represents the number of times something happens (e.g., the number of visits to the doctor).

All the methodological issues are illustrated by means of an empirical application to the analysis of diversification in sports practice, i.e., how many different sports are practiced by individuals. This specific feature of sports participation has received little attention in the sports economics literature.

Both the hurdle and the zero-inflated versions of the Negative Binomial model are performing much better than the standard Poisson and Negative Binomial models. In this particular exercise, taking into account the characteristics of the survey used in the empirical analysis, the hurdle model seems to be more adequate.

It is worth emphasizing the importance of the analysis of the marginal effects of the different explanatory variables in these models, given their non-linearity. This is an issue that usually does not receive too much attention in empirical work. In particular, when dealing with count data models, attention should be paid, not only to the marginal effects on the expected value of the dependent variable, but also to the marginal effects on the probabilities associated with the values the dependent variable can take. Most of the differences in the performance of the alternative models are more evident when analyzing the adjusted probabilities, since the distributional and the specification assumptions have more impact on the structure of the adjusted probabilities than in the expected value.

Finally, it is also relevant to mention some recent developments related to new models, which have proposed to deal with overdispersion (e.g., Altun 2019; Cahoy et al. 2021; Sellers and Premeaux 2021) and new proposals for clustered count data (e.g., Altinisik 2022).

References

Agrawal M, Sensarma R (2007) Determinants of merger activity: evidence from India. Int J Financ Serv Manag 2(4):277–288. https://doi.org/10.1504/IJFSM.2007.016285

Altinisik Y (2022) Addressing overdispersion and zero-inflation for clustered count data via new multilevel heterogeneous hurdle model. J App Stat 50(2):408–433. https://doi.org/10.1080/02664763.2022.2096875

Altun E (2019) A new model for over-dispersed count data: Poisson quasi-Lindley regression model. Math Sci 13(3):241–247. https://doi.org/10.1007/s40096-019-0293-5

Anokye NK, Pokhrel S, Buxton M, Fox-Rushby J (2012) The demand for sports and exercise: results from an illustrative survey. Eur J Health Econ 13(3):277–287. https://doi.org/10.1007/s10198-011-0304-4

Bridge MW, Toms MR (2013) The specialising or sampling debate: a retrospective analysis of adolescent sports participation in the UK. J Sport Sci 31(1):87–96. https://doi.org/10.1080/02640414.2012.721560

Cabane C, Lechner M (2015) Physical activity of adults: A survey of correlates, determinants and effects. J Econ Stat 235(4–5):376–402. https://doi.org/10.1515/jbnst-2015-4-504

Cahoy D, Di Nardo E, Polito F (2021) Flexible models for overdispersed and underdispersed count data. Stat Pap 62(6):2969–2990. https://doi.org/10.1007/s00362-021-01222-7

Cameron AC, Trivedi PK (1986) Econometric models based on count data: comparisons and applications of some estimators and tests. J Appl Econom 1(1):29–53. https://doi.org/10.1002/jae.3950010104

Cameron AC, Trivedi PK (2005) Microeconometrics: Methods and Applications. Cambridge University Press, New York. https://doi.org/10.1017/CBO9780511811241

Cameron AC, Trivedi PK (2014) Regression analysis of count data. Cambridge University Press, New York. https://doi.org/10.1017/CBO9781139013567

Cameron AC, Trivedi PK (2022) Microeconometrics using Stata. Volume II: Nonlinear models and causal inference methods, 2nd edn. Stata Press, Texas.

Dawson P, Downward P (2011) Participation, spectatorship and media coverage in sport: some initial insights. In: Andreff W (ed) Contemporary issues in sports economics: participation and professional team sports. Edward Elgar, Cheltenham, pp 15–42. https://doi.org/10.4337/9780857930385

Downward P, Muñiz C (2019) Sports participation. In: Downward P, Frick B, Humphreys BR, Pawlowski T, Ruseski JE, Soebbing BP (eds) The SAGE handbook of sports economics. SAGE Publications, London, pp 33–44

Dupuy JF (2018) Statistical methods for overdispersed count data. Elsevier, Oxford. https://doi.org/10.1016/C2017-0-00831-5

Feng CX (2021) A comparison of zero-inflated and hurdle models for modelling zero-inflated count data. J Stat Distrib Appl 8(1):1–19. https://doi.org/10.1186%2Fs40488-021-00121-4

Friendly M, Meyer D (2015) Discrete data analysis with R: visualization and modeling techniques for categorical and count data. CRC Press, Boca Raton

García J, Muñiz C, Rodríguez P, Suárez MJ (2016) Comparative analysis of sports practice by types of activities. Int J Sport Financ 11(4):327–348

García J, Suárez MJ (2020) Organised and non-organised after-school physical activity among children in Spain: the role of school-related variables. Eur Sport Manag Q 20(2):171–188. https://doi.org/10.1080/16184742.2019.1594329

García J, Suárez MJ (2021) Dimensions of sports participation: evidence from Mexico. In: Koning RH, Késenne S (eds) A modern guide to sports economics. Edward Elgar, Cheltenham, pp 226–239. https://doi.org/10.4337/9781789906530

García J, Suárez MJ (2023) The relevance of specification assumptions when analyzing the drivers of physical activity practice. Econ Model 119:106127. https://doi.org/10.1016/j.econmod.2022.106127

Geil P, Million A, Rotte R, Zimmermann KF (1997) Economic Incentives and Hospitalization in Germany. J Appl Econom 12:295–312. https://doi.org/10.1002/(SICI)1099-1255(199705)12:3%3C295::AID-JAE443%3E3.0.CO;2-X

Green JA (2021) Too many zeros and/or highly skewed? A tutorial on modelling health behaviour as count data with Poisson and Negative Binomial regression. Health Psyc Behav Med 9(1):436–455. https://doi.org/10.1080/21642850.2021.1920416

Harris MN, Zhao X (2007) A zero-inflated ordered probit model, with an application to modelling tobacco consumption. J Econom 141:1073–1099. https://doi.org/10.1016/j.jeconom.2007.01.002

Hausman J, Hall BH, Griliches Z (1984) Econometric models for count data with an application to the Patents-R&D relationship. Econometrica 52(4):909–938. https://doi.org/10.2307/1911191

Hilbe JM (2014) Modeling count data. Cambridge University Press, Cambridge. https://doi.org/10.1007/978-3-642-04898-2_369

Inan T (2021) Using poisson model for goal prediction in European football. J Hum Sport Exerc 16(4):942–955. https://doi.org/10.14198/jhse.2021.164.16

Jang TY (2005) Count data models for trip generation. J Transp Eng 131(6):444–450. https://doi.org/10.1061/(ASCE)0733-947X(2005)131:6(444)

Lee J, Park CG, Choi M (2016) Regular exercise and related factors in patients with Parkinson's disease: applying zero-inflated negative binomial modelling of exercise count data. Appl Nurs Res 30:164–169. https://doi.org/10.1016/j.apnr.2015.08.002

Lefèvre B, Nohara H, Nier O (2021) Sports practice in Japan and France: a comparative analysis. PLoS ONE 16(6):e0253435. https://doi.org/10.1371%2Fjournal.pone.0253435

Lefèvre B, Ohl F (2012) Consuming sports: distinction, univorism and omnivorism. Sport Soc 15(1):44–63. https://doi.org/10.1080/03031853.2011.625276

Lefèvre B, Routier G, Llopis-Goig R (2020) Sports participation in France and Spain: an international comparison of voraciousness for sport. Poetics 81:101429. https://doi.org/10.1016/j.poetic.2019.101429

Lord D, Geedipally SR, Guilkema SD (2010) Extension of the application of the Conway-Maxwell-Poisson models: analyzing traffic crash data exhibiting underdispersion. Risk Anal 30(8):1268–1276. https://doi.org/10.1111/j.1539-6924.2010.01417.x

McCullagh P (1980) Regression Models for Ordinal Data. J Roy Stat Soc B 42(2):109–142. https://doi.org/10.1111/j.2517-6161.1980.tb01109.x

Muñiz C, Rodríguez P, Suárez MJ (2014) Sports and cultural habits by gender: an application using count-data models. Econ Model 36:288–297. https://doi.org/10.1016/j.econmod.2013.09.053

Oliveira-Brochado A, Quelhas Brito P, Oliveira-Brochado F (2017) Correlates of adults' participation in sport and frequency of sport. Sci Sport 32(6):355–363. https://doi.org/10.1016/j.scispo.2017.03.005

Pohlmeier W, Ulrich V (1995) An econometric model of the two-part decision making process in the demand for health care. J Hum Resour 30(2):339–361. https://doi.org/10.2307/146123

Rhodes RE, Janssen I, Bredin SSD, Warburton DER, Bauman A (2017) Physical activity: health impact, prevalence, correlates and interventions. Psychol Health 32(8):942–975. https://doi.org/10.1080/08870446.2017.1325486

Sellers KF, Premeuax B (2021) Conway-Maxwell-Poisson regression models for dispersed count data. Wires Comput Stat 13(6):e1533. https://doi.org/10.1002/wics.1533

Slymen DJ, Ayala GX, Arredondo EM, Elder JP (2006) A demonstration of modelling count data with an application to physical activity. Epidemiol Perspect Innov 3:3. https://doi.org/10.1186/1742-5573-3-3

Sun J, Zhao X (2013) Analysis of panel count data. Springer, New York

Tang W, He H, Tu XM (2023) Applied categorical and count data analysis, 2nd edn. CRC Press, Boca Raton. https://doi.org/10.1201/9781003109815

WHO (2018) Global action plan on physical activity 2018–2030: More active people for a healthier world. https://apps.who.int/iris/bitstream/handle/10665/272722/9789241514187-eng.pdf?ua=1. Accessed 8 June 2023

Wilson P (2015) The misuse of the Vuong test for non-nested models to test for zero-inflation. Econ Lett 127:51–53. https://doi.org/10.1016/j.econlet.2014.12.029

Winkelmann R (2008) Econometric analysis of count data, 5th edn. Springer, Berlin. https://doi.org/10.1007/978-3-540-78389-3

Chapter 2
Binary and Ordinal Probit Regression: Applications to Public Opinion on Marijuana Legalization in the United States

Mohit Batham, Soudeh Mirghasemi, Manini Ojha, and Mohammad Arshad Rahman

Abstract This chapter presents an overview of a specific form of limited dependent variable models, namely, discrete choice models, where the dependent (response or outcome) variable takes values which are discrete and inherently ordered. Within this setting, the dependent variable may take only two values (such as 0 and 1) giving rise to binary models (e.g., probit and logit) or more than two values (say $j = 1, 2, \ldots, J$, where J is a small integer) giving rise to ordinal models (e.g., ordinal probit and ordinal logit). In these models, the primary goal is to model the probability of responses/outcomes conditional on the covariates. We connect the outcomes of a discrete choice model to the random utility framework in economics, discuss estimation techniques, and present the calculation of covariate effects and measures to assess model fitting. Some recent advances in discrete data modeling are also discussed. Following the theoretical overview, we utilize the binary and ordinal models to analyze public opinion on marijuana legalization and the extent of legalization in the United States. All computations are done in MATLAB. We

This book chapter was completed and accepted while the corresponding author was working as an Associate Professor in the College of Business, Zayed University, UAE.

Supplementary Information The online version contains supplementary material available at https://doi.org/10.1007/978-981-99-4902-1_2.

M. Batham
Walmart GTS, Bengaluru, India

S. Mirghasemi
Department of Economics, Hofstra University, Hempstead, USA
e-mail: Soudeh.Mirghasemi@hofstra.edu

M. Ojha
Jindal School of Government and Public Policy, O.P. Jindal Global University, Sonipat, India
e-mail: mojha@jgu.edu.in

M. A. Rahman (✉)
Department of Economic Sciences, Indian Institute of Technology Kanpur, Kanpur, India
e-mail: marshad@iitk.ac.in; arshadrahman25@gmail.com

D. Mukherjee (ed.), *Applied Econometric Analysis Using Cross Section and Panel Data*, Contributions to Economics, https://doi.org/10.1007/978-981-99-4902-1_2

obtain several interesting results including that past use of marijuana, belief about legalization and political partisanship are important factors that shape public opinion.

Keywords Discrete choice model · logit · Marijuana legalization · McFadden's R-squared · Pew research center

2.1 Introduction

This chapter will discuss settings in which the dependent variable we seek to model takes on a range of values that are restricted, broadly defined as **limited dependent variable models**. Within the class of limited dependent variables, a special case arises when the outcome is no longer a continuous measure but a discrete variable. Such data often arise when individuals make a choice from a set of potential discrete outcomes, thus earning the name **discrete choice** models. The most common case of such models occurs when y is a binary response and takes on the values zero and one, indicating whether or not the event has occurred, giving rise to **binary models**.[1] Consider, for example, participation in the labor force, whether or not an individual will buy a vehicle, or whether or not a country is part of free trade agreement. In other cases, y may take on multiple (more than two) discrete values, with no natural ordering. Consider, for example, the choice of brand of toothpaste or mode of transportation. These are referred to as **multinomial models**. We refer the readers to Train (2009) for a detailed discussion on multinomial models, their estimation and inference. Further, there could be situations where y takes on multiple (more than two) discrete values that are inherently ordered or ranked. For example, scores attached to opinion on surveys (oppose, neutral, support), classification of educational attainment, or ratings on bonds. These give rise to **ordinal models** or **ordered choice models**. In this chapter, we present binary and ordinal probit models along with a brief sketch on their logit counterparts, namely, binary and ordinal logit models.

Discrete choice models have their foundations in the theory of choice in economics, which itself is inherently related with the random utility model (Luce 1959; Luce and Suppes 1965; Marschak 1960). The random utility framework involves a utility maximizing rational individual whose objective is to choose an alternative from a set of *mutually exclusive* and completely *exhaustive* alternatives. The utilities attached with each alternative are completely known to the decision-maker and s/he chooses the same alternative in replications of the experiment. However, to a researcher the utilities are unknown, since s/he only observes a vector of characteristics (such as age, gender, and income) of the decision-maker, referred to as *representative utility*. This forms the systematic component. The unobserved factors form the stochastic part. The stochastic component is assigned a distribution,

[1] Binary models are special cases of both ordinal and multinomial models with more than two categories.

typically continuous, to make probabilistic statements about the observed choices conditional on the representative utility. The distributional specification implies that there exists a continuous latent random variable (or a continuous latent utility) that underlies the discrete outcomes.

When the set of alternatives or outcomes are inherently ordered or ranked, individual choice of a particular alternative can be associated as the latent variable crossing a particular threshold or cut-point. This latent variable threshold-crossing formulation of the ordered choices elegantly connects individual choice behavior and ordinal data models serve as a useful tool in the estimation process. While the theoretical support relates to choice and random utility theory, the econometric techniques are completely general and applicable when the ordering conditions of the data are met.

To understand the application of discrete choice models, we consider the case of legalization of marijuana in the United States (US). The debate around legalization of marijuana has been an important yet controversial policy issue. Marijuana has been proved to be effective in treatment of several diseases and a wealth of new scientific understanding regarding its medicinal benefits are documented in Berman et al. (2004), Wilsey et al. (2013), Abrams et al. (2003, 2007), Ellis et al. (2009), Johnson et al. (2010), McAllister et al. (2011), Guzmán (2003), Duran et al. (2010).[2] However, despite the medicinal benefits, smoking or consumption of marijuana is not completely benign and may cause harmful effects, especially associated with respiratory illnesses and cognitive development (Kalant 2004; Polen et al. 1993; Meier et al. 2012).[3] As a result, several surveys have been conducted to assess public opinion on the matter. For the purpose of this chapter, we specifically utilize poll data collected by the Pew Research Center for the periods 2013 and 2014 to demonstrate the application of binary and ordinal probit models. While there is an increasing trend in favor of legalizing marijuana based on public opinion, it is noteworthy to study these specific time periods given that the year 2013 marked the first time in more than four decades that majority of Americans favored legalizing the use of marijuana in the US (Dimock et al. 2013).

---

[2] The reader is directed to the website www.procon.org for a list of 60 peer-reviewed articles (http://medicalmarijuana.procon.org/view.resource.php?resourceID=000884) on the effect of marijuana in treatment of the above-mentioned diseases.

[3] A list of peer-reviewed articles on the public health consequences of marijuana can be obtained from the Office of National Drug Control Policy. Refer to https://www.whitehouse.gov/ondcp/marijuana.

2.2 Binary Models

Binary models are designed to deal with situations where the outcome (response or dependent) variable is dichotomous, i.e., takes only two values, typically coded as 1 for "success" and 0 for "failure." For example, the application presented in Sect. 2.6.1 models the response as a "success" if an opinion is in favor of legalization and a "failure" otherwise. While a binary model has a dependent variable that takes discrete values, the model can be conveniently expressed in terms of a continuous latent variable z_i[4] as follows:

$$z_i = x_i'\beta + \epsilon_i, \qquad \epsilon_i \overset{iid}{\sim} N(0, 1); \quad \forall\, i = 1, \cdots, n, \tag{2.1}$$

where x_i is a $k \times 1$ vector of covariates, β is a $k \times 1$ vector of unknown parameters, and n denotes the number of observations. Like most applications, the stochastic term ϵ is assumed to be *independently and identically distributed* (*iid*) as a standard normal distribution, i.e., $\epsilon_i \overset{iid}{\sim} N(0, 1)$ for $i = 1, \ldots, n$, which gives rise to a *binary probit model*. The latent variable z_i is related to the observed discrete response y_i as follows:

$$y_i = \begin{cases} 1 \text{ if } z_i > 0, \\ 0 \text{ otherwise.} \end{cases} \tag{2.2}$$

With only two responses, there is a single cut-point which is typically fixed at 0 for the sake of simplicity. A pictorial representation of the binary outcome probabilities for marijuana legalization is shown in Fig. 2.1. The figure also shows that the cut-point γ_1 is fixed at 0 to anchor the location of the distribution. Besides, the scale is fixed by assuming the variance of the normal distribution is 1. Both the restrictions are necessary to identify the model parameters (see Jeliazkov and Rahman (2012) for further details).

The likelihood for binary probit model can be expressed as

$$L(\beta; y) = \prod_{i=1}^{n} \left\{ \Pr(y_i = 0|x_i'\beta)^{(1-y_i)} \Pr(y_i = 1|x_i'\beta)^{y_i} \right\} = \prod_{i=1}^{n} \left\{ \Phi(-x_i'\beta)^{(1-y_i)} \Phi(x_i'\beta)^{y_i} \right\}, \tag{2.3}$$

where $\Phi(\cdot)$ denotes the *cumulative distribution function (cdf)* of a standard normal distribution. Given the likelihood in Eq. 2.3, the parameters β are estimated by maximizing the logarithm of the likelihood (log-likelihood) using numerical techniques such as the Newton–Raphson method or the BHHH procedure (Train 2009). The principle behind maximizing the likelihood—known as the maximum likelihood (ML) estimation—is to obtain those parameter values that are most probable to have produced the data under the assumed statistical model. Note that it is convenient to work with the log likelihood since logarithm being a monotonic function, the maxi-

---

[4] The continuous latent variable can be interpreted as the difference between utilities from choice 1 and 0, i.e., $z_i = U_{i1} - U_{i0}$, where U denotes utility (Jeliazkov and Rahman 2012).

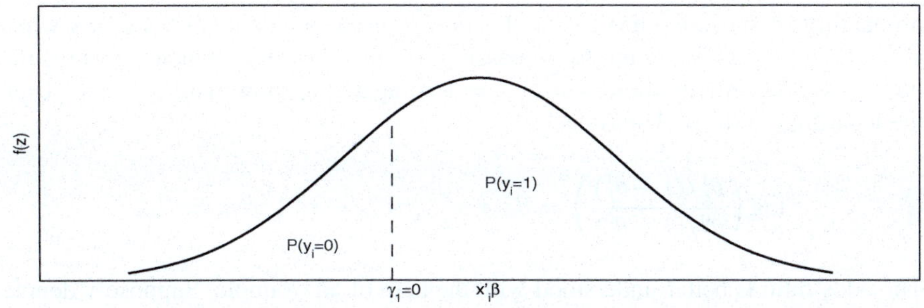

Fig. 2.1 The cut-point γ_1 divides the area under the curve into two parts, the probability of failure and probability of success. In our study, $\mathrm{P}(y_i = 0)$ and $\mathrm{P}(y_i = 1)$ correspond to probability of opposing and supporting marijuana legalization, respectively. Note that for each individual i, the mean $x_i'\beta$ and hence the probabilities, $\mathrm{P}(y_i = 0)$ and $\mathrm{P}(y_i = 1)$, will be different. *Source* authors' creation

mum of log-likelihood and the likelihood occurs at the same parameter values. Once the parameter estimates are available, we may calculate post-estimation constructs such as covariate effects and predicted probabilities. Measures for goodness of fit can also be calculated to assess model fitting. Readers interested in further details about binary data modeling may look into Johnson and Albert (2000, Chap. 3).

Thus far, we have described the binary probit model but the framework can be transformed into a binary logit model (or simply logit model) with the modification that the errors follow a logistic distribution (Hosmer et al. 2013). Like the normal distribution, the logistic distribution is symmetric but has heavier tails relative to a normal distribution. Both the location and scale restrictions apply to the logit model as before, but note that the variance is now fixed at $\pi^2/3$ as compared to 1 in a probit model. To obtain the logit likelihood, the normal *cdf* $\Phi(x_i'\beta)$ in Eq. (2.3) is replaced by the logistic *cdf*: $\Lambda(x_i'\beta) = \exp(x_i'\beta)/\left[1 + \exp(x_i'\beta)\right]$. We maximize the resulting log-likelihood to obtain the parameter estimates for the logit model.

The logit model is appealing to researchers in many fields (including epidemiologists) because of the ease in interpreting its slope coefficient. To see this, let $\theta_i = \Pr(y_i = 1|x_i'\beta)$ denote the probability of success and $x_{.,l}$ be a continuous covariate (or independent variable). Then the logarithm of the odds (log-odds) of success can be expressed as

$$\log\left(\frac{\theta_i}{1-\theta_i}\right) = x_i'\beta = x_{i,l}\,\beta_l + x_{i,-l}'\,\beta_{-l},$$

where $x_i = (x_{i,l},\, x_{i,-l})$, $\beta = (\beta_l,\, \beta_{-l})$, and $-l$ in the subscript denotes all covariates/parameters except the l-th covariate/parameter. If we differentiate the log-odds with respect to the l-th covariate, we obtain β_l. Therefore, the slope coefficient β_l represents the log-odds for a 1 unit change in the l-th covariate.

Similarly, the coefficient of an indicator variable (dummy or dichotomous variable) has an interesting interpretation. Let $x_{.,m}$ be an indicator variable, θ_i^1 be the probability of success when $x_{i,m} = 1$, and θ_i^0 be the probability of success when $x_{i,m} = 0$. Our goal is to find the expression for the odds-ratio, which measures the odds of success among those with $x_{i,m} = 1$ compared to those with $x_{i,m} = 0$. Then the logarithm of the odds-ratio is

$$\log\left(\frac{\theta_i^1/(1-\theta_i^1)}{\theta_i^0/(1-\theta_i^0)}\right) = \beta_m + x'_{i,-m}\beta_{-m} - x'_{i,-m}\beta_{-m} = \beta_m.$$

The odds-ratio is better understood with the help of an example. Suppose y denote the presence or absence of a heart disease and $x_{.,m}$ denote whether the person is a smoker or non-smoker. Then, an odds-ratio = 2 implies that heart disease is twice as likely to occur among smokers as compared to non-smokers for the population under study.

2.3 Ordinal Models

Ordinal regression models generalize the binary models by allowing the dependent variable to have more than two outcomes which are inherently ordered or ranked. Each outcome or category is assigned a score (value or number) with the characteristic that the scores have an ordinal meaning but hold no cardinal interpretation. Therefore, the difference between categories is not directly comparable. For example, the study presented in Sect. 2.6.2 codifies the public response to marijuana legalization as follows: 1 for "oppose legalization," 2 for "legal only for medicinal use," and 3 for "legal for personal use." Here, a score of 2 implies more support for legalization as compared to 1, but we cannot interpret a score of 2 as twice the support compared to a score of 1. Similarly, the difference in support between 2 and 1 is not the same as that between 3 and 2.

Similar to binary models, the ordinal regression model can be conveniently expressed in terms of a continuous latent variable z_i[5] as follows:

$$z_i = x_i'\beta + \epsilon_i, \qquad \forall\, i = 1, \cdots, n, \tag{2.4}$$

where the notations are identical to that of a binary model. If we assume that the errors are *iid* as a standard normal distribution, i.e., $\epsilon_i \overset{iid}{\sim} N(0, 1)$ for $i = 1, \ldots, n$; then we have an *ordinal probit model* (also known as *ordered probit model*). The latent variable z_i is related to the observed discrete response y_i as follows:

$$\gamma_{j-1} < z_i \le \gamma_j \;\Rightarrow\; y_i = j, \qquad \forall\, i = 1, \cdots, n;\; j = 1, \cdots, J, \tag{2.5}$$

[5] The continuous latent construct may represent underlying latent utility, some kind of propensity, or strength of preference (Greene and Hensher 2010).

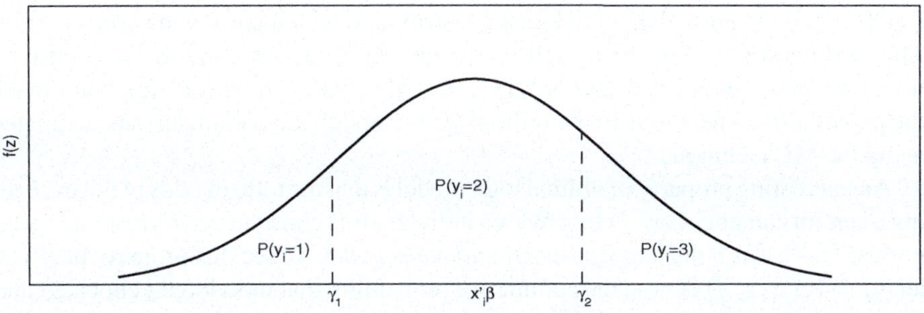

Fig. 2.2 The two cut-points (γ_1, γ_2) divide the area under the curve into three parts, with each part representing the probability of a response falling in the three response categories. The three probabilities $\text{P}(y_i = 1)$, $\text{P}(y_i = 2)$, and $\text{P}(y_i = 3)$ correspond to "oppose legalization," "legal only for medical use," and "legal for personal use," respectively. Note that for each individual i the mean $x_i'\beta$ will be different and so will be the category probabilities. *Source* Authors' creation

where $-\infty = \gamma_0 < \gamma_1 \cdots < \gamma_{J-1} < \gamma_J = \infty$ are the cut-points (or thresholds) and y_i is assumed to have J categories or outcomes. A visual representation of the outcome probabilities (for the case of marijuana legalization) and the cut-points are presented in Fig. 2.2. One may observe from Fig. 2.2 that different combinations of (β, γ) can produce the same outcome probabilities giving rise to parameter identification problem. We therefore need to anchor the location and scale of the distribution to identify the model parameters. The former is achieved by setting $\gamma_1 = 0$ and the latter by assuming $\text{var}(\epsilon_i) = 1$. Other identification schemes are possible and the reader is referred to Jeliazkov et al. (2008) and Jeliazkov and Rahman (2012) for details.

Given a data vector $y = (y_1, \cdots, y_n)'$, the likelihood for the ordinal probit model expressed as a function of unknown parameters (β, γ) is the following:

$$L(\beta, \gamma; y) = \prod_{i=1}^{n} \prod_{j=1}^{J} \Pr(y_i = j|\beta, \gamma)^{I(y_i=j)} = \prod_{i=1}^{n} \prod_{j=1}^{J} \Big[\Phi(\gamma_j - x_i'\beta) - \Phi(\gamma_{j-1} - x_i'\beta) \Big]^{I(y_i=j)}, \tag{2.6}$$

where $\Phi(\cdot)$ is the *cdf* of a standard normal distribution and $I(y_i = j)$ is an indicator function, which equals 1 if the condition within parenthesis is true and 0 otherwise. The parameter estimates for (β, γ) are obtained by maximizing the log-likelihood, i.e., logarithm of the likelihood given by Eq. (2.6), either using the Newton–Raphson method or BHHH procedure (Train 2009). Once the parameter estimates are available, they may be used to calculate the covariate effects, make predictions or assess model fitting. Interested readers may look into Greene and Hensher (2010) or Johnson and Albert (2000, Chap. 4) for a detailed review of ordinal data modeling.

Similar to binary models, the framework for ordinal probit model can be transformed into an *ordinal logit model* (or *ordered logit model*) by simply assuming that the error follows a logistic distribution (McKelvey and Zavoina 1975; McCullagh 1980). Therefore, for the model in Eq. (2.4), we now assume that $\epsilon_i \sim L(0, 1)$ for

$i = 1, \ldots, n$, where L denotes a logistic distribution with mean 0 and variance $\pi^2/3$. The likelihood for the ordinal logit model has the same structure as Eq. (2.6) with $\Phi(w)$ replaced by $\Lambda(w) = \exp(w)/[1 + \exp(w)]$, where w is the argument inside the parenthesis. Analogous to the ordinal probit model, the parameters are estimated using the ML technique.

An interesting property of ordinal logit model is that the ratio of odds of not exceeding a certain category (say j) for any two individuals is constant across response categories. This earns it the name *proportional odds model*. To see this property in effect, let $\theta_{ij} = \Pr(y_i \leq j)$ denote the cumulative probability that individual i chooses category j or below. For the ordinal logit model, this implies $\theta_{ij} = \exp(\gamma_j - x_i'\beta)/\big[1 + \exp(\gamma_j - x_i'\beta)\big]$, and $\theta_{ij}/(1 - \theta_{ij}) = \exp\big[\gamma_j - x_i'\beta\big]$, where the latter represents the odds for the event $y_i \leq j$. Accordingly, for any two individuals (say 1 and 2), the ratio of odds is

$$\frac{\theta_{1j}/(1 - \theta_{1j})}{\theta_{2j}/(1 - \theta_{2j})} = \exp\big[-(x_1 - x_2)'\beta\big]. \tag{2.7}$$

The odds-ratio presented in Eq. (2.7) does not depend on the response category j and is proportional to $(x_1 - x_2)$ with β being the constant of proportionality.

2.4 Covariate Effects and Model Fitting

In binary and ordinal models, the coefficients do not give covariate effects because the link function is non-linear and non-monotonic. Consequently, we need to calculate the covariate effect for each outcome. Let $x_{\cdot,l}$ be a continuous covariate, then the covariate effect for the i-th observation (or individual) in an ordinal probit model is calculated as

$$\begin{aligned} \frac{\partial \Pr(y_i = j)}{\partial x_{i,l}} &= -\beta_l \left[\phi(\gamma_j - x_i'\beta) - \phi(\gamma_{j-1} - x_i'\beta)\right] \\ &\simeq -\hat{\beta}_l \left[\phi(\hat{\gamma}_j - x_i'\hat{\beta}) - \phi(\hat{\gamma}_{j-1} - x_i'\hat{\beta})\right], \end{aligned} \tag{2.8}$$

where $\phi(\cdot)$ denotes the probability density function (*pdf*) of a standard normal distribution and $(\hat{\beta}, \hat{\gamma})$ are the ML estimates of the parameters (β, γ). The average covariate effect is computed by averaging the covariate effect in Eq. (2.8) across all observations. If the covariate is an indicator variable (say $x_{\cdot,m}$), then the covariate effect for the i-th observation on outcome j $(= 1, \ldots, J)$ is calculated as

$$\begin{aligned} &\Pr(y_i = j | x_{i,-m}, x_{i,m} = 1) - \Pr(y_i = j | x_{i,-m}, x_{i,m} = 0) \\ &= \left[\Phi(\gamma_j - x'^{\dagger}_i\beta) - \Phi(\gamma_{j-1} - x'^{\dagger}_i\beta)\right] - \left[\Phi(\gamma_{j-1} - x'^{\ddagger}_i\beta) - \Phi(\gamma_{j-1} - x'^{\ddagger}_i\beta)\right] \\ &\simeq \left[\Phi(\hat{\gamma}_j - x'^{\dagger}_i\hat{\beta}) - \Phi(\hat{\gamma}_{j-1} - x'^{\dagger}_i\hat{\beta})\right] - \left[\Phi(\hat{\gamma}_{j-1} - x'^{\ddagger}_i\hat{\beta}) - \Phi(\hat{\gamma}_{j-1} - x'^{\ddagger}_i\hat{\beta})\right], \end{aligned} \tag{2.9}$$

where $x_i^{\dagger} = (x_{i,-m}, x_{i,m} = 1)$ and $x_i^{\ddagger} = (x_{i,-m}, x_{i,m} = 0)$. The average covariate effect is calculated by averaging the covariate effect given in Eq. (2.9) across all observations. Note that for ordinal models, the sign of the regression coefficient translates unambiguously into the sign of covariate effect only for the lowest and highest categories of the response variable. Covariate effect for the middle categories cannot be known *a priori*.

For the binary probit models, the expressions for covariate effects simplify because with only two outcomes there is a single cut-point which is fixed at 0. For a continuous variable, the covariate effect is given by the expression

$$\frac{\partial \Pr(y_i = 1)}{\partial x_{i,l}} = \beta_l \, \phi(x_i'\beta) \simeq \hat{\beta}_l \, \phi(x_i'\hat{\beta}), \tag{2.10}$$

and the same for an indicator variable is given by the expression

$$\begin{aligned} &\Pr(y_i = 1|x_{i,-m}, x_{i,m} = 1) - \Pr(y_i = 1|x_{i,-m}, x_{i,m} = 0) \\ &= \Phi(x'^{\dagger}_i\beta) - \Phi(x'^{\ddagger}_i\beta) \simeq \Phi(x'^{\dagger}_i\hat{\beta}) - \Phi(x'^{\ddagger}_i\hat{\beta}), \end{aligned} \tag{2.11}$$

where all the notations have been explained in the previous paragraph. Once again, the average covariate effect is computed by averaging across all observations. While the discussion on covariate effects has considered binary and ordinal probit models because of their implementation in the applications, covariate effects for binary and ordinal logit models can be calculated analogously by replacing the normal *pdf*'s and *cdf*'s with the logistic *pdf*'s and *cdf*'s at appropriate places.

To assess the goodness of model fit, we calculate three measures: likelihood ratio (LR) test statistic, McFadden's R-squared (McFadden 1974), and hit-rate (Johnson and Albert 2000). For the null hypothesis $H_0 : \beta_2 = \ldots = \beta_k = 0$, the LR test statistic λ_{LR} is defined as follows:

$$\lambda_{LR} = -2[\ln L_0 - \ln L_{\text{fit}}] \overset{H_0}{\sim} \chi^2_{k-1}, \tag{2.12}$$

where $\ln L_{\text{fit}}$ is the log-likelihood of the fitted model and $\ln L_0$ is the log-likelihood of the intercept-only model. Under the null hypothesis, λ_{LR} follows a chi-square distribution with degrees of freedom equal to $k - 1$, i.e., the number of restrictions under the null hypothesis. So, we calculate the statistic λ_{LR} and compare it with χ^2_{k-1} for a given level of significance. If $\lambda_{LR} > \chi^2_{k-1}$, then we reject the null hypothesis. Otherwise, we do not reject the null hypothesis.

Another popular goodness-of-fit measure for discrete choice models is McFadden's R-squared (R^2_M), due to McFadden (1974). The McFadden's R-squared, also referred to as pseudo-R-squared or likelihood ratio index, is defined as follows:

$$R^2_M = 1 - \frac{\ln L_{\text{fit}}}{\ln L_0}. \tag{2.13}$$

The R_M^2 is intuitively appealing because it is bounded between 0 and 1, similar to the coefficient of determination (R^2) in linear regression models. When all slope coefficients are zero, the R_M^2 equals zero, but in discrete choice models R_M^2 can never equal 1, although it can come close to 1. While higher values of R_M^2 imply better fit, the value as such has no natural interpretation in sharp contrast to R^2 which denotes the proportion of variation in the dependent variable explained by the covariates.

While both LR test statistic and McFadden's R-squared are commonly used in applied studies, the hit-rate is relatively uncommon. The hit-rate (HR) is defined as the percentage of correct predictions, i.e., percentage of observations for which the model correctly assigns the highest probability to the observed response category. Mathematically, the HR can be defined as follows:

$$HR = \frac{1}{n}\sum_{i=1}^{n} I\left(\left(\max_{j}\,\{\hat{p}_{ij}\}_{j=1}^{J}\right) = y_i\right), \tag{2.14}$$

where $\hat{p}_{ij}$ is the predicted probability that individual i selects outcome j, and $I(\cdot)$ is the indicator function as defined earlier.

2.5 Some Advances in Discrete Choice Modeling

Till now, we have looked at binary and ordinal models and their Classical (or Frequentist) approach to estimation via the maximum likelihood technique, which only involves the likelihood function (say $L(\theta; y) \equiv f(y|\theta)$, where θ is the parameter vector). The Classical approach assumes that model parameters are unknown but have fixed values and hence the parameters cannot be treated as random variables. In contrast, Bayesian approach to estimation utilizes the Bayes' theorem,

$$\pi(\theta|y) = \frac{f(y|\theta)\pi(\theta)}{\int f(y|\theta)\pi(\theta)\, d\theta},$$

to update the belief/information about θ (considered a random variable) by combining information from the observed sample (via the likelihood function) and non-sample or prior beliefs (arising from previous studies, theoretical consideration, researcher's belief, etc.) represented by the prior distribution $\pi(\theta)$. Inference is based on the posterior distribution $\pi(\theta|y)$. Bayesian approach provides several advantages including finite sample inference, working with likelihoods which are difficult to evaluate, and advantages in computation. Interested readers may look into Greenberg (2012) for details on the Bayesian approach and Poirier (1995) for a comparison of Classical and Bayesian estimation methods.

The posterior density for binary and ordinal models does not have a tractable density and so the parameters cannot be sampled directly. While the Metropolis–Hastings (MH) algorithm (Metropolis et al. 1953; Hastings 1970) can be employed to sample the parameters, the standard and more convenient approach is to consider *data augmentation* (Tanner and Wong 1987). In this approach, the joint posterior density is augmented by a latent variable z and the augmented joint posterior $\pi(\theta, z|y)$ is written as

$$\pi(\theta, z|y) \propto \pi(\theta) f(z, y|\theta) = \pi(\theta) f(z|\theta) f(y|z, \theta).$$

For a binary probit model, $\theta = \beta$ and $f(y|z, \beta) \equiv f(y|z)$, whereas for an ordinal probit model $\theta = (\beta, \gamma)$ and $f(y|z, \beta, \gamma) \equiv f(y|z, \gamma)$. The two equivalencies arise because, given a latent observation z_i, y_i is known with certainty regardless of β for $i = 1, \ldots, n$. This de-linking of the likelihood function from β, made possible through data augmentation, simplifies the estimation procedure and allows sampling of β through a Gibbs process (Geman and Geman 1984)—a well-known Markov chain Monte Carlo (MCMC) technique. The latent variable z is sampled element-wise from a truncated normal distribution. For ordinal models, a monotone transformation of the cut-points, γ, is sampled using an MH algorithm. The MCMC algorithms for estimating binary and ordinal probit models outlined here were introduced in Albert and Chib (1993). Other notable references that describe the Bayesian modeling and estimation of binary and ordinal outcomes in great detail include Johnson and Albert (2000), Greenberg (2012), and Jeliazkov and Rahman (2012). Bayesian estimation of logit model is based on the same principle and presented in Holmes and Held (2006) and Jeliazkov and Rahman (2012).

The binary and ordinal models considered in this chapter, whether estimated using the Classical or the Bayesian techniques, provide information on the average probability of outcomes conditional on the covariates. However, interest on quantiles of the response variable as a robust alternative to mean regression has grown enormously since the introduction of quantile regression in Koenker and Bassett (1978). Quantile modeling gained further momentum with the development of Bayesian quantile regression by Yu and Moyeed (2001), where the authors create a working likelihood by assuming that the errors follow an asymmetric Laplace (AL) distribution (Yu and Zhang 2005). Binary quantile regression was proposed by Kordas (2006) and its Bayesian formulation was presented by Benoit and Poel (2010). Rahman (2016) introduced Bayesian quantile regression with ordinal responses and estimated the model using MCMC techniques. The corresponding R package *bqror* for estimating the quantile ordinal model is described in Maheshwari and Rahman (2023) along with the computation of marginal likelihood for comparing alternative quantile models. A flexible form of Bayesian ordinal quantile regression was proposed in Rahman and Karnawat (2019). Some recent researches on binary quantile regression in the panel/longitudinal set up include Rahman and Vossmeyer (2019) and Bresson et al. (2021). Two applied studies employing binary and ordinal quantile framework are Ojha and Rahman (2021) and Omata et al. (2017), respectively. Interested readers may explore the above-mentioned papers and references therein to develop a thorough understanding on binary and ordinal quantile modeling and their applications.

2.6 Applications: Public Opinion on Legalization of Marijuana in the United States

In the US, marijuana is illegal under the federal law as per the Controlled Substances Act of 1970. The Act classifies marijuana as a schedule I drug, i.e., a drug with no accepted medical value, high potential for abuse, and not safe to use even under medical supervision (Drug Enforcement Administration 2011). However, state laws pertaining to marijuana have evolved overtime. Up until 2016, 29 states had either legalized, allowed access for medical reasons or decriminalized its use (see Fig. 2.3). More legalization efforts are appearing in the remaining states of US. Such revisions in state laws represent a change in public attitude that is aptly reflected in survey data collected by independent polling agencies such as the Pew Research Center, General Social Survey and Gallup. Figure 2.4 shows an increasing trend in favor of legalizing marijuana based on public opinion. Besides, political standing on marijuana has also popularized the debate on its legalization and may have affected public opinion regarding it. The gradual growth in support of marijuana perhaps signals better public insight on the medicinal value of marijuana (Earleywine 2005) and the social cost of prohibition that includes illegal trade, racially skewed arrests of African Americans, and huge enforcement cost (Shepard and Blackley 2007).

While policies on marijuana use are in the early stages of formulation as states evaluate its costs and benefits (Winterbourne 2012), more states decriminalizing its use may cause a major policy shift at the federal level (Ferner 2015). In this regard,

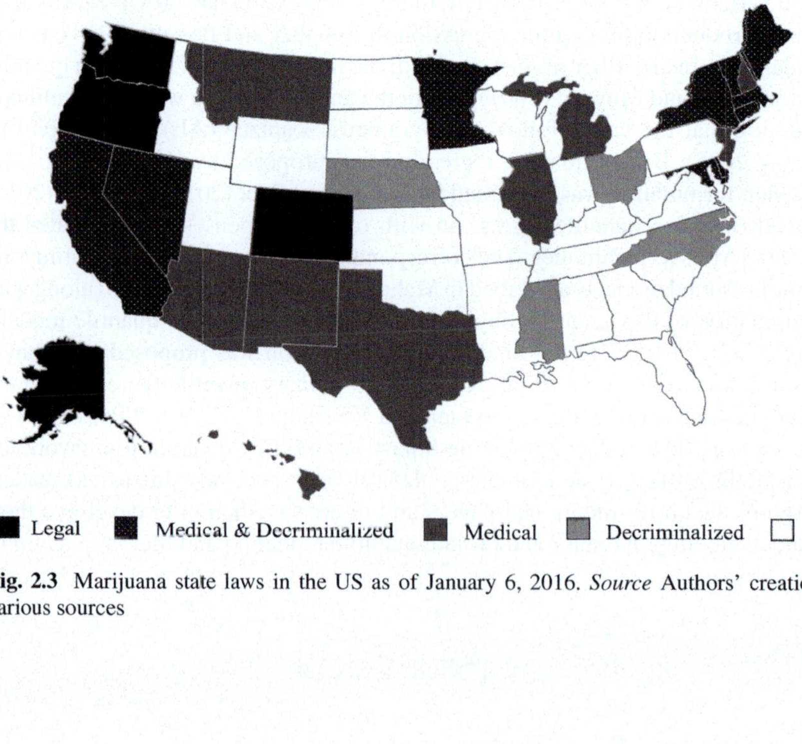

Fig. 2.3 Marijuana state laws in the US as of January 6, 2016. *Source* Authors' creation from various sources

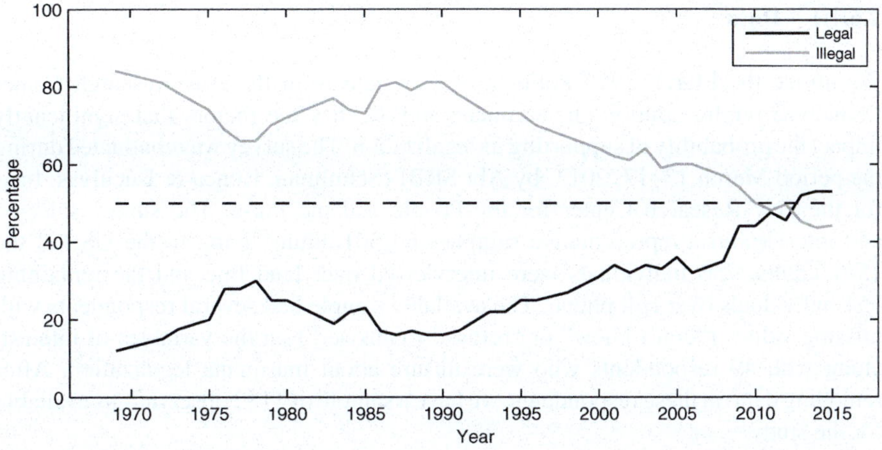

Fig. 2.4 Public opinion on marijuana legalization for the period 1969–2015. The black dashed line is the 50% benchmark. Data source: Pew Research Center, General Social Survey and Gallup. We have averaged the percentages for years with multiple surveys. The combined percentage of the two opinions is below 100 since on average 4% of respondents answered "don't know" or "refused to answer"

some scholars argue that public policies ought to be guided by public opinion such that mass opinion and democracy is upheld (Monroe 1998; Paletz et al. 2015). Besides, Shapiro (2011) cites a large number of studies to argue that public opinion influences government policy-making in the US. Therefore, it is imperative to study and identify the factors that significantly impact US public opinion toward marijuana legalization.

In the next section, we employ a binary probit model to analyze public opinion on marijuana legalization and thereafter implement the ordinal probit model to analyze public opinion on the extent of marijuana legalization. The choice of probit models over their logit counterparts is driven by practical considerations—probit models are tractable in univariate cases and can be generalized to multivariate and hierarchical settings (Jeliazkov et al. 2008). In contrast, logistic model based on logistic distribution cannot model correlations in multivariate settings.

2.6.1 Binary Probit Model—Marijuana Legalization

In this subsection, we summarize the March 2013 Political Survey data used for the study, estimate a binary probit model, present the results, model fitting diagnostics, and covariate effects.

2.6.1.1 Data

We utilize the March 2013 Political Survey data from the Pew Research Center to analyze public opinion on marijuana and identify the factors that significantly impact the probability of supporting its legalization. The survey was conducted during the period March 13–17, 2013, by Abt SRBI (Schulman, Ronca & Buculvas, Inc.) for the Pew Research Center for the People and the Press. The survey selected and interviewed a representative sample of 1,501 adults living in the US. Of the 1501 adults, 750 individuals were interviewed over land line and the remaining 751 individuals over cell phone. The available sample had several respondents with missing values ("don't know" or "refused to answer") on the variables of interest, along with 49 respondents who were unsure about marijuana legalization. After removing data on these respondents, we have a sample of 1182 observations available for the study.[6]

In this application, the dependent variable is the response to the question: "Do you think the use of marijuana should be made legal, or not?". The responses were recorded as "yes, legal" (i.e., favor legalization), "no, illegal" (i.e., oppose legalization), or "don't know or refused". We remove the last category as it constitutes missing responses. This makes the response variable binary and hence a binary probit model is utilized to analyze the response based on the following set of covariates: age, income, household size, past use of marijuana, gender, education, state of residence, race, party affiliation, and religion.

Age was recorded in years. Income (measured in US Dollars) was reported as belonging to 1 of 9 groups (0–10k, 10k–20k, $\cdots$, 40k–50k, 50k–75k, 75k–100k, 100k–150k, 150k, and above, where "k" denotes thousand). We convert income to a continuous variable by taking the mid-point of the first 8 income groups and impute 150k for the last group. Household size represents the number of members in the family. Past use of marijuana and gender are indicator variables in the model. Educational attainment of the respondents is classified into three categories and the category "high school and below" forms the base or reference category in the regressions. The variable "tolerant states" indicates if a respondent lives in 1 of the 20 states, where recreational usage is legal, possession is decriminalized and/or allowed for medical use only.[7] Race is classified into three categories and "White" race is used as the base category. The category "Other Races" comprises Asian, Hispanic, native American, Pacific Islanders, and remaining races. Party affiliation is also classified into three categories and Republican Party is used as the reference category. Religion is classified into five categories and "Protestant" is used as the base category. Here, the category "Conservative" comprises of respondents belonging to one of the following

[6] The data file ("Mar13Data.xlsx") and MATLAB codes file ("ProbitScript.m") for estimation and post-estimation constructs can be downloaded from the corresponding author's webpage: https://www.arshadrahman.com/Research.html.

[7] The list of tolerant states before the date of the survey includes Alaska, Arizona, California, Colorado, Connecticut, Delaware, Hawaii, Maine, Maryland, Massachusetts, Michigan, Montana, Nevada, New Jersey, New Mexico, Oregon, Rhode Island, Vermont, Washington, Washington DC. Source: https://www.whitehouse.gov/ondcp/state-laws-related-to-marijuana.

Table 2.1 Descriptive summary of the variables (March 2013 Political Survey)

Variable		Mean	Std.
Log age		3.86	0.40
Log income		10.64	0.98
Household size		2.72	1.44
	Category	Counts	Percentage
Past use		554	46.87
Male		570	48.22
Education	Bachelors and above	426	36.04
	Below bachelors	360	30.46
	High school and below	396	33.50
Tolerant states		374	31.64
Race	White	938	79.36
	African American	142	12.01
	Other races	102	8.63
Party affiliation	Republican	353	29.86
	Democrat	404	34.18
	Independent and others	425	35.96
Religion	Protestant	494	41.79
	Roman catholic	258	21.83
	Christian	138	11.68
	Conservative	72	6.09
	Liberal	220	18.61
Public opinion	Favor legalization	622	52.62
	Oppose legalization	560	47.38

religions: Buddhist, Hindu, Islam, Jew, Mormon, and orthodox church. The category "Liberal" comprises respondents who claim to be Agnostic, Atheist, Universalist, or nothing in particular. The descriptive statistics for all the variables are presented in Table 2.1.

Let us now look at the socio-demographic characteristics of a typical respondent in the sample. An average respondent is about 51 years old and s/he belongs to a household of size 3 with an annual income of 60,527 US Dollars. The sample is almost evenly split between males and females and 46.87% of respondents have a history of marijuana use. In the sample, the largest proportion of respondents (36.04%) have "bachelors and above" degree, followed by "below bachelors" degree (30.46%). A significant fraction of the respondents (31.64%) reside in states that have some favorable laws toward marijuana. The sample is predominantly White (79.36%) with a good representation (12.01%) of the African American population. Among the respondents, almost 30% consider themselves as Republican, about 34% declare themselves as Democrats and the remaining are Independent or belong to other parties. With respect to religious codification, the largest proportion (41.79%) is Protestants, followed by Roman Catholics (21.83%). A good proportion, 11.68%, declare themselves to be simply Christian. The Liberal category forms about 18.61% and the Conservatives have the lowest fraction at 6.09%.

2.6.1.2 Estimation

We estimate four different binary probit models and present the estimated coefficients and standard errors for each model in Table 2.2. To begin with, Model 1 considers a basic set of covariates that includes log age, income, past use of marijuana, gender, education categories, household size, and state of residence of the respondents. Subsequent models generalize Model 1 by adding more variables to the basic set of regressors. Specifically, Model 2 adds the race variable, Model 3 adds party affiliation to the list of variables in Model 2, and Model 4 incorporates religious denomination to the regressors in Model 3. A look at the model fitting measures in Table 2.2 reveal that all the four models have high LR statistic (see Eq. (2.12) in Sect. 2.4). Consequently, we reject the null hypothesis that the coefficients are jointly zero in each model. The two other goodness-of-fit statistics, McFadden's R^2 and hit-rate (defined in Eqs. (2.13) and (2.14), respectively), also show that all models provide a good fit, with each subsequent model providing a better fit than the previous model. For the best fitting model, i.e., Model 4, McFadden's R^2 is 0.15 and hit-rate is 69.03%. The latter implies that Model 4 correctly predicts more than 69% of the outcomes.

2.6.1.3 Results

We focus on the results from Model 4, since it provides the best model fit. Table 2.2 shows that log age has a negative coefficient and is statistically significant at 5% level.[8] This implies that young people are more supportive of marijuana legalization. This is not surprising since risk taking or deviant behavior is high among the younger population and is well documented in the literature (Brown et al. 1974). Moreover, Saieva (2008) reports a negative association between age and probability of supporting legalization, while Alfonso and Dunn (2007) and Delforterie et al. (2015) note that marijuana prevalence rate is higher among the younger population.

The coefficient for income is negative, but statistically insignificant as also documented in Nielsen (2007) and Saieva (2008). As such, we do not find a significant relationship between income and probability of supporting marijuana legalization. This is in disagreement with the hypothesis that economically weaker section will support legalization since marijuana is popular within the lower income group. Past use of marijuana may drive support for legalization, but this was not controlled either in Nielsen (2007) or Saieva (2008). Controlling for this variable in our models, we

[8] The default significance level is 5% and henceforth reference to significance level will be omitted.

Table 2.2 Estimation results for the binary probit model

	Model 1		Model 2		Model 3		Model 4	
	COEF	SE	COEF	SE	COEF	SE	COEF	SE
Intercept	1.74**	0.61	1.70**	0.64	0.11	0.66	0.51	0.69
Log age	–0.41**	0.11	–0.41**	0.11	–0.39**	0.11	–0.29**	0.12
Log income	–0.06	0.05	–0.06	0.05	–0.02	0.05	–0.03	0.05
Past use	0.81**	0.08	0.82**	0.08	0.82**	0.08	0.81**	0.08
Male	0.18**	0.08	0.17**	0.08	0.21**	0.08	0.17**	0.08
Bachelors and above	0.23**	0.10	0.23**	0.10	0.23**	0.11	0.21*	0.11
Below bachelors	0.19*	0.10	0.19*	0.10	0.24**	0.10	0.26**	0.10
Household size	–0.04	0.03	–0.05	0.03	–0.04	0.03	–0.03	0.03
Tolerant states	0.13	0.08	0.12	0.08	0.12	0.08	0.08	0.09
African American	..	..	–0.05	0.12	–0.26**	0.13	–0.14	0.13
Other races	..	..	0.12	0.14	0.03	0.14	0.02	0.15
Democrat	..	..	..	..	0.68**	0.10	0.57**	0.11
Other parties	..	..	..	..	0.48**	0.10	0.40**	0.10
Roman catholic	..	..	..	..	..	..	0.18*	0.10
Christian	..	..	..	..	..	..	–0.06	0.13
Conservative	..	..	..	..	..	..	0.44**	0.18
Liberal	..	..	..	..	..	..	0.66**	0.12
LR (χ^2) statistic	164.37		165.38		211.44		248.55	
Mcfadden's R^2	0.10		0.10		0.13		0.15	
Hit-rate	66.67		66.58		67.51		69.03	

$**\ p < 0.05$, $*\ p < 0.10$

find that the coefficient for past use is largest among all variables and highly significant. This finding provides support to the hypothesis that individuals who have used marijuana in the past strongly favor its legalization and the large coefficient value implies that past use is an important factor in favoring legalization. The coefficient for male is positive and significant, indicating that males are more supportive of legalizing marijuana as compared to females, a result also supported by Nielsen (2007) and Delforterie et al. (2015). Similarly, Rodríguez (2015) finds that boys are more likely to use marijuana during their adolescent years. Since past use is an important determinant for supporting legalization and marijuana use is more prevalent among males, it is not surprising to find that males are more supportive of legalization.

The indicator variables for higher education, i.e., "bachelors and above" and "below bachelors" have positive coefficients and are statistically significant (either at 10% or 5% significance level) relative to the base category, "high school and below". Thus, higher education leads to increased support for legalization possibly because a more educated individual can better understand the costs and medicinal benefits of marijuana. However, some studies have found that early use of marijuana leads to lower educational attainment and poor performance in school (Lynskey and Hall 2000; Van Ours and Williams 2009; Horwood et al. 2010). Household size has a negative effect, but the coefficient is not statistically significant. Similarly, the coefficient for "tolerant states" is positive, but insignificant. This implies that residing in 1 of 20 states that offers some relaxation on marijuana use/offence does not statistically increase the probability of supporting legalization.

The coefficient for African American and "Other Races" is not statistically different from the base category, White, with the exception of Model 3. The negative coefficient for African American, although insignificant, is rather surprising because one would expect African Americans to support legalization in order to curtail the large number of marijuana-related arrests from the African American community. In line with this, Chen and Killeya-Jones (2006) also examine the extent of marijuana use across race and find that marijuana use is higher among suburban White students compared to their African American counterparts. Moreover, Nasim et al. (2007) document the cultural orientation for African American young women and find that traditional religious beliefs and practices could be the reason behind less marijuana usage among African American.

Political affiliation often represents ideological differences toward any public policy and several poll studies conducted by Pew and Gallup have found that Republicans (Democrats) are more likely to oppose (favor) legalization of marijuana. We also arrive at a similar conclusion, with the coefficients for Democrat and "Other Parties" being positive and significant. This suggests that individuals having either political orientations are more supportive of legalization compared to Republicans and the result is consistent with Nielsen (2007). Lastly, we look at the effect of religious affiliations since religious beliefs sometime act as a protective factor against alcohol usage and smoking. The results show that the coefficient for Roman Catholic is positive and statistically significant at 10%, while coefficient for Christian is negative but statistically insignificant. In contrast, the coefficients for Conservative and Liberal are both positive and statistically significant and hence both groups are more supportive of legalization compared to Protestants. However, individual opinions often do not strictly adhere to religious codes and conducts, so these results may vary significantly across samples.

The above discussion suggests that the signs of the coefficients, except the race variables, are consistent with what one would typically expect. However, the coefficients by themselves do not give the covariate effects (see Sects. 2.2 and 2.3). Table 2.3 presents the average covariate effects for all significant variables, either at 5% or 10% level. Results show that an increase in age by 10 years decreases the probability of support by 1.9%. The highest positive impact comes from past use, which shows that an individual who has used marijuana is 28.5% more likely to support legalization

Table 2.3 Average covariate effects from Model 4

Covariate	ΔP (favor legalization)
Age, 10 years	–0.019
Past use	0.285
Male	0.057
Bachelors and above	0.068
Below bachelors	0.085
Democrat	0.188
Other parties	0.134
Roman Catholic	0.058
Conservative	0.143
Liberal	0.220

relative to someone who has never used it. Males are 5.7% more likely to support legalization relative to females. Higher education increases the probability of support and an individual with bachelors or higher degree (below bachelors) is 6.8 (8.5)% more likely to support legalization relative to an individual with a high school degree or below. Political affiliation to the Democratic Party increases the probability of support by 18.8%. Similarly, an individual who identifies themselves with Independent and other parties is 13.4% more likely to support legalization compared to a Republican. Finally, an individual who is Conservative (Liberal) is 14.3 (22)% more likely to support legalization relative to a Protestant.

2.6.2 Ordinal Probit Model—The Extent of Marijuana Legalization

The year 2013 was the first year in four decades that majority of Americans favored legalization of marijuana. While its support has grown overtime as shown in Fig. 2.4, it is important to distinguish between different levels of support. This distinction is crucial because support for personal use of marijuana is stronger than support for its medical use and has different policy implications. Individuals may opine to support marijuana for medicinal benefits, but not for personal use. The February 2014 Political Survey recorded individual response as a three-level categorical variable, which permits use of an ordinal probit model to study the effect of covariates on public opinion about the extent of legalization.

2.6.2.1 Data

The February 2014 Political Survey was conducted during February 14–23, 2014 by the Princeton Survey Research Associates and sponsored by the Pew Research Center for the People and the Press. In the survey, a representative sample of 1,821 adults living in the US were interviewed over telephone with 481 (1,340) individuals interviewed over land line (cell phone, including 786 individuals without a land line phone). The sampled data contain several missing observations and many respondents were unsure about their opinion on legalization. As before, we remove data on these respondents and are left with a sample of 1,492 observations for the study.[9]

The dependent variable in the model is the respondents' answer to the question, "Which comes closer to your view about the use of marijuana by adults?". The options provided were "It should not be legal," "It should be legal only for medicinal use," or "It should be legal for personal use." The fourth category labeled, "Don't know/Refused" is removed from the study. Similar to the March 2013 Survey, the February 2014 Survey also collected information on the age, income, household size, past use, gender, education, race, party affiliation, and religion. We use these variables as independent variables in the models. All the definitions and categories for the variables remain the same as in Sect. 2.6.1.1. We also include the indicator variable "tolerant states," with the definition modified to include Illinois and New Hampshire to the previous list of 20 states.[10] Finally, we include an additional variable, labeled "eventually legal," for which data was collected only in the February 2014 Survey. This variable indicates whether respondents expect marijuana to be legal irrespective of their individual opinion. We present the descriptive statistics for all the variables in Table 2.4.

Upon exploration of the socio-demographic characteristics of the current sample, we note that an average respondent is about 45.5 years old and s/he belongs to a household of size 3 with an annual income of 60,647 US Dollars. Thus, the typical respondent is about 6 years younger compared to the March 2013 data and approximately has the same household size and income. The percentage of males is higher in the current sample by 5%, but still close to a fair split between males and females. Similarly, the sample is almost evenly split between respondents who have used marijuana and those who have not. The largest proportion of respondents (36.93%) have "bachelors and above" degree, followed by "high school and below" degree (33.98%). A significant fraction of the respondents (37.27%) reside in states that have some favorable law on marijuana. Looking at the additional variable "eventually legal," note that 77.35% of the surveyed people expect marijuana to be legal irrespective of their opinion. Similar to the earlier data, the sample is predominantly White (77.01%) with a good representation (13.54%) of the African American

---

[9] The data file ("Feb14Data.xlsx") and MATLAB codes file ("OrdinalProbitScript.m") for estimation and post-estimation constructs are available at: https://www.arshadrahman.com/Research.html.

[10] Note that marijuana-related laws were passed in Illinois and New Hampshire after the March 2013 Political Survey, but before the February 2014 Political Survey.

Table 2.4 Descriptive summary of the variables (February 2014 Political Survey)

Variable		Mean	Std.
Log age		3.72	0.44
Log income		10.63	0.98
Household size		2.74	1.42
	Category	Counts	Percentage
Past use		719	48.19
Male		792	53.02
Education	Bachelors and above	551	36.93
	Below bachelors	434	29.09
	High school and below	507	33.98
Tolerant states		556	37.27
Eventually legal		1,154	77.35
Race	White	1149	77.01
	African American	202	13.54
	Other races	141	9.45
Party affiliation	Republican	333	22.32
	Democrat	511	34.25
	Independent and others	648	43.43
Religion	Protestant	550	36.86
	Roman Catholic	290	19.44
	Christian	182	12.20
	Conservative	122	8.18
	Liberal	348	23.32
Public opinion	Oppose legalization	218	14.61
	Legal only for medicinal use	640	42.90
	Legal for personal use	634	42.49

population. Party affiliation shows that 34.25% of the sample is comprised of Democrats, 22.32% Republicans, and the remaining fraction are "independent and others." With respect to religious classifications, the largest proportion of respondents are Protestant (36.86%), followed by Liberal (23.32%) and Roman Catholics (19.44%).

2.6.2.2 Estimation

The ordinal probit model results are presented in Table 2.5, which show the coefficient estimates and standard errors of four different models. The estimation of models follows a similar sequence as in Table 2.2. Model 5 is the base model and contains log age, log income, past use of marijuana, male, education categories, household size, tolerant states, and eventually legal. Model 6 adds the race categories to Model 5 and

Table 2.5 Estimation results for the ordinal probit model

	Model 5		Model 6		Model 7		Model 8	
	COEF	SE	COEF	SE	COEF	SE	COEF	SE
Intercept	1.26**	0.44	1.27**	0.45	0.83*	0.46	0.34	0.48
Log age	–0.44**	0.07	–0.45**	0.07	–0.45**	0.08	–0.35**	0.08
Log income	0.07*	0.03	0.07*	0.03	0.08**	0.03	0.09**	0.04
Past use	0.74**	0.06	0.73**	0.06	0.71**	0.06	0.69**	0.06
Male	0.06	0.06	0.06	0.06	0.07	0.06	0.06	0.06
Bachelors and above	0.26	0.08	0.26**	0.08	0.25**	0.08	0.24**	0.08
Below bachelors	0.06	0.08	0.05*	0.08	0.05	0.08	0.05	0.08
Household size	–0.04*	0.02	–0.04	0.02	–0.03	0.02	–0.02	0.02
Tolerant states	0.11*	0.06	0.13**	0.06	0.09	0.06	0.07	0.07
Eventually legal	0.58**	0.07	0.58**	0.07	0.56**	0.07	0.57**	0.07
African American	..	..	0.11	0.09	–0.01	0.10	0.03	0.10
Other races	..	..	–0.18*	0.11	–0.26**	0.11	–0.27**	0.11
Democrat	..	..	..	..	0.48**	0.09	0.44**	0.09
Other parties	..	..	..	..	0.40**	0.08	0.36**	0.08
Roman catholic	..	..	..	..	..	..	0.10	0.09
Christian	..	..	..	..	..	..	0.16	0.10
Conservative	..	..	..	..		..	0.09	0.12
Liberal	..	..	..	..	..	..	0.39**	0.09
Cut-point	1.43**	0.05	1.43**	0.05	1.45**	0.05	1.46**	0.05
LR (χ^2) statistic	316.27		321.47		356.99		377.02	
Mcfadden's R^2	0.10		0.11		0.12		0.12	
Hit-rate	57.77		57.44		59.11		58.91	

$** \ p < 0.05$, $* \ p < 0.10$

Model 7 adds party affiliation to the list of variables in Model 6. Finally, Model 8 contains all the variables in Model 7 and religious categories. The goodness-of-fit statistics are presented in the last three rows of Table 2.5. The LR statistics are large and each model fits better than the respective intercept model. The other two measures, McFadden's R^2 and hit-rate (defined in Eqs. (2.13) and (2.14), respectively), show that Model 7 and Model 8 outperform the remaining two models. Model 8 provides a better fit compared to Model 7 as per McFadden's R^2 (0.1187 compared to 0.1254), whereas Model 7 has a marginally better hit-rate compared to Model 8 (59.11% as opposed 58.91%). So, the model correctly predicts approximately 60% of observed outcomes.

2.6.2.3 Results

We focus on the results from Model 8 because it is the most general model, provides the best fit according to McFadden's R^2, and no variables change sign. The results indicate that log age has a negative effect on the support for personal use (third category) and is statistically significant at 5% level. Alternatively, log age has a positive effect on opposing legalization (first category) and is statistically significant. However, the effect of age on medicinal use only (second category) cannot be determined *a priori*. Henceforth, we shall only discuss the effect on personal use and the impact on opposing legalization will be opposite to that of personal use. As before, the default level of significance used is 5% and further discussion will omit reference to significance level.

We note that the coefficient for log income is positive and statistically significant. This implies that individuals with higher income are more likely to support legalization for personal use. Past use of marijuana has a statistically significant positive effect on the probability of supporting personal use of marijuana. Moreover, the coefficient for past use is largest among all the variables, a result which is similar to that obtained in the binary probit model. Contrary to the finding in Sect. 2.6.1.3, the coefficient for male is positive, but is not statistically significant. Thus, the current data do not confirm any role of gender on public opinion toward marijuana. Higher education is positively associated with support for personal use of marijuana. However, only the coefficient for "bachelors degree and above" is statistically significant. The coefficients for household size and "tolerant states" are not significant and conform to the results from the binary probit model. We find that "eventually legal" has a significant positive effect, indicating that if an individual expects marijuana to be legal irrespective of his or her opinion, then s/he is more likely to support legalization for personal use.

The race variables suggest that opinions of African Americans on personal use of marijuana are not significantly different compared to the Whites. Such a similarity of opinions across race was also observed in the binary probit model. In contrast, "Other Races" has a significant negative coefficient and is more opposed to legalization as compared to Whites. The coefficients for political party affiliations are in consonance with the results from Sect. 2.6.1.3. Affiliation to Democratic Party or "Other Parties" increases the support for personal use and the coefficients are significant. Lastly, religious affiliations do not show a strong effect. Here, only the Liberals are more supportive of personal use of marijuana, while the opinions of the remaining religious categories are not significantly different from the base category, Protestant.

We mentioned in Sect. 2.3 that the coefficients of the ordinal probit model only give the direction of impact for the first and last categories, but not the remaining categories. The actual covariate effects need to be calculated for all the categories. We

Table 2.6 Average covariate effects from Model 8

Covariate	ΔP (not legal)	ΔP (medicinal use)	ΔP (personal use)
Age, 10 years	0.015	0.012	–0.028
Income, $10,000	–0.005	–0.003	0.008
Past use	–0.129	–0.113	0.243
Bachelors and above	–0.045	–0.035	0.080
Eventually legal	–0.126	–0.060	0.186
Other races	0.059	0.031	–0.089
Democrat	–0.080	–0.066	0.147
Other parties	–0.070	–0.051	0.121
Liberal	–0.068	–0.066	0.134

compute the average covariate effects for all significant variables and present them in Table 2.6. From the table, note that past use, eventually legal, and identifying oneself as a Democrat are three variables with the highest impact on public opinion. Past use of marijuana increases support for personal use by 24.3% and decreases the support for medicinal use and oppose legalization by 11.3% and 12.9%, respectively. Similarly, a respondent who expects marijuana to be legal is 18.6% more likely to support marijuana for personal use. This increase comes from a decrease in probability for medicinal use and oppose legalization, which are 6.0% and 12.6%, respectively. In the same way, a respondent who is a Democrat is 14.7% more likely to favor personal use, and 6.6% and 8.0% less likely to favor medicinal use and oppose legalization, respectively. The covariate effects for the remaining variables can be interpreted similarly.

2.7 Concluding Remarks

This chapter presents an overview of two discrete choice models, namely, binary and ordinal probit models which are prevalent in different disciplines including economics, finance, and sociology. We use the binary and ordinal probit models as prototypes to derive the likelihood and outline the estimation procedure, but the approach is general and applicable to its logit counterparts. Some interesting aspects about interpreting the coefficients of logit models are emphasized. Since discrete choice models are non-linear, the coefficients do not represent covariate effects. We explain how to compute the covariate effects with continuous and binary (indicator) variables. Three model fitting measures, namely, likelihood ratio statistic, McFadden's R-squared, and hit-rate are also described. After the theoretical discussion, the models are employed in two applications on marijuana legalization in the United States.

In the first application, a probit model is employed to analyze public response to legalization ("oppose legalization" or "favor legalization") based on a host of individual and socio-economic variables. Data is taken from the March 2013 Political Survey collected by the Pew Research Center. The results show that age has a negative effect, but variables such as past marijuana use, male gender, and higher education have a positive effect on supporting legalization. Interestingly, past use of marijuana has the highest positive effect and increases the probability of support by 28.5%. In the second study, an ordinal probit model is employed to analyze ordered response to legalization ("oppose legalization," "legal for medicinal use," or "legal for personal use") using the February 2014 Political Survey data collected by the Pew Research Center. The results show that log age and "Other Races" (non-White and non-African American) negatively (positively) affect the probability of supporting personal use (oppose legalization) and the latter has the highest negative effect at 8.9%. Variables such as income, belief about legalization, and indicators for past use of marijuana, bachelors and above education, and affiliation to Democratic Party have a positive (negative) effect on personal use (oppose legalization). Among all variables, past use of marijuana has the highest positive effect on personal use at 24.3%.

The insights from these studies may assist policy-makers to better assess public preference regarding marijuana legalization (particularly, medical marijuana) and the factors associated with such preferences. For instance, our finding that higher education increases support for legalization implies that providing information on the medicinal findings on marijuana and emphasizing college and university education is likely to increase support for it. Our findings may also be helpful to various advocacy groups engaged in promoting or opposing unrestricted legalization of marijuana. A clear understanding of the underlying factors that drive an individual's opinion will help these groups better plan their campaigns. For example, since support for legalization is negatively related with age, groups opposing legalization may consider not campaigning among the youth as it is unlikely to yield support. Similarly, lobbies engaged in opposing legalization may optimize their time use on better possibilities than convince an individual or group with a history of marijuana use to oppose legalization.

References

Abrams DI, Hilton JF, Leiser RJ, Shade SB, Elbeik TA, Aweeka FT, Benowitz NL, Bredt BM, Kosel B, Aberg JA, Deeks SG, Mitchell TF, Mulligan K, Bacchetti P, McCune JM, Schambelan M (2003) Short-term effects of cannabinoids in patients with HIV-1 infection: a randomized, placebo-controlled clinical trial. Ann Intern Med 139(4):258–266

Abrams DI, Jay CA, Shade SB, Vizoso H, Reda H, Press S, Kelly ME, Rowbotham MC, Petersen KL (2007) Cannabis in painful HIV-associated sensory neuropathy. Neurol 68(7):515–521

Albert J, Chib S (1993) Bayesian analysis of binary and polychotomous response data. J Am Stat Assoc 88(422):669–679

Alfonso J, Dunn ME (2007) Differences in the marijuana expectancies of adoloscents in relation to marijuana use. Subst Use Misuse 42(6):1009–1025

Benoit DF, Poel DVD (2010) Binary quantile regression: a Bayesian approach based on the asymmetric Laplace distribution. J Appl Econ 27(7):1174–1188

Berman JS, Symonds C, Birch R (2004) Efficacy of two cannabis based medicinal extracts for relief of central neuropathic pain from brachial plexus avulsion: results of a randomised controlled trial. Pain 112(3):299–306

Bresson G, Lacroix G, Rahman MA (2021) Bayesian panel quantile regression for binary outcomes with correlated random effects: an application on crime recidivism in Canada. Empir Econ 60(1):227–259

Brown JW, Glaser D, Waxer E, Geis G (1974) Turning off: cessation of marijuana use after college. Soc Probl 21(4):527–538

Chen KW, Killeya-Jones LA (2006) Understanding differences in marijuana use among urban black and suburban white high school students from two U.S. community samples. J Ethn Subst Abus 5(2):51–73

Delforterie MJ, Cremers HE, Agrawal A, Lynskey MT, Jak S, Huizink AC (2015) The influence of age and gender on the likelihood of endorsing cannabis abuse/dependence criteria. Addict Behav 42:172–175

Dimock M, Doherty C, Motel S (2013) Majority now supports legalizing marijuana, Pew Research Center. Available: https://www.pewresearch.org/wp-content/uploads/sites/4/legacy-pdf/4-4-13-Marijuana-Release.pdf. Accessed 25 Jun 2023

Drug Enforcement Administration (2011) Drugs of abuse. Tech. rep., Drug Enforcement Administration, U.S. Department of Justice. http://www.dea.gov/docs/drugs_of_abuse_2011.pdf

Duran M, Pérez E, Abanades S, Vidal X, Saura C, Majem M, Arriola E, Rabanal M, Pastor A, Farré M, Rams N, Laporte JR, Capellá D (2010) Preliminary efficacy and safety of an oromucosal standardized cannabis extract in chemotherapy-induced nausea and vomiting. Br J Clin Pharmacol 70(5):656–663

Earleywine M (2005) Understanding marijuana: a new look at the scientific evidence. Oxford University Press, New York

Ellis RJ, Toperoff W, Vaida F, van den Brande G, Gonzales J, Gouaux B, Bentley H, Atkinson JH (2009) Smoked medicinal cannabis for neuropathic pain in HIV: a randomized, crossover clinical trial. Neuropsychopharmacol 34(3):672–680

Ferner M (2015) Obama: If enough states decriminalize marijuana, congress may change federal law. The Huffington Post, 17 March 2015. Accessed 25 Jun 2023

Geman S, Geman D (1984) Stochastic relaxation, Gibbs distributions, and the Bayesian restoration of images. IEEE Trans Pattern Anal Mach Intell 6(6):721–741

Greenberg E (2012) Introduction to Bayesian econometrics, 2nd edn. Cambridge University Press, New York

Greene WH, Hensher DA (2010) Modeling ordered choices: a primer. Cambridge University Press, Cambridge

Guzmán M (2003) Cannabinoids: potential anticancer agents. Nat Rev Cancer 3:745–755

Hastings WK (1970) Monte Carlo sampling methods using Markov chains and their applications. Biom 57(1):97–109

Holmes CC, Held L (2006) Bayesian auxiliary variable models for binary and multinomial regression. Bayesian Anal 1(1):145–168

Horwood LJ, Fergusson DM, Hayatbaksh MR, Najman JM, Coffey C, Patton GC, Silins E, Hutchinson DM (2010) Cannabis use and educational achievements: findings from three Australasian cohort studies. Drug Alcohol Depend 110(3):247–253

Hosmer DW, Lemeshaw S, Sturdivant RX (2013) Applied logistic regression, 3rd edn. John Wiley & Sons Inc, Hoboken, New Jersey

Jeliazkov I, Rahman MA (2012) Binary and ordinal data analysis in economics: modelling and estimation. In: Yang XS (ed) Mathematical modeling with multidisciplinary applications. John Wiley & Sons Inc., New Jersey, pp 123–150

Jeliazkov I, Graves J, Kutzbach M (2008) Fitting and comparison of models for multivariate ordinal outcomes. Adv Econ Bayesian Econ 23:115–156

Johnson JR, Burnell-Nugent M, Lossignol D, Ganae-Motan ED, Potts R, Fallon MT (2010) Multicenter, double-blind, randomized, placebo-controlled, parallel-group study of the efficacy, safety and tolerability of THC: CBD extract and THC extract in patients with intractable cancer-related pain. J Pain Symptom Manag 39(2):167–179

Johnson VE, Albert JH (2000) Ordinal data modeling. Springer, New York

Kalant H (2004) Adverse effects of cannabis on health: an update of the literature since 1996. Prog Neuro Psychopharmacol 28:849–863

Koenker R, Bassett G (1978) Regression quantiles. Econ 46(1):33–50

Kordas G (2006) Smoothed binary regression quantiles. J Appl Econ 21(3):387–407

Luce RD (1959) Individual choice behavior: a theoretical analysis. John Wiley & Sons, New York

Luce RD, Suppes P (1965) Preferences, utility and subjective probability. In: Luce RD, Bush RR, Galanter E (eds) Handbook of mathematical psychology, vol 3. John Wiley & Sons Inc., New York, pp 249–410

Lynskey M, Hall W (2000) The effects of adolescent cannabis use on educational attainment: a review. Addict 95(11):1621–1630

Maheshwari P, Rahman MA (2023) bqror: an R package for Bayesian quantile regression in ordinal models. R J 15(2):39–55

Marschak J (1960) Binary choice constraints on random utility indications. In: Arrow KJ (ed) Stanford symposium on mathematical methods in the social sciences. Stanford University Press, Stanford, CA, pp 312–326

McAllister SD, Murase R, Christian RT, Lau D, Zielinski AJ, Allison J, Almanza C, Pakdel A, Lee J, Limbad C, Liu Y, Debs RJ, Moore DH, Desprez P (2011) Pathways mediating the effects of cannabidiol on the reduction of breast cancer cell proliferation, invasion and metastasis. Breast Cancer Res Treat 129(1):37–47

McCullagh P (1980) Regression models for ordinal data. J R Stat Soc Ser B 42(2):109–142

McFadden D (1974) Conditional logit analysis of qualitative choice behavior. In: Zarembka P (ed) Frontiers in econometrics. Academic Press, New York, pp 105–142

McKelvey RD, Zavoina W (1975) A statistical model for the analysis of ordinal level dependent variables. J Math Sociol 4(1):103–120

Meier MH, Caspi A, Ambler A, Harrington H, Houts R, Keefe RSE, McDonald K, Ward A, Poulton R, Moffitt TE (2012) Persistent cannabis users show neuropsychological decline from childhood to midlife. Proc Natl Acad Sci 109(40):2657–2664

Metropolis N, Rosenbluth AW, Rosenbluth M, Teller AH, Teller E (1953) Equation of state calculations by fast computing machines. J Chem Phys 21:1087–1092

Monroe AD (1998) Public opinion and public policy, 1980–1993. Public Opin Q 62(1):6–28

Nasim A, Corona R, Belgrave F, Utsey SO, Fallah N (2007) Cultural orientation as a protective factor against tobacco and marijuana smoking for African American young women. J Youth Adolesc 36(4):503–516

Nielsen AL (2007) Americans' attitudes toward drug-related issues from 1975–2006: the roles of period and cohort effects. J Drug Issues 40(2):461–493

Ojha M, Rahman MA (2021) Do online courses provide an equal educational value compared to in-person classroom teaching? evidence from U.S. survey data using quantile regression. Educ Policy Anal Arch 29(85):1–25

Omata Y, Katayama H, Arimura TH (2017) Same concerns, same responses: a Bayesian quantile regression analysis of the determinants for nuclear power generation in Japan. Environ Econ Policy Stud 19(3):581–608

Paletz DL, Owen D, Cook T (2015) American government and politics in the information age. Flat World Knowledge

Poirier DJ (1995) Intermediate statistics and econometrics. The MIT Press, Cambridge

Polen MR, Sidney S, Tekawa IS, Sadler M, Friedman GD (1993) Health care use by frequent marijuana smokers who do not smoke tobacco. West J Med 158(6):596–601

Rahman MA (2016) Bayesian quantile regression for ordinal models. Bayesian Anal 11(1):1–24

Rahman MA, Karnawat S (2019) Flexible Bayesian quantile regression in ordinal models. Adv Econ 40B:211–251
Rahman MA, Vossmeyer A (2019) Estimation and applications of quantile regression for binary longitudinal data. Adv Econ 40B:157–191
Rodríguez AMi, (2015) Age, sex and personality in early cannabis use. Eur Psychiatry 30(4):469–473
Saieva AP (2008) Marijuana legalization: American's attitudes over four decades. M.S. thesis
Shapiro RY (2011) Public opinion and American democracy. Public Opin Q 75(5):982–1017
Shepard EM, Blackley PR (2007) The impact of marijuana law enforcement in an economic model of crime. J Drug Issues 37(2):403–424
Tanner MA, Wong WH (1987) The calculation of posterior distributions by data augmentation. J Am Stat Assoc 82(398):528–540
Train K (2009) Discrete choice methods with simulation. Cambridge University Press, Cambridge
Van Ours JC, Williams J (2009) Why parents worry: initiation into cannabis use by youth and their educational attainment. J Health Econ 28(1):132–142
Wilsey B, Marcotte TD, Deutsch R, Gouaux B, Sakai S, Donaghe H (2013) Low dose vaporized cannabis significantly improves neuropathic pain. J Pain 14(2):136–148
Winterbourne M (2012) United States drug policy: the scientific, economic, and social issues surrounding marijuana. http://web.stanford.edu/group/journal/cgi-bin/wordpress/wp-content/uploads/2012/09/Winterbourne_SocSci?_2012.pdf. Accessed 14 May 2015
Yu K, Moyeed RA (2001) Bayesian quantile regression. Stat Probab Lett 54(4):437–447
Yu K, Zhang J (2005) A three parameter asymmetric Laplace distribution and its extensions. Commun Stat Theory Methods 34(9–10):1867–1879

Chapter 3
Random Logit Model: An Application to US Soft Drink Differentiated Demand Estimation

Benaissa Chidmi

Abstract This chapter attempts to provide an overview of estimating demand for differentiated products using the random coefficient multinomial logit model, also known as the BLP model. The chapter discusses reasons for the BLP's superiority over traditional demand models, such as the AIDS models. It also describes recent development in the BLP-type literature, especially dealing with computational issues. In addition, the chapter covers the empirical process to estimate the iBLP model, starting with the numerical integration methods, simulation of observed and unobserved consumers' characteristics, contraction mapping, endogeneity, and the generalized method of moments (GMM) estimation, and the existing software and packages to estimate the random coefficient logit model. Finally, the chapter offers an empirical illustration for estimating differentiated demand for soft drinks.

Keywords BLP · Random coefficient logit · Differentiated demand · Soft drinks · Python pyblp

3.1 Introduction

The demand analysis constitutes a cornerstone to subsequent economic studies: price competition, market structure, and welfare estimation. Unlike the demand for homogeneous products, the demand for differentiated products presents the difficulty of the large number of brands analyzed. Firms produce horizontally differentiated products in imperfectly competitive markets to gain market power and brand loyalty. These products represent heterogeneous goods and are imperfect substitutes for each other. Consumer demand for differentiated goods is based on subjective tastes and preferences. Salty snacks (e.g., Lays Original, Pringles Sour Cream and Onion, and Doritos

Supplementary Information The online version contains supplementary material available at https://doi.org/10.1007/978-981-99-4902-1_3.

B. Chidmi (✉)
Department of Agricultural and Applied Economics, Texas Tech University, Lubbock, TX, USA
e-mail: benaissa.chidmi@ttu.edu

D. Mukherjee (ed.), *Applied Econometric Analysis Using Cross Section and Panel Data*, Contributions to Economics, https://doi.org/10.1007/978-981-99-4902-1_3

Nacho Cheese), ready-to-eat cereals (e.g., Multigrain Cheerios, Kellogg's Frosted Flakes, and Cookie Crisp Chocolate Chip Cookie Flavored Cereal), and carbonated soft drinks (e.g., Sprite, Mountain Dew, Dr. Pepper, Diet Coke, Pepsi Cola, and Sunkist) are a few examples of horizontally differentiated goods.

Researchers have approached the demand for differentiated products from two angles: the representative consumer model and the spatial or location model (Eaton and Lipsey 1989; Carlton and Perloff 1994). We assume in the representative consumer model that typical consumers regard a set of brands as equally good substitutes for one another. Consumer heterogeneity is generally ignored in these models. With the symmetry assumption, all products are treated as equal in competition with all other products, whether a representative consumer is used to capture aggregated demand for differentiated products or even if it can be assumed that consumer preferences differ (Eaton and Lipsey 1989). For example, Coca-Cola is an equally good substitute for Pepsi Cola, and also it is for Sprite. A slight change in the price of any product leads to a small change in demand for other products.

In spatial or location models, consumers perceive some brands as closer substitutes than others. Unlike the representative consumer model, location models include consumer heterogeneity in tastes and preferences. Consumers view the products as having a location or characteristics space, and the closer products in terms of location or characteristics space are better substitutes than others (Carlton and Perloff 1994). Therefore, consumers with different tastes and preferences have different preferred locations or characteristics (Eaton and Lipsey 1989). For instance, Coca-Cola Classic is a better substitute for Pepsi-Cola than Sprite. A product's demand may be independent of other products' prices since they are not close substitutes (Carlton and Perloff 1994).

The classical or traditional methods of demand, such as the linear expenditure model (Stone 1954), the Rotterdam model (Theil 1965; Barten 1966), the translogarithm model (Christensen et al. 1975), and the Almost Ideal Demand System (Deaton and Muellbauer 1980), present issues and challenges for analyzing demand for differentiated products. First of all, since a large number of products are analyzed, it creates a dimensionality problem. There is an exponential increase in parameters to be estimated. For example, if there are 60 brands to be analyzed, at least 3600 ($20^2 = 400$) parameters must be evaluated. Even with theoretical restrictions (symmetry, homogeneity, and adding-up restrictions), there would still be too many parameters to estimate.

Second, the traditional approach ignores consumer heterogeneity. In representative consumer models, only aggregate demand for a product can be estimated. In some cases, the aim is to explicitly model and estimate consumer behavior (Nevo 2011). Consumer heterogeneity is vital in estimating horizontally differentiated products because their demand depends on subjective taste and preferences. Omitting consumer heterogeneity leads to misinterpretations of market structure, product targeting, market segments, biased results, and wrong inferences concerning market strategies (Kamakura et al. 1996; Popkowski Leszczyc and Bass 1998; Chintagunta 2001; Gandhi and Nevo 2021).

3.1.1 Dimensionality Issue

One way to solve the dimensionality problem is aggregation. However, in this case, the substitution between different products cannot be estimated because of the individuals' aggregation. Regarding the industrial organization (IO) approach, product substitution is the heart of any study. Nevo (2011) points out that nearly all demand studies include some level of aggregation. Depending on the study's focus, the researcher has to decide on the aggregation level and whether the aggregation solves the issue of dimensionality.

Another way to solve the dimensionality problem is to impose symmetry. Spence (1976) and Dixit and Stiglitz (1977) propose the constant elasticity of substitution (CES) demand model. The utility from consumption of the J products is given by

$$u(q_1, q_2, \ldots, q_J) = \left(\prod_{j=1}^{J} q_j^{\rho}\right)^{\frac{1}{\rho}}, \tag{3.1}$$

where ρ is a constant parameter. The representative consumer's demand for a good, k, can be obtained from the above utility function using the following expression:

$$q_k = \frac{p_k^{\frac{-1}{(1-\rho)}}}{\sum_{j=1}^{J} p_j^{\frac{-1}{(1-\rho)}}} y, \tag{3.2}$$

where y is the representative consumer's income. We solve the dimensionality problem by imposing symmetry between the following restriction:

$$\frac{\partial q_k}{\partial p_j}\frac{p_j}{q_k} = \frac{\partial q_l}{\partial p_j}\frac{p_j}{q_l}, \tag{3.3}$$

for all j, k, and l. This implies that the cross-price elasticity of product k with respect to j is equal to the cross-price elasticity of product l with respect to the product j, which ignores how close substitutes are (Nevo 2011). Imposing symmetry necessitates strong assumptions, and the proposed models with symmetry restriction generally yield an appropriate fit for trade and macroeconomics data (Nevo 2011). However, in IO, the study of interest is to know the substitution between products, and with symmetry assumption, it is highly restricted.

A second approach to solve the dimensionality problem is to split the brands into smaller groups and use a flexible, functional form for demand estimation within each group. Here, we assume that the consumer categorizes expenditure into broad groups, and later the expenditure of a group is allocated to sub-groups of products. Each allocation stage depends on the total expenditure and prices of goods in a particular group (Nevo 2011). For example, Hausman et al. (1994) and Hausman (1996) use multistage budgeting by dividing the demand into a three-stage system for differentiated products, in the case of beer and ready-to-eat cereals (RTEC), respectively.

The authors use a similar structure where the top stage includes total demand for a particular product. In the middle stage, the interest is estimating demand for specific segments. Finally, the demand for brands is captured for a given segment in the lower level. One of the problems with this approach is the difficulty of dividing the categories into specific segments. For example, Cotterill et al. (1996), Ma (1996), and Cotterill and Haller (1997) divide RTEC demand into four categories (all family, taste enhanced wholesome, simple health, and children cereal), while Hausman (1996) divides the breakfast cereal brands into three groups (family, children, and adults). The difficulty of segmentation arises because some products may be multilayered, and the researcher may require a priori information about products.

3.1.2 Heterogeneity Issue

A second issue with the traditional demand approach is the representative consumer's assumption, which sidesteps the heterogeneity in consumer preferences that motivates product differentiation (Allenby and Rossi 1998). Consumers have different tastes and responses to the product's attribute offerings, including the prices. For instance, a slight change in the pricing of a Coca-Cola classic may induce a different reaction from two consumers with different observed and unobserved characteristics. For Allenby and Rossi (1998), marketers, and therefore marketing literature, consider consumer heterogeneity as the explanation of product differentiation, market segments and niches, and promotional activities, while for the representative consumer approach in economics, consumer heterogeneity is treated as a disturbance issue that econometricians should address appropriately but not stress. To incorporate consumer heterogeneity into the demand beyond the traditional fixed effect approach, researchers in the marketing and economics literature specify demand functions with random coefficients. The starting point is a consumer i with a demand for product j, specified as a function of prices and other demand shifters with random parameters as

$$q_{ij} = Z_j\theta_i + \alpha_i p_j + \varepsilon_{ij}, \quad i = 1, 2, \ldots, N; \quad j = 1, 2, \ldots J, \tag{3.4}$$

where Z_j is a vector of demand shifters, p_j the price of product j, and ε_{ij} represents the usual random error terms.

An essential feature of the above model is that the parameters θ_i and α_i account for the variation of consumers' tastes and preferences for the product characteristics. In the marketing and IO literature, this randomness in the tastes and preferences has been statistically approached in at least two different procedures. The first approach uses the Bayesian view in assuming the tastes, and preferences parameters (θ_i and α_i) follow some multivariate distribution (posterior distribution in the Bayesian jargon) the econometrician has to uncover using her prior belief and the likelihood function (e.g., Rossi and Allenby 1993; Rossi et al. 1995; Allenby and Rossi 1998; Li and Ansari 2014; Ebbes et al. 2015; Becker et al. 2018). The second approach specifies the random parameters θ_i and α_i as functions of some observed consumer's demographics (age and income, for example) in addition to an unobserved random variable, termed the unobserved consumer's characteristics (e.g., Berry 1994; Berry et al. 1995; Nevo 2001; Dubé 2004; Berto Villas-Boas 2007; Bonnet and Dubois 2010; Chidmi and Lopez 2007). Regardless of the method used, the outcome of the estimation of a random coefficient demand is a distribution of the taste parameters, providing a richer substitution pattern. Hence, instead of a single price elasticity, we obtain a distribution of this critical measure, depicting variation in consumers' price responsiveness.

3.1.3 Product Characteristic Mapping and Discrete Choice Models

Another approach to analyzing the demand for differentiated products is to view a brand or choice in an attribute rather than product space (Lancaster 1966; Gorman 1980). As mentioned earlier, some products are better substitutes in location (or spatial) models than others. Therefore, a bundle of product attributes is used for a substitutability measure instead of its number. Discrete choice models, such as logit, probit, nested logit, multinomial logit, multinomial probit, and mixed logit, are some applications for location models, and they can be used to estimate the demand for differentiated goods in characteristic space. The dimensionality problem, arising from analyzing many products, is solved by projecting the products onto a characteristic space instead of squaring the number of products, reducing the number of estimated parameters. Consumer heterogeneity can also be modeled by allowing the model parameters to vary with observed and unobserved consumer characteristics.

Discrete choice models are highly prevalent in estimating the demand for differentiated goods. The literature abounds on the applications of discrete choice models, notably the automobile industry (e.g., Berry et al. 1995; Goldberg 1995; Verboven 1996; Sudhir 2001; Xiao and Ju 2014), the ready-to-eat cereal industry (e.g., Nevo 2001; Chidmi and Lopez 2007; Zhu et al. 2016), the yogurt market (Berto Villas-Boas 2007; Bonnet and Bouamra-Mechemache 2019), the coffee market (e.g., Guadagni and Little 1983; Villas-Boas 2007; Draganska et al. 2010; Bonnet and Villas-Boas 2016), the fluid milk industry (e.g., Lopez and Lopez 2009; Chidmi and Murova 2011; Bonnet and Bouamra-Mechemache 2016; Hirsch et al. 2018; Li et al. 2018), the beer industry (e.g., Lopez and Matschke 2012; Toro-González et al. 2014), the smartphone industry (Hiller et al. 2018), and the carbonated soft drink industry (e.g., Mariuzzo et al. 2003; Dubé 2004; Mariuzzo et al. 2010; Lopez and Fantuzzi 2012; Bonnet and Réquillart 2013; Lopez et al. 2015; Liu and Lopez 2016).

3.2 Theoretical Framework for Discrete Choice Models

The discrete choice analysis is based on utility theory through the random utility model. For example, the seminal paper by Thurstone (2017) in the psychophysiology field states that an alternative j with correct stimulus level V_j is perceived with an error, that is, $V_j + e_j$. Marschak (1974) applies this perspective to economics, and the perceived stimulus level is interpreted as a utility with random elements. Marschak (1974) calls this process a random utility model (RUM) model. The random utility concept inspires McFadden to produce a series of seminal papers (see, for example, McFadden 1974, 1981, 1984) giving birth to the discrete choice analysis.

3.2.1 Random Utility Model

The starting point of discrete choice models is a consumer i choosing among J alternatives. Each alternative provides the consumer with an indirect utility U that is decomposed into a representative utility V and random disturbance terms ε (see, for example, Train 2009) as

$$U_{ij} = V_j + \xi_j + \varepsilon_{ij}. \tag{3.5}$$

The consumer chooses the alternative j if and only if $U_{ij} > U_{ik} \quad \forall j \neq k$. Given the econometrician observes the choices but does not observe the consumer's utility, she can only make probabilistic inferences about the consumer's choice. Hence, the probability, P, of choosing alternative j by consumer i can be written as

$$P_{ij} = Prob\big(U_{ij} > U_{ik} \quad \forall j \neq k\big). \tag{3.6}$$

This simplifies to

$$P_{ij} = Prob\big(\varepsilon_{ik} - \varepsilon_{ij} < V_{ij} - V_{ik} \quad \forall j \neq k\big), \tag{3.7}$$

which is a cumulative probability that we rewrite as

$$P_{ij} = \int_{\varepsilon} I\big[\big(\varepsilon_{ik} - \varepsilon_{ij} < V_{ij} - V_{ik} \quad \forall j \neq k\big)\big] f\big(\varepsilon_i\big) d\varepsilon_i, \tag{3.8}$$

where I, the indicator function, equals 1 if the expression in brackets is true and 0 otherwise, and f is the probability distribution of the random error terms ε_{ij}. To be specific, assume the decision-maker i is choosing among four alternatives. Her choice of alternative one, for instance, implies that

$$P_{i1} = Prob[U_{i1} > U_{i2}, U_{i1} > U_{i3}, U_{i1} > U_{i4}]$$
$$= Prob[\varepsilon_{i2} - \varepsilon_{i1} < V_{i1} - V_{i2}, \varepsilon_{i3} - \varepsilon_{i1} < V_{i1} - V_{i3}, \varepsilon_{i4} - \varepsilon_{i1} < V_{i1} - V_{i4}]$$
$$= \int_{-\infty}^{V_{i1}-V_{i2}} \int_{-\infty}^{V_{i1}-V_{i3}} \int_{-\infty}^{V_{i1}-V_{i4}} f(\varepsilon_{i2} - \varepsilon_{i1}) f(\varepsilon_{i3} - \varepsilon_{i1}) f(\varepsilon_{i4} - \varepsilon_{i1}) d(\varepsilon_{i2} - \varepsilon_{i1}) d(\varepsilon_{i3} - \varepsilon_{i1}) d(\varepsilon_{i4} - \varepsilon_{i1}). \tag{3.9}$$

So the resulting probability is a $(J - 1)$-dimensional integral.[1]

The choice of the functional forms for f will give rise to different discrete choice models. Hence, if the differences $\varepsilon_{ik} - \varepsilon_{ij}$ follow a multivariate normal distribution, then the integral in Eq. 3.9 becomes

$$P_{i1} = \int_{-\infty}^{V_{i1}-V_{i2}} \int_{-\infty}^{V_{i1}-V_{i3}} \int_{-\infty}^{V_{i1}-V_{i4}} \phi(\varepsilon_{i2} - \varepsilon_{i1}, \varepsilon_{i3} - \varepsilon_{i1}, \varepsilon_{i4} - \varepsilon_{i1}) d(\varepsilon_{i2} - \varepsilon_{i1}) d(\varepsilon_{i3} - \varepsilon_{i1}) d(\varepsilon_{i4} - \varepsilon_{i1}), \tag{3.10}$$

where ϕ indicates the multivariate normal distribution probability density function. In contrast, if the error terms ε_{ij} are $i.i.d.$ type 1 extreme value (EV) with the probability distribution function given by

$$f(\varepsilon_{ij}) = exp(-\varepsilon_{ij}) exp(-exp(-\varepsilon_{ij})), \tag{3.11}$$

then the error differences follow a logistic distribution, yielding the multinomial distribution, with the probability of choosing alternative j given by

$$P_j = \frac{e^{V_j}}{e^{V_1} + e^{V_2} + \cdots + e^{V_J}}. \tag{3.12}$$

Another popular distribution used is the generalized extreme value (GEV) distribution, with the cumulative distribution function given by

$$F(\varepsilon_1, \varepsilon_2, \ldots \varepsilon_J) = exp(-G(e^{-\varepsilon_1}, e^{-\varepsilon_2}, \ldots, e^{-\varepsilon_J})), \tag{3.13}$$

where the function G is chosen to ensure that F and f define cumulative and probability distribution functions $(CDF$ and $PDF)$. The nested logit model is obtained when

$$G(\varepsilon_{11}, \ldots, \varepsilon_{1K_1}, \ldots \varepsilon_{M1}, \ldots, \varepsilon_{MK_M}) \sum_{m=1}^{M} \left(\sum_{k=1}^{K_m} \varepsilon_{mk}^{1/\rho_m} \right)^{\rho_m} \tag{3.14}$$

for a choice set with M limbs, each with K_m branches.

For the random utility functional specification, the additive random utility is the widely used form, especially in the BLP model specification. However, researchers have explored other functional forms and approaches. For instance, Van Der Pol et al. (2014) compare the effects of choosing a linear, quadratic, or stepwise random utility on the patient's willingness to wait for hip and knee replacement in four Canadian

[1] The integral in Eq. 3.10 is written as a single integral for ease of presentation. A single integral will result only in the case of binary choices.

cities (Vancouver, Calgary, Regina, and Winnipeg). In addition, Fukuda and Yai (2010) use a smoothing spline-based semiparametric approach to analyze the travel mode choice for an interregional trip in the Netherlands. On the other hand, Walker and Ben-Akiva (2002) propose a generalized random utility model, encompassing the linear component, flexible disturbances, latent variables, latent classes, and a combination of revealed and stated preferences. In what follows, I will discuss only multinomial logit with random and non-random parameters with additive random utility.

3.2.2 *Discrete Choice Modeling*

The discrete choice literature, proposed by McFadden et al. (1973), McFadden (1981, 1984), solves the dimensionality issue by projecting the consumer choices onto a set of product attributes, giving smaller dimension than the number of products in the choice set. In addition, the consumer's heterogeneity is taken into account by allowing the parameters to vary with the consumer's observed and unobserved, therefore random, characteristics (see, for example, Cardell 1989; Berry et al. 1995; Nevo 2001), which solves the substitution pattern issues implied by the use of classical discrete choice models (logit, probit, and nested logit).

3.2.2.1 Multinomial Logit Model

Assume the indirect utility for choice j depends on the product price (p_j) and a set of observed (x_j) and unobserved (ξ_j) product characteristics. The resulting utility yields

$$U_{ij} = x'_j\beta + \alpha p_j + \xi_j + \varepsilon_{ij}, \tag{3.15}$$

where ε_{ij} represents the distribution of consumer preferences about the unobserved product characteristics, with a density $f(\varepsilon)$. The unobserved product characteristics represent all the factors that affect the demand for the product, observed by the seller and the buyer but not observed by the researcher. The unobserved product characteristics are modeled as part of the random error terms in the multinomial logit specification.[2] Keeping the same notation for the error terms, we get

$$U_{ij} = x'_j\beta + \alpha p_j + \varepsilon_{ij}. \tag{3.16}$$

[2] This implies a potential endogeneity problem that I will discuss later on.

Assuming ε_{ij} are independent and identically distributed as extreme value,[3] then the integral in Eq. (3.8) can be solved analytically and the market shares for the jth product (corresponding to the probability that the jth is chosen) are given by the following equation[4]:

$$s_j = \frac{\exp\left(x_j\beta + \alpha p_j + \xi_j\right)}{1 + \sum_{k=1}^{J} \exp\left(x_k\beta + \alpha p_k + \xi_k\right)}. \tag{3.17}$$

The multinomial logit model presents the advantage of being simple to implement. The estimation proceeds by the inversion proposed by Berry et al. (1995, hereafter BLP). For the logit model, the inversion is given by

$$\delta_j = \ln(s_j) - \ln(s_0) = x_j\beta + \alpha p_j + \xi_j, \tag{3.18}$$

where $s_0 = \frac{1}{1+\sum_{k=1}^{J}\exp\left(x_k\beta+\alpha p_k+\xi_k\right)}$ is the share of the outside good obtained by subtracting the sum of observed market shares of all the products in the choice set from 1. The utility of the outside option is normalized to zero, i.e., $U_{i0} = 0$. Note that the logit model is transformed to a simple linear regression where the natural logarithm of the ratio between the observed market shares of the brands in the choice set and outside good share is regressed on product characteristics and the price variables.

The price elasticities for the multinomial logit model are given by

$$\eta_{jk} = \frac{\partial s_j}{\partial p_k}\frac{p_k}{s_j} = \begin{cases} \alpha p_j(1 - s_j) & \text{if j = k} \\ -\alpha p_k s_k & \text{otherwise.} \end{cases} \tag{3.19}$$

Notice that the ratio of the logit market shares for any two brands j and l does not depend on brands other than j and l. That is, the relative odds of market shares of brand j over brand l are the same no matter what are the characteristics of the other brands. In the logit case, the ratio exhibits independence from irrelevant alternatives, or IIA (McFadden 1981; Train 2009). While the IIA property is appropriate in some cases, it is very restrictive in many cases. For instance, in the case of soft drinks, if Coca-Cola Classic and Sprite have similar market shares and if Pepsi-Cola decreases its price, the substitution from Coca-Cola Classic to Pepsi-Cola is the same as the substitution from Sprite to Pepsi-Cola. However, in real life, one would expect the substitution from Coca-Cola Classic to Pepsi-Cola to be more than from Sprite to Pepsi-Cola. In other words, the cross-price elasticity of product j with respect to product k is the same as the cross-price elasticity of product l with respect to product k, regardless of how close, in characteristics, the products are. In addition, the own-price elasticities are related to own prices. Therefore, a lower price implies lower elasticity (in absolute value), which gives an inaccurate measure of price-cost margins if the pricing equation is estimated.

---

[3] $f(\varepsilon_{ij}) = \exp\left(-\varepsilon_{ij}\right)\exp\left(-\exp\left(-\varepsilon_{ij}\right)\right)$.

[4] For an explicit derivation, see Cameron and Trivedi (2005), and Train (2009).

Nevertheless, the multinomial logit has been widely used in the fields of economics, marketing, transportation, psychology, and political sciences due to its simplicity and its straightforward interpretability. In the BLP context, the multinomial logit outcomes constitute excellent starting values for the more computationally cumbersome random coefficient logit. In contrast, one should be cautious using the multinomial logit outcomes to make inferences with real-world data due to the IIA property and the linearity in the odds ratio, as shown in Eq. 3.18.

3.2.2.2 BLP Model

The simplicity of the logit model allows the researcher to test how well the data is behaving. However, to overcome some of its significant limitations, one needs a more elaborate model, such as the BLP model, to allow for a more flexible substitution pattern and price elasticities.

In the BLP model (summarized here for exposition purposes), consumer heterogeneity enters the model by allowing the taste parameters to vary across the decision-maker i. The resulting indirect utility yields

$$U_{ij} = x_j \beta_i + \alpha_i p_j + \xi_j + \varepsilon_{ij}. \tag{3.20}$$

Note that taste parameters α_i and β_i are allowed to vary among consumers and therefore account for consumer heterogeneity. Consequently, we can decompose these parameters into a fixed component common to all consumers and a varying part that depends on the consumer's observed and unobserved characteristics. In economic and marketing literature, researchers adopt the following specification for the taste parameters:

$$\alpha_i = \alpha_0 + \alpha_1 D_{i1} + \alpha_2 D_{i2} + \cdots + \alpha_L D_{iL} + \gamma v_i, \tag{3.21}$$

and

$$\beta_i^c = \beta_0^c + \beta_1^c D_{i1} + \beta_2^c D_{i2} + \cdots + \beta_L^c D_{iL} + \lambda^c v_i^c, \tag{3.22}$$

where $D_{i1}, D_{i2}, \ldots, D_{iL}$ are L consumer's characteristics or demographics, such as income, age, education, and household size with an empirical distribution $h(D)$. v_i denotes the unobserved characteristics, typically assumed to follow a standard normal distribution. The subscript c in (3.22) is with respect to the product attribute c (e.g., sugar and calorie contents). For ease of presentation, assume we have two product attributes for brand j, x_{j1} and x_{j2}, and one consumer characteristic, D_{i1}, then Eq. (3.20) becomes

$$\begin{aligned}U_{ij} = \beta_0^1 x_{j1} + \beta_0^2 x_{j1} + \alpha_0 p_j \\ + \beta_1^1 x_{j1} D_{i1} + \beta_1^2 x_{j2} D_{i1} + \alpha_1 p_j D_{i1} \\ + \lambda^1 x_{j1} v_i^1 + \lambda^2 x_{j1} v_i^2 + \gamma p_j v_i + \xi_j + \varepsilon_{ij}.\end{aligned} \tag{3.23}$$

Adopting Nevo (2001) notation, we can rewrite the indirect utility equation as

$$U_{ij} = \delta_j\left(x_j, p_j, \xi_j; \theta_1\right) + \mu_{ij}\left(x_j, p_j, D_i, v_i; \theta_2\right), \tag{3.24}$$

with

$$\delta_j = \beta_0^1 x_{j1} + \beta_0^2 x_{j2} + \alpha_0 p_j + \xi_j \tag{3.25}$$

and

$$\mu_{ij} = \beta_1^1 x_{j1} D_{i1} + \beta_1^2 x_{j2} D_{i1} + \alpha_1 p_j D_{i1} + \lambda^1 x_{j1} v_i^1 + \lambda^2 x_{j1} v_i^2 + \gamma p_j v_i + \varepsilon_{ij}. \tag{3.26}$$

Aggregating over consumers in the market, the j market share corresponds to the probability of the brand being chosen. That is,

$$P_{ij} = \int_\varepsilon \int_v \int_D I\left[\left(D_i, v_i, \varepsilon_{ij}\right) : U_{ij} > U_{ik}\ \forall k \neq j\right] dH(D) dG(v) dF\left(\varepsilon_i\right). \tag{3.27}$$

The BLP model poses two challenges. First, the multidimensional integral in Eq. (3.27) has no closed-form solution and must be solved numerically. Second, information on the distribution of demographics is needed to compute the individual market shares. I will come back to these issues in the next section.

Assuming ε_{ij} are independent and identically distributed as extreme value, the brand j aggregate market share is given by

$$s_j\left(\delta_j, x_j, p_j; \theta, D, v\right) = \int_v \int_D \frac{\exp\left(\delta_j + \mu_{ij}\right)}{1 + \sum_{k=1}^J \exp\left(\delta_k + \mu_{ik}\right)} dH(D) dG(v). \tag{3.28}$$

Using Eq. (3.28), the price elasticities are given by

$$\eta_{jk} = \frac{\partial s_j}{\partial p_k} \frac{p_k}{s_j} = \begin{cases} \frac{p_j}{s_j} \int_v \int_D \alpha_i s_{ij}(1 - s_{ij}) dH(D) dG(v) & \text{if j = k} \\ -\frac{p_k}{s_j} \int_v \int_D \alpha_i s_{ij} s_{ik} dH(D) dG(v) & \text{otherwise,} \end{cases} \tag{3.29}$$

where s_{ij} represents the probability consumer i chooses brand j. Each consumer has a different price elasticity for each brand in this setting. The random coefficient model (BLP) offers many advantages over the multinomial logit model. First, the own-price elasticities depend now on the price sensitivity of the individuals in the sample and not on the functional form. Instead of being determined by the constant parameter α, the own-price elasticities are also determined by the unobserved and observed consumer characteristics. For a given brand, the aggregate price elasticities are obtained by averaging the price sensitivity of the individuals in the sample.

The second advantage is that for the BLP model, a priori segmentation of the market does not constrain the substitution patterns, allowing for flexible substitution between brands. If, for example, the price of a brand increases, consumers are more likely to switch to brands with similar characteristics. Further, individuals with similar characteristics tend to have similar purchasing patterns. As a result, the BLP model can help alleviate the independence from irrelevant alternative (IIA) issues encountered in the multinomial logit case.

Finally, the BLP model, by taking into account consumer heterogeneity taste, gives another explanation besides the price variation that accounts for the difference in market shares across markets and brands. By allowing for individual-specific preferences, the BLP model accounts for the varying sensitivities consumers have to changes in the choice set.

3.3 Empirical Estimation

This section covers the empirical process to estimate the integral in Eq. (3.28), starting with the numerical integration methods, simulation of observed and unobserved consumers' characteristics, contraction mapping, endogeneity, the generalized method of moments (GMM) estimation, and the existing software and packages to estimate the random coefficient logit model. This section is written as a companion-based tool to assist researchers in estimating the random coefficient multinomial logit model in food and agricultural marketing in the same spirit as Nevo (2000). It also provides literature extensions related to the original BLP model.

3.3.1 Integral Simulation

As mentioned above, the estimation of the taste parameters passes by the estimation of the integral in Eq. (3.28), which does not have a closed-form solution. Monte Carlo simulation remains one of the most widely used numerical methods to approximate integrals in the context of BLP-type models (see, for example, Berry et al. 1995; Nevo 2000, 2001; Berto Villas-Boas 2007; Bonnet and Bouamra-Mechemache 2019). Monte Carlo simulation is often used in numerical integration when the function being integrated is challenging to work with directly or when the region over which the integral is being taken is complex and cannot be easily divided into small subregions. In a Monte Carlo simulation of numerical integration, random samples are drawn from the region over which the integral is taken, and the integrand (integrated function) is evaluated at those points. The average of the function evaluations is then used as an approximation for the integral. The more samples a researcher draws, the more accurate the approximation will be. As an illustration, consider numerically solving the integral $\int_0^3 x^2 dx$. Given this integral has an analytical solution equal to 3, the following illustration shows how a Monte Carlo simulation approaches the true solution as the sample size increases. The following Python code allows us to compute the solution for different sample sizes.

Code Listing 3.1 Python code for Monte Carlo simulation to solve the integral of x^2 between a and b

```
    def monte_carlo_integration(n):
    sum_f = 0

    for _ in range(n):
        x = random.uniform(a, b)
        f_x = x**2
        sum_f += f_x

    average_f = sum_f / n
    integral_value = average_f
    return integral_value

# Sample sizes
N1 = 100
N2 = 1000
N3 = 10000
N4 = 100000
# Estimate the integral between a = 0 and b = 3, using the Monte Carlo simulation
estimated_integral = monte_carlo_simulation(0, 3, N)

print("Estimated value of the integral:", estimated_integral)
```

A generic algorithm for using Monte Carlo simulation to approximate the definite integral of a function $f(x)$ over a region R would proceed as follows:

The Monte Carlo simulation of the integral in Eq. (3.28) proceeds by generating N draws from the distribution of the observed (D_i) and unobserved (v_i) consumers' characteristics and approximating the brand j market share using the following equation[5]:

Algorithm 3.1 Generic Monte Carlo simulation

Choose the number of samples to draw, N.
Randomly generate N samples from the region R.
Evaluate the function $f(x)$ at each of the N samples.
Calculate the average of the function evaluations: $(f(x_1) + f(x_2) + \cdots + f(x_N))/N$
Multiply the average by the region's area R to obtain the approximation for the integral.

[5] For ease of presentation, I am using two product attributes and two consumers' characteristics.

$$s_j = \frac{1}{N}\sum_{i=1}^{N} s_{ij}$$
$$= \frac{1}{N}\sum_{i=1}^{N}\left[\frac{\exp\left(\delta_j + \beta_1^1 x_{j1} D_{i1} + \beta_1^2 x_{j2} D_{i1} + \alpha_1 p_j D_{i1} + \lambda^1 x_{j1} v_i^1 + \lambda^2 x_{j1} v_i^2 + \gamma p_j v_i\right)}{1 + \sum_{k=1}^{J} \exp\left(\delta_k + \beta_1^1 x_{k1} D_{i1} + \beta_1^2 x_{k2} D_{i1} + \alpha_1 p_k D_{i1} + \lambda^1 x_{k1} v_i^1 + \lambda^2 x_{k1} v_i^2 + \gamma p_k v_i\right)}\right]. \tag{3.30}$$

However, recently, some authors have warned against the Monte Carlo simulation in solving the integral in Eq. (3.28) as it brings in significant numerical inaccuracy and instability into the computations (Skrainka and Judd 2011). According to Skrainka and Judd (2011), Monte Carlo methods yield inaccurate point estimates, excessively tight standard errors, instability in the inner loop for inverting market shares, and poor convergence in most popular solvers. Besides, Knittel and Metaxoglou (2014) find substantial variation using 11 optimization algorithms, and data from Berry et al. (1995) and Nevo (2001). Moreover, Brunner (2017) reaches a similar conclusion by noting the simulation error propagates in the generalized method of moments (GMM) objective function.

To solve the issue of the error propagation due to errors in Monte Carlo integration, Brunner (2017) uses modified Latin hypercube sampling draws. Hence, the author finds the 95% confidence interval for the own-price elasticity between –24 and –3 with 50 Monte Carlo simulation draws. In contrast, the interval shrinks to values between –9 and –8 when 10,000 modified Latin hypercube sampling draws are used. Another way to improve the BLP-type model estimates is through the use of polynomial-based, monomial rules, and sparse grid integration quadrature methods (see, for example, Skrainka and Judd 2011). In the illustration below, I will use the Monte Carlo simulation method to solve the integral given in Eq. (3.28). However, agricultural and food marketing researchers are highly encouraged to explore recent development in numerical integration techniques.

3.3.2 Simulation of the Observed Unobserved Product Characteristics

The random-coefficient logit model presents the advantage of incorporating consumers' heterogeneity in taste parameters, resulting in a richer and more flexible substitution pattern. Consumer characteristics consist of observed and unobserved characteristics (to the researcher). Typically, the unobserved consumer characteristics are simulated from a theoretical distribution, such as the standard normal distribution (Nevo 2000; Berto Villas-Boas 2007; Chidmi and Lopez 2007; Bonnet and Bouamra-Mechemache 2019). Following is an example of a Python code to simulate and plot 1,000 observations from a standard normal distribution and 1,000 observations from a t-distribution with 5 °C of freedom.

Code Listing 3.2 Python code to simulate and plot 1,000 observations from a standard normal distribution t-distribution with 5 degrees of freedom

```
import numpy as np
from matplotlib import pyplot as plt
# Set the random seed for reproducibility
np.random.seed(42)

# Sample size
sample_size = 1000

# Simulate from the standard normal distribution
mean = 0
std_dev = 1
normal_sample = np.random.normal(mean, std_dev,
    sample_size)

# Simulate from the t-distribution
df = 5  # degrees of freedom
t_sample = np.random.standard_t(df, sample_size)

# Plot the two samples
figure = plt.figure()
ax0 = figure.add_subplot(121)
plt.hist(normal_sample, bins = 80)
plt.title('Normal distribution')
ax1 = figure.add_subplot(122)
plt.hist(t_sample, bins = 80)
plt.title('t distribution')
plt.show()
```

Observed consumer characteristics can come from various sources, including surveys, interviews, focus groups, online reviews, and purchase history. However, the most popular data sources for consumer characteristics are the Current Population Survey (CPS) of the United States Census Bureau and the panel data from IRI (Consumer Network) or AC Nielsen (HomeScan). Panel data include information on only the decision-makers that made the purchase. In contrast, using the CPS data allows the researcher to make the demand inferences for the entire market population (Berry et al. 1998).

3.3.3 Contraction Mapping and Fixed-Point Iteration

Once we numerically solve the integral in Eq. (3.28), we can use draws from the observed and unobserved consumer characteristics along with starting values for the parameters entering the deviation from the mean utility, μ_{ij}. We then use contraction mapping[6] to find a fixed-point solution by using the fixed-point iteration algorithm[7] to solve for the value of the mean utility, δ_j, that equates the observed market shares, S_j, and the computed market shares, s_j, given by Eq. (3.28). That is, given starting values for θ_2, we solve for the mean utility by inverting the following equality:

$$S_j = s_j\left(x_j, p_j, \delta_j; \theta_2\right). \tag{3.31}$$

Contraction mappings provide a means of guaranteeing that the fixed-point iteration will converge to a solution, as the distance between the current solution and the desired solution continuously decreases (see, for example, Istratescu 2001). Hence, we can retrieve the vector of mean utility valuations by using the following fixed-point iteration method:

$$\delta(\theta_2)^{w+1} = \delta^w + \ln S - \ln s\left(x, p, \delta^w; \theta_2\right) \tag{3.32}$$

where δ^w represents the wth iteration. We initiate the iteration using $\delta^0 = \ln s_{.} - \ln s_0 = \beta_0^1 x_{j1} + \beta_0^2 x_{j1} + \alpha_0 p_j$ estimated from the multinomial logit model. As an illustration, the following Python code illustrates how to solve the equation $x = 0.5 \times \sqrt{x} + 2$, using fixed-point iteration. Notice the solution converges to a fixed point after 12 iterations.

Code Listing 3.3 Python code to solve the equation $x = 0.5 \times \sqrt{x} + 2$, using fixed-point iteration

```
# Define the function
def f(x):
    return 0.5*x**0.5 + 2

# Initial guess
x = 0

# Number of iterations
num_iterations = 100

# Fixed-point iteration
for i in range(num_iterations):
    x = f(x)
    print(f"Iteration {i+1}: x = {x}")
```

With δ_j at hand, we can then retrieve the unobserved product characteristics as

$$\xi_j = \delta_j(\theta_2) - \beta_0^1 x_{j1} - \beta_0^2 x_{j2} - \alpha_0 p_j. \tag{3.33}$$

[6] A contraction mapping is a mapping between metric spaces that preserves contraction property. This means that the distance between two points (or elements) in the image space is always smaller than or equal to the distance between the same two points in the domain space.

[7] Fixed-point iteration is a method of finding a solution to a mathematical problem by iteratively applying a given function to its output, with the output of the function converging to a fixed point.

The unobserved product characteristics ξ_j act as the error terms of Eq. (3.33), and we can use any consistent estimator to estimate β_0^1, β_0^2, and α_0. In other words, the retrieved mean valuations δ_j represent the dependent variable, and the ξ_j represent the error terms in the following regression:

$$\delta_j(\theta_2) = \beta_0^1 x_{j1} + \beta_0^2 x_{j2} + \alpha_0 p_j + \xi_j. \tag{3.34}$$

To sum up, the numerical solution to the integral in Eq. 3.28 yielded the Monte Carlo simulation solution in Eq. 3.30. Using the mean utility from the multinomial logit results as starting values for δ_j and initial values for θ_2, we retrieve the mean utility valuation δ_j that equates the actual market shares to the predicted market shares using contraction mapping and fixed-point iteration on Eq. 3.30. Finally, we regress the obtained mean utility valuation δ_j on the price and product characteristics, using the generalized method of moments (GMM), given the potential endogeneity of the price and product characteristics.

3.3.4 *Endogeneity Issue and GMM Estimation*

Estimating the mean utility given in Eq. 3.34 presents the challenge of the potential endogeneity in prices and product characteristics, most likely correlated with the unobserved product characteristics ξ. This endogeneity implies the need to use instrumental variables (IV) to palliate potential biases in the results. Various instrumental variables have been used in the BLP literature, including characteristics of own and competing products (Berry et al. 1995), cost data (Berry et al. 1995; Nevo 2001; Hausman 1996; Berto Villas-Boas 2007; Chidmi and Lopez 2007), demographic characteristics, and market-level factors.

In choosing the instrumental variables, we have to keep in mind that the instrumental variables, call them Z, fulfill three conditions

$$\begin{aligned} E\left[Z'\varepsilon\right] &= 0 \\ E\left[Z'X\right] &\neq 0 \\ E\left[Z'Z\right] &< \infty. \end{aligned} \tag{3.35}$$

The first condition in Eq. 3.35 ensures that the IVs are uncorrelated with the model error or exogenous. As such, the model variables that are exogenous are part of the IV set, often termed as included exogenous variables. In addition, the instrumental variables also consist of excluded exogenous variables, that is, variables determined outside the dependent variable data-generating process. When the number of endogenous variables is higher than the number of excluded exogenous variables, the model is under-identified. The model is just-identified or over-identified when the number of excluded exogenous variables is equal to or higher than the number of endogenous variables, respectively. Only just- and over-identified models can be estimated, implying the need to have at least as many excluded exogenous variables as the endogenous ones.

The second condition in Eq. 3.35 ensures that the instrumental variables are relevant or highly correlated with the endogenous variables. Though the first condition is sufficient to ensure consistent estimation, some researchers have shown that weak instruments, that is, $E\left[Z'X\right]$ being close to zero, can yield inconsistent estimators and inaccurate statistical inference (Hahn and Hausman 2003). In addition, Hansen (2022) shows that the ordinary least-squares, the two-stage least-squares, and the limited information maximum likelihood estimators are inconsistent and remain random in large samples when the instrumental variables are weak. Therefore, it is imperative to use strong instruments to avoid weak instrument issues. Finally, the third condition ensures the IVs have a finite variance-covariance matrix.

In addition, the first condition in Eq. 3.35 offers the basis for the generalized method of moment estimation. The GMM is a generalization of the method moments, which is a technique for estimating parameters by matching population moments to sample counterparts. The GMM encompasses other econometric models, such as the ordinary least-squares (OLS), the instrumental variable, and the two-stage least-squares (2SLS) methods. The GMM, developed by Hansen (1982), enjoys its popularity because of its flexibility in accommodating linear and nonlinear data-generating processes with no distributional assumptions, as in the case of the maximum likelihood estimation. The moment conditions can come from the usual assumptions one makes, such as exogeneity, or from the economic theory. For instance, in the OLS regression $y = X\beta + e$, we often make the assumption of exogeneity, yielding the population moments $E\left[X'\varepsilon\right] = 0$ and the sample counterpart $\frac{1}{n}\sum_{i=1}^{n} x_i' e_i = 0$. For example, if the model is given by $y = \beta_1 + \beta_2 x_2 + \beta_3 x_3 + e$, we have the following sample moments given we assume $E\left[X'e\right] = 0$:

$$\begin{aligned}
\frac{1}{n}\sum_{i=1}^{n} e_i = 0 &\Rightarrow \frac{1}{n}\sum_{i=1}^{n} y_i - \beta_1 - \beta_2 x_{2i} - \beta_3 x_{3i} = 0 \\
\frac{1}{n}\sum_{i=1}^{n} x_{2i} e_i = 0 &\Rightarrow \frac{1}{n}\sum_{i=1}^{n} x_{2i}\left(y_i - \beta_1 - \beta_2 x_{2i} - \beta_3 x_{3i}\right) = 0 \\
\frac{1}{n}\sum_{i=1}^{n} x_{2i} e_i = 0 &\Rightarrow \frac{1}{n}\sum_{i=1}^{n} x_{3i}\left(y_i - \beta_1 - \beta_2 x_{2i} - \beta_3 x_{3i}\right) = 0.
\end{aligned} \tag{3.36}$$

When the number of moments is equal to the number of unknown parameters, as in the case of Eq. 3.36, the method of moments is the choice for parameter estimation. Now consider that $E\left[x_3 e\right] \neq 0$, and assume there are two instrumental variables, z_1 and z_2 that satisfy the conditions in Eq. 3.35. This implies the following sample moments:

$$
\begin{aligned}
\frac{1}{n}\sum_{i=1}^{n} y_i - \beta_1 - \beta_2 x_{2i} - \beta_3 x_{3i} &= 0 \\
\frac{1}{n}\sum_{i=1}^{n} x_{2i}\left(y_i - \beta_1 - \beta_2 x_{2i} - \beta_3 x_{3i}\right) &= 0 \\
\frac{1}{n}\sum_{i=1}^{n} z_{1i}\left(y_i - \beta_1 - \beta_2 x_{2i} - \beta_3 x_{3i}\right) &= 0 \\
\frac{1}{n}\sum_{i=1}^{n} z_{2i}\left(y_i - \beta_1 - \beta_2 x_{2i} - \beta_3 x_{3i}\right) &= 0.
\end{aligned} \tag{3.37}
$$

When there are more moments than parameters to be estimated, as in Eq. 3.37, we cannot find β estimates to equate all of the moments to zero. Rather, we try to find β estimates that make the moments as close to 0 as possible by minimizing a quadratic loss function given by

$$
\min_{\beta} Q(\beta) = \begin{bmatrix} \frac{1}{n}\sum_{i=1}^{n} e_i \\ \frac{1}{n}\sum_{i=1}^{n} x_{2i}e_i \\ \frac{1}{n}\sum_{i=1}^{n} z_{1i}e_i \\ \frac{1}{n}\sum_{i=1}^{n} z_{2i}e_i \end{bmatrix}' W \begin{bmatrix} \frac{1}{n}\sum_{i=1}^{n} e_i \\ \frac{1}{n}\sum_{i=1}^{n} x_{2i}e_i \\ \frac{1}{n}\sum_{i=1}^{n} z_{1i}e_i \\ \frac{1}{n}\sum_{i=1}^{n} z_{21}e_i, \end{bmatrix} \tag{3.38}
$$

where W is a weighting matrix. The generalized method of moments is more flexible because it allows the researcher to specify the optimal weighting matrix, implying a more efficient estimator than the 2SLS. We can have the following choice for W:

1. Identity matrix $W = I$: This gives equal weight to each moment condition. This is the 2SLS.
2. Optimal weighting matrix or a two-step weighting matrix: In this case, we start with $W = I$ and get $\hat{\beta}_{GMM}$. Then use the $\hat{\beta}_{GMM}$ to compute the new weighting matrix $\hat{W}$ and then the final $\hat{\beta}_{GMM}$.
3. Iterated GMM: Instead of two steps, we keep iterating between $\hat{\beta}_{GMM}$ and $\hat{W}$ until a convergence criterion is met.
4. Heteroscedasticity- and autocorrelation consistent weighting matrix. This will account for heteroscedasticity and autocorrelation, such as Eicker-White and Newey-West covariance estimators.

Going back to the BLP context, to estimate the set of parameters θ_1 and θ_2,[8] we interact with the error terms, ξ_j from Eq. 3.34 with a set of instrumental variables Z, such that $E\left[Z'\xi\right] = 0$ and $E\left[Z'p\right] \neq 0$. The generalized method of moments (GMM) estimator for $\theta = [\theta_1, \theta_2]$ is given by minimizing the following objective function:

$$
Q(\theta_1, \theta_2) = \left(\frac{1}{T}\xi(\theta_1, \theta_2)'Z\right) W \left(\frac{1}{T}Z'\xi(\theta_1, \theta_2)\right), \tag{3.39}
$$

[8] θ_1 represents the set of parameters entering δ_j, while θ_2 are the parameters entering μ_{ij}.

where T is the sample size and W is an optimal weighting matrix, which is the inverse of a consistent estimate of the moments. That is, $W = \left(E\left[Z'\xi\xi'Z\right]\right)^{-1}$.

3.3.5 *Estimation Flow, Algorithm, and Software*

To summarize, the estimation of the random-coefficient logit model or BLP model proceeds as follows:

1. Define the choice set, i.e., the number of brands J to be considered.
2. Define the market. For example, the market does not have to be a physical market; it could be weekly sales in the Dallas area. In other words, each week is a market.
3. Define the potential market size, M. The potential market size is equal to the per capita consumption during the period considered (weekly or monthly, for example) times the total population in the market.
4. Compute the observed potential market share for brand j as $S_j = \frac{Q_j}{M}$, where Q_j represents brand j total sales in the market.
5. Organize the data consisting of market shares, product characteristics, prices, and instrumental variables by market.
6. Prepare a sample of demographic data if using Current Population Survey for consumer demographics.

Following is the algorithm to estimate a BLP-type model:

Algorithm 3.2 BLP estimation algorithm

Generate N draws from the demographic sample (CPS, for example).

Generate N draws from the standard normal distribution. These draws represent the unobserved consumer characteristics.

Given starting values for θ_2 and δ_j, compute μ_{ij} using Eq. (3.26).

Solve for δ_j using the contraction mapping and fixed-point iteration method.

Retrieve the unobserved product characteristics $\xi_j = \delta_j - \beta_0^1 x_{j1} - \beta_0^2 x_{j2} - \alpha_0 p_j$.

Interact the retrieved unobserved product characteristics with the instrumental variables and form the GMM objective function.

Find θ_1 and θ_2 by minimizing the GMM objective function.

The estimation of the BLP-type models is possible either using a user-written code, such as Nevo's Matlab code, or packages from existing software, such as Stata (Vincent 2015), Python (Conlon and Gortmaker 2020a), and R (Brunner et al. 2017).

3.4 Illustration: US Soft Drink Differentiated Demand Estimation

For illustration, I use scanner data provided by Information Resources, Inc. (IRI) that includes weekly sales of carbonated soft drinks from January 2006 to December 2011 for the Dallas-Fort Worth metropolitan area. The data set consists of each brand's dollar sales, unit sales, volume equivalents, and universal product codes (UPC). In addition, I use the Current Population Survey to generate demographics.

The Market and the choice set
The choice set consists of twenty brands of carbonated soft drinks sold during 78 four-week periods between January 2006 and December 2011 in the Dallas-Fort Worth metropolitan area. Each four-week period constitutes one market, with a total of 78 markets, resulting in $20 \times 78 = 1,560$ observations. Table 3.1 lists the brands with their average market shares and average prices in \$/12 oz.

Table 3.1 Market shares and prices for selected carbonated drinks in Dallas metropolitan area, 2006–2011

Brand	Manufacturer	Market share (%)	Price (\$/12 oz)
Coke Classic	The Coca-Cola Co.	16.4468	0.2880
Dr Pepper	Dr Pepper Snapple Group	13.5843	0.2712
Diet Coke	The Coca-Cola Co.	7.3686	0.3000
Pepsi	PepsiCo	5.5919	0.2520
Sprite	The Coca-Cola Co.	4.3788	0.2940
Diet Dr Pepper	Dr Pepper Snapple Group	4.3275	0.2748
7-UP	Dr Pepper Snapple Group	2.6348	0.2592
Sunkist	Dr Pepper Snapple Group	2.3649	0.2640
Diet Pepsi	PepsiCo	1.9315	0.2676
Coke Zero	The Coca-Cola Co.	1.6455	0.3192
Mountain Dew	PepsiCo	1.5480	0.2856
Caffeine-Free Diet Coke	The Coca-Cola Co.	1.4939	0.2856
A & W Root Beer	Dr Pepper Snapple Group	1.4507	0.2676
Sprite Zero	The Coca-Cola Co.	0.9235	0.2844
Fanta	The Coca-Cola Co.	0.8294	0.2760
7-UP Diet	Dr Pepper Snapple Group	0.7601	0.2532
Caffeine-Free Diet Dr Pepeer	Dr Pepper Snapple Group	0.7516	0.2484
Royal Crown Cola	Dr Pepper Snapple Group	0.6534	0.2400
Canada Dry	Dr Pepper Snapple Group	0.5386	0.2760
A & W Cream Soda	Dr Pepper Snapple Group	0.2587	0.2652

Table 3.2 Product attributes and consumer characteristics summary statistics

	Mean	Std. dev.	Min.	Max.
Price ($/12oz)	0.2772	0.0300	0.1932	0.3708
Calories in 12-oz.	93.1	0	174	76.6861
Caffeine (mg) in 12-oz.	19.221	0	54.6	20.2261
Household income ($)	81,554.99	5,200	759,951	71,068.96
Number of persons under 15 years	0.8794	0	5	1.1376

The product attributes and consumer characteristics
Data for each brand's product characteristics comes from the nutritional fact labels provided by each company's website. In this illustration, I use calories and caffeine contents, and I assume that these characteristics remain the same during the data period.[9]

Demographic variables are collected from the Current Population Survey to allow for consumer heterogeneity, and 500 random draws are obtained for each market. The demographics used in this research are household income and the number of persons under 15 years old. In addition to observed demographics, households' unobserved characteristics are randomly generated (500 draws) from the standard normal distribution for each market. There are 78 markets and 500 draws for each market, hence, 39000 simulated households. Table 3.2 provides summary statistics for the product attributes and the consumer characteristics.

Instrumental variables
The last data consists of instrumental variables discussed in the previous section. Prices and product characteristics are potentially correlated with unobserved product characteristics, causing an endogeneity problem. Therefore, an instrumental variable method (IV) is necessary to provide consistent parameter estimates. This illustration uses input prices as instrumental variables for the price. Input prices include sugar prices, dextrose prices, the Federal Funds interest rate, producer price indices, employment cost index related to soft drink manufacturing, and gasoline prices from 2006 to 2011. Sugar and dextrose prices are obtained from the US Department of Agriculture (USDA), gasoline price is gathered from the US Energy Information Administration, and producer price indices and employment cost index for soft drinks, and the Federal Funds interest rate are retrieved from The Federal Reserve Bank of St. Louis.

Estimation using the Python pyblp package
To estimate the random coefficient multinomial logit using Python *pyblp* package, the data can be fed using two data sets. One data set consists of the market shares, the prices, the product characteristics, and the instrumental variables. The second data set consists of demographic draws. In this illustration, I use the household income

[9] Sugar content is excluded from the analysis because it gives similar information with calories.

and the number of persons under 15 years old. The following Python code imports the necessary packages and reads the two data into Python:

Code Listing 3.4 Python code to import the necessary packages and reads the two data into Python

```
import pandas as pd
import numpy as np
import scipy as sp
import pyblp
% Market data
market_data = pd.read_csv('blp_data.csv')
market_data.head()
% Demographic data
demogr_data = pd.read_excel('demo.xlsx')
demogr_data.head()
```

The market data is organized by market. In this illustration, the first twenty rows correspond to the twenty soft drink brands in Market 1, and so on. Similarly, the demographic data is also organized by market, with the first 500 rows corresponding to 500 draws of income and the number of persons under 15 years old in Market 1.

In the second step, the researcher provides the variables that linearly enter the indirect utility function, X_1, and the variables that are part of the deviation from the mean utility, X_2. Brand-specific effects should be entered in the linear part.

Code Listing 3.5 Python code to the BLP model

```
X1_formulation = pyblp.Formulation('0 + prices + cal + caff')
% If brand-specific effects are used, use the following line
% X_formulation = pyblp.Formulation ('0 + prices', absorb='C(Name)')
% where Name is the name of the brands in this illustration
X2_formulation = pyblp.Formulation('1 + prices + cal + caff')
product_formulations = (X1_formulation, X2_formulation)
```

The third step in the process is to select the integration method to compute the integral in Eq. (3.28) and the optimization algorithm to minimize the GMM objective function. Conlon and Gortmaker (2020b) provides extensive documentation regarding implementing the BLP-type model with the list of integration methods. In this illustration, I use the Monte Carlo method with $1,000$ draws for the integration method and the trust region routine to minimize the GMM objective function:

Code Listing 3.6 Python code to the numerical integration simulation

```
    mc_integration = pyblp.Integration('monte_carlo',
    size = 1000, specification_options = {'seed': 0})
    opt = pyblp.Optimization('trust-constr', {'gtol':
    1e-9}, compute_gradient = True)
    % where 'gtol' is the tolerance criterion to stop
    the GMM iteration.
\end{python}
\bigskip
The last part before the estimation is to provide the
    algorithm with starting values entering the
    deviation from the mean utility $\mu_{ij}$.
\begin{python}
    initial_sigma = np.diag([0.3302, 0.4526, 0.0163,
    0.2441])
    % This provides the starting values of the
    parameters of the interaction of the variables
    % in X2 % with the random draws (unobserved
    consumer characteristics)
    initial_pi = np.array([ [0.4819, 0.203], [0.8935,
    --0.2000], [--0.2506, 0.0511], [0.2650, --0.8091]
    ])
    % This provides the starting values of the
    parameters of the interaction of the
    % variables in X2 with the demographic variables
```

Finally, we put all the setups together and pass the problem to the solver chosen:

Code Listing 3.7 Python code to the numerical integration simulation

```
    blp_problem = pyblp.Problem( product_formulations,
    data, agent_formulation, agent_data, integration =
    mc_integration )

    blp_solution = blp_problem.solve(initial_sigma,
    initial_pi, optimization = opt)
```

3.4.1 Results

Table 3.3 presents the results of the random coefficient model multinomial logit model with the price and the calorie and caffeine contents as product characteristics. The second column gives the parameter estimates of the mean utility. In contrast, the second to the fifth columns have the parameter estimates of the deviation from the mean utility. For instance, 32.5201 in the fourth column is the parameter estimate of the interaction between the price and the number of persons under 15 years old. The fifth column estimates the variation of the unobserved consumer characteristics. The figures between parentheses are the parameter estimate standard errors.

Table 3.3 Random coefficient model parameter estimates

	Mean utility (δ_j)	Deviation from mean utility (μ_{ij})		
Variable	Linear part	Income	Number of children	Unobserved
Constant	Not included	0.85667	–0.96370	–0.8695
		(1.5742)	(2.9340)	0.3114***
Price	–23.1347***	3.5468	32.5201***	0.0000
	(6.6892)	(5.0321)	(9.1263)	(1.1151)
Calorie content	–0.0880	0.0279	0.0984	0.0366
	(0.1495)	(0.1397)	(0.0786)	(0.0397)
Caffeine content	0.8669*	–0.1664	–0.6109	0.0161
	(0.4855)	(0.4620)	(0.4188)	(0.1257)

*Significant at 10% level; ** significant at 5% level; *** significant at 1% level

Demand parameter estimates represented in Table 3.3 can also be written as follows:

$$\begin{cases} Price \quad \alpha_i = -23.1347 + 3.5468 Income_i + 32.5201 Children_i + 0.0000 v_i \\ Calorie \quad \beta_i^1 = -0.0880 + 0.0279 Income_i + 0.0984 Children_i + 0.0366 v_i \\ Caffeine \quad \beta_i^2 = 0.8669 - 0.1664 Income_i - 0.6109 Children_i + 0.0161 v_i. \end{cases} \tag{3.40}$$

These equations do not refer to single-point estimates. Instead, they provide a distribution of the parameter of interest. For example, since there are 39,000 simulated households (78 markets and 500 households in each market), there are 39,000 price parameter estimates. Figure 3.1 provides a distribution for the price responsiveness. The figure indicates the price parameter estimates are negative for all the households in the data, ranging from –22.8789 to –0.7982, with an average of –19.3128 and a standard deviation of 3.2278.

This heterogeneity in price responsiveness implies heterogeneity in price elasticities resulting in flexible substitution patterns. I use 20 brands in this illustration, implying 400 price elasticities per market and demographic draw or household. To summarize some of the results, the following figure shows the own-price elasticity boxplots of some brands (Fig. 3.2).

The boxplots indicate that popular brands, such as Coke Classic, Dr Pepper, and Pepsi, are less elastic than their diet versions, showing greater variability in the values of own-price elasticities. Finally, the *pyblp* Python package provides a parametric bootstrap function to construct the elasticities' 95% (Table 3.4).

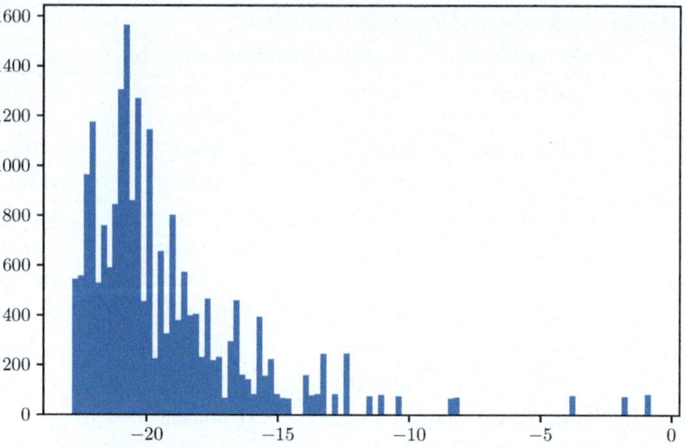

Fig. 3.1 Price parameter distribution

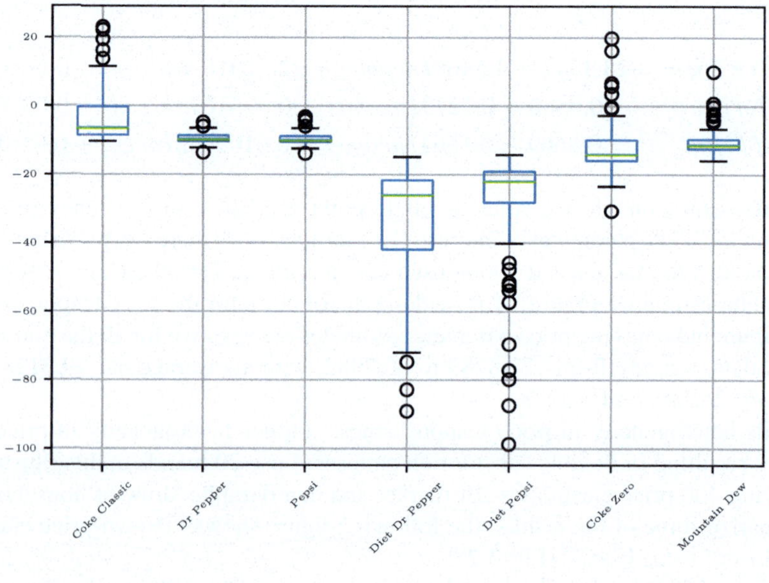

Fig. 3.2 Own-price elasticity boxplots

3.5 Concluding Remarks

This chapter attempts to provide an overview of estimating demand for differentiated products using the random coefficient multinomial logit model, also known as the BLP model. The BLP model presents at least two advantages over traditional demand system models, such as the AIDS model. First, the dimensionality problem arising

Table 3.4 Own-price elasticities 95% confidence interval

Brand	Lower bound bootstrap	BLP estimate	Upper bound bootstrap
Coke Classic	–8.9867	–17.5094	–3.2543
Dr Pepper	–9.5950	–14.7670	–4.321
Diet Coke	–24.8047	–25.5850	–4.1996
Pepsi	–9.5851	–15.8852	–4.5818
Diet Dr Pepper	–28.6167	–33.3638	–3.8906
Diet Pepsi	–25.8250	–29.8810	–3.3782
Coke Zero	–15.7129	–23.7851	–2.8789
Mountain Dew	–10.9672	–16.9472	–1.5773

from analyzing many products is solved by projecting the products onto a characteristic space, reducing the estimated parameters. Second, consumer heterogeneity is considered by allowing taste parameters to be random. This randomness is due to the randomness in the consumer's unobserved characteristics.

Though the BLP estimation is computationally challenging, the outcome is rewarding, allowing the researchers to estimate the demand appropriately. In this illustration, for instance, I considered 20 brands of soft drinks. However, in reality, consumer choices are made at lower levels of aggregation, such as package size. Brand manufacturers and retailers, whether shoppers tend to prefer larger package sizes over smaller ones (12-cane pack versus 6-can pack). This level of disaggregation will increase the number of products analyzed and, therefore, the number of parameters estimated using the traditional approach, hence the relevance of the BLP-type models in offering a richer and more flexible substitution pattern at the appropriate aggregation level.

Moreover, the BLP-type models' computational cost can be overcome with increasing computing capabilities and the recent development of software packages offering researchers huge savings on programming skills and time. For instance, the *pyblp* Python package offers several routines to estimate the random coefficient model and extends beyond the demand side by having the possibility to evaluate the supply side (marginal cost and markups), conduct merger, and welfare analysis, to name a few features.

Though the BLP model provides an efficient tool for the demand for differentiated goods, it is computationally challenging, requiring researchers to explore new techniques, especially in numerical integration and GMM optimization. Traditional optimization algorithms, like Newton's algorithm, often fail to converge to global optimal. In addition, most of the studies using BLP limit themselves to using a linear utility specification. While this specification is intuitive and easy to interpret, it may not accurately represent the real-world context. Adoption of nonlinear functional forms could introduce more flexibility and perhaps avoid flat zones during the optimization process. In the same line of thought, the generalized random utility model proposed by Walker and Ben-Akiva (2002) has the advantage of including flexible disturbances, latent variables, latent class, and a combination of revealed and stated preferences. This additional flexibility may bring an improvement in the first- and second-order conditions of the optimization process. In addition, future research could explore the development of nonparametric estimation and machine learning techniques to solve the BLP computational challenges. Finally, there are potential venues to focus on developing dynamic versions of the BLP model that account for time-dependent decision-making and market dynamics.

References

Allenby GM, Rossi PE (1998) Marketing models of consumer heterogeneity. J Econ 89(1–2):57–78
Barten AP (1966) Theorie en empirie van een volledig stelsel van vraagvergelijkingen. PhD thesis, Drukkerij Pasmans
Becker F, Danaf M, Song X, Atasoy B, Ben-Akiva M (2018) Bayesian estimator for logit mixtures with inter-and intra-consumer heterogeneity. Transp Res Part B: Methodol 117:1–17
Berry S, Levinsohn J, Pakes A (1995) Automobile prices in market equilibrium. Econ: J Econ Soc 841–890
Berry S, Levinsohn J, Pakes A (1998) Differentiated products demand systems from a combination of micro and macro data: autos again. Department of Economic, Yale University, New Haven, CT, Work paper
Berry ST (1994) Estimating discrete-choice models of product differentiation. RAND J Econ 242–262
Berto Villas-Boas S (2007) Vertical relationships between manufacturers and retailers: inference with limited data. Rev Econ Stud 74(2):625–652
Bonnet C, Bouamra-Mechemache Z (2016) Organic label, bargaining power, and profit-sharing in the French fluid milk market. Am J Agr Econ 98(1):113–133
Bonnet C, Bouamra-Mechemache Z (2019) "yogurt cartel" of private label providers in France: impact on prices and welfare
Bonnet C, Dubois P (2010) Inference on vertical contracts between manufacturers and retailers allowing for nonlinear pricing and resale price maintenance. Rand J Econ 41(1):139–164
Bonnet C, Réquillart V (2013) Impact of cost shocks on consumer prices in vertically-related markets: the case of the French soft drink market. Am J Agr Econ 95(5):1088–1108
Bonnet C, Villas-Boas SB (2016) An analysis of asymmetric consumer price responses and asymmetric cost pass-through in the French coffee market. Eur Rev Agric Econ 43(5):781–804
Brunner D (2017) Numerical integration in random coefficient models of demand. PhD thesis
Brunner D, Heiss F, Romahn A, Weiser C (2017) Reliable estimation of random coefficient logit demand models, vol 267. DICE Discussion Paper
Cameron AC, Trivedi PK (2005) Microeconometrics: methods and applications. Cambridge University Press, Cambridge
Cardell NS (1989) Extensions of multinomial logit: the hedonic demand model, the non-independent logit model, and the ranked logit model. Harvard University
Carlton DW, Perloff JM (1994) Modern industrial organization, 2005
Chidmi B, Lopez RA (2007) Brand-supermarket demand for breakfast cereals and retail competition. Am J Agr Econ 89(2):324–337
Chidmi B, Murova O (2011) Measuring market power in the supermarket industry: the case of the Seattle-Tacoma fluid milk market. Agribusiness 27(4):435–449
Chintagunta PK (2001) Endogeneity and heterogeneity in a probit demand model: estimation using aggregate data. Mark Sci 20(4):442–456

Christensen LR, Jorgenson DW, Lau LJ (1975) Transcendental logarithmic utility functions. Am Econ Rev 65(3):367–383
Conlon C, Gortmaker J (2020a) Best practices for differentiated products demand estimation with pyblp. RAND J Econ 51(4):1108–1161
Conlon C, Gortmaker J (2020b) Best practices for differentiated products demand estimation with PyBLP. RAND J Econ 51(4):1108–1161. https://doi.org/10.1111/1756-2171.12352. https://onlinelibrary.wiley.com/doi/abs/10.1111/1756-2171.12352
Cotterill RW, Haller LE (1997) An econometric analysis of the demand for RTE cereal: product market definition and unilateral market power effects. Technical report
Cotterill RW, Franklin AW, Ma LY (1996) Measuring market power effects in differentiated product industries: an application to the soft drink industry. Technical report
Deaton A, Muellbauer J (1980) An almost ideal demand system. Am Econ Rev 70(3):312–326
Dixit AK, Stiglitz JE (1977) Monopolistic competition and optimum product diversity. Am Econ Rev 67(3):297–308
Draganska M, Klapper D, Villas-Boas SB (2010) A larger slice or a larger pie? an empirical investigation of bargaining power in the distribution channel. Mark Sci 29(1):57–74
Dubé JP (2004) Multiple discreteness and product differentiation: demand for carbonated soft drinks. Mark Sci 23(1):66–81
Eaton BC, Lipsey RG (1989) Product differentiation. Handbook of industrial organization, vol 1, pp 723–768
Ebbes P, Liechty JC, Grewal R (2015) Attribute-level heterogeneity. Manage Sci 61(4):885–897
Fukuda D, Yai T (2010) Semiparametric specification of the utility function in a travel mode choice model. Transportation 37:221–238
Gandhi A, Nevo A (2021) Empirical models of demand and supply in differentiated products industries. In: Handbook of industrial organization, vol 4. Elsevier, pp 63–139
Goldberg PK (1995) Product differentiation and oligopoly in international markets: the case of the us automobile industry. Econ: J Econ Soc 891–951
Gorman WM (1980) A possible procedure for analysing quality differentials in the egg market. Rev Econ Stud 47(5):843–856
Guadagni PM, Little JD (1983) A logit model of brand choice calibrated on scanner data. Mark Sci 2(3):203–238
Hahn J, Hausman J (2003) Weak instruments: diagnosis and cures in empirical econometrics. Am Econ Rev 93(2):118–125
Hansen B (2022) Econometrics. Princeton University Press, Princeton
Hansen LP (1982) Large sample properties of generalized method of moments estimators. Econ: J Econ Soc 1029–1054
Hausman J, Leonard G, Zona JD (1994) Competitive analysis with differenciated products. Annales d'Economie et de Statistique 159–180
Hausman JA (1996) Valuation of new goods under perfect and imperfect competition. In: The economics of new goods, University of Chicago Press, pp 207–248
Hiller RS, Savage SJ, Waldman DM (2018) Using aggregate market data to estimate patent value: an application to united states smartphones 2010–2015. Int J Ind Organ 60:1–31
Hirsch S, Tiboldo G, Lopez RA (2018) A tale of two Italian cities: brand-level milk demand and price competition. Appl Econ 50(49):5239–5252
Istratescu VI (2001) Fixed point theory: an introduction, vol 7. Springer Science & Business Media
Kamakura WA, Kim BD, Lee J (1996) Modeling preference and structural heterogeneity in consumer choice. Mark Sci 15(2):152–172
Knittel CR, Metaxoglou K (2014) Estimation of random-coefficient demand models: two empiricists' perspective. Rev Econ Stat 96(1):34–59
Lancaster KJ (1966) A new approach to consumer theory. J Polit Econ 74(2):132–157
Li X, Lopez R, Yang S (2018) Energy-milk price transmission at the product brand level. Agric Econ 49(3):289–299

Li Y, Ansari A (2014) A Bayesian semiparametric approach for endogeneity and heterogeneity in choice models. Manage Sci 60(5):1161–1179
Liu Y, Lopez RA (2016) The impact of social media conversations on consumer brand choices. Mark Lett 27(1):1–13
Lopez E, Lopez RA (2009) Demand for differentiated milk products: implications for price competition. Agribus: Int J 25(4):453–465
Lopez RA, Fantuzzi KL (2012) Demand for carbonated soft drinks: implications for obesity policy. Appl Econ 44(22):2859–2865
Lopez RA, Matschke X (2012) Home bias in us beer consumption. Pac Econ Rev 17(4):525–534
Lopez RA, Liu Y, Zhu C (2015) Tv advertising spillovers and demand for private labels: the case of carbonated soft drinks. Appl Econ 47(25):2563–2576
Ma LY (1996) An econometric analysis of competition in a differentiated product industry: the United States ready-to-eat cereal industry. University of Connecticut
Mariuzzo F, Walsh PP, Whelan C (2003) Firm size and market power in carbonated soft drinks. Rev Ind Organ 23(3):283–299
Mariuzzo F, Walsh PP, Whelan C (2010) Coverage of retail stores and discrete choice models of demand: estimating price elasticities and welfare effects. Int J Ind Organ 28(5):555–578
Marschak J (1974) Binary-choice constraints and random utility indicators (1960). In: Economic information, decision, and prediction. Springer, Berlin pp 218–239
McFadden D (1974) The measurement of urban travel demand. J Public Econ 3(4):303–328
McFadden D (1981) Econometric models of probabilistic choice. In: Structural analysis of discrete data with econometric applications, p 198272
McFadden D et al (1973) Conditional logit analysis of qualitative choice behavior
McFadden DL (1984) Econometric analysis of qualitative response models. Handb Econ 2:1395–1457
Nevo A (2000) A practitioner's guide to estimation of random-coefficients logit models of demand. J Econ Manag Strat 9(4):513–548
Nevo A (2001) Measuring market power in the ready-to-eat cereal industry. Econometrica 69(2):307–342
Nevo A (2011) Empirical models of consumer behavior. Annu Rev Econ 3(1):51–75
Popkowski Leszczyc P, Bass FM (1998) Determining the effects of observed and unobserved heterogeneity on consumer brand choice. Appl Stoch Model Data Anal 14(2):95–115
Rossi PE, Allenby GM (1993) A Bayesian approach to estimating household parameters. J Mark Res 30(2):171–182
Rossi PE, McCulloch RE, Allenby GM (1995) Hierarchical modelling of consumer heterogeneity: an application to target marketing. In: Case studies in Bayesian statistics, vol II. Springer, Berlin, pp 323–349
Skrainka BS, Judd KL (2011) High performance quadrature rules: how numerical integration affects a popular model of product differentiation. SSRN, p 1870703
Spence M (1976) Product selection, fixed costs, and monopolistic competition. Rev Econ Stud 43(2):217–235
Stone R (1954) Linear expenditure systems and demand analysis: an application to the pattern of British demand. Econ J 64(255):511–527
Sudhir K (2001) Competitive pricing behavior in the auto market: a structural analysis. Mark Sci 20(1):42–60
Theil H (1965) The information approach to demand analysis. Econometrica (pre-1986) 32(1):67
Thurstone LL (2017) A law of comparative judgment. In: Scaling, Routledge, pp 81–92
Toro-González D, McCluskey JJ, Mittelhammer RC (2014) Beer snobs do exist: estimation of beer demand by type. J Agric Resour Econ 174–187
Train KE (2009) Discrete choice methods with simulation. Cambridge University Press, Cambridge
Van Der Pol M, Currie G, Kromm S, Ryan M (2014) Specification of the utility function in discrete choice experiments. Value Health 17(2):297–301

Verboven F (1996) International price discrimination in the European car market. RAND J Econ 240–268
Villas-Boas SB (2007) Using retail data for upstream merger analysis. joclec 3(4):689–715
Vincent DW (2015) The Berry-Levinsohn-Pakes estimator of the random-coefficients logit demand model. Stand Genomic Sci 15(3):854–880
Walker J, Ben-Akiva M (2002) Generalized random utility model. Math Soc Sci 43(3):303–343
Xiao J, Ju H (2014) Market equilibrium and the environmental effects of tax adjustments in china's automobile industry. Rev Econ Stat 96(2):306–317
Zhu C, Lopez RA, Liu X (2016) Information cost and consumer choices of healthy foods. Am J Agr Econ 98(1):41–53

Chapter 4
Quantile Regression and Decomposition Techniques: An Application to Nutritional Demand in India

Kompal Sinha

Abstract This chapter discusses the quantile regression technique and elaborates on the computation of parameter estimates in the context of cross-section quantile regression using rich nutrition data from rural India. The unique feature of estimating parameters at various quantiles of the distribution has several advantages: (a) it allows analyzing the relationship between variables beyond the mean; (b) it allows analyzing variables that are not independently and identically distributed; (c) it allows understanding the relationship between variables with non-linear relationships with the dependent variable. With India facing the double burden of overweight and malnutrition, using data for nutrition demand allows us to understand the benefits of using the quantile regression technique to study the distributional heterogeneity in the responsiveness of nutritional demand to the same covariates. The analysis finds the drivers of nutritional status to vary at various points of the nutritional demand highlighting heterogeneity in drivers of nutritional demand by nutritional status of households. Furthermore, to highlight the importance of a distributional analysis, we decompose the calorie consumption differential across quantiles to find tastes and preferences to dominate the differential for well-nourished households during first-generation reforms and undernourished households over second-generation reforms in India.

Keywords Quantile regression · Oaxaca-blinder · Counterfactual · Decomposition · Calorie demand

4.1 Introduction

An important characteristic of a rapidly developing economy such as India is the co-occurrence of poverty and affluence resulting in an inevitable co-existence of under-nutrition and over-nutrition. Rapid growth has brought about quick changes in

K. Sinha (✉)
Department of Economics, Macquarie Business School, Macquarie University, Sydney, Australia
e-mail: kompal.sinha@mq.edu.au

D. Mukherjee (ed.), *Applied Econometric Analysis Using Cross Section and Panel Data*, Contributions to Economics, https://doi.org/10.1007/978-981-99-4902-1_4

real wages and income, nature of work, technological innovation, access to amenities, improved transportation along with rapid modernization/westernization of its society. The responsiveness of nutritional intake (calorie demand) to these changing environmental factors would neither be as rapid, nor would it be uniform for the entire population. While increase in income would result in consumption of tastier foods (Behrman and Deolalikar 1989), the responsiveness of nutritional demand to changing environment would not be same across the calorie consumption distribution resulting in widening nutritional inequalities.

Recent literature has documented, both, a rise in overweight and obesity[1] and prevalence of under-nutrition[2] in India. While several studies that have analyzed nutritional trends in India and other developing countries (Deaton and Dreze 2009; Jha et al. 2009; Gaiha 1999; Subramanian and Deaton 1996; Behrman and Deolalikar 1987, 1989), most extant analyzes have essentially analyzed mean per capita calorie consumption (i.e., households with mean calorie consumption). From the policy perspective, it is important to understand nutrient consumption patterns while accounting for the inevitable consumption inequalities existing in any developing economy. A distributional analysis of the socioeconomic gradient in calorie distribution is of particular interest to policymakers struggling with the dual burden of undernourishment and obesity in India.

Poverty assessments[3] in India were originally based on a calorie norm and policy designed for people living below poverty line (BPL) to get access to food subsidies offered through the public distribution system (PDS). It is of immense policy interest to analyze whether access to these resources would influence calorie consumption patterns. The present paper analyzes how poverty benchmarking influenced calorie consumption patterns in India. Therefore, the main questions addressed by this paper are: Does the responsiveness of calorie consumption to various factors differs significantly for undernourished households and well-nourished households? What were the factors contributing toward the observed transition in calorie consumption and which households were most susceptible to this change? Whether setting poverty thresholds influence calorie consumption patterns around these benchmarks.

This chapter uses quantile regression techniques and decomposition techniques to analyze calorie consumption in India. Considering data from three rounds of the National Sample Survey (NSS), shows how this technique can be used for a distributional analysis to provide policy-relevant insights. *First*, we disaggregate the socioeconomic gradient in calorie demand/Quantile regression results for all three NSS rounds allows us to study the factors explaining the distributional variations in the demand for calories vary for undernourished households (at lower quantiles) and well-nourished households (at higher quantiles). For example, females as household heads started to have a significant influence on household's demand for calories

[1] "India facing obesity epidemic: experts." *The Hindu,* 2007, pp. 10–12.

[2] The prevalence of poor nutrition in a period of sustained economic growth has been discussed in Deaton and Dreze (2009).

[3] Poverty lines in India were originally based on the minimum per capita daily requirements of 2400 cal in rural areas and 2100 cal in urban areas.

in the post-reform period and the magnitude of this effect varied significantly for undernourished and well-nourished households. Household's access to clean cooking fuel resulted in an increasing effect on calorie consumption over NSS rounds.

Second, we use Oaxaca-Blinder decomposition and quantile regression decomposition techniques to quantify the contribution of factors toward changing calorie demand across time. Decomposition of calorie consumption gap over NSS rounds suggests that during the period of first-generation reforms (between 43rd and 50th round), calorie consumption increased for undernourished households and a decrease was primarily observed for well-nourished households resulting in a wider gap at higher quantiles. Quite interestingly calorie gap for the period of second-generation reforms (between the 50th and 61st rounds) was more pronounced for undernourished households who experienced a larger decline in calorie consumption. The distributional analysis across quantiles suggests that while for undernourished households both effect of distribution of covariates and tastes and preferences contributes toward explaining calorie differential, for well-nourished households the differential is completely dominated by tastes and preferences of households. The overall decline in calorie consumption (between 1987–1988 and 2004–2005) essentially started with well-nourished households initiating the transition toward tastier foods, with undernourished households resisting the transition to tastier foods till the period of second-generation reforms. This approach to study calorie consumption patterns in India would assist in understanding the path of nutritional transition. These issues hold potentially strong implications toward understanding how society adapts to changing environmental factors and which sections of the society are more susceptible to this change (Dubey and Palmer-Jones 2005).

The rest of this chapter is organized as follows. Section 2 presents a detailed discussion of the econometric model and specification of quantile regression and the decomposition methods. Section 3 explains the decomposition analysis and technique used for this analysis. Section 4 presents the results. Important conclusions and policy implications are drawn in Sect. 5.

4.2 Methodology

Existing literature on the analysis of demand for calorie focuses only on the mean, which statistically describes the effect of each covariate as a simple location shift (Melly 2005a, b). Recent empirical research has provided evidence to show that for data having outliers, the traditional conditional mean estimates do not give an efficient outcome. Yu et al. (2003) mention the "sample median is more robust to outliers than a sample mean for estimating the average location of population" and hence quantile regression is more stable than mean regression for analyzing data with outlying observation.

Consider a sample (y_i, x_i); $i = 1, 2 \ldots n$ from the population where x_i is a $\mathrm{K} \times 1$ vector of regressors. In the classical ordinary least square regression methodology, a dependent variable y is estimated as a function of independent variables x, and it is only necessary to know the conditional mean function, i.e., the function that describes how the mean of y changes with the vector of covariates x.

$$y_i = x_i{'}\beta + u_i \tag{4.1}$$

Simply said, it is the true value around which y fluctuates due to an accidental error u_i. The error is assumed to have exactly the same distribution irrespective of the values taken by the components of the vector x. This is known as a pure location shift model as it assumes the x vector affects only the location of the conditional distribution of y, neither its shape nor any other aspect of its distribution shape. With the additional assumption that the error terms are normally distributed, the least square methods give the maximum likelihood estimates of the conditional mean functions.

The econometrics literature has argued that the covariates may influence the conditional distribution of the response variable in ways other than just the location. These factors include, inducing multimodality, expand the dispersion of the response variable as in the models of heteroskedasticity, stretch one tail of the distribution, and/or compress the other tail of the distribution. All these issues can be addressed by performing quantile regressions.

Quantile regression models possess certain features that make this technique a better alternative than the ordinary least square model:

- Quantile regression models can be used to characterize the entire distribution of a dependent variable for a given set of regressors.
- A quantile regression model has a linear programming representation, which makes estimation easy.
- The objective function for quantile regression is the weighted sum of absolute deviations. This gives a robust measure of location and thereby the estimated coefficient is not sensitive to outlier observations of the dependent variable.
- Quantile regression estimators are more efficient than least square estimators if the distribution of the error term is non-normal.
- Potential different solutions at distinct quantiles may be inferred as differences in the response of the dependent variable to changes in the regressors at various points in the distribution of the dependent variable.
- Quantile regression is more stable than mean regression for analyzing contaminated data. Yu and Jones (1998) established that the variance of a typical kernel smoother is greater than the variance of a smooth quantile regression curve.

4.2.1 Quantile Regression

Before formally defining quantile regression the elementary definition of a sample quantile is explained. The word quantile is a synonym for percentile or fractiles and refers to the general case of dividing the reference population into four segments, a quintile divides the reference population into five parts and a decile divides the population into 10 segments. The median divides the population into two parts. In a sense, quantiles are related to the process of ordering and sorting. As a sample population mean is defined as a solution of minimizing the sum of squared residuals, the median is defined as the solution to minimizing a sum of absolute residuals. Suppose that the θth quantile of a population is m_θ where $0 < \theta < 1$ and F_N is the cumulative distribution function, in the population, of y then m_θ is defined as:

$$\theta = \Pr[y \leq m_\theta] = F_N(m_\theta) \tag{4.2}$$

For a sample the analogous expression for defining $\widehat{m_\theta}$ is:

$$\widehat{m_\theta} = \inf[\mathrm{y} : \mathrm{F_N(y)} \geq \theta] \tag{4.3}$$

These equations say that in a class of students, a student scores at the θth quantile of an exam if she performs better than the proportion θ of the reference group of students and worse than the proportion $(1 - \theta)$ of the reference group of students. The median would be represented by the case $\theta = 1/2$.

In the context of our analysis, the quantile regression framework allows covariates to have marginal effects (returns) that vary with household's position in the calorie consumption distribution.

4.2.2 The Model

The quantile regression model (QR, henceforth) was proposed by Koenker and Bassett (1978). This model can be understood as a natural extension of the mean Ordinary Least Squares (OLS) estimation of a conditional mean model with the difference that while OLS provides the effect of covariates as a location shift, conditional quantile regression is a linear function of observed heterogeneity, providing a detailed description of the conditional distribution.

Consider a sample (y_i, x_i); $i = 1 \ldots n$ from a population where x_i is an $K \times 1$ vector of regressors. Then, it is assumed that:

$$y_i = x_i{}'\beta_\theta + u_{\theta_i} \tag{4.4}$$

where u_{θ_i} is the error term such that $Quant_\theta[y_i|x_i] = x_i{}'\beta_\theta + u_{\theta_i} = 0$. Thus,

$$Quant_\theta[y_i|x_i] = x_i{}'\beta_\theta \tag{4.5}$$

where $Quant_\theta[y_i|x_i]$ represents the conditional quantile of y_i conditional upon the set of independent variables vector x_i. The assumption that $Quant_\theta\left[u_{\theta_i}|x_i\right] = 0$ implies that only the distribution term u_{θ_i} satisfies the assumption that the θth quantile of u_{θ_i}, i.e., $y_i - x_i{\prime}\beta_\theta$ conditional upon the vector of regressors is equal to zero. This can be expressed in terms of statistical probability theory for a given scalar τ as:

$$\Pr[y_i \leq \tau | x_i] = \Pr[x_i{\prime}\beta \leq \tau + u_{\theta_i} | x_i] = \Pr[u_{\theta_i} \leq \tau - x_i{\prime}\beta_\theta | x_i] = F_{u\theta}[\tau - x_i{\prime}\beta_\theta | x_i]$$

While no assumption is made regarding the distribution of the error term u_{θ_i}, the only assumption made is that the θth quantile of $y_i - x_i{\prime}\beta_\theta$ conditional upon the regressor vector x_i equals zero. This assumption is made to identify the intercept term in β_θ. The θth quantile regression result is the solution to the following minimization problem:

$$\min_\beta \frac{1}{n}[\sum_{i:y_i \geq x_i{\prime}\beta} \theta |y_i - x_i{\prime}\beta| + \sum_{i:y_i < x_i{\prime}\beta} (1-\theta)|y_i - x_i{\prime}\beta|] \tag{4.6}$$

The parameter space for β is B_θ and $B_\theta \subseteq \Re^k$. The above minimization problem can be written alternatively as:

$$\frac{1}{n}\min_\beta[\sum_{i=1}^{n}\left(\theta - \frac{1}{2} + \frac{1}{2}sgn(y_i - x_i{\prime}\beta)\right)(y_i - x_i{\prime}\beta)] \tag{4.7}$$

where, $sgn(u) = I(u \geq 0) - I(u \leq 0)$. The first-order condition corresponding to the above minimization problem is:

$$\frac{1}{n}\sum\nolimits_{i=1}^{n}\left(\theta - \frac{1}{2} + \frac{1}{2}sgn\left(y_i - x_i{\prime}\widehat{\beta_\theta}\right)\right)x_i = 0 \tag{4.8}$$

This minimization problem suggests the presence of a moment function $g(x_i, y_i; \beta) = \left(\theta - \frac{1}{2} + \frac{1}{2}sgn(y_i - x_i{\prime}\widehat{\beta_\theta})\right)x_i$. The asymptotic properties have been proved to hold in Koenker and Bassett (1978) have proved to hold the asymptotic properties. The results imply that for any error distribution for which the median is a more efficient estimator of location than the mean, the quantile regression estimator at the median, i.e., the Least Absolute Deviation (LAD) estimator is more efficient than the least square (OLS) estimator in the linear model. The quantile regression problem can be represented in a linear programming framework and can be solved by applying the simplex algorithm. The linear programming representation is very important as it has implicit implications (Buchinsky 1998). Firstly, the quantile regression estimator will be achieved in a finite number of simplex iterations. Secondly, due to the duality theorem a feasible solution is guaranteed. Thirdly, unlike the ordinary least square estimator the parameter estimate is robust to outliers. That is, if $y_i - x_i{\prime}\beta_\theta > 0$ then y is increased toward ∞; however, if $y_i - x_i{\prime}\beta_\theta < 0$ then y is decreased toward $-\infty$ and thus the solution $\widehat{\beta_\theta}$ remains unaltered.

4.2.3 Illustration Using STATA

Let us estimate the calorie demand equation using a sample dataset on calorie consumption across quantiles. The following steps should be followed in STATA:

(a) Load the dataset using the use filename command:
(b) Summarize the variables in the dataset using the sum command. Use the * to sum all variables in the dataset:
(c) Use the quantile regression command **qreg** followed by the dependent and independent variables. This command used without any options would estimate the median regression, i.e., estimate Eq. 4.5 for $\theta = \frac{1}{2}$.
(d) Install the command to graph quantile regression coefficients.
(e) Graph the coefficients of the quantile regression.

```
use "C: File location\filename.dta", clear
    sum *
    qreg y r
    ssc install grqreg
    grqreg, cons ci ols olsci
```

4.3 Decomposition Analysis

The changes that occur in the distribution structure of a variable over time or across subgroups can be better understood if the effects of various factors can be identified. Two seminal papers by Oaxaca (1973) and Blinder (1973) addressed the issue of wage differential/wage gap in the United States by proposing a method to quantitatively assess the source of male-female wage differentials. Specifically, they suggested that discrimination against females can be said to exist if the relative wage for males is more than the relative wage that would have prevailed if males and females were paid according to the same criteria. Commonly known as the Oaxaca-Blinder decomposition, this approach decomposes the difference between two group mean values into a component due to the difference between the group mean covariates characteristics and another component due to the difference in the returns to these characteristics. The author defines two alternative criteria of non-discrimination. The first criteria says that under non-discrimination the wage structure faced by females would also apply to males. Alternatively, the second criteria says that under non-discrimination the wage structure faced by males would also apply to females. In other words, the first criteria of defining non-discrimination assumes that in the absence of discrimination the females would on average receive the same wage as the presently receive, however, discrimination appears to exist in the form of males receiving more wage than what a non-discriminating market would award them. A similar analogy can be applied to understand the second assumption. Based on separate ordinary least square estimations of a wage structure for males and females, the wage differential between two groups is decomposed into:

- effects of discrimination.
- effects of differences in individual characteristics.

The author concludes that a substantial portion of the true male-female wage differential is attributable to the effects of discrimination. Ever since this seminal study by Oaxaca (1973) for male-female wage differential in the United States and the other study by Blinder (1973) in the same year, decomposition analysis has been widely used to address issues related to labor markets, the most important one being the application to wage differential.

The Decomposition techniques proposed by Oaxaca (1973) and Blinder (1973) were designed to decompose differences in distribution at a conditional mean of the dependent variable. Quantile regression decomposition techniques proposed by Machado and Mata (2005) (M&M, henceforth) technique extends the traditional Oaxaca-Blinder decomposition on the conditional mean of the dependent variable to the whole distribution of this variable. The M&M decomposition is based on the construction of a counterfactual distribution of the dependent variable (calorie demand in our case). This counterfactual distribution is decomposed to get a part explained by characteristics and a part explained by coefficients. The standard errors are estimated using bootstrap with 100 replications. We explain the Oaxaca-Blinder decomposition technique followed by the quantile regression decomposition technique next.

4.3.1 Oaxaca-Blinder Decomposition

Consider a sample $(y_i, x_i), i = 1...n$ from a population where x_i is an $KX1$ vector of regressors giving us an ordinary least square regression model as:

$$y_i = x_i{}'\beta + u_i \tag{4.9}$$

The Oaxaca-Blinder decomposition technique decomposes the change in the conditional mean of a variable in two steps. The first step is to estimate the OLS regression equations separately for the two distributions and then repeat the estimation for the pooled data, to represent the non-discrimination situation.[4] Ordinary Least Square (OLS) estimates for a variable y equations estimated for two scenarios A and B (these could be two subgroups like males and females in the Oaxaca (1973)) are:

$$y_A|\boldsymbol{x} = x_A{}'\beta^A + u_A \tag{4.10}$$

$$y_B|\boldsymbol{x} = x_B{}'\beta^B + u_B \tag{4.11}$$

[4] Neumark (1988) suggested that coefficients from a pooled regression analysis would serve as a good proxy in absence of any sort of personal tastes and preference.

where, y_A and y_B are vectors for two scenarios for which the decomposition analysis is to be conducted, X_A and X_B are row vectors of means of the explanatory variables for the two scenarios. The regression coefficient estimates are the column vectors $\widehat{\beta^A}$, $\widehat{\beta^B}$ and $\widehat{\beta^o}$ represent the coefficient estimates for the pooled regression analysis, respectively. While $\widehat{\beta^A}$ and $\widehat{\beta^B}$ are the rate of return to the X_A and X_B, $\widehat{\beta^o}$ is the estimate of the rate of returns to the independent variables that would exist in the absence of any discrimination (i.e., the non-discrimination situation). Combining Eqs. (4.7)–(4.9) and adding and subtracting the term $(X_A - X_B)\widehat{\beta^o}$ would result in decomposing the differential in Y into two factors as follows:

$$\overline{Y_A} - \overline{Y_B} = (X_A - X_B)\widehat{\beta^o} + [\overline{X_A}\left(\widehat{\beta^A} - \widehat{\beta^o}\right) - \overline{X_B}\left(\widehat{\beta^B} - \widehat{\beta^o}\right)] \quad (4.12)$$

The differential gap between the two groups A and B (on the left-hand side of this equation) is separated into two parts, the first part is explained by the characteristics or endowment (first term on the right-hand side) and the second part remains unexplained (second term on right-hand side). The gap explained by the difference in characteristics captures the difference in calorie consumption that would result if all households who varied only in their measured characteristics had the same level of calorie consumption. If this part is large in magnitude, then it can be concluded that most of the difference in per capita calorie consumption is explained by household characteristics only. The second expression on the right side of this equation is referred to as the unexplained part of the differential and is attributed to differences in tastes and preferences of households in the pre-reform year and post-reform year. This term captures the change in calorie consumption attributed solely to the unexplained factors involved in changes in calorie consumption which form the tastes, habits, and preferences of the households.

4.3.1.1 Illustration of Oaxaca-Blinder Decomposition Using STATA

Consider decomposing the differential between two groups, A and B as detailed in the framework explained in Eqs. 4.13–4.16 in Sect. 4.1. The command to estimate Oaxaca-Blinder decomposition in STATA is a **decompose**, a user-written program written by Ben Jann. The details of the command and explanation on how to use it are available in the program help file for this command. The following steps should be followed to estimate the Oaxaca-Blinder decomposition in STATA.

1. Install the program in STATA
2. Open the datasets for which decomposition analysis has to be carried out.
3. Estimate the OLS regression for the first group and save it as "high"
4. Estimate the OLS regression for the second group and save it as "low"
5. Use the STATA command decompose to get the decomposition.

```
ssc install decompose
    help decompose
```

```
use filename.dta, clear
recode group (A=0)(B=1), replace
reg y x1 x2 [weights=wts] if group == 0, robust
decompose, save(high)
reg y x1 x2 [weights =wts] if group== 1, robust
decompose, save(low)
reg y x1 x2 [weights =wts] if inlist(group, A, B)
decompose, lambda(lbda) detail
```

4.3.2 *Decomposition Across Quantiles*

The procedure adopted for decomposing the difference in similar distributions using quantile regression decomposition techniques was proposed by Machado and Mata (2005) (M&M, henceforth) extends the traditional Oaxaca-Blinder decomposition on conditional mean of the dependent variable to the whole distribution of this variable. The M&M decomposition is based on the construction of a counterfactual distribution of the dependent variable (calorie demand in our case). These counterfactuals are estimated as follows. Distribution of the dependent variable is estimated conditional on the independent variables using quantile regression at 100 quantiles. This conditional distribution of calorie consumption is thereby integrated over the set of independent variables to get the unconditional distribution.

Analysis of changing demand for calories in subsequent NSS rounds involves decomposing the calorie consumption gap between two rounds across quantiles to isolate the effect of differences in the distribution of covariates over rounds from differences in returns to these covariates by employing the M&M technique of quantile regression decomposition across the entire distribution. A counterfactual distribution is derived by taking the characteristics of distribution of the later NSS round and the coefficients estimated using observations with the previous NSS round to observe the distribution if the distribution in the later round had the same output function as the previous round. This counterfactual distribution is decomposed into a part explained by coefficients (i.e., effect of tastes and preferences) and a part explained by characteristics (effect of the covariates). In other words, the change in demand for calories between any two years can be decomposed into two components: one component due to differences in the distribution of returns between the two rounds and another component due to the differences in the distribution of covariates between the two rounds.

4.3.2.1 Application of Quantile Regression and Decomposition Methods to Estimate Demand for Calories

The quantile regression model can be estimated across the quantiles of log calorie distribution (Cal_i) in year *i*, conditional on a vector of covariates x_j ($i, j = $ 43rd, 50th, 61st round) as follows:

$$Q_\theta(Cal_i|X_i) = X_i\widehat{\beta_\theta^i}$$

which implies

$$Cal_i = X_i\widehat{\beta_\theta} + \varepsilon_\theta$$

with

$$Q_\theta(\varepsilon_\theta|X_i) = 0$$

where ε_θ is the error term of the θth conditional quantile which is assumed to be zero. The novelty of the quantile regression method is that QR results are sensitive outliers and heavy-tailed distributions and the only distributional assumption imposed is zero mean of error term (ε_θ). The QR coefficients represent the rate of return to the corresponding characteristics at the selected quantile of the conditional calorie consumption distribution in survey round *i.* A test of equality of coefficients across quantiles can be tested to confirm that the coefficients at each quantile are statistically different from each other.

The quantile regression decomposition methodology used in the present analysis is a modified procedure of the M&M technique proposed by Melly (2006). This procedure does not draw from a uniform distribution but estimates the conditional distribution using quantile regression for a large number of selected θ's and then the conditional distribution of the dependent variable is integrated over the range of explanatory variables. Thereby, integrating over all observations and overall quantiles, an estimator of the θth unconditional quantile of log (calorie consumption) is derived. This estimator for unconditional distribution is used to get the counterfactual distribution.

$$\begin{aligned} Q_\theta(Cal_i^{T2}, \beta^{T2}, \theta) - Q_\theta(Cal_i^{T1}, \beta^{T1}, \theta) &= [Q_\theta(X^{T2}, \beta_\theta^{T2}) - Q_\theta(X^{T2}, \beta_\theta^{T1})] \\ &+ [Q_\theta(X^{T2}, \beta_\theta^{T1}) - Q_\theta(X^{T1}, \beta_\theta^{T1})] \end{aligned} \tag{4.13}$$

where T1 is group 1 and T2 is group 2, Q_θ refers to the θth quantile (12) at various quantiles of the calorie consumption distribution, i.e., $\theta = 1$ to 100. The above equation separates the difference at each quantile of the unconditional distribution into a *coefficient effect* and a *characteristic effect*. The first term on the right-hand side of the above equation calculates the effect of differences in coefficients (effect of behavior, environment, tastes, and preferences), the *coefficient effect;* and the second term calculates the effect of differences in the distribution of characteristics (justified differential) and a *characteristics effect.*[5] The counterfactual distribution is estimated and the analysis at the various quantiles, the calorie demand equation is estimated at 100 quantiles of the calorie consumption distribution.

[5] For a more detailed description of this methodology see Melly (2006).

4.3.2.2 Illustration of Quantile Regression Decomposition Using STATA

Consider decomposition across the quantiles of calorie consumption discussed above. The command to estimate the decomposition of the differential in distributions using quantile regression is proposed by Melly (2005a, b). This technique is a generalization of the Oaxaca Blinder decomposition technique and is very similar to the Machado and Mata decomposition. The command to estimate quantile regression decomposition in STATA is **rqdeco**, a user-written program written by Blaise Melly based on the techniques proposed by M&M. Another command available to users is **cdeco**, which decomposes the change in the distribution of the covariates. The details of the command and explanation on how to use it are available in the program help file for these commands. The following steps should be followed to estimate the decomposition across quantiles in STATA.

1. Install the program for quantile regression decomposition in STATA
2. Open the datasets for which decomposition analysis will be carried out.
3. Estimate the quantile regression decomposition.
4. Display detailed results
5. Plot the results from the decomposition analysis

Decomposition analysis using **rqdeco**

net install rqdeco, from(https://raw.githubusercontent.com/bmelly/Stata/main/)

use filename.dta, clear

rqdeco y x, by(group) quantile(0.10) vce(boot)

grqreg × 1 × 2, ci ols olsci title(Figure1)

Decomposition analysis using **cdeco**:

net install counterfactual, from("https://raw.githubusercontent.com/bmelly/Stata/main/")

ssc install moremata

net install qrprocess, from(https://raw.githubusercontent.com/bmelly/Stata/main/)

use filename.dta, clear

cdeco y x [if] [in] [weight], group(varname) quantiles(0.10 0.25 0.5 0.75 0.95)

plotdeco all, legend('"order(1 "Observed difference" 2 "Explained component" 3 "Unexplained component")"') title("Quantile decomposition")

4.4 Data

Data for the present analysis was drawn from the 43rd, 50th, and 61st rounds of the National Sample Survey (NSS) for the rural sector in India. These surveys were conducted from June 1987 to July 1988, June 1993 to July 1994, and June 2004 to July 2005, respectively.[6] Covariates included in the analysis of calorie consumption include a host of variables. Monthly per capita expenditure (MPCE) is included to represent the household's income.[7] Farm harvest prices for three food grains, i.e., wheat, *bajra*(pearl millet), and gram (reported at 1987–1988 prices) are considered to account for the effect of prices of various commodities on households' demand for calories. Demographic, household characteristics, and environmental factors included in the analysis are, household size male equivalent[8] and characteristics of household head are represented by their gender, age, and literacy[9] level. Household's type of employment is included by considering whether the household is self-employed, agricultural labor, or other laborer. Household's social status (*SC/ ST*), household's religion in four categories, geographical dummies by grouping major states of India into BIMARU, Coastal or Non-coastal states.[10] The environmental factors have been addressed by including environmental variables in the analysis of 50th and 61st rounds only.[11] Household has access to clean cooking fuel if primary source of energy for cooking is gas (LPG, oil), biogas (gobar gas), kerosene, or electricity) and household has access to electricity, i.e., if a household has access to electricity). There has been discussion about movement of short-term and long-term measures of nutritional trends in India. The endogeneity between intake-focused nutritional status (calorie consumption) and outcome-focused nutrition (anthropometric nutrition) is addressed by pairing state-level anthropometric

[6] The data for the 55th NSS survey round was not included in the analysis because a new survey method was adopted, which makes consumption data structure for this round non-comparable with other NSS survey rounds. A detail of the problem is documented in Deaton (2003).

[7] Extant literature suggests expenditure, being a function of income, to be considered to be jointly determined with income (Strauss and Thomas, 1995) and act as a surrogate for household's per capita expenditure (PCE).

[8] An adult male is counted as 1, adult female is equivalent to 0.8 adult males and a child is equivalent to 0.5 adult male.

[9] The effect of education on the demand for nutrition and thereby health has been well documented by Behrman and Wolfe (1984). Education has both demand-side and supply-side effects on household behavior and there is a very high correlation between the demand for better health/nutrition and education. Education can improve the efficiency of an individual, in terms of producing investment in health and improving labor market productivity.

[10] BIMARU refers to the economically backward states of India which include Bihar, Maharashtra, Rajasthan, and Uttar Pradesh. The coastal states include West Bengal, Orissa, Andhra Pradesh, Tamil Nadu, Kerala, Karnataka, Maharashtra and Gujarat. Non-coastal states include Assam, Jammu and Kashmir, and Punjab.

[11] Information on accessibility to amenities (i.e., type of cooking fuel and do households have electricity) is only available for the 50th and 61st NSS rounds. To keep the analysis comprehensive the variables accounting for the effect of environmental variables are included only in the analysis of these two rounds.

measures of nutrition with household-level per capita calorie consumption. These state-level nutritional measures are—percentage of severely nourished children[12] in the state in the form of percentage underweight, percentage stunted, and percentage of children severely wasted in the state are included in the analysis.[13]

Calorie intake was computed using the information on food consumption provided in the surveys and converting the calorie content for each of the commodities consumed by the household following Gopalan et al. (1971). Using these calorie content factors, weights for calories were assigned to the reported food consumption data. Information on the nutrient content of each food provided in NSS data is multiplied by the quantity of food consumed in the last 30 days. Aggregating the calorie content of reported food consumption across commodities gives an estimate of the households' monthly calorie consumption.[14] Table 4.2 presents the distribution of per capita calorie consumption for rural households in India.

4.4.1 Descriptive Statistics

Table 4.1 displays summary statistics of selected variables considered in the analysis for all the three rounds. Per capita calorie consumption has declined from 2267.76 cal per day to 2032.32 cal per capita in 2004–05. The mean per capita calorie consumption in 1987–88 suggests that an average individual at the 75th percentile was adequately nourished. However, in all the three years rural households below the 50th percentile range are undernourished as per the recommendations of The Indian Council of Medical Research of a daily intake of 2400 Cal per person. In 1993–94, households at the 75th percentile have per capita calorie consumption close to the recommendation at 2416.31 Cal per day. In 2004–05, the 2400 Cal/day mark was achieved by households between the 75th and the 90th percentile suggesting deterioration in calorie consumption. This difference in calorie consumption pattern for these three years can be tested against each other to test whether the change in distribution of calorie consumption was statistically significant over each set of two years under consideration. A Kolmogorov-Smirnov test[15](KS) for equality of distributions gives a test statistic for the KS test, D-Stat, is 0.2852 with a *p-value* of

[12] These nutritional statistics are for children up to 48 months of age.

[13] Stunting (height for age is less) results from chronic undernutrition which retards linear growth. Wasting (weight for height is less) is a result of inadequate nutrition over a shorter period of time and underweight (weight for age is less) encompassed both.

[14] The nutrient content computed using this method converts the calorie content of the raw food commodity reported which does not account for the fact that calorie content of cooked food is different from raw food and is sensitive to the method of cooking.

[15] The KS test basically tests for the equality of two distributions by calculating cumulative frequencies for the two distributions. The KS test statistic, known as the D-Statistic, is based on the supremum of the absolute value of the difference in the cumulative density functions (CDF) of the two distributions (rescaled by the sample size). If the calculated D-stat is greater than the critical D-Stat, the null hypothesis equality of distribution is rejected. If the cumulative density function

0.00, implying that the null hypothesis of equality of distributions is not accepted and the calorie consumption distribution in 1987–88 and 1993–94 are statistically different from each other. The K-S statistic for 1993–94 and 2004–05 is 0.2387 again suggesting that the distributions are statistically different from each other. A t-test for the equality of means of the two distributions gives a t-statistic of 39.2883, rejecting the null hypothesis of equality of means of two distributions. While, this confirms the distribution of calorie consumption was indeed different in the two years, testing equality of means with the alternate hypothesis of the mean of 43rd round greater than the mean of 50th round, the null of equality of means could not be rejected. This implies that mean calorie consumption declined significantly after economic reform as previously observed by Dreze (2004). Therefore, it can be inferred that the calorie consumption pattern has changed significantly between the two NSS rounds. The factors that have contributed to this change and their proportion remain to be identified. In addition to the variables reported in Table 4.1, state-level anthropometric averages, state dummy, religion dummy, and household social status (SC/ST) dummy was included in the analysis.

Table 4.1 Summary statistics

Variable	NSS 43 round		NSS 50 round		NSS 61 round	
	Mean	Std. Dev	Mean	Std. Dev	Mean	Std. Dev
Price (wheat)	231.83	28.3	416.87	43.23	695.99	91.82
price_Bajra	188.24	27.89	308.8	44.41	489.51	108.68
price_gram	481.07	62.75	1003.68	127.1	1600.97	277.93
Ln(headage)	3.75	0.34	3.74	0.33	3.79	0.3
PC calorie cons	2267.76	608.26	2154.83	392.97	2032.32	564.77
Household size	5.61	2.78	5.22	2.51	5.23	2.57
Real MPCE	155.43	148.88	128.91	74.93	204.25	270.37

Table 4.2 Percapita calorie consumption by quantile

NSS round		Mean	10Q	25Q	50Q	75Q	90Q
43rd	(1987–88)	2158.13	1553.75	1906.45	2264.25	2620.18	2927.78
50th	(1993–94)	2098.54	1680.75	1956.67	2210.55	2416.31	2547.83
61st	(2004–05)	1948.86	1453.89	1685.8	1970.42	2298.47	2646.52

†: All numbers are Cal/day

for calorie consumption in 1987–88 is represented by $F_{cal}{}^{43}$, and that for 1993–94 is represented by $F_{cal}{}^{50}$ the null hypothesis to be tested is H_o: $F^{43}{}_{Cal} = F^{50}{}_{Cal}$.

4.5 Empirical Results

This section presents results for (a) the sources of inequality across quantiles of calorie consumption for each year (i.e., quantile regression results) and (b) sources of the gap in calorie consumption at various quantiles across years (i.e., quantile regression decomposition results).

4.5.1 Sources of Inequality in Calorie Consumption Across Quantiles

The entire analysis is done using log of calorie consumption to account for the fact that demand for calorie gap is varying across the distribution, i.e., being large at some points and small at other points. Log calorie consumption equation estimates using OLS and QR for three NSS rounds are presented in Tables 4.3, 4.4 and 4.5. This equation is estimated at 100 quantiles of the distribution, estimates for the entire distribution for all three NSS rounds are presented in Appendix A. Results for only 5 quantiles, i.e., 10th, 25th, 50th, 75th, and 90th quantiles are reported in these tables. The novelty of QR over OLS estimates is immediately apparent in the variation of estimated coefficients across quantiles of calorie consumption distribution. All independent variables except dichotomous variables have been converted into logarithms enabling coefficients for these variables to be interpreted as elasticities.

The conditional mean (OLS) estimates indicate an inverse relationship between calorie consumption and income, that is, change in income resulted in a decline in the per capita calorie consumption of households. In the 43rd round, a percentage increase in real per capita expenditure increased calorie consumption by 31 percentage points whereas in 50th and 61st rounds this effect was 26 percentage points and 13 percentage points respectively. QR estimates suggest that responsiveness to MPCE gradually declined across the calorie consumption distribution in the 43rd and 50th rounds, in 61st round it observed an increasing trend over quantiles. This suggests that responsiveness of calorie consumption to income was larger for undernourished households at bottom quantiles than for well-nourished households at upper quantiles in 1987–88 and 1993–94. However, in 2004–05, which represents a period of unprecedented economic growth, responsiveness of per capita calorie consumption to MPCE for undernourished households is smaller than that of well-nourished households. These results suggest that an increase in income increased the demand for calories of undernourished households during 43rd and 50th rounds, but, in the new millennium the responsiveness of undernourished households has reduced and that of well-nourished households has taken over.

A percentage point increase in prices of wheat increased demand for calorie across the quantiles of 43rd and 50th rounds and at higher quantiles of 61st round. Undernourished households responded negatively to prices of wheat in 61st round suggesting that increase in prices of superior goods reduced demand for calorie

Table 4.3 Quantile regression results: NSS 43rd round

Variable‡	Mean	Quantile				
		10th Q	25th Q	50th Q	75th Q	90th Q
ln(Real_ MPCE)	0.302***	0.312***	0.285***	0.261***	0.224***	0.165***
	(0.003)	(0.006)	(0.004)	(0.003)	(0.004)	(0.004)
Ln(Age Hhead)	−0.003	−0.016***	0.001	0.002	0.004	0.006
	(0.005)	(0.009)	(0.005)	(0.004)	(0.004)	(0.005)
ln(hhsize)	0.028***	0.047***	0.013***	0.003	−0.006**	−0.008***
	(0.003)	(0.007)	(0.004)	(0.003)	(0.003)	(0.002)
ln(Pr Bajra)	−0.135***	−0.164***	−0.082**	−0.057**	−0.044*	−0.049**
	(0.028)	(0.052)	(0.039)	(0.025)	(0.024)	(0.024)
ln(Pr Wheat)	0.181***	0.344***	0.141***	0.124***	0.067***	0.085***
	(0.036)	(0.055)	(0.036)	(0.036)	(0.022)	(0.029)
ln(Pr Grnut)	−0.04*	−0.27***	−0.121***	0.002	0.09***	0.113***
	(0.022)	(0.093)	(0.034)	(0.021)	(0.021)	(0.018)
Non SC/ST	−0.01***	−0.002	−0.01**	−0.017***	−0.013***	−0.014***
	(0.003)	(0.008)	(0.005)	(0.004)	(0.003)	(0.003)
Landown	-0.09***	−0.098***	−0.094***	−0.088***	−0.072***	−0.053***
	(0.009)	(0.016)	(0.008)	(0.009)	(0.007)	(0.007)
Self Emp	−0.016***	−0.03***	−0.027***	−0.03***	−0.025***	−0.021***
	(0.005)	(0.010)	(0.007)	(0.004)	(0.004)	(0.004)
Agri lab	−0.002	−0.037***	−0.015***	−0.014***	−0.008***	−0.004
	(0.004)	(0.008)	(0.006)	(0.005)	(0.003)	(0.003)
Female head	−0.004	−0.045***	−0.024***	−0.006	−0.003	0.006
	(0.005)	(0.012)	(0.008)	(0.005)	(0.006)	(0.006)
Literate head	−0.091***	−0.109***	−0.09***	−0.074***	−0.064***	−0.043***
	(0.012)	(0.013)	(0.011)	(0.009)	(0.008)	(0.011)
Bimaru	0.056***	0.036***	0.055***	0.06***	0.06***	0.045***
	(0.005)	(0.011)	(0.008)	(0.006)	(0.004)	(0.003)
Coastal	−0.043***	−0.124***	−0.056***	−0.017***	0.012***	0.015***
	(0.005)	(0.011)	(0.008)	(0.006)	(0.004)	(0.003)
Constant	6.196***	5.872***	6.154***	6.455***	6.77***	7.169***
	(0.027)	(0.050)	(0.028)	(0.027)	(0.028)	(0.028)
Number of obs	54154	54154	54154	54154	54154	54154
R2 (PseudoR2 for QR)	0.1602	0.1095	0.1048	0.1	0.089	0.0634

***: Significant at 1%. **: Significant at 5%. *: Significant at 10%

‡: Interaction terms, religion dummies not reported. Available with author

consumption in an era of economic growth. In 43rd round prices of inferior goods had a negative effect on calorie consumption for undernourished households, this effect became positive in 50th and 61st rounds.

An older household head had a positive effect on calorie consumption in the 43rd round whereas in the 50th and 61st rounds, this effect was negative. Household size had a positive effect at lower quantiles and gradually decreased across quantiles. This suggests that household size would increase demand for calories for poorly nourished households. This result does not hold for households with better nourishment at the top end of calorie consumption distribution. Households belonging to any of the four major religions (Hinduism, Sikhism, Islam, Christianity) did not influence calorie consumption significantly in 1987–1988 except for Islam at the bottom of distribution. This effect was statistically significant at bottom quantiles in the 50th and 61st rounds.

Demand for calorie consumption is influenced by the social status at lower quantiles more than at higher quantiles. This effect was statistically significant only for undernourished households in the 43rd round. In 61st round, social status had a negative effect on demand for calorie at all points of calorie consumption distribution. This effect was also larger for the undernourished households in comparison to well-nourished households. Belonging to upper social class (non-SC/ST) had a negative effect on demand for calories in 43rd and 61st rounds, the coefficient was statistically significant at bottom quantiles of 43rd round, insignificant across the entire distribution of 50th round and statistically significant at all quantiles of the 61st round. Therefore, belonging to an upper class rather than to the backward class had a negative effect on demand for calorie of undernourished households. This suggests that households belonging to upper classes reduced demand for calories more in comparison to SC/ST households.

Gender had a positive and significant effect across the calorie consumption distribution in the 61st round. In the 43rd and 50th rounds, this effect was negative and statistically significant for undernourished households at the 10th quantile. A female-headed household in 1987–88 had a negative effect on demand for calories and this effect was larger for well-nourished households than for undernourished households. In the 50th round, a female-headed household had a positive effect on calorie consumption and this effect was smaller for households at the top of the distribution than for households at the bottom of the distribution. Thereby, suggesting that well-nourished household with female heads increased demand for calories by a smaller amount than undernourished households with a female head. In the 61st round, a female household head had a positive and larger effect on calorie consumption at the top end of the distribution than at the bottom end. While having a female household head had a negative influence on calorie consumption of poorly nourished households in 43rd and 50th rounds, this effect was significant in 61st round. Gender of household did not have a significant effect in the pre-reform round (43rd) however this effect was positive in the post-reform rounds (50th and 61st rounds). Also, in the 61st round, the magnitude of this effect was larger than in 50th round. These results suggest that post-reform period has witnessed female empowerment resulting in a positive effect on household's demand for calories.

Table 4.4 NSS 50th round: regression results

Variable‡	Mean	Quantile				
		10th Q	25th Q	50th Q	75th Q	90th Q
ln(Real_ MPCE)	0.253***	0.26***	0.2***	0.149***	0.095***	0.048***
	(0.013)	(0.012)	(0.006)	(0.003)	(0.002)	(0.001)
Ln(Age Hhead)	−0.036***	−0.02**	−0.027***	−0.024***	−0.013***	−0.009***
	(0.006)	(0.009)	(0.006)	(0.004)	(0.003)	(0.002)
ln(hhsize)	0.048***	0.052***	0.026***	0.016***	0.006***	0.004***
	(0.005)	(0.008)	(0.004)	(0.003)	(0.002)	(0.002)
ln(Pr Bajra)	−0.048*	0.184***	−0.068***	−0.095***	−0.062***	−0.041***
	(0.026)	(0.034)	(0.020)	(0.013)	(0.011)	(0.008)
ln(Pr Wheat)	0.163***	0.15***	0.134***	0.12***	0.08***	0.044***
	(0.020)	(0.046)	(0.026)	(0.016)	(0.012)	(0.009)
ln(Pr Grnut)	−0.126***	−0.242***	−0.201***	−0.147***	−0.098***	−0.028***
	(0.022)	(0.037)	(0.022)	(0.015)	(0.012)	(0.009)
Non SC/ST	−0.006	−0.004	0.004	0.001	−0.001	0.0001
	(0.004)	(0.006)	(0.004)	(0.003)	(0.002)	(0.002)
Land own	−0.022***	−0.031***	−0.029***	−0.024***	−0.015***	−0.008***
	(0.004)	(0.008)	(0.005)	(0.003)	(0.002)	(0.002)
Self Emp	−0.002	−0.009	−0.007	−0.007	−0.004	−0.003
	(0.008)	(0.015)	(0.009)	(0.006)	(0.005)	(0.004)
Agri Lab	0.026***	0.023***	0.002	0.001	0.0002	0.001
	(0.005)	(0.008)	(0.005)	(0.003)	(0.002)	(0.002)
Female Head	0.018***	−0.008	0.014**	0.012***	0.013***	0.006**
	(0.007)	(0.012)	(0.007)	(0.005)	(0.004)	(0.003)
Literate Head	-0.018***	−0.002	−0.002	−0.007**	−0.005**	−0.004*
	(0.005)	(0.008)	(0.005)	(0.003)	(0.002)	(0.002)
Bimaru States	0.013*	−0.03**	−0.003	0.006	0.012***	0.001
	(0.007)	(0.013)	(0.008)	(0.005)	(0.004)	(0.003)
Coastal	0.026***	0.088***	0.002	−0.018***	−0.007*	−0.007**
	(0.007)	(0.012)	(0.007)	(0.005)	(0.004)	(0.003)
Clean Cook Fuel	−0.065***	−0.047***	−0.045***	−0.031***	−0.019***	−0.014***
	(0.009)	(0.016)	(0.009)	(0.006)	(0.005)	(0.004)
Electricity	−0.016	0.012	0.078*	−0.033	0.01	0.019
	(0.034)	(0.079)	(0.046)	(0.031)	(0.025)	(0.019)
Perc. Sev. Underweight†	0.007***	0.009***	0.005***	0.003***	0.002***	0.001***
	(0.001)	(0.001)	(0.001)	(0.000)	(0.000)	(0.000)
Perc. Sev. Stunting†	0.004***	0.012***	0.005***	0.002***	0.001**	0.0001
	(0.001)	(0.001)	(0.000)	(0.000)	(0.000)	(0.000)

(continued)

Table 4.4 (continued)

Variable‡	Mean	Quantile				
		10th Q	25th Q	50th Q	75th Q	90th Q
Per. Sev. Wasting†	−0.039***	−0.105***	−0.032***	−0.008***	-0.004***	0.0002
	(0.004)	(0.005)	(0.003)	(0.002)	(0.002)	(0.001)
Constant	6.415***	5.888***	6.601***	7.104***	7.385***	7.614***
	(0.081)	(0.118)	(0.066)	(0.043)	(0.034)	(0.025)
Number of obs	24305	24305	24305	24305	24305	24305
R2 (PseudoR2 for QR)	0.1349	0.1068	0.0898	0.0697	0.0454	0.0222

† : State level percentage children with −3 Standard Deviation for nutrition measure
‡: Interaction terms, religion dummies not reported. Available with author
***: Significant at 1%** : Significant at 5%* : Significant at 10%

The type of employment of the household had mixed effects across the calorie consumption distribution in all three rounds. For agricultural laborers demand for calories reduced across the distribution in 1987–88. In 1993–93, this effect was positive and statistically significant only at the 10th percentile. In 2004–2005 an agricultural laborer household responded positively at all quantiles.

Access to electricity did not have a statistically significant effect on demand for calories in both rounds (i.e., 50th and 61st) except for the 25th percentile in 1993–1994. However, access to clean cooking fuel had a negative and statistically significant effect in both rounds.[16] This effect was smaller for undernourished households than for well-nourished households in 1993–1994 implying that undernourished households reduced their demand for calorie consumption by a larger amount than their well-nourished counterparts. In comparison to 1993–1994 the effect of clean cooking fuel increased in magnitude by up to three times at each quantile in 2004–2005. This suggests that households with access to clean cooking fuel reduced calorie consumption by a larger amount at each quantile in 2004–05 than in 1993–1994. These effects of clean cooking fuel on calorie consumption can be suggestive of two facts. First, the use of clean cooking fuel rather than using traditional biomass (such as wood, animal dung, crop residue, etc.) helps retain more nutritive value of food resulting in cooked meals with better nutrient content, thereby reducing calorie consumption.[17] Second, negative effect of access to clean cooking fuel could suggest that using clean cooking fuel results in some expenditure being diverted toward the purchase of this fuel which would influence expenditure done on food commodities

[16] As previously discussed, due to data availability variables representing effect of environmental variables are included only in the analysis of the 50th and 61st rounds.

[17] It needs to be noted that due to data constraints, calorie consumption calculated in all studies on nutrition in India (including the present study) are based on the consumption of raw food material and it is well recognized that nutritive value of cooked food is dependent on the method of cooking (Sharma and Meenakshi 2007).

Table 4.5 Regression results: NSS 61st round

Variable‡	Mean	Quantile				
		10th Q	25th Q	50th Q	75th Q	90th Q
ln(Real_ MPCE)	0.166***	0.13***	0.136***	0.156***	0.193***	0.24***
	(0.005)	(0.006)	(0.004)	(0.003)	(0.003)	(0.005)
Ln(Age Hhead)	−0.06***	−0.03***	−0.048***	−0.07***	−0.077***	−0.087***
	(0.006)	(0.008)	(0.006)	(0.005)	(0.005)	(0.006)
ln(hhsize)	0.037***	0.018***	0.012***	0.012***	0.003	0.003
	(0.005)	(0.006)	(0.004)	(0.003)	(0.003)	(0.004)
ln(Pr Bajra)	0.025**	0.083***	0.059***	0.031***	0.008	−0.005
	(0.010)	(0.016)	(0.012)	(0.010)	(0.010)	(0.015)
ln(Pr Wheat)	0.044***	−0.178***	-0.07***	0.055***	0.113***	0.134***
	(0.016)	(0.023)	(0.018)	(0.016)	(0.017)	(0.025)
ln(Pr Grnut)	0.013	0.049***	0.007	0.029**	0.045***	0.055***
	(0.012)	(0.018)	(0.014)	(0.012)	(0.012)	(0.017)
Non SC/ST	−0.034***	−0.022***	−0.026***	−0.031***	−0.034***	−0.043***
	(0.003)	(0.005)	(0.003)	(0.003)	(0.003)	(0.005)
Land own	0.003	0.012	0.021	0.015	0.0001	−0.031*
	(0.012)	(0.018)	(0.013)	(0.012)	(0.012)	(0.017)
Self Emp	0.102***	0.098***	0.022	0.015	0.021	0.025
	(0.031)	(0.024)	(0.018)	(0.016)	0.016	(0.023)
Agri Lab	0.169***	0.139***	0.036*	0.052***	0.068***	0.104***
	(0.031)	(0.026)	(0.019)	(0.018)	(0.017)	(0.025)
Female Head	0.073***	0.028***	0.041***	0.057***	0.065***	0.079***
	(0.005)	(0.008)	(0.006)	(0.005)	(0.005)	(0.007)
Literate Head	−0.025***	−0.023**	−0.012*	−0.018***	−0.013**	−0.022**
	(0.006)	(0.009)	(0.007)	(0.006)	(0.006)	(0.009)
Bimaru States	0.024***	0.002	0.039***	0.046***	0.043***	0.041***
	(0.008)	(0.013)	(0.009)	(0.008)	(0.007)	(0.010)
Coastal	−0.03***	−0.116***	−0.063***	-0.015**	0.02***	0.051***
	(0.006)	(0.009)	(0.007)	(0.006)	(0.006)	(0.008)
Clean Cook Fuel	−0.111***	−0.115***	−0.106***	−0.106***	−0.119***	−0.129***
	(0.005)	(0.007)	(0.005)	(0.005)	(0.005)	(0.007)
Electricity	0.029	0.012	0.005	0.037	0.021	0.007
	(0.021)	(0.035)	(0.026)	(0.024)	(0.023)	(0.033)
Perc. Sev. Underweight†	0.003***	−0.005***	0.001	0.005***	0.007***	0.008***
	(0.001)	(0.001)	(0.001)	(0.001)	(0.001)	(0.001)
Perc. Sev. Stunting†	0.005***	0.005***	0.004***	0.004***	0.006***	0.007***
	(0.001)	(0.001)	(0.001)	(0.001)	(0.001)	(0.001)

(continued)

Table 4.5 (continued)

Variable‡	Mean	Quantile				
		10th Q	25th Q	50th Q	75th Q	90th Q
Per. Sev. Wasting†	−0.004***	0.003*	−0.005***	−0.007***	−0.007***	−0.008***
	(0.001)	(0.002)	(0.001)	(0.001)	(0.001)	(0.002)
Constant	6.465***	6.56***	6.762***	6.643***	6.526***	6.406***
	(0.060)	(0.074)	(0.054)	(0.048)	(0.047)	(0.069)
Number of obs	53355	53355	53355	53355	53355	53355
R2 (PseudoR2 for QR)	0.1084	0.0626	0.0676	0.0738	0.086	0.1048

†: State level percentage children with −3 Standard Deviation for nutrition measure
‡: Interaction terms, religion dummies not reported
***: Significant at 1%, ** : Significant at 5%, * : Significant at 10%

resulting in a reduced demand for calorie.[18] In either case, the negative effect of access to clean cooking fuel could be a strong contender in explaining the nutrition "puzzle" in India.

Other environmental factors, such as economic and nutritional status of the state of residence of households also exhibit some interesting patterns. To account for the effects of living in an unhealthy state, state-level statistics of anthropometric measures of health of children age have been included in our analysis. Living in a state with higher percentage of underweight and stunted children had a positive effect on calorie consumption. The magnitude of this effect is small, but it is relatively larger a lower quantiles of the distribution. Belonging to states with severely underweight children reduced calorie consumption for households at bottom quantiles in 61st round. For healthier households this effect is positive and increasing across quantiles. The effect of living in a state with higher percentage of severely wasted children is negative. Wasting is attributed to inadequate nutrition over short period and the effect of this variable is larger for poorly nourished households than their healthier counterparts in both 50th and 61st rounds. This result suggests that for households in states experiencing inadequate nutrition over shorter periods would reduce calorie consumption. Well-nourished households residing in states with severely underweight children would try to increase their calorie demand more in comparison to well-nourished households. Belonging to an economically backward state rather than belonging to non-coastal state had a positive statistically significant effect on calorie consumption. Coastal states had a negative and significant effect across quantiles in the 61st round.

Quantile regression results presented in this sub-section have thrown light on how socioeconomic and demographic factors have influenced calorie consumption

[18] This has been suggested in Deaton (2009) in the context of changing lifestyles influencing expenditure which in turn influences expenditure on food.

of undernourished and well-nourished households for each NSS round. How distributional patterns of calorie consumption for undernourished households and well-nourished households has changed over time? Whether this change can be explained by these covariates? How much of the observed change in calorie consumption can be attributed to these covariates is what is discussed next.

4.5.2 Explaining the Calorie Consumption Gap: Decomposition Results

For an assessment of the pattern of change in calorie consumption between NSS rounds simple quantile regression models of calorie consumption including NSS round dummy variables and a constant term are estimated for four groups of NSS rounds (i.e., 43rd and 50th round, 50th and 61st round, 43rd and 61st rounds and all three rounds together). Table 4.6 presents estimates for all these models. The coefficient on NSS round dummy represents the change in calorie consumption between rounds relative to the base case. The calorie consumption gap between 43rd and 50th round, (Panel 1 of Table 4.6) are highly significant and decreasing across quantiles. This gap is positive for lower quantiles and becomes increasingly negative for higher quantiles suggesting that the calorie consumption improved at lower quantiles in moving from NSS 43rd round to 50th rounds however for well-nourished household's calorie consumption declined between these two rounds. The gap was wider for well-nourished households at higher quantiles than for undernourished households at lower quantiles.

Calorie consumption gap over the period between 50th and 61st rounds (Panel 2) was increasing across the quantiles suggesting that in moving from 50th round to 61st round demand for calorie dropped at lower quantiles more than for higher quantiles and this effect was positive for the 90th quantile suggesting that while calorie consumption dropped severely for poorly nourished households it actually improved for highly nourished households. The gap was higher at the lower quantiles than at higher quantiles. The overall change in calorie consumption for the study period (between 43rd and 61st round (Panel 3, Table 4.6) is statistically significant and negative across the entire distribution. Demand for calories dropped across quantiles but this drop was larger for 50th and 75th quantile and smallest for 10th quantile suggesting that the fall in calorie consumption was lower for undernourished households than for overnourished household. The calorie consumption gap was smaller at lower quantiles and wider at higher quantiles. Considering the 43rd round as the base case (Panel 4) calorie consumption improved for lower quantiles in 50th round however the gap started to show for higher quantiles implying that only well-nourished households reduced calorie consumption. The undernourished people still showed an increase in consumption. This decline in calorie consumption continued at higher quantiles in the 61st round however the drop started to appear at lower quantiles too. The coefficients on the survey round dummies reflect differences

Table 4.6 Estimates of calorie consumption gap between NSS rounds

Ln (Percapita Calorie Con.) 10	10th Q	25th Q	50th Q	75th Q	90th Q
43rd and 50th round (Pane 1) (N = 78603)					
50th round dummy	0.100***	0.042***	−0.025***	−0.102***	−0.173***
	(0.004)	(0.003)	(0.002)	(0.001)	(0.001)
Base case	7.31***	7.537***	7.737***	7.907***	8.026***
	(0.003)	(0.002)	(0.001)	(0.001)	(0.001)
50th and 61st round (Pane 2) (N = 90289)					
61st round dummy	−0.161***	−0.165***	−0.123***	−0.048***	0.061***
	(0.002)	(0.002)	(0.001)	(0.001)	(0.002)
Base case	7.41***	7.579***	7.711***	7.805***	7.852***
	(0.003)	(0.001)	(0.001)	(0.001)	(0.001)
43rd and 61st round (Pane 3) (N = 120138)					
61st round dummy	−0.062***	−0.122***	−0.149***	−0.15***	−0.112***
	(0.004)	(0.001)	(0.001)	(0.001)	(0.002)
Base case	7.31***	7.737***	7.907***	7.907***	8.026***
	(0.003)	(0.001)	(0.001)	(0.001)	(0.001)
43rd, 50th and 61st round (Pane 4) (N = 144513)					
50th round dummy	0.1***	0.042***	−0.025***	−0.102***	−0.173***
	(0.005)	(0.003)	(0.002)	(0.001)	(0.001)
61st round dummy	−0.062***	−0.122***	−0.149***	−0.15***	−0.112***
	(0.003)	(0.002)	(0.002)	(0.002)	(0.002)
Base case	7.31***	7.537***	7.737***	7.907***	8.026
	(0.003)	(0.002)	(0.001)	(0.001)	(0.001)

Standard errors in parenthesis
Standard errors were estimated using bootstrap with 100 replications

in the distribution of covariates and their returns. These coefficients are the calorie gaps that would be decomposed next.

4.5.3 Machado-Mata Decomposition of the Calorie Consumption Differential

The calorie consumption gaps estimated in Table 4.6 are decomposed using the quantile regression decomposition technique into parts explained by the vector of covariates and a part explained by changes in tastes and preferences. Three sets of decompositions were carried out each representing a phase when the Indian economy has experienced economic reforms (1987–88 and 1993–94) and a period when India experienced unprecedented economic growth (1993–94–2004–05). The M&M technique involves estimating QRs across the distribution of Log (calorie consumption) for two rounds of NSS (say 43rd and 50th) followed by constructing the counterfactual distribution of NSS 43rd round using the distribution of covariates from NSS 50th round.

This counterfactual essentially estimates the distribution of log calorie consumption for NSS 43rd round that would have prevailed if the households in NSS 43rd round were endowed with the distribution of characteristics of households in NSS 50th round but received the returns that pertained to the NSS 43rd round. Then, a comparison of the counterfactual and empirical distribution of the contribution of differences in the distributions of covariates to the calorie consumption gap is estimated and the residual of this gap is attributed to the combined differences in the returns to these covariates.

Table 4.7 presents the results of calorie consumption decomposition between the 43rd and 50th, 50th and 61st, and 43rd and 61st rounds of NSS. Decomposition results for 5 quantiles are presented in this table, decomposition of calorie consumption across the entire distribution is presented in Appendix B. The coefficient effects (graphs B1, B3, B5, B7, and B9) show how behavior, environment and tastes and preferences influence calorie consumption. The decomposition of calorie consumption into a part attributed to differences in characteristics and the part attributed to differences in coefficients (Graphs B2, B4, B6, B8, and B10) show the contributions of the two effects across the distribution for all the three sets of decomposition.

Calorie Consumption Decomposition between 43rd and 50th round are presented in Table 4.3 (Panel 1) and Figures B1 and B2, suggesting that raw differential was positive and small at lower quantiles and negative and expanding for higher quantiles. That is, calorie consumption improved for undernourished households and fell for well-nourished households beyond the median quantile. The absolute calorie gap was highest (around 17%) at the 90th percentile, suggesting that well-nourished households reduced their calorie consumption over this period. Households at 10th and 25th quantile actually increased their calorie consumption over the period of first-generation reforms. The positive effect of characteristics at the 75th (0.025) and the 90th (0.027) quantiles indicates that for well-nourished household, if characteristics were rewarded the same in 1987–1988 and 1993–1994, then calorie consumption should have increased, not reduced. For undernourished households, the negative characteristics effect suggests that if household characteristics in the post-reform period were rewarded similarly to those in the pre-reform period, then calorie consumption should have fallen not risen. Improvement in calorie consumption for these households is explained by changes in coefficient effect suggesting that this change is due to discriminatory behavior of households, which is attributed to their changes in tastes and preferences. This fall in calorie consumption is explained by changes in the coefficient effect, i.e., how tastes and preferences of households have changed over the period of first-generation reforms. Effect of coefficients, presented in B1 suggests that over the reform period tastes and preferences (coefficient effect) had a much higher effect for undernourished households (at lower quantiles) but

Table 4.7 Calorie consumption gap: decomposition across quantiles

Rounds	10Q	25Q	50Q	75Q	90Q
NSS 43rd and 50th round					
Raw differential	0.1***	0.043***	−0.021***	−0.098***	−0.174***
	(0.003)	(0.002)	(0.001)	(0.001)	(0.001)
Characteristics	−0.132***	−0.064***	−0.001***	0.025***	0.027***
	(0.041)	(0.022)	(0.015)	(0.017)	(0.014)
Coefficients	0.232***	0.107***	−0.02***	−0.122***	−0.201***
	(0.003)	(0.002)	(0.001)	(0.001)	(0.001)
NSS 50th and 61st round					
Raw differential	−0.169***	−0.166***	−0.125***	−0.048***	0.06***
	(0.002)	(0.001)	(0.001)	(0.001)	(0.002)
Characteristics	−0.242***	−0.126***	−0.058***	−0.022***	−0.001***
	(0.041)	(0.022)	(0.015)	(0.011)	(0.007)
Coefficients	−0.074***	−0.04***	−0.068***	−0.026***	−0.061***
	(0.004)	(0.002)	(0.001)	(0.001)	(0.001)
NSS 43rd and 61st round					
Raw differential	−0.068***	−0.121***	−0.144***	−0.143***	−0.113***
	(0.002)	(0.001)	(0.001)	(0.001)	(0.002)
Characteristics	−0.121***	−0.043***	0.066***	0.112***	0.105***
	(0.070)	(0.046)	(0.032)	(0.028)	(0.020)
Coefficients	0.052***	−0.078***	−0.210***	−0.254***	−0.218***
	(0.003)	(0.002)	(0.001)	(0.001)	(0.001)

Standard Errors have been estimated using bootstrapping the results 100 times
Decomposition analysis was done at 100 quantiles of calorie consumption distribution
Standard errors in parenthesis

becomes close to zero at median and negative at higher quantiles suggesting a negative effect of coefficients at higher quantiles. Figure B2 suggests that, while coefficients effect was positive, the characteristics effect was negative at lower quantiles. At higher quantiles, coefficients explain a large amount of the differential and characteristics have a negative to zero effect. Therefore, the change in calorie consumption for households between 1987–88 and 1993–94 was dominated by their tastes and preferences at all points of the distribution. In fact, at the median quantile, the characteristics effect is statistically insignificant and the corresponding differential is completely explained by the coefficient effect. These results suggest that the calorie consumption gap over the period of first-generation reforms was dominated by the coefficients effect across all quantiles and the characteristics effect was negative at lower quantiles and became positive at higher quantiles.

Calorie Consumption Decomposition between 50th and 61st rounds are presented in Panel 2 of Table 4.7, and Figures B3 and B4 of Appendix B suggest that the calorie consumption differential was negative and widest at the bottom quantiles and was positive at the top quintiles while remaining negative for the intermediate quantiles. Undernourished households displayed larger changes in calorie consumption than their well-nourished counterparts. In fact, households at the 90th percentile actually increased calorie consumption between 1993–94 and 2004–05. For undernourished households, the characteristics effect is wide but becomes small in absolute terms across quantiles. Coefficient effect was positive and largest for the lowest quantiles but becomes negative and small for higher quantiles. The effect of coefficients was high for undernourished households at the lowest quantiles, falls sharply to become close to zero at the 40th quantile, subsequently picks up gradually till the 80th quantile and steeply increases after the 90th quantile resulting in a U-shape curve. This result suggests that tastes and preferences explain a large part of the calorie consumption gap for undernourished households (as also observed in the decomposition between 43rd and 50th rounds). The effect of characteristics is negative at the bottom quantiles but becomes larger and takes a flat shape for households beyond the 30th percentile. At the 10th and 25th percentile, the characteristics effect was statistically significant and dominated the calorie consumption gap. That is, covariates explain most of the change in calorie consumption whereas tastes and preferences account for a small part of the differential. At 50th and 75th quantile, where relatively well-nourished households are located, both returns to endowments and household's personal tastes and preferences contribute toward the calorie differential. For households at the 90th percentiles, changes in calorie consumption were completely explained by the coefficient effect and the characteristics effect is small and statistically insignificant. Therefore between 1993–1994 and 2004–2005 change in calorie consumption was completely explained by characteristics effect and coefficients have a small effect on explaining calorie differential. These results suggest that during the period both household tastes and preferences and characteristics contributed toward explaining the calorie gap for undernourished households. However, for well-nourished households at the higher end of calorie distribution, tastes and preferences explained the calorie consumption gap completely as an effect of characteristics becomes flat and stable.

Calorie Consumption Decomposition between 43rd and 61st round would explain the change in calorie consumption between a period when the Indian economy was dominated by Licence Raj (i.e., pre-reform period (1987–1988)) and a period of rapid economic growth (in 2004–2005). Decomposition results between 43rd and 61st rounds are presented in Panel 3 of Table 4.7 and Figures B5 and B6 of Appendix B. These results suggest that the raw differential was widest for well-nourished households at 90th quantile and smallest for undernourished households at the bottom quintiles suggesting that the overall fall in calorie consumption experienced by India in the last 25 years was largest for the well-nourished households.[19] While the characteristics effect (i.e., effect of covariates) explained a larger amount of differential for the undernourished households (−0.121), coefficient effect (i.e., effect of tastes and preferences) explained a larger part of the differential for well-nourished households (−0.218). The effect of coefficients is largest at the bottom quantiles ascertaining the importance of lifestyle factors/tastes and preferences for undernourished households. Around the 20th percentile this effect becomes negative suggesting that tastes and preferences explain larger part of the decline in calorie consumption experienced by India. While differences in distribution of characteristics or covariates between 1987–1988 and 2004–2005 mitigate the fall in calorie consumption at bottom quantiles, this effect becomes negligible and stable beyond the 20th quantile.

This decomposition analysis suggests that nutrition pattern in India over the three NSS rounds has undergone a phase of gradual transition wherein changing tastes and preferences has played a dominant role in explaining the calorie consumption differential. The observed decline in calorie consumption was initiated by well-nourished households changing their tastes and preferences in the period of first-generation reforms while households at the bottom of distribution had a positive differential. In the period of second generation reforms the largest decline in calorie consumption was for undernourished households and this decline was dominated by characteristics effect suggesting that undernourished households are more responsive to changing covariates than well-nourished households. Thus, for well-nourished households, tastes and preferences dominate calorie consumption patterns in all the three sets of decomposition. However, for undernourished households at bottom quintiles, tastes and preferences dominated the period of first-generation reforms, the period of second-generation reforms was dominated by effect of covariates. Therefore, differences in changing behavioral responses over time are responsible for the overall decline in calorie consumption observed in India.

4.6 Conclusion

Calorie consumption pattern in India during the last three decades has witnessed contrasting trends over time and across states. With both undernutrition and obesity becoming a public health concern economic growth has not benefitted nutrition

---

[19] An observation also made by Deaton and Dreze (2009).

inequality. Most econometric analysis of nutritional demand focuses on conditional mean within a parametric approach such as the ordinary least square (OLS) model. With the coexistence of undernutrition and obesity (over-nutrition) in a large country like India, estimating an OLS model would give an incomplete picture of the distributional pattern of nutritional demand. Utilizing quantile regression and decomposition techniques could provide important insights on the pattern of calorie consumption across the entire distribution of consumption. With the objective of highlighting the importance of a distributional analyses, this chapter provides a detailed overview of the quantile regression technique and decomposition techniques both at the mean and across quantiles. Taking the example of calorie demand in India, the chapter empirically models calorie demand at various points of the consumption distribution. We estimate quantile regressions and decomposing change in calorie consumption across time to decompose the change in calorie consumption differential into an explained and an unexplained component. The interpretation of the results across quantiles allows us to evaluate calorie demand at the extreme quantiles, where the risk of nutritional inadequacy is higher, i.e., undernourished households (lower quantiles) and overnourished households (higher quantiles).

The analysis reveals differences in factors affecting calorie consumption of undernourished households and well-nourished households with income affecting the responsiveness of calorie consumption to income more for undernourished households than for well-nourished households. Decomposition of calorie consumption gap across time reveals the importance households give to tastes and preferences for food depends heavily on their de facto nutritional status. The decline in demands for calorie consumption observed over the period of 1987–1988 to 2004–2005 essentially started at the highest quantile over the period 1988 to 1993–1994 and trickled down to the undernourished households between 1993–1994 and 2004–2005. Interestingly, while the coefficient effect became negative at higher quantiles over the period of first-generation reforms, this effect was positive and increased at the upper end of the distribution over the period of second-generation reforms suggesting that well-nourished households reduced calorie consumption due to changes in their tastes and preferences. The effect of tastes and preferences was more pronounced for well-nourished households than for undernourished households over 1987–88 and 2004–05. The advantage of using quantile decomposition techniques suggests that a unique nutrient policy in an economy where under- and overnutrition coexist would not be effective as factors influencing calorie consumption patterns differ for undernourished and well-nourished households. Economic policy designed to reduce undernutrition should focus on influencing the effect of the covariate as covariates effect dominated calorie consumption gap for undernourished households. However, policy designed to tackle overnutrition and obesity needs to focus toward educating the populace about the benefits of a healthy lifestyle which would gradually change tastes and preferences toward nutritional aspects of food (as coefficients effect dominates the calorie differential for well-nourished households).

4.7 Appendix A

See Figs. A.1, A.2, A.3 and A.4.

The graphs in this appendix have been plotted using the grqreg command in STATA.

See Figs. A.5, A.6, A.7 and A.8.

The graphs in this appendix have been plotted using the grqreg command in STATA.

See Figs. A.9 and A.10.

The graphs in this appendix have been plotted using the grqreg command in STATA.

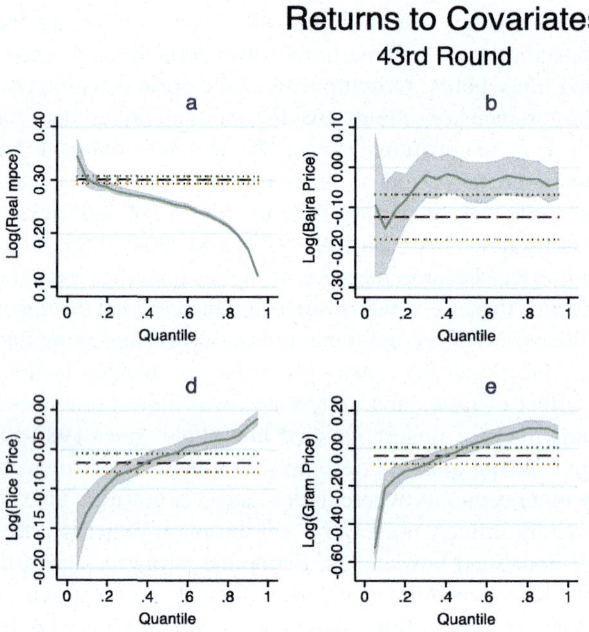

Fig. A.1 OLS and quantile regression results at 100 quantiles: returns to covariates for NSS 43rd round

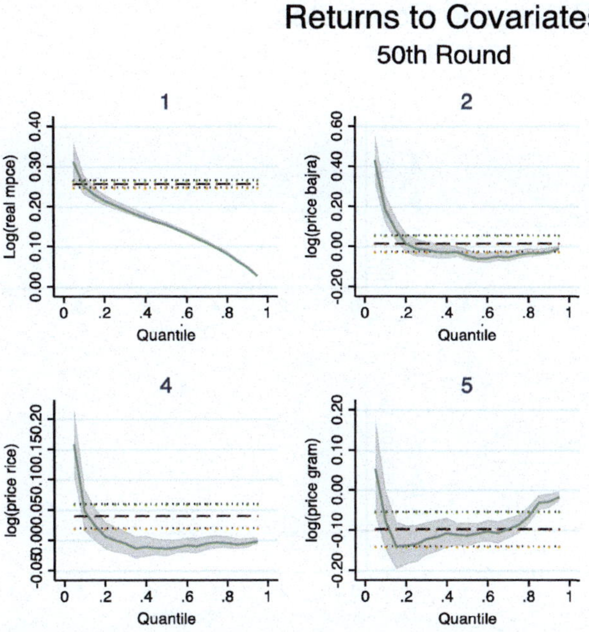

Fig. A.2 OLS and quantile regression results at 100 quantiles: returns to covariates for NSS 50th round

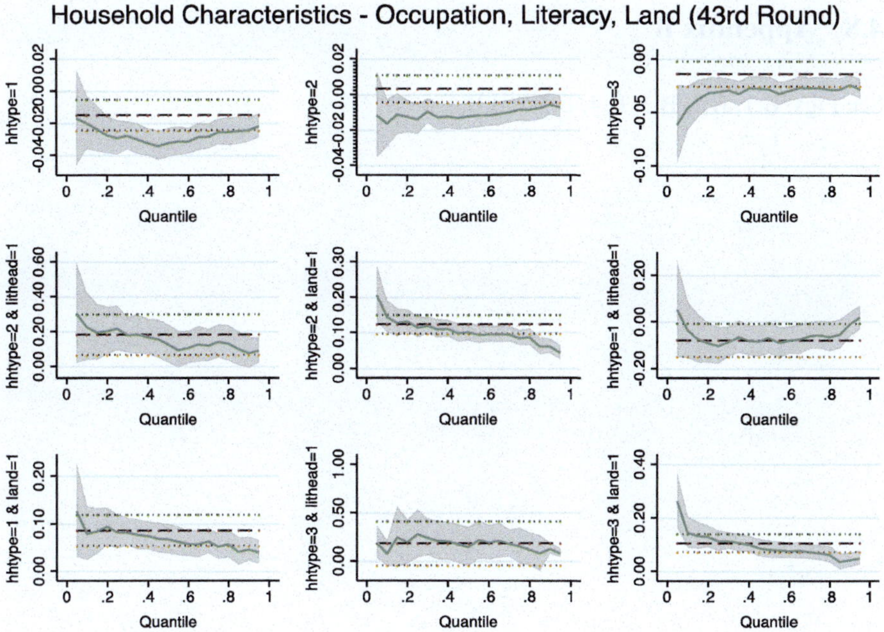

Fig. A.3 OLS and quantile regression results at 100 quantiles: covariate effect for NSS 43rd round

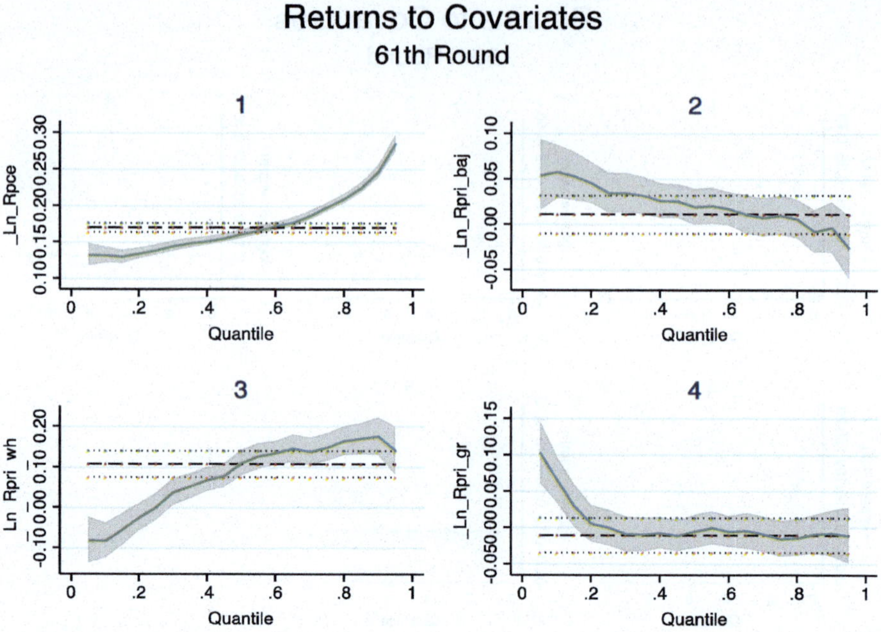

Fig. A.4 OLS and quantile regression results at 100 quantiles: returns to covariates for NSS 61st round

4.8 Appendix B

See Figs. B.1, B.2, B.3, B.4, B.5 and B.6.

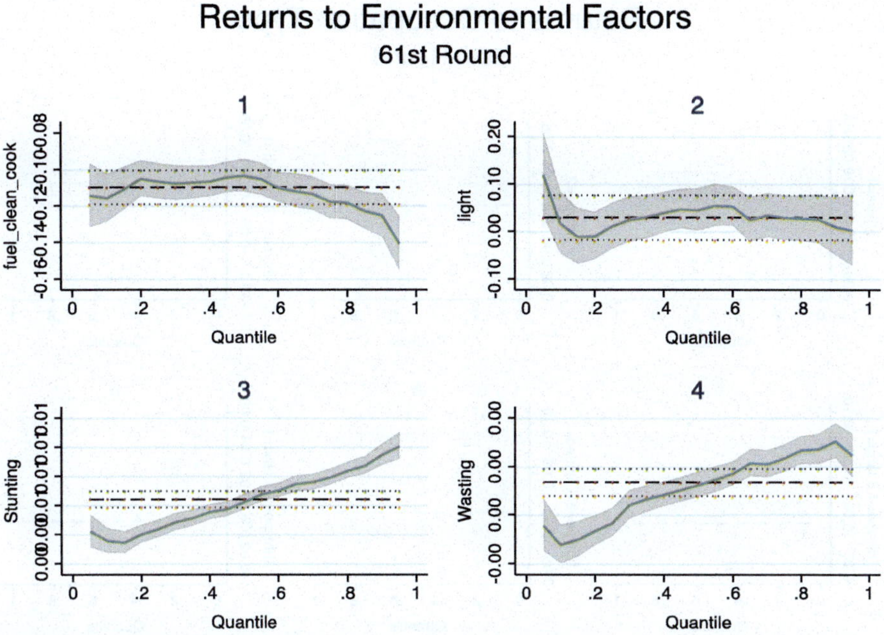

Fig. A.5 OLS and quantile regression results at 100 quantiles: returns to covariates for NSS 61st round

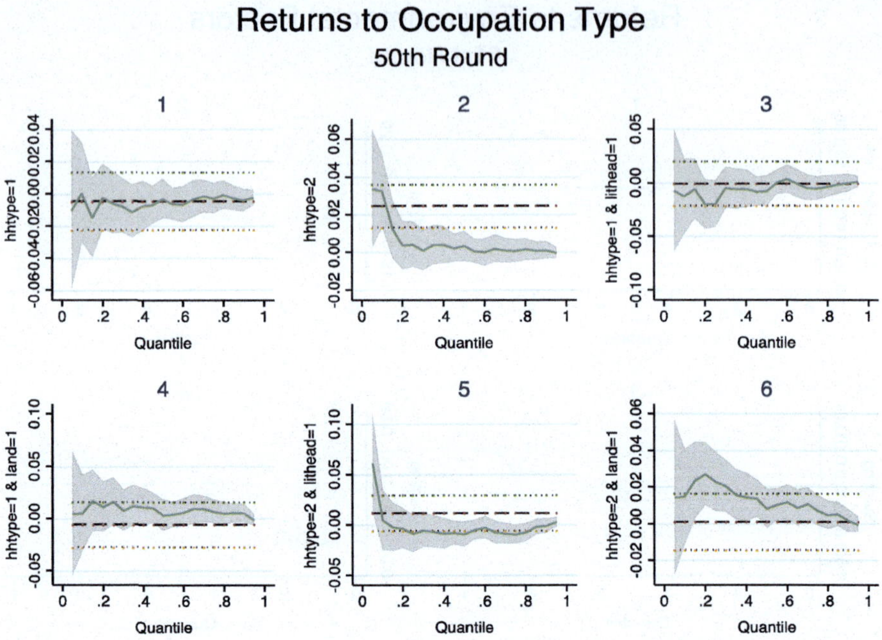

Fig. A.6 OLS and quantile regression results at 100 quantiles: returns to covariates for NSS 50th round

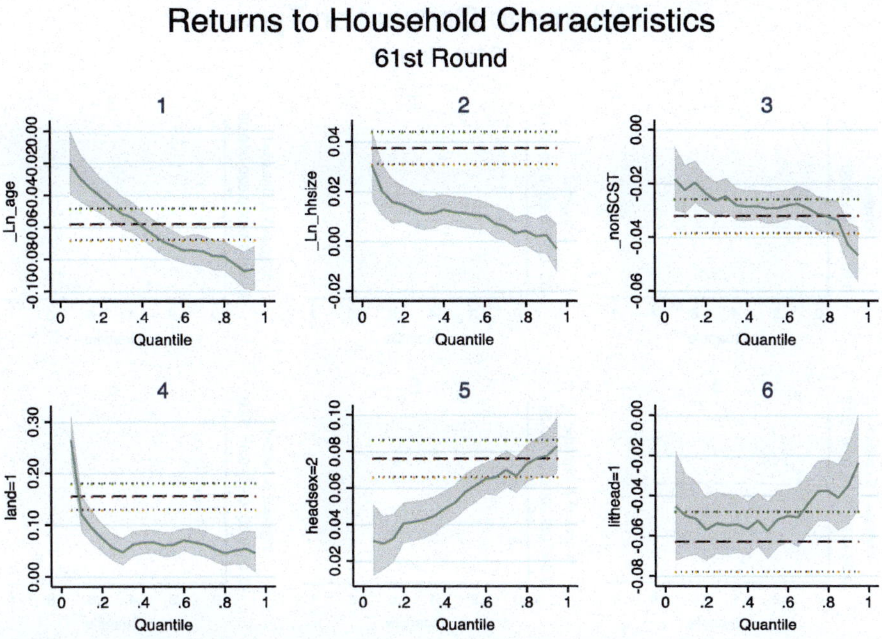

Fig. A.7 OLS and quantile regression results at 100 quantiles: returns to covariates for NSS 61st round

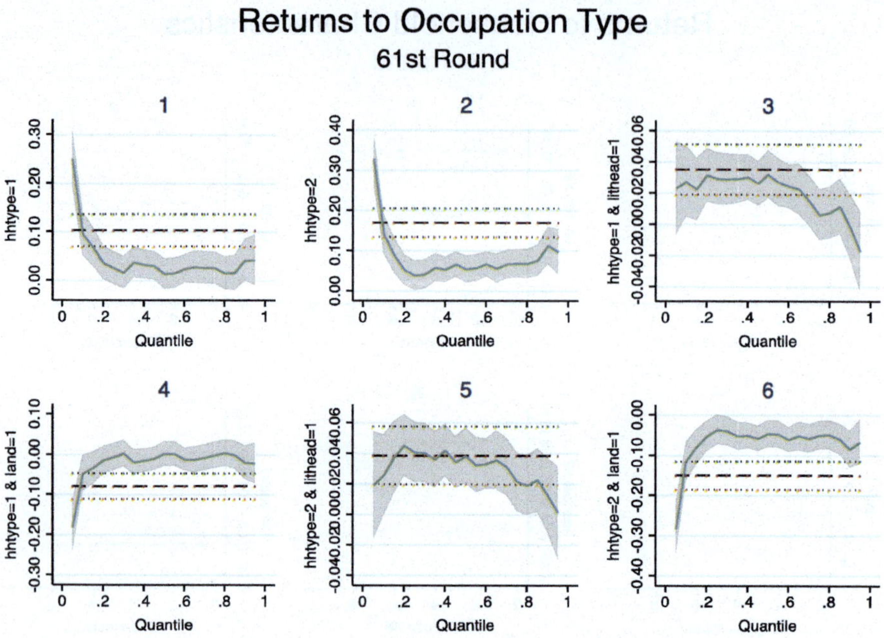

Fig. A.8 OLS and quantile regression results at 100 quantiles: returns to covariates for NSS 61st round

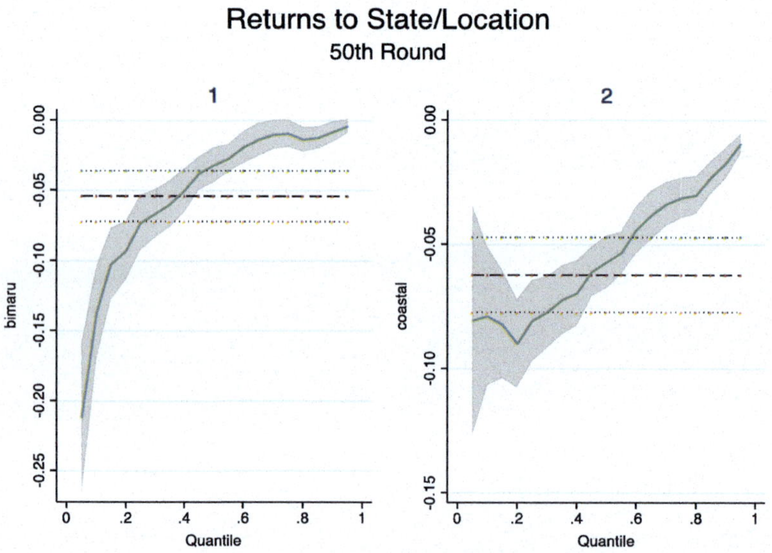

Fig. A.9 OLS and quantile regression results at 100 quantiles: returns to covariates for NSS 50th round

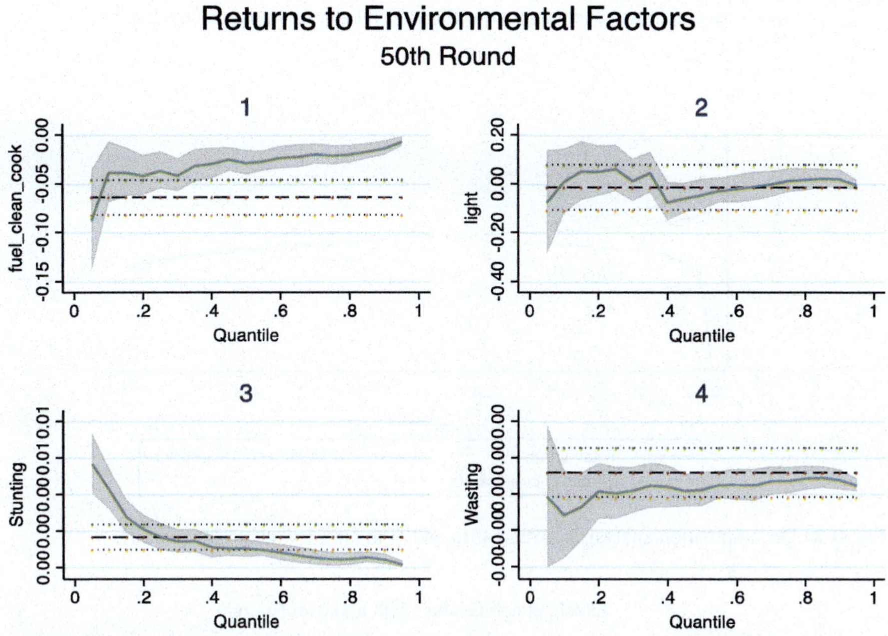

Fig. A.10 Quantile regression results at 100 quantiles: returns to environmental factors for NSS 50th round

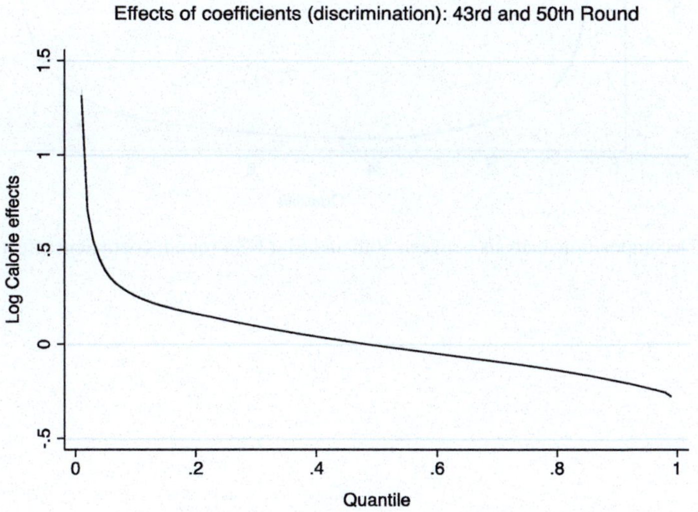

Fig. B.1 Decomposition analysis between 43rd and 50th NSS round: coefficient effect

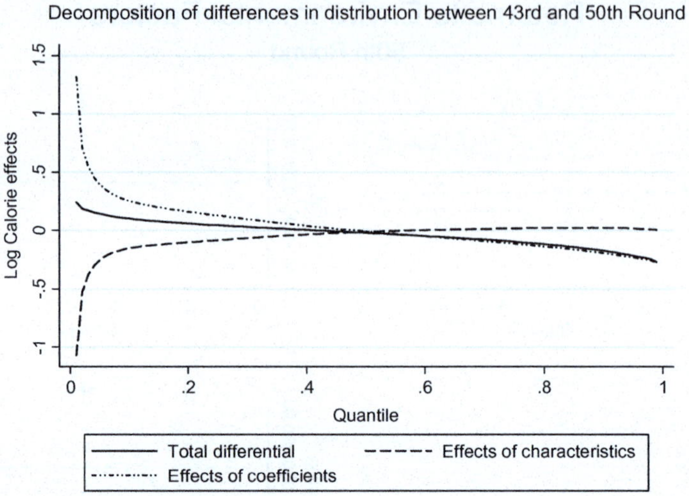

Fig. B.2 Decomposition analysis between 43rd and 50th NSS round at 100 quantiles

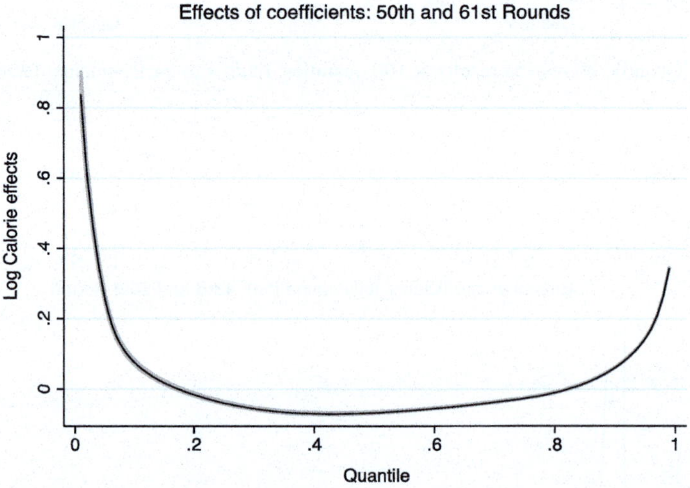

Fig. B.3 Decomposition analysis between 50th and 61st NSS round: coefficient effect

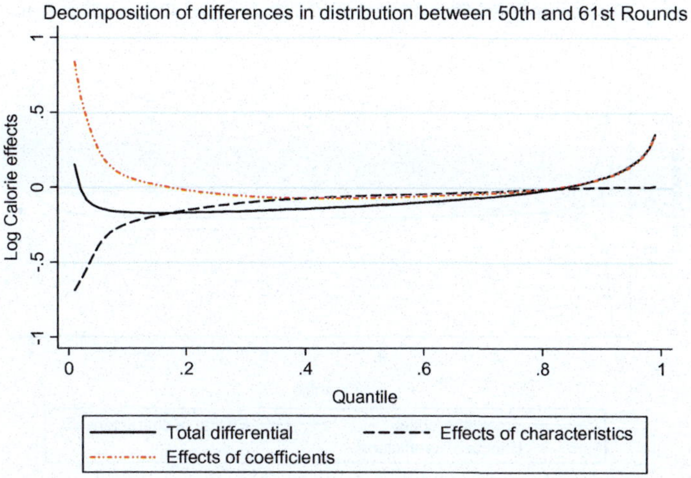

Fig. B.4 Decomposition analysis between 50th and 61st NSS round at 100 quantiles

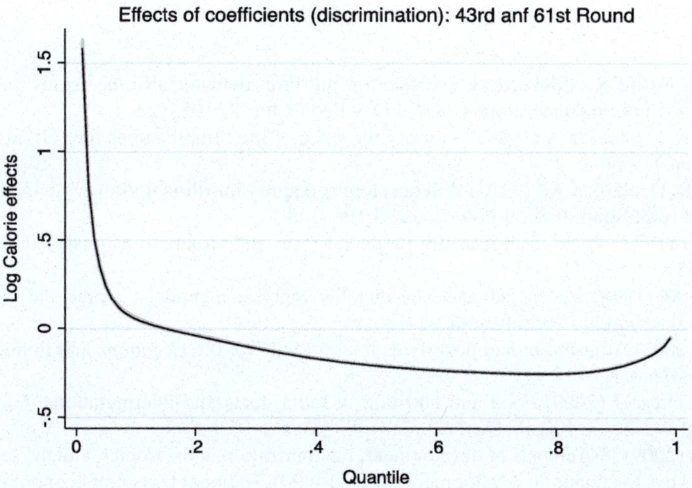

Fig. B.5 Decomposition analysis between 43rd and 61st NSS round: coefficient effect

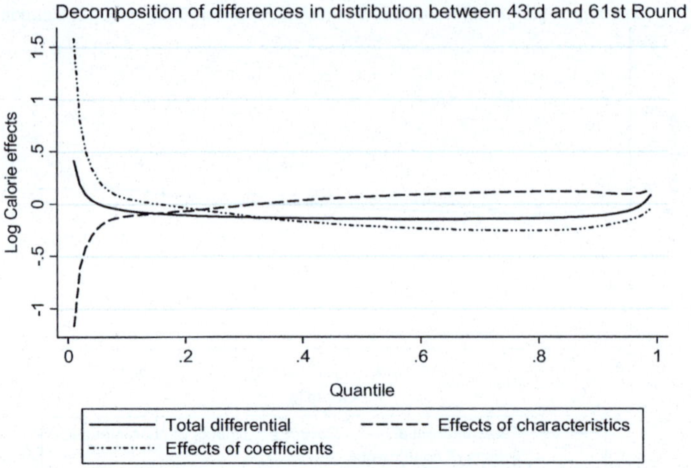

Fig. B.6 Decomposition analysis between 43rd and 61st NSS round at 100 quantiles

References

Behrman J, Wolfe B (1984) More evidence on nutrition demand: income seems overrated and women's schooling underemphasized. J Dev Econ 14(1–2):105–128

Behrman JR, Deolalikar A (1989) Is variety the spice of life? Implications for calorie intake. Rev Econ Stat 71:666–672

Behrman JR, Deolalikar AB (1987) Will developing country nutrition improvewith income? A case study of rural South India. J Polit Econ 95:108–138

Blinder AS (1973) Wage discrimination: reduced form and structural estimates. J Hum Resour 436–455

Buchinsky M (1998) Recent advances in quantile regression models: a practical guideline for empirical research. J Hum Resour 88–126

Deaton A (2003) Adjusted Indian poverty estimates for 1999–00. Economic and Political Weekly, pp 322–326

Deaton A, Dreze J (2009) Food and nutrition in India: facts and interpretations, Economic and Political Weekly, vol XLIV No 7

Deaton AS (2009) Instruments of development: randomization in the tropics, and the search for the elusive keys to economic development (No. w14690). National bureau of economic research

Deaton A, Kozel V (2005) Data and dogma: the great indian poverty debate. The World Bank Res Observ 20(2):177–199

Dreze J (2004) Don't forget India's poor. The Time Magazine. http://www.time.com/time/asia/covers/501041206/two_indias_vpt_dreze.html

Dubey A, Palmer-Jones R (2005). Prices, price index and poverty counts in India during 1980s and 1990s: calculation of unit value consumer price indexes, Artha Vijnana, vol XLVII, Nos 3–4, Sept–Dec 2005, pp 223–258

Gaiha R (1999) Food prices and income in India. Can J Dev Stud 20(1):31–58

Gopalan C, Shastri BVR, Balasubramanian SC (1971) Nutritive Value of Indian Foods. Hyderabad: National Institute of Nutrition

Jha R, Gaiha R, Sharma A (2009) Calorie and micronutrient deprivation and poverty nutrition traps in rural India. World Dev 37(5):982–991

Koenker R, Bassett G (1978) Regression quantiles. Econometrica 46(1):33–50

Machado JAF, Mata J (2005) Counterfactual decomposition of changes in wage distribution using quantile regression. J Appl Econom 20:445–465
Melly B (2005a) Public-private sector wage differentials in Germany: evidence from quantile regression empirical economics, vol 30, pp 505–20
Melly B (2005b) Decomposition of differences in distribution using quantile regression. Labour Econ 12(4):577–590
Neumark D (1988) Employers' discriminatory behavior and the estimation of wage discrimination. The J Hum Resour 23(3):279–295. https://doi.org/10.2307/145830
Oaxaca R (1973) Male-female wage differential in urban labour markets. Int Econ Rev 15:693–709
Strauss J, Thomas D (1995) Human resources: empirical modelling of household and family decisions. In: Behrman J, Srinivasan TN (Eds) Handbook of development economics, vol 3A, North-Holland, pp Chapter 34. Elsevier Science Publishers
Subramanian S, Deaton A (1996) Demand for food and calorie. J Polit Econ 104(1):133–162
Yu K, Jones M (1998) Local linear quantile regression. J Amer Stat Assoc 93(441):228–237

Chapter 5
Mixture Models: Identifying Consumption Classes in Post-liberalization India

Sudeshna Maitra

Abstract A mixture model is a probabilistic model that allows us to make inferences about the characteristics of sub-populations from observations on the overall population, without any information about the membership of individuals in the sub-populations or even the number of sub-populations. In this chapter, I present the theory of mixture models, and an application in which I identify consumption classes in urban India in 1999–00 (NSS). Suppose there are three sub-populations—a lower, a middle, and an upper consumption class—determined by the total number of different durables owned by households. I construct a three-component (or three-class) mixture model of household durable ownership, which is assumed to be distributed binomially by class. I then demonstrate the use of the Expectation Maximization (EM) algorithm to estimate the size of and mean durables owned by each class, as well as the probability that a household with a given number of durables belongs to a given class. Finally, I show how to assign households to classes using the mixture estimates, which allows further investigation of class-specific characteristics.

Keywords Consumption class · Binomial mixture model · EM algorithm

5.1 Introduction

A mixture model is a probabilistic model that allows us to make inferences about the characteristics of sub-populations from observations on the overall population, without any information about the membership of individuals in the sub-populations or even the number of sub-populations. In this chapter, I present an introduction to mixture models in a specific application—the identification of urban consumption

---

Supplementary Information The online version contains supplementary material available at https://doi.org/10.1007/978-981-99-4902-1_5.

S. Maitra (✉)
Department of Economics, York University, 4700 Keele Street, Toronto, ON M3J 1P3, Canada
e-mail: maitra@yorku.ca

D. Mukherjee (ed.), *Applied Econometric Analysis Using Cross Section and Panel Data*, Contributions to Economics, https://doi.org/10.1007/978-981-99-4902-1_5

classes (or sub-populations) in India after the widespread liberalization policies of 1991 came into effect.

Suppose that in the overall urban population, there are three sub-populations—a lower, a middle, and an upper class—determined by the total number of different durables owned by households. Can we identify the size and the (distinct) durable ownership pattern of each class—without specifically knowing the class membership of households—such that these, in combination, can generate the empirically observed durable ownership pattern in the entire urban population? Supposing that we could indeed identify classes in this way, how can we tell how many classes (or sub-populations) there are? How can we be sure that sub-populations exist in the first place?

A finite mixture model of durable ownership provides an intuitive framework for answering the questions posed above. In the following sections, I construct a three-component (or three-class) mixture model of household durable ownership, which is assumed to be distributed binomially by class. I then demonstrate the use of the Expectation Maximization (EM) algorithm (using data from the Indian National Sample Survey, urban sub-sample, 1999–00) to estimate the size of each class and the mean number of durables owned by each class, as well as the probability that a household with a given number of durables belongs to a given class. Also, I point to challenges that may arise in the interpretation of mixture estimates in general, and how to address them in our application so as to generate informative and meaningful estimates.

5.2 Finite Mixture Models

Consider a population of households where characteristic Y is distributed according to the density function $f(y)$.[1] Suppose now that there are n sub-populations in a population of households (where n is finite), and the characteristic Y in households from sub-population i follow the distribution $f_i(y)$, for each $i = 1, 2, \ldots, n$. Then,

$$f(y) = \sum_{i=1}^{n} \theta_i f_i(y) \tag{5.1}$$

where θ_i is the probability that any household belongs to sub-population i. Since households must belong to one of the n sub-populations, $\sum_{i=1}^{n} \theta_i = 1$. θ_i are referred

[1] A note on notation: throughout the paper, capital letters (e.g., Y) denote a variable that can take several values, while small letters (e.g., y) denote specific values. The only exception to this rule is the label N, which is used to denote sample size.

to as mixing probabilities. Equation (5.1) represents an n-component mixture model (McLachlan and Peel 2000).[2]

Note that the actual class membership of households is unknown. Let J denote the latent variable that represents the (unknown) class to which any household belongs, $J = 1, 2, \ldots, n$. Suppose that the joint distribution of characteristics Y and sub-population membership J is given by $\rho(y, j)$. Then $f(y)$ in (5.1) above clearly represents the marginal distribution of Y derivable from $\rho(y, j)$. Likewise, $f_i(y)$ represents the conditional distribution, or, the distribution of Y conditional on belonging to sub-population i. More explicitly, in the mixture setup[3]:

$$\rho(y, i) = \theta_i f_i(y) \tag{5.2}$$

for any $i = 1, 2, \ldots, n$, and

$$f(y) = \sum_{i=1}^{n} \rho(y, i) = \sum_{i=1}^{n} \theta_i f_i(y) \tag{5.3}$$

Additionally, using Bayes' Law, the conditional probability that any household with characteristic y belongs to class j is given by:

$$Pr(J = j/Y = y) = \frac{\theta_j f_j(y)}{\sum_{i=1}^{n} \theta_i f_i(y)} \tag{5.4}$$

for any $j = 1, 2, \ldots, n$.

Let us look at some numerical examples of mixture models such as in (5.1). For specificity, suppose $n = 2$ (viz., a two-component mixture model) and suppose that the sub-population densities $f_i(y; \mu_i, \sigma^2)$ are normal with parameters (μ_i, σ^2). What would the marginal density $f(y)$ look like for different mixing probabilities $\theta_1, 1 - \theta_1$? The graphs in Fig. 5.1, taken from McLachlan and Peel (2000), provide a visual illustration of what the marginal density looks like when it is a mixture of two normal densities.

Figure 5.1a plots the (marginal) density of a mixture of 2 components mixed in equal proportion. The densities of the 2 components are normally distributed with common variance 1. The mean of the first component is 0 throughout, while the mean of the second component is 1, 2, 3 and 4, respectively, in diagrams (i)–(iv). In Fig. 5.1b, the components are the same as above but they are mixed in proportions

[2] In (5.1), $f(y)$ and $f_i(y)$ refer to univariate distributions of a single characteristic Y. Mixture models may also apply to multivariate distributions $f(y_1, y_2, \ldots, y_k)$ and $f_i(y_1, y_2, \ldots, y_k)$ of k characteristics $(Y_1, Y_2, \ldots, Y_k)$. See McLachlan and Peel (2000).

[3] Recall the relationship between joint and marginal distributions: if $f(a, b)$ represents the joint probability of $A = a$ and $B = b$, then the marginal probability that $A = a$ is $\Pr(A = a) = \sum_x f(a, x)$ (where x represents all possible values that B can take).

0.75 (θ_1) and 0.25 (θ_2), respectively, instead of equal shares. Note how the shapes of the marginal densities are bimodal if the 2 components have sufficient separation (in terms of their means) between them. Note also (as in Fig. 5.1b(i)–(ii)), how an asymmetric density may be obtained by mixing 2 symmetric components, e.g., when the means of the component densities are close enough and the distinction between them is obscured by unequal mixing probabilities. Varying the number of components, means, variances and mixing probabilities can therefore generate a large range of shapes of the marginal density.

In Fig. 5.1, however, we have constructed the marginal distribution $f(y)$ by mixing two known component distributions $f_i(y; \mu_i, \sigma^2)$, that are normal. In empirical applications, the situation is reversed—we have at our disposal, an empirical distribution of y sampled from the population distribution $f(y)$, and we seek to determine

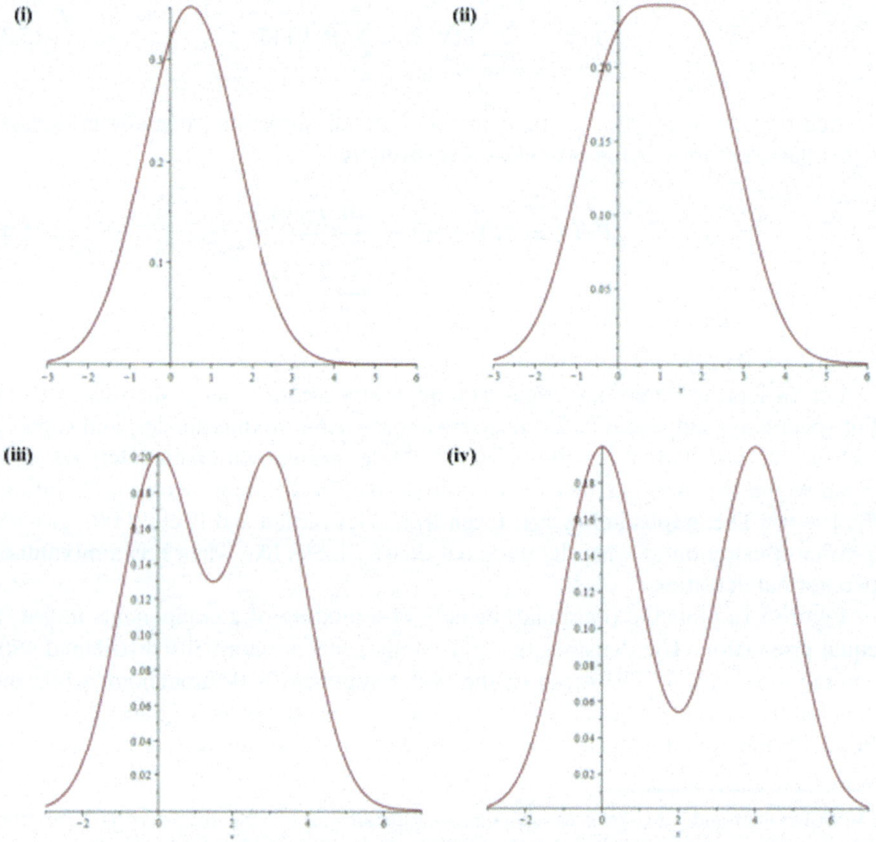

Fig. 5.1 **a** Plot of a mixture density of 2 univariate normal sub-populations (components) in equal proportions with common variance 1, and means 0 and (i) 1; (ii) 2; (iii) 3; (iv) 4. **b** Plot of a mixture density of 2 univariate normal sub-populations (components) in proportions 0.75 and 0.25 with common variance 1, and means 0 and (i) 1; (ii) 2; (iii); (iv) 4

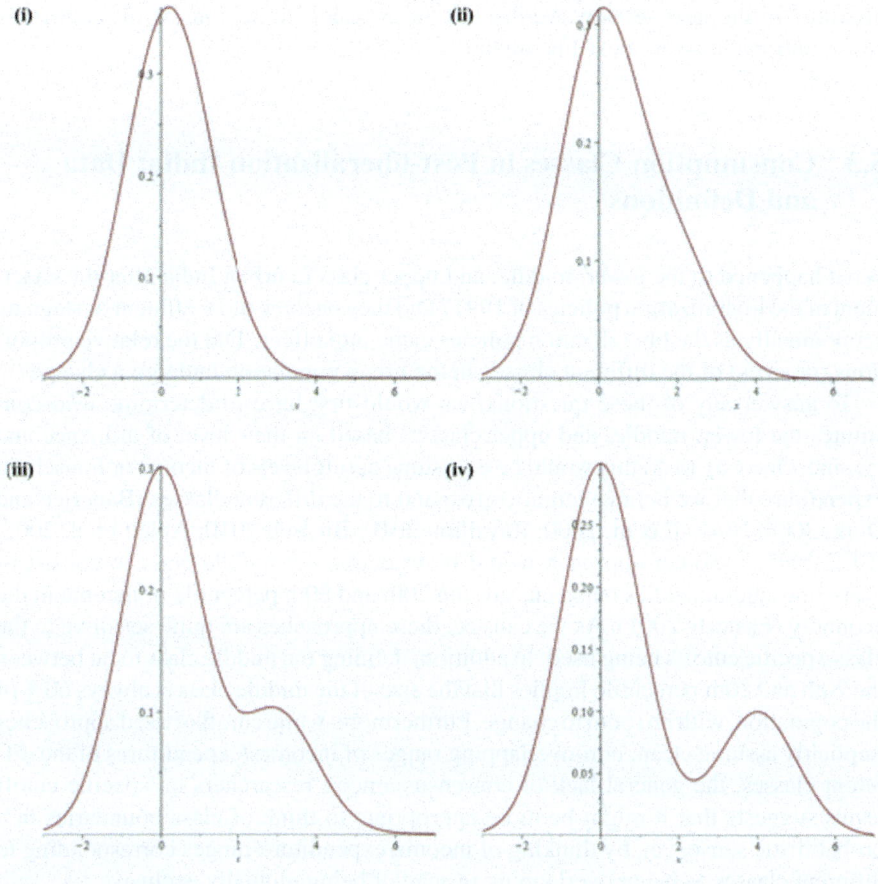

Fig. 5.1 (continued)

the size and characteristics of sub-populations (if any) that may have mixed to generate it. Given the flexibility of shapes that we have demonstrated can be obtained by mixtures, we could of course "fit" a mixture model to the data (using methods described in the sections below) assuming the existence of a certain number of sub-populations. But can we argue that sub-populations exist simply because they are able to "explain" our data? Consider, for example, the Pickering-Platt debate in the 1950s and 1960s about the patho-physiology of hypertension (McLachlan and Peel 2000). Platt (1963) claimed that the distribution of blood pressure was a two-component mixture of "hypertensive" and "normotensive" sub-populations. But Pickering (1968) argued that "hypertensive" was merely a label assigned to those with blood pressure readings in the upper tail of the distribution for a single population, viz., that the blood pressure distribution was not a mixture at all!

How then do we determine if there do indeed exist sub-populations that have mixed to generate our data? Furthermore, how many sub-populations (if any) exist in the mixture? In the next section, we discuss these issues in the context of identifying consumption classes in post-liberalization India.

5.3 Consumption Classes in Post-liberalization India: Data and Definitions

What happened to the lower, middle, and upper class in urban India after the enactment of the liberalization policies of 1991? Did they become more affluent or stagnate economically as the liberalization policies came into effect? Did the relative proportions (or sizes) of the different classes in the urban population undergo a change?

To answer any of these questions, we would first have to determine *who* constitutes the lower, middle, and upper classes, based on their level of affluence and income. One way to do this would be to assume cutoff levels of income or household expenditure that we believe might correspond to the different classes (Banerjee and Duflo 2008; Birdsall et al. 2000; Ravallion 2010; Birdsall 2010; Ablett et al. 2007; IBEF 2005). Another approach would be to define the middle class to consist of every household that lies between, say, the 20th and 80th percentile of income in the economy (Easterly 2001). As we can see, these approaches are quite sensitive to the class-specific cutoffs being used. In addition, defining the middle class to lie between the 20th and 80th percentile implies that the size of the middle class is always 60% of the population, with no room to change. Furthermore, while cutoffs-based approaches implicitly assume clean, non-overlapping ranges of incomes/expenditures of the different classes, the general lack of consensus among researchers on specific cutoff levels suggests that it might be more appropriate to think of class boundaries in a probabilistic sense, i.e., by thinking of income/expenditure-ranges corresponding to different classes as being overlapping instead of being mutually exclusive.[4, 5]

In addition to the larger problems associated with cutoffs-based approaches, there is a specific problem surrounding the measurement of household expenditures from the Indian National Sample Survey (NSS), 1999–00 survey. The recall period used for reporting expenditures in the 1999–00 NSS questionnaire was shorter than in previous years (Deaton and Kozel 2005). This could have resulted in higher total household expenditures reported in 1999–00 than in previous years, not due to any real increase in consumption but due to people being able to recall their more recent purchases with greater accuracy! To avoid running into this issue with measures of expenditure—especially when we compare our findings across previous rounds of NSS—we turn to a different measure of consumption to define classes, viz., durable

[4] See Sect. 5.6, where we discuss how a traditional clustering model such as the K-Means model would lead to a non-probabilistic assignments of households to classes.

[5] As Ravallion (2010) points out, some of the disagreement about cutoffs is due to the level of income of the countries concerned, viz., whether a developed or a developing economy. However, there does not appear to be a clear consensus on cutoffs even in studies that focus solely on developing nations.

ownership. Our measure of durable ownership is drawn from a survey question that asks respondents if a certain durable good is present in the household at the time of the survey. This measure is immune to the change in recall period, making our analysis robust to comparisons over the 1990s (Sect. 5.5.2).

Apart from the general ease (and reliability) of measurement of durable ownership, it is arguably also a good variable for measuring consumption standards of households over time. This is because durables are a store of utility that represents the stock component of household wealth rather than the flow component embodied in PCE. The ownership of durables assures the realization of a stream of consumption utility in the future periods. These characteristics make durables ownership a useful measure of consumption *standards*—a permanent, sustainable aspect of consumption (Bar-Ilan and Blinder 1988)—and, hence, an appropriate choice of variable for the identification of consumption classes.[6]

Our goal, therefore, is to derive a definition of classes—lower, middle, and upper—in urban India from the 55th Round of the National Sample Survey data (1999–00), using data on the durable ownership of households. Our underlying premise is only that higher classes enjoy a higher standard of living (or, are more affluent) than lower classes; no further specifications are made about who or what constitutes each class. In particular, we use the ownership of different durable goods by households to be a measure of the standard of living enjoyed therein.

We consider 12 specific durable goods in our analysis, as these have often been linked to middle class status in India in existing literature (Banerjee and Duflo 2008; Senauer and Goetz 2003)—viz., record player/gramophone, tape/CD player, radio, television, VCR/VCP, electric fan, washer, refrigerator, air conditioner, bicycle, motor cycle/scooter and motor car/jeep. We assume that owning a higher number of different durable goods indicates a higher standard of living. Hence, our variable of interest—call it Y—is the total number (out of 12) of different durable goods owned by households as reported in the urban sub-sample NSS, 1999–00 ($Y = 0, 1, 2, \ldots, 12$).

Note that the weight of different durable goods in the sum Y is the same regardless of the price of the good. This may appear to make Y an inadequate measure of affluence, except that there is a "natural weighting" involved in the definition of Y as a simple sum. An expensive item (such as an air conditioner) is more likely to occur in households with more total goods (i.e., higher value of Y) than a cheap item (such as a fan). So, even though it appears that a household with an air conditioner is treated the same as a household with a fan, this is only true when other factors are the same. We surmise that other factors are not the same in a household that has a fan and one that has an air conditioner, and that these dissimilarities will naturally place

[6] The approach adopted in this paper may, therefore, be considered a "dual" approach to the expenditure-cutoffs-based approach—here, durables ownership is used to identify the classes and the expenditure-ranges of the classes thus identified are subsequently explored (instead of using expenditures to identify classes in the first place). In addition, the mixture approach allows us to determine the *distribution* of households in any class over the relevant expenditures-range, instead of assuming that every household in this range belongs to this class with certainty, as in the cutoffs-based approach (Sect. 5.5.4 provides a further discussion of this point).

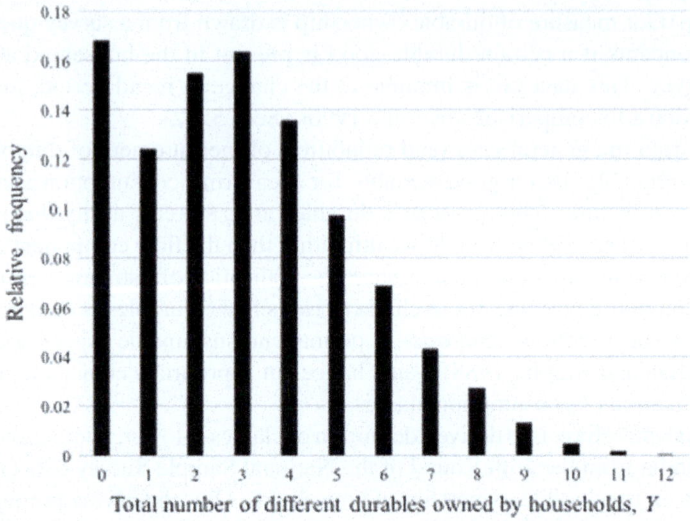

Fig. 5.2 Distribution of Y in urban NSS, 1999–00 (See Table A1(a) in the appendix for the tabular presentation of the data herein)

the ownership of more expensive durable items (air conditioners) in households with greater affluence (higher Y), even without using an explicitly higher weight on these premium goods. The same argument holds also for households owning different qualities of the same good (e.g., black-and-white vs. plasma tvs) as well as for households owning different numbers of units of the same durable good.

Figure 5.2 represents the distribution of Y in the sample of households in the urban round of NSS, 1999–00. It represents a draw from the distribution of Y in the urban population, viz., $f(y)$ in (5.1). What does the shape of the distribution tell us about the distribution of affluence in urban India?

The shape of the distribution in Fig. 5.2 reveals more than one mode, which we saw in Fig. 5.1, might be an indication that it is a mixture of component sub-population densities. But bimodality in itself is not sufficient to justify the existence of sub-populations. The concept of "class" is, however, more than a purely statistical phenomenon—it appears in historical as well as recent literature (Britannica 2022), as individual groups in the overall population that have distinct characteristics, as opposed to labels assigned to those with different levels of income or consumption (recall the Pickering-Platt debate, Sect. 5.2). In addition, Maitra (2021) shows that when households signal their social status in the marriage market with their observable durable ownership, then total durable expenditure levels of households segregate into clusters, interpretable as "classes". There is, therefore, historical evidence as well as an explicit economic modeling of the class phenomenon, suggesting that a mixture model with classes—as sub-populations—may indeed be an appropriate way to model the durables ownership distribution in Fig. 5.2. We will call the sub-populations "consumption classes" to underline the fact they are identified using a measure of consumption, viz., durable ownership.

This brings to us to the next question of *how many* classes could generate a distribution such as in Fig. 5.2. Should we look for 3 classes—a lower, a middle and upper—that describe the density in Fig. 5.2? Or more, given that there may be a lower middle class and an upper middle class? Note that in an extreme (and completely uninformative) scenario, we could assign each household in our sample (say, of size N) to its own class and achieve a perfect fit to the density in Fig. 5.2 using this N-component mixture model! To counter this phenomenon, we impose the criterion that the optimal number of classes is the *smallest* number of sub-populations that yields a good fit to the marginal density in Fig. 5.2. In other words, we iteratively estimate t-component mixture models, $t = 2, 3, \ldots$. The smallest value of t to provide a good fit to the marginal distribution (Fig. 5.2) is the appropriate number of classes that must constitute the urban population in 1999–00.

In Sect. 5.5.1, we show that the urban data from NSS 1999–00 is best described by 3 classes, which we will call a lower, a middle, and an upper class. In the next section, therefore, we will present the three-component mixture model used to identify the classes and estimate their size and characteristics.

5.4 A Three-Component Mixture Model to Identify Consumption Classes

Consider 12 durable goods and let Y represent the total number of these goods that a household owns at the time of interview, $Y = 0, 1, 2, \ldots, 12$. Households can belong to one of three classes—1, 2 or 3—which are defined by the pattern of durables ownership of members. Denote the density of Y within class i by $\phi_i(y)$ and the density of Y in the population by $f(y)$.[7] A Three-Component Mixture Model postulates the following:

$$f(y) = \pi_1\phi_1(y) + \pi_2\phi_2(y) + \pi_3\phi_3(y) \tag{5.5}$$

where π_1, π_2 and π_3 represent the proportions of class 1, 2 and 3 in the population, respectively ($\pi_1 + \pi_2 + \pi_3 = 1$).

To estimate the mixture model—i.e., to estimate the mixing probabilities π_i and the conditional distributions $\phi_i(Y)$—using maximum likelihood estimation (see Sect. 5.4.2), we make an assumption about the family of (discrete) density functions to which ϕ_i ($i = 1, 2, 3$) belong. We choose the family of binomial distributions, since binomial densities, depending on parameter values, are flexible enough to represent symmetric as well as skewed densities. This feature of binomials gives us the

[7] Remember that Y is a discrete variable, even though we use the term "density function" (and not "mass function") to describe its distribution throughout the chapter.

ability to capture potentially different shapes of different (class-specific) conditional densities of Y.

In particular, assume that a household owns each good with a fixed probability p_i, which depends on the class i (= 1, 2 or 3) to which it belongs. The ordering of the p_i's indicates which i (= 1, 2 or 3) corresponds to the lower, the middle and the upper class, respectively, since (by definition) $p_L < p_M < p_U$ (L: lower, M: middle, U: upper). Assume that each good is obtained independently by households. Hence the total number of goods owned by a class$-i$ household follows a binomial distribution with parameters 12 and p_i, i.e., $\phi_i(Y) \sim Binomial(12, p_i)$.

Note that we do not claim that households do indeed acquire each good independently and with the same probability. The assumption of binomial densities is a tool to approximate the shape of the conditional densities $\phi_i(Y)$. Think of the process as one of identifying the shapes of the conditional distributions $\phi_i(Y)$; the parameters p_i denote binomial densities that would successfully mimic these shapes.[8]

If the population is a (binomial) mixture of three classes, what is the probability of drawing a household in the sample with a certain level of ownership, say x? This probability—that of observing level x of durable ownership in a household in the sample—is given by:

$$Pr(Y = x; \pi_1, \pi_2, p_1, p_2, p_3) = \pi_1\phi_1(x; p_1) + \pi_2\phi_2(x; p_2) + \pi_3\phi_3(x; p_3) \quad (5.6)$$

where π_i represents the probability that the household we have drawn belongs to class i and $\phi_i(x; p_i)$ represents the (binomial) probability that a class$-i$ household owns x durables.

The expression in (5.6) can be used to derive the likelihood function of drawing a sample of size N with durable ownership levels $(y_1, y_2, \ldots, y_N)$. The likelihood function may then be maximized to obtain maximum likelihood estimates of the parameters, viz., those values of the parameters that would be most likely to have generated the sample we have drawn, viz., $(y_1, y_2, \ldots, y_N)$. However, maximum likelihood estimation can provide challenges in terms of parameter estimation and hypothesis testing for mixture models (McLachlan and Krishnan 1996). Calculating likelihoods for a sample based on a mixture model is complicated, and traditional numerical likelihood optimization techniques such as Newton–Raphson break down. Here, I will use the Expectations-Maximization (EM) algorithm for likelihood maximization (McLachlan and Krishnan 1996; Dempster et al. 1977; Hastie et al. 2001). The EM optimum coincides with the likelihood optimum but is reached (somewhat slowly) using iterated steps. The algorithm and its application to this analysis are described in Sect. 5.4.3.

[8] See footnote 10 on the drawbacks of allowing dependence in ownership of each good, or a different probability p_{ij} of ownership for each good i if in class j.

5.4.1 Identifiability and Observational Equivalence

Before attempting to estimate the binomial mixture model in (5.5)–(5.6), it is necessary to establish that the model is identifiable. In general, a parametric family of densities $f(y; \Psi)$ is identifiable if distinct values of the parameter Ψ determine distinct members of the family of densities $\{f(y; \Psi); \Psi \in \Omega\}$, where Ω is the specified parameter space (McLachlan and Peel 2000). In other words, a parametric family of densities $f(y; \Psi)$ is identifiable when $f(y; \Psi) = f(y; \Psi^*) \iff \Psi = \Psi^*$.

Blischke (1964) shows that a necessary and sufficient condition for identifiability of binomial mixtures is $h \geq (2r - 1)$, where h is the binomial parameter denoting the number of trials and r is the number of components in the mixture. In the current application, $h = 12$ (the number of durables) and $r = 3$ (the number of classes), so the condition for identifiability is easily satisfied. Hence the model (5.5) is identifiable.[9]

Note also the issue of observational equivalence known to plague mixture models in general. This means that even when the model is identified as defined above, there is observationally no difference between, for example, the parameter vector $(\pi_1, \pi_2, 1 - \pi_1 - \pi_2, p_1, p_2, p_3)$ and the vector $(\pi_2, \pi_1, 1 - \pi_1 - \pi_2, p_2, p_1, p_3)$. Observational equivalence makes it hard to uniquely map parameters to class (in the example above: is class 1 the lower class or class 2?). However, the very nature of the current application—the identification of a lower, a middle, and an upper class—provides a natural remedy for the issue, since, obviously, $p_L < p_M < p_U$ (L: lower class, M: middle class, U: upper class). Therefore, the ordering of the p_i estimates tells us which class is the lower class, which is the middle class and the upper class.[10]

5.4.2 Estimation: Maximum Likelihood and the Expectation-Maximization (EM) Algorithm

Having established identifiability, we now proceed to the estimation of the mixture model. From (5.6), we know the probability of observing a household with x durables in the sample. Recall that we have an independent and identically distributed sample of N households where household j is observed to own y_j durables ($j = 1, 2, \ldots, 12$). What is the likelihood of having drawn this sample of households with durables $(y_1, y_2, \ldots, y_N)$? The likelihood is obtained by multiplying (given independence) the probabilities in (5.6),

---

[9] In fact, a binomial mixture of up to 6 classes will be identifiable in our model with 12 durable goods, since $h \geq (2r - 1)$ is true for $h = 12$ and $r \leq 6$.

[10] If we had assumed different probabilities of ownership p_{ki} for each durable good k ($k = 1, 2, \ldots, 12$) given class i, we would be trying to estimate a vector of 12 probabilities for *each* class! The criterion for mapping 12-tuple vectors of probability estimates to the lower, middle, or upper class would not then be as straightforward as above.

$$L(y_1, y_2, \ldots, y_N; \pi_1, \pi_2, p_1, p_2, p_3) = \prod_{j=1}^{N}[\pi_1\phi_1(y_j; p_1) + \pi_2\phi_2(y_j; p_2) + (1 - \pi_1 - \pi_2)\phi_3(y_j; p_3)] \quad (5.7)$$

where subscript j denotes household j $(j = 1, 2, \ldots, N)$. The log likelihood function is then given by

$$\text{Log } L(y_1, y_2, \ldots, y_N; \pi_1, \pi_2, p_1, p_2, p_3) = \sum_{j=1}^{N}[\pi_1\phi_1(y_j; p_1) + \pi_2\phi_2(y_j; p_2) + (1 - \pi_1 - \pi_2)\phi_3(y_j; p_3)] \quad (5.8)$$

The goal of maximum likelihood estimation is to find the values of the parameters $(\pi_1, \pi_2, p_1, p_2, p_3)$ that maximize the likelihood (5.7) (hence, the log likelihood (5.8)) of having drawn the sample we have, viz., $(y_1, y_2, \ldots, y_N)$. This involves solving first and second-order conditions from (5.8) (obtained by taking partial derivatives with respect to the parameters and setting them equal to zero). It is hard, however, to obtain closed-form expressions for maximum likelihood estimates of the parameters from (5.7) or (5.8). The Expectation-Maximization (EM) algorithm is a tool used to simplify difficult maximum likelihood problems such as the above (McLachlan and Krishnan 1996; Dempster et al. 1977; Hastie et al. 2001) and is described in Sect. 5.4.3. The importance of the EM algorithm lies in its ability to find a path to the maximum likelihood point estimates where traditional numerical techniques typically fail.

5.4.3 Implementation of the EM Algorithm

Suppose that each household belongs to a particular class and let the dummy variables (δ_1, δ_2) represent the class membership of households, i.e., $\delta_1 j = 1$ if household j belongs to class 1 (0, otherwise), and $\delta_{2j} = 1$ if household j belongs to class 2 (0, otherwise).

Clearly, (δ_1, δ_2) are latent variables since the class memberships of households are unknown. Suppose, however, that (δ_1, δ_2) are known. Then the likelihood and log likelihood functions could be written as:

$$L_{EM}(y_1, y_2, \ldots, y_N; \pi_1, \pi_2, p_1, p_2, p_3) = \prod_{j=1}^{N}\{\pi_1\phi_1(y_j; p_1)\}^{\delta_{1j}}\{\pi_2\phi_2(y_j; p_2)\}^{\delta_{2j}}\{(1 - \pi_1 - \pi_2)\phi_3(y_j; p_3)\}^{(1-\delta_{1j}-\delta_{2j})} \quad (5.9)$$

and

$$
\begin{aligned}
&\text{Log } L_{EM}(y_1, y_2, \ldots, y_N; \pi_1, \pi_2, p_1, p_2, p_3) \\
&= \sum_{j=1}^{N} [\delta_{1j} log\{\pi_1 \phi_1(y_j; p_1)\} + \delta_{2j} log\{\pi_2 \phi_2(y_j; p_2)\} \\
&+ (1 - \delta_{1j} - \delta_{2j}) log\{(1 - \pi_1 - \pi_2)\phi_3(y_j; p_3)\}]
\end{aligned} \tag{5.10}
$$

If class memberships (δ_1, δ_2) were indeed known, it would be easy to find close-form expressions for maximum likelihood parameter estimates that maximize Log L_{EM} in (5.10) above. Since class memberships are not known, the EM algorithm computes the expected values of (δ_1, δ_2) conditional on the data (call these (γ_1, γ_2)), plugs these into (5.10) and computes the maximands. The procedure is iterated till convergence is obtained. The steps involved are outlined below (McLachlan and Krishnan 1996; Dempster et al. 1977; Hastie et al. 2001).

The EM Algorithm for a Three – Component Mixture Model

1. **Start with initial guesses for the parameters**: $(\pi_1^{(0)}, \pi_2^{(0)}, p_1^{(0)}, p_2^{(0)}, p_3^{(0)})$
2. **Expectation (E) step**: at the kth step, compute, as follows, the expected values $(\gamma_i^{(k)})$ of class membership conditional on the data $(y_1, y_2, \ldots, y_N)$. Note that since class memberships are binary, a household's expected value of class membership conditional on the data is also the estimated probability that a household belongs to class i conditional on the data. That is,

$$
\begin{aligned}
E(\delta_{ij}/(y_1, \ldots, y_N; \pi^{(k-1)}, p^{(k-1)}) &= Pr(\delta_{ij} = 1/Y = y_j; \pi^{(k-1)}, p^{(k-1)}) \\
&= \frac{Pr(\delta_{ij} = 1, Y = y_j/\pi^{(k-1)}, p^{(k-1)})}{Pr(Y = y_j/\pi^{(k-1)}, p^{(k-1)})} \\
= \frac{\pi_i^{(k-1)} \phi_i(y_j, p_i^{(k-1)})}{\pi_1^{(k-1)} \phi_1(y_j, p_1^{(k-1)}) + \pi_2^{(k-1)} \phi_2(y_j, p_2^{(k-1)}) + (1 - \pi_1^{(k-1)} - \pi_2^{(k-1)}) \phi_3(y_j, p_3^{(k-1)})}
\end{aligned} \tag{5.11}
$$

Therefore, the conditional expected values $(\gamma_i^{(k)})$ are given by the last term in (5.11) above, viz.,:

$$
\begin{aligned}
1\gamma_{ij}^{(k)} \\
= E(\delta_{ij}/(y_1, \ldots, y_N; \pi_1^{(k-1)}, \pi_2^{(k-1)}), p_1^{(k-1)}, p_2^{(k-1)}, p_3^{(k-1))} \\
= \frac{\pi_i^{(k-1)} \phi_i(y_j, p_i^{(k-1)})}{\pi_1^{(k-1)} \phi_1(y_j, p_1^{(k-1)}) + \pi_2^{(k-1)} \phi_2(y_j, p_2^{(k-1)}) + (1 - \pi_1^{(k-1)} - \pi_2^{(k-1)}) \phi_3(y_j, p_3^{(k-1)})}
\end{aligned} \tag{5.12}
$$

$i = 1, 2, 3; j = 1, 2, \ldots, N.$[11]

---

[11] The expression for the conditional probability in (5.11)–(5.12) follows from Bayes' Law (see Eq. (5.4)).

3. **Maximization (M) step**: at the kth step, compute the parameters as follows. These are the maximands of the EM-log-likelihood function in (5.10), when (δ_1, δ_2) are replaced by $(\gamma_1^{(k)}, \gamma_2^{(k)})$, viz., the expected values of class membership conditional on the data (calculated in the E step).[12]

$$\pi_i^{(k)} = \frac{1}{N}\sum_{j=1}^{N} \gamma_{ij}^{(k)} \tag{5.13}$$

$$p_i^{(k)} = \frac{1}{12}[\frac{\sum_{j=1}^{N} \gamma_j^{(k)} x_j}{\sum_{j=1}^{N} \gamma_j^{(k)}} \tag{5.14}$$

$i = 1, 2, 3.$

4. **Iterate steps 2 and 3 (the E and M steps)** till convergence is obtained in the estimates in (5.13)–(5.14).[13]

As output, the EM algorithm yields the following estimates[14]:

1. $\hat{\pi}_i$: estimates of the (unconditional) probability that any household belongs to class i; $i = 1, 2, 3$
2. $\hat{p}_i$: estimates of the probability with which a class$-i$ household owns a durable good; $i = 1, 2, 3$
3. $\hat{\gamma}_{ij}$: estimates of the (conditional) probability with which household j (with durable ownership y_j) belongs to class i; $i = 1, 2, 3$; $j = 1, 2, \ldots, N$.

The ownership probabilities $\hat{p}_i$ and the corresponding class-specific (binomial) densities $\phi_i(y, \hat{p}_i)$ answer our motivating question—who are the lower, middle, and upper class?—by identifying the distinct ownership patterns (densities) of the different classes. Moreover, the estimates of the unconditional probabilities $\hat{\pi}_i$—interpretable as estimates of class shares—tells us the sizes of the urban lower, middle, and upper classes in 1999–00. Finally, the estimated (conditional) probabilities of class membership, $\hat{\gamma}_{ij}$, along with $\hat{\pi}_i$ and $\hat{p}_i$, enable a random assignment of each household into a particular class. This allows a descriptive analysis of other class-specific household characteristics such as per capita monthly expenditures, education of household

---

[12] The expressions in (5.13) and (5.14) follow directly from the first order conditions of maximization of (5.10), with (δ_1, δ_2) replaced by $(\gamma_1^{(k)}, \gamma_2^{(k)})$.

[13] It is straightforward to write a computer program that iterates through the steps of the EM algorithm. The author's code written in STATA is available upon request.

[14] Standard errors of estimates are obtained by taking the square root of the diagonal elements of the (5×5) variance-covariance matrix $[I(\hat{\pi}_1, \hat{\pi}_2, \hat{p}_1, \hat{p}_2, \hat{p}_3)]^{-1}$. Denote the set of parameters by Ψ, viz., $\Psi = (\pi_1, \pi_2, p_1, p_2, p_3)$ and EM-generated estimates $\widehat{\Psi} = (\hat{\pi}_1, \hat{\pi}_2, \hat{p}_1, \hat{p}_2, \hat{p}_3)$. Then, the (5×5) information matrix is given by $I(\widehat{\Psi}) = -\frac{\partial^2 LogL_{EM}(\widehat{\Psi})}{\partial \Psi^2}$; the variance-covariance matrix is given by $[I(\widehat{\Psi})]^{-1}$.

heads, household types by employment, and so on (see Sect. 5.5.4). The next section presents the results.

5.4.4 Illustration of the EM Algorithm Using STATA

The supplemental material for this chapter includes an ado file called '*runembin1.ado*' that is programmed in STATA to estimate a three-component binomial mixture model using the EM algorithm. Here is an illustration of how to use the ado file to obtain estimates of the sizes and durable ownership densities of the three classes.

Before you use the STATA file provided, please refer carefully to the instructions accompanying the ado file. To call the ado file from your STATA application, please save it as a '*.ado*' file in STATA's designated folder on your computer.[15]

You will need to specify the following variables to use the ado file in your analysis:

1. the name of the variable in your dataset that contains total household durable ownership (e.g., specify 'Y', if Y represents the total number of durables (out of n) owned by households, $Y \in \{0, 1, 2, \ldots, n\}$)
2. $iter$; where $iter$ is the number of iterations of the E and M steps
3. n; where n is the total number of durables in your analysis (and definition of the variable in (5.1) above).

Below, I have provided a screenshot from STATA showing the commands and (a part of the) results' window. Please keep the following items in mind when running the code and interpreting the results:

1. clear the memory and load your dataset every time you call the ado file
2. the ado file is called by typing the name of the 'ado' file—'$runembin$1'—at the start of the command
3. after the name of the ado file, you must state (1) the name of the variable in your dataset that represents total durables owned, (2) the number of iterations and (3) the number of goods in your analysis, *in that order*. In our example, the variable that represents the total number of durables is called '*allgd*' in the dataset (urban NSS 1999–00); the number of iterations is 1000; and the number of durable goods used in the analysis is 12.
4. after typing the name of the ado file, please wait for a few minutes until the program finishes running. The final line of results in the STATA results' window (highlighted in blue in the figure below) will provide the estimated values of the parameters. Note that STATA lists the estimates under the headings *pi1_report*, *pi2_report*, *pi3_report*, *p1_report*, *p2_report*, *p3_report*, which represent, respectively, the EM-generated estimates $\hat{\pi}_1, \hat{\pi}_2, \hat{\pi}_3, \hat{p}_1, \hat{p}_2, \hat{p}_3$. The value reported under the heading *lkhd_report* provides the value of the likelihood function, when estimates take the values provided.

[15] Typing 'sysdir' in STATA will reveal the path to the folder for your personal ado files.

```
. runembin1 allgd 1000 12

      name:
       log:
  log type:
 opened on:

          x |      Freq.     Percent        Cum.
------------+-----------------------------------
          0 |      8,228       16.82       16.82
          1 |      6,063       12.39       29.21
          2 |      7,565       15.46       44.67
          3 |      8,001       16.35       61.03
          4 |      6,630       13.55       74.58
          5 |      4,744        9.70       84.28
          6 |      3,357        6.86       91.14
          7 |      2,090        4.27       95.41
          8 |      1,320        2.70       98.11
          9 |        632        1.29       99.40
         10 |        215        0.44       99.84
         11 |         70        0.14       99.98
         12 |          9        0.02      100.00
------------+-----------------------------------
      Total |     48,924      100.00
(bin=46, start=0, width=.26086957)
(48,924 missing values generated)
(48,924 missing values generated)
(48,924 missing values generated)

. . . .      . . .       ...

(1 real change made)
(1 real change made)
(1 real change made)
(0 real changes made)
(0 real changes made)
(0 real changes made)

     +---------------------------------------------------------------------------------+
     | pi1_re~t   pi2_re~t   pi3_re~t   p1_rep~t   p2_rep~t   p3_rep~t   lkhd_rep~t |
     |---------------------------------------------------------------------------------|
  1. | .2668857    .081986   .6511283   .1366463   .0285569   .8689333   -169450.02 |
     +---------------------------------------------------------------------------------+

        +---------------------------------------------------------------------------------+
        |      pi1         pi2        pi3         p1         p2         p3    lkhd_rep~t |
        |---------------------------------------------------------------------------------|
 1000.  | .6161444   .2034064   .1804492   .2510112   .0257142   .5249667   -105085.79 |
        +---------------------------------------------------------------------------------+

        +---------------------------------------------------------------------------------+
        | pi1_re~t   pi2_re~t   pi3_re~t   p1_rep~t   p2_rep~t   p3_rep~t   lkhd_rep~t |
        |---------------------------------------------------------------------------------|
 1000.  | .6161444   .2034064   .1804492   .2510112   .0257142   .5249667   -105085.79 |
        +---------------------------------------------------------------------------------+

      name:
       log:
  log type:
 closed on:
```

In the next section, we present and discuss the estimates obtained using urban NSS, 1999–00.

5.5 Results and Discussion

5.5.1 Estimates

The estimates produced by the EM algorithm from our data are presented in Table 5.1. The numbers in column (1) of Table 5.1 represent the population share of each class, $\hat{\pi}_i$. The middle class is estimated to constitute 62% of urban households. This is roughly equivalent to 17% of the total population, given that urban households accounted for about 28% of all Indian households in 2001 (2001 census; Indias-

Table 5.1 Estimates from a three-component mixture model using durable ownership Y. Urban sub-sample, Indian NSS, 55th Round (1999–00), N = 48,924 households

Sub-population (Class)	Mixture estimate (Std. error)		
	(1)	(2)	(3)
	Share of urban population	Probability of owning a good	Mean no. of goods owned (of 12)*
	$\bar{\pi}_i$	$\hat{p}_i$	$12\hat{p}_i$
Lower (L)	0.2034 (0.005)	0.0257 (0.002)	0.3084 (0.007)
Middle (M)	0.6161 (0.005)	0.251 (0.003)	3.012 (0.01)
Upper (U)	0.1804 (0.006)	0.5249 (0.004)	6.2988 (0.014)

* The 12 goods include 5 recreational goods (record player, radio, tv, vcr/vcp, tape/cd player), 4 household goods (electric fan, a/c, washer, fridge) and 3 transport goods (bicycle, motor bike/scooter, motor car/jeep)

tat, http://www.indiastat.com). The lower and upper classes are found to constitute 20 and 18% of urban households, respectively. Asymptotic standard errors (obtained from the information matrix) are small, supporting the existence of three classes in the population.

Column (2) reports estimates of the probability parameter p_i for each class $i = L, M, U$. Lower class households are found to own a good with 3% probability while middle and upper class households own a good with probabilities of 25% and 52% respectively. Small standard errors support three distinct patterns of durables consumption behavior.[16]

The mean number of durable goods (out of 12) owned by class$-i$ households is simply $12p_i$ (the mean of the binomial distribution for class i). These estimates are reported in Column (3) of Table 5.1. The lower, middle, and upper classes are found to own, on average, 0.3, 3 and 6.3 goods, respectively.

Figure 5.3 plots the binomial density functions ϕ_i at the estimated parameters $\hat{p}_i$ $(i = 1, 2, 3)$. It is the shape and structure of each density $\phi_i(y;\, \hat{p}_i)$ that identifies each class i in our analysis. The ownership density of the lower class and upper classes (binomials with probability parameters 0.03 and 0.52, respectively) are slightly positively skewed whereas that of the middle class is symmetric. Recall that we used the family of binomial functions in our mixture model for precisely this purpose—to allow for the estimation of different shapes of the different ϕ_i functions depending on the estimated parameters $\hat{p}_i$. Recall also that in estimating the densities ϕ_i, we made no explicit assumptions about *who* constitutes the classes other than that the three classes are different and that higher classes are more affluent than lower classes. The

[16] The estimates (standard errors) of the differences are as follows: $\hat{p}_L - \hat{p}_U = -0.5$ (0.004), $\hat{p}_L - \hat{p}_M = -0.23$ (0.002) and $\hat{p}_U - \hat{p}_M = 0.27(0.003)$ ($L \approx$ Lower; $M \approx$ Middle; $U \approx$ Upper).

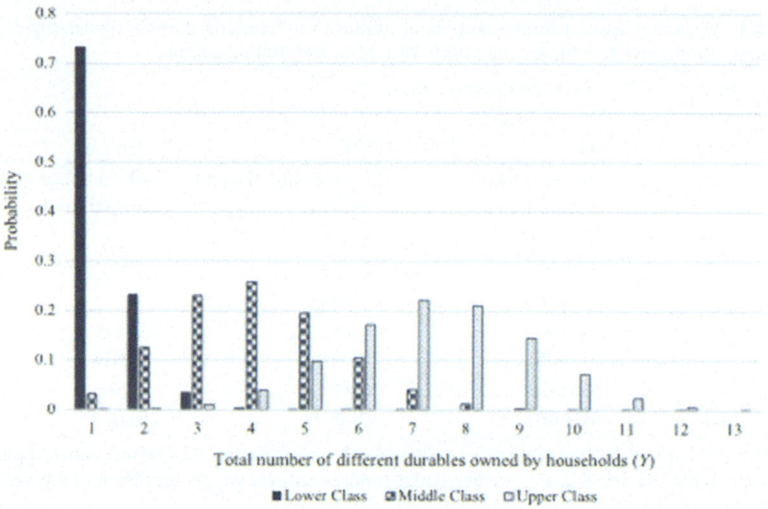

Fig. 5.3 Class-specific durable ownership densities estimated by the mixture model

criteria for class membership—viz., the location and shape of the densities ϕ_i—were instead delivered by the estimation process, based on natural clusters in the data.

Finally, note the overlapping sections of the density functions of the different classes, which indicate that the level of durables owned do not uniquely identify classes (as in cutoffs-based approaches). In Sect. 5.5.3, we will specifically calculate the probabilities with which a household with durables x belongs to each of the classes.

Let us now construct the ***predicted*** marginal density of durable ownership from our estimated parameters. If the population constitutes 3 classes in the proportions $(\hat{\pi}_1, \hat{\pi}_2, 1 - \hat{\pi}_1 - \hat{\pi}_2)$ and with densities $\phi_1(y; \hat{p}_1)$, $\phi_2(y; \hat{p}_2)$ and $\phi_3(y; \hat{p}_3)$, respectively, then what is the predicted probability of observing any level of durable ownership, say y^*, in this population? This is simply the expression in (5.6), with parameter values set equal to the estimates. That is,

$$\hat{Pr}(Y = y^*; \hat{\pi}_1, \hat{\pi}_2, \hat{p}_1, \hat{p}_2, \hat{p}_3) = \hat{\pi}_1\phi_1(y^*; \hat{p}_1) + \hat{\pi}_2\phi_2(y^*; \hat{p}_2) + \hat{\pi}_3\phi_3(y^*; \hat{p}_3) \tag{5.15}$$

$y^* = 0, 1, 2, \ldots, 12.$

Having calculated the predicted marginal density of Y as in (5.15), we can now answer the question: how well does the predicted marginal density match the observed marginal density of Y? Figure 5.4 plots the actual relative frequency of (Y) observations in the data along with the predicted values. The figure demonstrates a very good fit to the data.

Recall, from Sect. 5.3, our assertion that the number of classes that describe the data must be the smallest number of sub-populations that yield a good fit to the observed marginal density. Consider then the findings from a Two-Component (two

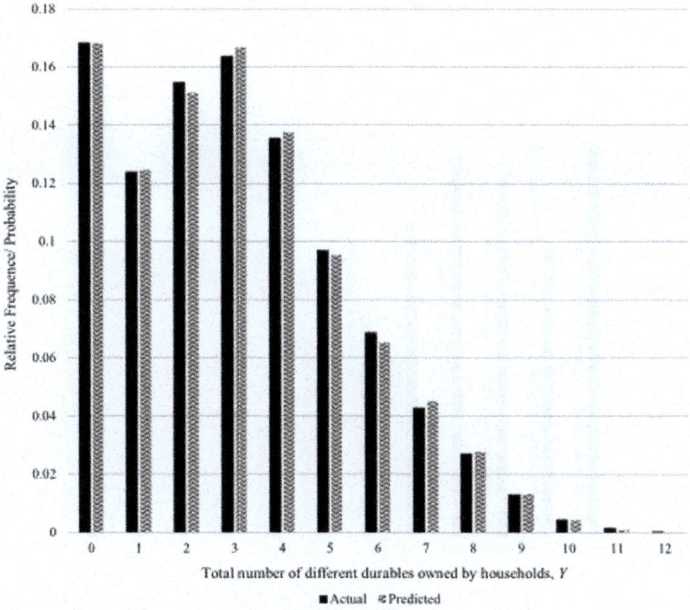

Fig. 5.4 Actual versus predicted distribution of Y

classes) Mixture Model fitted to the data by EM plotted in Fig. 5.5. The fit is visibly worse than that of the Three-Component Model. Hence, 3 appears to be the minimum number of classes that provide a good fit to the data.

5.5.2 *What Happened to Urban Consumption Classes in India, Post-liberalization?*

The ultimate goal of our analysis was to examine the fate of urban consumption classes in India—their sizes and characteristics—after the liberalization policies of 1991 came into effect. Maitra (2016, 2017) look at various aspects of this comparison using the mixture analysis outlined above, using the NSS rounds of 1993–94, 1999–00 and 2004–05. The use of durable ownership data—immune to known measurement issues in the NSS, 1999–00 round—to define the classes allows us to make credible comparisons across these rounds of data. Moreover, the mixture approach precludes the need to make arbitrary assumptions about who constitutes the classes in each survey year. These class-definitions are, in fact, delivered by the mixture approach, which uses natural clusters in the data in each round to identify class-specific conditional ownership densities $\phi_i(\widehat{p_i})$ in each survey year.

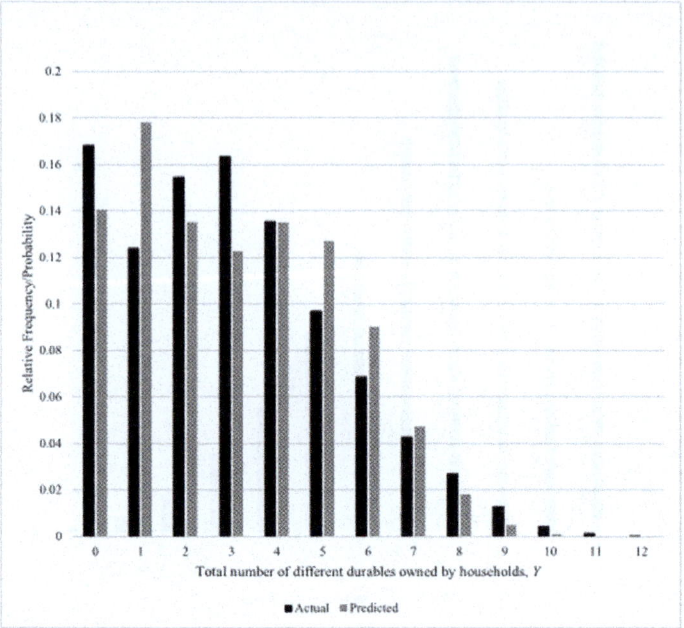

* Parameter Estimates, Two-Component (Binomial) Mixture Model, Urban NSS, 1999-00

Class	$\widehat{\pi}_i$	$\widehat{p}_i$	$12\widehat{p}_i$
Lower	0.4	0.1	1.08
Upper	0.6	0.4	4.52

Fig. 5.5 Two-component mixture model*: Actual versus predicted distribution of *Y*

Table 5.2 *Estimates from three-component mixture models, urban NSS subsamples, 1993-94, 1999-00 and 2004-05

Year	π_L	π_M	π_U	p_L	p_M	p_U
1993-94	0.324	0.647	0.029	0.085	0.313	0.644
1999-00	0.200	0.621	0.179	0.035	0.341	0.590
2004-05	0.161	0.603	0.235	0.079	0.340	0.627

*This table is reproduced from Maitra (2017)

Table 5.2 presents Maitra's (2017) mixture results for urban classes in the NSS rounds of 1993–94, 1999–00 and 2004–05.[17]

Notice the contraction in the size of the lower and middle classes over the decade 1993-94 to 2004-05, while the upper class grows larger over this time. In terms of class-definitions, the probability of durable ownership (p_L) of the lower class dropped dramatically between 1993-94 and 1999-00 but seems to have caught up again in

[17] The analysis presented in Table 5.2 uses a total of 8 (of the current 12) durable goods since these were the common items asked about in the questionnaires across all the survey years. The results for 1999–00 urban classes are very similar whether 8 or 12 durables are used. Also, 3 urban classes were found to be optimal in each of the years examined.

2004-05 to the original 1993-94 level. The upper class seems to have stagnated a bit over this time (p_U has not increased), while the middle class seems to be doing somewhat better over the period considered. Taken together, the estimates of class size and probabilities suggest a significant wave of upward class mobility among urban households in India in the 1990s.[18]

5.5.3 *Mixture-Estimated Probabilities of Class Membership ($\hat{\gamma}_i(y)$)*

Let us return to our baseline mixture estimates for 1999-00 in Table 5.1, where 12 durable goods are used in the definition of Y. The overlapping sections of the class-specific densities suggest that certain levels of durable ownership may be compatible with households in more than one class. Can we calculate the specific probability $\hat{\gamma}_i(y)$ that a household belongs to different classes i $(= 1, 2, 3)$ conditional on the number of durables y owned?[19] Using Bayes' Law, as in Eq. (5.4), we can derive these specific probabilities to be:

$$\hat{\gamma}_i(y) = \frac{\hat{\pi}_i \phi_i(y, \hat{p}_i)}{\hat{\pi}_1 \phi_1(y, \hat{p}_1) + \hat{\pi}_2 \phi_2(y, \hat{p}_2) + \hat{\pi}_3 \phi_3(y, \hat{p}_3)} \tag{5.16}$$

Figure 5.6 plots the probabilities $\hat{\gamma}_i(y)$ that a household belongs to different classes i $(= 1, 2, 3)$ conditional on the number of durables y owned. Evidently, households with low values of Y are most likely to belong to the lower class (class 1) whereas those with the highest values of Y are almost certain to belong to the upper class (class 3). Hence, unlike in previous studies that use the cutoffs-based approach, the current approach places households (arguably, more realistically) in different classes with a probability rather than with certainty.

In the next section, we will discuss how to use the estimated probabilities $\hat{\gamma}_i(y)$ to assign each household to a class. The assignment will allow us to look at characteristics (other than Y) of each class, further illuminating our understanding of who constitutes the different classes.

5.5.4 *Class Characteristics: A Descriptive Analysis*

We have shown that the mixture approach assigns households to different classes with a probability rather than with certainty. Using these (conditional) probability

---

[18] See Maitra (2016, 2017) for a detailed discussion of the implications of these estimates for poverty and inequality in India in the 1990s.

[19] Clearly, $\hat{\gamma}_1(y) + \hat{\gamma}_2(y) + \hat{\gamma}_3(y) = 1$ for any $y = 0, 1, 2, \ldots, 12$, since any household must belong to one of the 3 classes.

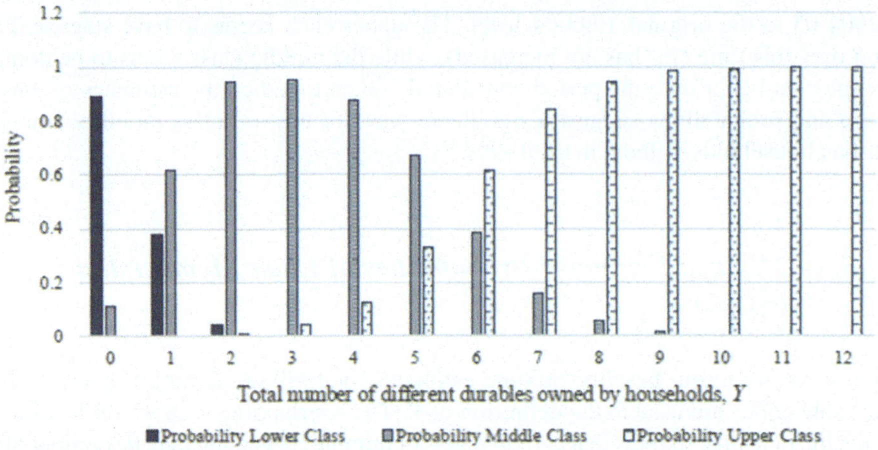

Fig. 5.6 Probability of class membership conditional on durables owned

estimates, it is possible to estimate the number of observations of each value of Y that belongs to each class. Based on this computation, we can randomly assign households to classes. Here is an example of how the assignment is performed. Suppose we estimate $\hat{\gamma}_1(0) = 0.6$, $\hat{\gamma}_2(0) = 0.1$ and $\hat{\gamma}_3(0) = 0.3$. This means that a household that owns none of the twelve durable goods (i.e., $Y = 0$) belongs to class 1 with probability 0.6, class 2 with probability 0.1 and class 3 with probability 0.3. Now suppose that in the dataset, there are 100 observations for $Y = 0$. We can randomly assign 60 of these 100 households with $Y = 0$ to class 1 (consistent with $\hat{\gamma}_1(0) = 0.6$), 10 to class 2 (consistent with $\hat{\gamma}_2(0) = 0.1$) and 30 to class 3 ($\hat{\gamma}_3(0) = 0.3$). The same procedure could be followed to randomly assign households to classes for each other value of Y (i.e., $Y = 1, 2, \ldots, 12$, respectively).[20]

Assigning a class to each household allows a descriptive analysis of the characteristics of each class. Below, in Tables 5.3, 5.4 and Figs. 5.7, 5.8, 5.9, 5.10, 5.11, 5.12, 5.13, 5.14, we will look at the durable ownership patterns for specific goods as well as a host of socioeconomic characteristics.

[20] But randomly assigning households to classes can lead to the same household being placed in different classes in different rounds of assignments (or draws)! This could result in different class-specific characteristics being obtained in different draws. To address this issue, we could repeat the procedure of random assignments multiple times. We could observe any characteristic, say Z, in the sample after each set m of random assignments ($m = 1, 2, \ldots, M$) and report the average values of these characteristics across all the draws $[\frac{1}{M}\sum_{m=1}^{M} z_m]$ along with the standard deviations $[\frac{1}{M}\sum_{m=1}^{M}(z_m - \frac{1}{M}\sum_{m=1}^{M} z_m)^2]^{0.5}$. This process of repeated draws (here, rounds of random assignments) from the same sample forms the essence of bootstrapping techniques (Hastie et al. 2001). (The results presented in Tables 5.3, 5.4 and Figs. 5.7, 5.8, 5.9, 5.10, 5.11, 5.12, 5.13, 5.14 are, however, obtained from a single draw as they serve a descriptive purpose.)

Table 5.3 Durable ownership by class in the urban sub-sample, NSS, 1999–00

Ownership by Durable Categories by Class in the Urban Sub-sample, NSS 1999-00, N = 48, 924 households

Category (Class)	Mean No. of Goods Owned by Households				Proportion of Households Owning At Least one Good in the Relevant Category, by Class			
	All (12 items)	Recreation Goods (5 items)	Household Goods (4 items)	Transport Goods (3 items)	All (12 items)	Recreation Goods (5 items)	Household Goods (4 items)	Transport Goods (3 items)
Lower (L)	0.31	0.12	0.11	0.07	0.27	0.12	0.11	0.07
Middle (M)	3.01	1.37	1.06	0.58	0.97	0.85	0.79	0.53
Upper (U)	6.30	2.51	2.52	1.27	1.00	1.00	0.99	0.87

Ownership of Individual Durable Goods by Class in the Urban Sub-sample, NSS 1999-00, N = 48, 924 households

Proportion of Households Owning the Relevant Good, by Class

Category (Class)	Recreational Goods					Household Goods				Transport Goods		
	Record Player	Radio	TV	VCR/ VCP	Tape/ CD Player	Electric Fan	Air Cond.	Washing Machine	Fridge	Bicycle	Motor Bike/ Scooter	Motor Car/ Jeep
Lower (L)	0.00	0.07	0.04	0.00	0.01	0.11	0.00	0.00	0.00	0.07	0.00	0.00
Middle (M)	0.01	0.39	0.68	0.02	0.27	0.77	0.07	0.04	0.18	0.43	0.14	0.01
Upper (U)	0.05	0.58	0.97	0.19	0.71	0.97	0.41	0.39	0.75	0.53	0.60	0.14

Table 5.4 Household characteristics, by class, in the urban sub-sample, NSS, 1999–00

Household Characteristics, by Class, in the Urban Sub-sample, NSS, (1999-00)

Category (Class)	Per Capita Monthly Household Expenditure in 2000 Rupees [2005 US$, PPP Converted]									Other Household Characteristics		
					Percentiles							
	Mean	Std. Dev.	Min.	Max.	25	50	75	90	99	Avg. No. of Meals Per Day Per Person (Mean)	Proportion of Literate Household Members (Mean)	Household Size (Mean)
Lower (L)	791.26	859.11	17	50528	423	625	981	1421	2791.43	2.34	0.64	3.97
	[65.53]	[71.15]	[1.41]	[4184.83]	[35.03]	[51.76]	[81.25]	[117.69]	[231.19]			
Middle (M)	961.79	1772.39	49	205987	532	762	1140	1663	3485	2.38	0.77	4.65
	[79.66]	[146.79]	[4.06]	[17060.27]	[44.06]	[63.11]	[94.42]	[137.73]	[288.63]			
Upper (U)	1469.57	1109.97	224	35612	842	1229	1777	2490.6	5390.08	2.41	0.88	5.12
	[121.71]	[91.93]	[18.55]	[2949.46]	[69.74]	[101.79]	[147.17]	[206.28]	[446.42]			

Addendum: Percentiles of Per Capita Monthly Expenditure (2000 Rupees) in the Entire Sample, N = 48, 921

Percentile	10	20	30	40	50	60	70	80	90	99
Value	392	490	584	686	801	940	1120	1377	1815	3799.56

Note: CPI inflation from 2000 to 2005: 1.215 (Indian Labour Bureau); PPP conversion rate INR/USD: 14.67 (ICP 2005)

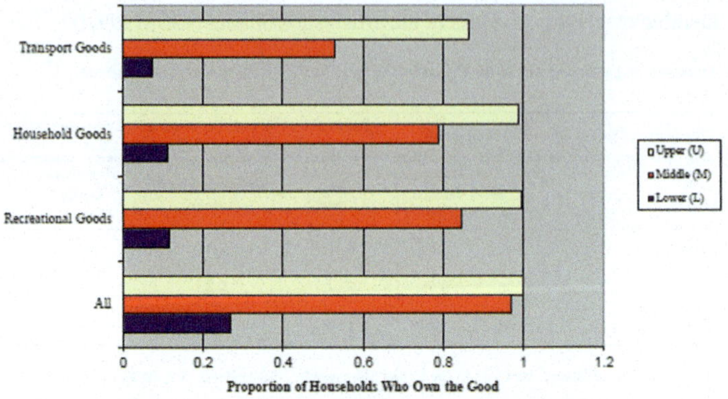

(a)

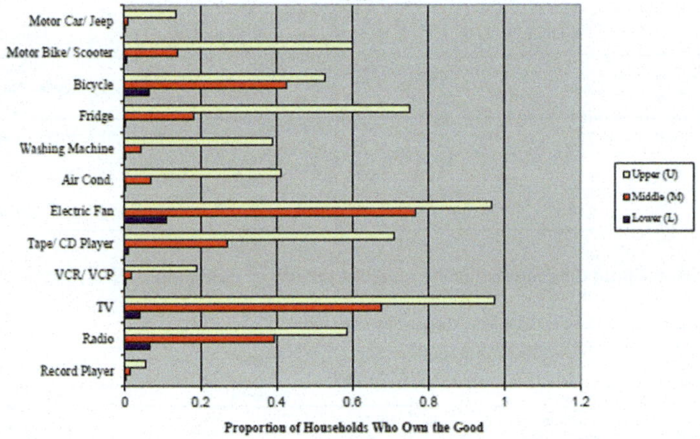

(b)

Fig. 5.7 (**a**) Ownership by durable categories by class, urban sub-sample, NSS 1990-00. (**b**) Ownership of individual goods by class, urban sub-sample, NSS 1990-00

Table 5.3 and Fig. 5.7 reveal the durables consumption patterns of households belonging to the three classes (assigned by the procedure described above). Recreational and household goods appear to be more commonly owned by all classes than are transport goods.[21] Of these, electric fans and televisions are most popular among the top two classes, whereas fans and bicycles are most popular among the lower class.

Table 5.4 reports the per capita monthly expenditures (PCE) of households in each assigned class. Note, yet again, that the fundamental difference between the cutoffs-based approach and the mixture approach lies in the postulated *distribution* of households: the cutoffs-based approach assumes every household with PCE in

[21] This could be partly attributable to the fact that, among the 12 goods considered, there are more recreational and household goods (5 and 4, respectively) than there are transport goods.

a certain range to belong to a particular class, whereas the mixture approach identifies classes whose expenditures are distributed over a PCE-range. Consequently, the ranges of PCE of different classes are overlapping instead of being mutually exclusive.

Keeping in mind this difference in approaches, how do the PCE of the mixture-identified classes roughly compare with those assumed by previous studies? Take the middle class, for example. The 1st and 99th percentiles of the daily per capita expenditure of the middle class identified here are about \$0.75 and \$9.62 (at 2005 PPP), with the median being \$2.10 (see Table 5.4: the addendum). Banerjee and Duflo (2008) define the middle class as having a daily per capita expenditure of \$2–\$4 or \$6–\$10 at 1993 PPP (roughly \$2.68–\$5.36 and \$8.04–\$13.40 at 2005 PPP). Ravallion's (2010) middle class has daily per capita expenditures of \$2–\$13 at 2005 PPP. [22] Also, the mean number of durables owned by the middle class as per Banerjee and Duflo's (2008) definition is found to be 3.77, which is very close to the mean durables ownership (3.01) of the middle class identified herein. The middle class as per Sridharan's (2004) definition is found to own on average 5.55 durables, a considerably higher figure.

The differences in distributional assumptions of the mixture versus the cutoffs-based approaches implies, furthermore, that estimates of any class characteristic that is sensitive to distribution could be very different based on which approach is used, even when the range of class-specific expenditures is comparable across approaches (as in Banerjee and Duflo 2008 or Ravallion 2010). As an example, consider the estimate of the *size* of the middle class as a proportion of urban households. Using Banerjee and Duflo's (2008) definition of middle class in our (NSS, 1999-00) sample, the size of the middle class is obtained to be 32%. Ravallion's definition yields a middle class of 56%. The mixture estimate obtained using the NSS, 1999-00 sample suggests a middle class that comprises 62% of urban households.[23]

Figure 5.8 plots the education levels of the household head, by class. The lower class has the highest component of illiterate heads (32%) whereas the upper class has the highest component of heads with a graduate degree (38%). Middle class household heads are most likely to have secondary education (18%) although grad-

---

[22] The cutoffs defined by Easterly (2001) and Birdsall et al. (2000) while not defined specifically for developing nations or India would capture only the lower end of middle class PCEs identified here. For instance, by Easterly's (2001) definition of the middle class (those lying between the 20th and 80th percentile of the consumption distribution), the daily PCE cutoffs would be \$1.35 and \$3.80 (2005 PPP-adjusted). Birdsall, Graham and Pettinato's (2000) definition (those lying between 75% and 125% of median income) would yield cutoffs of \$1.66 and \$2.76 (2005 PPP-adjusted). Birdsall's (2010) cutoff of \$10 and above (albeit for a definition of the "indispensable middle class") would exclude most of the middle class identified herein.

[23] It may not be informative to compare the size-estimates reported (implicitly) in Banerjee and Duflo (2008) and Ravallion (2010) with the mixture estimates obtained herein, since these estimates are derived using data from completely different years. Differences in size-estimates in these versus the current study may not be unambiguously attributed to the difference in approach, since the size of the middle class could be changing over time too. Sridharan's (2004) estimates, on the other hand, are comparable to the mixture estimates in this paper, since the data used therein correspond roughly to the same years (1998-99).

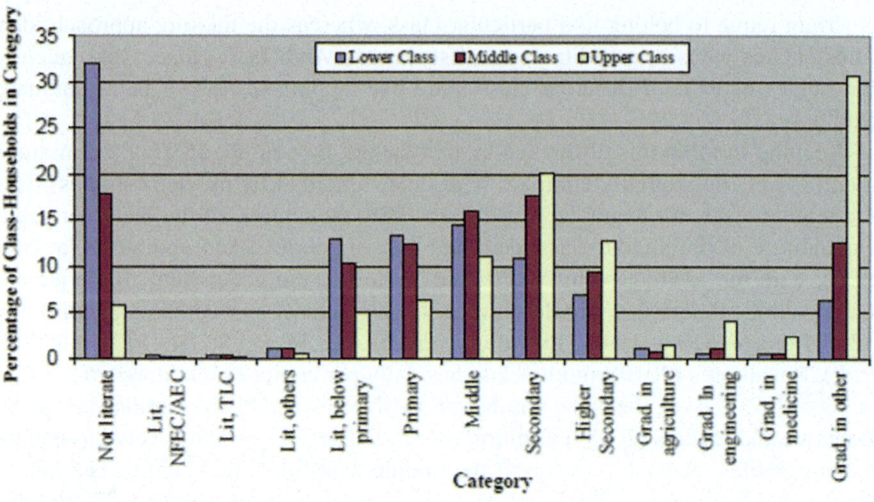

Fig. 5.8 Education of household head, by class

uates comprise a comparable component as well (15%). A large proportion (18%) of middle class heads appear to be illiterate. This finding appears surprising if the perception of the middle class as being largely white-collar workers is true. However, this finding would be consistent with an environment of active social mobility post-liberalization, characterized by a large influx of lower class members into the middle class.

Figure 5.9 presents a plot of household type by employment. Being an urban sample, the proportion of households who are self-employed in agriculture is negligible. The largest component of households in each class are wage/salary earners. This fact is also mirrored in Fig. 5.10 which plots sources of household income. Over 50% of households in each class have reported income in the past year from wages and salaries. Income from non-agricultural enterprises is reported by more than 30% of households in each class. A large proportion of households also report owning land. Income from interests and dividends is the third most highly reported source of income by the top two classes 15% and 7% of upper and middle class households, respectively. For the lower class, income from other sources is reported by considerably more households (12%) than is income from interests and dividends (2%).

Figures 5.11 and 5.12 present a summary of the primary sources of energy used in cooking and lighting. LPG is most commonly used for cooking among the top two classes; firewood and chips are most common among lower class households. For lighting, electricity is most common in all classes, although 25% of lower class households use kerosene as the primary source of energy.

Finally, Figs. 5.13 and 5.14 provide a summary of class composition by religion and social class. Hinduism is the religion of the majority in India, so it is not a surprise that Hindus constitute the largest component of all classes. However, Muslims, and

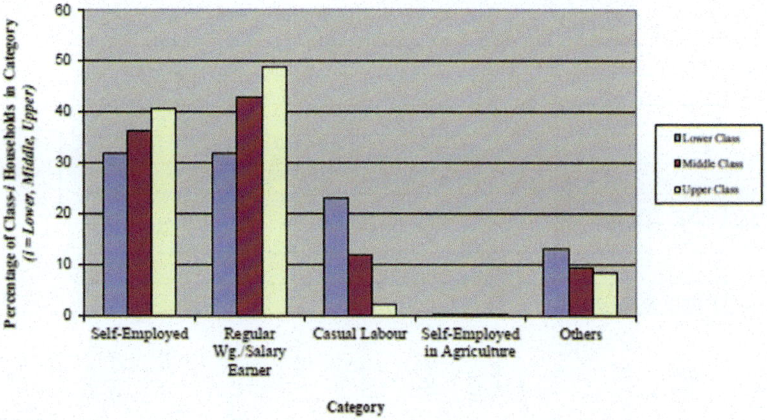

Fig. 5.9 Type of employment, by class

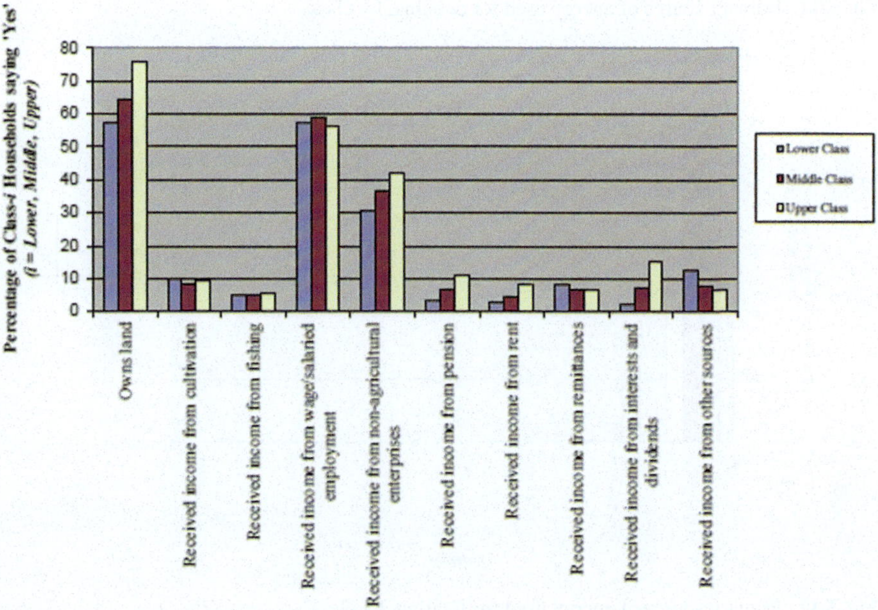

Fig. 5.10 Land ownership and source of income, by class

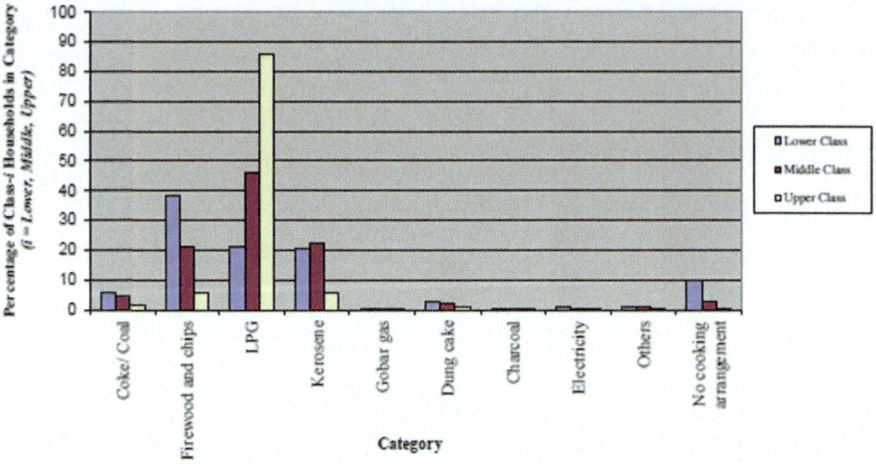

Fig. 5.11 Primary source of energy used for cooking, by class

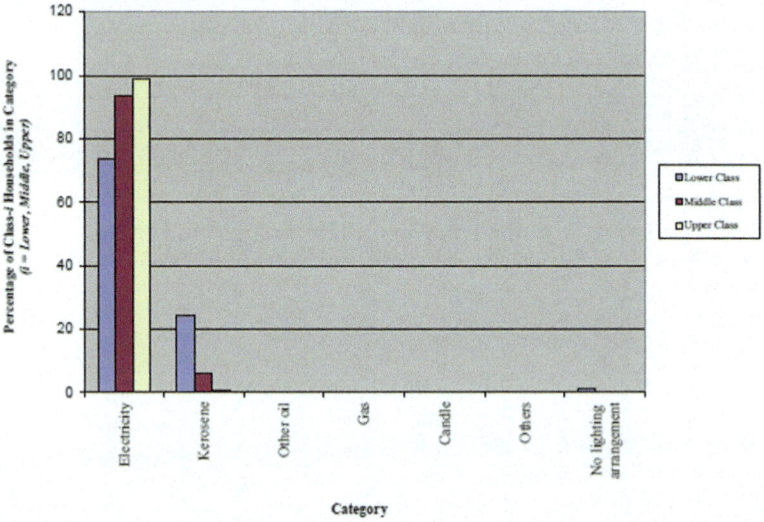

Fig. 5.12 Primary source of energy used for lighting, by class

Christians form a larger component of the lower class (18% and 11%, respectively) than the middle and upper classes (15% and 4% of the middle class while 10% and 4% of the upper class are Muslim and Christian, respectively). Scheduled Castes and Tribes also form a larger component of the lower than the middle and upper classes.

The descriptive analysis presented above demonstrates how the mixture estimates—computed using durable ownership data—may be used to assign households to classes (albeit probabilistically), which further permits an examination of class-specific characteristics *other* than durable ownership (per capita household

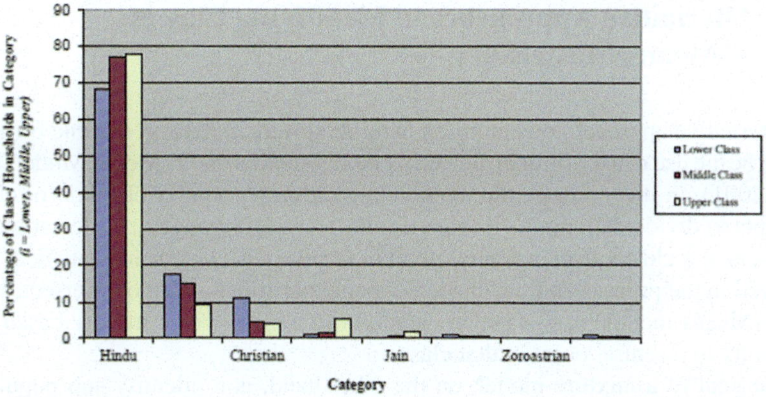

Fig. 5.13 Religion, by class

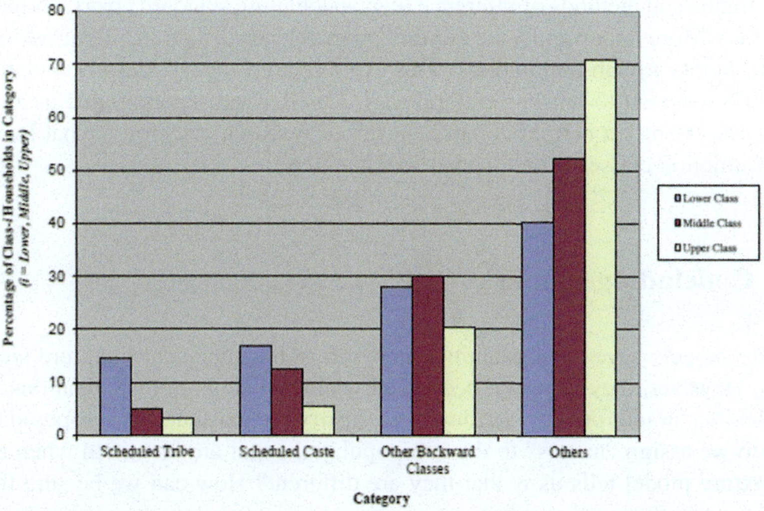

Fig. 5.14 Social group, by class

expenditure levels, for example). In this sense, our methodology presents a "dual" (or reverse) strategy for class identification as compared with traditional approaches that use expenditure cutoffs, primarily, to identify classes and then infer the durable ownership of classes from the expenditures-based classification.

5.6 Alternative Approaches to Identifying Classes: *K*-Means Clustering

An alternative approach to examining natural clusters in data on durable ownership would be the use of a traditional clustering model such as the *K*-Means Model (Hastie et al. 2001). In this method, the iterative algorithm to identify clusters (or classes) attempts to divide data points into partitions, so as to minimize the deviation of all members of a cluster from a central point in the cluster. There is no statistical model involved in the process and the clusters—being partitions—do not intersect. Hence, the *K*-Means method assigns each datapoint to a class with certainty based on its proximity to a central point in that class.

The goal of a mixture model, on the other hand, is to identify sub-populations with the help of a statistical model (here, binomial mixtures) so as to best fit the observed distribution of the data points. The use of a statistical model allows the use of traditional methods of inference (e.g., calculating standard errors, formulating tests, etc.). More importantly, the mixture process leads to a probabilistic assignment of data points to sub-populations. The overlapping "fuzzy" class boundaries are especially relevant to our current application as they are interpretable as zones of class "transitions", a natural component of our research question—what happened to consumption classes in India post-liberalization?

5.7 Concluding Remarks

Mixture models have been examined in depth in the statistical literature since the 1950s. However, they have not been used widely in economic applications due to complexities in interpretation. How do we justify the existence of sub-populations? How do we assign "names" to the sub-populations that are identified when all that the mixture model tells us is that they are different? How can we be sure that the estimates we obtain are unique?

In this chapter, I present and describe the technical aspects of a three-component binomial mixture model, which is then used to identify urban Indian consumption classes based on their total durable ownership. The approach is well-suited for this task as class-definitions emerge from the process—based on natural clusters in the data—instead of having to be specified by researchers. Interested readers are encouraged to consult the larger literature on mixture models and clustering methods (see the section below titled "Recommended Reading") for further discussions of the topic, including mixture analysis of more complex relationships within sub-populations.

An important goal of this chapter has been to provide a conceptual interpretation of the mixture process, so as to demonstrate how it may be used meaningfully despite the complexities of interpretation described above. Failing to understand or address the conceptual background for a mixture model comes with the danger of reducing it to an arbitrary procedure for data fitting with no real informational content. I hope the current demonstration underlines these lessons amply, and that it will inspire more studies that effectively use mixture models to illuminate economic phenomena.

Recommended Reading

- Everitt BS, Hand DJ (1981) Finite mixture distributions. Monographs on applied probability and statistics. Chapman and Hall, New York
- Hastie T, Tibshirani R, Friedman J (2001) Elements of statistical learning: data mining, inference and prediction. Springer series in statistics
- Maitra S (2021) On the theory and measurement of relative poverty using durable ownership data. Working Paper. https://www.sudeshnamaitra.com/Maitra_relative_poverty_Sep2021.pdf. Accessed 5 Jan 2022
- Maitra S (2017) Class matters: tracking urban inequality in post-liberalization India using a durables-based mixture model. App Econ Lett 24(17):1203–1207
- Maitra S (2016) The poor get poorer: tracking relative poverty in India using a durables-based mixture model. J Dev Econ 119:110–120
- Maitra S (2011) Who are the Indian middle class? A mixture model of class membership based on durables ownership. Working Paper. https://www.sudeshnamaitra.com/Maitra-middle-class-mixture-May2011.pdf. Accessed 5 Jan 2022
- McLachlan GJ, Krishnan T (1996) The EM algorithm and extensions. Wiley series in probability and statistics
- McLachlan GJ, Peel D (2000) Finite mixture models. Wiley series in probability and statistics.

References

Ablett J, Baijal A et al (2007) The bird of gold: the rise of India's consumer market. McKinsey Global Institute Report. https://www.mckinsey.com/featured-insights/asia-pacific/the-bird-of-gold. Accessed 5 Jan 2022

Banerjee A, Duflo E (2008) What is middle class about the middle classes around the world? J Econ Lit 22:3–28

Bar-Ilan A, Blinder AS (1988) The life cycle permanent-income model of consumer durables. Ann Econ Stat 9:71–91

Birdsall N (2010) The (Indispensable) Middle class in developing countries; or, the rich and the rest, not the poor and the rest. Center for Global Development Working Paper 207. https://papers.ssrn.com/sol3/papers.cfm?abstract_id=1693899. Accessed 5 Jan 2022

Birdsall N, Graham C, Pettinato S (2000) Stuck in the tunnel: is globalization muddling the middle class? Brookings Institution Center on Social and Economic Dynamics Working Paper No. 14. https://papers.ssrn.com/sol3/papers.cfm?abstract_id=277162. Accessed 5 Jan 2022

Blischke WR (1964) Estimating the parameters of mixtures of binomial distributions. J Amer Stat Ass 59:510–528

Britannica (2022) The editors of encyclopaedia. “social class”. Encyclopedia Britannica. https://www.britannica.com/topic/social-class. Accessed 5 Jan 2022
Deaton A, Kozel V (2005) Data and dogma: the great Indian poverty debate. World Bank Res Obs 20:177–199
Dempster AP, Laird NM, Rubin DB (1977) Maximum likelihood from incomplete data via the EM algorithm. J R Stat Soc Series B (Meth) 39:1–38
Easterly W (2001) The middle class consensus and economic development. J Econ Growth 6:317–335
Everitt BS, Hand DJ (1981) Finite mixture distributions monographs on applied probability and statistics. Chapman and Hall, New York
Hastie T, Tibshirani R, Friedman J (2001) Elements of statistical learning: data mining, inference and prediction. Springer series in statistics
India Brand Equity Foundation (IBEF) (2005) Economic indicators: India’s middle class dream takes shape. http://www.ibef.org/artdisplay.aspx?cat_id=391&art_id=5788. Accessed 5 Jan 2022
Indiastat. http://www.indiastat.com Accessed 5 Jan 2022
Maitra S (2021) On the theory and measurement of relative poverty using durable ownership data. Working Paper. https://www.sudeshnamaitra.com/Maitra_relative_poverty_Sep2021.pdf. Accessed 5 Jan 2022
Maitra S (2017) Class matters: tracking urban inequality in post-liberalization India using a durables-based mixture model. App Econ Lett 24(17):1203–1207
Maitra S (2016) The poor get poorer: tracking relative poverty in India using a durables-based mixture model. J Dev Econ 119:110–120
Maitra S (2011) Who are the Indian middle class? A mixture model of class membership based on durables ownership. Working Paper. https://www.sudeshnamaitra.com/Maitra-middle-class-mixture-May2011.pdf. Accessed 5 Jan 2022
McLachlan GJ, Krishnan T (1996) The EM algorithm and extensions. Wiley series in probability and statistics
McLachlan GJ, Peel D (2000) Finite mixture models. Wiley series in probability and statistics
Pickering G (1968) High blood pressure. Churchill, London
Platt R (1963) Heredity in hypertension. Lancet April: 899–904
Ravallion M (2010) The developing World’s bulging (but vulnerable) middle class. World Dev 38:445–454
Senauer B, Goetz L (2003) The growing middle class in developing countries and the market for high-value food products. Department of Applied Economics Working Paper, University of Minnesota. https://ageconsearch.umn.edu/record/14331/?ln=en. Accessed 5 Jan 2022
Sridharan E (2004) The growth and sectoral composition of India’s middle class: its impact on the politics of economic liberalization. India Rev 3:405–428

Chapter 6
Nonparametric and Semiparametric Regressions: An Empirical Investigation of Engel's Law in the Context of Brazil

Alexandre Nunes Almeida, Carlos Roberto Azzoni, and Tao Chen

Abstract The primary rationale for using nonparametric or semiparametric methods is to avoid limitations or misspecifications stemming from specific and erroneous functional forms, which can produce biased estimates. Most empirical studies in economics use parametric specifications to analyze the linear relationship between the dependent and independent variables of interest. Semi- or nonparametric regression models offer a significant advance, as they allow checking whether the estimated function is adequately specified according to the nature of the data. This chapter provides a brief theoretical discussion on the use of nonparametric and semiparametric models. It also contains a semiparametric application based on the well-known Engel's Law for food expenditures in the metropolitan regions of Brazil by using the R language programming. While the parametric model shows almost no difference in the implicit bias in the price index based on estimated Engel curves of households headed by the elderly vis-à-vis the non-elderly; for the same consumption group, the semiparametric estimators adopted for this exercise indicated that price indices overestimate the annual rate of increase in the cost of living and that the bias is marginally greater for the elderly compared to the non-elderly.

Keywords Kernel models · Engel curves · Consumer price index bias

Supplementary Information The online version contains supplementary material available at https://doi.org/10.1007/978-981-99-4902-1_6.

A. N. Almeida (✉)
Department of Economics, Administration and Sociology, Luiz de Queiroz College of Agriculture, University of São Paulo, Av. Pádua Dias, São Paulo 13418-000, Brazil
e-mail: alex.almeida@usp.br

C. R. Azzoni
Department of Economics, University of Sao Paulo, Av. Prof. Luciano Gualberto, 908, São Paulo 05508-010, Brazil
e-mail: cazzoni@usp.br

T. Chen
Big Data Research Lab and Department of Economics, University of Waterloo, 200 University Avenue West, Waterloo, ON N2L 3G1, Canada
e-mail: t66chen@uwaterloo.ca

D. Mukherjee (ed.), *Applied Econometric Analysis Using Cross Section and Panel Data*, Contributions to Economics, https://doi.org/10.1007/978-981-99-4902-1_6

6.1 Introduction

The number of applications of semi and nonparametric models based on kernel functions in many fields of economic research is still limited but it has increased in the last years. The new developments in estimators that handle both discrete and continuous data, along with faster processing power by modern computers and programming codes, which are easily adapted by the applied econometricians, have led to the popularity of kernel methods (Henderson and Parmeter 2015).

In addition, it is worth noting that the economic theory does not provide much guidance on the choice of the functional form for estimating any econometric model (Blundell and Duncan 1998; Yatchew 2003; Henderson and Parmeter 2015). According to Blundell and Duncan (1998), empirical economists have an obsession with linearity. This choice is justified because the parametric models are easy to interpret compared to nonparametric regressions (Henderson and Parmeter 2015). Notwithstanding, nonparametric or semiparametric models are a significant advancement. They allow verifying whether the specification of the functional form is adequate or not (Blundell and Duncan 1998; Blundell et al. 2003). The main reason for using nonparametric methods is to avoid mis-specifying the functional form, a problem that can result in biased estimates (Li and Racine 2007; Henderson and Parmeter 2015).

Henderson and Parmeter (2015) explain that while parametric estimators are considered global (as they use all points), semi- or nonparametric kernel estimators use a sample of data close to a point to adjust the estimation. A global estimator is then constructed based on this adjustment. The most significant advantage is that this procedure allows the researcher to focus on local peculiarities relating to the data while the unknown function (not determined a priori) is estimated. In summary, the mean value of the dependent variable is calculated based on specific values of each nonparametric independent variable, allowing the data to speak for themselves (Eubank 1999).

The rest of this chapter is organized as follows: The next section provides a brief overview of the theoretical background on nonparametric and semiparametric models, while Sect. 6.3 presents an application related to a semiparametric model based on the Engel Curve to estimate consumer price index bias using Brazilian data. Section 6.4 summarizes the major points discussed along with the chapter.

6.2 Theoretical Background on Nonparametric and Semiparametric Models

Most of the time, empirical researchers would like to conduct inference of Y conditioned on X, where Y is usually called the dependent variable, and X is independent variable or regressor. Both Y and X can be scalars or (column) vectors. It is well known that the best predictor of Y, in this regression setting, is the conditional expectation of Y given X, denoted by $\mathbb{E}[\mathrm{Y}|\mathrm{X}]$, equipped with a zero conditional mean identification condition for the residual ε:

$$\mathrm{Y} = \mathbb{E}[\mathrm{Y}|\mathrm{X}] + \varepsilon, \tag{6.1}$$

where $\mathbb{E}[\varepsilon|\mathrm{X}] = 0$ is assumed, to maintain causal interpretation. Therefore, model specification depends on the properties we impose on $\mathbb{E}[\mathrm{Y}|\mathrm{X}]$.

Parametric models assume that $\mathbb{E}[\mathrm{Y}|\mathrm{X}]$ is known, up to some finite-dimensional parameter (s) θ:

$$\mathrm{Y} = m(\mathrm{X}, \theta) + \varepsilon. \tag{6.2}$$

A leading example of a parametric model is the multiple linear regression model, probably the most widely used model in social science, in which $m(\mathrm{X}, \theta)$ is further restricted to be a linear function in θ. Then (6.2) takes the form.

$$Y = X'\theta + \varepsilon, \tag{6.3}$$

where θ is a vector of conformable size for $\mathrm{X}'\theta$.

Parametric models have many virtues. For instance, model interpretability is tractable. Again, if we use (6.3) as an example, the marginal (partial) effect of X on Y is exactly θ, which is very handy to researchers interested in policy implications. If $m(X,\theta)$ is smooth, another advantage of parametric models is their constant convergence rates, i.e., θ has some estimator converging to θ at a fixed rate, usually the root of the sample size, regardless of the dimension of θ. However, the validity of parametric models hinges upon a critical assumption: the functional form of $m(\mathrm{X}, \theta)$ we choose is a correct specification. There is no guarantee that we can conduct reliable inference if the choice of $m(\mathrm{X}, \theta)$ is wrong. Nonparametric approaches, on the other hand, overcome this misspecification problem.

When we do not parametrize $\mathbb{E}[\mathrm{Y}|\mathrm{X}]$, (6.2) becomes.

$$\mathrm{Y} = m(\mathrm{X}) + \varepsilon. \tag{6.4}$$

Following the convention, we let X be a random vector of continuous variable and x a realization of it:

$$m(x) = \mathbb{E}[\mathrm{Y}|\mathrm{X} = x] = \int y \frac{f_{\mathrm{Y,X}}(y, x)}{f_{\mathrm{X}}(x)} dy, \tag{6.5}$$

where $f_{\mathrm{Y,X}}(y, x)$ is the joint density of Y and X, and $f_{\mathrm{X}}(x)$ is the marginal density of X. An important insight from (6.5) is that if we can construct "good" density estimators, the nonparametric regressions will be almost immediate through the standard plug-in method by replacing $f_{\mathrm{Y,X}}(y, x)$ and $f_{\mathrm{X}}(x)$ in (6.5) with their kernel-based nonparametric density estimators, denoted by $\widehat{f}_{\mathrm{Y,X}}(y, x)$ and $\widehat{f}_{\mathrm{X}}(x)$ respectively.

Given its obvious importance, it is worth spending a couple of more pages helping the readers establish basic intuitions of kernel-based density estimation; for a detailed treatment of kernel-based density estimation, see Rosenblatt (1956), Parzen (1962) and Scott (1992).

For instance, consider a random sample X_j's, the kernel nonparametric density estimator defined as:

$$\widehat{f}_X(x) = \frac{1}{nb_n^S} \sum\nolimits_{(j=1)}^{n} K\left(\tfrac{X_j - x}{b_n}\right). \tag{6.6}$$

The above expressions and conditions might look abstract; however, through the following example, readers will be assured that kernel-based estimator is in fact a friendly and handy tool. Suppose X is a log-normal random variable with the mean of the underlying normal random variable being 0 and 0.5 for the standard deviation. In this case, (6.6) reduces to.

$$\widehat{f}_X(x) = \frac{1}{nb_n} \sum\nolimits_{j=1}^{n} K\left(\tfrac{X_j - x}{b_n}\right). \tag{6.6a}$$

If we choose k to be the density of a uniform random variable from $-1/2$ to 1/2, then this specific univariate kernel-based density estimator boils down to the traditional histogram, which coincides with the old wisdom: when we have a dataset, plot the histogram to obtain a general idea of its distribution (e.g., test scores). Now, for illustration purposes, suppose we have 100 independent random copies from this variable X with Fig. 6.1a being the scatter plot. Figure 6.1b is the corresponding histogram generated by the R programming language,[1] overlayed by the true density curve, which is in red.

If we enlarge the sample size to 1000 we get the results in Fig. 6.2:

We can see histogram is a reasonable estimator even if the sample size is as moderate as 100; when the sample size is 1000, the histogram virtually recovers the true density. Moreover, the kernel-based density estimation theory goes beyond histograms. The main reason is that a histogram, as a collection of bins, is not continuous.

Now, consider one of the most widely used kernel functions in the empirical literature, the Gaussian as:

$$k(u) = \frac{1}{\sqrt{2\pi}} e^{-u^2/2}$$

[1] For this chapter, we used the RStudio which provides a user-friendly and a powerful interface for working with econometric packages that are built in R programming language. For details see https://www.r-studio.com.

where $u = \left(\frac{X_j - x}{b_n}\right)$, b_n is the smooth parameter (to be discussed) and $k(\cdot)$ is a kernel function that satisfies the statistical properties of symmetry, integration to 1, and continuous differentiability (Henderson and Parmeter 2015).

When we add the estimator based on the Gaussian kernel to Fig. 6.1b, we obtain Fig. 6.3a. The blue curve, which is smooth, and the histogram are quite close to each other. This should not surprise us because both are kernel estimators. This observation reveals a fact that the choice of k is irrelevant, and we will come back to this momentarily. Let us provide a numerical example of how the blue curve is constructed at a specific point, x, 1.5, and then the readers will be able to recover the whole curve point-wisely over the region from sample minimum to sample maximum. For any fixed value of b_n, (6.6a) further reduces to:

$$\hat{f}_X(1.5) = \frac{1}{b_n}\frac{1}{n}\sum_{j=1}^{n}\frac{1}{\sqrt{2\pi}}e^{-\left(\frac{X_j - 1.5}{b_n}\right)^2/2}. \quad (6b)$$

The expression (6b) tells us that the estimated density at 1.5 is basically an average point rescaled by b_n. This rescaling compensates the fact that all the observations are measured by how far they are from the target point 1.5 in terms of b_n units, i.e., $\frac{X_j - 1.5}{b_n}$.

The main purpose of Fig. 6.3 is to discuss the bandwidth choice (the smooth parameter). In our example, the R programming language chooses the number of bins in a histogram as a multiple of 5 for an aesthetic reason. To accommodate that, we force the width of the bin in Fig. 6.3b to be 5 times the one in Fig. 6.3a and 1/5 for Fig. 6.3c. As we can see, when we increase the bandwidth, both kernel-based estimators become more "flattened out" and have less variations globally. On the other hand, when we shrink the bandwidth, they are more "jagged" and pick up the local variations.

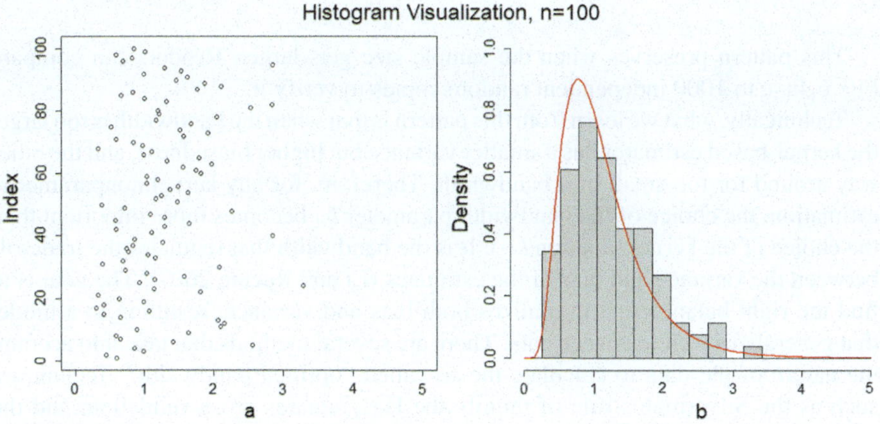

Fig. 6.1 The scatter plot (**a**) and the corresponding histogram and the true density curve (**b**) to 100 independent random copies. *Source* the authors

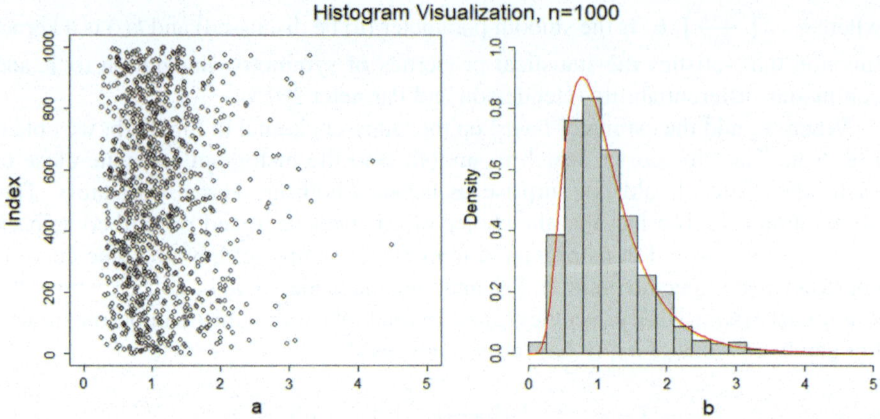

Fig. 6.2 The scatter plot (**a**) and the corresponding histogram and the true density curve (**b**) to 1000 independent random copies. *Source* the authors

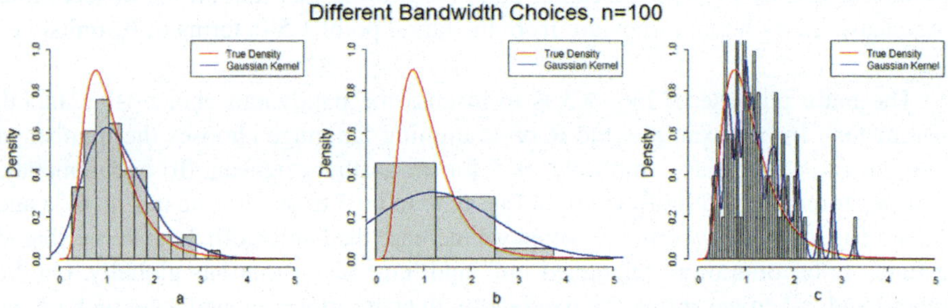

Fig. 6.3 The histograms, the true density curves, and Gaussian kernel density estimations based on different bandwidths to 100 independent random copies. *Source* the authors

This pattern preserves when the sample size gets larger. Readers can compare Fig. 6.4a–c to 1000 independent random copies to verify it.

Technically, what we learn from this pattern is that when the bandwidth is too large, the kernel-based estimator has a smaller variance but higher biasedness, and the other way around for too small of a bandwidth. Therefore, for any kernel nonparametric estimation, the choice of the bandwidth parameter b_n becomes more important than the choice of the kernel function $k(\cdot)$. It is the bandwidth that regulates the trade-off between the variance and bias of the estimates (Li and Racine 2007). The goal is to find the right balance that minimizes both bias and variance, resulting in a model that generalizes well to unseen data. There are several methods that take into account the nature of the data to calculate the so-called "optimal bandwidth." Techniques such as the Silverman's rule of thumb, the least squares cross-validation, and the maximum likelihood cross-validation are commonly employed in order to achieve

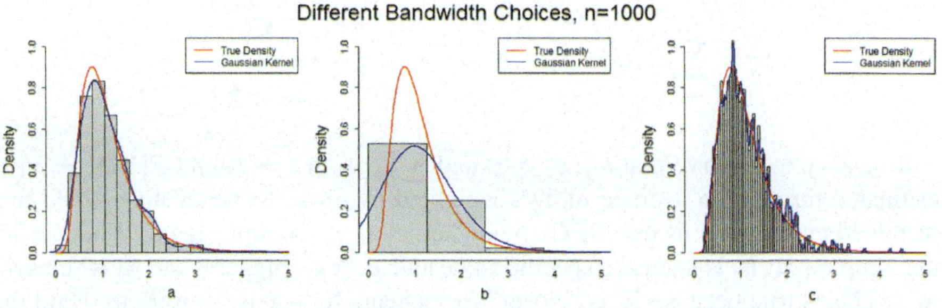

Fig. 6.4 The histograms, the true density curves, and Gaussian kernel density estimations based on different bandwidths to 1000 independent random copies. *Source* the authors

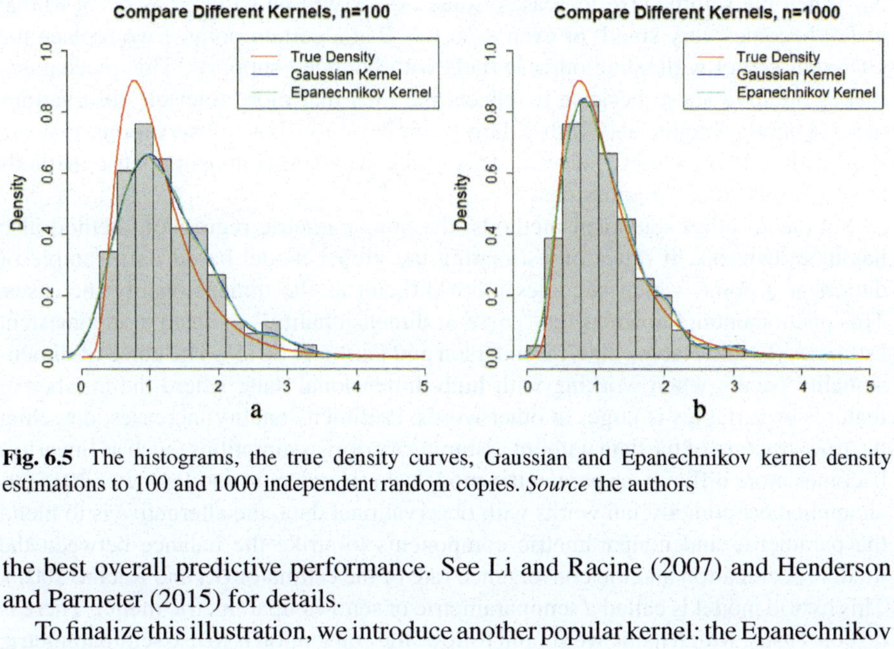

Fig. 6.5 The histograms, the true density curves, Gaussian and Epanechnikov kernel density estimations to 100 and 1000 independent random copies. *Source* the authors

the best overall predictive performance. See Li and Racine (2007) and Henderson and Parmeter (2015) for details.

To finalize this illustration, we introduce another popular kernel: the Epanechnikov Kernel as:

$$k(u) = 3/4(1 - u^2).$$

Figure 6.5a, b are Figs. 6.3a and 6.4a with the addition of the Epanechnikov Kernel-based estimator, plotted in green. Again, as we can see all three kernel-based estimators are quite close to each other.

With the knowledge from density estimation and kernel functions, we are ready to tackle the nonparametric regression based on Eq. 6.4 where:

$$\hat{m}(x) = \sum_{j=1}^{n} \omega_j(x) \cdot Y_j \quad \text{Where } \omega_j(x) = \frac{K\left(\frac{X_j - x}{b_n}\right)}{\sum_{i=1}^{n} K\left(\frac{X_i - x}{b_n}\right)}. \tag{6.7}$$

It is easy to observe that $\omega_j(x) \geq 0$ and $\sum_{j=1}^{n} \omega_j(x) = 1$, and $\mathbb{E}[Y|X = x]$ is estimated through an average of Y_j's weighted by ω_j's. To better understand this weighted average, let us use the Gaussian kernel as an example again. When fixing the sample size, b_n is fixed at a specific value and $\omega_j(x)$ is bigger when X_j is "closer" to x. This is true because X_j is "closer" to x means $X_j - x$ is "closer" to 0 and the kernel value is bigger if its argument is closer to 0. The term "closer" should be interpreted in an illustrative way because most of the time X is a vector.

As a result, Y_j is assigned with a higher weight than Y_i if X_j is "closer" to x than X_i. When the sample size increases, some $\frac{X_j - x}{b_n}$'s will be so large as $b_n \searrow 0$ that $\omega_j(x)$ becomes very small, or even $\omega_j(x) = 0$ at a certain point if we replace the Gaussian kernel with some other kernels with bounded supports. This mechanism makes intuitive sense because it reflects the idea that more relevant observations deserve more weight, and with a large sample, only those observations that are indeed close to the target x survive. This is also why kernel nonparametric methods are known as "local" regressions.

Similar to other statistical methods, the nonparametric regression method also has its drawbacks. It relies on estimating the global model based on a sample of data near a point, which becomes more difficult as the dimensionality increases. This phenomenon, known as the "curse of dimensionality," can lead to inconsistent estimates (Li and Racine 2007; Henderson and Parmeter 2015). The curse of dimensionality occurs when working with high-dimensional data, where the number of features or variables is large. In other words, as dimensionality increases, detecting the true structure of the data without assuming a priori assumptions (such as linearity) becomes more difficult, as parametric models do (Henderson and Parmeter 2015). If an applied econometrician works with observational data, the alternative is to blend the parametric and nonparametric components to strike the balance between the model specification and the convergence rate of the estimator (Li and Racine 2007). This hybrid model is called a semiparametric or semi-nonparametric model. There is no consensus, which name we should follow; the convention is to use semiparametric when the parameter of interest is finite dimensional.

Semiparametric models are the focus of this chapter. A general discussion of this type of model is inevitably too abstract. For interested readers, we refer to Ai and Chen (2003), where a general treatment is provided through a conditional moment restriction perspective. In this chapter, we use the partially linear model, which was studied by Robinson (1988), as an illustration:

$$Y = X'\theta_0 + m(Z) + \varepsilon, \tag{6.8}$$

where both $m(\cdot)$ and θ_0 are unknown. The empirical analysis of this chapter also adopts this model. Conceptually, $m(Z)$ functions as the "omitted variables" with flexible functional form in the presence of X so that the inference of the parameter of interest θ_0 is valid. Like in most of the semiparametric models, the usual two-step approach applies:

(1) First, we observe that (6.8) implies.

$$E[Y|Z] = E[X'|Z]\theta_0 + m(Z), \tag{6.9}$$

and the difference of (6.8) and (6.9) generates.

$$Y - E[Y|Z] = (X - E[X|Z])'\theta_0 + \varepsilon. \tag{6.10}$$

Note, (6.10) is an infeasible regression because both $\mathbb{E}[Y|Z]$ and $\mathbb{E}[X|Z]$ are unknown. However, we can replace $Y - \mathbb{E}[Y|Z]$and $X - \mathbb{E}[X|Z]$ by their nonparametric estimators $\widehat{m}(z)$, which renders a feasible version of (6.9).

(2) Once $\mathbb{E}[Y|Z]$ and $\mathbb{E}[X|Z]$ are estimated nonparametrically following (6.7), let $\hat{\theta}$ be the least square estimator of the feasible version of (6.10). The second step adopts a simple ordinary least squares (OLS) method to estimate $\hat{\theta}$.

Finally, in the context of semiparametric setup, we refer to Stein (1956) for the definition of efficient estimation of θ_0 in the presence of $m(\cdot)$ and Severini and Tripathi (2013) for a comprehensive treatment of it with many useful examples.

6.3 Application: A Semiparametric Engel Curve to Estimate Consumer Price Index Bias in Brazil

In this application, the objective is to analyze how changes in consumer price indices affect the consumption patterns of households headed by a person aged 60 or older[2] in relation to the non-elderly heads. More specifically, how the consumer pattern changes in the metropolitan regions of Brazil over time, based on the estimated Engel curves parametrically and semi parametrically.

Engel's law (1857) is an economic principle that states that the proportion of income spent on food decreases as income increases, while the proportion spent on other goods and services, such as housing, transportation, leisure activities, etc., increases (Deaton 1997). If the demand for a good grows as individuals or households become wealthier, the good is called a luxury good; if the demand decreases, the good is called a necessary good (Varian 2003). From this perspective, Engel's law provides a straightforward and powerful insight into the changing consumption patterns that occur as countries experience economic growth and development (Deaton 1997).

Empirical studies commonly adopt fully parametric specifications to estimate food and non-food Engel curves (Almeida et al. 2020). In addition, it is also noted

[2] In developing nations, any individual aged 60 years or more is considered—by definition—and elderly person (Camarano 2014).

that few works go further when looking for alternative methods that can adjust a form of demand function.

Bhalotra and Attfield (1998) conducted a semiparametric estimation of the Engel curve for rural Pakistan using a large household survey. They found that Engel curves for food, adult goods, and child goods are quadratic logarithmic; which implies that the commonly employed parametric functional forms for demand models are inappropriate.

Blundell and Duncan (1998) analyzed expenditures on alcoholic beverages and food in the United Kingdom between 1980 and 1982. The authors demonstrated that the format of the Engel curve, which reflects the proportion of spending on food, decreases as total household expenditure increases. Conversely, for alcoholic beverages, the Engel curve exhibited an inverted U-shape. Blundell et al. (1998) also utilized household surveys conducted in the United Kingdom between 1980 and 1982. They found that the linear specification was rejected for various consumption groups, including alcoholic beverages, clothing, transport, and other groups, when compared to their counterpart estimated nonparametric Engel curves.

Gong et al. (2005) employed a semiparametric model to estimate and identify variations in expenditure allocation among rural households in China, specifically focusing on food, education, and alcohol. The authors rejected the hypothesis of a linear relationship between food expenses and total household expenditures. Similar to Bhalotra and Attfield's (1998) findings, they also suggest that relying solely on fully parametric models would limit the power to obtain more accurate Engel curves.

In Brazil, Santana and Menezes (2009) estimated the Engel curve with a specific focus on education expenditures. They employed a semiparametric model, adjusting it to the data from the 2002–2003 Household Budget Survey. The model incorporated socioeconomic characteristics of household heads, demographic composition of household members, and household location as control variables. However, the authors did not conduct any analysis concerning the nonparametric variable (the total household expenses) and solely focused on the parametric coefficients.

More recently, Almeida et al. (2020) analyzed the shape of the Engel curve in Brazil, employing both parametric and nonparametric approaches based on data from Household Budget Surveys spanning the years 1987–2009. The authors observed that the results of the parametric models did not significantly differ from the nonparametric estimates on their mean values for various consumption groups. However, when they examined the nonparametric estimates of the Engel curve, significant differences in the allocation of total household expenditures to food and health-related personal expenses across different percentiles were observed, but not in other household expenses such as transportation, education, and housing.

In conclusion, the few studies mentioned provide valuable insights that underscore the importance of regularly reassessing the flexibility of the functional form used to estimate the Engel Curve.

The consumption of elderly people is of particular interest for this study. While most developed countries took almost 100 years to complete their respective fertility transition processes and the increase in life expectancy, it is worth noting that Brazil went through a similar process in just a quarter of a century (Camarano 2014). As a result, the rapid demographic transition resulted in the premature aging of the population. The Brazilian population pyramid began to present a more "rectangularized" configuration over time, catching up with the patterns of populations in developed countries (Camarano 2014).

There are various Brazilian studies on the consumption of health services and medications by the elderly (Loyola Filho et al. 2005; Silva et al. 2012; Duarte et al. 2012; Hernandes et al. 2012; Santos et al. 2013). However, analyzes focusing on the consumption patterns of elderly individuals are still scarce (Zanon et al. 2013; Almeida and Souza 2018; Travassos et al. 2021). As the aging of the population is taking place at a fast speed, the share of elderly individuals in the population is increasing, and the topic requires further attention by scholars and public policymakers.

Data

Data from Household Budget Surveys (*Pesquisa de Orçamentos Familiares*—POF), carried out by the Brazilian Official Statistics Office (IBGE) in 1996, 2003, 2009, and 2018, are used in the analysis. The period between 1996 and 2018 encompasses several important events influencing consumption patterns in Brazil. It involves a period with moderate inflation; the opening of the economy, with the consequent expansion of the spectrum of available goods; the reduction of income inequality; and the implementation of massive social programs (Azzoni and Almeida 2021).

The POF diagnoses the quality of life of Brazilian families based mainly on their household expenditure pattern (IBGE 2004). The surveys contain detailed information on households' expenditures on food, housing, transportation, education, health, hygiene, etc., and demographic and geographical information. The surveys interviewed 16,013 households in 1996; 48,470 in 2003; 55,970 in 2009, and 58,039 in 2018. The households are not necessarily repeated across surveys. Therefore, the data set do not follow a panel structure. As there is information on price indices of goods and services only for 11 urban agglomerations[3] in the country, the application is restricted to those areas. Prices expressed in BRL (Brazilian Real) were deflated by the respective price index[4] and converted to 2020 US$ PPP by the World Bank's conversion factors.[5]

This exercise aims to investigate the share of the family expenditure devoted to food products. Following Gorry and Scrimgeour (2018) and the related literature, only households spending between 20 and 80% on food items are included in the analysis. As a result, the sample consists of 29,057 households (11,917, 4,439, 5,882, and 6,819 for 1996, 2003, 2009, and 2018, respectively). Table 6.1 shows the descriptive statistics of the variables used in this exercise.

---

[3] Belém, Fortaleza, Recife, Salvador, Belo Horizonte, Rio de Janeiro, São Paulo, Curitiba, Porto Alegre, Brasília, and Goiânia.

[4] National Consumer Price Index - IPCA /IBGE. It includes a set of products and services sold in retail to families with income between 1 and 40 minimum wages, covering 90% of families in urban areas. https://www.ibge.gov.br/en/statistics/economic/prices-and-costs/17129-extended-national-consumer-price-index.html?=&t=o-que-e (Accessed September 23, 2020).

[5] Https://data.worldbank.org/indicator/pa.nus.ppp?view=chart.

Table 6.1 Summary statistics: means and standard deviations

Variable	Description	1996	2003	2009	2018
WFood	Food share (at home and outside) on total expenditure	0.31	0.27	0.27	0.26
		(0.15)	(0.14)	(0.14)	(0.13)
TotExp	Total expenditure per month (2020 US$ PPP)	1,258.75	1,305.06	1,188.12	1,450.55
		(1,436.32)	(1,344.07)	(1,239.27)	(1,447.25)
HHsize	Household size	4.08	3.67	3.36	3.03
		(2.00)	(1.78)	(1.67)	(1.48)
Elderly	= 1 if the head is elderly, 0 otherwise	0.19	0.18	0.23	0.27
		(0.40)	(0.39)	(0.42)	(0.44)
Age	Age of head	45.80	45.85	47.95	50.22
		(14.60)	(14.32)	(14.88)	(14.76)
Male	= 1 if the head is male, 0 otherwise	0.74	0.67	0.64	0.54
		(0.44)	(0.47)	(0.48)	(0.50)
North	= 1 if from North, 0 otherwise	0.10	0.08	0.07	0.02
		(0.30)	(0.27)	(0.26)	(0.15)
Northeast	= 1 if from Northeast, 0 otherwise	0.37	0.32	0.28	0.33
		(0.48)	(0.47)	(0.45)	(0.47)
Southeast	= 1 if from Southeast, 0 otherwise	0.26	0.33	0.39	0.41
		(0.44)	(0.47)	(0.49)	(0.49)
South	= 1 if from South, 0 otherwise	0.14	0.18	0.13	0.09
		(0.35)	(0.39)	(0.34)	(0.29)
Midwest	= 1 if from Midwest, 0 otherwise	0.13	0.09	0.13	0.14
		(0.33)	(0.28)	(0.34)	(0.34)

Note Standard deviations are between parentheses
Source the authors using data from Household Budget Surveys (POF/IBGE)

6.4 Methodology

Previous studies on consumption demand in Brazil use data from the IBGE's household expenditure surveys to estimate the Engel curve based on the seminal works of Working (1943) and Leser (1963). The specification of the functional form of the demand function is based on linear regression methods that associate the expenditure of a good (or group of goods) with total expenditure. For a specific good or service, these models use the following structure:

$$\omega_i = \alpha + \beta \ln(Y_i) + e_i \tag{6.11}$$

where ω_i is the portion spent on the specific good or service by family i, $\ln Y_i$ is the log of the total expenditure of family i, and the unobserved component e_i satisfies the following orthogonality condition $\mathbb{E}[\varepsilon_i|Y_i] = 0$ (Blundell and Duncan 1998). The coefficients α and β are parameters to be estimated.

Deaton and Muellbauer (1980) developed a procedure to estimate Eq. (6.11) as a demand model when information on the prices of goods and services is available. It is known as the "Price Independent Generalized Logarithmic-piglog." Alternatively, one can also estimate the model simultaneously using a demand system known as the Almost Ideal Demand System (AIDS), which is currently popular in empirical analyses. A demand system with n equations of Eq. (6.11) has the advantage of capturing consistently the mutual interdependence of a large number of goods, according to consumer choices, as well as their budget constraint (De Janvry and Saudolet 1995). In addition to satisfying all the assumptions of consumer theory, the AIDS model has a linear format as its main advantage, which facilitates the inclusion of constraints inherent to demand models, such as additivity, homogeneity, and symmetry (De Janvry and Saudolet 1995). Despite the advantages of the AIDS models, researchers identified a non-linear consumption behavior between poorer (necessary items) and richer (luxury items) individuals. In this case, Eq. (6.11) would no longer be appropriate (Banks et al. 1997; Blundell and Duncan 1998).

Banks et al. (1997) developed a demand system derived from the AIDS model, called the Quadratic Almost Ideal Demand System (QUAIDS). This model adds to Eq. (6.11) a quadratic term of the log of total expenditure. It allows measuring which goods would present a non-linear path of expansion of household expenditure. However, there is still no consensus on the suitable shape of the Engel curve that captures well-behaved consumer preferences and respects the nature of the data (Blundell et al. 2003). It is worth mentioning that the use of the AIDS or QUAIDS models without an a priori specification of the functional form has not been developed yet. Developing such a model is a promising avenue in the area of quantitative methods, particularly in the context of kernel nonparametric or semiparametric econometrics.

In this exercise, the method developed by Costa (2001) and Hamilton (2001) is followed to measure changes in the cost of living among non-elderly and elderly-headed households based on changes in prices. Costa and Hamilton use the overtime deviations of the Engel curve as an indirect measure of changes in the real cost of living and, therefore, in real income (Gorry and Scrimgeour 2018).

Suppose the demand function is appropriately specified and there are no systematic errors in the variables. In that case, there should be no systematic movement in the Engel curve from one year to the other (Hamilton 2001). The present simulation intends to estimate deviations in the Engel curve attributed to the bias in the price indices, which differ between households headed by the elderly or not. To date, Brzozowski (2006) for Canada and Gorry and Scrimgeour (2018) for the United States are the only studies assessing whether the consumer price index (CPI) is a good measure of inflation rates for families with senior citizens.

There is evidence that price indices generally do not always accurately track the true cost of living. Factors such as introducing new products and improvements in their quality, substitution effects, etc., may be more important for the elderly than non-elderly people (Brzozowski 2006). For instance, if the inclusion of new goods or services in the consumption list differs between elderly and non-elderly people, there will be a bias (Gorry and Scrimgeour 2018).

Except for Beatty and Larsen (2005), the works that estimate the changes in the cost of living mentioned above adopt the method developed by Hamilton (2001) and Costa (2001),[6] and use a fully parametric approach.[7] To illustrate the difference between parametric and semiparametric approaches, consider first the following fully parametric approach:

$$\omega_{ijt}^{f} = \alpha + \beta\left(log Y_{ijt} - log P_{jt}\right) + \sum_{t=1}^{T} \delta_t D_t + \gamma X_{ijt} + \varepsilon_{ijt} \tag{6.12}$$

where ω_{ijt}^{f} is the average share of expenditure on a given group of goods (e.g., food f) for family i in region j in period t; Y_{ijt} is the total nominal expenditure of family i in the period t given by the deflator P_{jt}. D_t is a year dummy variable, it absorbs all time-varying factors that shift the Engel curve that the regression equation does not capture (Gorry and Scrimgeour 2018). The estimated coefficient δ_t represents a change (bias) in the intercept from year to year. The vector X_{ijt} includes the household's geographic, demographic, and socioeconomic characteristics, and ε_{ijt} is the error term. The coefficients β and γ are also the parameters to be estimated.

Alternatively, consider a partially linear estimation of the Engel curve as follows:

$$\omega_{ijt}^{f} = \alpha + m\left(log Y_{ijt} - log P_{jt}\right) + \sum_{t=1}^{T} \delta_t D_t + \gamma X_{ijt} + \varepsilon_{ijt} \tag{6.13}$$

where Eq. (6.13) follows the same specification as Eq. (6.12) except that now $m(\cdot)$is an unknown function to be estimated nonparametrically. Robinson (1988) suggests the Local-Linear Least Squares (LCLS) method to estimate $m(\cdot)$. Alternatively, we can also resort to the Local-Linear Least-Squares (LLLS), another popular nonparametric estimator.[8]

Thus, assuming that measurement errors in price indices shift the Engel curve over time, the coefficient δ_t must represent $\beta\left(log Y_{ijt} - log P_{jt}^{*}\right)$ or $m\left(log Y_{ijt} - log P_{jt}^{*}\right)$ where P^{*} is the true cost of living (Hamilton 2001; Gorry and Scrimgeour 2018). Therefore, following Gorry and Scrimgeour (2018), the cumulative percentage deviation from the reported price index and the true cost of living in the period t can be computed from parametric and semiparametric models as:

---

[6] Hamilton (2001) and Costa (2001) present the complete derivation.

[7] Beatty and Larsen (2005) adopt the p-spline estimation of single-index models. They are nonparametric alternative estimators to the kernel regression, which is adopted by this chapter. Yatchew (2003) provides a comprehensive review of both estimators.

[8] A comprehensive review of theoretical and empirical foundations for both the LCLS and the LLLS estimators are beyond the scope of this chapter; for details see Li and Racine (2007) and Henderson and Parmeter (2015).

$$100\left(\exp\left(\frac{\delta_t}{\beta}\right)-1\right) \quad \text{or} \quad 100\left(\exp\left(\frac{\delta_t}{m(\cdot)}\right)-1\right) \tag{6.14}$$

It is possible to separate the bias in the consumer price index for different family groups by estimating the following parametric function:

$$\omega^f_{ijt} = \alpha + \beta\left(logY_{ijt} - logP_{jt}\right) + \sum_{t=1}^{T}\delta_t D_t + \sum_{t=1}^{T}\delta_t^{elderly} D_{ijt}^{elderly} + \gamma X_{ijt} + \varepsilon_{ijt} \tag{6.15}$$

or from a semiparametric model:

$$\omega^f_{ijt} = \alpha + m\left(logY_{ijt} - logP_{jt}\right) + \sum_{t=1}^{T}\delta_t D_t + \sum_{t=1}^{T}\delta_t^{elderly} D_{ijt}^{elderly} + \gamma X_{ijt} + \varepsilon_{ijt} \tag{6.16}$$

where $D_{ijt}^{elderly}$ it is a binary indicator that represents whether the family is headed by an elderly person. The cumulative percentage deviation of the price index for families with elderly people can then be estimated as:

$$100\left(\exp\left(\frac{\delta_t + \delta_{ijt}^{elderly}}{\beta}\right)-1\right) \quad \text{or} \quad 100\left(\exp\left(\frac{\delta_t + \delta_{ijt}^{elderly}}{m(\cdot)}\right)-1\right) \tag{6.17}$$

The main idea is that the Hamilton-Costa Engel curve method for estimating price index biases can overlook other sources of bias, such as preferences, which may change systematically over time and shift the Engel curve (Gorry and Scrimgeour 2018). This method for measuring changes in the cost of living of the elderly in relation to the non-elderly will differentiate any shift of the Engel curve at the population level that may occur for any reason (Brzozowski 2006).

6.5 Results

The critical variable of interest in the econometric analysis is the household's total nominal expenditure deflated by a Consumer Price Index. The model is estimated parametrically and semiparametrically. The dependent variable is the log of the share of the household expenditure allocated to food items. The appropriate price deflator is a specific price index for food and beverages (Gorry and Scrimgeour 2018). However, such a specific index is not available, and a general index covering all items of the consumption basket had to be used. Even considering that the amount of food consumption as a share of total expenditure is significant and covered 33–26% of families headed by the elderly and 30–26% by non-elderly between 1996 and

2018 (Fig. 6.6a), a word of caution is recommended. Figure 6.6b shows the total expenditure per month (2020 US$ PPP) for elderly and non-elderly heads.

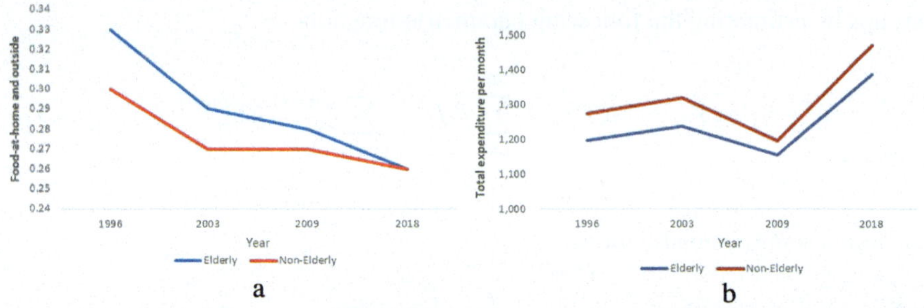

Fig. 6.6 Food consumption (at home and outside) as a share of total expenditure (**a**) and household total expenditure per month (2020 US$ PPP) (**b**) for elderly and non-elderly heads. *Source* the authors use data from Household Budget Surveys (POF/IBGE)

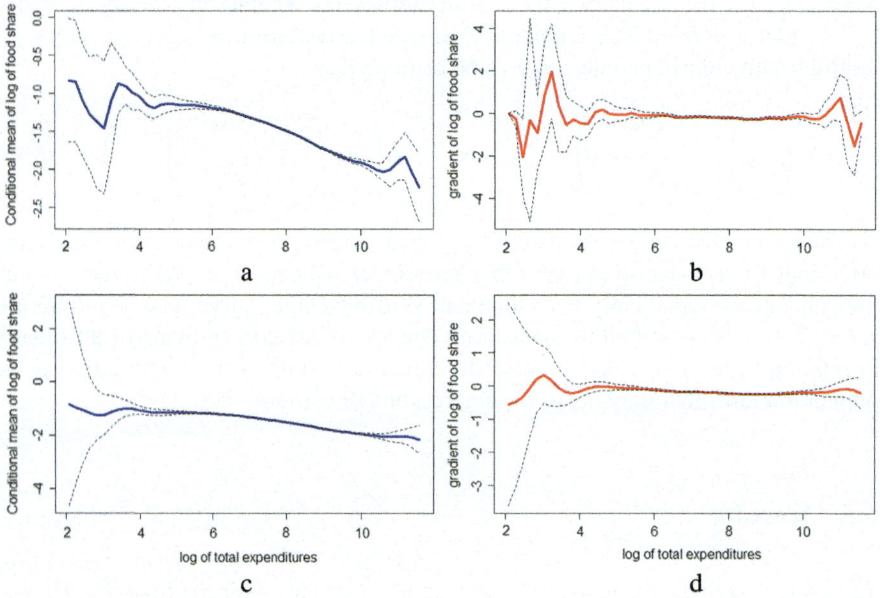

Fig. 6.7 reports conditional mean (**a**) and gradients (**b**) from the semiparametric model using the local-constant kernel estimator (column 2, Table 6.2); conditional mean (**c**) and gradients (**d**) of the semiparametric model using the local-linear kernel estimator (column 3, Table 6.2). The dashed lines indicate the 95% confidence intervals obtained from 399 (default) bootstrap replications. *Source* the authors

The starting point of all nonparametric and semiparametric estimators, as well as their recent developments, is the nonparametric estimator developed by Nadaraya (1964) and Watson (1964), based on kernel functions (Henderson and Parmeter 2015). The most used kernel functions are the Uniform, the Gaussian, and the Epanechnikov. In any nonparametric regression that uses kernel functions, the choice of the kernel is always more important than the choice of the kernel function itself (Li and Racine 2007). Gaussian kernel functions and techniques known as the cross-validation method to find the "optimal" bandwidth, as mentioned in Sect. 6.2, are adopted for this exercise. The "np" package of Hayfield and Racine (2008) built in R programming language is used for all semiparametric estimations. We start our estimations by using the following commands in blue:

```
rm(list=ls()) # Clear memory space (highly recommended for a new
RStudio script/project)
install.packages("np") # Installing R package of Hayfield and
Racine (2008) for nonparametric and #semiparametric regressions in
your RStudio
library(np) # Load the R Package to the current RStudio environment
# Uploading the data
data <- read.csv("C:/brazildata.csv") # Sample of 29,057 observa-
tions
#Reading variables from the uploaded data to the current RStudio
environment
lnwfood <-data$ln_w_food
lntotexp <-data$lntotexp
hhsize <-data$hhsize
age <-data$age
male <-data$male
year <-data$year
year96 <-data$du_1996
year03 <-data$du_2003
year09 <-data$du_2009
year18 <-data$du_2018
year96eld <-data$du_elder96
year03eld <-data$du_elder03
year09eld <-data$du_elder09
year18eld <-data$du_elder18
northeast <-data$northeast
southeast <-data$southeast
south <-data$south
midwest <-data$midwest
north <-data$north
```

Column (1) of Table 6.2 displays the results of a fully parametric model based on Eq. (6.15), while columns (2) and (3) display the results based on Eq. (6.16). Column (2) shows the results of a semiparametric estimator designed for pooled datasets called Local-Constant Least-Squares (LCLS). Column (3) shows the results of a semiparametric model designed for pooled datasets called Local-Linear Least-Squares (LLLS). The results will be discussed shortly afterward. Before, we illustrate the following R commands used to estimate the regressions.

Table 6.2 Engel curve estimates and consumer price index bias

	Dependent variable: log of food share		
	Parametric model	Semiparametric Kernel Models	
		Local-Constant	Local-Linear
	(1)	(2)	(3)
Log of TotExp	−0.188***	−0.180***	−0.189***
	(0.003)	(0.005)	(0.004)
HHsize	0.023***	0.022***	0.022***
	(0.002)	(0.002)	(0.002)
Age	0.001***	0.001***	0.001***
	(0.000)	0.1000)	(0.000)
Male	0.049***	0.049***	0.049***
	(0.006)	(0.006)	(0.069)
Dummy2003	−0.092***	−0.095***	−0.095***
	(0.009)	(0.009)	(0.009)
Dummy2009	−0.082***	−0.087***	−0.087***
	(0.008)	(0.008)	(0.008)
Dummy2018	−0.077***	−0.080***	−0.079***
	(0.008)	(0.008)	(0.008)
DummyElderly03	0.043**	0.038***	0.038***
	(0.019)	(0.019)	(0.019)
DummyElderly09	0.002	−0.001	−0.002
	(0.016)	(0.015)	(0.015)
DummyElderly18	− 0.041***	−0.046***	−0.046***
	(0.014)	(0.014)	(0.014)
North	0.074***	0.069***	0.069***
	(0.011)	(0.011)	(0.011)
Southeast	−0.092***	−0.093***	−0.093***
	(0.007)	(0.007)	(0.007)
South	−0.090***	−0.093***	−0.093***
	(0.009)	(0.009)	(0.009)
Midwest	− 0.112***	−0.112***	−0.112***

(continued)

Table 6.2 (continued)

	Dependent variable: log of food share						
	Parametric model	Semiparametric Kernel Models					
		Local-Constant			Local-Linear		
	(1)	(2)			(3)		
	(0.009)	(0.009)			(0.009)		
Constant	−0.003						
	(0.026)						
Observations	29,057	29,057			29,057		
R^2	0.153	0.156			0.156		
CPI Bias		25%	50%	75%	25%	50%	75%
Non-elderly bias	7.63	7.33	8.55	9.97	6.59	7.98	8.95
	(3.86)	(3.28)	(3.93)	(4.71)	(3.10)	(3.87)	(4.43)
Elderly bias	7.74	7.84	9.19	10.78	7.05	8.59	9.67
	(16.62)	(15.54)	(18.68)	(22.52)	(13.51)	(16.95)	(19.45)

Notes Columns 2 and 3 report the median of the gradient estimates for the log of the total expenditure per month variable. Percentile means of these estimates at the 25th, 50th, and 75th are used to estimate the CPI bias from Eq. (6.13) and (6.16). Standard errors are in parentheses. * $p < 0.10$, ** $p < 0.05$, *** $p < 0.01$
Source the authors

```
#####################################################
#1. Linear Model - fully parametric regression
#####################################################
model.ols <-lm(lnwfood ~ lntotexp + hhsize + age + male + year03
+ year09 + year18 + year03eld + year09eld + year18eld + north +
southeast + south + midwest)
print(summary(model.ols),digits=3)
##############################################################
# 2 Partially Linear Kernel Regression with Mixed Data Types - Local-
Constant Estimator
##############################################################
model.plm <-npplreg(lnwfood ~ hhsize + age + male + year03 + year09
+ year18 + year03eld + year09eld + year18eld + north + southeast +
south + midwest | lntotexp)
summary(model.plm)
print(coef(model.plm),digits=1)
print(coef(model.plm, errors = TRUE))
##############################################################
# 3 Partially Linear Kernel Regression with Mixed Data Types - Local-
Linear Estimator
##############################################################
model.plm.ll <-npplreg(lnwfood ~ hhsize + age + male + year03 +
year09 + year18 + year03eld + year09eld + year18eld + north +
southeast + south + midwest | lntotexp, regtype="ll")
summary(model.plm.ll)
print(coef(model.plm.ll),digits=1)
```

```
print(coef(model.plm.ll, errors = TRUE))
```

To make the results of these semiparametric models comparable with the parametric results, the gradient (partial effects) estimates of the nonparametric regressor (total monthly expenditures) at the 50th (median) percentile are reported in Table 6.2. The bootstrapped standard errors (with 399 replications as the default value) are also reported in parentheses. The following R commands are used to generate the partial effects and the standard errors.

```
###############################################################
# 2 Partially Linear Kernel Regression with Mixed Data Types - Local-
Constant Estimator
# Extracting the conditional mean and the gradients of the nonpara-
metric component
# Source: https://cran.r-project.org/web/packages/np/vignettes/
np_faq.pdf
###############################################################
y.sub <- lnwfood-model.matrix(~hhsize + age + male + year03 +
year09 + year18 + year03eld + year09eld + year18eld + north +
southeast + south + midwest)[,-1]%*%coef(model.plm)
model.sub <- npreg(y.sub ~ lntotexp, gradients=TRUE)
plm.se <- se(model.sub)
plm.grad <- gradients(model.sub)
quantile(plm.grad, probs = seq(0, 1, 1/4))
quantile(plm.se, probs = seq(0, 1, 1/4))
###############################################################
# 3 Partially Linear Kernel Regression with Mixed Data Types - Local-
Linear Estimator
# Extracting the conditional mean and the gradients of the nonpara-
metric component
# Source: https://cran.r-project.org/web/packages/np/vignettes/
np_faq.pdf
###############################################################
y.sub.ll <- lnwfood-model.matrix(~hhsize + age + male + year03
+ year09 + year18 + year03eld + year09eld + year18eld + north +
southeast + south + midwest)[,-1]%*%coef(model.plm.ll)
model.sub.ll <- npreg(y.sub.ll ~ lntotexp, gradients=TRUE,
regtype="ll")
plm.se.ll <- se(model.sub.ll)
plm.grad.ll <- gradients(model.sub.ll)
quantile(plm.grad.ll, probs = seq(0, 1, 1/4))
quantile(plm.se.ll, probs = seq(0, 1, 1/4))
```

Figure 6.7 shows nonparametric estimates of the conditional means and gradients of the log of the expenditure on food as a function of the log of total expenditure. The estimates come from the semiparametric models from both the local-constant and the local-linear estimators. They are obtained by running the following commands in the RStudio.

```
###############################################################
# 2 Partially Linear Kernel Regression with Mixed Data Types - local
constant estimator
```

```
################################################################
# Plotting the conditional mean estimates of the nonparametric term
par(mar=rep(5,4))
plot(model.sub, perspective=FALSE,plot.errors.method
="bootstrap", plot.errors.boot.num = 399, plot.behavior="plot-
data",
lwd=4,lty=1,  col="blue",xlab="log  of  total  expenditures",
ylab="Conditional mean of log of food share")
# Plotting the gradients estimates of the nonparametric term
plot(model.sub,plot.errors.method="bootstrap",
plot.errors.boot.num  =  399,gradients=TRUE,  lwd=4,lty=1,
col="red",
xlab="log of total expenditures", ylab="gradient of log of food
share")
################################################################
# 3 Partially Linear Kernel Regression with Mixed Data Types - local
linear
################################################################
# Plotting the conditional mean estimates of the nonparametric term
par(mar=rep(5,4))
plot(model.sub.ll, perspective=FALSE,plot.errors.method
="bootstrap",plot.errors.boot.num = 399, plot.behavior="plot-
data",
lwd=4,lty=1,  col="blue",xlab="log  of  total  expenditures",
ylab="Conditional mean of log of food share")
# Plotting the gradients estimates of the nonparametric term
plot(model.sub.ll,plot.errors.method="bootstrap",plot.errors
.boot.num = 399,gradients=TRUE, lwd=4,lty=1, col="red",
xlab="log of total expenditures", ylab="gradient of log of food
share"
```

Visually, the observed gradient estimates (Fig. 6.7b–d) seem to be similar. The conditional mean of the log of the share of food as a function of the log of the total household expenditure using the local-constant kernel estimator (Fig. 6.7a) seems to fall faster than the conditional mean of the log of the food share of the local-linear estimator (Fig. 6.7c). The question is: which one should we use? Both are very popular in applied work. Henderson and Parmeter (2015) suggest that the local-linear estimator holds more desirable theoretical and applied properties than the local-constant estimator. The former also provides a more accurate measurement of the conditional mean than the latter. A major difference between them lies in the amount of local information used by both and driven by the "optimal" bandwidths during the estimation (Henderson and Parmeter 2015).

Table 6.2 shows that the R^2 of the semiparametric models are almost identical to their parametric counterpart. The estimated parameters are also similar across the three models.

The bottom part of Table 6.2 shows the Consumer Price Index bias for non-elderly and elderly, based on Eqs. (6.14) and (6.17), respectively. The year dummy coefficients and their interactions with the elderly dummy are used to calculate the cumulative deviation of the CPI from the true cost of living, as discussed in the methodology (Gorry and Scrimgeour 2018). With just one exception, the parameters indicate a positive statistical relationship between the share of expenditure on food and household size, age, and gender of the head (=1 if male). The share of food for households in the South, Southeast, and Midwest regions is smaller than for households in the Northeast region (omitted variable); the North region shows the highest share.

Table 6.2 also shows that the partially linear models estimated by LLLS and LCLS estimators generate gradients of total expenditures at their medians that are similar to the one obtained from the fully parametric model. However, this finding does not hold for both semiparametric models across gradient percentiles, influencing the size of the CPI bias for both elderly and non-elderly.

In short, the parametric model shows almost no difference in the implied bias between elderly and non-elderly households (7.6% for non-elderly and 7.7% for elderly). The results are in line with the previous analyses that found that the CPI overstates the annual rate of increase in the cost of living and that the bias is marginally larger for the elderly, as compared to the non-elderly (Brzozowski 2006; Gorry and Scrimgeour 2018). This type of model produces a single result for the whole set of data, while the nonparametric models generate results for different parts of the distribution of the covariates when they are estimated nonparametrically. The results of the semiparametric models illustrate this difference. They indicate that the bias for the elderly is larger than for the non-elderly, in every part of the distribution. For instance, the local-linear estimator indicates biases of 6.6% for the non-elderly and 7% for the elderly at the 25th percentile of the expenditure distribution; 7.9 and 8.6% at the 50th percentile; and 8.9 and 9.6% at the 75th percentile. The local-constant estimator produces similar results.

Understanding the extent to which price indices capture changes in the cost of living is a crucial public policy issue, particularly among families with older people, who spend a larger part of their income on health services and medicines. Government indexes its programs with price indices to maintain a minimum standard of living for beneficiaries. An example is the minimum wage, which is adjusted yearly to compensate for inflation. Additionally, a significant part of social policy involves pensions and other cash transference programs to the growing population of long-lived individuals. Indexation is also present in contracts, wage negotiations, and as a critical indicator for monetary policy. Therefore, having more accurate estimates of price indices is of interest to economists, policymakers, and the general public (Gorry and Scrimgeour 2018).

6.6 Concluding Remarks

This chapter intended to contribute to the consolidation of an approach of quantitative methods on kernel semi and nonparametric econometrics in the field of consumer economics. The major rationale for using non- or semiparametric methods is to avoid limitations or misspecifications that can stem from specific functional forms, which can produce biased estimates.

In general, economic theory does not provide much guidance regarding the choice of functional form for estimation purposes and, in order to determine the real shape of a conditional mean relationship, nonparametric or semiparametric estimation are more appropriate than a linear regression (Blundell and Duncan 1998).

For policy analysis, a fully parametric model is preferable because it is easier to interpret than a nonparametric alternative (Henderson and Parmeter 2015). However, kernel models can be very helpful in identifying the true underlying structure of the data (Eubank 1999). In addition, for any non- or semiparametric estimation, the choice of the bandwidth parameter, which regulates the trade-off between variance and bias in the estimates, is always more important than the choice of the kernel function (Li and Racine 2007). Therefore, the correct choice either Silverman's rule of thumb or the cross-validation method to calculate the bandwidths is extremely recommended.

In summary, if there are deviations in the Engel curve, these provide an indirect measure of changes in the real cost of living for families. While the parametric Engel curve model produces a single result for the entire data set, nonparametric models generate results for different parts of the distribution of covariates. The results of the parametric model showed almost no difference in the implicit bias in the price index on food expenditures between the elderly and non-elderly (7.6% for non-elderly and 7.7% for elderly) between 1996 and 2018. However, for this same consumption group, the semiparametric estimators indicated biases of 6.6% for non-elderly and 7% for elderly in the 25th percentile of the distribution of family expenses; 7.9 and 8.6% at the 50th percentile; and 8.9 and 9.6% at the 75th percentile. The results clearly indicate that price indices overestimate the annual rate of increase in the cost of living. The bias is marginally larger for the elderly compared to the non-elderly. Therefore, the household's nominal expenditure (or income) on the Engel curve deflated by a price index shows a trend bias between the oldest relative to the youngest consumers. This prevents estimating the actual rate of improvement in living standards among these groups.

In conclusion, it is hoped that this material will awaken an important space for fostering research across different fields, while also contributing to the formation of future undergraduate and graduate students who end up taking an interest in nonparametric and semiparametric regressions.

Acknowledgements The first author thanks the "Conselho Nacional de Desenvolvimento Científico e Tecnológico" (CNPq-Brazil, Project 305415/2019-0) for the financial support.

References

Ai C, Chen X (2003) Efficient estimation of models with conditional moment restrictions with unknown functions. Econ 71(6):1795–1843

Almeida AN, Souza LRS (2018) Analysis of the consumption patterns in families with and without elderly members between 1987 and 2009 in the Metropolitan Regions of Brazil. J Pop Ag 11:1–31

Almeida AN, Amorim DIM, Azzoni CR, Tabosa FJS, Chagas ALS (2020) Gastos Domiciliares nas Regiões Metropolitanas: Uma Análise não Paramétrica Kernel usando Dados de Pseudo-Painel. Rev Bra Est Reg Urb 14(4):574–600

Azzoni CR, Almeida AN (2021) Mudanças nas Estruturas de Consumo e Custo de Vida Comparativo nas Regiões Metropolitanas: 1996–2020. Est Econ 51(1):529–563

Banks J et al (1997) Quadratic Engel curves and consumer demand. Rev Econ Stat 79(4):527–539

Beatty TKM, Larsen ER (2005) Using Engel curves to estimate bias in the Canadian CPI as cost of living index. Can J Econ 38(2):482–499

Bhalotra S, Attfield C (1998) Intrahousehold resource allocation in rural Pakistan: a semiparametric analysis. J App Econ 13(5):462–480

Blundell RW et al (2003) Nonparametric Engel curves and Revealed Preference. Econ 71(1):205–240

Blundell R, Duncan A (1998) Kernel regression in empirical economics. J Hum Res 13:62–87

Blundell R et al (1998) Semiparametric estimation and consumer demand. J App Econ 13:435–461

Brzozowski M (2006) Does one size fit all? The CPI and Canadian Seniors. Can Pub Pol 32(5):387–411

Camarano AA (2014) Introdução. In: Camarano AA (ed) Novo Regime Demográfico uma Nova Relação entre População e Desenvolvimento. IPEA, Rio de Janeiro, pp 15–39

Costa DL (2001) Estimating real income in the United States from 1988 to 1994: Correction CPI bias using Engel Curves. J Pol Econ 109(6):1288–1310

De Janvry A, Saudolet E (1995) Quantitative development policy analysis. The John Hopkins, Baltimore

Deaton A (1997) The analysis of household surveys: a microeconometric approach to development policy. The World Bank and the Johns Hopkins, Baltimore

Deaton A, Muellbauer J (1980) Economics and consumer behavior, Cambridge, New York

Duarte LR et al (2012) Hábitos de consumo de medicamentos entre idosos usuários do SUS e de plano de saúde. Cad De Sau Col 20(1):64–71

Eubank RL (1999) Nonparametric regression and spline smoothing. 2nd. Series Statistics: A Series of Textbooks and Monographs, CRC Press. doi.org/https://doi.org/10.1201/9781482273144

Gong X et al (2005) The effects of the gender of children on expenditure patterns in rural China: a semiparametric analysis. J App Econ 20:509–527

Gorry J, Scrimgeour D (2018) Using Engel curves to estimate consumer price index bias for the elderly. Cont Econ Pol 36(3):539–553

Hamilton BW (2001) Using Engel's law to estimate CPI bias. Am Econ Rev 91(3):619–630

Hayfield T, Racine JS (2008) Nonparametrics econometrics: The NP package. J Stat Soft 27(5):1–32

Henderson DJ, Parmeter CF (2015) Applied nonparametric econometrics, Cambridge, New York

Hernandes ESC et al (2012) Idosos com e sem plano de saúde e características sócio epidemiológicas associadas. Rev De Sau Pub 46(6):1030–1038

IBGE (2004) Instituto Brasileiro de Geografia e Estatística. Pesquisa de Orçamentos Familiares 2002–2003: primeiros resultados. Rio de Janeiro. https://biblioteca.ibge.gov.br/visualizacao/livros/liv81847.pdf. Accessed 20 July 2022

Leser CEV (1963) Forms of Engel Functions. Econ 31(4):694–703

Li Q, Racine J (2007) Nonparametrics Econometrics: Theory and Practice. Princeton, Princeton

Loyola Filho AI et al (2005) Estudo de base populacional sobre o consumo de medicamentos entre idosos: Projeto Bambuí. Cad Sau Pub 2(1):545–553

Nadaraya EA (1964) On estimating regression. Teor Veroy I Ee Prim 9:157–159

Parzen E (1962) On estimation of a probability density function and mode. Ann Math Stat 33(3):1065–1076
Robinson P (1988) Root-n-consistent semiparametric regression. Econ 56(4):931–954
Rosenblatt M (1956) Remarks on some nonparametric estimates of a density function. Ann Math Stat 27(3):832–837
Santana PJ, Menezes TA (2009) Diferenças raciais no padrão de gastos com educação: uma abordagem semiparamétrica. N Econ 19(3):383–405
Santos TRA et al (2013) Consumo de medicamentos por idosos, Goiânia, Brasil. Rev Sau Pub 47(1):94–103
Severini T, Tripathi G (2013) Semiparametric efficiency bounds for microeconometric models: a survey. Foun Tren Econ 6:163–397
Scott DW (1992) Multivariate density estimation: theory, practice, and visualization. Wiley, Hoboken
Silva A et al (2012) Utilização de medicamentos por idosos brasileiros, de acordo com faixa etária: um inquérito postal. Cad Sau Pub 28(6):1033–1045
Stein C (1956) Efficient nonparametric testing and estimation. In: Neyman J (ed) Proceedings of the Third Berkeley symposium on mathematical statistics and probability, vol 1. University of California Press, Berkeley and Los Angeles, pp 187–195
Travassos GF et al (2021) Consumption patterns and demand in households headed by the elderly: evidence from Brazil. Int J Soc Econ 48(5):657–674
Varian H (2003) Intermediate microeconomics, 6th edn. WW Norton & Company, New York
Watson GS (1964) Smooth Regression Analysis. Sank 26:175–184
Working H (1943) Statistical laws of family expenditure. J Am Stat Ass 38:43–56
Yatchew A (2003) Semiparametric Regression for the Applied Econometrician. In: Phillips PCB (ed) Themes in Modern Econometrics, Cambridge, Cambridge
Zanon RR et al (2013) Envelhecimento populacional e mudanças no padrão de consumo e na estrutura produtiva brasileira. Rev Bras Est Pop 30:45–67

Chapter 7
A Primer on Spatial Regression Models: Applications to Poverty and Inequality of Indian Districts

Somnath Chattopadhyay and Sandip Sarkar

Abstract The standard classical linear regression model (CLRM) assumption is that the observations are independent and identically distributed. This assumption is questionable whenever the units of analysis are spatially dependent. The first step for capturing spatial dependence is to define a spatial weight matrix, where the matrix elements capture pairwise spatial dependence between the units of analysis. Given the weight matrix, two main models that evolved in the literature are the spatial autoregressive (SAR) model and the spatial error model (SEM). SAR is much in line with the well-known autoregressive models frequently used in time series, where the outcomes of the dependent variable in a linear regression model depend on the outcomes of the neighboring regions. Estimating spatial autoregressive parameters and the parameters associated with other explanatory variables using least square methods will lead to an inconsistent estimator; hence needs to be taken care of with special attention. SEM, on the other hand, is applicable whenever the error term of the linear regression equation is spatially autocorrelated. If the error term exhibits such a pattern, then ignoring it would lead to a biased estimator of the standard errors of the parameters. Nevertheless, the coefficients will be consistent, which implies that, unlike SAR, if the sample size is large enough, then ignoring the SEM model and executing a linear regression will not be problematic. One can estimate the parameters of the SAR and SEM using either a maximum likelihood method or a generalized method of moments. In this chapter, we discuss the two methods at length. Furthermore, we also discuss how these models can be executed in the statistical software Stata 15.

Supplementary Information The online version contains supplementary material available at https://doi.org/10.1007/978-981-99-4902-1_7.

S. Chattopadhyay
Department of Economics, University of Burdwan, Kandra Radhakanta Kundu Mahavidyalaya, Burdwan, India

S. Sarkar (✉)
Department of Economics and Finance, BITS Pilani KK Birla Goa Campus, Goa, India
e-mail: sandips@goa.bits-pilani.ac.in

D. Mukherjee (ed.), *Applied Econometric Analysis Using Cross Section and Panel Data*, Contributions to Economics, https://doi.org/10.1007/978-981-99-4902-1_7

Keywords Spatial autoregressive models · Spatial error models · MLE · GMM · Moran's I

7.1 Introduction

A long-lasting theme in microeconomic theory is the problem of "*externality.*" Such issues are observed whenever the consumption or production of some individuals or firms affects another. Externality problems have become so common that it gets substantial space in standard undergraduate microeconomics textbooks (see Varian (2014), Nicholson and Snyder (2012), etc.). The standard assumption of the classical linear regression model that all observations are independent and identically distributed (*iid*), definitely will not hold in the presence of externalities. The *iid* assumption may also be challenged if the objective is to model the productions of different firms. This problem has been discussed in a celebrated paper by Nobel laureate Krugman (1991). He argues that a firm's output depends on that of another, mainly because firms face increasing returns to scale and thus are located in some specific zones of a country. Our objective in this chapter is to revisit the basics of spatial econometrics. We discuss some popular spatial econometric models and some crucial nitty–gritty that a researcher must consider while handling spatial data. We discuss the basic theory of spatial models from an econometrics perspective. Furthermore, we also illustrate how these models can be executed in Stata 15. This chapter will be helpful for beginners with prerequisite knowledge of econometrics and the statistical software Stata.

Spatial data represent data that have direct or indirect correspondence to the location on the surface of the earth. A spatial database has geographic information in terms of latitude and longitude embedded in it. While this configuration adds to the informational content, the same renders the data to be uniquely characterized by the presence of spatial dependence or spatial heterogeneity across the observations. Spatial dependence means that the value of an observation is influenced by its neighboring observations. Formally if i, j refers to individual observations (locations) and y_i is the value of the random variable of interest at location i, $y_i = f(y_j), i \neq j; i = 1, 2, \ldots, n$, y_j being the observation of the jth location. Spatial heterogeneity, on the other hand refers to structural variations in the relationships between variables under study over space. This means that although the explanatory variables may be the same, the effect of these on the dependent variable will vary for each point in space, yielding variable parameter estimates across observations (locations).

Spatial effect may be contrasted from temporal effect (correlation) in the sense that the latter is sequential and *unidimensional* in nature where the past influences the present while the dependence is conceived to be *multidimensional* in the cross-sectional spatial case with neighbors influencing the behavior of their neighbors and vice versa. The genesis of this spatial dependence may be linked intuitively with a fundamental notion in Geography, which says that nearby entities often share more similarities than entities, which are far apart, an idea which is known as Tobler's First Law of Geography. The essence of the above law is that "*everything is related to everything else, but nearby things are more related than distant things*" (Tobler 1970). This suggests that the strength of spatial dependence between observations should decline with the increase in the distance between these (observations). This also relates to situations involving spatially heterogeneous relationships between variables. It may be assumed that nearby observations should exhibit similar relationships in comparison to the distant objects which will behave the other way. Now, the strength of the spatial effect may be measured by quantifying the degree of spatial association between the observations. This may be obtained by constructing a spatial weight matrix W based on the spatial information as embedded in the data (i.e., the latitude and longitude), and subsequently computing the autocorrelation coefficient of the spatially dependent variable.[1] Just like autocorrelation measures the correlation of a variable with itself, spatial autocorrelation (ρ) does the same for the variable (Y) and its spatial lag (WY).[2]

In this chapter, we present a brief review on the main concepts of spatial econometrics that is crucial for beginners dealing with spatial data. We discuss two models in detail, namely, the Spatial Autoregressive (SAR) and Spatial Error Models (SEM) that economists take special interests in. SAR model is applicable whenever the dependent variable depends on its spatial lag. This model is like well-known Autoregressive models in time series econometrics. SEM on the other hand deals whenever the error term in a classical regression model depends on its lags. This is in fact much like the Moving Average process in time series models. One must note that if the data generating process is such that the outcomes of the dependent variable depend

[1] Corresponding to each observation, each row of W denotes its neighborhood status with other locations. For non-neighbors, $w_{ij} = 0$, while for neighbors the weights are either $w_{ij} = 1$ (binary weights), or a function of something else, such as $w_{ij} = 1/d_{ij}$ $(i \neq j)$, being the distance between observation i and observation j. The diagonal elements of a spatial weight matrix are conventionally set to zero and typically standardized such that the elements of a row sum to one (Anselin and Bera 1998, Gibson and Olivia 2007). Hence, the spatial weight matrix allows all the interactions between observation *i* and each of its neighbors to be parameterized in the form of a weighted average. Specifically, for the random variable of interest y, each element of the spatially lagged variable $Wy equals \sum_j w_{ij} y_j$, which is a weighted average of the y, values about point *i*.

[2] Estimates of spatial correlation helps in assessing whether the similarities in the values of the observations are coincidental or it comes as a fallout of the typical data structure (spatial structure). As emphasized by Tiefelsdorf (1998), spatial autocorrelation and spatial structure cannot exist independent of one another. The spatial structure cannot be empirically observed unless a significant correlated structure is present there. If the latter is true, the observed spatial distribution may be considered as the manifestation of the underlying spatial process. Spatial autocorrelation can take both positive and negative values. In the positive case, the value of a variable at a given location tends to be like the values of that variable in nearby locations. This means that if the value of some variable is low in each location, the presence of spatial autocorrelation indicates that nearby values are also low. On the other hand, negative spatial autocorrelation is characterized by dissimilar values in nearby locations. Rejecting the null hypothesis of no spatial correlation ($H_0 : \rho = 0$) means that spatial effect is present in the data. If we fail to reject the null, it can be inferred that spatial effect is absent, which in other words means that the spatial allocation of the observations is random.

on the outcomes of the neighbors then SAR is applicable. In such circumstances, if we ignore the spatial dependencies then we end up in a biased and inconsistent estimator of the regression parameters. If the error term depends on its spatial lag, then we have problems related to inconsistent estimates of the standard error. Therefore, the hypothesis testing exercises may be questionable. Nevertheless, if the sample size is long enough then ignoring the spatial dependencies of the error term may not be problematic. Apart from the SAR and SEM models, one model that economists take special interest in, is the spatial Durbin models (SDM). The spatial Durbin model is applicable whenever the spatial lag of the explanatory variable(s) affects the dependent variable. Note that one may include SAR, SEM, and SDM in a general model, with the same or different spatial weight matrices.

The models discussed in the previous paragraph can be estimated by the Maximum Likelihood methods (MLE) introduced in Anselin (1980). For further discussions, interested authors are referred to Anselin and Bera (1998), Lee (2004), and LeSage and Pace (2009). These models can also be estimated by the generalized method of moments (GMM). The MLE is computationally more challenging particularly when the number of spatial units is too high. GMM, on the other hand, does not suffer from such problems. Furthermore, after the influential article by Kelejian and Purcha (2010), GMM methods are more popular to correct for heteroskedasticity, and also in the context of modeling with some endogenous explanatory variables.

The rest of the article is organized as follows. In Sect. 7.2, we discuss the concept of spatial randomness, where we construct some simulated data without any spatial dependency. This section perhaps will help the readers to identify some situations where spatial models are inappropriate. Section 7.3 discusses the role of spatial weight matrix. In this section, we discuss the following three types of widely used weight matrices: contiguity weight matrices, inverse distance-based weight matrices, and economic distance-based weight matrices. In Sect. 7.4, we discuss the three spatial lag models SAR, SEM, and SDM; in a more technical way. Section 7.5 discusses the estimation methodologies of the spatial lag models. Section 7.6 presents an empirical illustration of these models with Indian data. We would like to highlight here that this section also illustrates the basics of executing spatial models in Stata 15. The next section discusses some advanced topics like: spatial models with higher order lags, spatial panel data models, and endogenous spatial weight matrices. Finally, we conclude this chapter in Sect. 7.7.

7.2 Spatial Weight Matrix

The first step for the formulation of any spatial econometric model is to specify the spatial weight matrix. This matrix captures the pairwise spatial dependence across all individuals. Therefore, if the number of observations is n (where $n > 1$), then the spatial weight matrix is nothing but a square matrix of order $n \times n$. Let $W = \{w_{ij}\}_{n\times n}$ be the spatial matrix. The i, jth row-column combination of the matrix (i.e., w_{ij}) captures the spatial dependence between i and j. If $w_{ij} = 0$, then there is no spatial dependence between i and j. On the contrary as w_{ij} increases then the spatial dependence between the i and j also increases. In many cases, the dependence between *i* and *j* is the same as that of *j* and *i*, therefore intuitively $w_{ij} = w_{ji}$ and thus W matrix, by construction is symmetric. However, for the sake of computation and interpretation of the result, we often need to consider a row-standardized weights matrix, which can be expressed as follows: $W^s = \left\{\frac{w_{ij}}{w_{i.}}\right\}_{n\times n}$, where $w_{i.} = \sum_{j\in\{1,2,\ldots,n\}} w_{ij}$. The advantage of using row-standardized matrix is that the elements of the matrix always belong in the closed interval [0, 1], and therefore the spatial lag can be expressed as the weighted average of the neighboring regions. In order to establish this point, we provide some numerical examples later in this section.

7.2.1 *Types of Spatial Weight Matrix*

Usually, it has been observed that there are three types of weight matrices typically used in spatial data analysis. These are contiguity, inverse distance, and economic distance-based weight matrices.

7.2.1.1 Spatial Contiguity Matrices

Spatial contiguity matrix is one of the most frequently used spatial weight matrices in the literature. The basic idea is that if two units (say, *i* and *j*) are neighbors, then $w_{ij} = 1$, else $w_{ij} = 0$. By neighbors, we mean here that *i* and *j* share a common geographic border. Usually, there are three types of contiguity-based weight matrices, namely, the (a) Rook contiguity, (b) the Queen contiguity, and (c) the Bishop Contiguity. In the rook contiguity matrix, vertices are excluded from the definition of neighbors. On the other hand, in Queen's contiguity, vertices are included. However, in Bishop's contiguity, which although is rare in practice, but includes only vertices of the spatial units of the analysis. To highlight the details, we consider the following six hypothetical regions in the graph:

Here, the vertices of A are B, D, F, and H. Therefore, of rook contiguity I, C, E, and G are the neighbors of A. On the other hand, by Queen contiguity everyone is a neighbor of A. Using the same logic, we can also define contiguity-based neighbors of other regions.

7.2.1.2 Inverse-Distance-Based Weight Matrices

The second most widely used spatial weight matrix is the inverse distance-based weight matrix. Following Tobler's law, one may assume that if any two regions *i* and *j* are far from each other, then their spatial dependencies will also be low. Similarly, if the two regions are close to each other, then their spatial dependencies will be high.

Thus, the *i, j*th element of the spatial weight matrix takes the following functional form: $w_{ij} = \frac{1}{d_{ij}}$ if $i \neq j$ and 0 otherwise. One can formulate other formulas in a similar fashion, for example , $w_{ij} = \frac{1}{d_{ij}^2}$.

The University of Texas has made access to geospatial data of many administrative regions of different countries across the globe. With such datasets, one can calculate the distance between two regions, very easily.

7.2.1.3 Economic-Distance-Based Weight Matrices

We can also formulate a spatial weight matrix based on the idea of economic distance. To illustrate its applications, think about the well-established trade network that operates at the global level. Two countries may be neighbors but they may not trade with each other. On the contrary, two countries may be trading partners in spite of the fact that they are located a thousand miles apart. For example, the United States of America is far from India, but USA is one of the dominant trading partners of India.

The fact is that in many cases, two regions though may be close in terms of geographical distance, do not necessarily give rise to an agglomeration of a certain economic phenomenon, while two regions far apart (geographically) behave quite similarly in respect of certain economic phenomenon. One has then, reason to believe that the economic distance between the regions is higher in the first case and lower in case of the latter. It follows that geographical and economic distances have different implications as regards interactions among regional units, the former identifying the similarities across contiguous regional units while the latter capturing the same among units with identical characteristics and economic structures. Case et al. (1993) have suggested the notion of economic distance as $w_{ij} = \frac{1}{|x_i - x_j|}$ if $i \neq j$, and 0 otherwise. X_I and x_j are observations of some meaningful socioeconomic characteristics of regions i and j such as per capita income or percentage of the population in each racial or ethnic group.[3]

7.2.1.4 Specification of a Spatial Weight Matrix

We must keep in mind the following issues while specifying the spatial weight matrix:

(1) All elements of the spatial weight matrix (i.e., w_{ij}) are exogenously given.
(2) Diagonal elements of a spatial weight matrix are always 0.

[3] The concept of distance may be fundamentally related to the notion of space. The latter is a multifaceted concept and cannot be explicitly defined, as such, that is suitable for all purposes. The Earth's surface with its complex physical variations represents the geographic space. The idea of a socioeconomic space is built upon a much higher level of generality compared to that of a geographic space. This denotes the total integrated social and economic space as coming out of the activities of the human community (Chojnicki, 1970).

(3) It is always better to consider a row-standardized spatial weight matrix, because in such cases, one can interpret the spatial parameters in a more meaningful way.
(4) The elements of the spatial weight matrix must be nonnegative and finite, and they should correspond to a proper metric. Sometimes formulations of the matrix may not be a proper matrix. For example, think of an economic distance-based weight matrix computed by the formula $w_{ij} = \frac{1}{|x_i - x_j|}$. If $x_i = x_j$, then w_{ij} is undefined. In such cases, we need to specify w_{ij} explicitly.

7.3 Spatial Lag Models

7.3.1 *The Concept of Spatial Lag*

Spatial lag of a variable y is defined as the value of y at its neighboring regions. If a certain region (say i) has only one neighbor (say j), then y_j is the spatial lag for y_i. On the other hand, if i has more than one neighbor, then the spatial lag of i is nothing but the average values of y at the neighboring regions, provided that we are using row-standardized spatial weight matrix.

We provide a numerical illustration of spatial lags using the following variable that contains data for three regions: $y = \begin{bmatrix} y_1 \\ y_2 \\ y_3 \end{bmatrix}$. Let the spatial dependence of these three regions be captured by the following rook-contiguity spatial weight matrix: $W = \begin{bmatrix} 0\,1\,0 \\ 1\,0\,1 \\ 0\,1\,0 \end{bmatrix}$. Thus, region 2 has two neighbors 1 and 3. On the other hand, regions 1 and 3 have one common neighbor "2". The row-standardized weights matrix of W can be written as follows: $W_1 = \begin{bmatrix} 0\,1\,0 \\ \frac{1}{2}\,0\,\frac{1}{2} \\ 0\,1\,0 \end{bmatrix}$. Therefore, the spatial lag of regions 1 and 3 are the same and equal to y_2, whereas spatial lag for individual 2 will be the average of y_1 and y_3. The spatial lags for all three regions are captured in the vector $W_1 y = \begin{bmatrix} y_2 \\ \frac{y_1 + y_3}{2} \\ y_2 \end{bmatrix}$. $W_1 Y$ is also referred to as the spatial effects of the first-order contiguous neighbors. Let us now discuss the idea of neighbor's neighbor. Region 1's neighbor is 2. Therefore regions 1's neighbor's neighbor are the neighbors of 2, which is 1 itself and 3. Similarly, region 2's neighbor's neighbor are the neighbors of 1 and 3, which happens only to be 2 itself. The second-order contiguous neighbor is captured in the following vector: $W_1^2 y = \begin{bmatrix} \frac{y_1+y_2}{2} \\ y_2 \\ \frac{y_1+y_2}{2} \end{bmatrix}$. For any finite k, we can easily extend this definition to the case of kth-order contiguous neighbors. Note that the notion of average will no longer be applicable if we do not consider row-standardized weight matrices. Interested readers can check this using the same numerical example, but using the weight matrix W instead of W_1.

7.3.1.1 Spatial *Versus* Temporal Lags

Spatial lag and temporal lags (i.e., lags frequently used in time series econometrics) have close resemblances. However, the movement of time is unidirectional; therefore, lag values in a time series model have only unidirectional causality. For example, in a standard AR (1) model $y_t = \rho y_{t-1} + \epsilon_t$ (where, ϵ is a white noise term) y_{t-1} is always exogenous, and the reverse causal model can be easily nullified. In fact, in many econometric exercises, the lagged values of a variable are often considered as a good instrument. In a spatial model, the effects of lags are bi-directional because if certain outcomes of i affect that of j, then the outcomes of j may also affect the outcomes of i. This bi-directional casualty creates a kind of simultaneity bias in some special cases. In this section, we give special attention to illustrate this point on the types of spatial regression models that need special attention for this classic endogenity problem.

7.3.2 Spatial Lag Dependence

7.3.2.1 Spatial Autoregressive Models

Like the $AR(1)$ model we can also define a Spatial Autoregressive (SAR) model of order 1 as follows:

$$y = \rho W y + X\beta + \epsilon \quad (7.1)$$

where W is a $n \times n$ spatial weight matrix, y is the dependent variable with n observations, X is a $n \times k$ matrix containing data on K explanatory variables, β is a $k \times 1$ vector of parameters, ϵ is a $n \times 1$ vector of error terms. We assume that X is of full column rank and there is no correlation between any of the elements of X and the error term. The error term also is assumed to satisfy all the standard OLS assumptions.

As discussed earlier, if W is a row standardized spatial weight matrix, then Wy is nothing but the weighted average of the neighboring regions. The estimate of ρ captures the neighborhood effect of the dependent variable. If the standard stationary conditions are satisfied (i.e., $0 \leq |\rho| \leq 1$), then we can rewrite Eq. (7.1) as follows:

$$y = (I - \rho W)^{-1} X\beta + (I - \rho W)^{-1}\epsilon \tag{7.2}$$

Equation (7.2) is also known as the reduced form model. We can further rewrite Eq. (7.2) as follows:

$$y = \left(1 + \rho W + \rho^2 W^2 + \ldots\right)(X\beta + \epsilon) \tag{7.3}$$

One can also write Eq. (7.1) as a spatial filter model as follows

$$y^* = (I - \rho W)\mathrm{y} = X\beta + \epsilon \tag{7.4}$$

The variable y^* may be interpreted as the spatially filtered version of y. The notion of spatial filter is very similar to the first difference operator frequently used in time series econometrics models. To highlight this, consider the following AR(1) model: $\mathrm{y_t} = \delta \mathrm{y_{t-1}} + \epsilon_t$. Here, ϵ_t is a white noise residual. In order to check the stationary of equation, we need to consider the first difference operator as follows:

$$\Delta y_t = y_t - y_{t-1} = \delta y_{t-1} + \epsilon_t \tag{7.5}$$

Notice the difference between Eqs. (7.4) and (7.5). The time series filtering as defined in Eq. (7.5) is quite straightforward, and it can be computed without much difficulty. However, the problem with Eq. (7.4) is that we need to estimate the parameter ρ in order to apply the spatial filter. Interestingly if $\rho = 0$ then there is no spatial dependence, and then Eq. (7.5) is nothing but a mere cross-sectional regression equation model.

We now discuss an important question. What happens if we ignore the spatial dependence among the observations? To be more precise, instead of applying the spatial filtering, suppose we go for a simple linear regression like $\mathrm{y} = X\beta + \epsilon$, i.e., we put $\rho = 0$ by force. In such cases, the parameters will be inconsistent. We multiply the Left-Hand Side (LHS) and Right-Hand Side (RHS) of Eq. (7.2) to get the following equation:

$$Wy = W(I - \rho W)^{-1} X\beta + W(I - \rho W)^{-1}\epsilon \tag{7.6}$$

Given Eq. (7.6), it is quite straightforward to check that $\mathrm{Cov(Wy, \epsilon)} \neq 0$. Hence, the standard CLRM assumption will be violated, i.e., some of the explanatory variables will be correlated with the error term. If we exclude Wy from the regression equation, then the presence of X on the RHS of Eq. (7.6) will create a kind of omitted variable bias in the regression equation defined in (1). Note that we can deal with this endogeneity either by using Maximum Likelihood Methods or by the Generalized Method of Moments (GMM). We discuss both the methodologies in the next section.

The advantage of the SAR model is that it captures the direct and indirect impacts of all the covariates used in the regression Eq. (7.1). To illustrate the decomposition, we first write the following expression of the conditional expectation:

$$E(y_i|x_l) = v_{ii}x_{li}\beta_l + \sum_{j=1,j\neq i}^{n} v_{ij}x_{lj}\beta_l \tag{7.7}$$

where v_{ij} is the ijth element of the matrix $V = (I_n - \rho W)^{-1}$.

The first term of Eq. (7.7) gives the direct effect of x_{li} on the outcome of individual i (i.e., y_i). This effect is also referred to as the own effect, since the change in a certain covariate in place *i* affects the outcome in the same place. The second term gives the indirect effect, which is also popularly referred to as the "*spill-over effects*." The rationality for calling this a spill-over effect is the fact that the change of x_l in region j effects the region *i*'s outcome. Therefore, differentiating Eq. (7.7), we w.r.t. x_l gives us the following expression:

$$\frac{\partial E(y_i|x_l)}{\partial x_l} = v_{ii}\beta_l + \sum_{j=1,j\neq i}^{n} v_{ij}\beta_l \tag{7.8}$$

The left-hand side of Eq. (7.8) is nothing but the marginal effect of x_l. The first term of the RHS in the same equation is nothing but the direct impact, whereas the second term is the spill-over effect. We have *n* different marginal effects for n different individuals. Therefore, a summary statistic of the marginal effects can be captured using the average marginal effects in the following fashion:

$$\text{Average Marginal Own Effects of } x_l = \frac{\beta_l \sum_{i=1}^{n} v_{ii}}{n} \tag{7.9}$$

$$\text{Average Marginal Spillover Effects of } x_l = \frac{\beta_l \sum_{i=1}^{n} \sum_{j=1,j\neq i}^{n} v_{ij}}{n} \tag{7.10}$$

We shall discuss in detail how the average marginal effects can be computed in the statistical software Stata 15.

7.3.2.2 Spatial Error Models

Another popular way of incorporating spatial dependencies is the Spatial Error Model (SEM), which captures spatial dependency only on the error term. To be more precise, the SEM model can be expressed by the following linear regression equation

$$y = X\beta + e \tag{7.11}$$

In the above equation, *e* is non-spherical, because it is spatially dependent in the following fashion:

$$e = \lambda We + \eta \tag{7.12}$$

In Eq. (7.12), λ stands for the spatial autoregressive coefficient of the error term. In general, it is assumed that η is a white noise type error term that satisfies all standard OLS assumptions. SEM model can also be expressed in the folllowing fashion:

$$y = X\beta + (I - \lambda W)^{-1}\eta \tag{7.13}$$

If, $0 < |\lambda| < 1$, then the model can also be expressed as follows:

$$y = X\beta + \left(1 + \lambda W + \lambda^2 W^2 + \ldots\right)\eta \tag{7.14}$$

Note that in the SEM model, consistency of the parameters β is not an issue. However, the estimates of the standard error will be inconsistent if estimated following the usual OLS methodology. Therefore, the hypothesis testing exercise will be questionable, unless special attention is taken care of. This is like any classic problem in the linear regression setup, whenever the error term is non-sperical, may be due to heteroskedasticity in the residual series. Note that, if the sample size is large enough, then we can ignore this problem.

Unlike the SAR model, there are no spillover effects here, and therefore, $\frac{\partial E(y_i|x_l)}{\partial x_l} = \beta_l$.

7.3.3 Spatial Durbin Model

In some cases, it is possible that the explanatory variables are spatially dependent. The model in that case looks like

$$y = X\beta + \gamma WZ + \epsilon \tag{7.15}$$

Here, Z is some explanatory variable(s). Thus, WZ is nothing but the effects of the neighboring values of the variable Z. Note that unless there is some systematic correlation between the error term and the explanatory variables, the estimated parameters will be consistent in general. This model in general can be estimated using standard approaches.

7.3.4 A General Model

A general spatial model will look like

$$y = \rho W_1 y + X\beta + \gamma W_2 Z + \epsilon + \lambda W_3 \epsilon \tag{7.16}$$

Although the above model looks very general, there are serious issues with working on such a general model. First, the interpretations of the spillovers are not straightforward. Secondly, the inclusion of spatial dependencies from so many directions may increase the chances of having more insignificant coefficients. Therefore, it is advised that unless there is a strong theoretical justification, it is better to avoid such models.

7.4 Estimation Techniques

In the literature, there are two widely used techniques for estimating the spatial models. The first is the Maximum Likelihood Method (MLE), and the second is the Generalized Method of Moments (GMM). In this section, we provide a brief discussion of both these methodologies.

7.4.1 *Maximum Likelihood Method (MLE)*

The method of Maximum Likelihood was introduced by the well-known geneticist and statistician R. A. Fisher in the 1920s. This method works well whenever the sample size is large enough. To illustrate the basics of MLE, let us consider X_1, X_2,...,X_n as random variables with joint pmf or pdf as $f(x_1, x_2, \ldots, x_n; \theta_1, \theta_2, \ldots, \theta_m)$, where $x_1, x_2, \ldots,$ and x_n are the observed values of the random variables X_1, X_2,..., and X_n, respectively. $\theta_1, \theta_2, \ldots, \theta_m$ are the parameters of interest. The maximum likelihood estimates $\widehat{\theta}_1, \widehat{\theta}_2, \ldots, \widehat{\theta}_m$ are those values of θ's such that $f\left(x_1, x_2, \ldots, x_n; \widehat{\theta}_1, \widehat{\theta}_2, \ldots, \widehat{\theta}_m\right) \geq f(x_1, x_2, \ldots, x_n; \theta_1, \theta_2, \ldots, \theta_m)$ for all $\theta_1, \theta_2, \ldots, \theta_m$. The procedure to the find the MLE estimators is usually by construction of the log-likelihood function, which is nothing but the joint distribution (i.e., the function f). If the observations are independent and identically distributed then $l = f\left(x_1, x_2, \ldots, x_n; \widehat{\theta}_1, \widehat{\theta}_2, \ldots, \widehat{\theta}_m\right) = \prod_{i=1}^{n} f_{X_i}(x_i, \theta_i)$, and therefore the log-likelihood function can be expressed as $\mathrm{L} = \ln(l) = \sum_{i=1}^{n} \ln(f_{X_i}(x_i, \theta_i)$. This simplification is not applicable in the spatial context because the observations are not *iid*.

7.4.1.1 MLE for the Spatial Autoregressive Model

To highlight how the MLE method works for a SAR model, we begin with the simple case without any spatial dependence (i.e., $\rho = 0$). Furthermore, we assume that the error term ϵ follows a multivariate normal distribution with zero mean and the variance–covariance (VARCOV) matrix Σ (i.e., $\epsilon \sim MVN(0, \Sigma)$). In that case, the log-likelihood function might be written as

$$L = -\frac{n}{2}\ln(2\pi) - \frac{1}{2}\ln(|\Sigma|) - \frac{1}{2}\epsilon'\Sigma^{-1}\epsilon \quad (7.17)$$

Assuming that there is no heteroskedasticity, $\Sigma = \sigma^2 I_n$, therefore $|\Sigma| = \sigma^2 n$. Thus, the first two terms are essentially constants and therefore maximizing the log-likelihood in Eq. (7.17) is nothing but a problem of minimizing the quadratic form $\frac{1}{2}\epsilon'\Sigma^{-1}\epsilon$.

Maximum Likelihood Method for the SAR model is also based on the multivariate normality of the error term. The error term for a SAR model can be expressed as follows: $\epsilon = (I - \rho W)y - X\beta$. Or, in other words, ϵ is a function of y. Let the function be $\epsilon = g(y)$. Using the rules of Jacobian, we can write $|J| = \left|\frac{\partial g}{\partial P}\right| = |I - \rho W|$. Notice that the value of this Jacobian is 1 in the case of linear regression equation models. Hence, transformation of variables from y to ϵ is straightforward in a classicial regression model setup. However, in the case of a SAR model, it is not. The multivariate normality assumption allows us to express the VARCOV matrix as follows: $|\Sigma| = \sigma^{\mathrm{n}} \times |I - \rho W|$, therefore $\ln(|\Sigma|) = \frac{\mathrm{n}^2}{2}\ln(\sigma^2) + \ln(|I - \rho W|)$. Using the notions of spatial filter (y^*) formally defined in Eq. (7.4), we may write: $\frac{1}{2}\epsilon'\Sigma^{-1}\epsilon = \frac{(y^*-X\beta)'(y^*-X\beta)}{2\sigma^2}$. Hence, the log-likelihood function for a SAR model can be expressed as follows:

$$L = -\frac{n}{2}\ln(2\pi) - \frac{n}{2}\ln(\sigma^2) - \ln(|I - \rho W| - \frac{(y^* - X\beta)'(y^* - X\beta)}{2\sigma^2}) \quad (7.18)$$

We would once again like to highlight the basic differences between the likelihood functions for the non-spatial and the spatial models defined in Eqs. (7.17) and (7.18), respectively. In Eq. (7.17), $\rho = 0$, and therefore the Jacobian term (i.e., $\ln(|I - \rho W|)$ disappears, and also $y^* = y$. Hence, the log-likelihood function defined in (7.17) is a special case of Eq. (7.18). Or, in other words, the log-likelihood for the OLS is a nested model of SAR. This property will help us in designing the model specification tests discussed later in Sect. 7.5.

One can further simplify the Likelihood function specified in Eq. (7.18) by considering a result from Ord (1975), where the author shows that $|I - \rho W|$ can be expressed as the Eigen values of the spatial matrix denoted by w_i in the following fashion:

$$|I - \rho W| = \prod_{i=1}^{n}(1 - \rho w_i) \quad (7.19)$$

Therefore, we can rewrite Eq. (7.18) as follows:

$$L = -\frac{n}{2}\ln(2\pi) - \frac{n}{2}\ln(\sigma^2) - \sum_{i=1}^{n}\ln(1 - \rho w_i) - \frac{(y^* - X\beta)'(y^* - X\beta)}{2\sigma^2} \quad (7.20)$$

To estimate the parameters from Eq. (7.20), we need to maximize the log-likelihood function. In general, these methods are dependent on numerical optimization techniques. We first estimate β and σ^2 from Eq. (7.20) for some given ρ (say ρ^*). Define $B = I - \rho^* W$. The first-order condition for maximizing Eq. (7.20) turns out as follows:

$$\widehat{\beta}_{ML} = \left(X'X\right)^{-1} X'By = \beta_0 - \rho^* \beta_L. \tag{7.21}$$

where $\beta_0 = \left(X'X\right)^{-1} X'y$ and $\beta_L = \left(X'X\right)^{-1} X'Wy$. Furthermore, the estimator of standard error can be expressed as follows:

$$\widehat{\sigma}^2_{ML} = \left(e_0 - \rho^* e_L\right)'\left(e_0 - \rho^* e_L\right) \tag{7.22}$$

where $e_0 = y - X\beta_0$, $e_L = y - X\beta_L$.

We now return to the problem of estimating ρ. For this exercise, we need to write the concentrated log-likelihood function (or profile likelihood function) as follows:

$$L = -\frac{n \ln\left[\frac{(e_0 - \rho^* e_L)'(e_0 - \rho^* e_L)}{n}\right]}{2} + \ln(|B|) = -\frac{n \ln\left[\frac{(e_0 - \rho^* e_L)'(e_0 - \rho^* e_L)}{n}\right]}{2} + \ln(I - \rho^* W) \tag{7.23}$$

Equation (7.23) is a function of a single parameter ρ^* that we can estimate from the same equation. Interestingly, the parameter space from this equation depends on the Eigen values of the spatial weights matrix. To be precise $\frac{1}{w_{\min}} < \rho < \frac{1}{w_{\max}}$, where $w_{\max}$ and $w_{\min}$ are the maximum and the minimum Eigen values, respectively. In the standard case, the weights matrix is row-standarized, where $w_{\max} > 1$, hence $\rho < 1$. However, the lower bound can be less than -1.

We are not presenting the estimates of the standard errors of the SAR parameters. Interested readers are referred to Anselin and Bera (1998) for this issue.

7.4.1.2 MLE for the Spatial Error Model

For the SEM model, the main problem is that the error term is non-spereical in nature. The VARCOV matrix for a spatial model (formally defined in Eq. 7.12) can be expressed as follows $E\left(ee'\right) = \sigma^2\left[(I - \lambda W)'(I - \lambda W)\right]^{-1}$. Let

$$G(\lambda) = \left[(I - \lambda W)'(I - \lambda W)\right]^{-1} \tag{7.24}$$

Therefore, $E\left(ee'\right) = \sigma^2 G(\lambda)$. Here, λ is a nuisance parameter, in the sense that it has no direct interest in itself. To be precise, unlike ρ in the SAR model, which illustrates the spatial dependency of the dependent variable, λ has no such intuitive appeal. Nevertheless, λ plays an important role in the context of estimating $\widehat{\beta}$. Recall that $\widehat{\beta}$ is consistent even if we ignore the spatial structure. However, the estimated standard errors of $\widehat{\beta}$ is inconsistent. In the rest of this section, we shall highlight the issue of estimating $\widehat{\beta}$ in a more efficient way following the MLE method.

The spatially filtered values of X, y, and e in the present context can be expressed as $\tilde{X} = (I - \lambda W)X$, $\tilde{y} = (I - \lambda W)y$, and $\tilde{e} = (I - \lambda W)(y - X\beta)$, respectively. Under normality assumption of the error term, the log-likelihood function can be expressed as follows:

$$\mathrm{L} = \ln(|G(\lambda)|) - \frac{n}{2}\ln(2\pi) - \frac{n}{2}\ln(\sigma^2) - \frac{\tilde{e}'G(\lambda)^{-1}\tilde{e}}{2\sigma^2} \tag{7.25}$$

The first-order conditions from Eq. (7.25) will lead us to familiar "*Feasible Generalized Least Square*" (FGLS) estimates of the parameters β and σ^2, conditioned on λ. Thus,

$$\widehat{\beta}_{FGLS} = \left[X'G(\lambda)^{-1}X\right]^{-1}X'G(\lambda)^{-1}y \tag{7.26}$$

From Eq. (7.24), we can easily derive $G(\lambda)^{-1} = \sigma^2[(I - \lambda W)'(I - \lambda W)]$, following which we can modify Eq. (7.26) as follows:

$$\widehat{\beta}_{FGLS} = \left[X'(I - \lambda W)'(I - \lambda W)X\right]^{-1}X'(I - \lambda W)'(I - \lambda W)y \tag{7.27}$$

We can rewrite Eq. (7.27) as follows:

$$\widehat{\beta}_{FGLS} = \left(\tilde{X}'\tilde{X}\right)^{-1}\tilde{X}'\tilde{Y} \tag{7.28}$$

The above estimator is also known as the spatial Cochrane–Orcutt estimator. The standard error of the estimates can be written as follows:

$$\widehat{\sigma}^2{}_{FGLS} = \sigma^2\left(\tilde{X}'\tilde{X}\right)^{-1} \tag{7.29}$$

Note that the estimators in Eqs. (7.28) and (7.29) are conditioned on λ. Therefore, it is necessary to estimate λ, which is not straightforward in this context, because if we regress $\hat{e} = \alpha + \lambda W\hat{e} + u$, the estimator $\widehat{\lambda}$ will be inconsistent. A consistent estimator of λ is possible in the same way we did for the SAR model, i.e., we write the concentrated log-likelihood, which is only a function of λ and then estimate it by standard numerical optimization techniques. We do not discuss the methodology here. Interested readers are referred to Anselin and Bera (1998).

7.4.2 Generalized Method of Moments

Method of moments (MOM) is the oldest estimation methodology. To illustrate the basics of MOM, consider X_1, X_2,...,X_n as random variables with joint pmf or pdf as $f(x_1, x_2, \ldots, x_n; \theta_1, \theta_2, \ldots, \theta_m)$, where $x_1, x_2, \ldots,$ and x_n are the observed values of the random variables X_1, X_2,..., and X_n, respectively, and $\theta_1, \theta_2, \ldots, \theta_m$ are the unknown parameters. The MOM estimators $\widehat{\theta}_1, \widehat{\theta}_2, \ldots, \widehat{\theta}_m$ are obtained by equating the first m sample moments to the corresponding population moments. Hence, there will be m equations and m unknowns. To be more precise, the kth equation is

$$E\left(X^k\right) = \frac{1}{n}\sum_{i=1}^{n} X_i^k \tag{7.30}$$

The Generalized method of moments (GMM) is applicable whenever the number of equations is more than the number of unknowns. A classic example is the case of a system of overidentified equation(s), in a simultaneous equation setup. In such cases, one may apply the standard two-stage least squares methods for consistent estimation of the parameters. If the number of equatuions is greater than the number of the parameters, then all equations will deliver a consistent estimator. However, GMM is an efficient way of estimating the unknown parameters. The basic idea for GMM is to minimize a weighted least square, where estimators with lower variance get more weightage compared to those estimators with higher variance. To be more precise, the optimization exercise is carried out in a way that the individual equations are weighted in accordance with the inverse of their variance. Note that given the variables are random in nature, and therefore we can also refer the equations as random equations and evaluate their variances accordingly. This methodology can be extended for the estimation of the parameters of an SEM model.

7.4.2.1 Spatial Autoregressive Models (GMM Framework)

MLE has two serious limitations. Firstly, MLE may be challenging particularly when the size of the matrix is large enough. For example, even if we simplify the likelihood equation using the Ord's formula expressed in Eq. (7.20), we still have to compute the n Eigen values of the weight matrix, which might be computationally challenging particularly when n is very large. Interested readers are referred to p. 514 of Kelejian and Prucha (1999), where this issue has been discussed at length. The second problem is that the MLE methodology is dependent on the strong distributional assumption of multivariate normality of the error term. Kelejian and Prucha (1999) have illustrated that in many practical situations, this assumption is questionable. The same authors are also one of the pioneers in developing the GMM estimating methodology for the SAR model.

The main problem in an SAR model is that the spatially lagged variable Wy and the error terms are correlated, which violates one of the basic CLRM assumptions. We have highlighted this problem by specifying the reduced form equation in Eq. (7.6), and then illustrating the rationale for $Cov(Wy, X) \neq 0$. An easy solution for this problem is to find some valid instruments of Wy. By valid instruments, we mean those instruments which are highly correlated with Wy, but uncorrelated with the error term. The first criterion is also known as the relevance of the instruments or the instruments are not weak, whereas the second criterion stands for the exogenetic condition of the instruments. Kelejan and Robinson (1993, p. 302) showed that such instruments can be constructed from the system itself. In fact, the set of instruments are $(WX, WX^2, \ldots)$. We now discuss the basic intuition of why such instruments are valid. We can rewrite Eq. (7.6) as follows

$$Wy = \left(1 + \rho W + \rho^2 W^2 + \ldots\right) X\beta + \left(1 + \rho W + \rho^2 W^2 + \ldots\right)\epsilon \qquad (7.31)$$

Given Eq. (7.27), it is quite straightforward to check that $Cov(WX, Wy) \neq 0$, $Cov\left(W^2X^2, Wy\right) \neq 0$, and so on. Furthermore, as long as the elements of X are exogeneous, the exogenity condition of the instruments can also be verified without much difficulties.

We now have a set of valid instruments which may be used for consistent estimation of the parameters of an SAR model using the two-stage least square (2SLS) methodology. Let the set of instruments be the matrix Q. Therefore, a consistent estimator of the parameters of the SAR model can be written as follows:

$$\widehat{\beta}_{2SLS} = \left[Z'Q(Q'Q)^{-1}Q'Z\right]^{-1} Z'Q(Q'Q)^{-1}Q'P \qquad (7.32)$$

where Z = [WP X]. The asymptotic variance turns out to be

$$Var\left(\widehat{\beta}_{2SLS}\right) = \sigma^2\left[Z'Q(Q'Q)^{-1}Q'Z\right]^{-1} \qquad (7.33)$$

where σ^2 is estimated from the residuals in the standard procedure.

7.4.2.2 Spatial Error Models (GMM Framework)

Recall the spatial error model as specified in Eqs. (7.11) and (7.12) are as follows: $y = X\beta + e$ where $e = \lambda We + \eta$. We need to make two crucial assumptions about η in order to apply the spatial GMM models to estimate the parameter vectors β and λ.

Assumption 7.1: η is independent and identically distributed with constant variance σ^2.

Assumption 7.2: The diagonal element of the matrix W is 0.

Following Assumption 7.2, we can also write the sum of the elements of the diagonal elements of W is also 0, i.e., $tr(W) = 0$.

Kelejian and Purcha (1998) were one of the pioneers in introducing the spatial GMM models, for the SEM model. The authors first introduced a concept that allows us to consistently estimate the parameter λ. Unlike the ML method, estimation of $\widehat{\lambda}$ is simple. However, the proof that $\widehat{\lambda}$ is consistent requires some advanced asypmtotic theories, and is thus omitted in this discussion. Readers interested in the proof are referred to Kelejian and Purcha (1998). On the basis of the two assumptions (Assumptions 7.1 and 7.2) we can write the following moment conditions:

$$E\left(\frac{\eta'\eta}{n}\right) = \sigma^2 \tag{7.34}$$

$$E\left(\frac{\eta' W' W\eta}{n}\right) = \frac{\sigma^2 tr(W'W)}{n} \tag{7.35}$$

$$E\left(\frac{\eta' W'\eta}{n}\right) = 0 \tag{7.36}$$

Equation (7.36) is a straightforward application of Assumption 7.1. Notice that the order of the matrix $\epsilon' W' W\epsilon$ is 1×1 i.e., it is a scalar. The RHS is also a scalar. To illustrate how we derive this expression consider $n = 2$, $\epsilon = \begin{bmatrix} \eta_1 \\ \eta_2 \end{bmatrix}$ and$W = \begin{bmatrix} 0 & w_{12} \\ w_{21} & 0 \end{bmatrix}$. In this example:

$$\eta' W' W\eta = [\,\eta_1\ \eta_2\,]\begin{bmatrix} 0 & w_{12} \\ w_{21} & 0 \end{bmatrix}\begin{bmatrix} 0 & w_{21} \\ w_{12} & 0 \end{bmatrix}\begin{bmatrix} \eta_1 \\ \eta_2 \end{bmatrix} = [\,\eta_1^2 w_{12}^2\ \eta_2^2 w_{21}^2\,] \tag{7.37}$$

Therefore, the LHS of Eq. (7.37) for the two variable cases can be expressed in the following fashion: $E\left(\frac{\eta' W' W\eta}{2}\right) = \frac{E(\eta_1^2 w_{12}^2) + E(\eta_2^2 w_{21}^2)}{2}$. Since W matrix is exogeneously given, it is non-stochastic, therefore we can always take the elements of W outside the expectation operator. Hence, $E\left(\frac{\eta' W' W\eta}{2}\right) = \frac{w_{12}^2 E(\eta_1^2) + w_{21}^2 E(\eta_2^2)}{2} = \frac{\sigma^2(w_{12}^2 + w_{21}^2)}{2}$. It is quite straightforward to check that $tr(W'W) = w_{12}^2 + w_{21}^2$. Hence, $E\left(\frac{\eta' W' W\eta}{2}\right) = \frac{\sigma^2 tr(W'W)}{2}$ that is what we get in Eq. (7.37). The same expression can be extended for any $n > 2$. Note that the example if $n > 2$, then the $tr(W'W)$ will also involve some cross-product terms.

The logic behind (7.38) is much in line with (7.37). The only difference is that, in the former, we have the matrix $W'W$, whereas for the latter, the matrix is W'. Since $W'W$ and W' are of the same orders, therefore we can write applying the rules $E\left(\frac{\eta' W'\eta}{n}\right) = \frac{\sigma^2 tr(W')}{n}$ and given the assumption $tr(W') = 0$, the third-moment condition is obtained easily.

Our objective is to now equate the sample and population monets. Note that from the regression equation $y = X\beta + e$, we can estimate the residual which we define as

$\hat{e}$. We know that $e = \lambda We + \eta$, which implies $\eta = (I - \lambda W)e$ is a kind of spatially filtered variable. Given we have predicted $\hat{e}$, therefore we can write $\hat{\eta} = \hat{e} - \lambda W\hat{e}$. We denote the first and second-order spatial lags of the residual as follows: $\hat{e}_L = W\hat{e}$ and $\hat{e}_{LL} = W\hat{e}_L$. Given $\hat{e}$ and W are known, therefore $\hat{e}_L$ and $\hat{e}_{LL}$ are also known. In order to get the sample counterparts of Eqs. (7.36), (7.37), and (7.38), we replace η by $\hat{\eta}$. After some simple matrix operations, we get the following three conditions:

$$\left(\frac{2\hat{e}'_L\hat{e}_L}{n}\right)\lambda - \left(\frac{\hat{e}'_L\hat{e}_L}{n}\right)\lambda^2 + \sigma^2 = \frac{\hat{e}'\hat{e}}{n} \tag{7.38}$$

$$\left(\frac{2\hat{e}'_{LL}\hat{e}_L}{n}\right)\lambda - \left(\frac{\hat{e}'_{LL}\hat{e}_{LL}}{n}\right)\lambda^2 + \frac{\sigma^2 tr(W'W)}{n} = \frac{\hat{e}'_L\hat{e}_L}{n} \tag{7.39}$$

$$\left(\frac{\hat{e}'_{LL}\hat{e} + \hat{e}'_L\hat{e}_L}{n}\right)\lambda - \left(\frac{\hat{e}'_{LL}\hat{e}_L}{n}\right)\lambda^2 = \frac{\hat{e}'_L\hat{e}}{n} \tag{7.40}$$

Notice that the RHS of the sample moment conditions specified in the above three equations are known. Hence. from these equations. we can solve for λ and σ^2. The main interest here is on the parameter λ. It can be shown that the estimated value of λ is consistent (Kelijan and Purcha 1998). Once we have a consistent estimator for λ (denoted by $\hat{\lambda}$), then in the next step, we can easily estimate the parameter vectors following a standard FGLS model. The formula turns out as follows:

$$\hat{\beta}_{FGLS} = \left[X'\left(I - \hat{\lambda}W\right)'\left(I - \hat{\lambda}W\right)X\right]^{-1} X'\left(I - \hat{\lambda}W\right)'\left(I - \hat{\lambda}W\right)y \tag{7.41}$$

The variance can be estimated using the estimated values of λ and σ^2 (i.e., $\hat{\lambda}$ and $\hat{\sigma}^2$)

$$Var\left(\hat{\beta}_{FGLS}\right) = \hat{\sigma}^2\left[\left(X - \hat{\lambda}WX\right)'\left(X - \hat{\lambda}WX\right)\right]^{-1} \tag{7.42}$$

Heteroskedasticity Problems in Spatial Error Models

One practical problem while dealing with SEM models is heteroskedasticity of the residual series. This problem arises naturally even when η is homoscedastic. This can be easily figured from the construction of the VARCOV matrix in the following expression[4]

$$E\left(ee'\right) = \sigma^2(I - \lambda W)(I - \lambda W)^{-1} \tag{7.43}$$

[4] Note that Eq. (7.38) can be derived by expressing the error term $e = \lambda We + \eta$ as $e = (I - \lambda W)^{-1}\eta$. We also need Assumption 7.1 (i.e., $E(\eta'\eta) = \sigma^2$).

Following the lines of Anselin and Bera (1998), Eq. (7.44) exposes the following two problems of SEM models: (a) SEM leads to a nonzero error covariance between every pair of observations, but decreases in magnitude with the order of contiguity, and (b) the diagonal elements are non-constant and therefore the regression model suffers from heteroskedasticity. Kelejian and Prucha (2010) have extended the GMM methods that address this problem. This is an important extension in the spatial literature and empirical researchers must include the heteroskedasticity correction suggested by these authors. The discussion of Kelejian and Prucha (2010)'s methodology is beyond the scope of the present chapter, and is thus omitted. Statistical software's like Stata 15 incorporates Kelejian and Prucha (2010)'s extension. We get back to incorporating the heteroskedasticity in the error term in the empirical illustrations section.

Estimation of Advanced Models by GMM

Note that Kelejian and Prucha (2010) also discuss how to estimate a SARSAR model like

$$y = \rho W_1 y + X\beta + \epsilon + \lambda W_2 \epsilon \tag{7.44}$$

In Eq. (7.46), we can estimate a model with spatial dependence not only in the dependent variable, but also in the error term. Such models will be computationally more challenging by the ML methods and are advised to be estimated using the GMM-based methods. The authors also extend the GMM methodology in the context where some of the X variables are correlated with the error term. We skip the details of these extensions in this chapter.

7.5 Model Specification Tests

Anselin (1980) broadly classifies specification tests into two types, namely, the diffuse tests, and the focused tests. The diffuse test detects the possible presence of spatial dependencies. One of the most widely used diffuse tests for checking the presence of special dependencies is the Moran's I. The test is very powerful and if it detects spatial dependency, we need to take care of some of the spatial models discussed in Sect. 7.5. Nevertheless, the problem with the diffuse test is that, it never allows us to identify whether the underlying model should be SAR, SEM, or some combination of SAR and SEM. For the latter, we need to concentrate more on the focused tests. The main idea here comes from the classic testing procedures between the constrained (restricted) and the unconstrained (unrestricted) models.

7.5.1 Diffuse Tests

We now discuss the widely used diffused test, namely, the Moran's I. To illustrate Moran's I, we consider the following regression equation: $y = X\beta + u$, where y is a $n \times 1$ vector, X is a $n \times k$ matrix containing all the explanatory variables, β is a parameter vector of $k \times 1$ vector of parameters, u may have some kind of spatial dependency, which we need to test, but we have to rely on the standard non-stochastic assumption for all the explanatory variables. Let $\widehat{u}$ denote the vector of estimated residuals. The Moran's I test statistics can be written as follows:

$$I = \left(\frac{\widehat{u}' W \widehat{u}}{\widehat{u}' \widehat{u}} \right) \times \frac{n}{S_0} \tag{7.45}$$

where $S_0 =$ trace of the matrix W. For a row standardized matrix $S_0 = n$. Therefore, the Moran's I test statistics for turns out to be: $I = \left(\frac{\widehat{u}' W \widehat{u}}{\widehat{u}' \widehat{u}} \right)$, which is nothing but the correlation coefficient between the residual and its spatial lag (i.e., $W\widehat{u}$). The functional form of the test statistics whenever W is row standardized, also bears a close resemblance with the Durbin-Watson test statistics for testing the presence of autocorrelation in time series variables. It may be noted here that the value of the index is contingent on the values of the weight matrix. Thus, the correlation coefficient is meaningful only when the weights matrix is specified correctly.

Under the null hypothesis of no global spatial autocorrelation, the expected value of I is given by $\mathrm{E(I)} = -\frac{1}{\mathrm{n}-1}$. If I is larger than its expected value, then the overall distribution of variable y can be seen as characterized by positive spatial autocorrelation, meaning that the value taken by y at each location i tends to be like the values taken by y at spatially contiguous locations. On the other hand, if I is smaller than its expected value, then the overall distribution of the variable can be seen as characterized by negative spatial autocorrelation, meaning that the value taken on by y at each location i tends to be different from the values taken on by y at spatially contiguous locations. Moran's I is an inferential statistic. Empirical distribution is compared with the theoretical distribution. Inference is based on the construction of z-scores, computed by subtracting E(I) from I and dividing the result by the standard deviation of I (denoted by $sd(I)$. Thus, $Z_I = \frac{I - E(I)}{sd(I)}$ is the test statistics, which follows standard normal distribution.

7.5.2 Focussed Tests

In general, there are three types of tests based on the MLE framework for executing the focused test; namely, the Wald, Likelihood Ratio, and the Lagrange Multiplier tests. In general, the principle of testing for these tests' statistics is based on the idea to distinguish between a constrained model and an unconstrained model. The null hypothesis for all these testing schemes there is no distinction between the constrained and the unconstrained model. Therefore, unless we reject the null, it is better to stick to the constrained model, since that is a model with higher degrees of freedom. Note that for all the three tests, the restricted model is the OLS.

7.5.2.1 Wald Test

We first discuss Wald's test. The null hypothesis for an SAR model is $\rho = 0$ whereas for an SEM model, the null hypothesis is $\lambda = 0$. Hence the restricted model for both SAR and SEM models is the OLS. Wald test is always formulated on the basis of the unrestricted model only. Wald test is routinely reported in Stata 15 and we also discuss how to interpret in the empirical sections of this paper. The functional form of the Wald test is based on the testing procedure for the multiple hypotheses of linear restrictions of the form $\mathrm{R}\beta = \mathrm{r}$, where R is a $q \times k$ $(k \geq q)$ matrix of known constraints and containing the restrictions, r is a $q \times 1$ known vector, and β is the parameter vector $k \times 1$. Let V be the variance-covriance matrix of β. The functional form of the test statistics can be written as follows:

$$W = (R\beta - r)'\left(RVR'\right)^{-1}(R\beta - r) \sim \chi_q^2 \tag{7.46}$$

A special case of the Wald statistics defined above is to test the null hypothesis $\rho = 0$ or $\lambda = 0$(i.e., the OLS model) against SAR and SEM, respectively. In such cases, the Wald statistics thus out to be the square of z statistics. Formally:

$$W = \frac{\rho^2}{asyVar(\rho)} \tag{7.47}$$

where $W \sim \chi^2(1)$ distribution. If we fail to reject the null hypothesis by the Wald test statistics, then we may conclude that statistically, there is not much distinction between the OLS and spatial model. Hence, it is better to use the OLS model in such cases.

7.5.2.2 Lagrange Multilier Test

The LM test (popularly known as the Score test) is based on the gradient or slope of the log-likelihood: $s(\theta) = \frac{\partial L(\theta)}{\partial \theta}$. The unrestricted parameter ($\widehat{\theta}$) is solved by setting the partial derivative of the log-likelihood function to be 0. Then, the score vector is evaluated under the unrestricted parameter (say $\widetilde{\theta}$). Let $s\left(\widetilde{\theta}\right)$ be the gradient vector evaluated at the null. If the restrictions are valid, then $s\left(\widetilde{\theta}\right)$ should also be close to zero. The score vector always has zero mean and the variance–covariance matrix is provided by the information matrix $I(\theta)$. The quadratic form $s'(\theta)I^{-1}(\theta)s(\theta)$

exhibits a χ^2 distribution. Furthermore, the same quadratic form at the null hypothesis $\theta = \tilde{\theta}$ can be written as follows:

$$LM = s'\left(\tilde{\theta}\right)I^{-1}\left(\tilde{\theta}\right)s\left(\tilde{\theta}\right) \sim \chi^2(q) \quad (7.48)$$

The advantage of the LM test is that each element is evaluated at the null hypothesis (i.e., $\theta = \tilde{\theta}$). This is completely opposite to that of the Wald test statistics.

7.5.2.3 Likelihood Ratio Test

In order to conduct the Likelihood Ratio (LR) test we need to run both the constrained and unconstrained models. The functional form of LR can be written as follows:

$$LR = 2(L_{OLS} - L_{UR}) \sim \chi_q^2 \quad (7.49)$$

where L_{OLS} and L_{UR} are the log likelihood obtained from the OLS (which is the restricted model) and the unrestricted models (either SAR or SEM model). Note that, for conducting the LR test, we need to estimate both the restricted and the unrestricted models. This is why it is also considered as a very powerful test compared to the Wald and LM tests.[5]

7.6 Empirical Illustrations

In this section, we illustrate how to apply spatial models using real-life data sets.

7.6.1 Data

The main variable required for the present exercise is income. We use data from National Sample Survey Organisation (NSSO). The survey provides a national representative sample at the all-India level. NSSO collects only monthly per capita consumption expenditure (MPCE) data and thus, MPCE is often considered as a proxy of per-capita income and all poverty-related statistics are computed using MPCE. NSSO conducts a program of quinquennial surveys on consumer expenditure and provides a time series of household consumer expenditure data, which is the prime source of statistical indicators of level of living, social consumption, and well-being, and the inequalities thereof.

[5] Greene (2003)

Note that there is a gap in standard of living between rural and urban India. In this chapter, we are going to use the ratio of poverty line as the difference of standard of living in rural and urban India. Data on poverty lines are available at the state level. Let z_{rs} and z_{us} be the rural and urban poverty lines for state s. We deflate the per-capita expenditures of urban India by the ratio $\frac{z_{rs}}{z_{us}}$. Therefore, all data points are converted in terms of the rural living standards. Furthermore, given everything has been converted in the scale of rural incomes, therefore, we may use the rural poverty line as the national poverty line. We use the transformed data set of MPCE and then compute: (a) Head Count Ratio (b) Gini Coefficient and (c) Per-capita expenditure at the district level. Note that some districts may not have adequate samples, for such cases, the estimated values of (a), (b), and (c) may not be consistent. Such problems can be addressed using Small Area Estimation techniques (see (Coondoo et al. 2011)). For the sake of simplicity and to remain focused on the current topic, we ignore this problem here.

7.6.2 *Graphical Illustrations*

In order to illustrate the main variables used for the present analysis consider a society with n individuals. The income (i.e., MPCE) of individual $i \in \{1, 2, \ldots, n\}$ is denoted by y_i where $y_I > 0 \forall i$. Let $z > 0$ denote the poverty line of society which is exogenously given. The Head Count Ratio (HCR) is defined as the percentage of individuals whose income is less than or equal to z. We use Gini as the measure of income inequality. It captures the interpersonal income differences of all individuals. For any income distribution $y = (y_1, y_2, \ldots, y_n) \in \mathbb{R}^n_{++}$ where $\mu(y) = \frac{\sum_{i=1}^n y_i}{n}$ is the mean income of y. Formally, Gini is defined as follows:

$$Gini(y) = \frac{\sum_{i=1}^n \sum_{i=1}^n |y_i - y_j|}{2n^2 \mu(y)} \tag{7.50}$$

Note that, if all individuals have equal income then there is no inequality in the society, therefore $Gini(y) = 0$. Further Gini is maximum $(Gini(y) \approx 1)$ if a single individual has access to all income and the rest of the individuals have zero income. Note that NSSO considers Monthly Per Capita Expenditure (MPCE) as a proxy of income. We use the same to compute Gini, HCR, and Per-capita expenditure (i.e., $\mu(y)$).

In Fig. 7.1, we present the Head Count Ratio for different districts of India. The more dark a region, higher the incidence of poverty in that region. For example, it can be figured out very easily that most of the high-density poverty regions are located in parts of Bihar and eastern regions of Uttar Pradesh. In fact, some parts of the north-eastern states also exhibit a high degree of poverty. On the contrary, the southern states are relatively richer. Thus, we may expect that poverty is spatially dependent. The spatial dependence may arise because of the fact that most of the

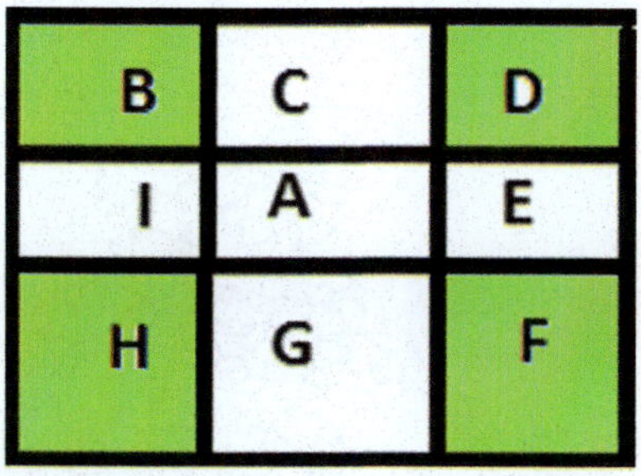

Fig. 7.1 Rook contiguity matrix of order 3

states are administrated by the same government. Furthermore, many other factors like unemployment rates, illiteracy, inflation, etc., are in general clustered in some specific regions and these factors play an active role in determining the poverty status of a region. For further illustrations on this issue, interested readers are referred to Sarkar and Das (2018) (Fig. 7.2).[6]

7.6.3 Detection of Spatial Dependence Using Moran's I

As discussed earlier, Moran's I is one of the most powerful statistics to detect the presence of spatial dependency. We first run the following regression

$$HCR_i = \beta_0 + \beta_1 Gini_i + \beta_2 MPCE_i + \epsilon_i \tag{7.51}$$

Assuming the error term is orthogonal to the explanatory variables and is also homoskedastic, our next objective is to test whether the error term exhibits any spatial dependence or not. We use Moran's I for this purpose. We present the results in Table 7.1.

It is quite straightforward to check that the coefficients associated lnMPCE and lnGini are highly significant and are also of appropriate signs. However, following the Moran's *I* test statistics, we may reject the null hypothesis that the error is independent and identically distributed. Therefore, we cannot reject the case of spatial dependencies. However, we do not know whether this spatial dependency can be handled by SAR, SEM, or some other spatial models. This is a classic problem of all diffuse tests, as discussed earlier. We need a focused test for this purpose. We discuss the results associated with the focus test later in this section.

[6] See Chattopadhyay et al. (2014) for another application of spatial regression analysis in the context of estimation of poverty using the NSS data (Using STATA).

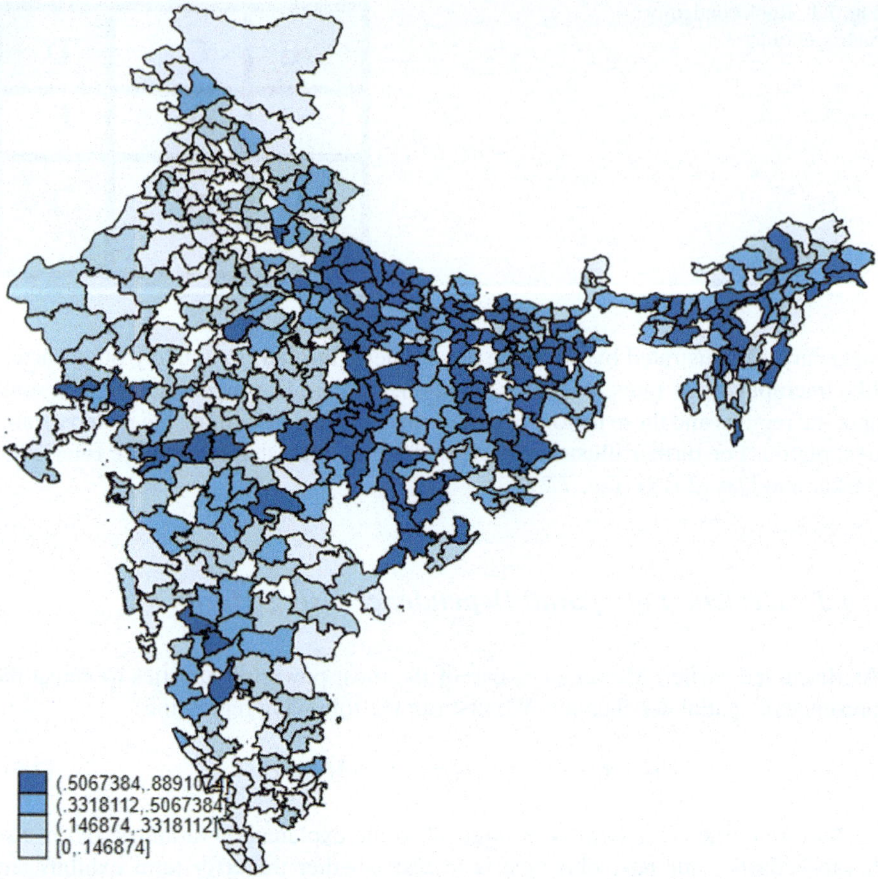

Fig. 7.2 Head count ratio across Indian districts

Table 7.1 Testing spatial dependency using Moran's I

Variables	Estimates
lnMPCE	−0.596(0.013)***
lnGini	0.235(0.020)***
Constant	3.931(0.089)***
Model diagnostics	
Number of Observations	521
R2	0.805
Adjusted R2	0.804
Morans test for spatial dependence	150.40***

7.6.4 Estimation of SAR Model

SAR model for this excrcise thus can be written as follows:

$$HCR_i = \beta_0 + \rho \sum_{j=1}^{n} w_{ij} HCR_j + \beta_1 Gini_i + \beta_2 MPCE_i + \epsilon_i \tag{7.52}$$

The above equation suggests that poverty in district i depends on a weighted average of the poverty of its neighboring districts and is also a linear function of some covariates. We choose the weight matrix using the otion of a contiguity distance-based matrix. The details of the calculation of weights are provided in the appendix. Parameters of Eq. (7.52) can be estimated either by the MLE or the GMM methods discussed earlier. Table 7.2 presents the results associated with the Maximum Likelihood methods.

Note that the spatial autoregressive term is positive and is highly significant. The value of the parameter is 0.346. Therefore, if the poverty of the neighborhood of region i increases by 1 unit, then the poverty of unit i may increase by 0.345 units. In order to interpret the coefficents, it is better to use the direct and indirect impacts, as specified earlier. We can also compute these impacts in Stata 15. These results are presented in the same table as direct, indirect, and total impacts. Note that the total impact for these estimates are nothing but the sum of the direct and indirect impacts. Tables 7.3 and 7.4, repeats the same results following GMM and GMM with heteroskedasticity correction. Since the results are more or less similar, we do not discuss these issues in detail

In Tables 7.2, 7.3, and 7.4 we also present two important Wald test statistics. Wald chi2(2), is a classic Wald test (see Eq. 7.41) where the null hypothesis is $H_0 : \rho = \beta_1 = \beta_2 = 0$. The null is rejected, in all the three tables, which implies at least one of the parameters is significant, however, which parameter is significant is not identified. To check the significance of the parameters, we need to go for the z

Table 7.2 Estimation of spatial autoregressive models ML

Variables	Estimates	Direct impact	Indirect impact	Total impact
lnMPCE	−0.556(0.017)***	−0.556***	−0.293***	−0.849***
lnGini	0.223(0.020)***	0.223***	0.118**	0.341***
_cons	3.553(0.133)***			
ρ	0.346(0.092)***			
$var(\rho)$	0.009(0.001)***			
Model diagnostics				
Number of observations:		521		
Wald chi2(2)		1672.89***		
Pseudo R2		0.804		
Wald test of error terms		470.55***		

Table 7.3 Estimation of spatial autoregressive models GMM

Variables	Estimates	Direct impact	Indirect impact	Total impact
lnMPCE	−0.570(0.017)***	−0.570***	−0.165*	−0.736***
lnGini	0.227(0.020)***	0.227***	0.066*	0.293***
ρ	3.685(0.137)***			
$var(\rho)$	0.225(0.096)***			
Model diagnostics				
Number of observations		521		
Wald chi2(2)		2209.94		
Pseudo R2		0.804		
Wald test of error terms		5.46**		

Table 7.4 Estimation of spatial autoregressive models GMM (Heteroskedasticity correction)

Variables	Estimates	Direct impact	Indirect impact	Total impact
lnMPCE	−0.570(0.019)***	−0.570***	−0.165*	−0.736***
lnGini	0.227(0.024)***	0.227***	0.066*	0.293***
ρ	3.685(0.157)***			
$var(\rho)$	0.225(0.097)***			
Model diagnostics				
Number of observations		521		
Wald chi2(2)		2178.58***		
Pseudo R2		0.804		
Wald test of error terms		5.44**		

tests. The spatial lag can be tested using $H_0 : \rho = 0$ or by the square of Z statistics. Notice that the Wald test presented at the bottom of the three tables is nothing but the approximate square of the Z value corresponding to the estimate of the spatial autoregressive parameter.

7.6.5 Estimation of SEM Model

The equation for the SEM model can be written as follows:

$$HCR_i = \beta_0 + \beta_1 Gini_i + \beta_2 MPCE_i + \eta_i \tag{7.53}$$

where $\eta_i = \epsilon + \lambda \sum_{j=1}^{n} w_{ij} \epsilon_j$.

Recall that the problem of SEM is not on an estimation of the parameter, rather estimation of the standard errors. We present the Stata output for the SEM model in Table 7.5.

The model suggests the presence of spatial dependence also in the error term. However, further introspections of the models are required to determine the model that will be a kind of best fit. One important discussion we would like to highlight here is that, unlike the SAR model, there are no direct and indirect impacts in the SEM model. In fact, the direct effect equals to the total impact in this context.

In Sect. 4.2.2.1, we discussed the advantages of estimating the SEM model using the GMM, in the sense that we can control heteroskedasicity problems to a large extent. To highlight this, we present the results associated with models without and with heteroskedasticity correction in Tables 7.6 and 7.7, respectively. It can be checked that the estimators are the same, but the standard errors are different. This is precisely what happens when we correct for non-spherical errors. The values of λ are slightly different.

Table 7.5 Maximum likelihood estimation of an SEM model

Variables	Estimates	Direct impact	Indirect impact	Total impact
lnMPCE	−0.600(0.015)***	−0.600***	0	−0.600***
lnGini	0.261(0.020)***	0.261***	0	0.261***
_cons	3.871(0.133)***			
λ	0.955(0.044)***			
$var(\lambda)$	0.008(0.001)***			
Number of observations		521		
Wald chi2(2)		1673.89***		
Pseudo R2		0.805		
Wald test of error terms		470.55***		

Table 7.6 SEM model without heteroskedasticity correction

Variables	Estimates	Direct impact	Indirect impact	Total impact
lnMPCE	−0.613(0.017)***	−0.613***	0	−0.613***
lnGini	0.271(0.020)***	0.271***	0	0.271***
λ	3.934(0.104)***			
$var(\lambda)$	2.734(0.480)***			
Number of observations	521			
Wald chi2(2)	1413.69***			
Pseudo R2	0.804			
Wald test of error terms	32.17***			

Table 7.7 SEM model with heteroskedasticity correction

Variables	Estimates	Direct impact	Indirect impact	Total impact
lnMPCE	−0.613(0.022)***	−0.613***	0	−0.613***
lnGini	0.271(0.024)***	0.271***	0	0.271***
λ	3.934(0.140)***			
$var(\lambda)$	2.724(0.476)***			
Number of observations	521			
Wald chi2(2)	776.76***			
Pseudo R2	0.804			
Wald test of error terms	33.01***			

7.7 Concluding Remarks

This chapter attempts to present the major issues related to spatial regression models. The chapter will be helpful for researchers handling spatial data for the first time. The concepts of spatial weights and the associated spatial lag operator, which allow for the formal specification of neighbors in space, have been highlighted with special care, so that beginners may appreciate the key distinction between spatial and temporal lags. Two key estimation methodologies in spatial econometrics, namely, the maximum likelihood approach as well as the generalized method of moments are discussed at length. We also highlight the details of model specification tests frequently used in spatial econometrics.

Nevertheless, by no means, this text is complete. Many challenging problems particularly in the context of panel data econometrics in a spatial framework have not been discussed much. Note that, as discussed multiple times in the main text that failing to model spatial dependencies of the dependent variable may lead to an inconsistent estimation of the parameters, particularly if the dependent variable exhibits spatial dependencies. However, there should be enough theoretical background for the execution of spatial models. Forcefully executing a spatial econometric model may lead to inconsistent estimators of the parameters and the standard errors.

Let us end this discussion with a brief mention of an advanced topic "endogenous spatial matrices," related to the theory and empirics presented in the chapter. Throughout this chapter, we assumed that the elements of the spatial weight matrix are exogenously given. However, researchers have made substantial progress in estimating the relationship between different spatial entries from the data itself. One major contribution in this context is by Basak et al. (2018), where the authors estimate the spatial interactions in the weights matrix using the notion of the Directed Acyclic Graph (DAG). DAG is very frequently used in the causal inference literature pioneered by Pearl et al. (2009). Interested readers may refer to Pearl et al. (2009) for a basic introduction to causal graphs and causal inference.

Appendix: Software Illustrations

Spatial Regression models can be executed in many softwares like R, Geodaspace, Stata 15, etc. In this short note, we discuss the basics of how to execute standard SAR and SEM models in Stata 15. To be more precise, we elaborate on how researchers can execute the models using the **SP** commands.

Formulation of the Weight Matrix and Declare the Data Set to Be Sp Spatial Data

Declare the dataset as spatial data. For this exercise, we need to specify the weights matrix. For incorporating a geographic distance-based matrix, we need to download Shapefile first, which provides coordinates of different regions. Based on these coordinates, one can easily compute the geographical distances. You can download shapefiles from this website https://geodata.lib.utexas.edu/catalog/stanford-sh819zz8121.

Once the shapefile is available, we need to convert it into.dta file that Stata can read. For example, "polbnda_ind.shp" is the file that contains data on Indian districts.

Use the following code for this

shp2dta using "polbnda_ind.shp", database("india_dist_data") coordinates("india_coordinates_dist.dta") genid(id) gencentroids(X) replace

The next two commands help us to formulate an inverse distance-based matrix and contiguity matrix:

spset id

spset, modify shpfile(india_coordinates_dist.dta)

spmatrix create idistance W, normalize(row) replace

spmatrix create contiguity Wc, normalize(row) second replace

Make sure you use the appropriate path for using the file *india_coordinates_dist.dta.*

spset is used for declaring the dataset as spatial data. Remember, for declaring dataset time series or panel data, we use a similar code called **xtset**.

Generating maps of different countries.

We have used the following codes to generate the map of India.

*spmap x using india_coordinates_dist.dta, id(id) fcolor(Blues) clnumber(5) legend(symy(*2) symx(*1) size(*1)) legorder(lohi) title("Fig. 7.1: Graphical Illustrations of Spatial Randomness", size(*0.8))*

Note that the dataset "*india_coordinates_dist.dta*" must be stored in the directory.

Estimation Using progress Stata 15 command:

Model	ML	GMM
SAR	spregress y x, ml dvarlag(Wc)	spregress y x, gs2sls dvarlag(W)
SAR (with heteroskedasticity correction)	NA	spregress y x, gs2sls dvarlag (W) heteroskedastic
SEM	spregress y x, ml errorlag(W) heteroskedastic	
SEM (with heteroskedasticity correction)	NA	spregress y x, gs2sls errorlag(W) heteroskedastic
SARSAR	spregress y x, ml dvarlag(W) errorlag(W2)	
Spatial Durbin	spregress y x, gs2sls ivarlag(W1: z) nolog	spregress y x, ml ivarlag(W1: z) nolog

References

Anselin L (1980) Estimation methods for spatial autoregressive structures. Regional Science Dissertation and Monograph Series 8. Field of Regional Science, Cornell University, Ithaca, N.Y

Anselin L, Bera AK (1998) Spatial dependence in linear regression models with an introduction to spatial econometrics. In: Ullah A, Giles DE (eds) Handbook of applied economic statistics. Marcel Dekker, New York, pp 237–289

Basak KG, Bhattacharjee A, Das S (2018) Causal ordering and inference on acyclic networks. Empir Econ 55:213–232

Case AC, Rosen HS, Hines JR (1993) Budget spillovers and fiscal policy interdependence: evidence from the states. J Public Econ 52(3):285–307

Chattopadhyay S, Majumder A, Jaman H (2014) Decomposition of inter-regional poverty gap in India: a spatial approach. Empir Econ 46(1):65–99

Chojnicki Z (1970) Distance concepts in socio-economic space analysis. http://igsegp.amu.edu.pl/wp-content/uploads/2018/05/Chojnicki_1970_a_EN-1.pdf

Coondoo D, Majumder A, Chattopadhyay S (2011) District-level poverty estimation: a proposed method. J Appl Stat 38(10):2327–2343

Gibson J, Olivia S (2007) Spatial autocorrelation and non-farm rural enterprises in Indonesia. In: 51st Conference on the Australian agricultural and resource economics society, 13–16 Feb 2007

Greene WH (2003) Econometric analysis. Pearson Education, India

Kelejian H, Prucha I (1998) A generalized spatial two-stage least squares procedure for estimating a spatial autoregressive disturbances. J Real Estate Finance Econ 17:99–121

Kelejian H, Prucha I (1999) A generalized moments estimator for the autoregressive parameter in a spatial model. Int Econ Rev 40:509–533

Kelejian HH, Prucha IR (2010) Specification and estimation of spatial autoregressive models with autoregressive and heteroskedastic disturbances. J Econ 157(1):53–67

Kelejian HH, Robinson DP (1993) A suggested method of estimation for spatial interdependent models with autocorrelated errors and an application to a county expenditure model. Pap Reg Sci 72:297–312

Krugman PR (1991) Geography and Trade. Cambridge, MA: MIT Press

LeSage J, Pace RK (2009) Introduction to spatial econometrics. Chapman and Hall/CRC

Nicholson W, Snyder CM (2012) Microeconomic theory: basic principles and extensions. Cengage Learning

Ord K (1975) Estimation methods for models of spatial interaction. J Am Stat Assoc 70:120–126

Pearl J (2009) Causal inference in statistics: an overview. Stat Surv 3:96–146

Sarkar S, Das S (2018) Interrelationship between poverty, growth, and inequality in India: a spatial approach. In: Dasgupta R (ed) Advances in growth curve and structural equation modeling: topics from the Indian statistical institute on the 125th birth anniversary of PC Mahalanobis. Springer, Singapore, pp 77–99

Tiefelsdorf M (1998) Modelling spatial processes: the identification and analysis of spatial relationships in regression residuals by means of Moran's I (Germany). Theses and dissertations (Comprehensive), vol 480. https://scholars.wlu.ca/etd/480

Tobler W (1970) A computer movie simulating urban growth in the detroit region. Econ Geogr 46(2):234–240

Varian HR (2014) Intermediate microeconomics with calculus: a modern approach. WW Norton & Company

Chapter 8
Hurdle Regression Models: An Application to Consumer Behavior in the United States

Fabrizio Carlevaro and Yves Croissant

Abstract Hurdle regression models are regression models where the dependent variable is left censored at zero, which is typically the case in household expenditure surveys. These models are of particular interest to explain the presence of a large proportion of zero observations for the dependent variable by means of censoring mechanisms, called hurdles. For the analysis of censored household expenditure data, up to three hurdles, expressing, respectively, a good selection mechanism, a desired consumption mechanism, and a purchasing mechanism, have been suggested by the econometric literature. This chapter presents the methodology for specifying single, double, or triple hurdle regression models based on these censoring mechanisms in a fully parametric form and to estimate them using the maximum likelihood method for random samples. Model evaluation and selection are tackled by means of goodness of fit measures and Shi's corrected Vuong tests. The practical use of this modeling methodology is illustrated with a real-world data set using an **R** package, especially developed for this purpose.

Keywords Limited dependent variable · Hurdle regression · Censored regression · Consumer demand · Household expenditure survey data

This chapter presents the econometric methodology coded in version 1.3-0 of the mhurdle **R** package (Croissant et al. 2021), first developed as part of a Ph.D. dissertation carried out by Hoareau (2009) at the University of Reunion under the supervision of professors Fabrizio Carlevaro and Yves Croissant. An application of this package is provided using a survey data set publicly available on the website of the Bureau of Labor Statistics of the U.S. Department of Labor: https://www.bls.gov/cex/.

Supplementary Information The online version contains supplementary material available at https://doi.org/10.1007/978-981-99-4902-1_8.

F. Carlevaro
Geneva School of Economics and Management, University of Geneva, Uni Mail Bd. du Pont-d'Arve 40, 1211 Geneva 4, Switzerland
e-mail: fabrizio.carlevaro@unige.ch

Y. Croissant (✉)
CEMOI, Faculty of Law and Economics, University of Reunion, 15 Av. René Cassin, CS 92003, 97744, Saint Denis Cedex 9, France
e-mail: yves.croissant@univ-reunion.fr

D. Mukherjee (ed.), *Applied Econometric Analysis Using Cross Section and Panel Data*, Contributions to Economics, https://doi.org/10.1007/978-981-99-4902-1_8

8.1 Introduction

Data collected by means of households' expenditure survey may present a large proportion of zero expenditures due to many households recording, for one reason or another, no expenditure for some items. Analyzing these data requires to model any expenditure with a large proportion of nil observations as a dependent variable left censored at zero.

Since the seminal paper of Tobin (1958), a large econometric literature has been developed to correctly deal with this problem of zero observations. In applied microeconometrics, different decision mechanisms have been put forward to explain the appearance of zero expenditure observations. The original Tobin's model takes only one of these mechanisms into account. With hurdle regression models, more mechanisms generating zero expenditure observations may be introduced in a consumer expenditure model. This chapter considers the three main zero expenditure-generating mechanisms suggested by the econometric literature to analyze the data provided by consumer expenditure surveys.

A good selection mechanism (hurdle 1). According to this mechanism, the consumer[1] first decides which goods to include in its choice set and, as a consequence, he can discard some marketed goods because he dislikes them (like meat for vegetarians or wine for non-drinkers) or considers them harmful (like alcohol, cigarettes, inorganic food, holidays in dangerous countries), among others.
This censoring mechanism has been introduced in empirical demand analysis by Cragg (1971). It allows to account for the non-consumption of a good as a consequence of a fundamentally non-economic decision motivated by ethical, psychological, or social considerations altering the consumer's preferences.

A desired consumption mechanism (hurdle 2). According to this mechanism, once a good has been selected, the consumer decides which amount to consume and, as a consequence of his preferences, resources and selected good prices, its rational decision can turn out to be a negative desired consumption level leading to a nil consumption.
The use of this mechanism, to explain the presence of zero observations in family expenditure surveys, was introduced by Tobin (1958). Its theoretical relevance has been later rationalized by the existence of corner solutions to the microeconomic problem of rational choice of the neoclassical consumer.[2] Cragg (1971)'s combination of this desired consumption mechanism and the selection mechanism leads to a double hurdle model which has been extended by Blundell and Meghir (1987) to the case where the two equations are correlated.

---

[1] The consumer we are referring to is that of the microeconomic theory, an abstract economic agent responsible for the decisions of a consumption unit that may be an individual, a family, and a household. According to the economic literature, we term this concept the "consumer" by convenience.

[2] For an elementary presentation of this issue see Sect. 10.2 of Amemiya (1985), and Chap. 4 of Pudney (1989) for a more comprehensive one.

A purchasing mechanism (hurdle 3). According to this mechanism, once a consumption decision has been taken, the consumer sets up the schedule at which to buy the good and, as a consequence of its purchasing strategy, a zero expenditure may be observed if the survey by which these data are collected is carried out over a too short period of time with respect to the frequency at which the good is bought.
This censoring mechanism has been introduced in empirical demand analysis by Deaton and Irish (1984). It allows to account for the non-purchase of a good not because the good is not consumed, but because it is an infrequently bought good or service. This is typically the case for durable or storable non-durable goods, but also for many infrequently bought services like health, leisure, education, and training services. Remarkably, this mechanism allows to derive from observed expenditures the rate of use of a durable good, the rate of consumption of a stored non-durable good, and the rate of purchase of an infrequently consumed non-storable non-durable good or service.

For each of these censoring mechanisms, a continuous latent variable is defined, indicating that censoring is in effect when the latent variable is negative. These latent variables are modeled as functions of explanatory variables and of a random disturbance, with a possible correlation between the disturbances of different latent variables in order to account for a possible simultaneity of the decisions modeled by censoring mechanisms. To model possible departures of the observed dependent variable from normality, as it is common with economic variables, we use transformations of this variable allowing to rescale non-normal random variables to normality. By combining part or the whole set of these censoring mechanisms, we generate a set of parametric models that can be used to explain censored expenditure data depending on the structural censoring mechanisms that a priori information suggests to be at work.

These formal models have been primarily developed to deal with censored household expenditure data, and numerous applications have been carried out in this field. Complementing a previous survey by Smith (2002), we give in the appendix a more updated overview of these studies. We note a late popularity of Cragg's approach, as the first applications of hurdle models are published in the late of 1980s, namely almost two decades after the publication of Cragg (1971)'s paper. Since then, a large variety of consumer demand models including one or two among the previous three censoring mechanisms are estimated. However, none of these studies use the three censoring mechanisms we consider, jointly. From the 1990s on, many studies account for deviations of the desired consumption relation to homoscedasticity and normality by modeling the standard error of this variable as a non-negative parametric function of some explanatory variables and by transforming its distribution to normality using either the logarithmic, the Box–Cox, or the inverse hyperbolic sine transformations. The estimation of a correlation coefficient between disturbances is also performed in several of these studies, with an increasing success over time, in terms of statistical significance of estimates.

The practical scope of hurdle regression models is not restricted to empirical consumer demand analysis but has been fruitfully used in other fields of economics. This includes labor economics, contingent valuation studies, finance, sport activities, internet use, gambling, and production.

Our hurdle regression models are specified as fully parametric models allowing estimation and inference within an efficient maximum likelihood framework. In order to identify a relevant model specification, we use goodness of fit measures for model evaluation as well as Vuong tests for discriminating between nested and non-nested models. Vuong tests remarkably permit to compare two competing models when neither of them contains the true mechanism generating the sample of observations. More precisely, such tests allow to assess which of the two competing models is closest to the true unknown model according to the Kullback–Leibler information criterion. Therefore, such tests are not intended, as classical Neyman–Pearson tests, to pinpoint the chimeric true model, but to identify, with respect to available observations, a best parametric model specification among a set of competing specifications. As a consequence, they can provide inconclusive results, which prevent from disentangling some competing models, and when they are conclusive, they don't guarantee an identification of the relevant model specification.

The chapter is organized as follows: Sect. 8.2 presents the rationale of our modeling strategy. Section 8.3 presents the theoretical framework for model estimation, evaluation, selection, and prediction. Section 8.4 illustrates the use of our hurdle regression models with a real-world data set of household expenditures using **R**'s mhurdle 1.3-0 package enabling the estimation, evaluation, selection, and prediction of our wide set of single, double, and triple hurdle regression models.

Sections 8.2 and 8.3 present the rationale of our modeling strategy in a formal manner. This might discourage uninitiated readers, unfamiliar with an advanced theory of econometrics and statistics. To these readers we suggest, in order to understand the rationale and the scope of the procedures presented in these sections, to refer to their applications based on a real-life data case within Sect. 8.4.

8.2 Modeling Strategy

Our modeling strategy is intended to model the level y of expenditures of a consumer for a given good or service during a given period of observation. For this purpose, we use up to three zero expenditure generating mechanisms, called hurdles, and a demand function.

8.2.1 Model Specification

Each hurdle is represented by a qualitative binary response model resting on one of the following three latent dependent variables relations:

$$\begin{cases} y_1^* = \beta_1^\top x_1 + z_1 \\ T(y_2^*) = \beta_2^\top x_2 + \sigma z_2 \\ y_3^* = \beta_3^\top x_3 + z_3 \end{cases} \tag{8.1}$$

where y_1^*, y_2^*, y_3^* stand for continuous latent dependent variables; x_1, x_2, x_3 for column-vectors of explanatory variables (called covariates in the followings); β_1, β_2, β_3 for column-vectors of the impact coefficients of the covariates on the latent dependent variables; and z_1, z_2, z_3 for standard normal random disturbances. Since variables y_1^* and y_3^* are never observed, contrary to y_2^*, the units of measurement of y_1^* and y_3^* are not identified. Hence, the disturbances in the corresponding binary response models are normalized by setting their variances equal to 1.

Relying on a Johnson (1949)'s proposal, $T(\cdot)$ denotes a differentiable one-to-one transformation intended to rescale a potentially not normally distributed random variable y_2^* into a normally distributed ones, with σ standard deviation. As the domain of definition of the inverse transformation $T^{-1}(\cdot)$ may be restrained to a subset of real numbers, the standard normal random disturbance z_2 is potentially truncated at the bounds of an interval $[B_1, B_2]$ with B_1 and/or B_2 finite. To account for heteroscedasticity of z_2, the standard deviation σ can be specified as a positive monotonic transformation of a linear function of a vector of covariates x_4, namely $\beta_4^\top x_4$. However, for notational simplicity, we will adopt in what follows the notation of a homoscedastic standard deviation σ rather than the more general one of a heteroscedastic standard deviation $\sigma(\beta_4^\top x_4)$.[3]

These equations model the hurdles, namely the sequence of binary decisions a consumer faces when buying a good. Each hurdle decision is coded by a binary variable I_j taking value 1 if $y_j^* > 0$ and 0 otherwise. Therefore, the outcome of each of such decisions is modeled as a probit model with outcome probabilities: $\mathrm{P}(I_j = 1) = \mathrm{P}(y_j^* > 0)$ and $\mathrm{P}(I_j = 0) = 1 - \mathrm{P}(y_j^* > 0)$.

By assuming that consumption and purchases are uniformly distributed over time, but, according to different timetables entailing a frequency of consumption higher than that of purchasing, we can also interpret the probability $\mathrm{P}(I_3 = 1) = \mathrm{P}(y_3^* > 0)$ as measuring the share of purchasing frequency with respect to that of consumption during the observation period. This allows to relate the observed level of expenditures y to the unobserved level of consumption y_2^* during the observation period, using the following identity:

$$y = \frac{T^{-1}(\beta_2^\top x_2 + \sigma z_2)}{\mathrm{P}(I_3 = 1)} I_1 I_2 I_3. \tag{8.2}$$

[3] For a practical application of this parametric model of heteroscedasticity, a functional form of $\sigma(\beta_4^\top x_4)$ written as $\exp\{\beta_{40}\Phi(\beta_4^\top x_4)\}$, where $\Phi(.)$ is the distribution function of the standard normal random variable, has been programmed in mhurdle. This functional form remains bounded with respect to any possible values of covariates x_4 and allows testing the assumption of homoscedasticity, $\sigma = \exp\{\beta_{40}/2\}$, by assessing the statistical non significance of parameter vector β_4 without an intercept.

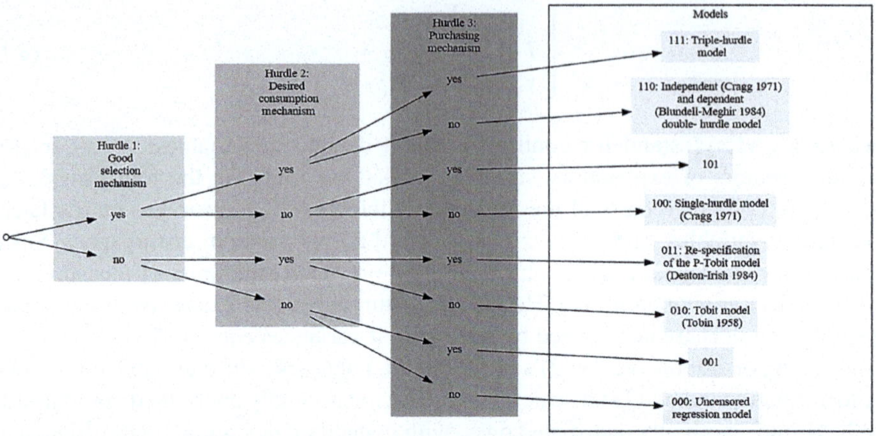

Fig. 8.1 The full set of special hurdle regression models encompassed by the formal framework (8.1)

This modeling strategy provides an explanatory framework where censoring of the observed dependent variables results from the effect of up to three different censoring mechanisms, namely: $I_1 = 0$ and/or $I_2 = 0$ and/or $I_3 = 0$.

A priori information (theoretical or real-world knowledge) may suggest that one or more of these censoring mechanisms are not in effect. For instance, we know in advance that all households purchase food regularly, implying that the first two censoring mechanisms are inoperative for food. In this case, the relevant model is defined by only two relations: one defining the desired consumption level of food, and the other the decision to purchase food during the observation period.

When the first and/or the third hurdles are supposed not to be in effect, the previous binary response models for I_1 and/or I_3 must be replaced by singular probability response models where $\mathrm{P}(I_1) = 1$ and/or $\mathrm{P}(I_3) = 1$. When the second hurdle is supposed not to be in effect, we must not only replace the binary response model explaining I_2 by a singular probability response model where $\mathrm{P}(I_2 = 1) = 1$ but also select a monotonic transformation $T(y_2^*)$ enforcing non-negative values to y_2^*.

Figure 8.1 outlines the full set of special models that can be generated by selecting which of these three mechanisms are in effect and which are not. It shows that eight different models can be dealt with by means of our modeling methodology. To use a mnemonic rule, we number the models by three binary digits, each of which indicates if a censoring mechanism is or is not in effect, using digits 1 and 0, respectively. For example, 011 indicates the model for which hurdle 1 (good selection mechanism) is not in effect, while hurdles 2 (desired consumption mechanism) and 3 (purchasing mechanism) are.

Among these models, one is not concerned by censored data, namely model 000. The latter model is only relevant for modeling uncensored samples. All the other models are potentially able to analyze censored samples by combining up to the three censoring mechanisms described above.

Some of these models have already been used in applied econometric literature. In particular, model 100 is a single-hurdle good selection model originated by Cragg (1971), which assumes independence between disturbances ϵ_1 and ϵ_2. The dependent version of this model may be viewed as a sample selection model in which only the desired consumption is observed, but differs from the model popularized by Heckman (1976) to illustrate linear regression model estimation given sample selection, in that desired consumption is generated by a demand model enforcing non-negative values on the latent variable y_2^*. Still, in many applications presented in the appendix, Heckman's sample selection model is used as a dependent single-hurdle good selection model in which a good selection decision is assumed to dominate good consumption decision. From our point of view, this model is theoretically misspecified to analyze a latent dependent variable that could take negative values while assuming that hurdle 2 is not in effect.

The double-hurdle model 110 combining independent good selection (hurdle 1) and desired consumption (hurdle 2) censoring mechanisms is also due to Cragg (1971). An extension of this double-hurdle model to dependent censoring mechanisms has been originated by Blundell and Meghir (1987).

Model 011 is a respecification of the P-Tobit model due to Deaton and Irish (1984), where $\mathrm{P}(I_3 = 1) = 1$ was specified as an unconstrained parameter which in their case generated inconsistent estimates greater than 1. It explains zero purchases by combining the desired consumption censoring mechanism (hurdle 2) with the purchasing censoring mechanism (hurdle 3). Model 001 is a single-hurdle model not yet used in applied demand analysis, where the censoring mechanism in effect is that of infrequent purchases (hurdle 3).

Among the original models encompassed by our general formal framework (8.1), models 101 is a double-hurdle model combining good selection (hurdle 1) and purchasing (hurdle 3) mechanisms to explain censored samples. Model 111 is an original triple-hurdle model formulated in Hoareau (2009). This model explains censored purchases either as the result of good rejection (hurdle 1), negative desired consumption (hurdle 2), or infrequent purchases (hurdle 3).

Cragg (1971) suggested two types of functional forms of the distribution of y_2^* enforcing non-negative values of y_2^*, namely the (inverse) log-normal distribution:

$$y_2^* = \exp\{\beta_2^\top x_2 + \sigma z_2\} \tag{8.3}$$

and the normal distribution left-truncated at 0:

$$y_2^* = \max\{0; \beta_2^\top x_2 + \sigma z_2\} = \beta_2^\top x_2 + \sigma \max\{B_1; z_2\} \tag{8.4}$$

where $\max\{B_1; z_2\}$ is a standard normal random variable left-truncated at $B_1 = -\beta_2^\top x_2/\sigma$.

To account for these two functional forms within our general formal framework (8.1), we consider in this chapter two transformations $T(y_2^*)$ which are special cases of a two parameters Box–Cox transformation generating a broad range of right skewed and J-shaped distributions, as shown by Carlevaro and Croissant (2020).

The first transformation is the identity transformation which generates an untruncated normal distribution of y_2^* when hurdle 2 is in effect, and the left-truncated normal distribution (8.4) when hurdle 2 is not in effect.

The second transformation is a slight generalization of the logarithmic transformation leading to the three parameters (inverse) log-normal distribution (8.3), namely:

$$T(y_2^*) = \ln(y_2^* + \alpha) \tag{8.5}$$

with α a location parameter which shifts the left-truncation bound of y_2^* toward negative or positive values according to the sign of α. As the inverse of this transformation is written as

$$y_2^* = \exp\{\beta_2^\top x_2 + \sigma z_2\} - \alpha \tag{8.6}$$

it turns out that this transformation allows to model skewed distributions of y_2^* according to a translated (inverse) log-normal functional form where the support of z_2 is untruncated. By the same token, testing the statistical non-significance of parameter α against the alternative $\alpha > 0$ amounts to testing the assumption that hurdle 2 is not in effect. Conversely, when $\alpha \leq 0$ the transformation (8.5) holds for $y_2^* \geq -\alpha$ meaning that $-\alpha$ stands for a "committed" consumption of a basic necessity, while $\alpha > 0$ typifies a luxury good whose consumption occurs only above a given income threshold.[4]

To derive the form of the probability distribution of the observable dependent variable y, we must still specify the joint distribution of the random disturbances entering the hurdle relations assumed to be in effect, and that of the demand function, which in turn depends on the domain of definition of transformation $T^{-1}(\cdot)$.

For trivariate hurdle models, where hurdles 1 and 3 are in effect (but not necessarily hurdle 2), the joint density function of z_1, z_2, and z_3 is a possibly truncated standard trivariate normal density function written as

$$\phi\left(z_1, z_2, z_3; \rho\right) / \Pi \tag{8.7}$$

where $\Pi = \Phi(B_2) - \Phi(B_1)$ with $\Phi(z)$ the distribution function of a standard univariate normal distribution, $\phi(z_1, z_2, z_3; \rho)$ the density function of a standard trivariate normal distribution with ρ the vector of the three symmetric correlation coefficients $\rho_{12}, \rho_{13}, \rho_{23}$ between the couples of normal standard random variables z_1 and z_2, z_1 and z_3, z_2, and z_3, respectively.

For bivariate hurdle models, where either hurdle 1 or hurdle 3 is not in effect, the joint density function of z_2 and z_1 or z_3 is a possibly truncated standard bivariate normal density function with a single correlation coefficient, ρ_{12} or ρ_{23}.

Finally, for the univariate hurdle model, where only hurdle 2 is in effect, the density function of z_2 is a possibly truncated standard univariate normal density function.

[4] This economic interpretation of α may justify to model this parameter as a function of some covariates, like household demographic characteristics.

While the assumption of correlated disturbances is intended to account for the interdependence between latent variables y_1^*, y_2^* and y_3^* unexplained by covariates x_1, x_2 and x_3, a priori information (theoretical or real-world knowledge) may also suggest to set to zero some or all correlations between the random disturbances entering these models, entailing a partial or total independence between model relations. The use of this a priori information generates, for each trivariate or bivariate hurdle model, a subset of special models all nested within the general model from which they are derived. For a trivariate hurdle model, the number of special models so derived is equal to seven, but, for a bivariate hurdle model, only one special model is generated, namely the model obtained by assuming the independence between the two random disturbances of the model.

8.2.2 *Probability Distribution of Censored Dependent Variable*

As for the standard Tobit model, the probability distribution of the observed censored variable y of our hurdle models is a discrete-continuous mixture, which assigns a probability mass $\mathrm{P}(y = 0)$ to $y = 0$ and a density function $f_+(y)$ to any $y > 0$, with:

$$\mathrm{P}(y = 0) + \int_0^\infty f_+(y)dy = 1. \tag{8.8}$$

To compute the probability mass $\mathrm{P}(y = 0) = 1 - \mathrm{P}(y > 0)$ and the density function $f_+(y)$, we must first establish the joint density function of the latent variables entering the hurdle model.

For trivariate hurdle models, the joint density function of latent variables y_1^*, y_2^*, and y_3^* can be derived from the density function (8.7) of variables z_1, z_2, and z_3 by means of the change of variables:

$$\begin{cases} z_1 = y_1^* - \beta_1^\top x_1 \\ z_2 = (T(y_2^*) - \beta_2^\top x_2)/\sigma \\ z_3 = y_3^* - \beta_3^\top x_3 \end{cases} \tag{8.9}$$

which leads to

$$f(y_1^*, y_2^*, y_3^*) = \frac{T^{'}(y_2^*)}{\sigma} \frac{\phi\left(y_1^* - \beta_1^\top x_1, (T(y_2^*) - \beta_2^\top x_2)/\sigma, y_3^* - \beta_3^\top x_3; \rho\right)}{\Pi}, \tag{8.10}$$

where $T'(y_2^*)$ stands for the derivative of $T(y_2^*)$.

To compute $\mathrm{P}(y > 0)$, we integrate this density function over the three-dimensional positive octant using the change of variables (8.9) and the symmetry property of density function (8.7). Performing this integration for a strictly increasing transformation $T(\cdot)$, which is the case for the identity and logarithmic transformations we focus in this paper, and z_2 truncated over the interval $[B_1, B_2]$ leads to:

$$\begin{aligned}
P(y > 0) &= \int_{-\beta_1^\top x_1}^{\infty} \int_{\frac{T(0)-\beta_2^\top x_2}{\sigma}}^{B_2} \int_{-\beta_3^\top x_3}^{\infty} \frac{\phi(z_1, z_2, z_3; \rho)}{\Pi} dz_1 dz_2 dz_3 \\
&= \int_{-\infty}^{\beta_1^\top x_1} \int_{-B_2}^{\frac{\beta_2^\top x_2 - T(0)}{\sigma}} \int_{-\infty}^{\beta_3^\top x_3} \frac{\phi(z_1, z_2, z_3; \rho)}{\Pi} dz_1 dz_2 dz_3 \\
&= \frac{\Phi(\beta_1^\top x_1, (\beta_2^\top x_2 - T(0))/\sigma, \beta_3^\top x_3; \rho) - \Phi(\beta_1^\top x_1, -B_2, \beta_3^\top x_3; \rho)}{\Pi}.
\end{aligned} \tag{8.11}$$

Note that, for a strictly decreasing transformation, as it is the case for some transformations of the Box–Cox family, the integration with respect to z_2 must be performed by reversing the direction of integration, from $(T(0) - \beta_2^\top x_2)/\sigma$ to B_1. By applying the theorem on the inversion of the integration limits of a definite integral, we obtain a closed form of the integral similar to that of formula (8.11) with the truncation value B_2 replaced by B_1.

Therefore, for z_2 left-truncated at $B_1 = -\beta_2^\top x_2/\sigma$, which is the case for the truncated normal distribution (8.4), this closed form for $P(y > 0)$ simplifies to

$$P(y > 0) = \frac{\Phi(\beta_1^\top x_1, (\beta_2^\top x_2 - T(0))/\sigma, \beta_3^\top x_3; \rho)}{\Phi(\beta_2^\top x_2/\sigma)}, \tag{8.12}$$

while for the untruncated normal and the translated (inverse) log-normal distribution (8.6) it is written as

$$P(y > 0) = \Phi(\beta_1^\top x_1, (\beta_2^\top x_2 - T(0))/\sigma, \beta_3^\top x_3; \rho). \tag{8.13}$$

To compute the density function $f_+(y)$ we first derive the joint density function of variables y_1^*, y and y_3^* by performing the change of variable $y_2^* = \Phi_3 y$ with $\Phi_3 = \Phi(\beta_3^\top x_3) = P(I_3 = 1)$ on the joint density function (8.10), which leads to

$$f(y_1^*, y, y_3^*) = \frac{\Phi_3 T'(\Phi_3 y)}{\sigma} \frac{\phi\left(y_1^* - \beta_1^\top x_1, (T(\Phi_3 y) - \beta_2^\top x_2)/\sigma, y_3^* - \beta_3^\top x_3; \rho\right)}{\Pi}. \tag{8.14}$$

We must then integrate this transformed density function over the positive quadrant of the bi-dimensional support of variables y_1^* and y_3^*. To this purpose, we rewrite this trivariate normal density function as the product of the marginal density function of y, written as

$$f(y) = \frac{\Phi_3 T'(\Phi_3 y)}{\sigma} \frac{\phi\left((T(\Phi_3 y) - \beta_2^\top x_2)/\sigma\right)}{\Pi}, \tag{8.15}$$

and of the conditional joint density function $f(y_1^*, y_3^* | y)$, which is bivariate normal with expectations, standard deviations, and correlation coefficient written as

$$\mu_{i|2}(y) = \beta_i^\top x_i - \rho_{i2}(T(\Phi_3 y) - \beta_2^\top x_2)/\sigma_{i|2}, \quad \sigma_{i|2} = \sqrt{1-\rho_{i2}^2}, \quad i = 1, 3$$
$$\rho_{13|2} = \frac{\rho_{13} - \rho_{12}\rho_{23}}{\sqrt{1-\rho_{12}^2}\sqrt{1-\rho_{23}^2}}. \tag{8.16}$$

Integrating this factorization of density function (8.14) with respect to positive values of y_1^* and y_3^* leads to the following closed form for $f_+(y)$:

$$\begin{aligned} f_+(y) &= f(y) \textstyle\int_0^\infty \int_0^\infty f(y_1^*, y_3^*|y) dy_1^* dy_3^* \\ &= f(y) \int_{-\frac{\mu_{1|2}(y)}{\sigma_{1|2}}}^{\infty} \int_{-\frac{\mu_{3|2}(y)}{\sigma_{3|2}}}^{\infty} \phi\left(z_1, z_3; \rho_{13|2}\right) dz_1 dz_3 \\ &= f(y)\Phi\left(\frac{\mu_{1|2}(y)}{\sigma_{1|2}}, \frac{\mu_{3|2}(y)}{\sigma_{3|2}}; \rho_{13|2}\right). \end{aligned} \tag{8.17}$$

The probability distribution of the observed censored variable y for the two correlated bivariate models 011 and 110 can be derived from formulas (8.11) and (8.17) of the correlated trivariate model by eliminating hurdles 1 and 3, respectively, while that of the univariate hurdle model 010 by eliminating hurdles 1 and 3.

8.3 Model Estimation, Evaluation, Selection, and Prediction

The econometric framework described in the previous section provides a theoretical background for tackling the problems of model estimation, evaluation, selection, and prediction within the statistical theory of classical inference. These statistical issues are tackled by assuming that the data at hand are those observed in a sample of individuals selected in a large population using a sampling design generating a data base having the features of a random sample.[5]

To appraise the results of a model estimation, two fundamental principles should be used, namely its economic relevance and its statistical and predictive adequacy. The first principle deals with the issues of the accordance of the model estimate with the economic rationale underlying the model specification and of its relevance for answering the questions for which the model has been built. These issues are essentially context-specific and, therefore, cannot be dealt with by means of generic criteria. The second principle refers to the issues of empirical soundness of an estimated model and of its ability to predict sample or out-of-sample observations. These issues can be tackled by means of measures of goodness of fit, by formal tests of

[5] Data provided by surveys conducted by official statistical offices usually fulfill such requirement, at least as far as the survey is performed according to a random sampling design where none of the model-dependent variables are used to design the sampling scheme. On this important issue see Chap. 24 of Cameron and Trivedi (2005).

significance based on the distribution of model parameter estimators, and by the quality of predictions provided by an estimated model, respectively.

8.3.1 Model Estimation

The full parametric specification of our hurdle regression models allows to efficiently estimate their parameters by means of the maximum likelihood principle. Indeed, it is well known from the classical estimation theory that, under the assumption of a correct model specification and for a likelihood function sufficiently well behaved, the maximum likelihood estimator is asymptotically efficient within the class of consistent and asymptotically normal estimators.[6]

For a random sample of n observations of the censored dependent variable y, it is easy to derive its likelihood function from the results set out in the previous Sect. 8.2.2. As these observations are all independently drawn from the same conditional (on covariates x_1, x_2, and x_3) discrete–continuous distribution, which assigns a conditional probability mass $\mathrm{P}(y = 0)$ to the observed value $y = 0$ and a conditional density function $f_+(y)$ to the observed values $y > 0$, the contribution of an observation y_i to this log-likelihood function can be written as

$$\ln L_i = \begin{cases} \ln \mathrm{P}(y_i = 0) & \text{if} \quad y_i = 0 \\ \ln f_+(y_i) & \text{if} \quad y_i > 0 \end{cases} \tag{8.18}$$

and the log-likelihood for the entire sample as

$$\ln L = \sum_{i=1}^{n} \ln L_i = \sum_{i|y_i=0} \ln \mathrm{P}(y_i = 0) + \sum_{i|y_i>0} \ln f_+(y_i). \tag{8.19}$$

A maximum likelihood estimate of the model parameters is obtained by numerically maximizing this function with respect to all the unknown model parameters entering this function. Algorithms used to perform this numerical optimization, as well as estimates of the asymptotic Fisher information matrix used for statistical inference, are described in the user manual of **R**'s mhurdle 1.3-0 package, enabling the estimation of the full set of hurdle regression models outlined in Fig. 8.1.

[6] For a rigorous statement of this property, see Amemiya (1985) Chap. 4. A more robust approach to classical statistical inference with respect to model specification errors will be presented later, in Sect. 8.3.3.

8.3.2 *Model Evaluation and Selection Using Goodness of Fit Measures*

To assess the goodness of fit of a hurdle regression model estimate, we cannot rely on a single measure, as a sample of censored observations of the dependent variable y consists of two sub-samples of incomparable observations, namely the sub-sample of zero observations and that of positive observations. The former is a sample of observations of a qualitative binary variable encoding the outcome of the censoring mechanisms at work, while the latter is a sample of observations of a quantitative variable measuring the outcome of the demand function, when this demand is uncensured. As a consequence, a measure of goodness of fit for each of these two samples of observations must be used, as the goodness of fit is not measured the same way in qualitative binary response models as in quantitative response models.

To this purpose, we reformulate a hurdle regression model as a two-part model. The first-part specifies a model for the censoring mechanism explaining the outcome of the qualitative binary variable:

$$d = \begin{cases} 0 \text{ if } & y = 0 \\ 1 \text{ if } & y > 0 \end{cases} \tag{8.20}$$

according to a probit model assigning the probability $\mathrm{P}(y = 0)$ to the censored observation ($d = 0$) and the probability $\mathrm{P}(y > 0) = 1 - \mathrm{P}(y = 0)$ to the uncensored observation ($d = 1$). Therefore, the log-likelihood for this first-part model is written as:

$$\ln L_0 = \sum_{i=1}^{n} [(1 - d_i) \ln \mathrm{P}(y_i = 0) + d_i \ln \mathrm{P}(y_i > 0)]. \tag{8.21}$$

The second-part specifies, for an uncensored observation of y, the demand model explaining the outcome of this quantitative variable according to the following conditional density function:

$$f(y|y > 0) = f_+(y)/\mathrm{P}(y > 0). \tag{8.22}$$

For this second-part model, the log-likelihood is written as

$$\ln L_+ = \sum_{i=1}^{n} d_i [\ln f_+(y_i) - \ln \mathrm{P}(y_i > 0)]. \tag{8.23}$$

Adding up the log-likelihoods of these two-part model leads to

$$\begin{aligned} \ln L_0 + \ln L_+ &= \textstyle\sum_{i=1}^{n} [(1 - d_i) \ln \mathrm{P}(y_i = 0) + d_i \ln f_+(y_i)] \\ &= \textstyle\sum_{i|y_i=0} \ln \mathrm{P}(y_i = 0) + \sum_{i|y_i>0} \ln f_+(y_i) = \ln L, \end{aligned} \tag{8.24}$$

meaning that the two-part model is entirely consistent with a single specification of a hurdle regression model.

To develop a measure of fit for binary response models which may be interpreted as a coefficient of determination R^2 in the linear regression model, Estrella (1998) suggests to rely on the relationship between R^2 and the classical likelihood-based test statistics, namely the likelihood ratio (LR), Wald (W), and Lagrange multiplier/score (LM) statistics. In the normal linear homoskedastic regression model, where such relationships hold exactly for the likelihood ratio statistics,[7] namely $-2\ln(L_c/L_u)$ with L_u the maximum value of the unconstrained likelihood, and L_c the maximum value of the likelihood constrained by the hypothesis of a model without covariates (intercept-only model), this relationship is written as

$$R^2 = 1 - \exp\{-A\} \tag{8.25}$$

with $A = -(2/n)\ln(L_c/L_u)$ the average value of the likelihood ratio statistic. Therefore, R^2 may be seen as a nonlinear rescaling of the average likelihood ratio statistics that takes values within the interval [0; 1]. The lower bound of this interval corresponds to the worst fit, when $L_u = L_c$ implying $A = 0$. The upper bound corresponds to the best fit, reached when the residuals of the linear homoskedastic regression model are all equal to zero, leading to a zero estimate of the variance of the random disturbances implying $L_u \to \infty$,[8] and accordingly $A \to \infty$. Between these two limits R^2 increases with A according to a rescaling of A determined by a differential equation written as

$$dR^2/(1 - R^2) = dA. \tag{8.26}$$

These properties of relationships (8.25) were adopted by Estrella (1998) as a set of requirements for developing a R^2 analog of the measure of fit for a binary response model. Taking into account that, contrary to the case of a normal linear regression model, for a binary response model the average likelihood ratio statistics A varies between 0 (when $L_u = L_c$) and an upper finite bound $B = -(2/n)\ln L_c$ (when $L_u = 1$), a R^2 analog for a binary response model is obtained by solving the differential equation:

$$dR^2/(1 - R^2) = dA/(1 - A/B) \tag{8.27}$$

with the initial condition $R^2(0) = 0$. This solution

$$R^2 = 1 - (1 - A/B)^B \tag{8.28}$$

provides a rescaling of the likelihood ratio statistic for the binary response model that satisfies the condition $R^2(B) = 1$ and converge toward the rescaling (8.25) when $B \to \infty$.

---

[7] For the Wald and Lagrange multiplier statistics such relationships hold only locally, in a neighborhood of the maintained hypothesis of an intercept-only model, and take another functional form.

[8] L_u is a power function of the residuals variance with negative exponent.

To conclude, in order to assessing the goodness of fit of the two parts of a hurdle regression model, we shall use the following R^2-rescaling of likelihoods L_0 and L_+:

$$R_0^2 = 1 - (\ln L_{0c} / \ln L_{0u})^{(2/n)\ln L_{0c}} \quad \text{and} \quad R_+^2 = 1 - e^{(2/n_+)\ln(L_{+c}/L_{+u})} \tag{8.29}$$

with $n_+ = \sum_{i=1}^{n} d_i$ the sample size of uncensored observations.

The estimation of an intercept-only hurdle regression model, where each linear function of covariates is set equal to its intercept parameter, is not generally possible in its original parametrization because, in the absence of covariates, many parameters are under-identified, and thus cannot be consistently estimated. Therefore, to compute the maximum values of the constrained likelihoods L_{0c} and L_{+c}, we must respecify the probability distribution of the dependent variable y by means of identifiable parameters. Such a respecification is cumbersome for correlated bivariate and trivariate hurdle regression models, but feasible for uncorrelated hurdles. Thus, we have opted for this definition of an intercept-only model, implying that the goodness of fit of a given multiple hurdle regression model is assessed by benchmarking it to the same naive model, regardless of the degree of correlation between the hurdles of the model.

In the general case of a trivariate hurdle model, the probability distribution of the observed censored variable y generated by an intercept-only independent hurdle model can be derived from formulas (8.11) and (8.17) by setting the correlation coefficients between random disturbances z_1, z_2, and z_3, equal to zero. This leads to the following simplified versions of these formulas:

$$P(y > 0) = \Phi_{10}\Phi_{30}\frac{\Phi((\beta_{20} - T(0))/\sigma) - \Phi(-B_2)}{\Pi} \tag{8.30}$$

$$f_+(y) = \Phi_{10}\Phi_{30}^2\frac{T'(\Phi_{30}y)}{\sigma}\frac{\phi((T(\Phi_{30}y) - \beta_{20})/\sigma)}{\Pi} \tag{8.31}$$

with β_{i0}, i=1,2,3 the intercepts of the three hurdles (8.1) and $\Phi_{i0} = \Phi(\beta_{i0})$, $i = 1, 2, 3$.

In a separate paper, in preparation, we show how to estimate this intercept-only hurdle model, and all his special cases, for the two transformations $T(y_2^*)$ considered in Sect. 8.2.1, namely, the identity transformation and the translated logarithmic transformation (8.5). Both transformations generate two similar families of hurdle regression models: the first family includes the four models where hurdle 2 is in effect, namely, models 111, 110, 011, and 010, while the second family comprises the three models where hurdle 2 is not in effect, namely, models 101, 100, and 001. Assuming the identity transformation leads to model y_2^* as a normal variate when hurdle 2 is in effect, and as a normal variate left-truncated at zero when hurdle 2 is not in effect. Therefore, in both the cases, the distribution of y_2^* of such an intercept-only hurdle model only depends on the two parameters β_{20} and σ. On the other hand, assuming the translated logarithmic transformation leads to model the presence or absence of hurdle 2 according to the sign of a third (location) parameter

α entering the distribution of y_2^*. Finally, the families of intercept-only independent hurdle models can be respecified by means of three identified parameters, namely Φ_0, $\mu = \beta_{20}/\Phi_{30}$, and $s = \sigma/\Phi_{30}$, when using the identity transformation, and by means of four identified parametrs, namely Φ_0, $a = \alpha/\Phi_{30}$, $m = \beta_{20} - \ln \Phi_{30}$, and σ, when using the translated logarithmic transformation. Whatever transformation is used, parameter Φ_0 is equal to $\Phi_{10}\Phi_{30}$ in models 111 and 101; to Φ_{10} in models 110 and 100; to Φ_{30} in models 011 and 001; to 1 in model 010.

Goodness of fit measures (8.29) can also be used for model selection, a decision problem dealing with the identification, among several model specifications used to explain the same dependent variable, of the one that is best suited to explain the sample of available observations. From this point of view, goodness of fit measures (8.29) allow to identify the model specification achieving the best in-sample fit.[9]

8.3.3 Model Selection Using Vuong Test

Model evaluation can also be tackled from the point of view of the model specification that is favored in a formal test comparing two model alternatives.

This second model selection criterion relies on the use of a test proposed by Vuong (1989). According to the rationale of this test, the "best" parametric model specification among a collection of competing specifications is the one that minimizes the Kullback–Leibler Information Criterion (KLIC), namely a measure of the distance between the conditional probability mass/density function[10] $f(y|x;\theta)$ of a possibly misspecified parametric model and that of the true unknown model denoted by $h(y|x)$, defined by the following formula:

$$KLIC = E\left[\ln\left(\frac{h(y|x)}{f(y|x;\theta_*)}\right)\right] = \int \ln\left(\frac{h(y|x)}{f(y|x;\theta_*)}\right) dH(y,x), \qquad (8.32)$$

where $H(y, x)$ denotes the distribution function of the true joint distribution of (y, x), and θ_* the probability limit with respect to $H(y, x)$ of the so-called quasi-maximum likelihood estimator $\hat{\theta}$ obtained by applying the maximum likelihood method when $f(y|x;\theta)$ is misspecified. Note that KLIC criterion takes a minimum value of 0 when there is a value θ_0 of parameter vector θ such that $f(y|x;\theta_0) = h(y|x)$ almost

---

[9] With small samples, the goodness of fit measure used for model selection must account for differences in the degree of model parametrization. Indeed, the value of goodness of fit measures (8.29) can be improved by increasing model parametrization, because model estimation is performed by maximizing the model likelihood function from which these goodness of fit measures functionally depend. Consequently, a penalty that increases with the number of model parameters should be added to formulas (8.29).

[10] For hurdle regression models, this conditional probability function is written as

$$f(y|x) = \mathrm{P}(y = 0|x)^{1-d} f_+(y|x)^d,$$

with d the binary variable (8.20).

everywhere,[11] meaning that the conditional probability function $f(y|x;\theta)$ is correctly specified. In contrast, the KLIC will take large values when $f(y|x;\theta)$ very poorly specifies the true conditional probability function $h(y|x)$. Thus, minimizing the KLIC criterion equals selecting the model specification for which the quantity:

$$E[\ln f(y|x;\theta_*)] = \int \ln f(y|x;\theta_*)dH(y,x) \tag{8.33}$$

is the largest. Therefore, given two competing models F_θ and G_π, with conditional probability functions $f(y|x;\theta)$ and $g(y|x;\pi)$ and parameter vectors θ and π of size K and L, respectively, Vuong suggests to discriminate between these models by testing the null hypothesis:

$$H_0 : E[\ln f(y|x;\theta_*)] = E[\ln g(y|x;\pi_*)] \Longleftrightarrow E\left[\ln\left(\frac{f(y|x;\theta_*)}{g(y|x;\pi_*)}\right)\right] = 0,$$

meaning that the two models are equivalent in the sense that they are equally distant from the true unknown model according to the KLIC measure, against either:

$$H_f : E[\ln f(y|x;\theta_*)] > E[\ln g(y|x;\pi_*)] \Longleftrightarrow E\left[\ln\left(\frac{f(y|x;\theta_*)}{g(y|x;\pi_*)}\right)\right] > 0,$$

meaning that model F_θ is better than G_π in the sense that F_θ is less distant than G_π from the true unknown model according to the KLIC measure, or:

$$H_g : E[\ln f(y|x;\theta_*)] < E[\ln g(y|x;\pi_*)] \Longleftrightarrow E\left[\ln\left(\frac{f(y|x;\theta_*)}{g(y|x;\pi_*)}\right)\right] < 0,$$

meaning that specification F_θ is worse than G_π in the sense that F_θ is more distant than G_π from the true unknown model according to the KLIC measure.

The quantity $E[\ln f(y|x;\theta_*)]$ is unknown but it can be consistently estimated, under some regularity conditions, by $1/n$ times the log-likelihood evaluated at the quasi-maximum likelihood estimator for θ. Hence:

$$LR(\hat{\theta},\hat{\pi}) = \frac{1}{n}\sum_{i=1}^{n} \ln \frac{f(y_i|x_i;\hat{\theta})}{g(y_i|x_i;\hat{\pi})} \tag{8.34}$$

is a consistent estimator for $E\left[\ln(f(y|x;\theta_*)/g(y|x;\pi_*))\right]$.

Therefore, an obvious test of H_0 consists in verifying whether an LR-based statistics differs from zero. The distribution of such a statistics can be worked out even when the true model is unknown, as the quasi-maximum likelihood estimators $\hat{\theta}$ and

[11] By "almost everywhere" we mean: for all points of the support of the true distribution of (y,x) except those for which the probability $P_H[(y,x) : f(y|x;\theta_0) \neq h(y|x)] = 0$.

$\hat{\pi}$ converge in probability to the pseudo-true values θ_* and π_*, respectively, and have asymptotic normal distributions centered on these pseudo-true values.

In his seminal paper, Vuong (1989) suggests to use different LR-based statistics according to the relation linking the two competing models, which may be nested, meaning that $f(y|x;\theta_*) = g(y|x;\pi_*)$ almost everywhere, strictly non-nested, meaning that $f(y|x;\theta_*) \neq g(y|x;\pi_*)$, or overlapping, meaning that $f(y|x;\theta_*) = g(y|x;\pi_*)$ almost everywhere but none of these models is nested in the other.

In a recent paper, Shi (2015) has criticized Vuong testing procedures by showing that they can generate severe size distortions in finite samples. She develops a new test statistics that corrects these size distortions and universally applies to nested, strictly non-nested, and overlapping models.

The rationale of Shi test statistics consists in correcting two finite sample size distortions present in the following test statistics used by Vuong to discriminate between two strictly non-nested models:

$$T_{LR} = \frac{\sqrt{n}\,LR(\hat{\theta},\hat{\pi})}{\hat{\omega}}, \tag{8.35}$$

with $\hat{\omega}^2$ a sample analogue consistent estimator of the variance of the asymptotic distribution of the statistics T_{LR} numerator, which is $N(0,\omega^2)$ under hypothesis H_0.

Using a local asymptotic theory instead of the pointwise asymptotic theory on which the Vuong test is based, she suggests a modified Vuong test, called a non-degenerate Vuong test, based on the following statistics:

$$T_{LR}^{mod} = \frac{\sqrt{n}\,[LR(\hat{\theta},\hat{\pi}) + \mathrm{tr}(\hat{V})/2n]}{\sqrt{\hat{\omega}^2 + c\,\mathrm{tr}(\hat{V}^2)/n}} \tag{8.36}$$

where $\mathrm{tr}(\hat{V})$ is a consistent estimator of $\mathrm{tr}(V) = \mathrm{tr}(A_F^{-1}B_F) - \mathrm{tr}(A_G^{-1}B_G)$, with A_F and B_F the Hessian and the gradient versions of the asymptotic Fisher information matrix of the model F_θ, and A_G and B_G those of the model G_π.

Note that, for a model where these two versions of the asymptotic Fisher information matrix are identical, and therefore the information identity $A + B = O$ holds, $\delta = -\mathrm{tr}(A^{-1}B) = \mathrm{tr}(I)$ is equal to the number of model parameters. This suggests to consider δ as a measure of the degree of the model parametrization. This measure increases with the number of model parameters and with the discrepancy of the information identity resulting from the nonlinearity of the model with respect to its parameters. As a consequence, the finite sample bias of the $LR(\hat{\theta},\hat{\pi})$ statistics under hypothesis H_0 is given by $(-\delta_F + \delta_G)/(2n)$. It will be negligible for models of similar degree of parametrization, but negative and of possibly significant magnitude when model F_θ is more heavily and nonlinearly parameterized than model G_π. By adding to $\hat{\omega}^2$ the positive constant term $c\,\mathrm{tr}(\hat{V}^2/n)$, with c a positive constant chosen according to a data-dependent method,[12] the modified Vuong statistics also prevents

[12] Except for nested models, where c is set equal to zero.

its denominator from taking values close to zero with non-negligible probability, which contributes to create a fat tail for the distribution of T_{LR}.

To completely remove the asymptotic size distortion, Shi proposes to compute a simulated critical value $\mathrm{cv}(a)$, which has a well-controlled asymptotic size, in the sense that, asymptotically and for any $c \geq 0$, the probability of rejecting H_0 when it is true is upper bounded by a.[13] By systematically changing the value of a in order to equalize the simulated critical value $\mathrm{cv}(a)$ to the observed value of statistic T_{LR}^{mod}, it is possible to derive a simulated p-value allowing to perform a non-degenerate Vuong test at any controlled asymptotic size level.

For non-nested models the test is two-sided. It is carried out by rejecting H_0 if the simulated p-value is less than the selected size level a, and in favor of either H_f if $T_{LR}^{mod} > 0$, or of H_g if $T_{LR}^{mod} < 0$.

For nested models, the test is one-sided, because according to the KLIC criterion the nested model cannot be closer to the true unknown model than the nesting model. Supposing that model G_π is nested into model F_θ, the test is carried out by rejecting H_0 in favor of H_f if the simulated p-value is less than the selected size level a. Note that this test is a robust alternative to the usual LR-test for testing the statistical significance of a priori restrictions on the parameters of model F_θ, in the sense that it allows the unrestricted model to be misspecified.

But how do we proceed when we need to compare a set of model alternatives, which is the typical situation we face in econometric studies? To solve this problem, we suggest to start by computing Shi's test statistics (8.36) for every pair of models to be assessed. Then, to define a binary relation of strict preference between pairs of models F_θ and G_π, using a Simon (1943) symmetric test, namely a binary choice between these models where none of these models is privileged as a null hypothesis of a classical asymmetric Neyman–Pearson test. The test is carried out by rejecting model G_π in favor of model F_θ when the value of Shi's statistics is positive, and conversely by rejecting F_θ in favor of G_π when the value is negative.[14]

For a set of m model alternatives, the $m(m-1)/2$ values of Shi's test statistics can be visualized as the elements of a triangular double-entry table whose rows represent the first $m-1$ model alternatives and whose columns the last $m-1$ ones. From this table, we can infer a strict preference ordering of the m model alternatives using the transitivity[15] property of the binary relation of strict preference. To this purpose, it is useful to represent the strict preference relations of the table as a graph where the vertices represent the models and a directed arc between two vertices the strict preference between the two corresponding models. The first top-ranked model of the strict preference ordering is identified by looking for the source vertex of the graph, namely the vertex of the graph with no directed arcs inwards. The second top-ranked

[13] For a two-sided test this size is $P[|T_{LR}^{mod}| > \mathrm{cv}(a)|H_0]$, and for a one-sided test $P[T_{LR}^{mod} > \mathrm{cv}(a)|H_0]$.

[14] For nested models, Simon's approach always leads to favor the nesting (unrestricted) model over the nested (restricted) one.

[15] Transitivity expresses the consistency of choices which a symmetric model selection test leads to $M_1 \succ M_2$ and $M_2 \succ M_3 \Rightarrow M_1 \succ M_3$, where $M_i \succ M_j$ means that model M_i is strictly preferred to model M_j according to a symmetric test of model selection.

model is identified by looking for the source vertex of the subgraph obtained by suppressing the first source vertex and its directed arcs outwards, and so on until the graph is exhausted.

By applying an asymmetric Neyman–Person testing procedure, where the null hypothesis of equivalence of the two contrasted models is privileged over that of selecting one of these two models, we define a binary relation of weak preference between pairs of models M_1 and M_2, written as $M_1 \succeq M_2$, meaning: *model M_1 is weakly preferred to model M_2 according to an asymmetric test of model selection.* It is a transitive preference preorder[16] which may uncover a symmetric and transitive binary relation of equivalence or "indifference" when $M_1 \succeq M_2$ and $M_2 \succeq M_1$, denoted by $M_1 \sim M_2$, and a transitive binary relation of strict preference denoted as before by $M_1 \succ M_2$, when $M_2 \complement \succeq M_1$ with $\complement \succeq$ the complementary binary relation of $\succeq$.

The number of equivalent models uncovered by an asymmetric test of model selection will obviously depend on the value pre-assigned to the size of the test. When this value is greater than the largest p-value of the tests performed on all pairs of contrasted models, the preference preorder between pairs of models only includes strict preference relationships, because all the null hypotheses of these tests will be rejected. In contrast, when this value is less than the smallest p-value of these tests, the preference preorder only includes equivalence relationships, because none of the null hypotheses of these tests will be rejected. Thus, by progressively decreasing the size of the test from the maximum value of the p-values, we restructure the set of models endowed with the binary relation of weak preference into a quotient set provided with the strict preference relation $\succ$ but with a dimension fewer than that of the set of models. Thus, by decreasing the size of the test, the dimension of the quotient set will also decrease until it includes a single equivalence class of all the contrasted models. For this reason, it is important to avoid to pre-assign a too small size to an asymmetric test of model selection, because it can deprive the test of any discriminating power.

8.3.4 Prediction and Partial Effects

Prediction, based on a regression model relating an outcome random variable y to a set of covariates x, deals with the choice of a function of model covariates providing, for a given value of x, a point estimate $\tilde{y}$ of y whose prediction error $e = y - \tilde{y}$ is minimized according to some measure of the expected loss generated by the prediction error. In econometrics, it is conventional to specify a quadratic loss e^2 which leads to choose, as an optimal predictor of y given x, the conditional mean function $E[y|x]$ which minimizes the mean-square loss $E[e^2|x]$, called the best mean-square error predictor of y.

---

[16] Note that this weak preference ordering is antisymmetric only between nested models.

As defined by identity (8.2), the outcome variable y of a hurdle regression model is a mixture of a qualitative and a quantitative variable whose expectation has no actual meaning, the zero-value of y denoting the numerical value taken by the binary dummy variable d when the observation of the latent variable y_2^* is censored. Therefore, for a predictive purpose, one must disentangle the qualitative component of y from its purely quantitative component. This can be done by solving the prediction problem of y in the framework of the two-part respecification of a hurdle regression model presented in Sect. 8.3.2.

The first part of this model explains the outcome of the qualitative component of y using the binary variable d, whose best mean-square error predictor is given by

$$E[d|x] = 0 \times \mathrm{P}(y = 0) + 1 \times \mathrm{P}(y > 0) = \mathrm{P}(y > 0), \tag{8.37}$$

with $\mathrm{P}(y > 0)$ specified by formulas (8.11), (8.12), (8.13).

The second part of the model explains the outcome of the quantitative component of y taking positive real values according to the density function (8.22). Accordingly, the best mean-square error predictor of $y > 0$ is given by

$$E[y|y > 0, x] = \int_0^\infty y \frac{f_+(y)}{\mathrm{P}(y > 0)} dy = \frac{E[y|x]}{\mathrm{P}(y > 0)}, \tag{8.38}$$

with $f_+(y)$ specified by formula (8.17).

For the special cases of identity and logarithmic transformations $T(\cdot)$ which we restrict to in this chapter, closed analytical forms for $E[y|x]$ can be established.[17]

For the identity transformation $T(y_2^*) = y_2^*$, this analytical closed form for the correlated trivariate hurdle model with density function $f_+(y)$ specified by formula (8.17) is written as

$$E[y|x] = \frac{\Phi_{123}}{\Phi_3} \beta_2^\top x_2 + \frac{\sigma}{\Phi_3} \left(\phi_2 \Phi_{13|2} + \rho_{12} \phi_1 \Phi_{23|1} + \rho_{23} \phi_3 \Phi_{12|3}\right), \tag{8.39}$$

where

$$\Phi_{123} = \Phi\left(\beta_1^\top x_1, \frac{\beta_2^\top x_2}{\sigma}, \beta_3^\top x_3; \rho\right), \quad \Phi_3 = \Phi\left(\beta_3^\top x_3\right),$$

$$\phi_i = \phi(\beta_i^\top x_i), \quad i = 1, 3, \quad \phi_2 = \phi\left(\frac{\beta_2^\top x_2}{\sigma}\right),$$

$$\Phi_{ij|k} = \Phi\left(\frac{\mu_{i|k}}{\sigma_{i|k}}, \frac{\mu_{j|k}}{\sigma_{j|k}}; \rho_{ij|k}\right), \quad i \neq j \neq k, \quad \mu_{i|k} = \beta_i^\top x_i - \rho_{ik} \beta_k^\top x_k, \quad k = 1, 3,$$

$$\mu_{i|2} = \beta_i^\top x_i - \rho_{i2} \frac{\beta_2^\top x_2}{\sigma}, \quad \sigma_{i|k} = \sqrt{1 - \rho_{ik}^2}, \quad \rho_{ij|k} = \frac{\rho_{ij} - \rho_{ik}\rho_{jk}}{\sigma_{i|k}\sigma_{j|k}}.$$

[17] Proofs for the analytical forms (8.39) and (8.40) are available from the authors.

Similarly, a closed analytical form for $E[y|x]$ can be established in the case of the logarithmic transformation $T(y_2^*) = \ln(y_2^* + \alpha)$ for the correlated trivariate hurdle model:

$$E[y|x] = \frac{e^{\beta_2^\top x_2 + \frac{1}{2}\sigma^2}}{\Phi_3} \Phi\left(\beta_1^\top x_1 + \rho_{12}\sigma, \frac{\beta_2^\top x_2 - \ln\alpha}{\sigma} + \sigma, \beta_3^\top x_3 + \rho_{23}\sigma; \rho\right) - \frac{\alpha}{\Phi_3}\Phi_{123}, \tag{8.40}$$

with $\Phi_{123} = \Phi(\beta_1^\top x_1, (\beta_2^\top x_2 - \ln\alpha)/\sigma, \beta_3^\top x_3; \rho)$.

From these formulas, we can easily derive the corresponding ones for correlated bivariate models 011 and 110 by eliminating hurdles 1 and 3, respectively, as well as the one of the univariate model 010 by eliminating hurdles 1 and 3.

The partial effects we consider refer to the change in the value of predictors (8.37) and (8.38) generated by a ceteris paribus change of a model covariate, that is, by keeping the value of the other model covariates unchanged, as in a laboratory experiment.[18]

The definition of the partial effect of a covariate x_0 on these predictors, depends on the scale of measurement of x_0. When x_0 is a continuous variable, the partial effect of x_0 on the predictor (8.37) or (8.38) is the first derivative of the predictor with respect to x_0, namely the rate of change in the value of the predictor generated by a ceteris paribus infinitesimal increase of x_0.

Similarly, if x_0 is a count variable measuring the size of a population of individuals or objects which can only vary by integers, the partial effect will be defined as the change in the predictor brought about by a ceteris paribus unit increase of x_0.

When x_0 is a qualitative variable that can be in one and only one of $H \geq 2$ different mutually exclusive and exhaustive situations called modalities, it is usual to code it as a column-vector x_0 of H dummy variables $d_h, h = 1, \ldots, H$, taking values $d_g = 1$ and $d_h = 0, \forall h \neq g$, when the observed modality of x_0 is the one indexed by g. Yet, this dummy coding of a qualitative variable has a drawback, because the H dummy variables are linearly related by the constraint $\sum_{h=1}^{H} d_h = 1$. As a consequence, the impact coefficients of these H dummy variables are not identified when the vector β_i to which these coefficients pertain does contain an intercept term. To avoid this inconvenience, it is customary to suppress from x_0 one of the modalities, the discarded modality playing the role of a "reference modality" with respect to which the impact of each of the $H - 1$ remaining modalities, called contrast, is measured.

So far, point prediction and partial effects have been tackled by assuming the value of the model parameters to be known. However, to be operational, these formulas must be quantified by means of an estimate of these theoretical parameters. Using the maximum likelihood estimate $\hat{\theta}$ of the model parameters θ presented in Sect. 8.3.1 provides an implied maximum likelihood estimator for a column-vector $h(\theta)$ of best mean-square error predictors (8.39), (8.40), and/or partial effects of these predictors, namely $h(\hat{\theta})$. This estimator is, as $\hat{\theta}$, a consistent and asymptotically normal esti-

[18] In econometrics, these effects are often called "marginal", to emphasize the size of the change affecting the manipulated covariate when it is continuous. We prefer to use the term "partial", which also encompasses the ceteris paribus change of a discrete or a qualitative covariate.

mator for $h(\theta)$ whose asymptotic distribution can be derived from a linearization of $h(\hat{\theta})$ around θ, called the "delta method", which leads to the following asymptotic variance–covariance matrix of $h(\hat{\theta})$: $(1/n)(\partial h/\partial\theta^\top)I_A(\theta)^{-1}(\partial h/\partial\theta^\top)^\top$, with $I_A(\theta)$ the asymptotic Fisher information matrix.

It is worth commenting on how to present the estimate of partial effects which are representative of the available sample. To this purpose, it is customary to compute either the "partial effect for the sample average individual", by fixing the model covariates to their sample mean, or the "average partial effect in the sample", by computing the mean of the sample partial effect values. The first estimate has a meaningful interpretation when all covariates are quantitative, but must be assessed for sub-samples of average individuals when some model covariates are qualitative and define a set of distinct representative individuals. More informative would be to characterize the shape of the distribution of a partial effect by displaying its histogram or computing other indicators like the bounds of the distribution range, the standard deviation and some quantiles.

8.4 Application

To illustrate the use of our hurdle regression models in consumer demand analysis, we use a survey conducted by the Bureau of Labor Statistics of the U.S. Department of Labor, called "Interview Survey". This survey collects data from 27,659 households on all their expenditures on a quarterly basis. There is very few attrition in the survey as the large majority of enrolled households respond to the four quarterly interviews and their expenditures are therefore observed for 12 consecutive months. The micro-data files of the survey are publicly available on the website of the Bureau of Labor Statistics and may be downloaded and used without permission.

Among the numerous goods available in this data set, we choose to explain the good called "fees and admissions", a subset of entertainment expenditures labeled `fees` in the data set. We selected a sample of quarterly observations for which at least one month is within the year 2019, leading to a sample size of 7,548 observations, for which 42% are uncensored. The overall sample average expenditure is 184 US$ and 434 US$ for the uncensored sample of observations.

The dependent variable is defined as the quarterly household expenditure for `fees` rescaled by dividing it by its sample geometric mean of 175 US$, in order to have a null sample mean when using the translated logarithmic transformation (8.5), as is the case in our application. So defined, the dependent variable as well as the location parameter α are pure numbers, namely dimensionless magnitudes without an explicit unit of measurement, because the ratio of a quarterly household expenditure for `fees` (Y) to its sample geometric mean ($\bar{Y}_G$) can be written as a product of ratios of the same magnitude, namely:

Table 8.1 Descriptive statistics of the distribution of model variate and covariates in the sample

	Age (years)	Education (years)	Living (proportion)	Size (persons)	Income (US$)	Fees (US$)
Minimum	16	7.0		1.0	1	2
1st-Quantile	36	12.0		1.0	28278	69
Median	52	13.0		2.0	52878	175
Mean	52	13.6	0.899	2.4	71554	434
3rd-Quantile	65	15.0		3.0	93298	440
Maximum	88	17.0		11.0	606740	21124

$$y = Y/\bar{Y}_G = \prod_{i=1}^{n_+} (Y/Y_i)^{1/n_+}, \tag{8.41}$$

with Y_i, $i = 1, ..., n_+$ the sample nonzero observations of Y.

To explain these observations, we use the following covariates as determinants of hurdle 1 (good selection mechanism) or of hurdle 3 (purchasing mechanism):

age: age of the household reference person (years);
education: education of the household reference person (years);
size: size of the household (number of persons);
living: binary indicator of a household living in a metropolitan statistical area (0 = no, 1 = yes);

and the following covariate as determinant of the level of desired consumption, and of hurdle 2 (desired consumption mechanism), when it is in effect:

income: household annual income (kUS$), net from estimated taxes in the last 12 months, per equivalent adult computed according to the OECD definition, namely: 1 unit for the first adult aged 18 years or over, 0.7 units for the other adults aged 18 years or over, 0.5 units for persons aged less than 18 years.

Table 8.1 presents some descriptive statistics characterizing the shape of the distribution of these covariates in the sample, as well as that of the uncensored values of the dependent variable `fees`. By comparing the median to the mean, we note a strong symmetry of the distributions of covariates `age`, `education`, and `size`, and a strong right asymmetry of dependent variable `fees` and of covariate `income` used as determinant of the uncensored values of `fees`. Furthermore, the vast majority (90%) of households in the sample live in metropolitan areas.

8.4.1 Model Estimation, Evaluation, and Selection

Our modeling strategy consists in estimating all the trivariate and bivariate hurdle regression models by assuming either a full dependence or a full independence between the disturbances of the model. As suggested by the shape of the distribution of the uncensored dependent variable in the sample, we rescale this right-skewed distribution into a normally distributed one by assuming a translated logarithmic transformation (8.5). These model specifications are codified as in Figure 1 by 3 binary digits indicating which censoring mechanisms are or are not in effect, preceded by the capital letter `L` identifying the translated logarithmic transformation functional form applied to the dependent variable, and followed by letters `D` or `I` depending on whether the random disturbances of the model are assumed to be dependent (correlated) or independent (uncorrelated). This leads to estimate the following eight models: L111D, L111I, L101D, L101I, L110D, L110I, L100D, and L100I.

To identify for which of the hurdle 1 or 3 the covariates `age`, `education`, `living`, and `size` are the more relevant determinants, we estimated two versions of these eight models: one including all the covariates in hurdle 1, and the other including all the covariates in hurdle 3. It is the first version of the models, whose estimates are presented in Table 8.2, which proved to be the most relevant specification.[19] It is worth noting that the logarithm of covariate `income` has been introduced as a determinant of the level of desired consumption in order to interpret its regression coefficient as a constant elasticity of the Engel curve, when hurdle 2 is not in effect. Also, an estimate of model L111D couldn't be obtained, therefore it is not reported in Table 8.2.

Using the p-values of parameter estimates, reported in parenthesis in Table 8.2, we can perform a significance test for each estimated parameter using the classical Wald test. Unfortunately, all these p-values, to a single exception, are so small that every single coefficient results to be highly significant whichever the value of its estimate. The same result is obtained by testing the significance of a single or a set of parameters using any classical likelihood-based test for nested models.

These unconvincing results are due to tests performed with a very large sample under the optimistic hypothesis of a well-specified unrestricted model, which can lead to underestimate the probability of rejecting the restricted model when it is true, and thus entailing the risk of unduly favoring the use of the unrestricted model. To avoid such size distortions of the classical likelihood-based tests, it is wise to use Shi's non-degenerate Vuong test for nested models, which represents a robust approach, regarding a possible error in specification of the nesting model, for testing the statistical significance of a priori restrictions on model parameters, as pointed out in Sect. 8.3.3.

---

[19] The second version of the models was discarded based on a series of Shi tests, each one contrasting the two versions of the same model specifications differing only in the presence of the four covariates in hurdle 1 or hurdle 3. This series of tests rejected all the model versions with covariates in hurdle 3 with a very low p-value (0 for the first 3 digits).

Table 8.2 Hurdle regressions model estimates with covariates included in hurdle 1

	Trivariate models			Bivariate models			
	L111I	L101D	L101I	L110D	L110I	L100D	L100I
Good selection mechanism							
Intercept	−2.866 (0.000)	−3.431 (0.000)	−3.169 (0.000)	−2.574 (0.000)	−2.866 (0.000)	−3.160 (0.000)	−2.920 (0.000)
Age	−0.012 (0.000)	−0.007 (0.000)	−0.011 (0.000)	−0.007 (0.000)	−0.012 (0.000)	−0.007 (0.000)	−0.009 (0.000)
Education	0.222 (0.000)	0.217 (0.000)	0.227 (0.000)	0.191 (0.000)	0.222 (0.000)	0.198 (0.000)	0.199 (0.000)
Living	0.449 (0.000)	0.388 (0.000)	0.395 (0.000)	0.392 (0.000)	0.449 (0.000)	0.360 (0.000)	0.350 (0.000)
Size	0.110 (0.000)	0.134 (0.000)	0.091 (0.000)	0.132 (0.000)	0.110 (0.000)	0.118 (0.000)	0.076 (0.000)
Desired consumption mechanism							
Intercept	−1.961 (0.000)	−1.117 (0.000)	−1.946 (0.000)	−1.233 (0.000)	−1.962 (0.000)	−0.685 (0.000)	−1.818 (0.000)
ln(income)	0.557 (0.000)	0.408 (0.000)	0.498 (0.000)	0.478 (0.000)	0.557 (0.000)	0.407 (0.000)	0.498 (0.000)
α	0.412 (0.000)			0.457 (0.000)	0.413 (0.000)		
Purchasing mechanism							
Intercept	3.864 (0.764)	0.742 (0.000)	1.169 (0.000)				
Random disturbances							
σ	1.150 (0.000)	1.417 (0.000)	1.275 (0.000)	1.359 (0.000)	1.150 (0.000)	1.465 (0.000)	1.275 (0.000)
ρ_{12}		−0.590 (0.000)		−0.702 (0.000)		−0.662 (0.000)	
ρ_{13}		0.870 (0.000)					
ρ_{23}		−0.121 (0.399)					
Goodness of fit measures							
N	7548	7548	7548	7548	7548	7548	7548
δ	11.4	12.7	10.0	12.3	11.4	10.0	8.2
N_o	4346	4346	4346	4346	4346	4346	4346
N_+	3202	3202	3202	3202	3202	3202	3202
R_o^2	0.156	0.133	0.135	0.156	0.156	0.132	0.134
R_+^2	0.073	0.152	0.103	0.113	0.073	0.150	0.103
ln(likelihood)	−9917.8	−9865.5	−9948.5	−9850.1	−9917.8	−9873.5	−9949.9

In parenthesis, p-value of Wald's statistical test of significance of the above coefficient estimate

Table 8.3 Shi tests of model equivalence by pair of models

	L101D	L100D	L111I	L110I	L101I	L100I
L110D	0.81 (0.425)	**1.16** (0.011)	5.62 (0.000)	**5.87** (0.000)	4.27 (0.000)	**4.46** (0.000)
L101D		**1.97** (0.000)	2.19 (0.037)	2.19 (0.036)	**6.21** (0.000)	**6.14** (0.000)
L100D			1.91 (0.071)	1.91 (0.071)	5.38 (0.000)	**5.69** (0.000)
L111I				**0.06** (0.565)	**1.56** (0.000)	**1.58** (0.002)
L110I					1.55 (0.146)	**1.58** (0.001)
L101I						**0.29** (0.219)

In parenthesis, p-value of Shi's statistical test of models equivalence
In bold figures, Shi's statistical test value of nested models

Based on the results of Shi tests presented in Table 8.3 for every possible pair of models of Table 8.2, and reported in bold figures for nested models, we can test the significance of a single parameter by testing the equivalence of a pair of nested models differing only with respect to the tested parameter. Taking, as an example, the case of parameter α, this test can be carried out using three pairs of nested models, namely: L101I nested into L111I, L100D nested into L110D, and L100I nested into L110I. All these tests reject the equivalence of the two models and therefore accept the significance of parameter α with small p-values, but not as small as with the classical Wald test, in particular for the pair of correlated models L100D nested into L110D with p-value = 0.011.

More interesting is the possibility to rigorously test the non-relevance of the purchasing mechanism (hurdle 3), which is formally obtained by letting the intercept of this hurdle become ∞. This test cannot be performed as a classical likelihood-based test, except by choosing an arbitrary high value of the Intercept for the restricted model. Using a Shi test, it can be carried out with three pairs of nested models, namely: L110I nested in L111I, L100D nested in L101D, and L100I nested in L101I. The first and third tests accept the equivalence of pair of models with a high p-value of 0.565 and 0.219, respectively, while the second test rejects the equivalence at an extremely low p-value of 0.000. The marked difference between these test results is explained by the differences existing between the respective nesting models. For the first and third tests, the nesting model assumes a full independence of the three model disturbances, while, for the second test, the disturbances of the nesting model are fully dependent. By the same token, these contrasting results show the huge size distortions which a classical likelihood-based test using an especially misspecified unrestricted model can lead to.

To avoid such pitfalls when confronted with a set of model alternatives, as in our case, it is wise to preorder the specified model alternatives by a binary relation of weak preference, as explained at the end of Sect. 8.3.3. The set of model alternatives which we rely on is represented by the seven models of Table 8.2. Therefore, by applying Simon's symmetric testing procedure, we first define a binary relation of strict preference between the 21 pairs of these 7 model alternatives. This binary relation can be visualized using a double-entry table, like Table 8.3, where the value of the test statistic is replaced by the symbol $\succ$ of strict preference oriented from a row-model F toward a column-model G when the value of Shi's statistic (8.36) is positive, meaning that model F is strictly preferred to model G, and oriented in the opposite direction when the value is negative, meaning that model G is strictly preferred to model F.

Using this table, we can draw a graph whose vertices represent the seven models and where a directed arc between two vertices represents the strict preference between the two corresponding models. From this graph, we can derive the strict preference ordering of our seven models implied by the transitivity property of the relation of strict preference between pairs of models. The first preferred model of this ordering is identified by looking for the source vertex of this graph with no directed arcs inwards, which turns out to be model L110D. The second preferred model of the ordering is identified by looking for the source vertex of the subgraph obtained by suppressing the first source vertex and all its directed arcs outwards, which is model L101D; and so on until the exhaustion of the graph. This procedure leads to the following strict preference ordering of our seven models: L110D $\succ$ L101D $\succ$ L100D $\succ$ L111I $\succ$ L110I $\succ$ L101I $\succ$ L100I. Note that presenting the results of Shi tests for every pair of models in a double-entry table with models ranked on rows and columns according to this ordering of strict preference, as done in Table 8.3, generates a table where all Shi's test statistic values are positive.

This ordering of the estimated models by strict preference shows the prevalence of the assumption of correlated versus that of uncorrelated disturbances in explaining the sample observations, but it says nothing about how distant these models are from the true unknown data distribution. To tackle this issue, we need to use an asymmetric Neyman–Person testing procedure where the null hypothesis of equivalence of two confronted models, according to the KLIC criterion, is tested in order to infer a possible preorder through a binary relation of weak preference between pairs of models.

To uncover the pairs of models which are equivalent, we need to pre-assign a size to this test of model equivalence. Looking at Table 8.3, where the p-values of Shi's statistical tests of model equivalence are reported in parenthesis, we can see that when the size of the test is greater than 0.565, the largest p-value of the table, the Shi test rejects the equivalence for all pairs of models, and therefore the preference preorder between pairs of models only includes strict preference relationships. But, by progressively decreasing the size of the test from this value, we restructure the set of models endowed with the binary relation of weak preference into a quotient set endowed with the strict preference relation $\succ$, but with a dimension fewer than that of the set of models. Thus, by lowering the test size down to a standard level of 0.05, we progressively accept the equivalence of models: L111I and L110I (test size between 0.565 and 0.425); L110D and L101D (test size between 0.425 and 0.219);

L101I and L100I (test size between 0.219 and 0.146); L110I and L101I (test size between 0.146 and 0.071); L100D and L111I (test size of 0.05). Using the transitivity of the binary relation of equivalence, it turns out that the 5 last ranked models L111I, L110I, L101I, and L100I are all equivalent, according to a test size of 0.05. This finally leads to a quotient set composed of only two equivalence classes, ordered by strict preference as follows: {L110D, L101D} $\succ$ {L100D, L111I, L110I, L101I, L100I}.

Note that performing the test with a size less than 0.011 will lead to accept the equivalence of models L110D and L100D, and consequently to identify a quotient set with a single equivalent class including all the contrasted models.

The analysis of the goodness of fit measures presented in Table 8.2 allows to shed light on the assumptions that impact the quality of fit, in explaining each of the two sub-samples of incomparable observations at hand, namely the sub-sample of zero-qualitative censored observations and that of positive-quantitative uncensored observations.

Starting with the top-ranked model L110D by order of preference, where hurdles 1 and 2 are in effect but not hurdle 3, we observe a goodness of fit for the censored sub-sample of observations ($R_0^2 = 0.156$) better than that of the sub-sample of uncensored observations ($R_+^2 = 0.113$). The opposite is observed for the second top-ranked model L101D where hurdles 1 and 3 are in effect but not hurdle 2, as well as for its nested model L100D where only hurdle 1 is in effect. For these models indeed, the goodness of fit for the censored sub-sample of observations ($R_0^2 = 0.133$ & 0.132) is worse than that of the sub-sample of uncensored observations ($R_+^2 = 0.152$ & 0.150). The same form of goodness of fit inversion, but with weaker values of R_+^2, is observed between model L111I with its nested model L110I, where hurdle 2 is in effect, and model L101I with its nested model L100I, where hurdle 2 is not in effect.

To understand this issue, we must refer to the two-part model reformulation of our hurdle regression models, described in Sect. 8.3.1, on which the goodness of fit measures R_0^2 and R_+^2 are based, and more precisely to its regression relation. For all our estimated models, this relation is written as

$$y_2^* = \exp\{\beta_{20} + \beta_{21}\ln(\text{income}) + \sigma z_2\} - \alpha \tag{8.42}$$

and represents the household Engel curve for `fees`, namely, the household demand for `fees` as an increasing function of household income ($\beta_{21} > 0$). When hurdle 2 is assumed not to be in effect, the parameter α is set equal to 0, and therefore the demand for `fees` is positive for any positive value of the income covariate. In contrast, when hurdle 2 is assumed to be in effect, the parameter α is estimated, and if the estimated value is positive, which is the case for all our estimated models with this assumption, the demand for `fees` (8.42) may generate negative values for some low-income levels. As a consequence, the households of our sample having such low-income levels will be considered as having a nil consumption of `fees`. They will contribute to improve the goodness of fit of the first part model, by adding the income covariate to the other hurdle determinants, but, to the expense of the goodness of fit of the second part model, by decreasing the sample size of income observations used to assess this regression model.

Note that the existence of a negative correlation between the random disturbance z_2 and those of the other hurdles will reduce the impact of hurdle 2 activation on the deterioration of the goodness of fit of the regression relation, as is shown by comparing the R^2_+ of a dependent model with its independent counterpart. Therefore, assuming correlated instead of uncorrelated random disturbances seems to significantly improve the goodness of fit of the household Engel curve for `fees`.

8.4.2 The Shape of the Engel Curve and its Partial Effects

The previous evaluation of our estimated models presented in Table 8.2, based on a preordering of weak preference between pairs of models, has uncovered two best equivalent models according to the KLIC criterion, namely, models L110D and L101D. But a more detailed analysis of these two model estimates, based on the goodness of fit measures R^2_0 and R^2_+, has revealed a quite marked difference of goodness of fit of their main structural relation (8.42) to the sample of uncensored observations. Therefore, in the following, we analyze the shape of the Engel curve of these two model estimates and the responses to their covariates to highlight their differences and similarities.

For this purpose, we consider two versions of the Engel curve, namely the average desired Engel curve, $E[y_2^*|x]$, and the average observable Engel curve, $E[y|y > 0, x]$.

The first of these Engel curves is a function of covariate `income` only, written as

$$E[y_2^*|\text{income}] = e^{\beta_{20}+\frac{1}{2}\sigma^2}\text{income}^{\beta_{21}} - \alpha. \tag{8.43}$$

For model L101D, where $\alpha = 0$ by assumption, the estimated average desired Engel curve for this model is a constant elasticity function of `income`, namely a positive increasing and concave function of `income` on $\mathbf{R}_+$, as the estimated income elasticity is equal to 0.408. For model L110D instead, where $\alpha > 0$, the Engel curve (8.42) is a constant elasticity function of `income`, but is vertically translated by the quantity $-\alpha$ toward lower values of y_2^*. Therefore, contrary to the Engel curve of model L101D, this Engel curve takes negative values when `income` is less than a threshold solution of the equation $E[y_2^*|\text{income}] = 0$, namely for an income equal to $\exp\{\frac{\ln\alpha-\beta_{20}-\sigma^2/2}{\beta_{21}}\}$, which represents a minimum household income level giving access to the consumption of `fees`, considered as a luxury good. Assessing this income threshold using the parameter estimates of model L110D presented in Table 8.2 leads to an annual per equivalent adult income value, net from estimated taxes, of 371 US$. Such a ridiculous low-income level suggests that the shape of the average desired Engel curve of model L110D differs in practice from that of model L101D only by the value of its parameter β_{21}, slightly higher in model L110D

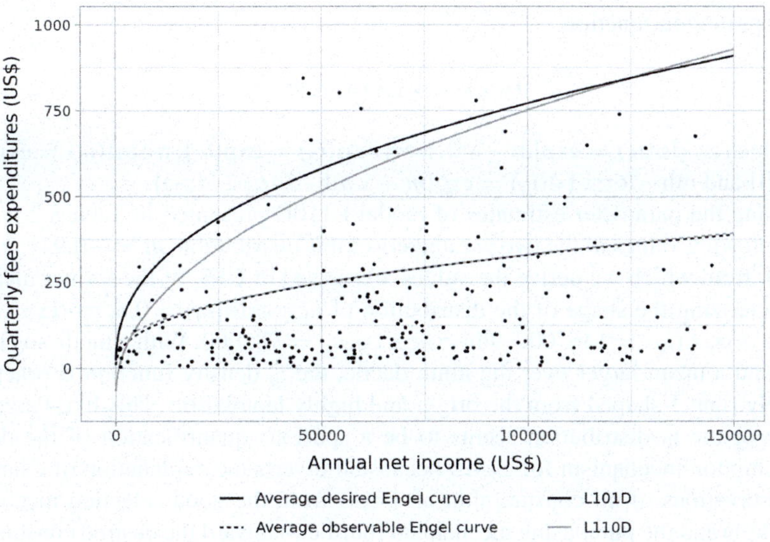

Fig. 8.2 Engel curves

(0.478) than in model L101D (0.408), implying a concavity of the average desired Engel curve of model L101D greater than for model L110D, and by a vertical shift of this less concave curve of –80 US$, as shown in Fig. 8.2.

To understand this result, we analyze the distribution, within the household population, of individual income thresholds giving access to `fees` consumption. Such distribution is that of the values of `income`, say i_0, which sets to 0 the household Engel curve for `fees` (8.42), when $\alpha > 0$ and $\beta_{21} > 0$, namely:

$$i_0 = \exp\{m - sz_2\} \tag{8.44}$$

with $m = (\ln\alpha - \beta_{20})/\beta_{21}$ and $s = \sigma/\beta_{21}$. It is a log-normal random variable whose distribution can be easily derived from that of the random disturbance $-z_2$ using the inverse of relation (8.44), functionally relating variable $-z_2$ to variable i_0 by the one-to-one relation:

$$-z_2 = (\ln i_0 - m)/s. \tag{8.45}$$

As z_2 is a standard random variable with density function $\phi(z_2)$, the density function of $-z_2$ is $\phi(-z_2) = \phi(z_2)$ and its distribution function $\Phi(z_2)$. Performing change of variable (8.45) therefore leads to a random variable i_0 with density function

$$f(i_0) = \phi\left((\ln i_0 - m)/s\right)/(i_0 s) \tag{8.46}$$

and distribution function

$$F(i_0) = \Phi\left((\ln i_0 - m)/s\right) \tag{8.47}$$

for which $\texttt{mode}(i_0) = \exp\{m - s^2\}$, $\texttt{median}(i_0) = \exp\{m\}$, $\texttt{mean}(i_0) = \exp\{m + (s^2/2)\}$ and nth-$\texttt{decile}(i_0) = \exp\{m + s\, n\text{th-}\texttt{decile}(z_2)\}$.

Using the parameter estimates of model L110D presented in Table 8.2 leads to the following values of the two parameters of this distribution, $m = -0.941$ and $s = 2.843$, from which we derive the values, expressed in US$, of the former measures characterizing the shape of the distribution of i_0: $\texttt{mode}(i_0) = 0.8$, $\texttt{median}(i_0) = 2,563$, $\texttt{mean}(i_0) = 146,000$, 9th-$\texttt{decile}(i_0) = 98,000$. With a mode so close to zero and a mean larger over the ninth decile, the i_0 density function is practically entirely right J-shaped from the origin and highly leptokurtic. This like-Pareto-law shape of the i_0 distribution seems to be a spurious quantification of the desired consumption mechanism for `fees` because it diverts the explanation of a large set of observations of nil consumption of `fees` from the good selection mechanism (hurdle 1) and the purchasing mechanism (hurdle 3) toward the desired consumption mechanism (hurdle 2), even for households benefitting from very high-income levels, who can therefore afford the consumption of `fees`. On this ground, we conclude that model L101D provides a better theoretical explanation of our data set than model L110D while providing a similar quality of overall empirical adequacy to our sample of observations.

The second Engel curve we consider, namely the average observable Engel curve for `fees`, defined by formula (8.38) as the expectation of a non-zero household expenditure for `fees`, is not only a function of the single covariate `income` but also of the covariates `age`, `education`, `size`, and `living`, used as determinants of hurdle 1, as a non-zero expenditure for `fees` presumes that the household has previously included `fees` in its basket of goods. For models L101D and L110D, this Engel curve written as $E[y|x]/\mathrm{P}(y > 0)$ can be derived from formula (8.13), for $\mathrm{P}(y > 0)$, and from formula (8.40), for $E[y|x]$.

In model L101D, $\alpha = 0$ implying $\ln \alpha = -\infty$, which leads to

$$\mathrm{P}(y > 0) = \Phi(\beta_1^\top x_1, \infty, \beta_{30}; \rho_{13}) = \Phi(\beta_1^\top x_1, \beta_{30}; \rho_{13}) \tag{8.48}$$

$$E[y|x] = E[y_2^*|\text{income}]\frac{\Phi(\beta_1^\top x_1 + \rho_{12}\sigma, \beta_{30} + \rho_{23}\sigma; \rho_{13})}{\Phi(\beta_{30})} \tag{8.49}$$

with $\beta_1^\top x_1 = \beta_{10} + \beta_{11}\,\text{age} + \beta_{12}\,\text{education} + \beta_{13}\,\text{living} + \beta_{14}\,\text{size}$, $E[y_2^*|\text{income}]$ defined by formula (8.43) with α set equal to 0 and β_{30} the intercept of hurdle 3. Therefore, the average observable Engel curve for `fees` of model L101D is written as

$$E[y|y > 0, x] = E[y_2^*|\text{income}]\frac{\Phi(\beta_1^\top x_1 + \rho_{12}\sigma, \beta_{30} + \rho_{23}\sigma; \rho_{13})}{\Phi(\beta_1^\top x_1, \beta_{30}; \rho_{13})\Phi(\beta_{30})}. \tag{8.50}$$

It appears to be proportional to the average desired Engel curve by a factor of proportionality which, for our model estimate, is less than 1 whatever the value of covariates x_1, because the estimates of the correlation coefficients ρ_{12} and ρ_{23} are all negative and that of $\Phi(\beta_{30})$ close to one.

In model L110D, hurdle 3 is not in effect, implying $\beta_{30} = \infty$ and $\Phi(\beta_{30}) = 1$, which leads to

$$P(y > 0) = \Phi\left(\beta_1^\top x_1, \frac{\beta_2^\top x_2 - \ln\alpha}{\sigma}, \infty; \rho_{12}\right) = \Phi\left(\beta_1^\top x_1, \frac{\beta_2^\top x_2 - \ln\alpha}{\sigma}; \rho_{12}\right) \tag{8.51}$$

$$\begin{aligned} E[y|x] = {} & \left(E[y_2^*|\text{income}] + \alpha\right) \Phi\left(\beta_1^\top x_1 + \rho_{12}\sigma, \tfrac{\beta_2^\top x_2 - \ln\alpha}{\sigma} + \sigma; \rho_{12}\right) \\ & - \alpha\Phi\left(\beta_1^\top x_1, \tfrac{\beta_2^\top x_2 - \ln\alpha}{\sigma}; \rho_{12}\right) \end{aligned} \tag{8.52}$$

with $\beta_2^\top x_2 = \beta_{20} + \beta_{21}\ln(\text{income})$. Therefore, the average observable Engel curve for `fees` of model L110D may be written as

$$E[y|y > 0, x] = \left(E[y_2^*|\text{income}] + \alpha\right) \frac{\Phi\left(\beta_1^\top x_1 + \rho_{12}\sigma, \frac{\beta_2^\top x_2 - \ln\alpha}{\sigma} + \sigma; \rho_{12}\right)}{\Phi\left(\beta_1^\top x_1, \frac{\beta_2^\top x_2 - \ln\alpha}{\sigma}; \rho_{12}\right)} - \alpha. \tag{8.53}$$

It appears to be a proportion of a constant elasticity function of `income` vertically translated by the quantity $-\alpha$ toward lower values of y. As a ratio of two normal bivariate distribution functions, this proportion is a decreasing function of the covariate `income` toward the ratio $\Phi(\beta_1^\top x_1 + \rho_{12}\sigma)/\Phi(\beta_1^\top x_1)$, when income $\to \infty$, whose value is always less than 1 whatever the value of covariates x_1, because the estimate of the correlation coefficient ρ_{12} is negative for model L110D. When income $\to 0+$, this proportion becomes ∞ but the product of the constant elasticity function times this proportion tends toward α. These limits can be analytically proven for the special case of model L010, but only numerically computed for model L110D.

To compare the shape of these two average observable Engel curves for `fees`, we drew in Fig. 8.2 their profile for a representative household `living` in a metropolitan area, as 90% of households in the sample, and whose `size` (2 persons), `age` (52 years) and `education` (13 years) of the reference person have the median value in the sample. Both curves are practically identical over the vast range of `income` of Fig. 8.2, with small discrepancies only for income values beneath 10,000 US$, confirming the difficulty to choose between these two models on a purely statistical basis. In Fig. 8.2, we also added the scatter diagram of the uncensored sample of observations for the representative household considered, in order to assess the empirical adequacy of our observable Engel curves for `fees`.

Table 8.4 Partial effects

Covariate (unit change)	L110D		L101D	
	E(Y | $Y > 0$)	P($Y > 0$)	E(Y | $Y > 0$)	P($Y > 0$)
Age (+1 year)	−1.373 (0.642)	−0.002 (0.001)	−1.490 (0.752)	−0.002 (0.001)
Education (+1 year)	36.784 (16.639)	0.056 (0.013)	47.404 (23.258)	0.067 (0.017)
Living (from 0 to 1)	69.507 (33.557)	0.118 (0.028)	74.878 (38.059)	0.122 (0.026)
Size (+1 person)	25.201 (11.514)	0.039 (0.009)	28.893 (14.336)	0.042 (0.010)
Income (+10^3US$)	6.169 (70.671)	0.005 (0.014)	5.963 (46.233)	0.000 (0.000)

Finally, we present in Table 8.4 the partial effects of a ceteris paribus change of each covariate of models L101D and L110D on the quantities P($Y > 0$) and E($Y|Y > 0$). The ceteris paribus change we consider is, for each sample observation, the unit change of the observed value of covariates indicated in the first column of Table 8.4. This table reports the average partial effect in the sample, namely the mean of the sample partial effect values, and beneath, in brackets, the standard deviation of the sample partial effect values.

As expected, both models provide sample average partial effects similar in sign and magnitude. Because the estimate of parameter β_{21} is slightly higher in model L110D than in model L101D, the sample average partial effect of covariate `income` on non-zero expenditures for `fees` is a little higher in model L110D than in model L101D. Conversely, the same partial effect of the other four covariates is higher in magnitude in model L101D than in model L110D, to compensate the lower partial effect of `income` in model L101D.

8.5 Concluding Remarks

Hurdle regression models aim at estimating regression models using samples of observations with a large proportion of zeros for the regression-dependent variable. They can be viewed as two-part models. The first part specifies a model for the censoring mechanism explaining whether the dependent variable has been observed or not. The second part specifies the regression model conditional upon the dependent variable being observed.

For the analysis of household expenditure surveys, three main censoring mechanisms based on paradigms of the consumer's behavior have been extensively used in applied econometrics. These censoring mechanisms, called hurdles, are (i) an economic decision mechanism for the desired level of consumption which, when negative, leads to a nil consumption (Tobin 1958); (ii) a non-economic decision mechanism for a good rejection or selection motivated by ethical, psychological or social considerations (Cragg 1971); and (iii) an economic or non-economic decision mechanism for the time–frequency at which the desired quantity of a selected good is bought or consumed (Deaton and Irish 1984).

This chapter provides a unified framework allowing to specify these three hurdles separately or jointly for a single equation demand analysis. A possible interdependence between these hurdles is modeled by assuming a correlation between the random disturbances of the three hurdle relations. Moreover, despite the particular area of application which the mentioned censoring mechanisms stem from, the practical scope of hurdle regression models doesn't seem to be restricted to empirical demand analysis, as proved by the applications in many other fields of economics.

In order to provide an operational and efficient statistical framework, our hurdle regression models are specified in a fully parametric form, allowing statistical estimation and testing within the maximum likelihood inferential framework. Tools for model evaluation and selection are provided, based on extensions of the classical coefficient of determination and on Shi's corrected Vuong tests for discriminating between nested or non-nested possibly misspecified models.

In order to practically implement this modeling methodology, a mhurdle **R** package has been developed, which has proved operational and robust when applied to a wide variety of real-world data. Extensions and improvements of this software are still ongoing, in particular in order to implement more flexible functional forms than the basic ones presented in this chapter, which can be used to enforce non-negative values to the regression-dependent variable.

8.6 Appendix: Literature Overview of Applied Papers on Consumer Demand Analysis Using Hurdle Regression Models

Table 8.5 outlines the main features of hurdle regression models used in the applied econometric literature to analyse household expenditure survey data left censored at zero.

Table 8.5 Main features of hurdle regression models used to analyse household expenditure survey data left censored at zero

Ref	Goods	Hurdles			Distribution of y_2^*(a)	Skedasticity	Sample size	% of zeros	Correlation (b, c)
		h1	h2	h3					
Cheng and Capps (1988)	Finfish and shellfish	■	□	□	Log-normal	□	9422	72–83	–0.69(**), 0.04
Haines et al. (1988)	Milk, bread	■	□	□	tr. normal	□	5406	43–71	
Jones (1989)	Cigarettes	■	□	□	Normal	□	1565	40	ns
Jones (1989)	Cigarettes	■	■	□	Normal	□	1565	40	ns
Popkin et al. (1989)	Milk, bread	■	□	□	tr. normal	□	1068–5406	na	
Reynolds (1990)	Fresh vegetables	■	□	□	tr. normal	□	3368	32	
Blaylock and Blisard (1992)	Cigarettes	■	■	□	normal	□	2962	61	ns
Gould (1992)	Cheese	□	■	■	Normal	□	5017	59	0.22(***)
Blaylock and Blisard (1993)	Wine	■	■	□	Normal	□	916	80	ns
Blaylock and Blisard (1993)	Wine	■	□	□	Normal	□	916	80	ns
Yen (1993)	Food away from home	■	□	□	Box–Cox	■	4199	12	
Blisard and Blaylock (1993)	Butter	■	■	□	Normal	□	5000	na	

Table 8.5 (continued)

Blisard and Blaylock (1993)	Butter	□	■	■	Normal	□	5000	na	
Yen (1994)	Alcohol	■	□	□	Box–Cox	■	4245	72	
Gao et al. (1995)	Rice	■	■	□	IHS	■	4273	67	0.24 (***)
Yen et al. (1995)	crawfish	■	■	□	Box–Cox	□	915	78	
Yen and Su (1995)	Butter	■	■	□	Normal	■	8083	81	
Yen and Su (1995)	Butter	□	■	■	Normal	■	8083	81	
Yen (1995)	Alcohol	■	□	□	Box–Cox	□	4538	88	
Yen (1995)	Alcohol	■	□	□	IHS	□	4538	88	
Wang et al. (1996b)	Eggs	■	■	□	Normal	□	1492	na	
Garcia and Labeaga (1996)	Cigarettes	■	■	□	Normal	□	23669	41	ns
Garcia and Labeaga (1996)	Cigarettes	■	□	□	Normal	□	23669	41	
Yen and Huang (1996)	Finfish	■	■	□	IHS	■	4066	74	
Yen and Jones (1996)	Cigarettes	■	■	□	Box–Cox	□	3801	57	–2.63* (***)
Su and Yen (1996)	Pork	■	■	□	IHS	■	4198	30	
Su and Yen (1996)	Pork	□	■	■	IHS	■	4198	30	
Burton et al. (1996)	meat	■	■	□	Box–Cox	□	na	na	ns

Table 8.5 (continued)

Yen and Jensen (1996)	Alcohol	■	■	□	IHS	■	9552	54	
Wang et al. (1996a)	Alcohol	■	■	□	Normal	□	ns	ns	0.77 (***)
Yen et al. (1996)	Egg	■	■	□	IHS	□	4230	58	4.72* (***)
Yen and Jones (1997)	Cheese	■	■	□	IHS	□	4245	18	ns
Yen (1999)	Cigarettes	■	□	□	tr. Normal	□	5814	75	
Bertail et al. (1999)	Home produced food	■	■	□	Normal	□	6121	76	0.20 (ns)
Burton et al. (2000)	Meat	■	■	□	Box–Cox	□	na	na	ns
Jones and Yen (2000)	Beef	■	■	□	Box–Cox	□	4150	15	–0.45 (***)
Angulo et al. (2001)	Alcohol	■	■	□	Normal	■	15087	na	
Angulo et al. (2001)	Alcohol	■	□	■	Normal	■	15087	na	
Newman et al. (2001)	Meat	■	■	□	IHS	□	7112–7332	15–68	
Newman et al. (2003)	Prepared meals	■	■	□	IHS	■	7112–7332	51–57	
Newman et al. (2003)	Prepared meals	□	■	■	IHS	■	7112–7332	51–57	
Mutlu and Gracia (2004)	Food away from home	■	■	□	Normal	■	12430	61	
Chaze (2005)	Health services	■	■	□	Box–Cox	□	9295	23	–0.15 (ns)

Table 8.5 (continued)

Yen (2005)	Cigarettes	■	□	□	tr. normal	□	4921–4672	75–78	–0.88, –0.59 (***)
Yen (2005)	Cigarettes	■	■	□	Normal	□	4921–4672	75–78	–0.71, –0.88 (***)
Zhang et al. (2008)	Fresh organic product	■	□	□	Log-normal	□	6916	42	0.90 (***)
Fuller et al. (2007)	Dairy products	■	■	□	Normal	□	314	na	0.35, 0.56 (***)
Aristei and Pieroni (2008)	Cigarettes	■	■	□	Box–Cox	■	27499	67	ns
Aristei et al. (2008)	Alcohol	■	■	□	normal	□	134515	41	0.12 (***)
Aristei et al. (2008)	Alcohol	■	□	□	Normal	□	134515	41	0.14 (***)
Keelan et al. (2009)	Food service	■	■	□	Box–Cox	□	7526–7877	47–56	
Aristei and Pieroni (2009)	Cigarettes	■	■	□	Box–Cox	□	47777	40	0.23 (***)
Okunade et al. (2010)	Healthcare	■	■	□	Normal	□	98632	28	–0.27 (***)
Brouhle and Khanna (2012)	Eco-labeled market	■	■	□	normal	□	2483–2933	na	
Brouhle and Khanna (2012)	Eco-labeled market	■	□	□	Normal	□	2483–2933	na	
Crowley et al. (2012)	Lottery	■	■	□	Normal	■	3082	55	

`na` means that the information was not in the article. A black box in columns `h1-h2-h3` indicates that the relevant hurdle is taken into account, and in column `skedasticity`, heteroscedasticity is taken into account.

(a) `IHS` stands for inverse hyperbolic sine transformation and `tr.normal` for truncated normal distribution.

(b) A starred value indicates a covariance estimate.

(c) (*), (**), and (***) indicate that the correlation coefficient or the covariance estimate is significant at the 10%, 5%, or 1% level, respectively; `ns` that it is non-significant at the 10% level

References

Amemiya T (1985) Advanced econometrics. Harvard University Press, Cambridge (MA)
Angulo AM, Gil JM, Gracia A (2001) The demand for alcoholic beverages in Spain. Agric Econ 26(1):71–83
Aristei D, Pieroni L (2008) A double-hurdle approach to modelling tobacco consumption in Italy. Appl Econ 40(19):2463–2476
Aristei D, Pieroni L (2009) Addiction, social interactions and gender differences in cigarette consumption. Empirica 36(3):245–272
Aristei D, Perali F, Pieroni L (2008) Cohort, age and time effects in alcohol consumption by Italian households: a double-hurdle approach. Empir Econ 35(1):29–61
Bertail P, Caillavet F, Nichele V (1999) A bootstrapped double hurdle analysis: consumption of home-produced food. Appl Econ 31(12):1631–1639
Blaylock JR, Blisard WN (1992) Self-evaluated health status and smoking behaviour. Appl Econ 24(4):429–435
Blaylock JR, Blisard WN (1993) Wine consumption by US men. Appl Econ 25(5):645–651
Blisard N, Blaylock J (1993) Distinguishing between market participation and infrequency of purchase models of butter demand. Am J Agr Econ 75(2):314–320
Blundell R, Meghir C (1987) Bivariate alternatives to the Tobit model. J Econom 34:179–200
Brouhle K, Khanna M (2012) Determinants of participation versus consumption in the Nordic Swan eco-labeled market. Ecol Econ 73:142–151
Burton M, Dorsett R, Young T (1996) Changing preferences for meat: evidence from UK household data, 1973–93. Eur Rev Agric Econ 23(3):357–370
Burton M, Dorsett R, Young T (2000) An investigation of the increasing prevalence of nonpurchase of meat by British households. Appl Econ 32(15):1985–1991
Cameron AC, Trivedi PK (2005) Microeconometrics: Methods and Applications. Cambridge University Press, New York
Carlevaro F, Croissant Y (2020) On the use of the Box-Cox transformation in censored and truncated regression models. Model Assist Stat Appl 15:197–214
Chaze JP (2005) Assessing household health expenditure with Box-Cox censoring models. Health Econ 14(9):893–907
Cheng H, Capps OJ (1988) Demand analysis of fresh and frozen finfish and shellfish in the United States. Am J Agr Econ 70(3):533–542
Cragg JG (1971) Some statistical models for limited dependent variables with applications for the demand for durable goods. Econometrica 39(5):829–44
Croissant Y, Carlevaro F, Hoareau S (2021) mhurdle: multiple hurdle models. https://CRAN.R-project.org/package=mhurdle. (R package version 1.3-0)
Crowley F, Eakins J, Jordan D (2012) Participation, expenditure and regressivity in the Irish lottery: evidence from Irish household budget survey 2004–05. Econ Soc Rev 43(2):199–225
Deaton A, Irish M (1984) A statistical model for zero expenditures in household budgets. J Public Econ 23(1–2):59–80
Estrella A (1998) A new measure of fit for equations with dichotomous dependent variables. J Bus Econ Stat 16(2):198–205
Fuller FH, Beghin JC, Rozelle S (2007) Consumption of dairy products in urban China: results from Beijing, Shangai and Guangzhou. Aust J Agric Resour Econ 51(4):459–474
Gao X, Wailes EJ, Cramer GL (1995) Double-hurdle model with bivariate normal errors: an application to U.S. rice demand. J Agric Appl Econ 27(2):363–376
Garcia J, Labeaga JM (1996) Alternative approaches to modelling zero expenditure: an application to Spanish demand for tobacco. Oxford Bull Econ Stat 58(3):489–506
Gould BW (1992) At-home consumption of cheese: a purchase-infrequency model. Am J Agr Econ 74(2):453–459
Haines PS, Guilkey DK, Popkin BM (1988) Modeling food consumption decisions as a two-step process. Am J Agr Econ 70(3):543–552

Heckman J (1976) Sample selection bias as a specification error. Econometrica 47(1):153–161
Hoareau S (2009) Modélisation économétrique des dépenses de consommation censurées. PhD thesis, Faculty of Law and Economics, University of Reunion
Johnson N (1949) Systems of frequency curves generated by methods of translation. Biometrika 36(1–2):149–176
Jones AM (1989) A double-hurdle model of cigarette consumption. J Appl Economet 4(1):23–39
Jones AM, Yen ST (2000) A Box-Cox double-hurdle model. Manch Sch 68(2):203–221
Keelan CD, Henchion MM, Newman CF (2009) A double-hurdle model of Irish households' food service expenditure patterns. J Int Food Agribus Mark 21(4):269–285
Mutlu S, Gracia A (2004) Food consumption away from home in Spain. J Food Prod Mark 10(2):1–16
Newman C, Henchion M, Matthews A (2001) Infrequency of purchase and double-hurdle models of Irish households' meat expenditure. Eur Rev Agric Econ 28(4):393–419
Newman C, Henchion M, Matthews A (2003) A double-hurdle model of Irish household expenditure on prepared meals. Appl Econ 35(9):1053–1061
Okunade AA, Suraratdecha C, Benson DA (2010) Determinants of Thailand household healthcare expenditure: the relevance of permanent resources and other correlates. Health Econ 19(3):365–376
Popkin BM, Guilkey DK, Haines PS (1989) Food consumption changes of adult women between 1977 and 1985. Am J Agr Econ 71(4):949–959
Pudney S (1989) Modelling individual choice. The econometrics of corners, kinks and holes. Basil Blackwell, Oxford and New York
Reynolds A (1990) Analysing fresh vegetable consumption from household survey data. South J Agric Econ 22(2):31–38
Shi X (2015) A nondegenerate Vuong test. Quant Econ 6:85–121
Simon H (1943) Symmetric tests of the hypothesis that the mean of one normal population exceeds that of another. Ann Math Stat 14(2):149–154
Smith M (2002) Handbook of applied econometrics and statistical inference, Marcel Dekker, New-York, chap On specifying double hurdle models
Su SJB, Yen ST (1996) Microeconometric models of infrequently purchased goods: an application to household pork consumption. Empir Econ 21(4):513–533
Tobin J (1958) Estimation of relationships for limited dependent variables. Econometrica 26(1):24–36
Vuong QH (1989) Likelihood ratio tests for selection and non-nested hypotheses. Econometrica 57(2):397–333
Wang J, Gao XM, Wailes EJ, Cramer GL (1996a) U.S. consumer demand for alcoholic beverages: cross-section estimation of demographic and economic effects. Rev Agric Econ 18(3):477–489
Wang Q, Jensen HH, Yen ST (1996) Impact of cholesterol information on the US egg consumption: evidence from consumer survey data. Appl Econ Lett 3(3):189–191
Yen ST (1993) Working wives and food away from home: the Box-Cox double hurdle model. Am J Agr Econ 75(4):884–895
Yen ST (1994) Cross-section estimation of US demand for alcoholic beverage. Appl Econ 26(4):381–392
Yen ST (1995) Alternative transformations in a class of limited dependent variable models: alcohol consumption by US women. Appl Econ Lett 2(8):258–262
Yen ST (1999) Gaussian versus count-data hurdle models: cigarette consumption by women in the US. Appl Econ Lett 6(2):73–76
Yen ST (2005) Zero observations and gender differences in cigarette consumption. Appl Econ 37(16):1839–1849
Yen ST, Huang CL (1996) Household demand for finfish: a generalized double-hurdle model. J Agric Resour Econ 21(2):220–234
Yen ST, Jensen HH (1996) Determinants of household expenditures on alcohol. J Consum Aff 30(1):48–67

Yen ST, Jones AM (1996) Individual cigarette consumption and addiction: a flexible limited dependent variable approach. Health Econ 5:105–117
Yen ST, Jones AM (1997) Household consumption of cheese: an inverse hyperbolic sine double-hurdle model with dependent errors. Am J Agr Econ 79(1):246–251
Yen ST, Su SJ (1995) Modeling U.S. butter consumption with zero observations. Agric Resour Econ Rev 24(1):47–55
Yen ST, Dellenbarger LE, Schupp AR (1995) Determinants of participation and consumption: the case of crawfish in South Louisiana. J Agric Appl Econ 27(1):253–262
Yen ST, Jensen HH, Wang O (1996) Cholesterol information and egg consumption in the US: a nonnormal and heteroscedastic double-hurdle model. Eur Rev Agric Econ 23(3):343–356
Zhang F, Huang CL, Lin BH (2008) Modeling fresh organic produce consumption: a generalized double-hurdle model approach. Agribusiness 24(4):510–522

Chapter 9
Conditional Mixed Process Modeling: Applications from the Agriculture Sector in Ghana

Yazeed Abdul Mumin, Benjamin Musah Abu, and Paul Kwame Nkegbe

Abstract Economists are often faced with situations in which the data generating processes are not continuous and unbounded. This is further complicated by the increasing need to model several and mixed (dependent) variables in a system, either as a system seemingly unrelated regressions, or in a more general system of simultaneous equations. However, few econometric models have been developed to handle such empirical questions and many other complex developments in the Stata ecosystem. The Conditional Mixed Process (CMP) Stata package was developed to respond to the increasing complexity of multi-equation, multi-level empirical research. CMP primarily fits a system of seemingly unrelated equations where the dependent variables are conceived as independent but with correlated errors. It is also flexible in fitting considerably larger class of simultaneous equation frameworks where dependent variables are considered endogenous and appear as explanatory variables in the other models, and in recursive settings. The CMP allows mixing of models in a multi-equation system. With the mixed process not being recursive but fully observed, the CMP relies on a maximum likelihood estimation and thereby circumvents the multistage, less efficient, routines of mixed models estimation. This chapter discusses the CMP with Stata implementation and application to data on Ghanaian agriculture.

Keywords Conditional mixed process · SUR models · Recursivity · Survival analysis · Ghana

---

Supplementary Information The online version contains supplementary material available at https://doi.org/10.1007/978-981-99-4902-1_9.

Y. Abdul Mumin · B. M. Abu
Department of Agricultural and Food Economics, University for Development Studies, Tamale, Ghana

P. K. Nkegbe (✉)
Department of Applied Economics, University for Development Studies, Tamale, Ghana
e-mail: pnkegbe@uds.edu.gh

D. Mukherjee (ed.), *Applied Econometric Analysis Using Cross Section and Panel Data*, Contributions to Economics, https://doi.org/10.1007/978-981-99-4902-1_9

9.1 Introduction

Economic issues and phenomena come from several aspects of life and in multiple ways and forms. Thus, economists are often faced with situations in which the data generating processes are not continuous and unbounded. Historically, the development of econometric models was based on continuous and unbounded dependent variables. However, in recent times, especially dictated by real empirical events, the monopoly of continuous and unbounded variables has been broken. In addition to this, current empirical developments are increasingly becoming convoluted, especially imposed by the increasing need to model several and mixed (dependent) variables in a system, either as a system seemingly unrelated regressions, or in a more general system of simultaneous equations.

For instance, agricultural economists have long studied the association between productivity, improved crop varietal adoption, and climate smart agricultural practices. In this case, whereas productivity is a continuous variable which can be estimated in a classical linear regression model, adoption of improved crop variety and climate smart practices are not continuous but either binary or discrete variables. Hence these will need to be estimated either by a binary regression model or a multinomial regression model. A similar situation arises in the agricultural commercialization literature proposed by Burke et al. (2015), who conceived of agricultural commercialization at three stages. The first stage involves farmers being categorized into producers and non-producers and requires a probit model to evaluate the determinants. In the second stage, producers are classified in an ordered fashion into net-buyers, autarkic, and net-sellers, which requires an ordered probit model to evaluate the determinants. In the third stage, the dependent variable is quantity bought or sold, and this requires a log-normal model to fit the determinants. The challenge of this empirical work is that the three stages are to be estimated in a multi-equation system simultaneously. Therefore, using standalone models of probit, ordered probit, and log-normal does not fit the objective of the analysis. A host of other empirical studies (e.g., Mottaleb et al. 2022; Nkegbe and Abdul Mumin 2022; Alhassan et al. 2020; Agbanyo and Peprah 2021; Sekyi et al. 2017; Makate et al. 2016; Roodman and Morduch 2014) raise this multi-equation simultaneous systems situation.

The complication posed by these empirical studies is not necessarily the challenge, but rather the rarity of econometric models to handle these and many complex developments (see Roodman 2011). Few econometric models have been developed to handle such empirical questions in the Stata ecosystem. For instance, the *movestay*, *switch_probit*, *ivtobit*, and *heckprob* commands have been developed to handle empirical issues that were not previously possible with official Stata commands. But even these user-written commands are developed to handle specific empirical issues. To provide a package that has the capability to respond to increasing complexity of multi-equation, multi-level empirical research and fill the void of rare econometric models, Roodman (2011) developed the Conditional Mixed Process (CMP) Stata package. In fact, "*cmp is the first general Stata tool for this class of models, and even it could be extended much further*" (Roodman 2011:160). CMP primarily fits a system of seemingly unrelated equations where the dependent variables are conceived as independent but with correlated errors. It is also flexible in fitting considerably larger class of simultaneous equation frameworks where dependent variables are considered endogenous and appear as explanatory variables in the other models, and in recursive settings. The CMP allows mixing of models in a multi-equation system. With the mixed process not being recursive but fully observed, the CMP relies on a maximum likelihood estimation and thereby circumvents the multistage, less efficient, routines of mixed model estimation.

Though the motivation for developing CMP is not to replicate existing commands (both official Stata and user-written), it does well to provide the platform to match these commands. For example, CMP replicates a host of existing commands including *probit*, *oprobit*, *mprobit*, *mvprobit*, *ivprobit*, *biprobit*, *triprobit*, *tobit*, *bitobit*, *mvtobit*, *intreg*, *heckman*, *heckprob*, *truncreg*, *treatreg*, among others. At its best, CMP permits the mixing of different models in multi-equation system that is not otherwise possible within existing Stata official and user-written commands. For example, a study that assumes correlated errors of credit access (measured as a dummy variable), credit constraints (measured as a dummy variable) and agricultural commercialization (measured as a continuous variable) and aims to simultaneously examine the determinants of these variables is not possible with existing Stata commands. In standalone modelling, a probit model can provide the determinants of credit access and credit constraints, and ordinary least squares (OLS) can provide the determinants of agricultural commercialization, but these standalone models break the assumption of correlated errors of these respective models. CMP provides the mechanism to simultaneously model these three phenomena and provides an estimate of the correlation between the error terms. Associated with the multi-equation capability is the ability to fit different models that have different observations (i.e., the models can be conditioned on the data). Further, CMP helps overcome the challenges of estimating models that were hitherto difficult to estimate.

The motivation for this chapter, thus, stems from discussing the CMP Stata package and demonstrating its usefulness in fitting multi-equation and mixed models with application to data on Ghanaian agriculture.

9.2 Econometric Theory of Seemingly Unrelated Regression (SUR) Models

Seemingly unrelated regression (SUR) or seemingly unrelated regression equation (SURE) models comprise a set of regression models, each model having its own dependent and explanatory variables. They are seemingly unrelated because no dependent variable is treated as endogenous in the other set of models, but their error terms may be correlated. While SUR models can be estimated separately (i.e., as standalone equations), simultaneous modeling accounts for the joint estimation of their correlated errors, thus improving efficiency (see Roodman 2011).

The basic theoretical econometric specification of a SUR system is stated as:

$$y^* = \boldsymbol{x}'\boldsymbol{\beta} + \varepsilon'$$

$$\mathrm{y} = g(y^*) = \{g_1(y^*), \ldots, g_J(y^*)\}' \tag{9.1}$$

$$\varepsilon|X \sim \text{i.i.d.}N(0, \Sigma)$$

where β is a matrix of coefficients, y and ε are random vectors, $\boldsymbol{x}$ is a vector of explanatory variables and g is a link function. It is important to note that equations can vary by the number of X.

9.2.1 Bivariate Model

A common SUR model is the bivariate probit model. The specification of a bivariate probit model is stated as:

$$y_1^* = \theta_1 + \varepsilon_1$$

$$y_2^* = \theta_2 + \varepsilon_2$$

$$\mathrm{y} = g(y^*) = \left(1\{y_1^* > 0\}, 1\{y_2^* > 0\}\right)' \tag{9.2}$$

$$\varepsilon = (\varepsilon_1, \varepsilon_2)' \sim N(0, \Sigma)$$

$$\Sigma = \begin{vmatrix} 1 & \rho \\ \rho & 1 \end{vmatrix}$$

where $\theta_1 = \beta_1 X$ and $\theta_2 = \beta_2 X$ just to simplify the equations. Assume that $y_{i1} = y_{i2} = 0$, then the likelihood function is specified as:

$$L_i(\beta_1, \beta_2, \rho; y_i|x_i) = \int_{-\infty}^{-\theta_{i1}} \int_{-\infty}^{-\theta_{i2}} \phi\{(\varepsilon_1, \varepsilon_2)'; \Sigma\} d\varepsilon_2 d\varepsilon_1 = \Phi\{(-\theta_{i1}, -\theta_{i2})'; \Sigma\} \tag{9.3}$$

However, if we assume that $y_{i1} = y_{i2} = 1$, then the likelihood function is specified as:

$$L_i(\beta_1, \beta_2, \rho; y_i|x_i) = \int_{-\theta_1}^{\infty}\int_{-\theta_2}^{\infty} \phi\{(\varepsilon_1, \varepsilon_2)'; \Sigma\}d\varepsilon_2 d\varepsilon_1 = \Phi\{(\theta_{i1}, \theta_{i2})'; \Sigma\} \tag{9.4}$$

In general, the likelihood function of the bivariate probit is stated as:

$$L_i(\beta_1, \beta_2, \rho; y_i|x_i) = \Phi\{(q_1\theta_{i1}, q_2\theta_{i2})'; \Sigma\} \tag{9.5}$$

where $q_j = 2y_{ij} - 1$. The bivariate probit is a SUR model but not a mixed model since there are two probit models.

9.3 CMP and its Benefits

CMP (conditional mixed-process) is a multipurpose and flexible command that fits a variety of multi-equation, conditional mixed-process, and multi-level estimators and thus equations. Multi-equation implies CMP fits typical SUR, instrumental variables (IV) and simultaneous equation systems. Mixed process implies that a system of simultaneous equations can take on different dependent variables. That is, it can fit, for example, a three-stage model—first stage probit, second stage ordered probit, and third stage continuous model. Conditional implies that different equations in a multi-equation model can have different observations. For example, in the study of Burke et al. (2015), the first stage fits a model of farmers who produced a crop and the second stage models whether producers are net-sellers, net-buyers or autarkic. Thus, the set of observations for the second stage is lower since it only concentrates on producers. Recursive implies that in a multi-equation modeling framework, the dependent variable in the first equation can be an explanatory variable in the second equation in that order, but not the reverse.

1. Multi-equation estimation: CMP can estimate multiple equation models such as the Seemingly Unrelated (SUR) systems, instrumental variables (IV) systems, and some simultaneous-equation systems in which the dependent variable of each equation enters the other equations as a linear (latent) function.
2. Conditional (recursive) mixed-process estimators: CMP can estimate different equations with different types of dependent (i.e., continuous, binary, discrete, interval, etc.) variables, which makes it a "mixed process." Similarly, it can fit a model where the model or type of response variable depends on the data or observation.
3. Multi-level multiprocess estimation: CMP can estimate models where the random coefficients and effects can be modeled in hierarchical levels. In estimating such models, the multi-level nature of CMP accounts for unit level unobserved traits whereas the multi-equation ability of the model allows for random effects at one given level to be correlated across equations.

Table 9.1 CMP's equation types and their expressions

Model type	Expression	
	Number	Statement
Observation not in equation	0	$cmp_out
Observation in equation with unobserved dependent variable		$cmp_missing
Continuous	1	$cmp_cont
Left-censored (tobit)	2	$cmp_left
Right-censored (tobit)	3	$cmp_right
Probit	4	$cmp_probit
Ordered probit	5	$cmp_oprobit
Multinomial probit	6	$cmp_mprobit
Interval-censored	7	$cmp_int
Truncated	8	$cmp_trunc
Rank-ordered	9	$cmp_roprobit
Fractional probit	10	$cmp_frac

To install the CMP package, the user should connect to the internet and type "ssc install cmp" into the Stata command window and execute. Stata will install the package. The ghk2() Mata function, which implements the GHK multivariate normal simulator, must be installed separately for CMP to function. After installation, the user can learn initial details about CMP by typing and executing "*help cmp*" or "*h cmp*" in the command window. The various equations and their expressions accepted by CMP are presented in Table 9.1.

9.3.1 Stata Illustration of Bivariate Probit Model

Credit and crop market participation are two important decisions of agricultural farm households. Credit access stimulates technology adoption that boosts productivity and increases marketable surpluses for sale to raise crop income. Thus, estimating the determinants of credit and crop market participation decisions has been of interest to agricultural economists. In this example, we estimate a bivariate probit model of households' credit decisions (cred) and participation in maize market (maize_part1) because of the possibility that unobserved factors may drive correlation between household credit and crop market participation decisions. Based on the data at hand (see Tables 9.9 and 9.10 in the Appendix), we aim to estimate the empirical models:

$$\begin{aligned} cred_i = {} & \alpha_0 + \alpha_1 hhage_i + \alpha_2 hhsex_i + \alpha_3 edyears_i + \alpha_4 hhsize_i + \alpha_5 hhloc_i \\ & + \alpha_6 remit_i + \alpha_7 commmnet_i + \alpha_8 mfag_i + \alpha_9 mtrd_i + \alpha_{10} ptpass_i \\ & + \alpha_{11} commbank_i + \alpha_{12} econact_i + \alpha_{13} chemfert_i \end{aligned}$$

$$+ \alpha_{14} commextoff_i + e_i \tag{9.6a}$$

$$\begin{aligned} maize\_part1_i = {} & \beta_0 + \beta_1 hhage_i + \beta_2 hhsex_i + \beta_3 edyears_i + \beta_4 hhsize_i \\ & + \beta_5 hhloc_i + \beta_6 remit_i + \beta_7 commmnet_i + \beta_8 mfag_i + \beta_9 mtrd_i \\ & + \beta_{10} ptpass_i + \beta_{11} commbank_i + \beta_{12} econact_i \\ & + \beta_{13} chemfert_i + \beta_{14} commextoff_i + \beta_{15} maize\_fsize\_ha_i + v_i \end{aligned} \tag{9.6b}$$

The basic assumption is that $cov(e_i, v_i) \neq 0$. The command for implementing the models using "cmp" is (see Table 9.11 in the Appendix for corresponding "biprobit" command):

```
cmp (cred = hhage hhsex edyears hhsize hhloc remit commmnet mfag mtrd
ptpass commbank econact chemfert commextoff) (maize_part1 = hhage
hhsex edyears hhsize hhloc remit commmnet mfag mtrd ptpass comm-
bank econact chemfert commextoff maize_fsize_ha) if maize_prod ==
1, ind($cmp_probit $cmp_probit)
```

The "if maize_prod == 1" instructs Stata to restrict the analysis to only households that produced maize. Because both credit (cred) and market participation (maize_part1) are dummy variables, we add the indicator options $cmp_probit and $cmp_probit to inform Stata that both models should be estimated using probit models. The results from implementing the commands are presented in Table 9.2.

The coefficient of rho is negative and statistically significant at the 1% significance level. This implies that unobserved factors that increase households' probability of credit access decrease their probability of market participation. CMP also allows for the estimation of the marginal effects of these binary models. This is done by using the "margins" command and specifying the equation number. The marginal effects of the models estimated using the following commands are presented in Table 9.3.

```
margins, dydx(*) predict(eq(#1) pr)
margins, dydx(*) predict(eq(#2) pr)
```

The results show that household head's sex (hhsex) has a negative and statistically significant effect. The estimate shows that probability of obtaining credit decreases by 0.05 with a household head being male (relative to a female-headed household, the reference group). For further reading on empirical application of the bivariate probit, see Salazar et al. (2019) and Torres et al. (2016).

Table 9.2 Bivariate probit regression

Variable	"cmp"		"biprobit"	
	Credit	Sold maize	Credit	Sold maize
Age of head	−0.002 (0.002)	0.000 (0.001)	−0.002 (0.002)	0.000 (0.001)
Sex of head	−0.290*** (0.068)	0.088 (0.054)	−0.290*** (0.068)	0.088 (0.054)
Years of education of head	0.027*** (0.006)	0.014*** (0.005)	0.027*** (0.006)	0.014*** (0.005)
Household size	0.015* (0.009)	−0.032*** (0.007)	0.015* (0.009)	−0.032*** (0.007)
Household resides in rural area	0.158* (0.086)	0.216*** (0.065)	0.158* (0.086)	0.216*** (0.065)
Received cash remittance	0.335*** (0.055)	0.060 (0.044)	0.335*** (0.055)	0.060 (0.044)
Mobile phone network in community	0.111 (0.068)	0.145*** (0.050)	0.111 (0.068)	0.145*** (0.050)
Membership of cooperatives and fbos	0.015 (0.124)	−0.214** (0.090)	0.015 (0.124)	−0.214** (0.090)
Navigable road to community	−0.026 (0.083)	0.606*** (0.067)	−0.026 (0.083)	0.606*** (0.067)
Public transport availability	−0.083 (0.072)	0.449*** (0.053)	−0.083 (0.072)	0.449*** (0.053)
Bank in community	−0.008 (0.100)	0.172** (0.070)	−0.008 (0.100)	0.172** (0.070)
Major economic activity in community	−0.008 (0.108)	0.024 (0.082)	−0.008 (0.108)	0.024 (0.082)
Use of chemical fertilizer in community	0.297*** (0.086)	−0.277*** (0.059)	0.297*** (0.086)	−0.277*** (0.059)
Agric extension office in community	−0.434*** (0.106)	0.442*** (0.065)	−0.434*** (0.106)	0.442*** (0.065)
Maize farm size		0.057*** (0.009)		0.057*** (0.009)
Constant	−1.670*** (0.183)	−1.267*** (0.145)	−1.670*** (0.183)	−1.267*** (0.145)
Observations	4606		4606	
Wald chi-square/LR chi-square	983.440***		861.971***	
Rho	−0.121***		−0.121***	
LR test of rho = 0			11.156***	

Note * $p < 0.1$, ** $p < 0.05$, *** $p < 0.01$; Standard errors in parentheses
Source Produced using the GLSS7 Data

Table 9.3 Marginal effect after cmp bivariate probit regression

Variable	Credit		Sold maize	
	Marginal effect	Std. error	Marginal effect	Std. error
Age of head	−0.000	0.000	0.000	0.000
Sex of head	−0.046***	0.011	0.028	0.017
Years of education of head	0.004***	0.001	0.004***	0.001
Household size	0.002*	0.001	−0.010***	0.002
Household resides in rural area	0.025*	0.014	0.068***	0.021
Received cash remittance	0.054***	0.009	0.019	0.014
Mobile phone network in community	0.018	0.011	0.046***	0.016
Membership of cooperatives and fbos	0.002	0.020	−0.068**	0.028
Navigable road to community	−0.004	0.013	0.191***	0.021
Public transport availability	−0.013	0.012	0.142***	0.016
Bank in community	−0.001	0.016	0.054**	0.022
Major economic activity in community	−0.001	0.017	0.007	0.026
Use of chemical fertilizer in community	0.048***	0.014	−0.088***	0.018
Agric extension office in community	−0.070***	0.017	0.140***	0.020
Maize farm size			0.018***	0.003
Observations	4606		4606	

Note * $p < 0.1$, ** $p < 0.05$, *** $p < 0.01$; Standard errors in parentheses
Source Produced using the GLSS7 Data

9.4 CMP and Other SUR Models

9.4.1 Mixed-Process Uncensored Model

To illustrate a mixed SUR model, an example of an uncensored-probit model is shown. This implies the first equation is a linear model and the second equation is a probit model. The structure of this mixed SUR model is specified as:

$$y_1^* = \theta_1 + \varepsilon_1$$

$$y_2^* = \theta_2 + \varepsilon_2$$

$$\mathrm{y} = g(y^*) = \left(y_1^*, 1\{y_2^* > 0\}\right)' \tag{9.7}$$

$$\varepsilon = (\varepsilon_1, \varepsilon_2)' \sim N(0, \Sigma)$$

$$\Sigma = \begin{vmatrix} \sigma_{11} & \sigma_{12} \\ \sigma_{12} & 1 \end{vmatrix}$$

where θ_1 and θ_2 are as defined earlier. If, for example, $y_i = (y_{i1}, 0)'$ is observed, the likelihood function is specified as:

$$L_i(\beta_1, \beta_2, \Sigma; y_i|x_i) = \int_{-\infty}^{-\theta_2} \phi\{(y_{i1} - \theta_{i1}, \varepsilon_2)'; \Sigma\} d\varepsilon_2 \quad (9.8)$$

This function shows the usefulness of CMP because no classical statistical function in econometric software can directly estimate it. CMP factorizes $\phi\{(\varepsilon_1, \varepsilon_2); \Sigma\}$ into probability distribution functions for ε_1 and $\varepsilon_2|\varepsilon_1$ that yields:

$$\phi\{(\varepsilon_1, \varepsilon_2); \Sigma\} = \phi(\varepsilon_1; \sigma_{11})\}\phi\left(\varepsilon_2 - \frac{\sigma_{21}}{\sigma_{11}}\varepsilon_1; 1 - \frac{\sigma_{21}\sigma_{12}}{\sigma_{11}}\right)$$

Symmetrically, $\sigma_{21} = \sigma_{12}$. If this factorized function is substituted into initial equation, it yields:

$$L_i(\beta_1, \beta_2, \Sigma; y_i|x_i) = \int_{-\infty}^{-\theta_2} \phi(y_{i1} - \theta_{i1}; \sigma_{11})\phi\left\{\varepsilon_2 - \frac{\sigma_{21}}{\sigma_{11}}(y_{i1} - \theta_{i1}); 1 - \frac{\sigma_{21}\sigma_{12}}{\sigma_{11}}\right\} d\varepsilon_2$$

$$= \phi(y_{i1} - \theta_{i1}; \sigma_{11}) \int_{-\infty}^{-\theta_2} \phi\left\{\varepsilon_2 - \frac{\sigma_{21}}{\sigma_{11}}(y_{i1} - \theta_{i1}); 1 - \frac{\sigma_{21}\sigma_{12}}{\sigma_{11}}\right\} d\varepsilon_2$$

$$= \phi(y_{i1} - \theta_{i1}; \sigma_{11})\Phi\left\{-\theta_2 - \frac{\sigma_{21}}{\sigma_{11}}(y_{i1} - \theta_{i1}); 1 - \frac{\sigma_{21}\sigma_{12}}{\sigma_{11}}\right\} \quad (9.9)$$

With this simplified function, which is a product of a normal probability density and cumulative normal density functions, classical functions can be used to estimate it in econometric software. This specific example of a two-equation mixed model provides the foundation for any type of mixed model. For all equation types, including continuous (i.e., linear), Tobit, probit, ordered probit, multinomial probit, interval-censored, truncated, rank-ordered, and fractional probit, mixed modeling dictates that different equations are developed in a multi-equation and estimated simultaneously in a SUR fashion (i.e., jointly estimating the error terms of the respective models).

9.4.1.1 Stata Illustration

Taking inspiration from the credit-crop market participation models, we apply CMP to model the determinants of credit, yield, and market participation of maize farmers in a mixed probit-uncensored model. In this setting, credit and market participation are binary, and maize yield is a continuous variable. Using `$cmp_probit`, `$cmp_cont`, and `$cmp_probit` respectively indicate that the first equation (i.e., credit model) should be fitted with a probit, the second equation (i.e., yield) should be fitted with OLS and the third equation (i.e., market participation) should be fitted with a probit model, which makes the system a mixed process. The empirical specifications of the three models are:

$$\begin{aligned} cred_i = {} & \alpha_0 + \alpha_1 hhage_i + \alpha_2 hhsex_i + \alpha_3 edyears_i + \alpha_4 hhsize_i + \alpha_5 hhloc_i \\ & + \alpha_6 remit_i + \alpha_7 commmnet_i + \alpha_8 mfag_i + \alpha_9 mtrd_i + \alpha_{10} ptpass_i \\ & + \alpha_{11} commbank_i + \alpha_{12} econact_i + \alpha_{13} maize\_fsize\_ha_i \\ & + \alpha_{14} regiondum_i + e_i \end{aligned} \tag{9.10a}$$

$$\begin{aligned} myield_i = {} & \gamma_0 + \gamma_1 hhage_i + \gamma_2 hhsex_i + \gamma_3 edyears_i + \gamma_4 hhsize_i + \gamma_5 hhloc_i \\ & + \gamma_6 remit_i + \gamma_7 commmnet_i + \gamma_8 mfag_i + \gamma_9 mtrd_i + \gamma_{10} ptpass_i \\ & + \gamma_{11} commbank_i + \gamma_{12} econact_i + \gamma_{13} chemfert_i \\ & + \gamma_{14} commextoff_i + \gamma_{15} maize\_fsize\_ha_i + \gamma_{16} regiondum_i + \varsigma_i \end{aligned} \tag{9.10b}$$

$$\begin{aligned} maize\_part1_i = {} & \beta_0 + \beta_1 hhage_i + \beta_2 hhsex_i + \beta_3 edyears_i + \beta_4 hhsize_i + \beta_5 hhloc_i \\ & + \beta_6 remit_i + \beta_7 commmnet_i + \beta_8 mfag_i + \beta_9 mtrd_i + \beta_{10} ptpass_i \\ & + \beta_{11} commbank_i + \beta_{12} econact_i + \beta_{13} chemfert_i \\ & + \beta_{14} commextoff_i + \beta_{15} maize\_fsize\_ha_i + \beta_{16} regiondum_i + v_i \end{aligned} \tag{9.10c}$$

Again, the basic assumption is that $cov(e_i, \varsigma_i, v_i) \neq 0$. The command for implementing the models using "cmp" is:

```
cmp (cred = hhage hhsex edyears hhsize hhloc remit commmnet mfag mtrd
ptpass commbank econact maize_fsize_ha regiondum) (myield = hhage
hhsex edyears hhsize hhloc remit commmnet mfag mtrd ptpass commbank
econact chemfert commextoff maize_fsize_ha regiondum) (maize_part
= hhage hhsex edyears hhsize hhloc remit commmnet mfag mtrd ptpass
commbank econact chemfert commextoff maize_fsize_ha regiondum) if
maize_prod == 1, ind($cmp_probit $cmp_cont $cmp_probit) nolog
```

The results from this command are reported in Table 9.4.

In contrast to single-equation models, CMP provides the standalone models of credit, yield, and market participation before estimating the multi-equation model of the three. The rho parameters measure the correlation among the respective error terms. Thus, rho_12 provides the estimate of the correlation between the error terms of Eq. 9.10a (credit model) and Eq. 9.10b (yield model). rho_13 measures the correlation between the error terms of Eqs. 9.10a and 9.10c (market participation model) and rho_23 measures the correlation between the error terms of Eqs. 9.10b and 9.10c. The extra parameters not shown in Table 9.4 (i.e., lnsig_2, antanhrho_12, antanhrho_

Table 9.4 Determinants of credit, yield and market participation

Variable	Access to credit	Maize yield	Sold maize
Age of head	−0.002 (0.002)	0.587 (1.055)	−0.001 (0.001)
Sex of head	-0.277^{***} (0.068)	84.674^{**} (41.569)	0.170^{***} (0.056)
Years of education of head	0.028^{***} (0.006)	−0.587 (3.675)	−0.003 (0.005)
Household size	0.014 (0.009)	−7.400 (5.092)	-0.025^{***} (0.007)
Household resides in rural area	0.158^{*} (0.085)	−56.050 (48.599)	0.185^{***} (0.066)
Received cash remittance	0.335^{***} (0.055)	1.999 (33.925)	0.024 (0.044)
Mobile phone network in community	0.141^{**} (0.067)	41.911 (39.240)	0.189^{***} (0.050)
Membership of cooperatives and fbos	−0.031 (0.122)	209.235^{***} (72.429)	-0.265^{***} (0.092)
Navigable road to community	−0.055 (0.083)	29.792 (49.143)	0.687^{***} (0.069)
Public transport availability	−0.122 (0.074)	−21.560 (43.928)	0.312^{***} (0.055)
Bank in community	−0.146 (0.094)	4.569 (56.725)	0.185^{***} (0.071)
Major economic activity in community	0.045 (0.106)	-243.245^{***} (62.333)	0.069 (0.084)
Maize farm size	0.006 (0.011)	-23.798^{***} (7.976)	0.061^{***} (0.009)
Household in southern Ghana	−0.009 (0.062)	167.382^{***} (37.481)	0.501^{***} (0.049)
Use of chemical fertilizer in community		160.174^{***} (45.963)	-0.202^{***} (0.059)
Agric extension office in community		137.683^{***} (52.958)	0.445^{***} (0.065)
Constant	-1.487^{***} (0.174)	725.716^{***} (107.537)	-1.527^{***} (0.150)
Observations	4606	1636	1636
Wald-statistic	1154.366^{***}		
Rho_12	0.024		
Rho_13	-0.118^{**}		
Rho_23	0.224^{**}		

Note * $p < 0.1$, ** $p < 0.05$, *** $p < 0.01$; Standard errors in parentheses
Source Produced using the GLSS7 Data

13, antanhrho_23) ensure that infeasible estimates for their respective parameters are eliminated. For example, once sigma cannot be negative, lnsig is estimated to ensure that sigma is not negative. Since the first and third equations are probit models, the marginal effects of their respective parameters can be estimated just as we did in the bivariate probit example with the `margins, dydx(*) predict(eq(#1) pr)` and `margins, dydx(*) predict(eq(#3) pr)`, respectively. For further reading on the application of mixed models, see Sekyi et al. (2017).

Agricultural commercialization literature developed from the background of a two-stage modeling approach. That is, farm households make the decision to sell and then decide the quantity to sell. However, Burke et al. (2015) challenged the two-stage approach by arguing that the first decision of farm households is the decision to produce a particular crop before making participation and sale quantity decisions. This birthed the triple-hurdle modeling approach. We estimate a triple-hurdle model of agricultural commercialization of farmers inspired by the work of Burke et al. (2015). Originally, the first stage is a model of farmers who produced a crop, the second stage is a model of whether producers are net-sellers, net-buyers or autarkic and the third stage is a model of the quantity sold. However, the second stage modeled here is whether farmers sold maize or not. Thus, the first and second stages are fitted with a probit and the third stage is fitted with a fractional model. The empirical models are specified as:

$$\begin{aligned} maize\_prod_i = {} & \alpha_0 + \alpha_1 hhage_i + \alpha_2 hhsex_i + \alpha_3 edyears_i + \alpha_4 hhsize_i \\ & + \alpha_5 hhloc_i + \alpha_6 remit_i + \alpha_7 commmnet_i + \alpha_8 mfag_i + \alpha_9 mtrd_i \\ & + \alpha_{10} ptpass_i + \alpha_{11} commbank_i + \alpha_{12} econact_i \\ & + \alpha_{13} chemfert_i + \alpha_{14} commextoff_i + e_i \end{aligned} \tag{9.11a}$$

$$\begin{aligned} m\_part1_i = {} & \beta_0 + \beta_1 hhage_i + \beta_2 hhsex_i + \beta_3 edyears_i + \beta_4 hhsize_i + \beta_5 hhloc_i \\ & + \beta_6 remit_i + \beta_7 commmnet_i + \beta_8 mfag_i + \beta_9 mtrd_i + \beta_{10} ptpass_i \\ & + \beta_{11} commbank_i + \beta_{12} econact_i + \beta_{13} chemfert_i + \beta_{14} commextoff \\ & + \beta_{15} maize\_fsize\_ha_i + \varsigma_i \end{aligned} \tag{9.11b}$$

$$\begin{aligned} maize\_hcifrac_i = {} & \delta_0 + \delta_1 hhage_i + \delta_2 hhsex_i + \delta_3 edyears_i + \delta_4 hhsize_i \\ & + \delta_5 hhloc_i + \delta_6 remit_i + \delta_7 commmnet_i + \delta_8 mfag_i + \delta_9 mtrd_i \\ & + \delta_{10} ptpass_i + \delta_{11} commbank_i + \delta_{12} econact_i + \delta_{13} chemfert_i \\ & + \delta_{14} commextoff_i + \delta_{15} maize\_fsize\_ha_i + \tau_i \end{aligned} \tag{9.11c}$$

The command for implementing the triple-hurdle model is:

```
cmp (maize_prod = hhage hhsex edyears hhsize hhloc remit commmnet
mfag mtrd ptpass commbank econact chemfert commextoff) (maize_
part1 = hhage hhsex edyears hhsize hhloc remit commmnet mfag
mtrd ptpass commbank econact chemfert commextoff maize_fsize_ha)
(maize_hcifrac = hhage hhsex edyears hhsize hhloc remit commmnet
mfag mtrd ptpass commbank econact chemfert commextoff maize_fsize_
ha), ind($cmp_probit $cmp_probit $cmp_frac) tech(dfp bhhh) nolog
```

Table 9.5 reports the results of the triple-hurdle model.

The expression `tech(dfp bhhh)` is Stata's standard maximization option which is added to help the estimation achieve convergence. Without it, the default tech(nr), which specifies the use of Newton–Raphson (NR) algorithm, failed to achieve convergence. The other algorithms available are tech(bhhh), which specifies the use of Berndt-Hall-Hall-Hausman (BHHH) algorithm, tech(dfp), which specifies the use of Davidon-Fletcher-Powell (DFP) algorithm and tech(bfgs), which specifies the use of Broyden-Fletcher-Goldfarb-Shanno (BFGS) algorithm. In this example, "dfp" and "bhhh" are used together since "tech()" allows the use of more than one algorithm. As indicated earlier, the rho parameters are estimated to show the correlations among the error terms of the respective models. The marginal effects can then be estimated for each equation using the command `margins, dydx(*) predict(eq(#...) pr)` with the equation number specified just after the hash symbol (#).

9.4.2 Recursive Systems

Just like the maximum likelihood SUR, the cmp can consistently estimate parameters of a recursive (either mixed or not) simultaneous system model that is fully observed. Such a model will normally have clearly defined stages where the right-hand side of the equation for the first endogenous variable includes only exogenous variables and the endogenous variables (i.e., the left-hand size of preceding equations) will appear on the right-hand side of each successive equation. This forms a simultaneous equation model commonly referred to in the econometrics literature as the triangular system (Greene 2012). The name is derived from the recursivity of the model where the equations are arranged in a way that the coefficients of the endogenous variables in one another's equations form a triangular matrix. Recursive models have clearly defined stages with one or more equations in each stage. To specify this, we can modify the SUR system specified earlier as:

$$y_1^* = \boldsymbol{x}'\boldsymbol{\beta}_1 + \varepsilon_1,$$

$$y_2^* = \boldsymbol{x}'\boldsymbol{\beta}_2 + \delta_{12}y_1 + \varepsilon_2,$$

$$y_3^* = \boldsymbol{x}'\boldsymbol{\beta}_3 + \delta_{13}y_1 + \delta_{23}y_2 + \varepsilon_3, \tag{9.12}$$

$$\varepsilon|X \sim \text{i.i.d.}N(0, \Sigma)$$

$$\Sigma = \begin{vmatrix} 1 & \rho \\ \rho & 1 \end{vmatrix}$$

Table 9.5 Triple-hurdle model of agricultural commercialization

Variable	Produced maize	Sold maize	Maize commercialization index
Age of head	0.001 (0.001)	−0.000 (0.001)	0.001 (0.001)
Sex of head	0.341*** (0.034)	−0.202*** (0.042)	0.093 (0.445)
Years of education of head	−0.025*** (0.003)	0.024*** (0.003)	0.006 (0.043)
Household size	0.057*** (0.005)	−0.056*** (0.005)	−0.024 (0.102)
Household resides in rural area	0.370*** (0.037)	−0.146*** (0.045)	0.068 (0.440)
Received cash remittance	0.028 (0.030)	−0.004 (0.033)	−0.013 (0.045)
Mobile phone network in community	−0.029 (0.039)	0.127*** (0.039)	−0.087 (0.113)
Membership of cooperatives and fbos	−1.858*** (0.042)	1.270*** (0.057)	−0.191 (2.747)
Navigable road to community	0.458*** (0.050)	−0.015 (0.049)	−0.000 (0.417)
Public transport availability	−0.211*** (0.045)	0.398*** (0.042)	0.099 (0.555)
Bank in community	0.053 (0.044)	0.049 (0.052)	0.252*** (0.072)
Major economic activity in community	0.424*** (0.044)	−0.265*** (0.052)	0.106 (0.565)
Use of chemical fertilizer in community	0.050 (0.040)	−0.171*** (0.043)	−0.151 (0.230)
Agric extension office in community	0.005 (0.044)	0.301*** (0.049)	0.023 (0.241)
Maize farm size		0.056* (0.031)	0.042 (0.058)
Constant	−1.010*** (0.085)	0.711*** (0.102)	0.012 (1.516)
Observations	14,009	1636	1636
Wald-statistic	6299.817***		
Rho_12	−0.985***		
Rho_13	0.160		
Rho_23	−0.167		

Note * $p < 0.1$, ** $p < 0.05$, *** $p < 0.01$; Standard errors in parentheses
Source Produced using the GLSS7 Data

A case in point is the two-stage probit (in which $y = f(y^*) = (1[y_1^* > 0], 1[y_1^* > 0])')$ which can be expressed following the bivariate probit model by adding the dependent variable in the first stage as an independent variable in the second stage as expressed in Eq. (9.12) above. Here ρ measures the endogeneity of the dependent variable in the first stage as an explanatory variable in the second stage. If we again assume that $y_{i1} = y_{i2} = 0$, then the likelihood function is specified as:

$$L_i(\beta_1, \beta_2, \delta, \rho; y_i|x_i) = \int_{-\infty}^{-\theta_{i1}} \int_{-\infty}^{-\theta_{i2}} \phi_{\varepsilon_1}(\varepsilon_1)\phi_{\varepsilon_2|\varepsilon_1}(\varepsilon_2)d\varepsilon_2 d\varepsilon_1 \tag{9.13}$$

Recursive equation systems emanate in two principal means. The first is the most popular case of limited-information procedure where it is only the final stages that are fully specified while the preceding stages are instrumented to account for endogeneity. Cases in point are the 2SLS and related linear models such as the 3SLS which produce consistent estimates, even in the presence of heteroscedasticity, if the dependent variable of the final stage is continuous and unbounded (Roodman 2011). However, if the dependent variable of the final stage is not continuous and bounded, such a limited-information approach could produce inefficient estimates. A simple example is the two-stage probit model and mixed-process system where the dependent variable in the final stage is not continuous and bounded. This results in the second instance, which is the full-information approach. The full-information case does not omit any variable and the structural model in this case is inherently recursive and completely specified, leading to recursive system of equations. Here CMP handles such recursive systems and produces consistent estimates by explicitly modeling any censoring and estimating the equations as a system.

9.4.2.1 Stata Illustration

Let us now replicate the procedure of Alhassan et al. (2020) by estimating their recursive set up. The main objective of their study was to use a simultaneous modeling approach to test whether credit affects maize yield, and whether maize yield in turn affects market participation. Here, unlike the mixed-process uncensored example, credit is added to the yield model as an explanatory variable and yield is added to the market participation model as an explanatory variable. The empirical model is specified as:

$$\begin{aligned} cred_i =& \alpha_0 + \alpha_1 hhage_i + \alpha_2 hhsex_i + \alpha_3 edyears_i + \alpha_4 hhsize_i + \alpha_5 hhloc_i \\ &+ \alpha_6 remit_i + \alpha_7 commmnet_i + \alpha_8 mfag_i + \alpha_9 mtrd_i + \alpha_{10} ptpass_i \\ &+ \alpha_{11} commbank_i + \alpha_{12} econact_i \& + \alpha_{13} maize\_fsize\_ha_i \\ &+ \alpha_{14} regiondum_i + e_i \end{aligned} \tag{9.14a}$$

$$myield_i = \gamma_0 + \gamma_1 hhage_i + \gamma_2 hhsex_i + \gamma_3 edyears_i + \gamma_4 hhsize_i + \gamma_5 hhloc_i$$

$$+\gamma_6 remit_i + \gamma_7 commmnet_i + \gamma_8 mfag_i + \gamma_9 mtrd_i + \gamma_{10} ptpass_i$$
$$+\gamma_{11} commbank_i + \gamma_{12} econact_i + \gamma_{13} chemfert_i + \gamma_{14} commextoff_i$$
$$+\gamma_{15} regiondum_i + \gamma_{16} cred_i + \varsigma_i \tag{9.14b}$$

$$maize\_part_i = \beta_0 + \beta_1 hhage_i + \beta_2 hhsex_i + \beta_3 edyears_i + \beta_4 hhsize_i$$
$$+\beta_5 hhloc_i + \beta_6 remit_i + \beta_7 commmnet_i + \beta_8 mfag_i + \beta_9 mtrd_i$$
$$+\beta_{10} ptpass_i + \beta_{11} commbank_i + \beta_{12} econact_i + \beta_{13} chemfert_i$$
$$+\beta_{14} commextoff_i + \beta_{15} regiondum_i + \beta_{16} myield_i + v_i \tag{9.14c}$$

The corresponding command to implement the models in Stata is:

```
cmp (cred = hhage hhsex edyears hhsize hhloc remit commmnet mfag mtrd
ptpass commbank econact maize_fsize_ha regiondum) (myield = hhage
hhsex edyears hhsize hhloc remit commmnet mfag mtrd ptpass commbank
econact chemfert commextoff maize_fsize_ha regiondum cred) (maize_
part = hhage hhsex edyears hhsize hhloc remit commmnet mfag mtrd
ptpass commbank econact chemfert commextoff regiondum myield) if
maize_prod == 1, ind($cmp_probit $cmp_cont $cmp_probit) nolog
```

The results of the models are presented in Table 9.6. The corresponding marginal effects for the non-linear models (i.e., Eqs. 9.14a and 9.14c) can then be estimated using the procedure specified previous under the triple-hurdle model.

9.4.3 Conditional Modeling

Conditional modeling is a common situation in agriculture in Africa. For instance, in a fertilizer application training program, we may have a situation where the observed outcome and the model will depend on the data. In this case, in evaluating the effect of the training program on fertilizer application or yield, the equation modeling the determinants of uptake of the training can be dropped for areas where the program was not offered. Similarly, evaluating the effect of a government subsidy program on farm productivity and income, will require a model of determinants of participation in the subsidy program for both areas where farmers had access to the subsidy and areas where farmers do not have access. In either case, the model is conditional on the data.[1] Such generalization does not affect the consistency of the SUR likelihoods for completely observed recursive systems as discussed earlier (Roodman 2011). Two conditional modeling that is commonly applied in studies of the agricultural sector in Africa are the Heckman selection model and the switching regressions.

The classical Heckman selection model is where the variable of interest (i.e., the quantity of fertilizer applied) is modeled only when the selection (i.e., training on fertilizer application) is completely observed.

[1] "Conditional" means that the model can vary by observation.

Table 9.6 Determinants of credit, yield and market participation with recursivity

Variable	Access to credit	Maize yield	Sold maize
Age of head	−0.002 (0.002)	0.835 (1.093)	−0.000 (0.001)
Sex of head	−0.287*** (0.065)	136.834*** (43.413)	0.165*** (0.049)
Years of education of head	0.027*** (0.006)	−5.800 (3.847)	−0.003 (0.004)
Household size	0.014* (0.008)	−8.829* (5.275)	−0.020*** (0.006)
Household resides in rural area	0.206** (0.083)	−79.157 (50.408)	0.102* (0.060)
Received cash remittance	0.281*** (0.054)	−54.667 (35.700)	0.026 (0.039)
Mobile phone network in community	0.143** (0.063)	15.432 (40.712)	0.150*** (0.045)
Membership of cooperatives and fbos	−0.097 (0.118)	213.863*** (75.003)	−0.082 (0.089)
Navigable road to community	−0.062 (0.078)	42.845 (50.892)	0.511*** (0.077)
Public transport availability	−0.102 (0.070)	3.512 (45.556)	0.212*** (0.055)
Bank in community	−0.105 (0.090)	36.473 (58.566)	0.143** (0.064)
Major economic activity in community	0.083 (0.101)	−250.403*** (64.510)	−0.081 (0.077)
Maize farm size	0.025*** (0.010)	−47.375*** (6.563)	
Household in southern Ghana	−0.043 (0.060)	159.258*** (38.743)	0.430*** (0.047)
Use of chemical fertilizer in community		154.067*** (45.704)	−0.059 (0.059)
Agric extension office in community		133.705** (52.776)	0.386*** (0.062)
Access to credit		1044.280*** (114.443)	
Maize yield			−0.001*** (0.000)
Constant	−1.471*** (0.167)	668.955*** (111.123)	−0.670*** (0.207)
Observations	4606	4606	1636
Wald chi-square	1171.196***		
Rho_12		−0.491***	

(continued)

Table 9.6 (continued)

Variable	Access to credit	Maize yield	Sold maize
Rho_13		−0.102***	
Rho_23		0.709***	

Note * $p < 0.1$, ** $p < 0.05$, *** $p < 0.01$; Standard errors in parentheses
Source Produced using the GLSS7 Data

$$y_i^* = x_i'\beta + \varepsilon_i$$

$$d_i^* = z_i'\gamma + v_i$$

$$d_i = 1 \text{ if } d_i^* > 0;\ d_i = 0 \text{ otherwise} \tag{9.15}$$

$$y_i = \left(y_i^*, 1\{d_i^* > 0\}\right)'$$

$$(\varepsilon_i, v_i) \sim N(0, \Sigma)$$

$$\Sigma = \begin{vmatrix} \sigma_{\varepsilon\varepsilon} & \sigma_{\varepsilon v} \\ \sigma_{\varepsilon v} & \sigma_{vv} \end{vmatrix} \text{ and } (\varepsilon_i, v_i), v_i) \text{ are independent of } z_i$$

Given these assumptions, the parameters of the model are estimated by maximizing the average log likelihood function specified as:

$$L_i(\beta, \gamma, \Sigma; y_i|x_i) = \frac{1}{N}\sum_{i-1}^{N}\left\{d_i \times \ln\left[\int_{-(z_i'\gamma)}^{\infty} \phi_{\varepsilon v}\left\{\left(y_i - x_i'\beta, v_i\right)'\right\}dv_i\right]\right.$$
$$\left. +(1 - d_i) \times \left[\ln\int_{-(z_i'\gamma)}^{\infty}\int_{-\infty}^{\infty} \phi_{\varepsilon v}\{(\varepsilon_i, v_i)'\}d\varepsilon_i dv_i\right]\right\} \tag{9.16}$$

The switching regression on the other hand can combine two or more models for the same dependent variable, and the data will then determine which of the models applies to which observations. In fact, it is a system of equations with non-overlapping samples. In our example of the government's fertilizer subsidy program on yields, a model can be estimated for participants in the program and another model estimated for non-participants in the program.

In the endogenous switching regression model, we can express the observed outcomes, y_0 and y_1 in their respective subsamples as:

$$\begin{aligned} y_0 &= x_i'\beta_0 + \varepsilon_0 \quad \text{if } d_i = 0 \\ y_1 &= x_i'\beta_1 + \varepsilon_1 \quad \text{if } d_i = 1 \end{aligned} \tag{9.17}$$

The selection model can be expressed as

$$d_i^* = z_i'\gamma + v_i \tag{9.18}$$

$$d_i = 1 \text{ if } d_i^* > 0 \text{ and } 0 \text{ if otherwise}$$

$$(\varepsilon_0, \varepsilon_1, v_i) \sim TVN(0, \Sigma)$$

$$\Sigma = \begin{bmatrix} \sigma_{\varepsilon 00} & . & \sigma_{\varepsilon 0 v} \\ . & \sigma_{\varepsilon 11} & \sigma_{\varepsilon 1 v} \\ \sigma_{\varepsilon 0 v} & \sigma_{\varepsilon 1 v} & \sigma_{vv} \end{bmatrix} \text{ and} (\varepsilon_0, \varepsilon_1, v_i) \text{ are independent of } z_i$$

where $\text{var}(\varepsilon_0) = \sigma_{\varepsilon_{00}}$, $\text{var}(\varepsilon_1) = \sigma_{\varepsilon_{11}}$, $\text{var}(v_i) = \sigma_{vv}$, $\text{cov}(\varepsilon_0, v_i) = \sigma_{\varepsilon_0 v}$ and $\text{cov}(\varepsilon_1, v_i) = \sigma_{\varepsilon_1 v}$. Given that the outcomes in the two regimes are not simultaneously observed, the $\text{cov}(\varepsilon_0, \varepsilon_1)$ is expressed as undefined. Following the assumption of the distribution of the error terms, we can express the log likelihood function of the model as:

$$\ln L_i(\beta, \gamma, \Sigma; y_i | x_i) = \frac{1}{N}\sum_{i-1}^{N}\left\{ d_i \left(\ln\left[\Phi\left(\frac{(z_i'\gamma + \rho_1\varepsilon_1/\sigma_{\varepsilon_1})}{\sqrt{1-\rho_1^2}} \right) \right] + \ln\left[\phi(\varepsilon_1/\sigma_{\varepsilon_1})/\sigma_{\varepsilon_1}\right] \right) \right.$$

$$\left. +(1-d_i)\left(\ln\left[1 - \Phi\left(\frac{(z_i'\gamma + \rho_0\varepsilon_0/\sigma_{\varepsilon_0})}{\sqrt{1-\rho_0^2}} \right) \right] + \ln\left[\phi(\varepsilon_0/\sigma_{\varepsilon_0})/\sigma_{\varepsilon_0}\right] \right) \right\} \tag{9.19}$$

where ρ is the correlation coefficient between ε_j and v_i, $(j = 0, 1)$, Φ is the cumulative normal distribution function, ϕ is the normal probability density function.

In estimating these models, studies in the past have used a two-step estimator where a probit model of the probability of participating in the selection (e.g., the fertilizer training) is estimated in the first stage, and a second-stage regression is then estimated for the fertilizer application or yield model. However, the maximum likelihood approach which makes it possible to estimate these two equations as a system has clear advantage and efficiency gains. Thus, cmp framework relies on this maximum likelihood approach and implements the systems approach for the traditional Heckman selection models as well as other combination forms of these conditional models.

9.4.3.1 Stata Illustration: Heckman Sample Selection

We examine the Heckman selection model by estimating household maize market participation and the extent of maize market participation. Whereas maize market participation is a dummy variable, extent of market participation is a fraction. We estimate the model using the cmp command below (see Table 9.11 in the Appendix for corresponding "heckman" command). Results are presented in Table 9.7.

```
cmp (maize_hcifrac = hhage hhsex edyears hhsize hhloc remit commmnet
mfag mtrd ptpass commbank econact commextoff) (maize_part = hhage
hhsex edyears hhsize hhloc remit commmnet mfag mtrd ptpass comm-
bank econact maize_fsize_ha chemfert commextoff) if maize_prod ==
1, ind(selectvar $cmp_probit) tech(dfp bhhh) quietly
```

The statistically significant LR chi-square shows the model is well fitted. Our interest is the rho since this is the parameter reported by the cmp about the correlation in unobservables between the selection and the outcome equations. The rho is 0.74 for both the cmp and the Heckman models, which is negative and statistically significant. This implies that unobserved factors that increase the likelihood of participation in maize market decrease the intensity of market participation. The "sold maize" panel presents estimates of the maize market participation decisions and the 'maize commercialization index' presents estimates of the market participation intensity model. We also see that the estimates of the two equations are same for the cmp and the Heckman model.

9.4.4 *Multilevel Multiprocess Models: Survival Analysis*

We begin discussion of this section with an introduction into the basics of survival/ duration and hazard regression models before dwelling on the multilevel multiprocess model, and how such situations can be handled by the CMP model.

9.4.4.1 Basics of Duration/Hazard Regression Model

Duration or survival analysis involves modeling of time-to-event situations where the occurrence of an event is divided into several mutually exclusive domains of time periods or intervals (Jenkins 2005). Over time, some agents move while others do not move between these time domains. Several instances of this exist and examples include time-to-event in agents' marriage states (i.e., single, married, cohabiting, separated, divorced), and time-to-adoption of a particular agricultural innovation or technology among others. In each state of marriage or adoption, the patterns for each agent are defined by the time spent within the state, and the date of transition (if any) between states. In the case of the time-to-adoption of agricultural technology, we can define two states (non-adopter, adopter) and the time (either in years, months or days)

Table 9.7 Heckman selection model

Variable	"cmp"		"Heckman"	
	Maize commercialization index	Sold maize	Maize commercialization index	Sold maize
Age of head	0.000 (0.000)	0.000 (0.001)	0.000 (0.000)	0.000 (0.001)
Sex of head	0.013 (0.017)	0.087 (0.054)	0.013 (0.017)	0.087 (0.054)
Years of education of head	0.001 (0.001)	0.014*** (0.005)	0.001 (0.001)	0.014*** (0.005)
Household size	−0.007*** (0.002)	−0.031*** (0.007)	−0.007*** (0.002)	−0.031*** (0.007)
Household resides in rural area	−0.018 (0.021)	0.200*** (0.065)	−0.018 (0.021)	0.200*** (0.065)
Received cash remittance	−0.012 (0.014)	0.054 (0.043)	−0.012 (0.014)	0.054 (0.043)
Mobile phone network in community	−0.053*** (0.015)	0.159*** (0.049)	−0.053*** (0.015)	0.159*** (0.049)
Membership of cooperatives and fbos	0.047* (0.028)	−0.208** (0.090)	0.047* (0.028)	−0.208** (0.090)
Navigable road to community	−0.104*** (0.028)	0.595*** (0.067)	−0.104*** (0.028)	0.595*** (0.067)
Public transport availability	−0.006 (0.019)	0.444*** (0.053)	−0.006 (0.019)	0.444*** (0.053)
Bank in community	0.079*** (0.020)	0.166** (0.069)	0.079*** (0.020)	0.166** (0.069)
Major economic activity in community	0.014 (0.024)	0.036 (0.081)	0.014 (0.024)	0.036 (0.081)
Agric extension office in community	−0.042** (0.019)	0.435*** (0.064)	−0.042** (0.019)	0.435*** (0.064)
Maize farm size		0.061*** (0.008)		0.061*** (0.008)
Use of chemical fertilizer in community		−0.320*** (0.052)		−0.320*** (0.052)
Constant	0.896*** (0.069)	−1.240*** (0.143)	0.896*** (0.069)	−1.240*** (0.143)
Observations	1636	4606	1636	4606
Wald chi-square/ LR chi-square	1046.400***		78.272***	

(continued)

Table 9.7 (continued)

Variable	"cmp"		"Heckman"	
	Maize commercialization index	Sold maize	Maize commercialization index	Sold maize
Rho	-0.737^{***}		-0.737^{***}	
Lambda			-0.215^{***}	
LR test of indep. eqn			28.984^{***}	

Note * $p < 0.1$, ** $p < 0.05$, *** $p < 0.01$; Standard errors in parentheses
Source Produced using the GLSS7 Data

spent within a state (e.g., as a non-adopter) with the passage of time, t, is termed as the spell durations or survival times. A survival time can be censored or not. It is censored if the duration spell observed, began or ended within some time interval where the total duration spell is unknown. For instance, if the time-to-adoption was observed among farmers for 10 years and it is the case that some of these agents had not adopted the technology after the 10th year, then the duration spell of those agents will be considered as being censored. Censoring can be contrasted with truncation in survival analysis, where truncated survival time data arises when there is systematic exclusion of survival times from the sample, resulting in the sample selection being dependent on the survival time itself (Jenkins 2005).

To present the duration/survival regression framework, we define the length of a spell for an agent (such as a farmer) as the realization of a random variable T with a probability density and cumulative distribution functions as $\phi(t)$ and $\Phi(t)$, respectively. Here, the length of spell can be continuous or discrete. Given the cumulative distribution function, which is also referred to as failure function, the survival function can be expressed as $S(t) = 1 - \Phi(t)$ in which t is the time elapsed since entry into the duration spell at time 0. Thus, if the failure function is expressed as:

$$\Pr(T > t) = \Phi(t), \tag{9.20}$$

then the survival function can be expressed as

$$\Pr(T > t) = 1 - \Phi(t) \equiv S(t) \tag{9.21}$$

Given that the probability density function is the slope of the cumulative distribution function, the density function can be deduced as:

$$S(t) = \lim_{\Delta t \to 0} \frac{\Pr(t \le T \le t + \Delta t)}{\Delta t} = \frac{\partial \Phi(t)}{\partial t} = -\frac{\partial S(t)}{\partial t} \tag{9.22}$$

where Δt is an infinitesimal time interval and $\phi(t)\Delta t$ is an unconditional probability of surviving up to exactly time t (that is, leaving the given state in a very small interval of time $(t, t + \Delta t)$). Thus, given $\phi(t)\Delta t$ and the survival function, $S(t)$, defined as the probability of living in the spell (i.e., surviving) up to time t, then the hazard rate, $h(t)$, can be specified as:

$$h(t) = \frac{\phi(t)}{1 - \Phi(t)} = \frac{\phi(t)}{S(t)}. \tag{9.23}$$

which generally represents the likelihood of exiting from the time interval $(t, t+\Delta t)$, given that one survives up to time t. In our adoption scenario or giving birth to a child in a household, this shows the probability of adoption (i.e., exiting the spell), given that the agent had not adopted (i.e., surviving) up to time t, or the likelihood of giving birth to a child in the household given that the household has been waiting without a child until time t.

Unobserved individual effects are a common phenomenon in empirical economic analysis and the survival analysis framework has also taken this concern in what is usually referred to as "frailty" in bio-medical and related disciplines. In the childbirth example, frailty is an unobserved likelihood of experiencing events that are favorable to giving birth to a child. When we assume the existence of such unobserved heterogeneities, we can generally express the hazard regression model as:

$$S(t, X|\beta, e) = [S(t, X)]^e \tag{9.24}$$

where the survival function is expressed as depending on observed time variant (e.g., age, household size) and in-variant (e.g., sex) characteristics, X, and an unobserved individual effect, e, assumed to be greater than zero ($e > 0$), has a mean normalized to unity for identification ($E(e) = 1$), finite variance greater than zero ($\sigma^2 > 0$) and distributed independently of time and the observed variables. If we assume a specific distribution for the frailty term, which summarizes the variance of this term, we can write the likelihood function, based on the parameters of the distribution, by integrating out the individual heterogeneities (frailty).

To do this, we specify the survivor function in terms of the variance and not the frailty terms as:

$$S_e(t, X) = S\big(t, X|\beta, \sigma^2\big), \tag{9.25}$$

and then

$$S_v(t, X) = \int_0^\infty [S(t, X)]^e g(e)de \tag{9.26}$$

where $g(e)$ is the density function for e which is assumed to be a Gamma distribution with a mean of one and variance of σ^2.

9.4.4.2 Multilevel Multiprocess Models

The multilevel multiprocess models basically consist of equations of hazards (i.e., time-to-event) that account for individual-specific heterogeneities. Such models can account for selection bias due to unobserved individual traits. In Africa, the family is a major source of labor for farm activities, especially for poor households and in areas where the labor market is not well developed. Hence, this can lead to situations in which engaging in farming activities by the household can have an effect (i.e., either speedup or delay) the time of having babies in the household. The general form of the multilevel multiprocess involves hazard equations expressed as:

$$y_{it}^0 = \beta^0 x_{it}^0 + \varepsilon_i^0 \tag{9.27}$$

$$y_{it}^1 = \beta^1 x_{it}^1 + \varepsilon_i^1$$

where i indexes individuals and t indexes time episodes (i.e., duration spells in the survival analysis framework). The vector of explanatory variables, x, may include time-variant and different forms of duration dependencies. The ε's are individual specific error terms which are assumed to be correlated, making the equations seemingly unrelated (Bartus 2012). Multilevel multiprocess models can be simultaneous hazards equations (where the time of occurrence of an event depends on both the observed characteristics and the time of occurrence of another event), and/or hazard equations with sample selection (in which the hazard of an event is estimated using the sample of observations that experienced another event). Finally, a multilevel multiprocess can be a hazard model with endogenous explanatory variable where the hazard of an event is explained by an endogenous binary variable. The latter case expresses the example we have above about household childbirth decisions and engagement in an agricultural activity. In particular, the hazard of wives giving birth and engagement in agriculture can be expressed in the hazard models with endogenous variables as:

$$y_{it} = \alpha m_{it} + \beta^0 x_{it}^0 + \varepsilon_i^0 \tag{9.28}$$

$$m_{it}^* = \beta^1 x_{it}^1 + \varepsilon_i^1$$

where y_{it} represents childbirth in the household and m_{it} denotes, for instance, maize production. The other variables are as previously defined.

9.4.4.3 Stata Illustration

We present the multilevel multiprocess model by estimating hazard models of the effect of household maize production (maize prod) on the speed of having a child in the household. We first merge the household level dataset in memory with the individual level dataset of the GLSS7 that contains information about specific household members, their years of birth and ages. Merging the two files increases the units of observation to 59,864. Multilevel multiprocess requires a multiprocess data format. We do this by first creating a dataset of durations with a failure indicator to show whether an event occurred or not. For instance, the duration will be the years of a woman until her first birth, until her second birth, and so on, whereas the failure indicator is coded 1 any time a woman in the household gives birth or 0 if otherwise (i.e., censored). But we first show a cross-section of the data to use.

```
list hid s1q4yy Dur birth in 1/10, sep(5)
```

The command above displays data on year of birth, duration, and failure indicator (i.e., birth) of the first 10 observations, and the sep(5) is an option instructing Stata to insert a horizontal line in to separate every 5 observations (Fig. 9.1).

In this dataset, it took the woman in the second household 36 years to have her first child and the woman in the fifth household 22 years to have her first child. Also, the "birth" column shows there are 7 failures and 3 censored observations in all.

The second step in setting up the multiprocess data structure is to define the dependent variables for each process. CMP uses interval-censored regressions for multilevel multiprocess data, and this requires two dependent variables in which one

```
list hid s1q4yy Dur birth in 1/10, sep(5)

     +-----------------------------------+
     |      hid   s1q4yy   Dur   birth |
     |-----------------------------------|
  1. | 70001/02     2003     1       1 |
  2. | 70001/02     2002     4       1 |
  3. | 70001/02     1997     4       1 |
  4. | 70001/02     1993    36       1 |
  5. | 70001/02     1992     0       0 |
     |-----------------------------------|
  6. | 70001/05     2000     3       1 |
  7. | 70001/05     1997     3       1 |
  8. | 70001/05     1994    22       1 |
  9. | 70001/05     1993     0       0 |
 10. | 70001/06     1992     0       0 |
     +-----------------------------------+
```

Fig. 9.1 Screenshot of list command and results

defines the lower and the other defines the upper limits. For the process of birth duration, the limits are generated in Stata as:

```
gen lw_bduration = cond(birth==1,ln(Dur-.9),ln(Dur))
```

This command instructs Stata to generate the lower limit variable (lw_bduration) as a conditional function conditioned on failing (birth==1), natural log of duration minus 0.9, and the natural log of duration. The next command generates the upper limit variable (hi_bduration) also as a conditional function conditioned on failing, natural log of duration, and a large positive number 999.

```
gen hi_bduration = cond(birth==1,ln(Dur) , 999 )
```

Once these two limits are created and with our maize production variable being a dummy, we are set to estimate our multilevel multiprocess models.

We first estimate the models of time until birth and maize production separately in which the hazard of birth is modeled as dependent on maize production. The syntax for this first model is:

```
cmp(lw_bduration hi_bduration = maize_prod hhage hhsex edyears
hhsize hhloc remit commmnet mfag mtrd ptpass commbank), ind($cmp_
int)
```

In this model, both the lower and upper limits are stated as the dependent variables and the option ind($cmp_int) instructs Stata to estimate an interval regression. The output reports the number of observations used in the estimation as 35,958 and the log likelihood in Table 9.8 (column 1). The LR chi-squared at 12 degrees of freedom and the associated probability of 0.0000 indicates the model is well fitted.

The coefficient of maize production measures the effect of participation in maize production by a household on the speed of having a child in the household. The negative coefficient of 0.015 shows that households which participate in maize production wait less (i.e., participation reduces the duration) to having a child in the household (column 1).

To control for the effect of unobserved factors, we can do this by either estimating the birth duration equation and the model of maize production participation jointly or treating maize production as an endogenous regressor and estimate this recursively. In the following example, we implement the latter by specifying both the duration and the maize production equations as in Eq. (9.28). To obtain the hazard model with endogenous explanatory variable, we must use the following command:

Table 9.8 Duration of having a child and maize production, multilevel multiprocess

	(1)	(2)	(3)
	Low birth duration	Low birth duration	
	High birth duration	High birth duration	Produced maize
Produced maize	−0.015* (0.009)	−0.077*** (0.026)	
Age of head	0.010*** (0.000)	0.010*** (0.000)	−0.000 (0.001)
Sex of head	1.394*** (0.010)	1.401*** (0.010)	0.108*** (0.005)
Years of education of head	0.004*** (0.001)	0.003*** (0.001)	−0.007*** (0.001)
Household size	0.006*** (0.001)	0.007*** (0.001)	0.009*** (0.001)
Household resides in rural area	0.017* (0.009)	0.024*** (0.009)	0.092*** (0.005)
Received cash remittance	0.004 (0.007)	0.004 (0.007)	−0.003 (0.004)
Mobile phone network in community	−0.015* (0.009)	−0.017* (0.009)	−0.016*** (0.005)
Membership of cooperatives and fbos	−0.002 (0.010)	−0.035** (0.017)	−0.395*** (0.004)
Navigable road to community	0.008 (0.011)	0.018 (0.012)	0.127*** (0.006)
Public transport availability	−0.001 (0.010)	−0.007 (0.010)	−0.076*** (0.005)
Bank in community	−0.001 (0.009)	−0.001 (0.009)	−0.003 (0.006)
Major economic activity in community			0.116*** (0.006)
Constant	1.325*** (0.019)	1.350*** (0.022)	
Observations	35,958	35,958	
LR chi-square	18,212.254	37,664.506	
p-value	0.000	0.000	
Rho_12		0.071*** (0.027)	

Standard errors in parentheses
Source Produced using the GLSS7 Data
* $p < 0.1$, ** $p < 0.05$, *** $p < 0.01$

```
cmp(lw_bduration hi_bduration= maize_prod hhage hhsex edyears
hhsize hhloc remit commmnet mfag mtrd ptpass commbank) (maize_prod
= hhage hhsex edyears hhsize hhloc remit commmnet mfag mtrd ptpass
commbank econact), ind($cmp_int $cmp_probit)
```

The model has now featured two indicator options for the interval regression, $cmp_int, and probit regression, $cmp_probit. It also reports the standalone models, which have been omitted in the presentation. The information below column 2, Table 9.8, consists of the number of observations used, and the LR chi-squared and its probability of significance (i.e., Prob > chi2). The LR chi-squared is very high and with a probability of 0.0000 suggesting that the model is well fitted. The bottom row reports the rho_12 which gives information about the correlation between the error terms of the two equations. Of much importance is the rho which is positive and statistically significant. This implies that unobserved factors that increase the likelihood of a household participating in maize production also delay the hazard of childbirth in the household. Column 3 presents the estimates for maize production participation (maize production). In the hazard model, the estimate of maize production is negative and statistically significant at the 1% level, which implies that when a household participates in maize production it increases the hazard of childbirth in the household. Estimates in column 3 of Table 9.8 are marginal effects obtained by using the command margins, `dydx(*) predict(eq(#2) pr)`.

9.5 Concluding Remarks

In this chapter, we have demonstrated the close relationship between the CMP and SUR and shown how the CMP is able to implement various types of SUR models theoretically and with Stata illustrations. The CMP has been used to estimate models of recursive nature, mixed-process models, conditional models where the model depends on the observations as well as multilevel multiprocess models. In all these, CMP produces estimates that are the same as the Stata in-built commands for each of these models. However, a major limitation of CMP is when it comes to the implementation of switching regression models where CMP has not routine commands to be able to handle them. This is a potential area for future research in the development of codes or estimation routines for the implementation of switching regressions using CMP. This will be an important contribution towards enhancing the flexibility in estimating such models given the difficulty of the "movestay" or "selmlog" in handling complex models.

Appendix

See Tables 9.9, 9.10 and 9.11.

Table 9.9 Variables and their measurement

Variable	Description	Measurement
hhage	Age of head	Number of years
hhsex	Sex of head	Dummy: 1 = if male; 0 otherwise
edyears	Years of education of head	Number of years attended school
hhsize	Household size	Number of people in household
hhloc	Household resides in rural area	Dummy: 1 = if yes; 0 otherwise
remit	Received cash remittance	Dummy: 1 = if yes; 0 otherwise
mfag	Membership of cooperatives and fbos	Dummy: 1 = if yes; 0 otherwise
mtrd	Navigable road to community	Dummy: 1 = if yes; 0 otherwise
ptpass	Public transport availability	Dummy: 1 = if yes; 0 otherwise
commbank	Bank in community	Dummy: 1 = if yes; 0 otherwise
commmnet	Mobile phone network in community	Dummy: 1 = if yes; 0 otherwise
econact	Major economic activity in community	Dummy: 1 = if agriculture; 0 otherwise
chemfert	Use of chemical fertilizer in community	Dummy: 1 = if yes; 0 otherwise
commextoff	Agric extension office in community	Dummy: 1 = if yes; 0 otherwise
cred	Access to credit	Dummy: 1 = if yes; 0 otherwise
myield	Maize yield	Output per hectare
maize_fsize_ha	Maize farm size	Hectare
maize_prod	Produced maize	Dummy: 1 = if yes; 0 otherwise
maize_part	Sold maize (any crop producers)	Dummy: 1 = if yes; 0 otherwise
maize_part1	Sold maize (only maize producers)	Dummy: 1 = if yes; 0 otherwise
maize_hcifrac	Maize commercialization index	Sale value / Output value
regiondum	Household in southern Ghana	Dummy: 1 = if yes; 0 otherwise

Table 9.10 Descriptive statistics of variables

Variable	Sample	Mean	S.D	Min	Max
hhage	14,009	46.24	15.91	15	99
hhsex	14,009	0.688	0.463	0	1
edyears	14,009	6.472	5.357	0	19
hhsize	14,009	4.200	2.867	1	28
hhloc	14,009	0.570	0.495	0	1
remit	14,009	0.353	0.478	0	1
mfag	14,009	0.516	0.500	0	1
mtrd	14,009	0.831	0.374	0	1
ptpass	14,009	0.757	0.429	0	1
commbank	14,009	0.348	0.476	0	1
commmnet	14,009	0.724	0.447	0	1
econact	14,009	0.701	0.458	0	1
chemfert	14,009	0.730	0.444	0	1
commextoff	14,009	0.206	0.404	0	1
cred	14,009	0.076	0.264	0	1
pstatus	14,009	1.636	0.670	0	2
myield	4,606	743.7	1.062	0	16,473
maize_fsize_ha	6,637	0.687	1.703	0	97.13
maize_prod	14,009	0.329	0.470	0	1
maize_part	6,637	0.246	0.431	0	1
maize_part1	4,606	0.355	0.479	0	1
maize_hcifrac	1,636	0.568	0.246	0.00313	1
regiondum	14,009	0.610	0.488	0	1

Table 9.11 Commands

Model	Command
"biprobit"	`biprobit (cred = hhage hhsex edyears hhsize hhloc remit commmnet mfag mtrd ptpass commbank econact chemfert commextoff) (maize_part1 = hhage hhsex edyears hhsize hhloc remit commmnet mfag mtrd ptpass commbank econact chemfert commextoff maize_fsize_ha) if maize_prod = = 1`
"heckman"	`heckman: heckman maize_hcifrac hhage hhsex edyears hhsize hhloc remit commmnet mfag mtrd ptpass commbank econact commextoff if maize_prod = = 1, select(maize_part = hhage hhsex edyears hhsize hhloc remit commmnet mfag mtrd ptpass commbank econact maize_fsize_ha chemfert commextoff)`

References

Agbanyo R, Peprah JA (2021) National health insurance and the choice of delivery facility among expectant mothers in Ghana. Int J Health Econ Manag 21:27–49. https://doi.org/10.1007/s10754-020-09288-w

Alhassan H, Abu BM, Nkegbe PK (2020) Access to credit, farm productivity and market participation in Ghana: a conditional mixed process approach. Margin—The J Appl Econ Res 14(2):226–246. https://doi.org/10.1177/0973801020904490

Bartus T (2012) Can multilevel multiprocess models be estimated using Stata? a case for the cmp command. 10th German Stata Users Group Meeting, Berlin

Burke WJ, Myers RJ, Jayne TS (2015) A triple-hurdle model of production and market participation in Kenya's dairy market. Am J Agric Econ 97(4):1227–1246. https://doi.org/10.1093/ajae/aav009

Greene WH (2012) Econometric analysis, 7th ed. Pearson Education, Inc. USA

Jenkins SP (2005) Survival analysis. Unpublished manuscript. Institute for Social and Economic Research, University of Essex, UK

Makate C, Wang R, Makate M, Mango N (2016) Crop diversification and livelihoods of smallholder farmers in Zimbabwe: adaptive management for environmental change. Springerplus 5. https://doi.org/10.1186/s40064-016-2802-4

Mottaleb KA, Kruseman G, Snapp S (2022) Potential impacts of Ukraine-Russia armed conflict on global wheat food security: a quantitative exploration. Glob Food Secur 35. https://doi.org/10.1016/j.gfs.2022.100659

Nkegbe PK, Abdul Mumin Y (2022) Impact of community development initiatives and access to community markets on household food security and nutrition in Ghana. Food Policy 113:102282. https://doi.org/10.1016/j.foodpol.2022.102282

Roodman D (2011) Fitting fully observed recursive mixed-process models with cmp. Stata J 11(2):159–206. https://doi.org/10.1177/1536867X1101100202

Roodman D, Morduch J (2014) The impact of microcredit on the poor in Bangladesh: revisiting the evidence. J Dev Stud 50(4):583–604. https://doi.org/10.1080/00220388.2013.858122

Salazar C, Jaime M, Pinto C, Acuña A (2019) Interaction between crop insurance and technology adoption decisions: the case of wheat farmers in Chile. Aust J Agric Resour Econ 63:593–619. https://doi.org/10.1111/1467-8489.12307

Sekyi S, Abu BM, Nkegbe PK (2017) Farm credit access, credit constraint and productivity in Ghana: empirical evidence from northern savannah ecological zone. Agric Finance Rev 77(4):446–462. https://doi.org/10.1108/AFR-10-2016-0078

Torres AP, Marshall MI, Alexander CE, Delgado MS (2016) Are local market relationships undermining organic fruit and vegetable certification? A bivariate probit analysis. Agric Econ 48(2):197–205. https://doi.org/10.1111/agec.12326

Chapter 10
Multivariate Tobit Model: An Application to Farmer Adoption of Soil Erosion Practices in El Salvador

Taeyeon Yoon, Charles Rhodes, and Deep Mukherjee

Abstract This chapter talks about the appropriate modeling framework for mixed discrete-continuous random variables which is popularly called the Tobit model and its extension the multivariate Tobit model which is essentially a Seemingly Unrelated Regression or multi-equation Tobit system. The model is illustrated through an empirical application on technology adoption problem in agriculture. In developing countries, failures of programs to formulate technological prescriptions for soil conservation raise doubt about the effectiveness of large-scale public interventions. Many farmers abandon program practices soon after an intervention ends. Is this crucial evidence that farmers engage in strategic adoption behaviors just for program incentives, and that public intervention is inept? Most such criticisms rely on secondary and/or cross-sectional data—which are of limited use for tracing adoption behaviors during and after public intervention. This study uses two-period data for participants in the Environmental Program for El Salvador, during and after the intervention. To model dynamics between multiple adoption decisions—which differ across two periods and four viable practices—eight Tobit models are jointly estimated in Stata software using the Geweke-Hajivassiliou-Keane simulator.

Keywords Multivariate tobit · Seemingly unrelated regression · Adoption-abandonment · Soil conservation

---

This work is based on Yoon (2013) and more than 50% of its content uses sections from Yoon (2013).

T. Yoon (✉)
Assistant Professor, Department of International Economics and Trade, Sun Moon University, Asan, South Korea
e-mail: tay07001@sunmoon.ac.kr

C. Rhodes
Independent Scholar, Washington, USA

D. Mukherjee
Associate Professor, Department of Economic Sciences, Indian Institute of Technology Kanpur, Kanpur, India

D. Mukherjee (ed.), *Applied Econometric Analysis Using Cross Section and Panel Data*, Contributions to Economics, https://doi.org/10.1007/978-981-99-4902-1_10

10.1 Introduction

The original Tobit model was proposed to handle zero-censored observations of a nonnegative continuous variable (e.g., household expenditure) with several observations taking value zero (Tobin 1958). A non-negative dependent variable y and regressors (or, covariates) can be used to characterize a connection using the initial Tobit regression model. Several types of variations are possible with the Tobit model, all of which can be produced by varying where and when censoring occurs (Amemiya 1984). In applied microeconometric investigations, a surge in the use of multi-equation counterpart of the Tobit model is seen in the last two decades.

Let us define the multivariate Tobit (MVT) model in which Y is a vector of non-negative dependent variables with covariates X. It is assumed that the data are generated as follows: $Y = max(Y^*, 0)$, where Y^* is a random vector with the multivariate normal (MVN) distribution with mean $X\beta$ and covariance matrix Σ, 0 is a vector of zeros, and the operator *max* is applied component-wise. The MVT model is essentially a Seemingly Unrelated Regression or M-equation Tobit system (Amemiya 1974). Hence, MVT model is also known as Seemingly Unrelated Tobit Regression (SUTR) model. The linear regression form of SUTR model, for the ith observation (i = 1, 2, … N), can be written as follows.

$$Y_{1i}^* = X_{1i}\beta_1 + \varepsilon_{1i}, Y_{1i} = \max(0, Y_{1i}^*)$$

$$Y_{2i}^* = X_{2i}\beta_2 + \varepsilon_{2i}, Y_{2i} = \max(0, Y_{2i}^*)$$

$$\cdots$$

$$Y_{Mi}^* = X_{Mi}\beta_M + \varepsilon_{Mi}, Y_{Mi} = \max(0, Y_{Mi}^*)$$

$$\varepsilon|\tau_i \sim MVN(0, \tau_i\Sigma)$$

Here, Y^* and τ are unobservable latent variables, ε is Gaussian error, Σ is $M \times M$ positive definite matrix, and $\tau_i \sim IG(\frac{v}{2}, \frac{2}{v})$. For brevity and simplicity, the variables can be stacked in the following way,

$$Y_i^* = \begin{pmatrix} Y_{1i}^* \\ \cdots \\ Y_{Mi}^* \end{pmatrix}, Y_i = \begin{pmatrix} Y_{1i} \\ \cdots \\ Y_{Mi} \end{pmatrix}, X_i = diag(X_{1i}, \ldots, X_{Mi}), \beta = \begin{pmatrix} \beta_1 \\ \cdots \\ \beta_M \end{pmatrix}, \varepsilon_t = \begin{pmatrix} \varepsilon_{1i} \\ \cdots \\ \varepsilon_{Mi} \end{pmatrix}$$

$$Y^* = \begin{pmatrix} Y_1^* \\ \cdots \\ Y_N^* \end{pmatrix}, Y = \begin{pmatrix} Y_1 \\ \cdots \\ Y_N \end{pmatrix}, X = \begin{pmatrix} X_1 \\ \cdots \\ X_N \end{pmatrix}, \tau = \begin{pmatrix} \tau_1 \\ \cdots \\ \tau_N \end{pmatrix}.$$

Like any other regression problem, the econometrician aims to estimate the parameters β, Σ, v from the data Y and X. For easy manipulation, the latent scale is assumed to follow an inverted Gamma distribution $IG(\frac{v}{2}, \frac{2}{v})$ so that $\varepsilon_i's$ marginal distribution follows multivariate t distribution with parameters Σ and v.

In contrast with single-equation Tobit, the M-variate SUTR model may show various forms of censoring, offering 2^M possible patterns. For some individual i, let us rearrange the order of variables so that the first M_u dependent variables are intact but the last $M_c = M - M_u$ variables are censored to zero. The subscript "u" and subscript "c" denote the uncensored block and the censored block, respectively. Thus, $M_c = 0$ and $M_u = 0$ correspond to the cases of no censoring and all censoring, respectively. For analytical tractability, the variables for an individual i are partitioned in the following manner.

$$Y_i^* = \begin{pmatrix} Y_{ui}^* \\ Y_{ci}^* \end{pmatrix}, Y_i = \begin{pmatrix} Y_{ui} \\ Y_{ci} \end{pmatrix}, X_i = \begin{pmatrix} X_{ui} & \\ & X_{ci} \end{pmatrix}, \beta = \begin{pmatrix} \beta_u \\ \beta_c \end{pmatrix}, \Sigma = \begin{pmatrix} \Sigma_{\mathrm{uu}} & \Sigma_{\mathrm{uc}} \\ \Sigma_{\mathrm{cu}} & \Sigma_{\mathrm{cc}} \end{pmatrix}$$

There are four techniques for estimating the SUTR model: Maximum Simulated Likelihood (MSL); Heckman Two Steps; Expectation Maximization algorithm; and Bayesian Posterior Simulator. In this chapter, we focus on the first approach. The corresponding log-likelihood function is $logL = \sum_{i=1}^{N} lnp(Y_{ui}, Y_{ci})$ where,

$$\begin{aligned} p(Y_{ui}, Y_{ci}) &= \int_0^\infty \int_{-\infty}^0 p(Y_{ui}^*, Y_{ci,}^*, \tau_i) dY_{ci}^* d\tau_i \\ &= p(Y_{ui}^*). \int_0^\infty \int_{-\infty}^0 p(\tau_i | Y_{ui}^*) p(Y_{ci}^* | Y_{ui}^*, \tau_i) dY_{ci}^* d\tau_i. \end{aligned}$$

The likelihood function associated with the MVT model is intricate, so direct maximization is difficult and time consuming. It is tough to calculate the integral $\int_0^\infty \int_{-\infty}^0 p(\tau_i | Y_{ui}^*) p(Y_{ci}^* | Y_{ui}^*, \tau_i) dY_{ci}^* d\tau_i$, which belongs to the c.d.f of the "multivariate generalized t-distributions family" (Arslan 2004), as the integral does not have a close-form solution. The Geweke-Hajivassiliou-Keane (**GHK**) simulator (Geweke 1991; Börsch-Supan and Hajivassiliou 1993; Keane 1994) is a popular choice for evaluating probabilities of multivariate normal distribution and is used to solve the MVT model via MSL approach. Readers interested in application of MVT model, may refer to Cornick et al. (1994) and Dribe and Stanfors (2009).

10.2 The Use of MVT in Modelling Farmers' Technology Adoption Behaviour

Soil erosion is recognized to be the single most important environmental degradation problem (Ananda and Herath 2003). This problem is particularly threatening to developing countries' sustainable development (Albaladejo et al. 2021). Land degradation constrains development of the agricultural sector, the primary economic and employment generating sector for many developing countries.

Responding to the problem, governments and international donor organizations have been financing massive land-improvement expenditures in developing countries in recent decades, to formulate technological prescriptions for soil conservation (**SC**). Many success stories are associated with SC programs, but there are many failures and overall progress has been slow. Among the reasons for failure, many papers cite the apparent reluctance of farmers to undertake and maintain new SC practices (e.g., Amsalu and De Graaff 2007). Farmers often reject or abandon practices promoted by SC programs, even when they perceive that these practices have profit potential (Knowler 2003). Experience from past failures has turned researchers' attention from technologies to the farmers themselves, i.e., to the factors and constraints that farmers consider when deciding whether to adopt SC practices.

Case studies from around the world report farmers abandoning SC practices or maintenance as soon as program incentives are withdrawn. There is a substantive break between program intentions and final adoption rates; the source of the break is not clearly identified. As such, existing literature has not carefully identified how farmers actually behave during and after SC programs (Smith and Weinberg 2004).

The absence of panel data in SC adoption studies has curtailed the ability to characterize dynamics in farmer decision processes (Doss 2006). Farmers do not commit to a range of SC practices all at once, and may undergo a complex decision process, involving information gathering and the evaluation of available alternatives. Public intervention may play a critical role in the SC adoption process by easing farmers' financial constraints and providing information about new technologies. But then we must consider that adoption decisions may be influenced in periods during and after public intervention. Panel data can be used to reveal the dynamics between adoption decisions, and provide useful information about farmer adoption behaviors.

In the past, logit and probit models have been used extensively in SC adoption studies. Dichotomous models such as logit and probit are appropriate when any technology must be adopted either in full or not at all (Doss 2006). Farmers, however, undertake a range of SC practices, presenting a decision structure best characterized by a continuous (rather than dichotomous) variable. Thus, the dichotomous models may ignore important behavioral information in farmer adoption decisions.

A further modeling problem arises because farmers often decide not to adopt a certain SC practice, even when they have full information about the practice. They may judge a practice to be unprofitable, judge constraints to implementation to be too high, or may substitute with other practices. Accordingly, the adoption data include a cluster of zero values indicating non-adoption. The zero values will lead an Ordinary Least Squares regression model to produce biased and inconsistent estimation results, which will worsen as the fraction of zeros increases (Cameron and Trivedi 2005). In our sample, the average fraction for non-adoptions across eight adoption choices runs to 50%, necessitating a procedure to handle the censored values at zero.

10.3 MVT or SUTR Model Applied to Adoption-Disadoption Case

A Tobit model reflects continuous and censored aspects of the adoption intensities. Given two periods in which any of four practices may be chosen, each of eight decisions corresponds to a single Tobit model. By jointly estimating eight Tobit models, we may identify correlations between all the decisions.

An appropriate methodology to estimate eight Tobit models simultaneously is a multivariate Tobit model. This is a straightforward conceptual extension of a univariate Tobit model. Beginning with the univariate Tobit model, consider the limiting case that the m-th SC practice in a single period is the only available choice for farmers. Now extend this model to the multivariate Tobit model for a total of M practices over two periods. The standard Tobit model for adoption intensity of the m-th practice can be represented by the two following equations. First, a latent variable is described by a linear function of a set of explanatory variables and an error term:

$$y_m^* = \beta_m x + \varepsilon_m \tag{10.1}$$

where y_m^* is the latent (unobservable) adoption intensity, and represents the net expected utility from adopting the m-th practice rather than staying with existing farming practices only. x is a $(k \times 1)$ vector of explanatory variables, each of which may influence an adoption decision. β_m is a $(1 \times k)$ vector of the coefficients, and ε_m is an error term following a normal distribution with variance σ_m^2, such that $\varepsilon_m \sim N(0, \sigma_m^2)$. The second equation describes the observable adoption intensity that a farmer applies to the m-th practice:

$$y_m = \begin{cases} y_m^* & \text{if } \; y_m^* > 0 \\ 0 & \text{if } \; y_m^* \leq 0 \end{cases} \tag{10.2}$$

where y_m denotes the incompletely observed value of the latent adoption intensity y_m^*. Equation (10.2) describes the censoring process when observing latent adoption intensity. A farmer does not adopt the practice when the expected utility from adopting the practice would be less than or equal to that from existing practices, resulting in a non-positive net expected utility. The net expected utility is represented by the latent adoption intensity, but we cannot observe negative values for the latent adoption intensity. We can only observe zero values. Because the negative values of y_m^* are set to zero, the density of y_m masses at zero. For $y_m > 0$ the density of y_m is the same as that of y_m^*, but for $y_m = 0$ the density is discrete, with mass equal to the probability of observing $y_m^* \leq 0$. Thus, the density of y_m for constructing a likelihood function can be written as:

$$f(y_m) = f(y_m^*)^d F(y_m^*)^{1-d} \tag{10.3}$$

where $f(y_m)$ indicates the density function of y_m, which is composed of the density function of y_m^*, depicted as $f(y_m^*)$, and the cumulative density function (**cdf**) of y_m^*, depicted as $F(y_m^*)$. d is an indicator variable, $d = 1\{y_m > 0\}$. Because in a Tobit model the latent variable y_m^* is assumed to follow a normal distribution, the likelihood function in the univariate Tobit model is simply written as the product of the normal density and the normal cumulative density:

$$L(\beta_m, \sigma_m^2) = \phi(\varepsilon_m | \beta_m, \sigma_m^2)^d \Phi\left(-\frac{\beta_m x}{\sigma}\right)^{1-d} \tag{10.4}$$

where $L(\cdot)$ denotes the likelihood function from the density of y_m, and $\phi(\cdot)$ and $\Phi(\cdot)$ are the normal density and the normal cumulative density functions respectively.

Since a multivariate generalization of the Tobit model manifests no irregularities (Lee 1993), the multivariate Tobit model for multiple practices can simply be extended from the univariate Tobit model above (Amemiya 1974). In applying the multivariate Tobit model, the latent variable equation in (10.1) is extended to a system of equations with M latent dependent variables:

$$Y^* = \beta x + \varepsilon \tag{10.5}$$

where Y^* is an $(M \times 1)$ vector that represents the adoption intensities of M practices, half of which are chosen in each of two periods. β is an $(M \times k)$ vector of coefficients, and ε is an $(M \times 1)$ vector of error terms distributed as multivariate normal with an $(M \times M)$ variance-covariance matrix Σ, $\varepsilon \sim N(0, \Sigma)$. If the off-diagonal elements of Σ are non-zero, there may be efficiency gains in estimating the M Tobit models jointly (Cameron and Trivedi 2005).

In the second equation (10.2), observed adoption intensities (y_m) belong to one of two regimes, the limit regime $(y_m^* \leq 0)$ and the non-limit regime $(y_m^* > 0)$. Likewise, there are in total 2^M different regimes for M practices. The 2^M regimes are identified using an indicator variable D^j $(j = 1, \ldots, 2^M)$ where D^j equals 1 if a farmer belongs to the j-th regime; 0 otherwise. For example, D^1 represents the regime where a farmer adopts all M practices, D^2 where a farmer adopts only the first practice, and D^3 where a farmer adopts only the first two practices, and so on. Maximum likelihood estimation for the multivariate Tobit model is straightforward after identifying the different 2^M regimes.

For farmers who adopt all M practices ($D^1 = 1$), the multivariate Tobit model has the same structure as an SUR model, so the likelihood function simply becomes the multivariate normal density function (ϕ):

$$L^{D^1=1}(\beta, \Sigma) = (2\pi)^{-\frac{M}{2}}|\Sigma|^{-\frac{1}{2}}\exp\left[-\frac{1}{2}\left(\varepsilon'\right)(\Sigma)^{-1}(\varepsilon)\right] = \phi(\varepsilon|\beta, \Sigma). \quad (10.6)$$

For other regimes, the likelihood function in (10.6) is modified to accommodate censoring. Farmers belong to the h-th regime ($D^h = 1$) if they do not adopt the first p of M available practices. The likelihood function for these farmers is:

$$\begin{aligned} L^{D^{h=1}}(\beta, \Sigma) &= \int_{-\infty}^{-\beta_1 x} \ldots \int_{-\infty}^{-\beta_p x} (2\pi)^{-\frac{M}{2}}|\Sigma|^{-\frac{1}{2}} exp[-\frac{1}{2}(\varepsilon')(\Sigma)^{-1}(\varepsilon)]d\varepsilon_p \ldots d\varepsilon_1 \\ &= \int_{-\infty}^{-\beta_1 x} \ldots \int_{-\infty}^{-\beta_p x} \phi(\varepsilon^{1h}, \varepsilon^{2h}|\beta, \Sigma)d\varepsilon_p \ldots d\varepsilon_1 \end{aligned} \quad (10.7)$$

where $\varepsilon^{1h} = (\varepsilon_1, \ldots, \varepsilon_p)$ and $\varepsilon^{2h} = (\varepsilon_{p+1}, \ldots, \varepsilon_M)$. The variance-covariance matrix Σ comprises three partial matrices: $\Sigma^{11h} = cov(\varepsilon^{1h})$, $\Sigma^{12h} = cov(\varepsilon^{1h}, \varepsilon^{2h})$, and $\Sigma^{22h} = cov\left(\varepsilon^{2h}\right)$. Then, given that $E\left(\varepsilon^{1h}\right) = E\left(\varepsilon^{2h}\right) = 0$, the conditional density of ε^{1h} on ε^{2h} can be defined as:

$$\varepsilon^{1h}|\varepsilon^{2h} \sim N(\varepsilon^h, \Sigma^h) \quad (10.8)$$

where $\varepsilon^h = \Sigma^{12h}\left(\Sigma^{22h}\right)^{-1}\varepsilon^{2h}$ and $\Sigma^h = \Sigma^{11h} - \Sigma^{12h}\left(\Sigma^{22h}\right)^{-1}\Sigma^{12h}$. Based on (10.8) and on Bayes' theorem, the joint density in (10.7) can be decomposed into two conditional densities:

$$\phi\left(\varepsilon^{1h}, \varepsilon^{2h}|\beta, \Sigma\right) = \phi\left(\varepsilon^{1h}|\beta, \varepsilon^h, \Sigma^h\right)\phi\left(\varepsilon^{2h}|\beta, \Sigma^{22h}\right). \quad (10.9)$$

So, the likelihood function in (10.7) can be simplified to a product of the density function and the cumulative density function just as in the likelihood function for the univariate Tobit model in (10.4) (Pudney 1989):

$$\begin{aligned} L^{D^{h=1}}(\beta, \Sigma) &= \phi\left(\varepsilon^{2h}|\beta, \Sigma^{22h}\right)\int_{-\infty}^{-\beta_1 x} \ldots \int_{-\infty}^{-\beta_p x} \phi(\varepsilon^{1h}|\beta, \varepsilon^h, \Sigma^h)d\varepsilon_p \ldots d\varepsilon_1 \\ &= \phi\left(\varepsilon^{2h}|\beta, \Sigma^{22h}\right)\Phi(\varepsilon^{1h}|\beta, \varepsilon^h, \Sigma^h) \end{aligned} \quad (10.10)$$

By combining the two likelihood functions in (10.6) and (10.10) to account for all censoring combinations, we finally derive the log-likelihood function for the multivariate Tobit model:

$$ln\, L(\beta, \Sigma) = \sum_{\{D^1=1\}} ln\, \phi(\varepsilon|\beta, \Sigma) + \sum_{h=2}^{2^M} \left[\sum_{\{D^h=1\}} \{ln\, \phi\left(\varepsilon^{2h}|\beta, \Sigma^{22h}\right) + ln\, \Phi(\varepsilon^{1h}|\beta, \varepsilon^h, \Sigma^h)\} \right] \tag{10.11}$$

The first two terms on the right-hand side of (10.11) are simply a multivariate normal density. The third term describes a multivariate normal cumulative density, evaluated using integration. Up to M choices are made by a farmer, but these must be integrated for each choice not to adopt. However, the cdf of a multivariate normal distribution does not have a closed-form solution, and a trivariate normal cdf is the limit for numerical methods (Cameron and Trivedi 2005). Our study examines eight SC practices, and so requires eight-fold integral evaluation. Bayesian methods using Gibbs sampling and simulation methods using Monte Carlo integration are commonly used as alternatives to high-dimensional multivariate normal integration.

We apply the Geweke-Hajivassiliou-Keane (**GHK**) simulator, a very popular importance sampling simulator for Monte Carlo integration over a region of the multivariate normal distribution. The GHK simulator truncates the multivariate normal density to the conditional standard normal densities using the Cholesky decomposition, and takes random draws from these truncated standard normal densities, then recursively computes multivariate probabilities (Layton 1995). This simulator has a number of desirable properties for multivariate normal limited-dependent-variable models (Börsch-Supan and Hajivassiliou 1993). First, the simulated probabilities are unbiased and are bounded within the (0, 1) interval. Second, the simulator is a continuous and differentiable function of the parameters. Hajivassiliou et al. (1996) tested 13 different simulation techniques and found the GHK simulator to outperform all others in keeping a good balance between accuracy and computational cost.

The simulated cdf for censored adoption intensities then replaces the third term in (10.11). Maximizing the simulated log-likelihood with respect to the elements of β and Σ is now achievable using a conventional maximum likelihood algorithm. Additionally, correlations across periods and/or practices can be statistically tested using elements in the error matrix. For example, a complementary effect between the i-th practice and the j-th practice can be tested using the (i, j) element ρ_{ij} from the estimated variance-covariance matrix $\widehat{\Sigma}$.

10.4 Study Site and Data

This study focuses on an SC project that concluded in 2004—the Environmental Program of El Salvador (PAES). The thrust of this project was to increase farm-household income through improved soil productivity, adoption of conservation technologies, and diversification of cultivars. With training and technical assistance, PAES used some half of its budget as incentives to promote farmer adoption, including in-kind as agricultural inputs (seeds, plants, agrochemicals, tools), and payments for construction of SC structures. The level of incentive disbursals was gauged to commitment levels that farmers submitted as plans before their program participation. Farmers who received the incentives were required to follow technical recommendations specific to the plans they submitted. Farmers chose among SC practices based on their access to labor and capital.

The data used in this study were obtained from on-the-spot surveys, which were conducted on representative samples of small-scale farm households in two sub-projects, PAES-1 and PAES-3.[1] The northern and western parts of the country that both sub-projects cover are generally classified as land unsuitable for cultivation due to severe land degradation (Fig. 10.1) (Pagiola and Dixon 1997). The original survey was conducted in 2002 for 353 beneficiary farmers, 175 from PAES-1 and 177 from PAES-3, all of whom were randomly selected from records provided by implementing agencies. From the 353 beneficiaries surveyed in 2002, 260 were randomly selected for re-survey in 2005 after the project finished in 2004. After excluding 23 households, 20 that had ceased farming, and 3 that did not respond to the primary questions in the 2005 survey, the final data set employs 237 households over two periods.[2] The resulting balanced two-period panel data set allows us to trace farmer decision behaviors concerning SC adoption during and after public intervention in PAES.

The survey items include information on adoption intensities of eleven SC practices that PAES promoted. Residue management, the most widely adopted practice, was implemented on most of the sample farming area during both periods.[3] With a scarcity of contrasting examples, it may be meaningless to analyze farmer adoption decisions on residue management. The six least commonly adopted practices—green manure, infiltration pits, zero/minimum tillage, grass barriers, stone walls, and conservation trees—were adopted by fewer than ten farmers. For our analysis, we use the four most widely adopted SC practices after residue management: live barriers, dead barriers, individual terraces, and contour ditches. In addition, the data provides rich information on a range of adoption factors. Table 10.1 presents definitions and descriptive statistics for these factors, which are used as explanatory variables in our estimation. Apart from the factors in three typical categories[4]—farmer characteristics, farm characteristics, and project characteristics—the 2005 survey adds a few variables to describe characteristics of the towns where farmers reside, as a proxy for

---

[1] PAES is viewed as three separate projects, PAES-1, PAES-2, and PAES-3, since each one was implemented in a different area by a different international consortium.

[2] In fact, a separate survey of PAES non-participants in El Salvador was also conducted in 2005. This survey was originally designed to generate observations for a control group to the 2005 survey group used here. But out of 324 surveyed farmers, only 28 adopted live barriers, 22 dead barriers, 9 contours ditches, and none individual terraces. Such a large-portion of non-adopters makes it impractical to directly compare this group with the 2005 participants in our sample in any meaningful way, using Tobit modeling.

[3] Out of 237 sample farmers, 204 in 2002 and 226 in 2006 adopt residue management, applying the practice to 87 and 96% of their cultivated area for each year.

[4] Factors affecting SC adoption decisions are generally classified into three main groups: farmer characteristics (e.g., schooling, age, gender); farm characteristics (e.g., land tenure, plot size, slope, access to credit); and project characteristics (e.g., program participation, financial incentives, extension assistance) (Bravo-Ureta et al. 2006).

Fig. 10.1 El salvador soil conservation program areas—PAES-1 & PAES-3

market access. In contrast, the project characteristic variables are generally available only in 2002, i.e., during the PAES period, so their coefficients in 2005 estimation are expected to demonstrate residual effects of services that PAES provided. Likewise, a "Perception" variable is collected only in 2002, representing farmers' recognition of soil erosion problems.

10.5 Empirical Results

10.5.1 Farmer Adoption Rates

Across the 237-farmer sample, farmers on average adopt more than two practices out of the four in both periods. Table 10.2 gives a general description of the four practices, along with the number of adopters and average adoption intensities. Live barriers are cost-effective practices for soil conservation because they can use gradual bio-terraces rather than cut-and-fill steep terracing that requires machines or significant manual labor (Cocchi 2004). In El Salvador, live barriers traditionally have been the most frequently used (McReynolds et al. 1994), so plant species and planting guides for live barrier use are well-established for each regional zone (FAO 2000). Accordingly, Salvadoran smallholders can put in live barriers without worrying much about investing in new technologies. More than three-fourths of farmers have adopted live barriers. Dead barriers and contour ditches are classified as conservation structures,

Table 10.1 Description and summary statistics of adoption factors

Variable name	Description	2002	2005
Farm characteristics			
Land	Natural logarithm of farm size (Mz)	0.40 (0.70)	0.41 (0.64)
Tenure	Average tenure rate of all plots, 1 if the farmer own each plot, 0 otherwise	0.65 (0.42)	0.74 (0.40)
Slope	Average slope rate of all plots, 1 if slope of each plot is greater than 15 degrees, 0 otherwise	0.58 (0.48)	0.66 (0.47)
Distance	Distance from house to the nearest plot (km)	0.93 (1.54)	1.12 (1.39)
Livestock	1 if the ratio of livestock sales to total farming sales is greater than 0.3, 0 otherwise	0.17 (0.38)	0.23 (0.42)
Hired labor	1 if the farmer uses hired labor for his/her farming, 0 otherwise	0.73 (0.44)	0.95 (0.23)
Credit	1 if the farmer uses financial credit for his/her farming, 0 otherwise	0.24 (0.43)	0.31 (0.46)
Farmer characteristics			
Age	Age of the household head (years)	48.63 (14.63)	52.66 (14.02)
Education	1 if schooling years of the household head is higher than 6, 0 otherwise	0.19 (0.40)	0.16 (0.37)
Family members	Number of family members who are older than or equal to 14	3.43 (1.77)	3.66 (1.69)
Off-farm income	1 if the household earns off-farm income, 0 otherwise	0.52 (0.50)	0.32 (0.47)
Organization	1 if the farmer participates in organizations, 0 otherwise	0.51 (0.50)	0.52 (0.50)
Perception	1 if the farmer perceives soil erosion to be a problem on his/her fields, 0 otherwise	0.86 (0.35)	–
Project characteristics			
PAES	1 if the farm belongs to PAES-1, 0 otherwise	0.49 (0.50)	–
Years	Number of years involved with PAES	2.71 (0.85)	4.24 (0.96)
Visits	1 if PAES technicians visit the farm at least once a month, 0 otherwise	0.55 (0.50)	–
Incentive	1 if the farmer receives more than three types of incentives from PAES, 0 otherwise	0.80 (0.40)	–
Teach	1 if the farmer has taught what s/he learned from PAES to others, 0 otherwise	0.54 (0.50)	–
Town characteristics			
Carton	Number of residents in the town that the farmer lives in	–	447.17 (457.84)

(continued)

Table 10.1 (continued)

Variable name	Description	2002	2005
City	Distance from the town to the nearest city (km)	–	1.15 (0.90)
Road	1 if the road to the nearest city is a primary one, 0 otherwise	–	0.14 (0.34)

Note The numbers in the last two columns indicate the average values for the variables, and the parenthetic numbers below the averages denote standard deviations

Table 10.2 Description of soil conservation practices and adoption rates during and after PAES

SC practice	Description	2002	2005
Live barriers	Live Barriers are strips of vegetation planted along a contour. They serve to anchor the soil in place with their roots, and to slow the movement of flowing water down-slope with their stems and leaves	178 (343.5)	195 (300.7)
Dead barriers	Dead Barriers function similar to live barriers, the difference being that they are composed of rocks, plant residues, or other non-living materials	80 (175.7)	102 (254.3)
Individual terraces	Individual terraces are constructed to provide a level platform for the growth of an individual tree, and generally are used in combination with another type of conservation structure, such as a contour ditches	117 (65.5)	81 (58.6)
Contour ditches	Contour ditches serve many of the same purposes as contour barriers. In addition, they completely stop down-slope water movement as water collects in the ditch	93 (278.2)	106 (255.6)

Note The numbers in parentheses below the number of adopters in the last two columns indicate the average adoption intensity among farmers who adopted each SC practice. Units are in meters, except for individual terraces (the number of terraces built)

due to the high cost and labor requirements for their installation and maintenance (Knowler 2004). Construction of individual terraces also necessitates a lot of manual labor, and individual terraces are often implemented with contour ditches because the small platforms by themselves do not appreciably control surface water movement (Crozier 1985). As a result, the three practices that require extensive investment are not as easily adopted by resource-poor farmers as live barriers—at least without careful scrutiny of their potential for economic return.[5] Compared to live barriers, adoption rates for the three resource-intensive options are relatively lower, with each adopted by less than half of farmers in both periods.

[5] Only three in-sample farmers cultivate more than five hectares and over 80% of agricultural production comes from two subsistence crops, maize and beans. Most of the smallholders may not have enough resources to invest in SC practices for themselves, particularly in the more expensive dead barriers, individual terraces, and contour ditches.

Our study suggests that a public intervention provides a necessary intermediate process to final SC adoption after the intervention, so farmer adoption behavior in 2002 is expected to differ from that in 2005. Nevertheless, in Table 10.2, we detect no significant differences between the survey years, for adopter numbers or average intensities. While these aggregate numbers are commonly used to assess SC projects (e.g., Bewket 2007), they cannot identify individual adoption behaviors. There is no guarantee that adopters in 2002 continue to use a certain practice in 2005. Our two-period panel data allows us to trace individual adoption decisions for two survey periods. Table 10.3 classifies the 237 farmers into four groups, based on their adoption decisions in both periods. If farmers adopted a certain practice in 2002, and maintained it at half or more of the 2002 coverage through 2005, we define them as **early-adopters**. The 2002 adopters failing to so maintain are **abandoners**. Farmers who did not adopt a certain practice in 2002, but did in 2005, are **late-adopters**. **Non-adopters** did not adopt a certain practice in either period.

Unapparent in Table 10.2, there were in fact significant changes in farmer adoption behaviors after PAES expired. Out of 117 farmers adopting individual terraces in 2002, as many as 79 farmers removed or stopped maintaining more than half their terracing trees by 2005. Planting individual trees for a level platform occupies considerable land space, particularly when terracing a steep slope. For farmers who depend on small plots, land loss due to individual terracing can seriously threaten their livelihood, so often after public support ceases they reclaim for cultivation land lost during the 2002 PAES. Dead barriers and contour ditches requiring high-cost maintenance were also abandoned by almost half of the 2002 adopters. In contrast, farmers prefer live barriers relative to other practices—two-thirds of farmers maintained their live barriers through 2005. The grasses in live barriers serve as valuable forage for animals, or for human consumption in the case of sugar cane or lemon grass. In addition to low maintenance costs, these additional benefits may encourage smallholders to maintain live barriers even without public support.

In sum, soon after PAES ended, half of participating farmers had abandoned at least half of the practices that they adopted in 2002. In contrast, over thirty percent of 2005 adopters had not implemented certain practices in 2002. Practices newly launched by late-adopters mostly offset the practices discarded by abandoners, resulting in the close aggregate numbers we find in Table 10.2. Because of the high abandonment rates among 2002 adopters, we cannot definitively rule out the possibility that some farmers behaved strategically during program participation, just to earn promised incentives. PAES determines the amount of incentive available to

Table 10.3 Classification of farmers adopting soil conservation practices

SC practices	Early adopters	Abandoners	Late adopters	Non-adopters
Live barriers	115	63	41	18
Dead barriers	44	36	50	107
Individual terraces	38	79	32	88
Contour ditches	50	43	37	107

each farmer based on the conservation plan the farmer reports before their SC investments. This may incentivize farmers to overstate the amount necessary to get them to adopt, without fully considering their available labor and capital, or farming conditions. Strategic inflation of the payments farmers are willing to accept may explain the much lower abandonment rates for live barriers compared to the other three SC practices with high installation costs.

Why many in-sample farmers changed their adoption decision just after PEAS expired is still unclear. Their apparently capricious behavior may indicate a transitional process before final adoption, or, as many case studies point out, may indicate the inevitability of withdrawal for investments that were primarily strategic. To get a clearer understanding of farmer adoption behavior, we widen focus from adoption decisions themselves to endogenous factors affecting a farmer's environment. By regressing potential adoption factors on farmer adoption intensities, we identify the distinct effects of these factors on each type of farmer adoption decision. Furthermore, controlling for these effects allows us to identify the dynamics between decisions, including intervention correlations and interaction correlations between decisions to adopt multiple SC practices.

10.5.2 Empirical Model

The 237 farmers in PAES decide how much they adopt each of the four practices in 2002 and 2005. As a result, a total of eight adoption intensities are observed: four in 2002 and four in 2005. For example, out of the 237 farmers, 178 farmers in 2002 and 195 in 2005 adopt 343.5 and 301.1 m of live barriers, respectively, on average. The remaining 59 and 42 farmers decide not to adopt because the utility they gain from adoption is equal to or less than zero ($y_m^* \leq 0$), in which case their intensities are observed to be zero ($y_m = 0$). The distribution of adoption intensities in 2002 and 2005 for a total of 237 farmers, including these non-adopters, is shown in Fig. 10.2. These intensities are censored to the left around zero, resulting in a spike at zero in the distribution in Fig. 10.2. The censored portion of these adoption intensity distributions is appropriately reflected by the introduction of the cdf in the Tobit model ($F(y_m^*)^{1-d}$), otherwise yield a biased estimator. Along with histograms, Fig. 10.2 shows the normal distribution of live barrier intensities estimated by assuming a distribution censored at zero. In both distributions, 23.9 and 17.0% of the samples are censored to zero, respectively, and estimating the mean while ignoring these censored features leads to overestimates of 74.2 and 55.3 m, respectively.

The above results are simply estimates of the mean with only a constant term, so an empirical model with potential adoption factors as explanatory variables is shown in (10.12) below.

$$\begin{aligned} y_{i,t}^* = \beta_{i.t}^0 + \beta_{i,t}^{Farm} X_{i,t}^{Farm} + \beta_{i,t}^{Farmer} X_{i,t}^{Farmer} + \beta_{i,t=2002}^{Project} X_{i,t=2002}^{Project} \\ + \beta_{i,t=2005}^{Town} X_{i,t=2005}^{Town} + \varepsilon_{i.t} \end{aligned} \tag{10.12}$$

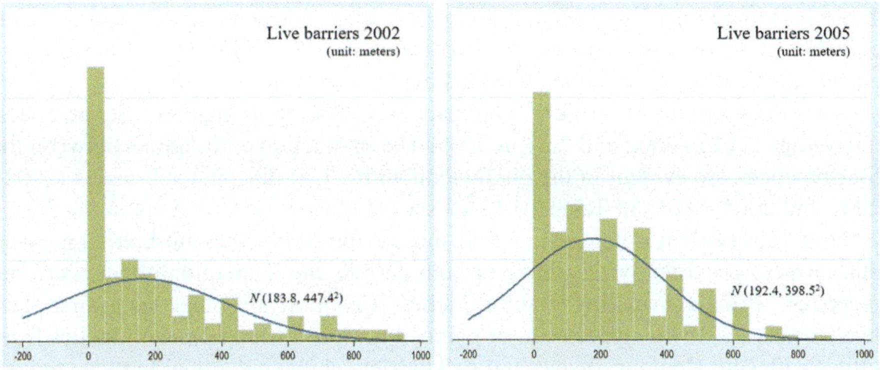

Fig. 10.2 Histograms of adoption intensity for live barriers in 2002 and 2005

where the superscripts $Farm$, $Farmer$, $Project$, and $Town$ refer to the factors categorized by each of the four characteristics in Table 10.1.[6] The subscripts i denote the four SC Practices: live barriers, dead barriers, individual terraces, and contour ditches, and t denotes 2002 and 2005, respectively. i and t take on four and two values, respectively, so that a total of eight adoption intensities ($y^*_{i,t}$) are estimated simultaneously with correlations in the error term ($\varepsilon_{i,t}$).

10.5.3 *Estimation of Factors Affecting Farmer Adoption Rates*

The dynamics between the eight adoption decisions are examined using the estimated variance-covariance matrix, whose elements are presented in Table 10.4, after converting them to correlation coefficients. The four diagonal coefficients in the upper-rightmost sub-box (2002 rows and 2005 columns) describe the intervention correlations between two sequential decisions, made for the same practices across two periods. All four coefficients present positive signs and are strongly significant at the one percent level, except for individual terraces. The positive signs suggest that experience implementing a certain practice in 2002 may positively impact the decision to adopt the practice in 2005. Alternatively, the expectation that adopting a certain practice will ultimately benefit the farm may motivate experimentation in 2002. However, the significantly positive intervention correlations appear to contradict the mass exodus of adopters evident in Table 10.3. The large number of abandoners and late-adopters may provoke negative signs or at least insignificant correlations between the two sequential decisions. Table 10.3 examines individual adoption decisions in both periods, but does not consider adoption factors, such as those presented in

[6] In Table 10.1, project characteristic is limited to 2002 ($t = 2002$) and town characteristic is limited to 2005 ($t = 2005$) except for 'Years'.

Table 10.1 that potentially influence these decisions. The unobserved residuals after controlling for the effects of these factors demonstrate highly significant positive correlations between the sequential decisions.

Around two-thirds of farmers simultaneously adopt more than two SC practices, on average 2.14 in 2002 and 2.21 in 2005. The interaction correlations between the four practices are evident in the coefficients in the two diagonal sub-boxes (2002–2002 and 2005–2005) in Table 10.4. All six off-diagonal coefficients in the 2002–2002 sub-box present identical signs with those in the 2005–2005 sub-box, suggesting that farmers consistently recognize in both periods the interaction effects between practices.[7] Prior to installing contour ditches, it is often advantageous to first plant live barriers above the upper edge of planned contour lines to prevent ditches from filling with soil. Contour ditches and live barriers above individual terraces protect fruit trees on the terraces by filtering surface flow and keeping the vertical elements from eroding. Such complementary effects between live barriers, individual terraces, and contour ditches drive the positive and mostly significant estimates for the 12 correlation coefficients they share in both periods. Contour ditches function similarly to dead barriers, except that the ditches completely stop down-slope water movement. In addition, just as contour ditches demand high labor costs to dig and maintain, the construction of dead barriers also requires a lot of manual labor if enough rocks are not available, suggesting a substitution effect. On the other hand, the interaction correlations in 2005 tend to be more significant than those in 2002. This implies that farmers accumulate more information about the interaction effects between the practices, and/or they give more consideration to the effects when making final adoption decisions after the intervention.

In addition to information about the correlations between the eight adoption decisions from the estimated variance-covariance matrix, our multivariate modeling provides efficiency gains over a system of eight univariate specifications.[8] Figures 10.3 and 10.4 present STATA code to produce estimation results for the univariate Tobit model and the mutivariate Tobit model, respectively.[9] Table 10.5

---

[7] Aside from the intervention and interaction correlations, the off-diagonal coefficients in the 2002-row and 2005-column sub-box describe correlations of elements mixed to determine intervention and interaction correlations. These off-diagonal elements correlate adoption decisions across two periods and four different practices. The signs and significance of the 12 mixed coefficients mostly follow those of the interaction correlations, suggesting that farmers consistently recognize the interaction effects independent of the three-year gap.

[8] Assessing the fitness of two different types of Tobit modeling is not straightforward, since Tobit estimators do not generate sums of squared errors or values. But the likelihood ratio test in Table 10.4 suggests statistically strong joint-significance for the correlation coefficients, so multivariate modeling is more appropriate than modeling independently, guaranteeing an efficiency gain from cross-correlation coefficients.

[9] In Fig. 10.2, "ll(0)" means left-censored at 0. In Fig. 10.3, "draws" specifies the number of pseudo-random standard uniform variables and "adoonly" prevents using the STATA plugin to perform the intensive numerical calculations. You can refer to the STATA manual for specific instructions on using those commands.

Table 10.4 Correlation coefficient estimates from the multivariate tobit model

SC practices		2002					2005							
		Live barriers	Dead barriers	Individual terraces	Contour ditches		Live barriers		Dead barriers		Individual terraces		Contour ditches	
2002	Live barriers	1.000	−0.046	0.080	0.171	**	0.191	***	−0.176	**	0.091		0.277	***
	Dead barriers		1.000	−0.054	−0.097		−0.096		0.346	***	−0.144		−0.099	
	Individual terraces			1.000	0.138	*	0.153	**	−0.004		0.021		0.212	***
	Contour ditches				1.000		0.131		−0.272	***	0.214	**	0.458	***
2005	Live barriers						1.000		−0.139		0.124	*	0.365	***
	Dead barriers								1.000		−0.034		−0.201	**
	Individual terraces										1.000		0.252	***
	Contour ditches												1.000	

Note Likelihood Ratio Test (H0: all correlation coefficients are zero): (28) = 113.73 (Prob. > = 0.00)
* Significant at the ten percent level; ** at the five percent level; *** at the one percent level

```
/* Univariate Tobit */

local X_2002 `farm_2002' `household_2002' `project_2002' `town'
local X_2005 `farm_2005' `household_2005' `project_2005' `town'

quietly tobit live_2002 `X_2002', ll(0)
estimates store live_2002
quietly tobit dead_2002 `X_2002', ll(0)
estimates store dead_2002
quietly tobit ter_2002 `X_2002', ll(0)
estimates store ter_2002
quietly tobit ditch_2002 `X_2002', ll(0)
estimates store ditch_2002
quietly tobit live_2005 `X_2005', ll(0)
estimates store live_2005
quietly tobit dead_2005 `X_2005', ll(0)
estimates store dead_2005
quietly tobit ter_2005 `X_2005', ll(0)
estimates store ter_2005
quietly tobit ditch_2005 `X_2005', ll(0)
estimates store ditch_2005

estimates table live_2002 dead_2002 ter_2002 ditch_2002 ///
  live_2005 dead_2005 ter_2005 ditch_2005, b(%7.3f) se(%7.3f) t(%7.2f) p(%7.2f)
```

Fig. 10.3 STATA code for the Univariate Tobit model

```
/* Multivariate Tobit */

mvtobit (live_2002=`X_2002') (dead_2002=`X_2002') (ter_2002=`X_2002') (ditch_2002=`X_2002') ///
        (live_2005=`X_2005') (dead_2005=`X_2005') (ter_2005=`X_2005') (ditch_2005=`X_2005'), ///
        draws(16) seed(10101) nrtol(1e-2) adoonly
```

```
Fitting univariate models (Tobit or continuous) to get starting values

Maximum # of censored equations is 8

Draws (Halton/pseudo random) are being made:

Created 16 Halton draws per equation for 8 dimensions. Number of initial draws dropped per dimension = 0 . Primes used:

   2   3   5   7  11  13  17  19

Iteration 0:   log likelihood = -7436.6548  (not concave)
Iteration 1:   log likelihood = -7436.4224  (not concave)
Iteration 2:   log likelihood = -7435.4258  (not concave)
```

Fig. 10.4 STATA code and results window for the multivariate tobit model

presents estimates of 168 coefficients from the eight-variate Tobit model.[10] In comparison with the estimates from the univariate models (see Table 10.6 in the Appendix), the estimates in Table 10.5 differ on average by 0.23 standard errors, and eight estimates show opposite signs. The degree of efficiency gain from multivariate modeling depends on the significance of the off-diagonal elements in the estimated variance-covariance matrix. As demonstrated in Table 10.4, the eight adoption decisions are strongly correlated with each other, resulting in noticeable differences between the estimates from multivariate versus univariate modeling.

[10] We leave out the estimation results of the constants in the eight adoption models, to save space and concentrate on the characteristic categories, but all eight estimate sets show statistically significant results at the five percent level.

Table 10.5 Coefficient estimates from the multivariate tobit model

Variable	2002								2005							
	Live barriers		Dead barriers		Individual terraces		Contour ditches		Live barriers		Dead barriers		Individual terraces		Contour ditches	
Farm characteristics																
Land	17.013		−9.345		21.811		63.620		106.254	**	221.823	***	24.002	**	43.593	
Tenure	−85.123		47.602		33.903		128.186	*	42.263		32.948		24.898		31.737	
Slope	25.368		82.635		−7.636		18.613		123.586	*	143.219	**	16.379		92.978	*
Distance	43.332	**	−3.995		−27.795	**	−0.499		4.007		−56.668	**	−15.823	**	−29.364	*
Livestock	21.668		−3.042		79.617	*	−100.311		183.233	***	−33.791		−38.915	**	−88.574	*
Hired labor	−56.998		−61.924		19.927		−27.850		270.345	*	259.017	*	38.153		167.800	*
Credit	−79.839		51.265		−55.966	*	21.123		12.310		105.650	*	−5.641		140.712	***
Farmer characteristics																
Age	3.437	*	2.759	*	2.578	***	0.158		0.768		7.403	**	0.249		1.334	
Education	157.572	**	−2.863		54.088	*	86.966		57.525		82.540		26.698		17.978	
Family members	0.833		−0.190		−8.536		−13.971		7.210		−48.332	***	5.940		−30.163	**
Off−farm income	−63.408		−8.025		33.494		−52.771		105.816		119.866	*	−17.815		151.890	***
Organization	94.298	*	−6.322		57.544	**	124.452	**	−83.105		−11.141		1.700		−84.069	*
Perception	195.228	**	206.363	***	11.796		328.983	***	63.816		90.499		20.663		113.700	

(continued)

Table 10.5 (continued)

Variable	2002								2005							
	Live barriers		Dead barriers		Individual terraces		Contour ditches		Live barriers		Dead barriers		Individual terraces		Contour ditches	
Farm characteristics																
Project characteristics																
PAES	−159.798	**	178.526	***	72.121	***	147.449	**	−50.881		161.196	**	−12.033		80.300	
Years	121.752	***	62.600	**	−4.029		−18.874		−14.892		61.251		2.859		−8.880	
Visits	45.399		3.963		42.818	*	47.716		98.401		149.029	**	30.190	*	115.960	**
Incentive	162.291	**	−73.574		57.710	*	245.940	***	83.923		−228.449	*	−14.204		74.887	
Teach	49.784		96.047	*	58.566	**	−25.371		71.488		−85.363		−3.454		−85.728	
Town characteristics																
Carton	−0.001		−0.099	*	−0.057	**	0.139	**	−0.023		−0.022		−0.008		0.023	
City	−20.159		−9.580		−44.128	**	−12.785		−99.915	***	55.154		−4.456		−61.657	**
Road	−0.036		−24.286		38.063		30.780		−49.170		17.993		45.853	**	155.852	**

Note Log likelihood = −7136.73, Wald (168) = 433.03 (prob. ≥ 0.00)
* Significant at the ten percent level; ** at the five percent level; *** at the one percent level

Table 10.6 Coefficient estimates from the Univariate Tobit model

Variable	2002								2005							
	Live barriers		Dead barriers		Individual terraces		Contour ditches		Live barriers		Dead barriers		Individual terraces		Contour ditches	
Farm characteristics																
Land	13.122		−9.838		19.966		65.145		112.601	**	226.069	***	24.110	**	52.458	
Tenure	−58.001		48.852		42.323		158.394	**	39.344		15.215		25.155		33.674	
Slope	28.567		68.441		−6.509		16.391		142.569	**	130.188	*	22.728		120.550	**
Distance	39.886	**	2.097		−27.584	***	−7.007		−6.093		−42.948	*	−18.158	**	−58.294	***
Livestock	−28.495		8.887		65.817	**	−180.220	**	148.138	**	7.325		−47.039	**	−161.716	***
Hired labor	−54.299		−85.148	*	14.539		−17.751		321.623	**	148.667		57.619		311.728	**
Credit	−32.849		44.674		−43.941		63.640		8.116		140.839	*	−12.750		121.117	**
Farmer characteristics																
Age	3.746	*	2.525		2.522	***	0.728		0.833		6.251	***	0.209		0.566	
Education	187.596	***	−5.485		61.624	**	131.258	*	64.405		56.779		31.406		10.639	
Family members	8.488		−0.669		−6.043		−8.469		2.373		−45.019	**	6.252		−34.588	**
Off-farm income	−55.079		−13.533		33.823		−41.937		100.390		120.326	*	−19.240		140.546	***
Organization	93.103		−21.178		54.309	**	144.229	**	−67.741		−13.026		4.155		−73.397	
Perception	195.892	**	219.561	***	10.125		338.401	***	61.751		63.562		27.178		130.022	
Project characteristics																
PAES	−165.252	**	174.298	***	72.413	***	158.354	**	−49.748		160.464	**	−10.320		96.526	
Years	117.719	***	48.977	*	−7.310		−17.201		−3.581		64.438	*	3.709		5.835	

(continued)

Table 10.6 (continued)

Variable	2002								2005							
	Live barriers		Dead barriers		Individual terraces		Contour ditches		Live barriers		Dead barriers		Individual terraces		Contour ditches	
Farm characteristics																
Visits	45.326		−0.609		42.714	*	47.111		98.272		129.266	*	31.963	*	114.381	**
Incentive	164.459		−66.736		58.970	*	249.589	***	77.220		−207.387	***	−16.961		62.942	
Teach	48.121		106.960	**	62.028	**	−36.159		63.815		−76.623		−3.314		−71.139	
Town characteristics																
Carton	−0.003		−0.099	*	−0.057	*	0.127	**	−0.030		−0.019		−0.009		0.022	
City	−18.962		−9.665		−44.858	***	−13.869		−96.556	**	43.085		−3.799		−70.144	**
Road	10.102		−40.678		40.221		76.566		−42.774		5.254		49.886	**	187.732	**
Log likelihood	−1350.00		−629.73		−798.93		−736.79		−1484.79		−817.42		−551.04		−824.90	
LR test (21)	78.96	***	40.51	***	73.12	***	71.40	***	54.05	***	74.53	***	39.89	***	67.88	***

Note * Significant at the ten percent level; ** at the five percent level; *** at the one percent level

Despite the advantages of being able to estimate the variance-covariance matrix and improving efficiency, estimating three or more tobit models at once, as in this study, is a very time-consuming task. The STATA "mvtobit" command used in this study improves on the existing GHK simulator by pivoting integrals over a wider range to reduce variability in simulated probabilities and by using Mata code to perform multiple processors simultaneously.[11] In addition to the "mvtobit" code in Fig. 10.3, You can speed up the calculation by using the "atrho0" option, which specifies the starting values for the standard deviation and correlation directly, or the "cmp" command, which is more commonly used for models that share a multivariate normal distribution.[12]

From the estimation results for 21 adoption factors in four categories, we derive which factors significantly correlate with farmer choice in their eight different adoption decisions, which differ by whether or not they get public support, and which of four practices they consider implementing. While using data from identical panels of farmers for both years, the factors present substantially different estimates in each year, with over half of the factors in 2002 rejected (at the five percent significance level) by the null hypothesis that they are equal to 2005 factors. Statistically significant factors also vary between the 2002 and 2005 estimates. Thirty-three factors are significant at least at the ten percent level in 2002, and roughly the same number, 32, in 2005. Among these significant factors, only five factors are common in both years, and two of these five display opposite signs. The substantial difference between the two periods suggests that the determinants of and/or constraints to farmer adoption decisions differ significantly in 2002 and 2005, so farmer adoption behaviors diverge during and after public intervention.

Estimation for the eight adoption models is conducted on the same 237 farmers, but results present unique estimates for each of the eight models. The most striking differences in Table 10.5 are found between the 2002 and 2005 periods, i.e., during and after PAES, rather than between categories of variable types. In each period, the factors that farmers consider carefully seem to differ clearly. In general, for 2002 adoption decisions, factors related to PAES or to intermediate behaviors expected during the PAES period, such as "Perception", "PAES", and "Incentives", result in significant estimates. In contrast, for 2005 adoption decisions, factors directly associated with farm income, including farming conditions, input constraints, and market accessibility, produce most of the significant estimates. The 2005 factors include "Land", "Livestock", "Off-farm Income", and "Road". As a result, with few exceptions, including 'Visits' and 'Age,' almost all adoption factors have statistically significant impacts in only one of the two years, so their effects generally seem limited to a single period.

[11] The reader is referred to Gates (2006) for the basic operating algorithms of the GHK simulator and its application within the STATA program.

[12] The reader is referred to Roodman (2011) for the theoretical background of the "cmp" command and specific examples of its use in SUR, probit and tobit type models.

Farmers also carefully consider the characteristics specific to each SC practice. The significant factors in Table 10.5 vary widely across the four practices, particularly in the 2005 estimation. The four practices are broadly classified as vegetative technologies and structural technologies. Structural technologies—dead barriers and contour ditches—generally require more expensive inputs but are more effective conservation tools. Farmers who invest in cash crops expect more benefits from soil conservation, so may prefer these two structures. This preference for two input-intensive structures is revealed as distinctively significant estimates in factors related to farming inputs, such as "Credit", "Family members", and "Off-farm income". Distinct farmer preferences arising from SC practice characteristics mostly manifest in 2005 decisions. Farmer consideration of SC practice characteristics only in 2005 would suggest that during the PAES period, farmers accumulated enough knowledge about these characteristics to apply that knowledge to their own farming, and/or they became fully comfortable acting on that knowledge only after the intervention period.

10.6 Discussion

Many case studies report developing country farmers abandoning SC practices when public support ends. Critics cite this abrupt behavior as crucial evidence that substantial (usually direct) incentives offered by SC projects induce strategic behavior as farmers adopt merely to qualify for promised incentives. By this argument, immediate abandonment is also a rational behavior consistent with maximizing benefits post-project. Public intervention is further criticized for drawing farmers' attention from learning new technologies best for them, to technologies associated with attractive giveaways, ultimately wasting resources (e.g., Bodnár et al. 2006).

Our empirical analysis of PAES in El Salvador presents fairly similar results to other case studies reporting disappointing intervention effects. In Table 10.3, almost half the farmers who adopted the four SC practices abandoned at least half the practices soon after PAES expired. Moreover, these "abandoners" were concentrated in resource-intensive practices, such as dead barriers, individual terraces, and contour ditches. For example, among 117 farmers adopting individual terraces in 2002, 79 were abandoners in 2005, and of these 79, 68 went so far as to demolish their entire terraces and reclaim the lost growing area. Robust abandonment behavior supports the criticism that farmers strategically choose expensive practices to procure promised program rewards, then simply discard the practices soon after reward incentives stop.

Estimation results also support incentive program critics in some ways. Farm characteristic factors are generally not significant determinants of behavior in 2002, and a few even show unexpected signs.[13] Farmers appear to adopt SC practices blindly, spurred by project agents and public support, without ever considering viability of the

[13] For example, dead barriers can be constructed during fallow periods, so we may expect adoption without any break in a farmer's cultivation cycle. While farmers with enough farming plots to rotate thus may prefer dead barriers, 'Land' in dead barriers presents a negative sign in 2002. Fruit trees are typically planted on individual terraces, so dairy-oriented farmers may not be interested in individual

practices. Critics usually cite aggregate data about adoption rates or adopter numbers or single-period survey data mostly collected after an SC project concludes. Critics' conclusions or suspicions—that strategic behavior by farmers dooms public intervention to impotence—may be plausible based on the limited data. The PAES drew similar suspicions in many circles, as half the participants abandoned SC practices soon after PAES expired. The 2005 estimates of project factors mostly presented insignificant or negative effects from PAES intervention. However, aggregate data cannot identify individual farmer behavior, and cannot exclude effects from adoption factors. This work demonstrates that aggregating data and excluding adoption factors can alter results in telling ways. Table 10.2, relying on aggregate numbers, in fact presents a set of inferences about farmer adoption behaviors and intervention effects that directly conflict with results presented in Tables 10.3 and 10.4, investigating individual adoption rates, and including adoption factors, respectively. Single-period data are also at risk for presenting results that conflict depending on whether the data were collected during or after an intervention. For example, Bravo-Ureta et al. (2006) empirically demonstrated positive intervention effects using survey data collected during an intervention period. The project factors in PAES also indicated many significant intervention effects in 2002.

Conflicting perceptions about the efficacy of public intervention may derive in part from characteristics unique to each SC project, but more importantly may derive from a difference in the adoption decision criteria farmers use during compared to after public intervention. Farmers may experiment with SC practices preferentially recommended during an SC program because they may have little prior knowledge of new practices and can reduce economic risk by receiving public support. However, after the program ends, farmers must shoulder the full economic risk alone, so potential risks and benefits may become their top priorities when ultimately choosing SC practices (Marra et al. 2003). It simply follows that data collected during an intervention period are expected to present more significant intervention effects than data collected after the period. In the same context, many farmers are likely to reverse the adoption decisions they experiment with during an intervention when the program ends, because their priorities or criteria for choosing SC practices change after the intervention.

Our PAES data set covers a period during PAES intervention and a period after, allowing us to avoid conclusions based on half a story—as data constraints have unfortunately made the standard in the field. In spite of clues from PAES like those cited typically as evidence of strategic behavior by farmers, much evidence refutes these criticisms, suggesting that farmers participate for practical purposes, i.e., to actively learn about new SC practices during the intervention, with the intention of utilizing effective practices to augment farm income later.

First, one-third of farmers newly launched SC practices after PAES expired in 2005, with late adopters consistently adopting all four practices (Table 10.3). Farmers

---

terraces, preferring to keep every square meter for grazing. Contrary to this expectation, the 2002 estimate of 'Livestock' indicates a significantly positive sign for individual terraces. 'Land' and 'Livestock' recover their expected signs in the 2005 estimation, along with statistical significance.

strategically adopting certain practices may strategically abandon them after public support ceases, but would not subsequently invest in other new practices without further support. Late-adopting farmers may be risk averse—reluctant to sacrifice short-term returns for the less certain benefits of new practices—but may be prepared to adopt new practices after they gather enough information.

Second, the intervention correlations present positive signs for all four practices, significant at the one percent level, except for individual terraces. Assuming identical effects from adoption factors in both years, if a farmer adopts a certain practice in 2002 and then abandons the practice in 2005, or does not adopt in 2002 and then first adopts it in 2005, the correlation between the two sequential adoption decisions is estimated to be negative. The large number of abandoners and late adopters shown in Table 10.3, on average forty percent of in-sample farmers, strongly suggests negative (or at least insignificant) intervention correlations may result, but in fact for all four practices, positive intervention correlations manifest. The perhaps counterintuitive correlations indicate that adoption factors impact farmer adoption decisions differently in each period. Even allowing for the different effects, statistically significant unobserved factors drive the positive correlations between sequential decisions, indicating a positive link between experimental adoptions during intervention and ultimate adoptions after intervention.

Third, the 2005 estimates demonstrate convincingly that, in their adoption decisions after PAES, farmers carefully considered the specific characteristics of each SC practice, mostly relating to farm income. These include all seven farm factors, "Family members" and "Off-farm income" in farmer factors, and "City" and "Road" in town factors. Out of 44 coefficients across eleven factors, 25 estimates are statistically significant. Moreover, the signs and significance levels for the coefficients fairly accurately reflect the distinct characteristics of each practice, and each practice's expected compatibility with the farmers' environment. For example, dairy-oriented farmers, possibly less interested in soil conservation, may exceptionally welcome live barriers as forage sources. The 2005 coefficients for "Livestock" complied exactly with expectation, presenting significantly positive estimates for live barriers at the one percent level, but negative estimates for other practices. The relative advantage of conservation structures for cash-crop farming was captured by the 2005 estimates for the four input factors—"Hired labor", "Credit", "Family members", and "Off-farm income". These input factors presented significant estimates in 2005 only for dead barriers and contour ditches, reflecting properly that cash-crop farming aggressively utilizes credit, off-farm income, and hired labor.

In their adoption decision after PAES, farmers also have carefully considered interaction effects between the four SC practices. Live barriers, individual terraces, and contour ditches are often installed together to complement their disadvantages. In contrast, two conservation structures may compete with each other for labor and capital. The 2005 correlation coefficients in Table 10.4 capture unobserved factors, reflecting interaction effects between the four practices. The three complementary practices present positive and significant estimates, with negative and significant estimates for dead barriers and contour ditches.

Marketing campaigns aim to inform consumers about the existence and characteristics of new products, to induce consumers to differentiate between new products and existing ones, so that consumers might subsequently try the new products and change their brand loyalty. Similarly, the role of a public intervention is to provide farmers opportunities to learn about new SC practices, to help them recognize the characteristics of new practices, and to gain confidence in their practicality. Empirical evidence for practical application of SC practices suggests that, although many farmers changed their adoption decisions soon after PAES ended, PAES had noteworthy intervention effects on its participants, guiding many to ultimately adopt SC practices.[14]

10.7 Concluding Remarks

Farmer adoption decisions diverge based on whether decisions are made during or after an intervention, and on which management practices are chosen. In fact, divergent decisions of either type influence each other. Farmer decision behaviors thus should be understood within a larger view that includes all available adoption alternatives, as well as dynamics between alternatives. Unfortunately, almost all previous studies on SC adoption, including empirical studies criticizing public intervention, depend on fragmentary information from single-period survey data or aggregate time-series data. This chapter applies multivariate Tobit model to analyze the adoption-disadoption of SC practices in one of the hot-spots of soil erosion.

This study instead uses two-period data from 237 PAES participants in El Salvador, covering periods during and after PAES intervention, and all SC practices promoted by PAES. For empirical application, we basically retrace the steps of previous studies, introducing typical adoption factors and modeling adoption decisions under a Tobit framework, but we also extend research focus from a single adoption decision to eight adoption decisions—across two periods and four dominant SC practices. Eight Tobit models, one for each decision, are estimated simultaneously to embody and identify dynamics between the decisions, using a GHK simulator to evaluate an eight-variate normal cumulative density.

By examining farmer adoption decisions as a whole—during and after the PAES intervention, for all four practices, and the correlations between the decisions—this study draws an all-encompassing conclusion about farmer adoption behavior that may explain widely divergent adoption behaviors. Farmers may pass through an intermediate learning-process during an intervention, while collecting information about new practices and evaluating these practices. After the intervention ends, farmers apply practical knowledge to their own plots, and assume full risk. Decision

[14] In fact, a separate survey of PAES non-participants in El Salvador, also conducted in 2005, reported much lower adoption rates for all four practices than among participants in our sample—out of 324 surveyed farmers, only 28 adopted live barriers, 22 dead barriers, 9 contours ditches, and none individual terraces.

criteria that farmers use for experimental adoption during an intervention in principle differs from criteria for practical adoption after the intervention. Two distinct groups of adoption factors result, one exclusively influencing farmer adoption decisions during each period. Thus, adoption in one period does not guarantee adoption in the other period—and some farmers abandon certain practices after an intervention.

Acknowledgements The authors thank Emeritus Professor Boris Bravo-Ureta [Department of Agricultural and Resource Economics, University of Connecticut] for his procurement and sharing of data used in this chapter.

This research was funded by the National Research Foundation of Korea Grant funded by the Korean Government (NRF-2022S1A5C2A03093594).

References

Albaladejo J, Díaz-Pereira E, de Vente J (2021) Eco-holistic soil conservation to support land degradation neutrality and the sustainable development goals. CATENA 196, Article 104823

Amemiya T (1974) Multivariate regression and simultaneous equation models when dependent variables are truncated normal. Econometrica 42:999–1012

Amemiya T (1984) Tobit models: a survey. J Econ 24(1–2):3–61

Amsalu A, De Graaff J (2007) Determinants of adoption and continued use of stone terraces for soils and water conservation in an Ethiopian highland watershed. Ecol Econ 61:294–302

Ananda J, Herath G (2003) Soil erosion in developing countries: a socio-economic appraisal. J Environ Manag 68:343–353

Arslan O (2004) Family of multivariate generalized t distributions. J Multivar Anal 89(2):329–337

Bewket W (2007) Soil water conservation intervention with conventional technologies in northwestern highlands of Ethiopia: acceptance and adoption by farmers. Land Use Policy 24:404–416

Bodnár R, Schrader T, Campen WV (2006) How project approach influences adoption of SWC by farmers, examples from southern mali. Land Degrad Develop 17:479–494

Börsch-Supan A, Hajivassiliou V (1993) Smooth unbiased multivariate probability simulators for maximum likelihood estimation of limited dependent variable models. J Econ 58:347–368

Bravo-Ureta BE, Solís D, Cocchi H, Quiroga RE (2006) The Impact of soil conservation and output diversification on farm income in central American hillside farming. Agric Econ 35:267–276

Cameron AC, Trivedi PK (2005) Microeconometrics: methods and applications. Cambridge University Press, New York

Cocchi H (2004) Soil conservation, output diversification and farm income: evidence from hillside farmers in central America. Department of Agricultural and Resource Economics, University of Connecticut

Cornick J, Cox TL, Gould BW (1994) Fluid milk purchases: a multivariate Tobit analysis. Am J Agric Econ 76(1):74–82

Doss CR (2006) Analyzing technology adoption using microstudies: limitations, challenges, and opportunities for improvement. Agric Econ 34:207–219

Dribe M, Stanfors M (2009) Does parenthood strengthen a traditional household division of labor? evidence from Sweden. J Marriage Fam 71(1):33–45

FAO.: Manual on integrated soil management and conservation practices. FAO Land and Water Bulletin 8, Rome, Italy (2000)

Gates R (2006) A Mata Geweke–Hajivassiliou–Keane multivariate normal simulator. Stata J 6(2):190–213

Geweke J (1991) Efficient simulation from the multivariate normal and Student-t distributions subject to linear constraints and the evaluation of constraint probabilities. In: Computing science and statistics: Proceedings of the 23rd Symposium on the Interface, Fairfax Station, VA: Interface Foundation of North America, pp 571–578

Hajivassiliou V, McFadden D, Ruud P (1996) Simulation of multivariate normal rectangle probabilities and their derivatives: theoretical and computational results. J Econ 72:85–134

Keane PK (1994) A computationally practical simulation estimator for panel data. Econometrica 62(1):95–116

Knowler DJ (2003) Explaining the financial attractiveness of soil and water conservation: a meta-analysis model. In: The 2003 soil and water conservation society's annual conference, Spokane, Washington, 26–30

Knowler DJ (2004) The economics of soil productivity: local, national and global perspectives. Land Degrad Develop 15:543–561

Layton DF (1995) Specifying and testing econometric models for stated preference surveys. Unpublished doctoral dissertation. Department of Economics, University of Washington

Lee L (1993) Asymptotic distribution of the maximum likelihood estimator for a stochastic frontier function model with a singular information matrix. Econ Theory 9(3):413–430

Marra M, Pannell DJ, Ghadim AA (2003) The economics of risk, uncertainty and learning in the adoption of new agricultural technologies: where are we on the learning curve? Agric Syst 75:215–234

McReynolds S, Johnston TM, Geisler CE (1994) Factors affecting land use and soil management practices in El salvador. In: Lutz E et al (eds) Economic and institutional analyses of soil conservation projects in central America and the Caribbean. The World Bank, Washington, D.C., pp 191–200

Pagiola S, Dixon JA (1997) Land degradation problems in El salvador. In: El Salvador Rural Development Study, Report no. 16253-ES. Washington, D. C: World Bank

Roodman D (2011) Fitting fully observed recursive mixed-process models with cmp. Stata J 11(2):159–206

Smith K, Weinberg M (2004) Measuring the success of conservation programs. Amber Waves 2(4):14–19

Tobin J (1958) Estimation of relationships for limited dependent variables. Econometrica 26(1):24–36

Yoon T (2013) Economics of Sustainable Natural Resource Management. Ph.D. Dissertation, University of Connecticut

Part II
Panel Analysis

Chapter 11
Propensity Score Matching and Difference-In-Difference Estimator for Impact Evaluations: A Case Study from Zimbabwe

Michée Arnold Lachaud

Abstract Development banks, non-governmental organizations, and international institutions regularly implement projects in low-income countries to assist them in their development process. These projects, often called "programs," are of different natures and target different sectors in the economy, as well as different aspects of society or different demographic groups. This chapter discusses econometric methods based on panel data to evaluate the impact of such programs. Those who participate or benefit from these programs are called the *beneficiaries*. Often, the evaluation consists of comparing the change in a target outcome (e.g., income) between the beneficiaries and a *control group*, often called *the counterfactual*. To do so, both groups should be *comparable*; therefore, careful attention should be paid when choosing both the *beneficiaries* and the *counterfactual*, while avoiding selection bias. This chapter further discusses the sampling strategy for selecting both groups, including the calculation of the sample size, propensity score matching methods to define the final evaluation sample, and ways to handle potential selection bias in panel data using difference-in-difference techniques. The chapter also shows implementation of these techniques in Stata software using a case study and data from the "Training for Rural Economic Empowerment (TREE)" program implemented in Zimbabwe in 2010 by the International Labour Organization.

Keywords Difference-in-Difference · Propensity score matching · Program evaluation

---

M. A. Lachaud (✉)
College of Agriculture and Food Sciences, Florida Agricultural and Mechanical University, Tallahassee, FL, USA
e-mail: michee.lachaud@famu.edu

D. Mukherjee (ed.), *Applied Econometric Analysis Using Cross Section and Panel Data*, Contributions to Economics, https://doi.org/10.1007/978-981-99-4902-1_11

11.1 Introduction

One of the missions of development banks, non-governmental organizations, and several international institutions is to implement projects in low-income countries to assist them in their development process. The primary objective of these projects, often called "programs," is to change an outcome such as *higher yields*, *productivity*, *gross margins*, *income*, *profits*, *better health care*, *education*, *consumption*, or *well-being* in general. Assessing whether implemented programs achieve their intended goals is an important policy question for these organizations before deciding to replicate them, scale them up, make needed adjustments, or simply stop them. Another equally important policy question that is often overlooked is whether these programs are cost-effective, i.e., their objectives could neither have been achieved with a lower cost, nor more could have been done with the amount of money allocated. The objective of this chapter is to discuss how to use panel data, propensity score matching and difference-in-difference non-experimental methods to evaluate the impact of a program and its cost-effectiveness.

The people who benefit from a program are called *beneficiaries,* the *treated group,* or simply *treated.* The *causal* impact of the program on its beneficiaries is what is being evaluated, so the million-dollar question without relaxing the *ceteris paribus* assumption is what the outcome would have been for beneficiaries had they not participated in the program. One could think of comparing outcomes of treated subjects with and without the program; unfortunately, these same individuals cannot be observed in two different states of nature during the same timeframe, i.e., participation and non-participation in the program. This leads to probably the most challenging task in evaluation using non-randomized methods, which is to find a group of individuals who do not benefit from the program and who are as comparable as possible to the beneficiaries before the program implementation. This group is often called *counterfactual*, *control*, or *untreated*. The evaluation consists of contrasting changes due to the program in a set of targeted outcomes between beneficiaries and the counterfactual. The mean difference in outcomes between these two groups is known as the *treatment effect* or *average treatment effect* (ATE) and captures the program impact. The outcomes are derived from a *theory of change* or *logic model of intervention*, which is a framework that illustrates the different steps and specific pathways of the program, and how, at a strategic level, the program leads to changes in the targeted outcomes.[1]

An evaluation is used to address specific questions related to a program's design, implementation, execution, and results. According to Imas and Rist (2009), an evaluation addresses three types of question: *descriptive*, which is related to what is taking place, the process, conditions, organizational relationships, and stakeholder views; *normative*, which consists of subjectively contrasting what is or should be

[1] See Connell and Kubisch (1998), Sullivan and Stewart (2006), and more recently Mayne (2017) for more detail about the theory of change.

taking place where the program is implemented; and finally *causative*, which examines whether the program has a causal impact on those who participate in it, i.e., whether it makes a significant difference in the outcome(s) of interest. The latter is the question addressed by an impact evaluation.

There are all kinds of programs or projects depending on the targeted sector(s) in the economy (e.g., agriculture, microfinance, employment). Once a program is implemented, it takes some time, in most cases years, before any effects can be observed, depending on the nature of the program and the sector of the economy. Another challenge in evaluating a program is that there are many other factors, policies, and projects in place, including unobserved heterogeneity, that can affect the targeted outcomes, and thus make it difficult to directly attribute changes to the specific program being evaluated.

A non-randomized evaluation involves at least two rounds of data collection: one before its implementation, *baseline data*, and another during the time of the evaluation, *endline data*. When baseline data are collected on both beneficiaries and the control group, it is a *prospective evaluation*, which is the ideal situation for an evaluation. Nevertheless, when baseline information is collected only on beneficiaries, one faces a *retrospective evaluation* at the endline, i.e., collecting baseline data on controls at the same time as collecting endline data on both groups. The results of a retrospective evaluation rely largely on the accuracy of the memory of the individuals in the control group. The longer the time between the collection of the baseline and endline data in a retrospective evaluation, the higher the likelihood of having biased estimates.

The analysis presented in this chapter is based on difference-in-difference (DID) and propensity scores matching (PSM), two statistical and econometric methods used to define the full sample and conduct the evaluation. The former is used is used to properly gauge the impact of the program by accounting for unobserved characteristics between the two groups whereas the latter is used to match individuals, i.e., to find comparable treated and untreated subjects based on observable attributes.

Empirically testing or establishing causal relationships between variables is a difficult exercise, requires strong statistical and econometric techniques. This chapter is designed to present the theoretical framework required for such evaluations and discusses empirical techniques and skills that are needed but often overlooked. The empirical application relies on the "Training for Rural Economic Empowerment" (TREE) program, implemented in Zimbabwe in 2010 by the International Labour Organization (ILO), as a case study to illustrate the different steps needed to conduct an impact evaluation (Lachaud et al. 2018). Section 11.2 presents the DID approach, which is a panel data method that can be used to estimate the treatment effect when unobserved time-invariant heterogeneity across treated and controls is present. Section 11.3 discusses the advantages of using PSM and the assumptions under which this approach yields unbiased estimates. Section 11.4 briefly presents the TREE program implemented in Zimbabwe by ILO. The sampling strategy for TREE is briefly discussed in Sect. 11.5, which illustrates how to use the statistical software package Stata to perform PSM and estimate the DID model. Section 11.6 presents the results of the evaluation.

The methods discussed in this chapter are general and can answer impact evaluation questions as well as broader questions related to different types of intervention. They are used to empirically test the causal effect of the ILO TREE's intervention on income, household consumption, child welfare, and health expenses on the beneficiaries and to assess whether TREE was cost-effective.

11.2 Difference-In-Difference (DID) or Double Difference (DD)

Difference-in-Differences (DID) Methods are based on panel data and often used when a program or development project cannot be randomly assigned.[2] Basically, DID methods consist of comparing chronological changes in the program outcomes between treated (the beneficiaries) and untreated subjects (non-beneficiaries). In an impact evaluation, causal relationships between the program implemented and the outcome variable(s) are critical. In the presence of characteristics as potential regressors that the evaluator cannot observe, one can rely on DID estimation to obtain causal effects. By using DID methods, one can account for time-invariant differences in characteristics between both groups: innate ability, personality, specific attributes such as risk aversion or effects of specific regulations or policies across different regions where the program is implemented.

One of the key assumptions of DID methods is that unobserved characteristics between treated and non-treated for program participation are time-invariant, thus, can be considered as fixed effects and will be differentiated out when estimating the impact of the program. Some evaluation questions that require accounting for unobserved time-invariant characteristics include: do beneficiaries report higher income than non-beneficiaries because of the program implementation, or would they have reported higher incomes for other unobserved causes? These questions can be addressed by DID methods. The time required to observe a difference between outcomes between treated and controls due to a program implementation often leads to the use of an unbalanced panel dataset or a repeated cross-sectional dataset as beneficiaries can drop out of the program and people from both groups can move to a different location. However, DID methods can accommodate these issues if the composition of individuals of both groups is stable over time (Caliendo and Kopeining 2008).

There are several other factors that may affect a program's outcome. For instance, in developing countries, it is common that several projects from the international community (e.g., The World Bank, the U.N., USAID) along with national projects are implemented at the same time making it difficult to evaluate a specific program as all these projects can affect the program's targeted outcome. Thus, the difference

[2] A cross-sectional dataset consists of a sample of statistical units taken at a given point in time. Whereas a time series data are observations on variables over time. A panel dataset consists of a time series for each cross-sectional statistical unit.

in income between and after the implementation of the program does not capture the causal impact of a program over time. Using DID methods allows addressing this issue as discussed below.

In addition, unobserved factors across areas where the program is implemented can also affect the program's outcomes. To better understand how the DID method works, let us consider the TREE training program that was implemented by ILO in 2010 in Zimbabwe to improve marketable skills of its beneficiaries with the objective of increasing income of the beneficiaries. Comparing income across Zimbabwe districts where TREE was implemented and not, will not either provide the causal impact of the program because of non-randomization, i.e., there are likely geographical reasons or unobserved heterogeneity across districts that can explain why some districts were selected and others were not, not known to the evaluator, which would affect the observed difference in outcomes over time. This is known as the selection bias problem, which is beyond the scope of this chapter.

The DID method also known as the double difference method allows addressing the two aforementioned issues. On one hand, the DID compares outcomes of beneficiaries before and after being enrolled in the program (*the first difference*), hence, accounts for time-invariant factors since this is a within group comparison. On the other hand, it accounts for time-varying factors by comparing outcomes of non-treated experiencing similar environmental conditions with treated before and after the implementation of the program (*the second difference or second counterfactual difference).*

Finally, by subtracting the second difference from the first, DID compares situations before and after the program's implementation and differences between beneficiaries and non-beneficiaries over time. Simply stated, applying DID to TREE will compare changes induced by TREE in income of treated with those who do not benefit from the program. It is worth noting that to use DID methods, baseline and endline data for the outcome under study is needed for both treated and controls.

More practically, suppose that the average annual income (Y) for those who were selected to participate in the TREE program goes from $Y_b^T = \$1{,}000$ before the program implementation (baseline) to $Y_e^T = \$2{,}500$ after the program implementation (endline). By contrast, the average annual income for the control group goes from $Y_b^C = \$1{,}400$ (baseline) to $Y_e^C = \$2{,}200$ (endline). How to apply the DID method to calculate the impact of TREE? There are three steps in applying the DID method. First, one must compute the *first difference* which is the difference between the income of the beneficiaries before and after the program implementation, i.e., $\Delta Y^T = Y_e^T - Y_b^T = \$1{,}500$. Next, we calculate the *second difference* which captures the observed difference in income for the control group after the program implementation: $\Delta Y^C = Y_e^C - Y_b^C = \$800$. Finally, the impact of TREE using the DID method is obtained by subtracting the *second difference* from the *first difference*: $DID = \left(Y_e^T - Y_b^T\right) - \left(Y_e^C - Y_b^C\right) = \$700$ suggesting that the average income of TREE beneficiaries has increased by an amount of \$700 due to the program implementation.

More formally assuming a panel data setting with an available baseline dataset where $T = 0$ and endline dataset with $T = 1$ after the program implementation and let us denote P_i as the program status of a specific individual where $P_i = 1$ for beneficiaries and $P_i = 0$ otherwise. Let us denote Y_{its} the income (assumed outcome) of individual i (treated or control) at time t, thus:

$$Y_{its} = \begin{cases} Y_{it1} & if\, P_s = 1 \\ y_{0it} & if\, P_s = 0 \end{cases} \tag{11.1}$$

Obviously, one cannot observe an individual i in both statuses (s) simultaneously, i.e., in the program and not in the program. Thus, in practice one observes only one state. The DID framework assumes an additive structure for the outcome of the comparison group as follows (Angrist and Pischke 2009):

$$E(Y_{0it}|\alpha_i, X_{it}, T) = \alpha_i + X_{it}\prime\beta + \lambda T_t \tag{11.2}$$

where α_i captures an individual specific effect, X is a vector of observed individual's attributes, and T is a time-dummy variable. Equation 11.2 implies that without the implementation of the program, income is determined by the sum of individual unobserved and observed characteristics and a time effect that is common across individuals.

As explained by Angrist and Pischke (2009), DID methods assume that the causal effect of program participation is additive and constant and thus:

$$E(Y_{1it}|\alpha_i, X_{it}, T) = E(Y_{0it}|\alpha_i, X_{it}, T) + \gamma \tag{11.3}$$

where γ captures the causal effect of program participation. DID is a version of the linear fixed effects panel data model that does not require repeated observations on the same decision-making unit and thus is a good fit for an impact evaluation as it is common in such studies for beneficiaries to drop out of the program or targeted controls to be unreachable.

The DID model can be formulated as follows:

$$Y_{it} = \alpha_i + \delta P_{it} + \lambda T_t + \gamma P_{it} T_t + X_{it}\prime\beta + \varepsilon_{it}, \quad i = 1, .., n; t = 1, 2 \tag{11.4}$$

where this model contains program and time effects and an interaction term for beneficiaries after program participation. Besides the parameters associated to the vector of observed characteristics, the other parameters as related to the conditional mean function of the two main effects $E(Y_{it}|P_i, T)$ that need to be estimated can be expressed as follows:

$$\alpha_i = E(Y_{it}|P_i = 0, T_t = 0) = \delta(P_i = 0) + \lambda(T_t = 0) \tag{11.5}$$

$$\delta = E(Y_{it}|P_i = 1, T_t = 0) - E(Y_{it}|P_i = 0, T_t = 0) = \delta(P_i = 1) - \delta(P_i = 0) \tag{11.6}$$

$$\lambda = E(Y_{it}|P_i = 0, T_t = 1) - E(Y_{it}|P_i = 0, T_t = 0) = \lambda(T_t = 1) - \lambda(T_t = 0) \tag{11.7}$$

$$\begin{aligned}\gamma = &\{E(Y_{it}|P_i = 1, T_t = 1) - E(Y_{it}|P_i = 1, T_t = 0)\} \\ &- \{E(Y_{it}|P_i = 0, T_t = 1) - E(Y_{it}|P_i = 0, T_t = 0)\}\end{aligned} \tag{11.8}$$

This framework is quite flexible compared to the fixed effects models because it is easier to add other regressors including additional time periods and treatments. It is worth noting that one cannot calculate the ATE discussed in the introduction without full randomization as one cannot observe the difference in targeted outcomes with and without program participation. Instead, as explained above, by constructing a counterfactual and using the approach developed in Duflo et al. (2007), one can compute the conditional ATE on the treated (ATET) as the impact of the program, which can be expressed as follows:

$$ATET = E\left[Y_i^T|\alpha_i, X_i, T_t = 1, P_i = 1\right] - E\left[Y_i^C|\alpha_i, X_i, T_t = 0, P_i = 1\right] \tag{11.9}$$

where Y_i^T and Y_i^C are income for treated subjects and controls, respectively, and all the other variables are as previously defined. Notice that Eq. 11.9 is equivalent to what DID methods do which is estimating the impact of the program by comparing changes in average outcome changes between beneficiaries and controls between the two time periods relative to their conditions at the baseline and thus can be rewritten as:

$$DID = E\left(Y_e^T - Y_b^T|P_s = 1\right) - E\left(Y_e^C - Y_b^C|P_s = 0\right) \tag{11.10}$$

which is subtracting the *second difference* from the *first difference* as discussed above.

11.3 Combining Evaluation Methods

The DID approach discussed above is one of the non-experimental methods used in evaluation when randomization is not possible. A critical question is whether the impact estimates and statistical inferences are similar to those produced by a randomized controlled trial (RCT), i.e., can DID methods replicate findings from experimental designs? This question addresses two issues. First, the internal validity of the program's impact of non-experimental designs in terms of causal effects. Second, their external validity in terms of generalizing the results. Notice that the DID framework discussed above is similar to the linear fixed effects panel data estimators (see Eq. 11.5). Ferraro and Miranda (2017) assess the capability of this approach to replicate the results of a RCT and they find that the use of linear fixed effects panel data estimator alone fails to produce similar results. The authors point out a few strong assumptions of the linear fixed effects panel data estimator that are often overlooked and are likely to produce biased estimates. The DID methods are based on similar assumptions. First, like the linear fixed effects panel data estimator DID assumes that treated and controls *exhibit common mean responses to common shocks*. Second, the *treatment effect is additive and constant* (see Eq. 11.4), and this is known as the assumption of homogeneous treatment responses. The violation of this assumption will lead to biased estimates because the linear fixed effects panel data estimator overweighs groups with larger variance of treatment conditional on other covariates and underweights those with smaller conditional variances (see Gibbons et al. 2018 for a more detailed discussion). Third, the *linearity and additive and constant treatment effect* may not hold if unobserved time-invariant characteristics that affect the outcomes of the program are highly imbalanced between treated and controls. For instance, if a beneficiary's choice to participate in TREE is highly correlated with her inner ability and, on average, the inner ability is higher for treated than non-treated units and plays a critical role in determining the income distribution across units. Finally, the assumption of lagged dependent variables that do not belong to the model. Nevertheless, Ferraro and Miranda (2017) show that by combining panel data and propensity score matching methods, one can obtain similar estimates and inferences to those from an RCT. Matching methods are discussed in the next sub-section.

Combining matching methods with panel data estimators is not enough to guarantee non-biased estimates or generate similar results to experimental methods. To illustrate, Wichman and Ferraro (2017) extend the design of Ferraro and Miranda (2017) discussed above by using a group of untreated units that are more comparable to the treated subjects while combining matching methods and panel data estimators and find the results of the linear fixed effects panel data fail to reproduce similar findings to the RCT approach. Specifically, they find that the results of Ferraro and Miranda (2017) were sensitive to the sample choice. When using non-experimental methods for evaluation, it is highly recommended to increase the number of untreated units from which one will draw the group of comparison because it will improve the evaluation design (Heckman et al. 1997). Another important finding from Wichman and Ferraro (2017) is that one needs to be cautious about making certain assumptions without testing them when using non-experimental methods. In particular, the *conditional bias stability* assumption which states that at the baseline conditional on the observed characteristics outcomes of treated and controls have similar trends and are stable across post-program periods. This assumption seems to fail in Ferraro and Miranda (2017) and may explain why these authors were able to reproduce results that are similar to the RCT. The bottom line here is that the choice of an appropriate sample is critical, and it is necessary to replicate the results using different methods and studies before deciding to implement a program somewhere else.

11.4 Propensity Score Matching (PSM)

A robust method for program evaluation is to use randomization, in which treated subjects and controls have the same expected outcomes in the absence of the program. As such, one can control for selection bias since treatment assignment would not be correlated with outcomes. When randomized evaluations cannot be implemented, one can rely on partial randomization methods such as matching to compare treated and untreated subjects and define the counterfactual. Assuming that a large sample of non-beneficiaries exists, this group can be matched with beneficiaries using a set of observed similar characteristics. By matching the two groups, one can construct the counterfactual if participation in the program depends solely on these observed attributes. The average treatment effect of the program can be calculated as the mean difference in outcomes between the two groups. In practice, evaluators use the PSM method to avoid the so-called "*curse of dimensionality*" which consists of matching the two groups on too many characteristics.

PSM matches beneficiaries to controls based on a propensity score, which is the probability of participating in the program conditional on their respective observed characteristics. Those who are not matched are often dropped from the full sample retained for the evaluation analysis (Rosenbaum and Rubin 1983). The implicit assumption is that only the observed characteristics serve as selection criteria for program participation.

PSM is a statistical sampling method and can be viewed as a second-best solution that mimics randomization by identifying a control group that is as comparable to the treatment group at the baseline in terms of *observed characteristics* that are not affected by the program. The common practice is to collect data on both groups before the implementation of the program to construct the baseline sample. Data collected at the baseline on treated and untreated groups are used to determine the sample size and construct the counterfactual.

More formally, denote $P_i = 1$ the program status of treated (T) and $P_i = 0$ that of the individuals in the control group (C), and X_i is a vector of observed characteristics that includes individuals' attributes that are likely to be time-invariant and unlikely to be affected by the program. The propensity score, which is the probability of all individuals (treated and non-treated) participating in the program, is a function of their observed characteristics X given by $P(X) = Prob(P = 1|X)$, which is the same for both groups. This probability serves as the criterion to define the counterfactual, and its validity to properly match individuals from treated and controls depends on the following two key assumptions (see Rosenbaum and Rubin 1983 for more discussion):

Conditional Independence Assumption (CIA)

The conditional independence assumption (CIA), also called *un-confoundedness*, *ignorability*, *exogenous selection*, and *selection on observables assumption*, states that after controlling for the observed characteristics, the potential outcomes of the program are independent of treatment assignment (Rosenbaum and Rubin 1983). If one denotes Y_i as the outcome of the program as before, CIA implies:

$$\left(Y_i^T, Y_i^C\right) \perp P_i | X_i \tag{11.11}$$

That is, program participation depends solely on observed characteristics X_i and after controlling for such characteristics for both treated subjects and controls, both groups are similar in their remaining attributes except for participation in the program. In other words, conditional on the vector of observed characteristics, assignment to treatment can be considered now to be random, thus there is no more problem of self-selection bias. The difference in outcomes between both groups is the causal treatment effect or ATE. For the estimation of ATET instead of ATE, one can use a weaker assumption:

$$Y_i^C \perp P_i | X_i \tag{11.12}$$

Though the conditional independence assumption depends on the nature of the program, it is worth highlighting that it is a very strong one, often violated, and requires large enough data on observed characteristics. When participation in the program is also influenced by unobserved characteristics, PSM alone is not enough to establish causality effects between outcome variables and program participation. One solution to this problem is to combine PSM with DID, as illustrated in the empirical section.

Common Support Assumption (CSA)

The common support is known as the range of propensity scores where there are treated and controls. To apply PSM, the existence of a common support is necessary. That is:

$$0 < P(P_i = 1 | X_i) < 1. \tag{11.13}$$

Equation (11.13) ensures that treated and controls conditional on observables have comparable observations neighbouring the propensity score distribution (Heckman and Smith 1999). As before, to compute ATET, a weaker assumption is needed:

$$P(P_i = 1 | X_i) < 1 \tag{11.14}$$

The common support assumption (CSA) assumes that there is enough overlap in the observed characteristics between treated and control to construct comparable groups (Rosenbaum and Rubin 1983).

Finally, if both assumptions CIA and CSA hold, one can compute the PSM estimator for ATET as the mean differences in outcomes over the common support area using the propensity scores of treated as weights for the matched untreated subjects as follows (Khandker et al. 2010):

$$ATET = \{E[Y_i^T | P_i = 1, P(X)] - E[Y_i^C | P_i = 0, P(X)]\} \tag{11.15}$$

In practice, the propensity score is unknown, but can be estimated using a probit or a logit model, as illustrated in the empirical section below using the statistical software package Stata.

11.5 Implementation of the PSM Framework

Once the final sample of treated and untreated groups at the baseline is constructed with all possible observed characteristics and the inclusion of a dummy variable for program participation, one can follow the following steps to apply PSM:

- *Step 1: Estimate the propensity scores.*

First, estimate the propensity scores using a logit or a probit model by regressing a binary variable (program participation) on the set of observed characteristics:

$$Beneficiary_i = X_i\prime\beta + \varepsilon_i \tag{11.16}$$

where Beneficiary is the dichotomous dependent variable equal to 1 for being a beneficiary and 0 otherwise. The vector X is a set of covariates that includes participant attributes such as age, gender, years of schooling, household size, involvement in other economic activities and any other observed characteristics unaffected by the program depending on the nature of the program under study. Predicted values of the equation above can be computed after the regression and represent the propensity scores that are equivalent to the probability of being a beneficiary considering both groups and the set of observed covariates. If the participation variable is a categorical variable with more than two categories, a multinomial probit or logit model can be used to estimate the propensity scores (Caliendo and Kopeinig 2008).

- *Step 2: Determine the region of common support and balancing tests.*

The results of the Logit/Probit model make it possible not only to calculate propensity scores but also to determine the common support area which is the second step in applying PSM. Recall that this area ensures that individuals with similar characteristics have a positive probability of being both beneficiaries or non-beneficiaries. As shown in Fig. 11.1, this area can be easily defined where distributions of the propensity scores for treated and controls overlap. An example is provided in the empirical application. Individuals who are not matched are often dropped from the sample as no comparisons can be made.

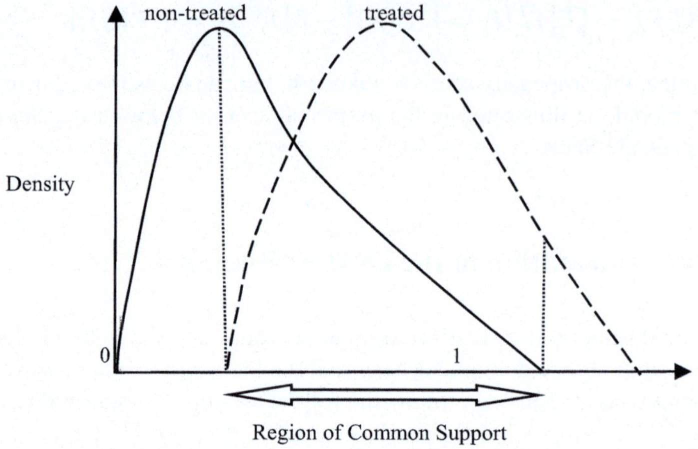

Fig. 11.1 Region of common support

Balancing properties test whether treated and non-treated subjects who have similar propensity scores are equivalent in terms of distribution of their observed characteristics. Having similar or same propensity scores do not guarantee that both groups are similar in terms of observed characteristics and this issue arises when a proper functional was not used to estimate the participation model. Thus, balancing tests are often recommended to check whether similar propensity scores are based upon similar observed characteristics and thus distributions of treated and matched untreated are the same:

$$\widehat{Prob}(X|P_i = 1) = \widehat{Prob}(X|P_i = 0) \quad (11.17)$$

- *Step 3: Matching beneficiaries and non-beneficiaries*

Matching consists of providing different weights to subgroups of treated and untreated. There are different algorithms that can be used to match beneficiaries and non-beneficiaries and the results may vary in function of the algorithm used. A discussion of the advantages and disadvantages of the most used in the empirical application is provided.

11.6 The Training for Rural Economic Empowerment (TREE) Project in Zimbabwe: A Case Study

Zimbabwe is a predominantly rural country, divided into 59 districts and 1,200 wards or municipalities, where approximately 68% of the population lives in rural areas and the economy is dominated by agriculture. Poverty is more prevalent for people living in rural areas, where 76% are poor compared to 38.2% in urban areas, and incomes in the agricultural sector are lower compared to other sectors in the economy. The average annual net cash income in the country was approximately US$ 2,545 per household in 2011, and nearly 62% of households are classified as poor, while 16.2% are very poor according to the poverty datum line analysis (Zimstat 2013).

The need to generate positive outcomes for low-income populations across economic sectors including agriculture is a common denominator among most developing countries, which often rely on non-governmental organizations (NGOs) and other international entities to assist governments to address such development issues. Zimbabwe is a good empirical example. To promote income generation in Zimbabwe, ILO implemented the TREE project in 2010 with three main phases and goals. The first component of TREE's logic model consisted of establishing partnerships with policymakers and other stakeholders in the country to reinforce and increase institutional capacity. Nine main activities were identified across selected districts: beekeeping, horticulture, cattle fattening, potato production, green jobs (mainly the use of solar energy), poultry production, piggery, dairy farming, and fish farming. These activities can be understood as part of three groups: *crop production, livestock,* and *green jobs.* This component sought to promote income generation in rural areas through the creation of new economic and employment opportunities (ILO 2013). The second component aimed at reinforcing managerial skills by delivering marketable and vocational skills, core work, and business skills to increase knowledge and best management practices, including in the adoption of new technologies to increase income. The third component provided financial support to the beneficiaries to facilitate start-up processes for any income-generating activities they chose to undertake. These objectives are directly linked to TREE's logic model or theory of change (see Lachaud et al. 2018 for more details).

In summary, TREE was a rural market program for youths aged between 18–32 years old who were unemployed and vulnerable (e.g., disabled orphans). From 2010–2014, the program had a total of 2,173 direct beneficiaries. The working assumption was that after four years of TREE implementation, it would be possible to capture and isolate its impacts on income, which is the primary outcome of the project.

11.6.1 Sampling Strategy

To evaluate the program, data need to be collected at the baseline and endline on treated and non-treated subjects to construct the full sample. The evaluator needs a sampling strategy, which depends on aspects such as the nature of the program, how it was implemented, and the selection criteria of the beneficiaries. There is no silver bullet for the sampling design (see Iarossi 2006 for a literature review). For TREE, this study conducted a multi-stage survey by randomly selecting the districts, then the wards, and finally the beneficiaries (see Lachaud et al. 2018 for more detail). Determining the appropriate sample size is a critical component of the sampling strategy, needed to ensure adequate statistical power to identify reliable and significant effects of the program on the outcome of interest. The sample size could be limited due to budget constraints. Nevertheless, the evaluator must be careful in balancing the trade-off between a smaller sample and statistical power.

According to Wassenich and Muñoz (2007), the sample size can be based on four parameters: (i) the expected effect of the program on the outcome (e.g., the mean difference in income between TREE beneficiaries and controls), (ii) the standard deviation of the outcome distribution, (iii) the confidence level, and (iv) the statistical power. The first two parameters can be obtained from the baseline dataset when treated subjects and controls are assumed to be similar. The third and fourth parameters can be determined using common statistical techniques as explained below. Specifically, the sample size can be determined using Eq. 11.18:

$$N = \frac{4\sigma^2(Z_\alpha + Z_\beta)^2}{E^2} \tag{11.18}$$

where N represents the total sample size, E is the expected impact effect of TREE on beneficiaries compared to non-beneficiaries, σ^2 is the standard deviation of the income distribution of the beneficiaries at the baseline, and $Z_{\alpha/2}$, Z_β are the critical value of a confidence interval (two-tailed test = 1.96 for 95% confidence) and the critical value of the statistical test (two-tailed test = 1.282 for 90% power), respectively, assuming that income is normally distributed.

The income distribution for beneficiaries at the baseline was US$ 61.3 per month with a standard deviation of US$ 52.0. The expected effects of a program can be approximated using stakeholders' expertise, program implementers' expectations, or the impact of similar programs. In TREE's case, it was expected that a successful program would increase income levels by at least 15%. Plugging these values into Eq. 11.18 leads to a sample size of approximately 1,010, i.e., 505 beneficiaries and 505 controls. It is customary or recommended to adjust the sample size to account for *cluster effects*, *attrition*, and other *design effects* depending on the sampling design. For the TREE project, we assume an intra-cluster correlation (ρ) equal to 0.05 and randomly select 10 youths per ward (m) due to logistical constraints[3]:

$$N_{adjusted} = N[1 + \rho(m - 1)] \tag{11.19}$$

Thus, the adjusted sample size is equal to 1,465. Finally, accounting for the possibility of future attrition and data losses, as is common with survey data, the study assumes a 25% *safeguard*, which leads to a total sample size equal to 1,831, which is rounding to 2,000. The safeguard is also grounded on the need to over-sample given the uncertainty associated with the exercise of matching, where one may lose considerable data due to a lack of common support. An equal allocation of the total

[3] The intra-cluster correlation (ρ) measures the degree to which beneficiaries within a ward tend to be closer to each other, i.e., they have similar characteristics, which thus decreases the statistical power.

sample, which is the standard procedure between treated and controls yields a sample size of 1,000 youths per group.

11.6.2 TREE Dataset and Stata Illustration

It is highly recommended to collect *baseline* data on both beneficiaries and non-beneficiaries. An evaluator may face a situation in which project implementers fail to define the counterfactual and thus do not collect data on the control group. A possible solution for the evaluator is to conduct a retrospective survey, which consists of simultaneously collecting baseline and endline data on the control group during the aforementioned endline data collection process.

The TREE evaluators for ILO faced a similar situation and had to conduct a retrospective survey in 2015 to collect data for the year 2011 for the control group. Data were collected in 11 districts distributed across four provinces in Zimbabwe. Table 11.1 shows the final unmatched sample size, which includes 2,277 observations: 1,219 controls and 1,058 treated. The controls include 617 women and 602 men, while the respective gender distribution for beneficiaries is 534 women and 524 men.

The preparation of the final sample for the evaluation involves data cleaning, curation, and transformation. After opening the dataset, generated from baseline and

Table 11.1 Distribution of beneficiaries and non-beneficiaries per district

		Number of observations			
District	Province	Treated	Control	Male	Female
Chimanimani	Manicaland	77	228	166	139
Mutare Rural	Manicaland	29	39	21	47
Mutasa	Manicaland	36	179	109	106
Nyanga	Manicaland	156	293	205	244
Mt Darwin	Mashonaland	147	0	73	74
Murehwa	Mashonaland	77	0	43	34
Mutoko	Mashonaland	188	164	204	148
Shamva	Mashonaland	58	139	86	111
Nkayi	Matebeleland	131	177	125	183
Gokwe South	Midlands	114	0	72	42
Gweru Rural	Midlands	45	0	22	23
Total	4	1,058	1,219	1,126	1,151
Treated				524	534
Control				602	617

Source Lachaud et al. (2018)

endline surveys, in the software package Stata, the command *describe variables list* can be used to obtain information about the variables in the dataset:

```
. describe prog_status gender educ household_size  vulnerability marital income_year district

Variable       Storage   Display    Value
    name          type    format    label      Variable label
-----------------------------------------------------------------------------------------------------
prog_status     str10    %10s                  Participating in the Program: 1=Y, 0=N
gender          str6     %9s                   Gender is male: 1=Y, 0=N
educ            str10    %10s                  level of Education
household_size  byte     %8.0g                 Number of people in the household
vulnerability   str10    %10s                  Type of Disability
marital         str9     %9s                    Marital Status
income_year     float    %9.0g                 Profits and salary reported by respondents
district        str10    %10s                  Name of the district where the respondents live
```

For example, the dummy variable *prog_status* was created during data collection to identify beneficiaries (*prog_status* = 1) and non-beneficiaries (*prog_status* = 0). One can use the following command: *tabulate prog_status, generate(BENEF)* to transform *prog_status* into a new variable, *"BENEF,"* for beneficiaries and to have an idea about the distribution of treated subjects and controls in the full sample size (baseline and endline). The command generates two variables in the dataset: *BENEF1*, which equals 1 for treated and 0 otherwise, and *BENEF2*, which equals 0 for treated and 1 for non-treated.

```
. tabulate prog_status, generate(BENEF)

 Prog_Status |      Freq.     Percent        Cum.
-------------+-----------------------------------
  Beneficiar |      2,116       46.46       46.46
     Control |      2,438       53.54      100.00
-------------+-----------------------------------
       Total |      4,554      100.00
```

The variables *educ*, *vulnerability*, *marital*, and *district* are categorical variables, whereas household size and income are continuous variables. More details about the definition of these variables can be found in Table 11.2.

Before estimation, categorical variables need to be transformed into dummy variables. The following Stata command can be used to do so, creating a dummy for each category in the dataset:

tabulate gender, generate(gender)
tabulate marital, generate(marital)
tabulate vulnerability, generate(vulnerability)
tabulate educ, generate(educ)

Table 11.2 Definition of variables

Variable	Unit	Definition
BENEF	Dummy	1 if the respondent is a beneficiary of TREE
YEAR	Dummy	0 = 2011, 1 = 2014
Gender	Dummy	1 if the respondent is a female
Marital status	Categorical	1 = Married, 2 = Single, 3 = Divorced, 4 = separated, 5 = Widowed
Vulnerability	Categorical	1 = Disabled, 2 = Ill, 3 = Able bodied, 4 = Disabled and ill
Education	Categorical	1 = None, 2 = Primary, 3 = O Level, 4 = All levels above O Level (A Level, Certificate, Diploma, and Degree)
Income	US dollars	Profits plus wages generated by respondents
Health expenses	US dollars	Expenditures on health of the household
Children welfare	US dollars	Expenditures on children (education, health, and other expenses)
Consumption	US dollars	Expenditures on cooking items, fuel, and electricity

```
. tabulate gender, generate(gender)

     Gender |      Freq.     Percent        Cum.
------------+-----------------------------------
     Female |      2,301       50.54       50.54
       Male |      2,252       49.46      100.00
------------+-----------------------------------
      Total |      4,553      100.00

. tabulate marital, generate(marital)

Marital_sta |
        tus |      Freq.     Percent        Cum.
------------+-----------------------------------
   Divorced |        111        2.46        2.46
    Married |      2,400       53.09       55.54
  Separated |         47        1.04       56.58
     Single |      1,918       42.42       99.00
    Widowed |         45        1.00      100.00
------------+-----------------------------------
      Total |      4,521      100.00

. tabulate vulnerability, generate(vulnerability)

Vulnerabili |
         ty |      Freq.     Percent        Cum.
------------+-----------------------------------
 Able bodie |      4,288       94.78       94.78
   Disabled |         38        0.84       95.62
 Disabled a |         53        1.17       96.79
        Ill |        145        3.21      100.00
------------+-----------------------------------
      Total |      4,524      100.00
```

```
. tabulate educ, generate(educ)

   level of |
  Education |      Freq.     Percent        Cum.
------------+-----------------------------------
 Certificat |        107        2.39        2.39
       None |        201        4.49        6.88
    O Level |      3,275       73.20       80.08
    Primary |        891       19.92      100.00
------------+-----------------------------------
      Total |      4,474      100.00
```

11.6.3 PSM and DID Illustration by Using Stata

As explained above, there are three main steps to implement PSM. First, estimate the propensity scores using a logit or a probit model. This study applied the PSM approach by estimating the following logit model using baseline data for beneficiaries and non-beneficiaries:

$$BENEF_{it} = f(Gender, Household\, size, Marital\ Status, Vulnerability\, status) + \varepsilon_{it} \tag{11.20}$$

where all the variables are as defined in Table 11.2 and ε_{it} is the error term of the econometric model that captures residuals such as noise in the data, error measurement, and misspecification or functional form issues.

PSM was estimated using the Stata *psmacth2* command, which was created by Leuven and Sianesi (2015). Because PSM is based on baseline data, the study used the following Stata commands to separate beneficiaries and control from baseline and endline:

gen treatment1_1 = BENEF1 = = 1 & year = = 1
gen treatment1_2014 = max(treatment1_1), by(id)
*gen treatment1_year = treatment1_2014*year*

The first command generates a dummy variable (*treatment1_1*) equal to 1 for treated at the baseline (year = 1 or 2011) and 0 otherwise. The second command generates a dummy variable (*treatment1_2014*) equal to 1 for treated at the endline (year = 2014) and 0 otherwise. The last command generates the key variable for the evaluation, which is the interaction between year and the variable treatment. In this example, the Logit model estimation was carried out with a very few observable characteristics. The evaluator needs to ensure that all available data on observable characteristics that are susceptible to influence participation in the program are accounted for without causing the curse of dimensionality. The option *"in 1/2262"* in the command implies that only baseline data are considered, i.e., observations 1 to 2,262 are from year 2011. Another command option is to replace *"in 1/2262"* by *"if year = = 1"* in the *psmacth2* command. One must sort by year in Stata using the command *"sort year"* before the estimation.

```
. psmatch2 BENEF1 gender1 household_size marital1 marital2 marital3 marital4 vulnerability1 vulnerability2 vulnerabilit
> y3  in 1/2262,  logit common noreplacement ate

Logistic regression                                     Number of obs =  2,233
                                                        LR chi2(9)    = 335.26
                                                        Prob > chi2   = 0.0000
Log likelihood = -1375.4571                             Pseudo R2     = 0.1086

------------------------------------------------------------------------------------
        BENEF1 | Coefficient  Std. err.      z    P>|z|     [95% conf. interval]
---------------+--------------------------------------------------------------------
       gender1 |  -.3080388   .0950692   -3.24   0.001    -.4943711   -.1217066
household_size |   .0498138   .0247315    2.01   0.044     .0013409    .0982866
      marital1 |  -2.012839   .7505645   -2.68   0.007    -3.483918   -.5417595
      marital2 |  -.5808363    .620547   -0.94   0.349    -1.797086    .6354135
      marital3 |  -1.922191   .8710525   -2.21   0.027    -3.629422   -.2149593
      marital4 |  -2.221953   .6222282   -3.57   0.000    -3.441498   -1.002408
vulnerability1 |   .9713452   .2903828    3.35   0.001     .4022054    1.540485
vulnerability2 |   1.026207   .6262303    1.64   0.101    -.2011816    2.253596
vulnerability3 |  -.7542203   1.193508   -0.63   0.527    -3.093453    1.585013
         _cons |   .3114749   .6516748    0.48   0.633    -.9657842    1.588734
------------------------------------------------------------------------------------

. tab _support treatment1 in 1/2262

  psmatch2: |
     Common |      treatment1
    support |         0          1 |     Total
------------+----------------------+----------
Off support |       152          7 |       159
 On support |     1,037      1,037 |     2,074
------------+----------------------+----------
      Total |     1,189      1,044 |     2,233
```

The *psmatch2* command generates a list of post-estimation new variables in the dataset that can be useful for the evaluator, including:

- *_treated*, which is a dummy variable that equals 1 and 0 for treated and non-treated, respectively.
- *_support*, which is another dummy variable that takes the value of 1 if the subject is on the common support and 0 otherwise.
- *_pscore*, which is the estimated propensity score; and
- *_weight*, which in the calculation depends on the algorithm used. For instance, for the NNM, it is defined as the "frequency with which the observation is used as a match" whereas for the Kernel algorithm it is an overall weight given to the matched observation.

The second step is to determine the region of common support in which propensity scores for treated subjects and controls overlap. The balancing test is one of the most common statistical techniques used after PSM to gauge the balance of covariate distribution between treated and controls, i.e., to check if the mean values of observable attributes for these two groups are the same after matching (Leuven and Sianesi 2015). The following command can be used after *psmatched2* to identify beneficiaries and non-beneficiaries who are on common support:

```
. tab _support treatment1

  psmatch2: |
     Common |      treatment1
    support |         0          1 |     Total
------------+----------------------+----------
Off support |         0          7 |         7
 On support |     1,189      1,037 |     2,226
------------+----------------------+----------
      Total |     1,189      1,044 |     2,233
```

The results yield a dataset that includes 1,189 controls and 1,037 beneficiaries that are on common support. Thus, all these observations satisfy the common support condition. Then, one can examine whether the values of the observable characteristics of treated and non-treated subjects are, on average, equal at the baseline after matching.[4] This is the so-called balancing property, which tests the null hypothesis that the mean values of the variables for beneficiaries and non-beneficiaries do not differ after matching (Becker and Ichino 2002). The following *pstest, both* command in Stata can be used to check the balancing property after estimating the logit or probit model for PSM by assessing the comparability of both groups before and after matching. The "*pstest, both*" command does so by computing, for each variable, *t-tests* for equality of means in the two samples, the associated standardized percentage bias between the two before and after matching, the variance ratio for the continuous variable (household size) of beneficiaries over controls. The command also calculates a set of overall measures of covariate imbalance: *pseudo* R^2 from the logit estimation, the *mean and median bias*, the *Rubin's B*, *Rubin's R* (see Rubin 2001 for more detail).

[4] Notice that the *psmatch2* Stata command also matches the data while estimating the Logit model.

```
. pstest, both

----------------------------------------------------------------------------------
                    Unmatched |       Mean               %reduct |     t-test    |  V(T)/
Variable              Matched | Treated Control    %bias  |bias| |    t    p>|t| |  V(C)
------------------------------+----------------------------------+---------------+--------
gender1                    U  |    .5    .48936      2.1          |   0.50  0.619 |     .
                           M  |    .5    .51952     -3.9    -83.5 |  -0.87  0.385 |     .
                              |                                  |               |
household_size             U  | 4.8465   4.6579      8.7          |   2.03  0.042 |   0.95
                           M  | 4.8465   4.8241      1.0     88.1 |   0.23  0.819 |   0.93
                              |                                  |               |
marital1                   U  | .02323    .0311     -4.8          |  -1.12  0.262 |     .
                           M  | .02323   .02214      0.7     86.1 |   0.16  0.870 |     .
                              |                                  |               |
marital2                   U  |  .7202    .3748     74.0          |  17.23  0.000 |     .
                           M  |  .7202   .71799      0.5     99.4 |   0.11  0.913 |     .
                              |                                  |               |
marital3                   U  | .00909   .01637     -6.5          |  -1.50  0.135 |     .
                           M  | .00909   .00662      2.2     66.0 |   0.62  0.533 |     .
                              |                                  |               |
marital4                   U  | .23535   .57365    -73.4          | -17.03  0.000 |     .
                           M  | .23535    .2401     -1.0     98.6 |  -0.25  0.804 |     .
                              |                                  |               |
vulnerability1             U  | .97778   .93617     20.6          |   4.70  0.000 |     .
                           M  | .97778   .97864     -0.4     97.9 |  -0.13  0.896 |     .
                              |                                  |               |
vulnerability2             U  | .00707   .00736     -0.3          |  -0.08  0.935 |     .
                           M  | .00707   .00678      0.3      1.2 |   0.08  0.938 |     .
                              |                                  |               |
vulnerability3             U  | .00101   .00491     -7.2          |  -1.62  0.105 |     .
                           M  | .00101   .00126     -0.5     93.7 |  -0.16  0.870 |     .
----------------------------------------------------------------------------------
* if variance ratio outside [0.88; 1.13] for U and [0.88; 1.13] for M

-----------------------------------------------------------------------------------
 Sample    | Ps R2   LR chi2   p>chi2   MeanBias   MedBias      B      R     %Var
-----------+-----------------------------------------------------------------------
 Unmatched | 0.108    328.48    0.000     22.0       7.2      82.0*   0.74     0
 Matched   | 0.001      1.66    0.996      1.2       0.7       5.8    1.12     0
-----------------------------------------------------------------------------------
* if B>25%, R outside [0.5; 2]

.
end of do-file
```

The results above are based on *student-t* statistical tests conducted before and after matching. The differences between treatment and control groups are significantly reduced. In all cases, the null hypothesis, that the mean values of all the variables/categories for beneficiaries and non-beneficiaries do not differ after matching, cannot be rejected at the almost 1% significance level except for the gender variable. In other words, controls and beneficiaries are similar in terms of observables at the baseline after matching.

The examples above serve to illustrate how PSM can be applied but the choice of the covariates depends on the evaluator and the nature of the program. One can use graphs to visualize the distribution of the observed characteristics before and after matching to check the balancing test. For instance, in the example below, only four variables are used to match and check the balancing test: *gender, income (outcome variable), household size and the number of bedrooms.*

The Stata commands below are then used:

psmatch2 BENEF1 gender1 household_size income_year rooms_no in 1/2262, radius caliper(0.04) logit ate (results are not reported).

Then, the following Stata commands are used to check the balancing properties before and after matching and yield the following graph:

*twoway (kdensity _pscore if _treated==1) (kdensity _pscore if _treated==0, ///
lpattern(dash)), legend(label(1 "treated") label(2 "control")) ///
xtitle("propensity scores BEFORE matching") name(before, replace)*

*twoway (kdensity _pscore if _treated==1 [aweight=_weight]) ///
(kdensity _pscore if _treated==0 [aweight=_weight] ///
, lpattern(dash)), legend(label(1 "treated") label(2 "control")) ///
xtitle("propensity scores AFTER matching") name(after, replace)*

grc1leg before after, ycommon

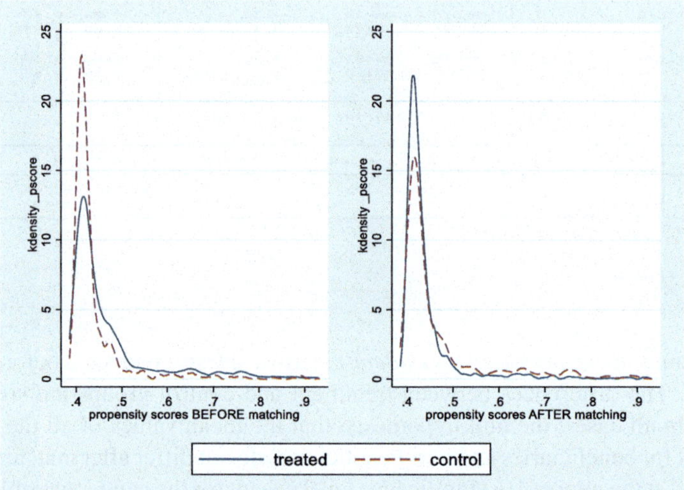

These results clearly show after matching the distributions of the observed characteristics are closer after matching than before even though as expected both have similar trends at the baseline and thus the *conditional bias stability* may hold.

Finally, it is worth noting that different algorithms can be used to match samples and *psmatch2* can implement a variety of them. The most common include *nearest-neighbour matching* (NNM), which consists of matching each treated to the non-beneficiary who has the closest propensity score. This criterion can be performed with replacement (non-beneficiary is a match for different beneficiaries) or without replacement (one non-beneficiary per matching). The Stata command below implements the "1-to-1" nearest neighbour without replacement criterion to match beneficiaries with controls.

Second, assess the balancing properties to test whether treated and non-treated subjects who have similar propensity scores are equivalent in terms of distribution of their observed characteristics, i.e., they are on common support. Finally, match treated and non-treated who are on common support to define the full and comparable sample for the evaluation.

It is also worth noting that NNM does not minimize the distance in propensity scores between treated and its closest non-treated, so it can lead to improper matches.

Caliper or radius matching (CRM) is an improvement over NNM as it is a matching method with replacement that minimizes the distance between propensity scores for treated subjects and their closest non-treated counterparts by putting a threshold on the maximum propensity score distance within a certain range. In this case, the study uses a caliper width of 0.04 which is the range within which the propensity scores must fall to be considered a valid match. A wider caliper width may lead to a greater sample size but decrease balance between groups and yield bias in the estimates of program effects (Cochran and Rubin 1973; Wang et al. 2013).

The following Stata commands elucidate the use of this matching algorithm:

```
. psmatch2 BENEF1 gender1 household_size marital1 marital2 marital3 marital4 vulnerability1 vulnerability2 vulnerabilit
> y3  in 1/2262, radius caliper(0.04)  logit ate

Logistic regression                                     Number of obs =  2,233
                                                        LR chi2(9)    = 335.26
                                                        Prob > chi2   = 0.0000
Log likelihood = -1375.4571                             Pseudo R2     = 0.1086

-------------------------------------------------------------------------------
        BENEF1 | Coefficient  Std. err.      z    P>|z|     [95% conf. interval]
---------------+---------------------------------------------------------------
       gender1 |  -.3080388   .0950692    -3.24   0.001    -.4943711   -.1217066
household_size |   .0498138   .0247315     2.01   0.044     .0013409    .0982866
      marital1 |  -2.012839   .7505645    -2.68   0.007    -3.483918   -.5417595
      marital2 |  -.5808363    .620547    -0.94   0.349    -1.797086    .6354135
      marital3 |  -1.922191   .8710525    -2.21   0.027    -3.629422   -.2149593
      marital4 |  -2.221953   .6222282    -3.57   0.000    -3.441498   -1.002408
vulnerability1 |   .9713452   .2903828     3.35   0.001     .4022054    1.540485
vulnerability2 |   1.026207   .6262303     1.64   0.101    -.2011816    2.253596
vulnerability3 |  -.7542203   1.193508    -0.63   0.527    -3.093453    1.585013
         _cons |   .3114749   .6516748     0.48   0.633    -.9657842    1.588734
-------------------------------------------------------------------------------

. tab _support treatment1 in 1/2262

 psmatch2: |
    Common |      treatment1
   support |         0          1 |     Total
-----------+----------------------+----------
Off suppor |         1          1 |         2
On support |     1,188      1,043 |     2,231
-----------+----------------------+----------
     Total |     1,189      1,044 |     2,233
```

Moreover, *stratification and interval matching* (SIM) partitions the common support of the propensity score into intervals and evaluates the impact within each interval by taking the mean difference in outcomes between treated and control observations. The most common implementation of stratification is five equal frequency intervals, which eliminates approximately 90% of the initial bias due to the observed variables (Cochran 1968; Rosenbaum and Rubin 1983). SIM works well when there is a linear relationship between propensity and outcome. For non-linear relationships, Hullsiek and Louis (2002) propose choosing strata that balance the variances of the stratum-specific estimates.

Kernel and local linear matching (KLLM) is a non-parametric matching method that resolves a critical problem found when using NNM, CRM, and SIM, which is that relatively small sample size can affect statistical power because only a few numbers of treated and non-treated subjects fall within the common support. To avoid this problem, KLLM uses a weighted average of all controls to match all treated (see Caliendo and Kopeinig 2008; Ravallion 2008 for a review of literature on these methods). The following Stata method shows how to implement the KLLM method:

```
. psmatch2 BENEF1 gender1 household_size marital1 marital2 marital3 marital4 vulnerability1 vulnerability2 vulnerabilit
> y3, kernel logit ate

Logistic regression                                     Number of obs =  4,459
                                                        LR chi2(9)    = 601.42
                                                        Prob > chi2   = 0.0000
Log likelihood = -2778.0341                             Pseudo R2     = 0.0977

------------------------------------------------------------------------------
        BENEF1 | Coefficient  Std. err.      z    P>|z|     [95% conf. interval]
---------------+--------------------------------------------------------------
       gender1 |  -.2563233   .0670156    -3.82   0.000    -.3876714   -.1249752
household_size |   .0127338   .0144484     0.88   0.378    -.0155846    .0410523
      marital1 |  -1.336607   .3861592    -3.46   0.001    -2.093465   -.5797488
      marital2 |  -.4042283   .3337987    -1.21   0.226    -1.058462    .2500052
      marital3 |  -1.453978   .4529357    -3.21   0.001    -2.341715   -.5662401
      marital4 |  -1.947975   .3369006    -5.78   0.000    -2.608288   -1.287662
vulnerability1 |   1.162669   .2117911     5.49   0.000     .7475661    1.577772
vulnerability2 |   1.004758   .4211013     2.39   0.017     .1794142    1.830101
vulnerability3 |    .057121   .5024576     0.11   0.909    -.9276777     1.04192
         _cons |  -.1445534   .3764289    -0.38   0.701    -.8823405    .5932337
------------------------------------------------------------------------------
```

11.6.4 The Economic Impact of TREE on Its Beneficiaries

Once obtained the final matched sample, the study used the following DID framework to estimate the impact of TREE on income:

$$y_{it} = \alpha_0 + \alpha_1 BENEF_{it} + \alpha_2 YEAR_{it} + \alpha_3 BENEF_{it} \times YEAR_{it} + \alpha_4 GENDER_{it} + \alpha_5 EDUC_{it} + \alpha_6 DISTRICT_{it} + \varepsilon_{it} \tag{11.21}$$

where all the variables are defined as before, the dependent variable, y, is income, and ε_{it} is a standard error term.

The following Stata command can be used to estimate the DID regression:

```
. xtreg Income year  BENEF BENEF_YEAR    gender1  Education1 Education2 Education3  district1 district2 district3 district4 district5 district6 district7 district8 district9 district10

Random-effects GLS regression                   Number of obs     =      4,388
Group variable: id                              Number of groups  =      2,194

R-squared:                                      Obs per group:
     Within  = 0.1431                                         min =          2
     Between = 0.1582                                         avg =        2.0
     Overall = 0.1518                                         max =          2

                                                Wald chi2(17)     =     775.57
corr(u_i, X) = 0 (assumed)                      Prob > chi2       =     0.0000

------------------------------------------------------------------------------
      Income | Coefficient  Std. err.      z    P>|z|     [95% conf. interval]
-------------+----------------------------------------------------------------
        year |   321.8508   57.40756     5.61   0.000     209.3341    434.3676
       BENEF |   217.5536   71.36738     3.05   0.002     77.67607    357.4311
  BENEF_YEAR |    788.833   84.46047     9.34   0.000     623.2935    954.3725
     gender1 |  -164.5827   48.37827    -3.40   0.001    -259.4024   -69.76307
  Education1 |  -583.7166    189.415    -3.08   0.002    -954.9632   -212.4699
  Education2 |  -977.5814   161.6042    -6.05   0.000     -1294.32    -660.843
  Education3 |   -701.203   154.3708    -4.54   0.000    -1003.764   -398.6418
   district1 |   24.79715   109.3095     0.23   0.821    -189.4456    239.0399
   district2 |  -522.0591   143.0276    -3.65   0.000     -802.388   -241.7302
   district3 |  -122.5972   194.3412    -0.63   0.528    -503.4989    258.3045
   district4 |   835.9369   132.9102     6.29   0.000     575.4377    1096.436
   district5 |  -226.7878   176.4331    -1.29   0.199    -572.5903    119.0146
   district6 |   182.5137   167.5294     1.09   0.276    -145.8378    510.8653
   district7 |   157.9701   115.9195     1.36   0.173    -69.22807    385.1682
   district8 |  -20.52058   106.1399    -0.19   0.847     -228.551    187.5098
   district9 |  -275.0273   108.3608    -2.54   0.011    -487.4106   -62.64394
  district10 |   -134.524   101.6175    -1.32   0.186    -333.6907    64.64267
       _cons |   1148.657   180.4723     6.36   0.000     794.9383    1502.377
-------------+----------------------------------------------------------------
     sigma_u |  546.82337
     sigma_e |   1379.317
         rho |  .13582174   (fraction of variance due to u_i)
------------------------------------------------------------------------------
```

The constant, α_0, from Eq. 11.21 is the *estimated income* for the *control group at the baseline* (2011), i.e., approximately US$1,149. By contrast, the estimated income for the beneficiaries at the baseline is given by $\alpha_0 + \alpha_1$, thus, US$1,471. In addition, it is worth noting that α_2 captures the increase in income in both groups by factors unrelated to the program during the 2011–2014 period ($217.5). The key variable of interest that captures the causal impact of the program on its beneficiaries is α_3, which suggests that from 2011 to 2014, TREE increased the income of its beneficiaries by US$ 789 dollars in comparison to non-beneficiaries. The results also suggest substantial heterogeneity in the income distribution at the baseline; on average, women were significantly worse off than men in terms of income in 2011.[5] As expected, more educated farmers were able to take greater advantage of the program. Furthermore, beneficiaries from districts such as Mount Darwin, Mutare Rural, and Mutasa started the program with some comparative advantages compared to other districts, in particular Gokwe South and Nkayi (see Table 11.1).

In addition, the study estimates the impact of TREE on three more indicators: child welfare, health, and consumption, by applying similar Stata commands as shown below:

[5] In this regression, the gender1 dummy-variable is 1 if it the individual is a woman and 0 otherwise.

```
. xtreg Child_Welfare year  BENEF BENEF_YEAR   gender1  Education1 Education2 Education3  district1 district2 district3 district4 district5 district6 district7 district8 district9 district10

Random-effects GLS regression                   Number of obs     =      2,828
Group variable: id                              Number of groups  =      1,717

R-squared:                                      Obs per group:
     Within  = 0.1127                                         min =          1
     Between = 0.0710                                         avg =        1.6
     Overall = 0.0820                                         max =          2

                                                Wald chi2(17)     =     271.25
corr(u_i, X) = 0 (assumed)                      Prob > chi2       =     0.0000

------------------------------------------------------------------------------
Child_Welf~e | Coefficient  Std. err.      z    P>|z|     [95% conf. interval]
-------------+----------------------------------------------------------------
        year |   119.6363   31.44592     3.80   0.000     58.00343    181.2692
       BENEF |   125.3281    42.5463     2.95   0.003     41.93884    208.7173
  BENEF_YEAR |   225.8786   43.39148     5.21   0.000     140.8328    310.9243
     gender1 |   40.15129   29.26298     1.37   0.170     -17.2031    97.50568
  Education1 |  -295.2712   112.7982    -2.62   0.009    -516.3516   -74.19078
  Education2 |  -331.0175   100.7818    -3.28   0.001    -528.5461   -133.4888
  Education3 |  -243.1592   96.67775    -2.52   0.012    -432.6441   -53.67426
   district1 |  -62.76432   64.51069    -0.97   0.331     -189.203    63.67432
   district2 |  -42.81106   83.15409    -0.51   0.607    -205.7901     120.168
   district3 |   29.50037   115.6938     0.25   0.799    -197.2553     256.256
   district4 |  -169.6391    72.9337    -2.33   0.020    -312.5865    -26.6917
   district5 |  -280.2424    98.4449    -2.85   0.004    -473.1909   -87.29398
   district6 |  -289.4418   106.6318    -2.71   0.007    -498.4362   -80.44733
   district7 |   27.83569   68.25394     0.41   0.683    -105.9396     161.611
   district8 |  -105.8251   59.11983    -1.79   0.073    -221.6978    10.04764
   district9 |  -142.3369    64.6935    -2.20   0.028    -269.1338   -15.53995
  district10 |  -142.2242   57.44326    -2.48   0.013    -254.8109   -29.63748
       _cons |   727.5221    109.385     6.65   0.000     513.1314    941.9127
-------------+----------------------------------------------------------------
     sigma_u |  409.75319
     sigma_e |  533.65163
         rho |  .37089563   (fraction of variance due to u_i)
------------------------------------------------------------------------------
```

The evidence suggests that, during the 2011–2014 period, TREE increased the expenses devoted to child welfare for beneficiaries by US$ 240 compared to the control group.

```
. xtreg Health year  BENEF BENEF_YEAR    gender1  Education1 Education2 Education3  district1 district2 district3 district4 district5 district6 district7 district8 district9 district10

Random-effects GLS regression                   Number of obs     =      4,388
Group variable: id                              Number of groups  =      2,194

R-squared:                                      Obs per group:
     Within  = 0.0109                                         min =          2
     Between = 0.0714                                         avg =        2.0
     Overall = 0.0443                                         max =          2

                                                Wald chi2(17)     =     189.75
corr(u_i, X) = 0 (assumed)                      Prob > chi2       =     0.0000

------------------------------------------------------------------------------
      Health | Coefficient  Std. err.      z    P>|z|     [95% conf. interval]
-------------+----------------------------------------------------------------
        year |    9.01482   15.99715     0.56   0.573    -22.33901    40.36865
       BENEF |   35.20948   19.29191     1.83   0.068    -2.601968    73.02092
  BENEF_YEAR |   99.41111   23.54622     4.22   0.000     53.26137    145.5608
     gender1 |  -3.980222   12.84358    -0.31   0.757    -29.15318    21.19273
  Education1 |   82.23894   51.07658     1.61   0.107    -17.86931    182.3472
  Education2 |  -23.40432    43.3528    -0.54   0.589    -108.3743    61.56561
  Education3 |  -35.33674   41.43225    -0.85   0.394    -116.5425    45.86898
   district1 |  -208.0038   29.03823    -7.16   0.000    -264.9177   -151.0899
   district2 |  -228.7277   37.98561    -6.02   0.000    -303.1781   -154.2772
   district3 |  -240.9084   51.60263    -4.67   0.000    -342.0477   -139.7691
   district4 |  -132.9749   35.28833    -3.77   0.000    -202.1388   -63.81106
   district5 |    -188.25   46.84037    -4.02   0.000    -280.0554   -96.44455
   district6 |  -217.3056   44.48365    -4.89   0.000    -304.4919   -130.1192
   district7 |  -145.7347   30.78212    -4.73   0.000    -206.0665   -85.40282
   district8 |  -145.0406   28.18104    -5.15   0.000    -200.2744   -89.80672
   district9 |  -227.9499   28.78144    -7.92   0.000    -284.3605   -171.5393
  district10 |  -203.8644   26.98153    -7.56   0.000    -256.7472   -150.9816
       _cons |   278.6436   48.34446     5.76   0.000     183.8902     373.397
-------------+----------------------------------------------------------------
     sigma_u |  118.21179
     sigma_e |  383.10701
         rho |  .08693289   (fraction of variance due to u_i)
------------------------------------------------------------------------------
```

Likewise, TREE was able to increase household health expenses of beneficiaries by US$ 107.8 compared to non-beneficiaries.[6]

[6] This change in beneficiaries' income, health and children welfare corresponds to an increase of 77%, 31.2% and 38.9% respectively with respect to non-beneficiaries.

```
. xtreg Consumption year  BENEF BENEF_YEAR   gender1  Education1 Education2 Education3  district1 district2 district3 district4 district5 district6 district7 district8 district9 district10

Random-effects GLS regression                   Number of obs     =      4,388
Group variable: id                              Number of groups  =      2,194

R-squared:                                      Obs per group:
     Within  = 0.0242                                         min =          2
     Between = 0.0410                                         avg =        2.0
     Overall = 0.0324                                         max =          2

                                                Wald chi2(17)     =     144.88
corr(u_i, X) = 0 (assumed)                      Prob > chi2       =     0.0000

------------------------------------------------------------------------------
 Consumption | Coefficient  Std. err.      z    P>|z|     [95% conf. interval]
-------------+----------------------------------------------------------------
        year |   30.48863   29.09665     1.05   0.295    -26.53977    87.51702
       BENEF |   132.7564    34.0517     3.90   0.000     66.01633    199.4965
  BENEF_YEAR |  -44.62024   42.84552    -1.04   0.298    -128.5959    39.35543
     gender1 |   16.54324   22.22991     0.74   0.457    -27.02658    60.11305
  Education1 |   336.8717   89.74717     3.75   0.000     160.9705    512.7729
  Education2 |  -118.2959   75.77888    -1.56   0.119    -266.8197    30.22801
  Education3 |  -103.6237   72.45547    -1.43   0.153    -245.6338    38.38646
   district1 |  -158.9962   50.29194    -3.16   0.002    -257.5666   -60.42585
   district2 |  -210.6186   65.77149    -3.20   0.001    -339.5283   -81.70884
   district3 |  -204.3847   89.32999    -2.29   0.022    -379.4683   -29.30113
   district4 |  -105.5353   61.08303    -1.73   0.084    -225.2559     14.1852
   district5 |  -154.3815   81.07316    -1.90   0.057    -313.2819    4.519026
   district6 |  -198.7467   77.00621    -2.58   0.010    -349.6761   -47.81733
   district7 |  -143.3178   53.29151    -2.69   0.007    -247.7672   -38.86835
   district8 |  -32.39006   48.78121    -0.66   0.507    -127.9995    63.21934
   district9 |  -161.6363   49.83944    -3.24   0.001    -259.3199   -63.95284
  district10 |  -117.7571   46.70699    -2.52   0.012    -209.3012   -26.21311
       _cons |   266.9136   84.40873     3.16   0.002     101.4755    432.3517
-------------+----------------------------------------------------------------
     sigma_u |   136.2597
     sigma_e |  700.33928
         rho |  .03647383   (fraction of variance due to u_i)
------------------------------------------------------------------------------
```

Finally, there is no evidence that TREE increased the consumption of its beneficiaries when compared to non-beneficiaries in terms of food consumption, fuel, and electricity. The estimated coefficient associated with consumption, α_3, is negative and not statistically significant. One plausible explanation is these goods or fuel sources are not considered normal goods, or that TREE beneficiaries devoted income surplus to buy assets or meet other expenses instead of consumption of the bundle of food and services considered.

11.6.5 Financial Return Analysis

The previous section addressed the question of whether the program achieved its goals, i.e., increasing the well-being and, in particular, the targeted outcomes of its beneficiaries compared to those who did not participate in the program. In other words, it answers the question of whether to continue, adjust, or stop the program. Another critical question is whether the program implementation was too expensive, in the sense the same impact could have been obtained at a lower cost, or with the allocated money, more people or districts could have benefited from it. These are legitimate questions to address before making decisions about replicating the program somewhere else.

Administrative costs and local consultant fees for implementing a project can be quite expensive for justifiable and unjustifiable reasons. A good evaluator must stay away from all kinds of politics, remain objective, and act as a scientist. Different financial indicators such as the net present value (NPV), the benefit–cost ratio (B/C), and the internal rate of return (IRR) of the project can be used to evaluate its cost-effectiveness. The NPV is the discounted net cashflows of the project using a predetermined discount or interest rate, which represents the opportunity cost of capital. A positive NPV indicates a profitable project, with higher values leading to greater profitability. B/C represents the ratio of the discounted inflows divided by the discounted outflows. This ratio must equal 1 for the project to be economically viable and the higher the value above 1, the better. Finally, the IRR is the discount rate that yields an NPV equal to zero and represents the return on the project (Boardman et al. 2011).

The cost-effectiveness analysis presented here focuses only on expenses related to the training and business development components of the program, given the data received from the ILO field office in Zimbabwe. A few pieces of information about the ILO project are needed to conduct this analysis: cash inflow, cash outflow, number of beneficiaries, and assumptions about the interest rate. The average impact of TREE on beneficiaries in terms of incremental income is US$ 789 for the 2011–2014 period, or an average of US$ 197.25 per year compared to non-beneficiaries.[7] Using this information, one can calculate the cash inflows of the project for the 2011–2014 period, which is the estimated benefit generated by the program per beneficiary per year (US$ 197.25) multiplied by the number of TREE beneficiaries. The annual cash outflows of TREE were provided by the ILO field office in Zimbabwe. All these data are shown in Table 11.3. The net-cashflow is the difference between the inflows and outflows, and the NPV is the discounted value. The cost-effectiveness analysis considers four scenarios, as shown in Table 11.3: two scenarios with 12%, 6% discount rates (Scenarios 1 and 2) and another two with a 6% discount rate and an additional two (Scenario 3) and four (Scenario 4) years.

Table 11.3 depicts the results of the NPV, B/C, and IRR analyses. Scenario 1 assumes a discount rate of 12% and estimates 2,173 beneficiaries during the 2010–2014 period of the project. Under Scenario 1, NPV is negative, and the B/C ratio is less than 1. Thus, the study conducted a sensitivity analysis considering a discount rate of 6% (Scenario 2), and NPV was still negative while the B/C ratio was still less than one. That is, the TREE project was not profitable for investors, policymakers, international donors, and specifically the ILO during the 2010–2014 period with 12% and 6% discount rates.

The results were surprising and unexpected by the ILO field office in Harare, Zimbabwe, and also in Switzerland where ILO is headquartered. This is the advantage of not only estimating the impact of the project but also assessing its cost-effectiveness, as ILO intended to replicate this project in several other African countries as well as in Latin America and the Caribbean.

Given the negative NPV generated by the program for the 2010–2014 period, the study next investigated how many years of cash inflows are needed for TREE to pay off. Benefits of the project in terms of additional income are assumed to continue into the future, which could be for several years. The study also assumed in this context that there is no additional cost related to training and business development and that the number of beneficiaries is fixed.

Finally, under Scenario 4 with a discount rate again of 6%, and assuming four years of benefits beyond the end of the program, the evidence showed a non-negative

[7] Different sub-samples are used in this chapter to calculate these numbers for confidentiality issues without loss of generality in terms of methodological approaches.

Table 11.3 Cash flows ($1,000 US), NPV, B/C and IRR

Year	Outflow	Beneficiaries	Inflow	Netflow	Beneficiaries	Inflow	Netflow
Scenario 1 (discount rate = 12%)					Scenario 2 (discount rate = 6%)		
2010	74.4	134	26.4	($48.0)	134	26.4	($48.0)
2011	783.5	438	86.4	($697.1)	438	86.4	($697.1)
2012	270.1	873	172.2	($97.9)	873	172.2	($97.9)
2013	626.4	1664	328.2	($298.2)	1664	328.2	($298.2)
2014	461.5	2173	428.6	($32.9)	2173	428.6	($32.9)
Total	$2,216		1041.9	($1,174.1)		1041.9	($1,174.2)
NPV				($981.6)			($1,069.2)
B/C				0.43			0.45
Scenario 3 (discount rate = 6%)					Scenario 4 (discount rate = 6%)		
2010	74.4	134	26.4	($48.0)	134	26.4	($48.0)
2011	783.5	438	86.4	($697.1)	438	86.4	($697.1)
2012	270.1	873	172.2	($97.9)	873	172.2	($97.9)
2013	626.4	1664	328.2	($298.2)	1664	328.2	($298.2)
2014	461.5	2173	428.6	($32.9)	2173	428.6	($32.9)
2015	0	2173	428.6	428.6	2173	428.6	428.6
2016	0	2173	428.6	428.6	2173	428.6	428.6
2017	0				2173	428.6	428.6
2018	0				2173	428.6	428.6
Total			1,971.33	($244.7)		2,861.18	645.13
NPV				($446.8)			$108
B/C				0.8			2.5
IRR(%)							8.1

Note Beneficiaries are the number of beneficiaries. Monetary indicators are in thousands of US$. Values between parentheses are negative

NPV.[8] In this case, the IRR is equal to 8.1%. Thus, the results show that the program needed at least four additional years without additional administrative and local consulting costs if benefits were to pay off. These results show that assessing the impacts of a program on beneficiaries is not enough and gauging whether it was well implemented and executed by targeting the right people and reaching the optimal number of beneficiaries is fundamental because the goal of a program should merely be to marginally improve the targeted outcomes for beneficiaries but doing the best one could do given the available resources.

[8] It worth noting that with scenario 3, TREE was still not profitable.

References

Angrist JD, Pischke JS (2009) Mostly harmless econometrics: an empiricist's companion. Princeton University Press

Becker SO, Ichino A (2002) Estimation of average treatment effects based on propensity scores. Stand Genomic Sci 2(1):358–377

Boardman A, Greenberg D, Vining A, Weimer D (2011) Cost-benefit analysis: concepts and practice, 4th edn. Pearson Education, Upper Saddle River, NJ

Caliendo M, Kopeinig S (2008) Some practical guidance for the implementation of propensity score matching. J Econ Surv 22(1):31–72

Cochran WG (1968) The effectiveness of adjustment by subclassification in removing bias in observational studies. Biometrics, 295–313

Cochran W, Rubin D (1973) Controlling Bias in Observational studies. Sankyha 35(4):417–446

Connell JP, Kubisch AC (1998) Applying a theory of change approach to the evaluation of comprehensive community initiatives: progress, prospects, and problems. New Approach Eval Community Initiat 2(15–44):1–16

Duflo E, Glennerster R, Kremer M (2007) Using randomization in development economics research: a toolkit. Handb Dev Econ 4:3895–3962

Ferraro PJ, Miranda JJ (2017) Panel data designs and estimators as substitutes for randomized controlled trials in the evaluation of public programs. J Assoc Environ Resour Econ 4(1):281–317

Gibbons CE, Suárez Serrato JC, Urbancic MB (2018) Broken or fixed effects? J Econom Methods 8(1):20170002

Heckman JJ, Smith JA (1999) The pre-programme earnings dip and the determinants of participation in a social programme. Implications for simple programme evaluation strategies. Econ J 109(457):313–348

Heckman JJ, Ichimura H, Todd PE (1997) Matching as an econometric evaluation estimator: evidence from evaluating a job training programme. Rev Econ Stud 64(4):605–654

Hullsiek KH, Louis TA (2002) Propensity score modeling strategies for the causal analysis of observational data. Biostatistics 3(2):179–193

Iarossi G (2006) The power of survey design: a user's guide for managing surveys, interpreting results, and influencing respondents. World Bank Publications

Imas LGM, Rist RC (2009) The road to results: designing and conducting effective development evaluations. World Bank Publications

International Labour Organization (2013) Training for rural economic empowerment knowledge-sharing workshop. Report, Addis-Ababa

Khandker SR, Koolwal GB, Samad HA (2010) Handbook on impact evaluation: quantitative methods and practices. World Bank Publications, Washington, DC

Lachaud MA, Bravo-Ureta BE, Fiala N, Gonzalez SP (2018) The impact of agri-business skills training in Zimbabwe: an evaluation of the Training for Rural Economic Empowerment (TREE) programme. J Dev Eff 10(3):373–391

Leuven E, Sianesi B (2015) PSMATCH2: stata module to perform full mahalanobis and propensity score matching, common support graphing, and covariate imbalance testing. Statistical Software Components, Boston College Department of Economics, USA. http://ideas.repec.org/c/boc/bocode/s432001.html

Mayne J (2017) Theory of change analysis: building robust theories of change. Can J Program Eval 32(2):155–173

Ravallion M (2008) Evaluating anti-poverty programs. Ch. 59. In: Schultz T, Strauss J (eds) Handbook of development economics. Elsevier, Amsterdam, Holland, pp 3787–3846

Rosenbaum PR, Rubin DB (1983) The central role of the propensity score in observational studies for causal effects. Biometrika 70(1):41–55

Rubin DB (2001) Using propensity scores to help design observational studies: application to the tobacco litigation. Health Serv Outcomes Res Method 2(3):169–188

Sullivan H, Stewart M (2006) Who owns the theory of change? Evaluation 12(2):179–199

Wang Y, Cai H, Li C, Jiang Z, Wang L, Song J, Xia J (2013) Optimal caliper width for propensity score matching of three treatment groups: a Monte Carlo study. PLoS ONE 8(12):e81045
Wassenich P, Muñoz J (2007) Data for impact evaluation. Poverty reduction and economic management. In: Thematic group on poverty analysis, monitoring and impact evaluation. The World Bank, Washington, DC
Wichman CJ, Ferraro PJ (2017) A cautionary tale on using panel data estimators to measure program impacts. Econ Lett 151:82–90
ZimStat (2013) Poverty and poverty datum line analysis in Zimbabwe. Report, Harare, Zimbabwe

Chapter 12
Panel Probit Models Applied to Stated Preference Auctions: A Cost Discovery for Ecosystem Services through Wetland Restoration in the Canadian Prairies

Manikarnika Kanjilal, Wiktor Adamowicz, Scott Jeffrey, and James Unterschultz

Abstract This chapter presents a brief discussion on panel probit models and their estimation using an application in non-market valuation. Agricultural producers' willingness to accept (WTA) for environmental conservation on agricultural land is the "true" cost of beneficial management practices (BMPs) but is also unobservable. In this study, producers' WTA for restoring wetlands on their currently active farmland is estimated using stated preference (SP) methods and panel probit models in NLogit 5.0 based on the results of an in-person survey of 29 producers with farms located over four rural municipalities in Alberta and Saskatchewan. The producers' WTA indicates that adoption of wetland restoration BMP imposes net private costs on the producers with significant within- and between-sample heterogeneity in costs. Own WTA is less than inferred WTA across all models indicating social desirability bias. The findings indicate that policy interventions in terms of compensation payments are required to encourage the uptake of wetland restoration BMP in Alberta and Saskatchewan. SP auctions could be employed as a valid and

This work is based on Kanjilal (2015) and more than 50% of its content uses sections from Kanjilal (2015) with or without paraphrasing: this is further indicated in each section.

James Unterschultz: Deceased November 11, 2015.

W. Adamowicz · S. Jeffrey · J. Unterschultz
Department of Resource Economics and Environmental Sociology, University of Alberta, 515 General Services Building, Edmonton, AB T6G 2H1, Canada
e-mail: vic.adamowicz@ualberta.ca

S. Jeffrey
e-mail: scott.jeffrey@ualberta.ca

M. Kanjilal (✉)
Government of Alberta, Ministry of Technology and Innovation, 9942 108 Street, Edmonton, AB T5K 2J5, Canada
e-mail: manikarnika.kanjilal@gov.ab.ca

D. Mukherjee (ed.), *Applied Econometric Analysis Using Cross Section and Panel Data*, Contributions to Economics, https://doi.org/10.1007/978-981-99-4902-1_12

cheaper cost discovery tool compared to reverse auctions for facilitating wetland policy and design of compensation packages.

Keywords Agriculture · Valuation · Wetland restoration · Random effects probit

12.1 Introduction

When asked to describe their research in a polite elevator conversation with a minister, a researcher in panel probit models and wetland restoration might say: "our work shows that people are different – heterogenous – and this difference should be taken into account in wetland policy. One size does not fit all – especially when it comes to designing compensation for wetland restoration".

Panel probit is about heterogeneity. Panel data are a dataset of cross-sectional data with a longitudinal dimension. The data have a natural grouping. The cross-sectional data could represent persons or agricultural farms or businesses or countries with various attributes. The longitudinal dimension could be time (e.g., individuals surveyed over a period of time) or a discrete change of state (e.g., sales data for Winter, Spring, Summer, Fall seasons) or multiple responses from the same individual. While the grouped nature of the data has implications for the econometric model in terms of how errors are correlated across the observations, panel data are appropriate for use in analyzing heterogeneity across cross-sectional units. This offers great flexibility in modelling differences in behavior across individuals. This is especially the case when the observed choices are likely correlated within an individual (i.e., the group) due to latent, individual-specific preference parameters.[1] When the economic outcome of interest is a choice variable driven by a latent preference structure of an individual and when multiple observations are available for each individual (i.e., the group), a panel probit or logit model fits the theoretical framework of the probability model underlying the observed choice.

The structure of models with panel data varies depending on assumptions about heterogeneity. Random effects (RE) characterize heterogeneity. In RE, unobserved heterogeneity is uncorrelated with included regressors (i.e., they are group-specific but time- or period-invariant). This means in the regression equation, individual-specific constant terms that capture heterogeneity are randomly distributed across the sample. This is an appropriate view if sampled cross-sectional units are drawn from a large population. Given this consideration, a RE panel model maybe appropriate in analyzing behavioral data from sample surveys, including stated preference (SP) studies, thus offering greater external generalizability of the results than fixed effects (FE).[2] This feature of RE models make them appropriate for SP studies that may

[1] More detailed discussion on panel data is provided by Greene (2008). For discussion on use of panel data for choice models see Loomis (1997).

[2] In FE unobserved individual effects are correlated with the regressors, unlike RE.

involve multiple choice responses for the same contingent valuation (CV) problem.[3] These types of data could also be analyzed using logit models, but the RE probit provides the advantage of capturing the heterogeneity.

This paper provides an application of panel RE probit models for data on agricultural producer behavior obtained from a SP auction to estimate producers' willingness to accept (WTA) compensation—a measure of the "true" cost of adopting wetland restoration beneficial management practice (BMP) in active farmland. In doing so, it accounts for the heterogeneity in cost of BMP adoption and the corresponding preferred compensation which has implications for policy and compensation design for wetland restoration in the Western Canadian Prairie region.

Section 12.2 describes the policy issue and the gap in the empirical literature addressed by this analysis. Section 12.3 describes the conceptual framework of the choice problem faced by the agricultural producers that underlies the econometric models. Section 12.4 presents a brief literature review. Section 12.5 presents data, methods, and model results and Sect. 12.6 discusses the findings.

12.2 Policy Issue[4]

BMPs are farming practices aimed at reducing the negative impact of agriculture on the surrounding environment and can be thought of as an example of institutional and participatory mechanisms that generate non-market ecosystem services (ES).[5] The impact of agricultural production practices on the environment is an important policy issue. Evaluation and development of appropriate policy requires economic evaluation of the land use change. This necessitates estimation of the costs of adopting agricultural BMPs (Pannell 2008).

Agricultural producers' WTA for environmental conservation on agricultural land is unobservable. There are various ways to approximate this value; for example, by using various SP instruments (Espinosa-Goded et al. 2010; Yu and Belcher 2011; Lindhjem and Mitani 2012; Trenholm et al. 2013), by examining financial costs of BMP adoption by agricultural producers (e.g., Cortus et al. 2011; Jeffrey et al. 2014), as well as by eliciting WTA estimates in a reverse auction (Hill et al. 2011). However, limited information is available in a Canadian context regarding the WTA associated with ES produced through agricultural BMPs.

[3] Alberini et al. (1994) provide a discussion of multiple dichotomous choice (DC) responses and Loomis (1997) addresses combining responses to CV and actual behavior questions.

[4] This section draws heavily from Kanjilal (2015).

[5] Boyd and Banzhaf (2007) define ES as "..components of nature, directly enjoyed, consumed, or used to yield human well-being".

The policy instruments traditionally used in the Canadian prairie pothole region to induce voluntary wetland restoration by producers and landowners can be characterized as flat-rate or cost-share policies which are administratively set, fixed-payment offers.[6] However, agricultural producers are heterogeneous agents in terms of their preferences and risk perceptions. There is also significant heterogeneity with respect to farm characteristics, such as soil productivity, enterprise mix, crop rotation, existing number of wetlands in their land, etc. These factors influence producers' private costs of supplying ES through adoption of BMPs. In the presence of heterogeneity in the cost of providing ES, a flat rate policy, unlike an auction, would tend to over-compensate some low-cost suppliers and fail to encourage participation among comparatively high-cost suppliers of ES. It would also not be cost-effective from the policy makers' perspective. In order to achieve efficiency and cost-effectiveness of the policy to incentivize producers to adopt wetland restoration programs, the heterogeneity in the cost of service provision needs to be recognized. It is an efficient strategy from the policy makers' perspective to identify the low-cost suppliers of the wetland service. It also helps in identifying the "true cost" of wetland restoration and determining the optimal investment required for wetland conservation.

The use of conservation auctions represents one method to address this issue. This type of auction involves multiple sellers who each submit bids indicating the amount of compensation they are willing to accept for providing an ES. In a typical conservation auction, bids are ranked in terms of the compensation amount and environmental benefit index (EBI) (e.g., Hill et al. 2011) to identify the low-cost winners, given program budget and/or the environmental target. While the design and effectiveness of conservation auctions are widely explored (e.g., Iho et al. 2014; Kits et al. 2014; Boxall et al. 2013; Schilizzi and Latacz-Lohmann 2012), the application of conservation auctions in Canada, real or experimental, is fairly limited. Examples of Canadian studies include Hill et al. (2011) in the Assiniboine river watershed in Saskatchewan, a conservation incentive program in the East Interlake Conservation District in Manitoba (Noga and Adamowicz 2014; EICD 2015), and Boxall et al. (2013) in South Tobacco Creek in Manitoba. Novak (2017) and Lloyd-Smith (2018) are more recent applications.

The main objective of this work was to use SP methods to investigate the heterogenous cost of adoption of wetland restoration BMP by agricultural producers in the black soil regions of Central Alberta and South-eastern Saskatchewan. SP auctions with the inferred valuation method (IVM) (discussed below) offer an alternative

[6] At the time of the study, in Alberta, compensation for landowners for wetland restoration was available on a 70% cost-share basis with a maximum funding of $50,000 through On-Farm Stewardship Programs under Growing Forward 2 (AARD 2015). In Saskatchewan, the Lower Souris Watershed Committee provided local producers an incentive of a one-time, $2000 per acre payment for every acre of re-established slough under the Saskatchewan Wetland Restoration Program and the National Wetland Conservation Fund (LSW 2015). The Committee also offered to build and install the drainage plugs themselves. An additional one-time incentive program of up to $2000 per acre for wetland restoration was available to the producers in the Pipestone Creek Watershed, a sub-watershed of Lower Souris Watershed area that contains the site of this study, under the Pipestone Phosphorous Reduction Program.

approach to identify the central tendencies of and the heterogeneity in the cost of adoption of a wetland restoration BMP. Median WTAs and the distributions of WTAs obtained for the two samples from the two case study sites in Western Canada address the issue of limited availability of empirical findings in the valuation literature regarding agricultural producers' preference for compensation for adopting BMPs.

A secondary objective was to compare the findings of this paper with the salient bids received by Hill et al. (2011) in a reverse auction in Saskatchewan to determine if the stated WTA is comparable with the salient bids. Comparability of stated WTA with salient bids would indicate potential for using SP as an ex-ante cost discovery method for a PES program that can provide policy makers with information on the cost of supply of ecosystem services.

12.3 Conceptual Framework[7]

The conceptual framework for most studies focusing on producer or landowner WTA for environmental conservation is the random utility model (RUM). Assuming the producer is maximizing utility, the indirect utility for the ith producer is given by $V(\Pi_i, X_i, \varepsilon_i)$ where Π_i is the profit of the farm-household, X_i is the vector of individual characteristics and ε_i is the error term. A producer would participate in a wetland restoration BMP if the utility from participation and the compensation is greater than the utility from the status quo. Therefore, $V_1(\Pi_{i1} + \text{Bid}, X_i, \varepsilon_{i1}) > V_0(\Pi_{i0}, X_i, \varepsilon_{i0})$ where subscript 1 indicates participation in the BMP, subscript 0 indicates status quo and Bid refers to the compensation amount. The probability of the ith producer accepting a bid amount as compensation for participation in a restoration program (i.e., probability of a "Yes" answer to the stated preference question) is given by:

$$\text{Prob}\,(\text{Yes}_i) = \text{Prob}[V_{1i}(\Pi_{i1} + \text{Bid}, X_i, \varepsilon_{i1}) > V_{0i}(\Pi_{i0}, X_i, \varepsilon_{i0})] \tag{12.1}$$

If it is assumed that utility is additively separable in deterministic and stochastic preference components, then,

$$\begin{aligned}\text{Prob}\,(\text{Yes}_i) &= \text{Prob}[V_{1i}(\Pi_{i1} + \text{Bid}, X_i) + \varepsilon_{i1} > V_{0i}(\Pi_{i0}, X_i) + \varepsilon_{i0}] \\ &= \text{Prob}[V_{1i}(\Pi_{i1} + \text{Bid}, X_i) - V_{0i}(\Pi_{i0}, X_i) > \varepsilon_{i0} - \varepsilon_{i1}]\end{aligned} \tag{12.2}$$

If the random term is specified as $\varepsilon_{i1} - \varepsilon_{i0} = \varepsilon_i$, then

$$\text{Prob}\,(\text{Yes}_i) = \text{Prob}[V_{1i}(\Pi_{i1} + \text{Bid}, X_i) - V_{0i}(\Pi_{i0}, X_i) + \varepsilon_i > 0] \tag{12.3}$$

---

[7] This section is taken from Kanjilal (2015) without paraphrasing.

Assuming the deterministic component of utility to be linear in profit (farm income) and covariates,

$$V_{ji} = \beta_i X_i + \gamma_i(\Pi_i) \tag{12.4}$$

$$\text{Therefore,}\quad V_{1i} - V_{0i} = (\beta_1 - \beta_0) \cdot X_i + \gamma_1 \cdot \text{Bid} \tag{12.5}$$

assuming that the marginal utility of income stays constant across states and farm income does not change across states (Haab and McConnell 2002). This implies

$$\begin{aligned} \text{Prob}\,(\text{Yes}_i) &= \text{Prob}[(\beta_1 - \beta_0) \cdot X_i + \gamma \cdot \text{Bid} + \varepsilon_i > 0] \\ &= \text{Prob}[\beta \cdot X_i + \gamma \cdot \text{Bid} + \varepsilon_i > 0] \end{aligned} \tag{12.6}$$

where $\beta = (\beta_1 - \beta_0)$. Given data on producers' acceptance of compensation, farm characteristics and producer attributes, the above model could be empirically developed to determine the welfare impact of BMP adoption.

12.4 Literature Review[8]

While a growing proportion of SP studies (e.g., Horne 2006; Ruto and Garrod 2009; Espinosa-Goded et al. 2010; Kaczan 2011; Trenholm et al. 2013) employ choice experiments (CE) or conjoint analysis to explore WTA estimation in the context of conservation agriculture and PES, a limited number of SP studies have used CV (e.g., Whittington and Pagiola 2011). Most of the CE approaches focus on the marginal value of the attributes of the contract and not on the actual WTA for the overall contract. Within this limited literature, a number of studies attempted to understand landowners' willingness to participate in the Conservation Reserve Program (CRP) or Conservation Reserve Enhancement Program (CREP) of the USDA CREP program using a CV framework (e.g., Lohr and Park 1995; Cooper and Osborn 1998; Kingsbury and Boggess 1999; Vanslembrouck et al. 2002; Amigues et al. 2002; Shaikh et al. 2007; Bateman et al. 1996; Yu and Belcher 2011; Lindhjem and Mitani 2012). Adamowicz et al. (2019) used an SP survey designed as a stochastic payment card with multiple payment options similar to this work to estimate WTA for landowners' participation in agroforestry program and cost for land conversion.

From the literature review, a few observations can be made. A myriad of preference elicitation survey frameworks have been used. Most of the studies focused on estimation of WTA along with exploring the effects of various covariates deemed relevant for the ecosystem service provision problem at hand. The commonly used covariates in these studies are prior knowledge and participation in conservation programs (e.g., Lynch et al. 2002; Yu and Belcher 2011); stewardship behavior among the farmers

[8] This section draws heavily from Kanjilal (2015).

(e.g., Amigues et al. 2002); flexible vs. fixed payment (e.g., Dupraz et al. 2003); farm production potential and size of holdings (e.g., Dupraz et al. 2003; Lindhjem and Mitani 2012), income risk reduction (e.g., Shaikh et al. 2007; Southgate et al. 2009), preference for status quo, transaction cost and flexibility (e.g., Horne 2006; Ruto and Garrod 2009; Porras and Hope 2005). Only a handful of studies compared estimated WTA with revenue from current production activity (e.g., Amigues et al. 2002; Shaikh et al. 2007) and with land rental rates (e.g., Yu and Belcher 2011). Kaczan (2011) and Dupraz et al. (2003) discussed the issue of incentive compatibility and inherent biases in the SP models. While Dupraz et al. (2003) claimed that similarity of the contingent conservation scenario with the existing conservation programs kept hypothetical bias in responses to a minimum, Kaczan (2011) used a cheap talk script and IVM to control for the hypothetical and social desirability biases. Finally, a very small number of studies discussed or explored the issue of heterogeneity of WTA across farmers and the implications for policy (e.g., Ruto and Garrod 2009; Horne 2006; Lindhjem and Mitani 2012; Espinosa-Goded et al. 2010; and Kaczan 2011).

12.5 Data and Methods[9]

12.5.1 Survey of Agricultural Producers: Instrument Design

The literature on the estimation of WTA for provision of ES and land use change using various SP techniques informed the choices made in the current analysis in terms of preference elicitation design that generated a panel data set for which a binomial choice model is ideal.

The main objective of the study was to achieve the best approximation of the true cost of BMP adoption by inducing agricultural producers to reveal their WTA. Since auctions (e.g., uniform pricing format using first or second price as determinant of price) can be incentive-compatible, a survey instrument framed like an auction was designed for its efficiency in eliciting preference in an acceptably incentive-compatible manner.

A major concern with SP studies is the potential that responses are not incentive-compatible since the respondents face no real consequence of their actions or choices. This may lead to them answering the SP questions strategically to skew the results or without paying much attention to the trade-off or problem posed by a SP question. This issue may manifest as hypothetical bias or social desirability bias. Hypothetical bias can take the form of a discrepancy between their real WTA and stated WTA (Bishop and Heberlein 1979; Li et al. 1996; Welsh and Poe 1998; Ready et al. 2010; Nape et al. 2003). Social desirability bias is observed when a respondent receives utility out of saying that their WTA for a good is less than they would actually accept in an actual transaction (Lusk and Norwood 2009). Entem et al. (2021) explored

[9] This section draws heavily from Kanjilal (2015).

biases in a SP survey designed to estimate willingness to pay (WTP) for "morally charged goods". They used a CE in the form of binary-choice, referendum-style SP task presented to multiple referent groups to elicit non-use values of species-at-risk conservation programs and compare biases in the WTP estimates.

There is a significant literature on the distinction between real versus hypothetical WTA and methods to reconcile these two estimates. Although some studies indicate that the distinction between real versus hypothetical scenarios may not significantly influence choice models, there is an abundance of evidence to the contrary. However, the number of WTA studies that discuss the issue of hypothetical bias or discuss issues with various SP valuation techniques (e.g., List and Gallet 2001; Harrison 2007; Carson and Groves 2007) are limited compared to the huge number of WTP studies that deal with these issues.

Social desirability bias (Lusk and Norwood 2009) or warm glow (Becker 1974; Andreoni 1990) or other-regarding behavior (Charness and Rabin 2002) may be attributed to people's utility from conforming with social norms.[10] Alternatively, it may arise from an interviewer effect in an in-person SP study whereby the respondents tend to answer in a way that they feel would please the interviewer. Identifying hypothetical bias or social desirability bias or an interviewer bias from warm glow in the context of an SP survey is often difficult (Carson, Flores and Meade 2001). Entem et al. (2021) found that social desirability bias could be greater than other survey biases such as hypothetical bias.

Lusk and Norwood (2009) noted that a possible cause of social desirability bias is that people receive utility out of their responses to the SP question. Lusk and Norwood (2009) go on to suggest that one way to mitigate this bias would be to ask the respondents how they think another person would value the good in question. If respondents are asked to value a good on behalf of another person, they use their own values as a reference point but do not receive any utility out of providing a "pleasing" answer or a picking a normative answer. The indirect questioning reduces the incentive to provide socially desirable answers and thus reduces social desirability bias and hence hypothetical bias. Lusk and Norwood (2009) noted that the advantage of this IVM is that not only does it help to mitigate the social desirability bias but also does not depend on a particular elicitation format. Kaczan (2011) used IVM in estimating the preference for PES design for reducing deforestation in Usambara, Tanzania but did not find significant evidence of social desirability bias. However, in an experimental study, Stachtiaris et al. (2013) found that IVM helps mitigate social desirability bias in valuation problems with low commitment cost and high normative motivations. Entem et al. (2021) noted that in a WTP context, IVM may overestimate social desirability bias if respondents derive utility from painting themselves in a good light (i.e., suggesting lower WTP for other respondents).

To deal with hypothetical bias and strategic response, an auction-like design was used in this study with a cheap talk script followed by multiple bids and uncertain

[10] The experimental literature that deals with modelling or testing observed altruism under laboratory conditions includes Andreoni and Miller (2002), Rutström and Williams (2000), and McKelvey and Palfrey (1992).

response options. The hypothetical wetland restoration program involved restoring seven acres of wetland for a period of 12 years. A seven-acre restoration plan was chosen to match the average number of wetland acres offered for restoration per bid in the Hill et al. (2011) study. The respondents were presented with a list of 11 bids ranging from \$0 to \$1280 per acre per year for restoration on their best cropland (referred to as Crop-Own scenario henceforth). The bids were presented with a "no skew" design such that the presented bid amounts were: baseline, 100% higher and lower than baseline, 75% higher and lower than baseline, 50% higher and lower than baseline, 25% higher and lower than baseline and 10% higher and lower than baseline. The baseline bid value was based on the average cropland bid of \$643/acre/year (in 2009 dollars) as received by Hill et al. (2011) and rounded down to \$640/acre/year.[11] The respondents were also asked to complete the same preference elicitation tasks for a typical farmer in their area (referred to as Crop-Inferred scenario henceforth).[12] The legend for the valuation scenarios was constructed using province ID (AB for Alberta or SK for Saskatchewan), type of land (C for cropland), and valuation method used (Own or Inferred). For instance, ABCO stands for Alberta-Cropland-Own valuation scenario.

For each bid amount, four response categories were provided. The respondents had the option of indicating whether they would "definitely not accept", "probably not accept", "probably accept" and "definitely accept" the presented bid amount as compensation. The response categories were re-defined during the analysis as "definitely no", "probably no", "probably yes" and "definitely yes", respectively. The own and inferred valuation questions for restoration in cropland are presented in Fig. 12.1.

12.5.2 Survey Results[13]

12.5.2.1 Producer Characteristics

Obtaining a large sample of respondents proved challenging. However, similar studies in the study area also reported very low response rate (e.g., Hill et al. 2011). All 29 respondents in this study were male (aged 35–70 years in Alberta and 28–66 years in Saskatchewan) with an equal split between high school graduates and individuals holding Bachelor's degree or diploma. Of the 15 Alberta respondents, 11 (73%) worked full time in the farm (with farm income constituting 50–100% of total income) and four (27%) worked only part time (with farm income constituting

[11] This amount was not adjusted to 2014 dollars.

[12] If a producer had pastureland suitable for wetland restoration, they were also asked to indicate their preference for compensation for restoring wetland on owned pasture. However, the pasture results are not discussed in this paper.

[13] The three part survey collected farm enterprise details, such as land use details, crops grown, yields, fertilizer and chemical costs, number of livestock, grazing and feeding days, WTA responses for restoration in cropland and pasture, and socio-economic data.

Suppose you were asked to submit a sealed bid that represents the amount that you will be willing to accept in compensation for participating in the program. The agency would select the winning bids by choosing the lowest bids according to their budget.

1.1. Please indicate whether you would be interested in restoring wetlands on 7 acres of your best cropland for each of the following compensation amounts in Table 1.1. Please note that the land given up for wetland restoration would not be available for agricultural purposes for the next **12 years**.

Table 1.1. For **7 acres** of wetland in your **annual cropland**

Amount	Definitely not accept	Probably not accept	Probably accept	Definitely accept
$0 /acre/year				
$160 /acre/year				
$320 /acre/year				
$480 /acre/year				
$576 /acre/year				
$640 /acre/year				
$704 /acre/year				
$800 /acre/year				
$960 /acre/year				
$1120 /acre/year				
$1280 /acre/year				

1.4. Do you think a typical farmer in your area would be willing to participate in such a program?
Yes/No

1.5. How much compensation do you think they would be willing to accept if you think they would participate in restoring 7 acres of wetland in their best cropland? For each amount please indicate if you think **a typical farmer in your area** would definitely accept, probably accept, probably not accept or definitely not accept, in exchange for the restoration of the wetland.

Table 1.5. For **7 acres** of wetland in the **annual cropland of a typical farmer**

Amount	Definitely not accept	Probably not accept	Probably accept	Definitely accept
$0 /acre/year				
$160 /acre/year				
$320 /acre/year				
$480 /acre/year				
$576 /acre/year				
$640 /acre/year				
$704 /acre/year				
$800 /acre/year				
$960 /acre/year				
$1120 /acre/year				
$1280 /acre/year				

Fig. 12.1 Stated Preference questions for restoration in cropland–(Crop-Own scenario in the top panel and Crop-Inferred scenario in the bottom panel) from Kanjilal (2015)

45–60% of total income). Nine respondents in Saskatchewan (64%) were employed full time in the farm (70–100% of their income came from the farm) and five (36%) worked in the farm on a part time basis (farm income constituted 20–50% of total income). Five producers (33.3%) in Alberta were members of conservation and stewardship groups and five producers belonged to recreational hunting or fishing organizations. Three producers (21.4%) in Saskatchewan were members of recreational hunting or fishing organizations and only one (7%) belonged to a conservation stewardship organization.

12.5.2.2 Farm Characteristics

Most of Alberta (n = 9; 60%) and Saskatchewan (n = 9; 64%) respondents reported cropping as the main enterprise. Four Alberta respondents (27%) had cow-calf as their main enterprise. Two farms in Alberta (13%) and five in Saskatchewan (36%) reported a mix of crop and cow-calf as their main enterprise.

Significant variability was observed among the producers in terms of the farm characteristics in both the study sites (Table 12.1). The average woodland and wetland areas on Saskatchewan farms were significantly less than for the Alberta farms. This is corroborated by the past land use changes reported by the Saskatchewan farms compared to their Alberta counterparts. Over the past 12 years (2001–2013), the extent and frequency of land use change (e.g., undertaking wetland drainage projects or clearing of woodland for extending the existing cropland area) was higher for the producers in Saskatchewan (n = 8; mean 243.5 acres; range 18–820 acres) than in Alberta (n = 5; mean 15.4 acres; range 2–40 acres). The average number of permanent and seasonal wetlands was also less than that reported by the Alberta farms.

Table 12.1 Farm characteristics

	Alberta (n = 15)		Saskatchewan (n = 14)	
Description	Mean (s.d.)	Range	Mean (s.d.)	Range
Total farm size (acres)	3524 (2601)	500–11040	3713 (2674)	160–8800
Woodland area (acres)	100 (159)	0–600	70 (80)	0–200
Wetland area (acres)	144 (225)	0–940	63 (56)	0–200
Number of livestock	149 (274)	0–1120	105 (149)	0–550
Number of permanent waterbodies	34 (71)	1–285	28 (53)	0–210
Number of seasonal wetlands	23 (32)	2–108	18 (32)	0–126
Number of temporary/ephemeral wetlands	29 (28)	0–100	55 (105)	0–420

12.5.2.3 Distribution of Valuation Responses

In the ABCO scenario, 13% of respondents always picked "definitely no". These included the non-responses. Approximately 46% of respondents answered in uncertain terms ("probably no" and "probably yes") for the lowest positive bid of $160/acre/year. 80% of respondents switched to "definitely yes" at bid levels of $960 and higher. 7% of participants were uncertain about the highest bid presented and picked "probably yes". Except for the non-responses, for bid levels of $800 or higher, all respondents picked "probably yes" or "definitely yes".

For the ABCI scenario, 20% of respondents in Alberta did not pick any bid: they indicated that in their opinion a typical farmer would not participate in a similar wetland restoration project. For the lowest positive bid, 53% picked "definitely no" and 27% picked the uncertain response categories. For the highest three bids, all respondents picked either "definitely yes" or "definitely no" indicating that beyond a bid threshold there was no uncertainty when they were making these inferred choices. Compared to the ABCO scenario, respondents in the inferred scenario seemed more comfortable picking a certain response or rejecting a bid.

In the SKCO scenario, at the lowest positive bid ($160/acre/year), approximately 92% answered "probably no" or "definitely no" and 7% answered, "definitely yes". 7–50% of respondents used the uncertain response categories for various bid amounts. 7% of respondents picked "definitely no" at the highest bid amount and all other picked either "definitely yes" or "probably yes".

In the SKCI scenario, the lowest bid for a "definite yes" response was $480/acre/year. 7–57% of respondents used the uncertain response categories for this scenario. 21% responded "definitely no" at the highest bid amount and 78% responded either "definitely yes" or "probably yes".

12.5.3 *Econometric Methods and Results*

The choice to participate in the restoration program was conceptualized as one guided by a RUM framework, as described in Sect. 12.3. This implies that a respondent only chooses a bid when the indirect utility from the adoption of restoration program and acceptance of the bid amount equals the indirect utility of the status quo.

As for each respondent, multiple choices were observed, RE probit models were estimated to obtain central tendencies of WTA.[14] The SP auction design for eliciting the WTA takes the form of a multiple-bounded choice question. For $k = 11$ bids presented to a respondent for each valuation scenario, the latent WTA is conceptualized to reside in any one of the $k + 1 = 12$ intervals. The bid interval where the

[14] An ordinary least squares (OLS) estimation of the midpoint of the switching intervals was conducted to identify the univariate distribution of WTA and obtain farm-specific predicted WTAs. Kernel density estimators were also obtained to graphically present the distributions of WTAs based on the midpoint analyses. Kanjilal (2015) presents the midpoint estimates and the distributional comparisons.

respondent switched from a "definitely no" to "definitely yes" response identifies the relevant bounds of the latent WTA. The statistical information underlying each respondent's choice when presented with multiple bids helps improve the efficiency of the discovery of the latent WTA. The RE probit models do not assume that a single WTA value underlies the choices the respondents are making for each sequence of presented bids, and allow WTAs at each bid level to be correlated to each other.[15]

12.5.3.1 RE Probit

The RE probit model was fitted assuming certainty in response. Following Welsh and Poe (1998) and Alberini et al. (2003), the "probably yes" and "probably no" answers were treated as "definitely no". This involved re-coding the response data as a binary choice where "definitely yes" is 1 and all other responses are coded as 0. The choice data thus captured a repeated dichotomous choice (DC) for 11 bids in own valuation scenario and 11 bids in inferred valuation scenario. Given that respondents expressed their choice for 11 bid amounts in each of the relevant valuation scenarios with some "NA"s, the own, inferred and combined choice data resulted in an unbalanced panel data.

The structural RE model is given by:

$$\begin{aligned} Z_{it} &= \beta X_{it} + \gamma \cdot \text{Bid} + u_i + \eta_{it} \\ Y_{it} &= 1 \quad \text{if } Z_{it} > 0 \\ Y_{it} &= 0 \quad \text{otherwise} \end{aligned} \tag{12.7}$$

where Z_{it} = vector of latent variable, Y_{it} = vector of observed indicator variable, X_{it} = vector of explanatory variables, β = vector of coefficients, i = individuals and t = number of responses per person.

As noted earlier, an RE model assumes that for each respondent the answers to each bid question are correlated. It therefore allows estimation of the correlation coefficients between responses. As prescribed in the literature (Greene 2008), Butler and Moffitt's (1982) method of reformulating the likelihood function using quadrature approximation method has been adopted for estimation of the RE models using NLogit 5.0.[16]

To test if the own choices are significantly different than the inferred choices about adoption of the restoration program, partial RE probit models (using only bid and the intercept as explanatory variables) were estimated separately for both the study sites using own valuation data and inferred valuation data. The same models were also estimated using a combination of own and inferred valuation data. The

[15] In contrast, the midpoint analysis explicitly treats only the switching interval as relevant and assumes that a single WTA represented by the exact midpoint of the switching interval is the relevant latent WTA measure.

[16] A similar analysis can be done in Stata using **xtprobit** command or in R using a RE probit estimator as used by Peng and Van den Bulte (2023-forthcoming).

```
|-> regress; lhs=one; rhs=one; panel; str=farmid$
======================================================
| No variables specified. Stratification and count  |
| variables were created. Ngroup =        14         |
| Full sample with missing data  =       286         |
| Stratification variable is        _STRATUM         |
| Count variable for N(i) is        _GROUPTI         |
======================================================
```

Fig. 12.2 Grouping in NLogit 5.0–Alberta Own and Inferred scaenario; screenshot of software output from Kanjilal (2015)

producer's decision to accept the bids was regressed only on the bid amounts which were re-scaled by dividing the bids by 1000. In the partial models with combined own and inferred data, the models were restricted to have the same intercept to explain both own and inferred choices. The socio-demographic variables were not included in the partial RE probit models because of the small sample size. The observations with non-response were removed before estimating the models. The effective sample sizes are reported with each estimated model.

In NLogit 5.0, response groups were created using identifying number for each respondent (FARMID) (Fig. 12.2). An example output for the Alberta Own and Inferred scenario using pooled own and inferred response data is in Fig. 12.3.

The command ***regress; lhs = one; rhs = one; panel; str = farmid$*** asked the model to use FARMID as grouping variable. **_GROUPTI** indicated a panel dataset. **Ngroup = 14** indicated number of groups created as there are 14 respondents in this subsample. **Full sample with missing data = 286** indicated an unbalanced panel as it is not a multiple of 14.

Running the model using the command **probit;** generated the coefficient estimates, significance levels and diagnostics for a binomial probit model and then the desired RE Probit model along with marginal effects. **Pds = GROUPTI;** indicated a panel dataset. **Hpt = 20;** was used to request the model to use Hermite quadrature with 20 points for implementing Butler and Moffitt's (1982) method of reformulating the likelihood function.

As RE probits are nonlinear models, the regression coefficients are not the marginal effects, which are reported separately by the software with a note on how they are calculated (e.g., Nlogit output in Fig.12.3 notes that marginal effects are calculated at the mean). Marginal effect of the *k*th regressor (X_k) at the mean is given by:

$$\frac{\partial}{\partial x_k} Pr\left(Y_{i,t} = 1 | X_{i,t}, Bid\right) = \frac{\beta_k}{\sqrt{1+\sigma_u^2}} \varnothing \left(\frac{\alpha + X_{i,t}\beta + Bid.\gamma}{\sqrt{1+\sigma_u^2}} \right) \quad (12.8)$$

where $\varnothing\left(\frac{\alpha+X_{i,t}\beta+Bid.\gamma}{\sqrt{1+\sigma_u^2}}\right)$ is the standard normal cumulative density function at mean values of $X_{i,t}$ and *Bid*, and σ_u^2 is the variance of the random heterogeneity captured in u_i. A full derivation of marginal effects is presented in Bland and Cook (2019).

```
|-> probit; lhs=acptcrop; rhs=one, cropbid;Pds=_GROUPTI;Margin;Hpt=20$
Normal exit:    5 iterations. Status=0, F=      119.2708
-----------------------------------------------------------------------------
Binomial Probit Model
Dependent variable              ACPTCROP
Log likelihood function       -119.27081
Restricted log likelihood     -191.46616
Chi squared [   1](P= .000)    144.39070
Significance level               .00000
McFadden Pseudo R-squared       .3770658
Estimation based on N =     286, K =   2
Inf.Cr.AIC   =     242.5 AIC/N =    .848
------ LM test for Random Effects -----
ChiSqd.[1]    11.406     P value   .00073
--------+--------------------------------------------------------------------
        |               Standard            Prob.         95% Confidence
ACPTCROP|  Coefficient    Error       z    |z|>Z*           Interval
--------+--------------------------------------------------------------------
        |Index function for probability
Constant|    -1.60390***   .21027    -7.63  .0000    -2.01602   -1.19178
 CROPBID|     3.14910***   .32540     9.68  .0000     2.51133    3.78687
--------+--------------------------------------------------------------------
***, **, * ==>  Significance at 1%, 5%, 10% level.
-----------------------------------------------------------------------------
Normal exit:    9 iterations. Status=0, F=      71.90735
-----------------------------------------------------------------------------
Random Effects Binary Probit Model
Dependent variable              ACPTCROP
Log likelihood function        -71.90735
Restricted log likelihood     -119.27081
Chi squared [   1](P= .000)     94.72692
Significance level               .00000
(Cannot compute pseudo R2.  Use RHS=one
to obtain the required restricted logL)
Estimation based on N =     286, K =   3
Inf.Cr.AIC   =     149.8 AIC/N =    .524
Unbalanced panel has       14 individuals
- ChiSqd[1] tests for random effects -
LM    ChiSqd    11.406     P value   .00073
LR    ChiSqd    94.727     P value   .00000
Wald ChiSqd   560.738     P value   .00000
--------+--------------------------------------------------------------------
        |               Standard            Prob.         95% Confidence
ACPTCROP|  Coefficient    Error       z    |z|>Z*           Interval
--------+--------------------------------------------------------------------
Constant|    -4.25646***   .43747    -9.73  .0000    -5.11389   -3.39904
 CROPBID|     7.37567***   .52421    14.07  .0000     6.34823    8.40310
     Rho|      .87743***   .03705    23.68  .0000      .80481     .95006
--------+--------------------------------------------------------------------
***, **, * ==>  Significance at 1%, 5%, 10% level.
-----------------------------------------------------------------------------
-----------------------------------------------------------------------------
Partial derivatives of E[y] = F[*] with
respect to the vector of characteristics
They are computed at the means of the Xs
Observations used for means are All Obs.
--------+--------------------------------------------------------------------
        |     Partial     Standard            Prob.         95% Confidence
ACPTCROP|      Effect       Error       z    |z|>Z*           Interval
--------+--------------------------------------------------------------------
 CROPBID|     1.01665***   .07836    12.97  .0000      .86307    1.17023
--------+--------------------------------------------------------------------
***, **, * ==>  Significance at 1%, 5%, 10% level.
-----------------------------------------------------------------------------
```

Fig. 12.3 Example output in NLogit 5.0–Alberta Own and Inferred scaenario; screenshot from authors

Bland and Cook (2019) also discussed and demonstrated how econometric software may (or, in case of Stata, used to) calculate the predicted probability of $Y_{it} = 1$ at the median and not the mean, which also leads to a difference in marginal effects calculated as derivatives of the predicted probabilities.

While marginal effects are important to communicate economic significance of the results of RE probits in general, in this work, the welfare measures are the key measures of interest as they show the magnitude of the attribute of interest in monetary terms. For the linear utility function the expected compensating variation for the probit model is the ratio of coefficients as the expected value of the error term is zero (Haab and McConnell 2002). Note that while there is a scale (variance) associated with the error, this cancels out in the ratio. Because of the small sample size, reasonable expectation that individuals' responses to the bids are correlated given the instrument design, and the primary focus on the ratio of coefficients, any adjustment of the coefficients following Arulampalam (1999) for a comparison with pooled probit model was not done. The ratio of the coefficients in this case provides a measure of the median and "mean" or expected value of WTA, the main output of interest of this model, given the assumption of a linear utility function. The median WTA was obtained as a ratio of the attribute coefficients to the bid coefficients fitted at the mean of the explanatory variables. For a partial model with only bid and no covariates, the median WTA is given by the ratio of the intercept coefficient to the bid coefficient.

Likelihood ratio (LR) tests for statistically significant difference between two sets of valuation data/models indicated that the hypothesis of the own and inferred preferences being the same could be rejected for both Alberta and Saskatchewan subsamples (Table 12.2).[17] Respondents indicated that their own preferences were significantly different than that of a typical farmer in their area. In the ABCO model, the intercept and the bid variable were significant at 5% level. In the ABCI model, only the correlation coefficient (ρ) was significant and neither the intercept or bid were significant. The individual models for the Saskatchewan subsample based on only own valuation or inferred valuation data lacked significance of the bid variable and had large standard errors. This is potentially attributable to the limited sample size and the latent nature of the dependent variable.

Although the LR tests with partial RE probit models suggested that data from two valuation methods ideally should not be pooled, another set of models were estimated using combined own and inferred valuation data, dummy variables for the type of valuation method and an interaction between bid and the type of valuation method as a separate assessment (Table 12.3).

Estimating the RE probit models was instructive as the coefficient of correlation (ρ) between responses was found to be statistically significant across almost all of the specifications and was of high magnitude. The high and significant ρ observed

---

[17] For the Alberta subsample, LR $= -2\{-71.9074-(-34.2232-28.9185)\} = 17.5314$ with degrees of freedom (d.f.) = 3. This is greater than the LR critical value at 1% level of significance. For the Saskatchewan sub-sample, LR $= -2\{-89.8627-(-28.8198-29.969)\} = 62.1478$ which is greater than the LR critical value with 3 degrees of freedom at 1% level of significance.

Table 12.2 Partial RE probit models

2a. Alberta	Own and inferred			ABCO[d]			ABCI[e]		
	Coefficients		S.E	Coefficients		S.E	Coefficients		S.E
Constant	−4.25646	***	0.43747	−7.90126	**	3.99845	−15.55960		11.62255
CROPBID[a]	7.37567	***	0.52421	17.38230	**	8.33656	24.03240		17.98130
ρ^b	0.87743	***	0.03705	0.97347	***	0.02481	0.97554	***	0.03286
LL[c]	−71.90735			−34.22317			−28.91851		
Restricted LL	−119.27081			−65.36877			−52.70168		
No. of obs.	286			154			132		
No. of indiv.	14			14			12		
AIC	149.8			74.4			63.8		
WTA	577.10		38.84	454.56		26.01	647.44		18.12
2b. Saskatchewan	Own and Inferred			SKCO[d]			SKCI[e]		
	Coefficients		S.E	Coefficients		S.E	Coefficients		S.E
Constant	−2.72057	***	0.55099	−14.57870		13.04959	−14.18320		11.13718
CROPBID[a]	4.38085	***	0.24848	19.88050		19.04767	18.50720		14.41018
ρ^b	0.72292	***	0.11540	0.98512	***	0.02440	0.98615	***	0.02140
LL[c]	−89.86274			−28.81980			−29.96900		
Restricted LL	−133.75293			−63.47837			−68.77105		

(continued)

Table 12.2 (continued)

No. of obs.	264			132			132		
No. of indiv.	12			12			12		
AIC	185.7			63.6			65.9		
WTA	621.01		108.38	733.32		50.42	766.36		20.49

[a]Presented bid for restoration in cropland (in $/acre/year)/1000
[b]coefficient of correlation between responses
[c]Log-likelihood estimate
[d]Crop-Own scenario
[e]Crop-Inferred scenario
***Significant at 1% level
**Significant at 5% level
*Significant at 10% level

Table 12.3 RE probit model with combined own and inferred data

	Alberta			Saskatchewan		
	Coefficients		S.E	Coefficients		S.E
Constant	−5.13861	***	0.92099	−2.82775	***	0.95851
CROPBID[a]	8.02450	***	1.30470	4.23329	***	0.75920
OWN[b]	−0.16285		0.82957	−0.05402		0.85280
CROPBID*OWN[c]	2.34456		1.46297	0.93186		0.99887
Rho[d]	0.91412	***	0.03674	0.73734	***	0.12161
LL[e]	−65.08064			−86.57676		
Restricted LL	−118.07045			−132.24942		
AIC	140.20			183.20		
No. of obs.	286			264		
No of indiv.	14			12		
WTA_Own	511.28		24.75	557.93		92.44
WTA_Inferred	640.36		35.00	667.98		132.26

[a]Presented bid for restoration in cropland (in \$/acre/year)/1000
[b]Dummy for type of valuation – 1 if own, 0 if inferred
[c]Interaction of CROPBID and OWN
[d]Coefficient of correlation between responses
[e]Log-likelihood estimate
***Significant at 1% level
**Significant at 5% level
*Significant at 10% level

in all of the RE probit models indicated that multiple responses should be treated as dependent on each other or correlated. This implies that the WTA amounts underlying the response at each bid level are correlated.

In the specifications with the combined own and inferred valuation data (Table 12.3), the bid variable (CROPBID) had a positive and significant coefficient at a 1% level which implies that the probability of participation in the BMP would increase with the amount of compensation. The dummy variable OWN had a negative coefficient which indicates that the probability of participation is lower in the OWN scenario than in the Inferred scenario. This indicates that respondents infer that a typical farmer in the study area in Alberta is more likely to participate in this type of wetland restoration programs. However, the coefficients of this OWN variable and its interaction with CROPBID were not significant. The positive coefficient of CROPBID*OWN interaction implies that higher compensation would lead to higher probability of respondents' own participation compared to the participation of a typical farmer. This suggests that the respondents perceive that higher compensations are needed to persuade them to participate than would be needed to impact the decisions of others. The higher coefficients on CROPBID*OWN imply a higher probability of accepting (at any bid level), indicating a lower mean/median WTA overall. When asked about their own WTA, landowners said that they would need less compensation than "their neighbours" —signaling social desirability or warm glow effect. Own WTA was found to be less than inferred WTA thus indicating the presence of social desirability bias for both sub-samples.[18]

12.6 Discussion[19]

To the best of our knowledge, no previous studies exist that look into producers' welfare impact of wetland restoration BMP in the Western Canadian Prairie region using SP methods. To address this gap in the empirical literature, agricultural producers' WTA for restoring naturally occurring wetlands in their cropland was elicited at two case study sites in Alberta and Saskatchewan using SP methods. The study accounted for the heterogeneity in cost of BMP adoption and the corresponding preferred compensation by eliciting distributions of WTAs as it was hypothesized that the failure to do so would have implications for the popularity and success of a wetland restoration compensation program. Finally and most importantly, the study generated welfare impact estimates that would make it possible to investigate the relationship of these estimates with alternative estimates of cost such as farm-level wealth impact of wetland restoration and bids obtained in a previous reverse auction in Saskatchewan (Hill et al. 2011), and also use the estimates in a cost transfer exercise.

Quite a few observations persist across the various models fitted for elicitation of median WTA even though the econometric analyses were limited and challenged by data limitations. Use of a panel data ensured comparatively higher accuracy and efficiency in estimation of WTA than using a single DC variable, especially in a small sample. As noted earlier, the RE probit model is best suitable for analyzing correlation in responses within-individual—in this case an experimentally designed covariate matrix of WTA bids. The other advantages of using RE probit over a logit model were that it allowed accounting for heterogeneity in responses and also allowed external generalizability important for a sample-based study with broader policy implications.

Own WTA is found to be less than inferred WTA, indicating the likely presence of social desirability bias. This result is robust across model specifications. Median

[18] A "full" model with bid and covariates such as area under annual crops, number of seasonal wetlands and area of past land use change along with the interaction terms was also fitted for both subsamples. Very low significance of the covariates and high standard errors were obtained in these "full" model specifications. Given the concern that some of these covariates were potentially endogenous and the low significance, it was noted that the full RE probit model may not be suitable especially with such small datasets.

The distribution of actual responses revealed that even at the higher bid amounts the proportion of definitely yes responses were less than 100%. This indicated a potentially skewed distribution of preferences. To check if a non-linear specification would improve significance of the explanatory variables, a lognormal RE probit model was also estimated. However, it led to very high standard errors for crop scenarios and hence was considered not a good fit.

[19] This section draws heavily from Kanjilal (2015).

Table 12.4 Comparison of WTA Values ($/acre/year)

Models	Median (S.E.)	S.D	Median (S.E)	S.D
	ABCO[a]		ABCI[b]	
Partial RE probit	454.56 (26.01)	57.53	647.44 (18.12)	41.61
Partial RE probit with Interaction	511.28 (24.75)	96.44	640.36 (35.00)	124.62
	SKCO[c]		SKCI[d]	
Partial RE probit	733.32 (50.42)	50.30	766.36 (20.49)	54.03
Partial RE probit with Interaction	557.93 (92.44)	193.61	667.98 (132.26)	236.22

[a] Alberta-Crop-Own scenario
[b] Alberta-Crop-Inferred scenario
[c] Saskatchewan-Crop-Own scenario
[d] Saskatchewan-Crop-Inferred scenario

WTA is higher in Saskatchewan than in Alberta indicating between-sample variability observed in the stated WTA. This may reflect a bias in the sample since a bigger percentage of the Alberta sample were members of conservation groups or were involved with some wetland conservation programs already. This may also be due to the fact that the sampled producers in Alberta have reportedly invested significantly less resources in past drainage activities. The historical and current policy differences in the two case study areas as well as availability of alternative land use leases (e.g., oil and wind turbine agreements) may also contribute to potentially significant differences in producer preferences for wetland restoration projects across the two sites.

Results suggest that the cost of adoption of BMP is fairly heterogeneous within sample as well as across samples from the two sites. The large standard deviations indicate high dispersion in the WTA relative to the median. The observed heterogeneity of WTA estimates suggests that a one-size-fits-all compensation package for wetland restoration BMP might be inefficient. The cost heterogeneity and corresponding need for targeted policy was also noted by Boxall et al. (2013) although they employed a conservation auction experiment. The following (Table 12.4) summarizes the estimated median WTA values from various RE probit models described above.[20]

The RE probit models present a range of median WTAs, indicating that elicited WTA is dependent on model specification. This leads to the issue of identifying the specification that fits the data best. The level of significance of the variables in the partial models with interaction is higher than the partial models fitted with separate own and inferred data although the standard errors are higher as well. It is difficult to say whether the higher significance is due to the pooled nature of the data used. However, a higher standard error of the median WTA indicates lower precision of the measured central tendencies in terms of the ability to predict the population mean.

[20] Only numerical comparisons between WTA estimates are made using the values in Table 12.4. However, no tests of statistical equality of means were conducted due to the small sample size.

By this criterion, the partial RE probit model fitted with separate own and inferred valuation data seems to be the best fit.

If inferred valuation WTA estimates are to be highlighted as the true underlying estimates, as they are corrected for social desirability bias, then the median WTA obtained for ABCI and SKCI scenarios represent the required average compensation in Alberta and Saskatchewan, respectively. A producer in Alberta would require an average compensation of $647.44/acre/year and a producer in Saskatchewan would require $766.36/acre/year for restoring wetlands in cropland.

Although estimated fair market values were used by Hill et al. (2011) to screen bids that were too high and would be more suitable for a "revolving purchase"[21] scheme, average farmland values may not be the best comparison for the estimated WTA as the SP auction was presented for a finite time period.[22] Nonetheless, For a similar comparison, farmland values were obtained from FCC (2015) for the study site rural municipalities (RMs) for comparison with the WTA estimates. The mean farmland values in all three study site RMs in Alberta ($1695.65/acre in Beaver, $1799.55/acre in Vermillion River and $1792/acre in Wainwright) are higher than the mean farmland value in Moosomin ($1263.00/acre) (FCC 2015).[23] In general, estimated WTA values are considerably less than the average farmland values in the study areas.

The SP auction was presented to the producers as a 12-year program. It is possible that producers viewed the participation in the wetland restoration program as a rental arrangement. In the open-ended comments sought in the survey about the program and producers' choices in the SP auction, one respondent indicated that he considered his chosen bids to be sufficient as they are at par with the rental rates in the area. Another respondent indicated that he chose the higher bids as they are comparable with oil lease and wind turbine agreements. Therefore, the observed heterogeneity in bids may also be driven by the available substitute PES schemes in the area apart from the opportunity cost from agricultural production. A future study could further explore these aspects of anchoring of WTAs.

As the small sample size in this study limited the scope of fitting complex econometric models for the estimation of WTA, it was especially interesting to see whether the results were consistent with salient bids received by Hill et al. (2011). Hill et al. (2011) reported that in their reverse auction in the Assiniboine river watershed in Saskatchewan with two rounds, the range of submitted cropland bid in the second

---

[21] A revolving purchase conservation scheme refers to an alternative method of restoring wetland which involves outright purchase of land in which wetland restoration is conducted by the restoration agency. The land is resold in the market after a conservation easement is put in place (Hill et al. 2011; DUC 2015).

[22] Farmland values are expressed in $/acre and elicited WTA values are in $/acre/year and, thus, they may not be directly comparable.

[23] The mean farmland value in Moosomin ($1263.00/acre) was based on 4 records (FCC 2015). FCC (2014) reported that Saskatchewan experienced the highest growth in average farmland values at 28.5% in 2013 and Alberta experienced an increase of 12.9%. It may be that growth of farmland values rather than the magnitude played a bigger role in a higher median WTA for the Saskatchewan sample.

round was \$619.2–\$666.7/acre/year in 2009 dollars although none of the cropland bids were finally approved.[24] The range of all submitted cropland bids as received by Hill et al. (2011) was \$83.33–\$1000.00/acre/year in 2009 dollars (\$91.58–\$1099.06/acre/year in 2014 dollars).[25] Out of 17 cropland bids received by Hill et al., only three bids were at the maximum of \$1099.06/acre/year (2014 dollars), with the rest being no greater than \$734.74/acre/year (2014 dollars). The median WTA for Saskatchewan in this study is approximately 4.39% higher than the highest revised bid received by Hill et al. (2011) after converting to 2014 dollars.[26]

The key finding of this analysis is that it is possible to obtain information on cost variability for adoption of wetland restoration BMP as observed by Hill et al. (2011) using a SP auction although a reverse auction not only discovers cost but implements the restoration. It is re-assuring to see that the median WTA values for cropland from the partial models corrected for social desirability bias roughly match the actual bids submitted in the reverse auction conducted by Hill et al. (2011). The cost of a PES program can be assessed ex ante using SP to provide policy makers with information on the cost of supply of ecosystem services. It is much more difficult and expensive to implement a reverse auction. Even though the sample size was small, the respondents in this study spent a considerable amount of time discussing the details of the proposed wetland restoration scenarios as if they were real. This is most likely due to the fact that at the time of this work, wetland restoration agencies such as Ducks Unlimited and Alternative Land Use Services (ALUS) were actively restoring wetlands in these areas and thus the designed scenarios seemed realistic and credible. The elicited range of farm-specific bids indicates the variability in costs of provision of the ES through wetland adoption and potentially allows a restoration agency to identify the low-cost suppliers of the service even without an EBI measure. In the context of existing flat-rate policies for encouraging adoption of BMPs and low rate of uptake, this observed variability in cost may indicate that targeting low-cost suppliers of ES may improve rate of adoption of these BMPs.

12.7 Concluding Remarks

The current study faced data limitations while exploring producers' motivation for participating in restoration programs and hence could not tease out the source of heterogeneity in the cost of adoption. With sufficient data availability, a formal analysis using latent class model or random coefficients model would allow identifying the sources of this heterogeneity and help design a better targeted wetland restoration

[24] Approved bids refer to successful bids that were selected after the second round in the reverse auction and led to actual restoration.

[25] The authors received permission to use the first-round bids received by Hill et al. (2011) for comparison and validation of the findings of this study.

[26] The rates of inflation for 2014–2021 period using the annual average all-item consumer price index (CPI) are 13% and 12% for Alberta and Saskatchewan respectively.

policy. A future analysis would involve exploration of the relationship of estimated WTA in this study and the impact of BMP adoption on farm level cash flow to understand the relationship of the stated and revealed measures of cost.

Acknowledgements This study was funded by the Watershed Evaluation of Beneficial Management Practices (WEBs) research project of Agriculture and Agri-Food Canada, Farm Credit Canada (FCC) and Sustainable Prosperity.

References

Adamowicz W, Calderon-Etter L, Entem A et al (2019) Assessing ecological infrastructure investments. PNAS 116(12):5254–5261. https://doi.org/10.1073/pnas.1802883116

Alberta Agriculture and Rural Development (AARD) (2015) On-farm stewardship program. http://www.growingforward.alberta.ca/Programs/index.htm?contentId=ON_FARM_STEWD_PRG&useSecondary=true&active=yes. Accessed June 2015

Alberini A, Boyle K, Welsh M (2003) Analysis of contingent valuation data with multiple bids and response options allowing respondents to express uncertainty. J Environ Econ Manag 45(1):40–62

Alberini, A, Kanninen B, Carson R (1994) A general model for double-bounded discrete choice contingent valuation data. Paper presented at the AERE Session of the ASSA Meetings, Boston MA, January 1994

Amigues JP, Boulatoff (Broadhead) C, Desaigues B et al (2002) The benefits and costs of riparian analysis habitat preservation: a willingness to accept/willingness to pay contingent approach. Ecol Econ 43:17–31

Andreoni J (1990) Impure altruism and donations to public goods: a theory of warm-glow giving. Econ J 100:464–477

Andreoni J, Miller J (2002) Giving according to GARP: an experimental test of the consistency of preferences for altruism. Econometrica 70(2):737–753

Arulampalam W (1999) A note on estimated coefficients in random effects probit models. Oxford Bull Econ Stat 61(4):597–602

Bateman IJ, Diamand E, Langford IH et al (1996) Household willingness to pay and farmers' willingness to accept compensation for establishing a recreational woodland. J Environ Plan Manag 39(1):21–43

Becker GS (1974) A Theory of social interactions. J Polit Econ 82(6):1063–1093

Bishop RC, Heberlein TA (1979) Measuring values of extramarket goods: are indirect measures biased? Am J Agric Econ 926–930

Bland JR, Cook AC (2019) Random effects probit and logit: understanding predictions and marginal effects. Appl Econ Lett 26(2):116–123

Boxall PC, Perger O, Weber M (2013) Reverse auctions for agri-environmental improvements: Bid selection rules and pricing for beneficial management practice adoption. Can Public Policy 39(S2):S23–S36

Boyd J, Banzhaf S (2007) What are ecosystem services? The need for standardized environmental accounting units. Ecol Econ 63:616–626

Butler JS, Moffitt R (1982) A computationally efficient quadrature procedure for the one-factor multinomial probit model. Econometrica 761–764

Carson RT, Groves T (2007) Incentive and informational properties of preference questions. Environ Resour Econ 37(1):181–210

Carson RT, Flores NE, Meade NF (2001) Contingent valuation: controversies and evidence. Environ Resour Econ 19:173–210

Charness G, Rabin M (2002) Understanding social preferences with simple tests. Q J Econ 817–869
Cooper J, Osborn TC (1998) The effect of rental rates on the extension of conservation reserve program contracts. Am J Agr Econ 80:184–194
Cortus BG, Jeffrey SR, Unterschultz JR et al (2011) The economics of wetland drainage and retention in Saskatchewan. Can J Agric Econ 59:109–126
Ducks Unlimited Canada (DUC) (2015) Revolving land program. http://www.ducks.ca/what-we-do/your-land/prairie-programs/rlp/. Accessed Aug 2015
Dupraz P, Vermersch D, Henry De Frahan B et al (2003) The environmental supply of farm households: a flexible willingness to accept model. Environ Resour Econ 25(2):171–189
East Interlake Conservation District (EICD) (2015) Conservation incentive program information sheet #1. http://www.eicd.ca/assets/informationpackage.pdf. Accessed 15 July 2015
Entem A, Lloyd-Smith P, Adamowicz W (2021) Using inferred valuation to quantify survey and social desirability bias in stated preference research. Am J Agric Econ 1–19
Espinosa-Goded M, Barreiro-Hurlé J, Ruto E (2010) What do farmers want from agri-environmental scheme design? A choice experiment approach. J Agric Econ 61(2):259–273
Farm Credit Canada (FCC) (2014) 2013 Farmland values report. https://www.fcc-fac.ca/fcc/about-fcc/corporate-profile/reports/farmland-values/farmland-values-report-2013.pdf. Accessed 26 Apr 2015
Farm Credit Canada (FCC) (2015) Farmland values. Obtained through personal communication with JP Gervais, Chief Agricultural Economist, Regina, Saskatchewan, April 2015
Greene WH (2008) Econometric analysis, 7th edn. Prentice Hall, New Jersey
Haab TC, McConnell KE (2002) Valuing environmental and natural resources: the econometrics of non-market valuation. Edward Elgar Publishing
Harrison GW (2007) Making choice studies incentive compatible. In: Kanninen B (ed) Valuing environmental amenities using stated choice studies. Springer, The Netherlands, pp 67–110
Hill MRJ, McMaster DG, Harrison T et al (2011) A reverse auction for wetland restoration in the Assiniboine river watershed, Saskatchewan. Can J Agric Econ 59(2):245–258
Horne P (2006) Forest owners' acceptance of incentive based policy instruments in forest biodiversity conservation-A choice experiment based approach. Silva Fennica 40(1):169–178
Iho A, Lankoski J, Ollikainen M et al (2014) Agri-environmental auctions for phosphorus load reduction: experiences from a Finnish pilot. Aust J Agric Resour Econ 58(2):205–222
Jeffrey SR, Koeckhoven S, Trautman D et al (2014) Economics of riparian beneficial management practices for improved water quality: A representative farm analysis in the Canadian Prairie region. Can Water Resour J 39(4):449–461
Kaczan D (2011) Designing an incentive program to reduce on-farm deforestation in the East Usambara Mountains, Tanzania. Dissertation, University of Alberta
Kanjilal M (2015) Agricultural producers' costs of adoption of wetland restoration beneficial management practice: estimation and spatial transferability. Dissertation, University of Alberta
Kingsbury L, Boggess W (1999) An economic analysis of riparian landowners' willingness to participate in Oregon's conservation reserve enhancement program. Selected Paper for the Annual Meeting of American Agricultural Economics Association, August 1999
Kits GJ, Adamowicz WL, Boxall PC (2014) Do conservation auctions crowd out voluntary environmentally friendly activity? Ecol Econ 105:118–123
Li C, Löfgren K, Hanemann WM (1996) Real versus hypothetical willingness to accept: the Bishop and Heberlein model revisited. http://www.researchgate.net/profile/Chuan-Zhong_Li/publication/4729310_Real_versus_hypothetical_willingness_to_accept__the_Bishop_and_Heberlein_model_revisited/links/02e7e52552cc9c798a000000.pdf. Accessed Sept 2012
Lindhjem H, Mitani Y (2012) Forest owners' willingness to accept compensation for voluntary conservation: a contingent valuation approach. J For Econ 18(4):290–302
List JA, Gallet CA (2001) What experimental protocol influence disparities between actual and hypothetical stated values? Environ Resour Econ 20(3):241–254
Lloyd-Smith P (2018) Fish, time, and water: essays on environmental resource trade-offs. Dissertation, University of Alberta

Lohr L, Park TA (1995) Utility consistent discrete-continuous choices in soil conservation. Land Econ 71:474–490

Loomis JB (1997) Panel estimators to combine revealed and stated preference dichotomous choice data. J Agric Resour Econ 233–245

Lower Souris River Watershed (LSW) (2015) Lower Souris watershed newsletter. Spring 2015. http://www.lowersourisriverwatershed.com/files/LSW_Newsletter_-_Spring_2015.pdf. Accessed June 2015

Lusk JL, Norwood FB (2009) An inferred valuation method. Land Econ 85(3):500–514

Lynch L, Hardie I, Parker D (2002) Analyzing agricultural landowner's willingness to install streamside buffers. WP02–02. The University of Maryland, College Park Department of Agricultural and Resource Economics

McKelvey R, Palfrey TR (1992) An experimental study of the centipede game. Econometrica 60:803–836

Nape S, Frykblom P, Harrison GW et al (2003) Hypothetical bias and willingness to accept. Econ Lett 78(3):423–430

Noga W, Adamowicz WL (2014) A study of Canadian conservation offset programs- lessons learned from a review of programs, analysis of stakeholder perceptions, and investigation of transactions costs. Sustainable Prosperity. University of Ottawa

Novak L (2017) A reverse auction for wetland restoration in Southern Alberta. Dissertation, University of Alberta

Pannell DJ (2008) Public benefits, private benefits, and policy mechanism choice for land-use change for environmental benefits. Land Econ 84(2):225–240

Peng J, Van den Bulte C (2023) Participation vs. effectiveness in sponsored tweet campaigns: a quality-quantity conundrum. Management Science (forthcoming)

Porras I, Hope RA (2005) Using stated choice methods in the design of payments for environmental services schemes. Edinburgh, IIED. http://www.dfid.gov.uk/R4D/PDF/Outputs/Forestry/R8174Usingstatedchoicemethodsreport.pdf

Ready RC, Champ PA, Lawton JL (2010) Using respondent uncertainty to mitigate hypothetical bias in a stated choice experiment. Land Econ 86(2):363–381

Ruto E, Garrod G (2009) Investigating farmers' preferences for the design of agri-environmental schemes: a choice experiment approach. J Environ Plan Manag 52(5):631–647

Rutström EE, Williams MB (2000) Entitlements and fairness: an experimental study of distributive preferences. J Econ Behav Organ 43:75–89

Schilizzi S, Latacz-Lohmann U (2012) Evaluating conservation auctions with unknown bidder costs: the Scottish fishing vessel decommissioning program. Land Econ 88(4):658–673

Shaikh SL, Sun L, van Kooten GC (2007) Are agricultural values a reliable guide in determining landowners' decisions to create forest carbon sinks? Can J Agric Econ 55:97–114

Southgate D, Haab T, Lundine J et al (2009) Payments for environmental services and rural livelihood strategies in Ecuador and Guatemala. Environ Dev Econ 15:21–37

Stachtiaris S, Drichoutis A, Klonaris S (2013) Preference reversals in contingent and inferred valuation methods. Eur Rev Agric Econ 40(2):379–404

Trenholm R, Anderson T, Lantz V et al (2013) Landowner views on wetland enhancement and restoration in and adjacent to the Credit River Watershed. Research report prepared for Credit Valley Conservation, Mississauga, ON

Vanslembrouck I, Van Huylenbroeck G, Verbeke W (2002) Determinants of the willingness of Belgian farmers to participate in agri-environmental measures. J Agric Econ 53(3):489–511

Welsh MP, Poe GL (1998) Elicitation effects in contingent valuation: comparisons to a multiple bounded discrete choice approach. J Environ Econ Manag 36(2):170–185

Whittington D, Pagiola S (2011) Using contingent valuation in the design of payments for environmental services mechanisms: a review and assessment. MPRA Paper No. 32730, posted 10. August 2011 / 14:46, http://mpra.ub.uni-muenchen.de/32730/

Yu J, Belcher K (2011) An economic analysis of landowners' willingness to adopt wetland and riparian conservation management. Can J Agric Econ 59:207–222

Chapter 13
Sample Selection Models for Panel Data: Application to Labor Force Participation in India

Sutirtha Bandyopadhyay and Soham Sahoo

Abstract This chapter explores existing empirical methods to tackle sample selection bias in a panel data framework. In the first part of the chapter, we illustrate the theoretical foundations for estimating regression models where sample selection can potentially lead to bias and inconsistency in the estimates, with a special focus on the Heckman model. We explain the challenges of applying a standard selection model in the panel data framework, especially when fixed effects are used to aid in causal inference. We discuss the incidental parameters problem that arises in this context, as the selection model relies on a maximum likelihood estimation. We then discuss the solutions to this problem. In the second part of the chapter, we demonstrate a practical application of the method using data from India. We focus on the estimation of a standard wage regression when labor force participation is an endogenous decision. By applying the techniques covered in the first section of the chapter, we extend the study utilizing panel data.

Keywords Sample selection bias · Heckman model · Panel data · Female labor force participation · MGNREGS

Supplementary Information The online version contains supplementary material available at https://doi.org/10.1007/978-981-99-4902-1_13.

S. Bandyopadhyay
Indian Institute of Management Indore, Indore, India
e-mail: sutirthab@iimidr.ac.in

S. Sahoo (✉)
Indian Institute of Management Bangalore, Bengaluru, India
e-mail: soham.sahoo@iimb.ac.in

D. Mukherjee (ed.), *Applied Econometric Analysis Using Cross Section and Panel Data*, Contributions to Economics, https://doi.org/10.1007/978-981-99-4902-1_13

13.1 Introduction

Selection bias occurs in econometric analysis when the sample is not chosen randomly from the population of interest. A non-random sample fails to provide an appropriate description of the underlying population. Therefore, tackling sample selection bias is crucial in modern-day econometric analysis for making causal inferences. In this chapter, we discuss the possible causes of sample selection bias and ways to solve the problem, emphasizing on panel data. The sample selection issue in panel data requires special attention as one needs to solve the endogeneity caused by omitted unobserved time-invariant factors and the sample selection problem simultaneously. This chapter details the alternative methodologies (Wooldridge 1995; Rochina-Barrachina 1999) widely used by empirical practitioners to account for sample selection bias in panel data. An empirical application in the Indian context supports our theoretical discussion. Using panel data at the individual level from a nationally representative household survey, we examine the impact of a rural workfare program implementation on female labor income. This empirical exercise illustrates the sample selection problem in panel data setup and shows how suitable statistical techniques address the issue.

There is rich empirical literature that addresses the panel data sample selection problem. Using the German Socio-Economic Panel, Oaxaca and Choe (2016) analyzed wage decomposition methodology in the context of panel data sample selection. Ahn (2004) applied a non-parametric panel data sample selection model to remove bias caused by non-random selection in the medical claims data. Using the German Socio-Economic Panel data, Dustman and Rochina-Barrachina (2007) compared alternative panel estimators for estimating the wage returns to the experience of females. D'Addio et al. (2002) used panel data sample selection models to investigate whether unemployment traps exist and are significant in the transition from unemployment into employment in Belgium. Other important and notable contributions to the application of the panel data sample selection model include Semykina and Wooldridge (2018), Knoef and Bean (2015), and Chinnakum et al. (2013).

We discuss the different approaches while focusing on methods that have wide applicability. Especially, our empirical application in the second part of the chapter utilizes models that are easily implementable using data from developing countries. We follow Wooldridge (1995) to show that accounting for sample selection, the rural workfare program does not seem to have any impact on wage rate, although it does increase the likelihood of employment participation of women in rural India. This application relates to several studies in the literature that seek to explain the low female labor force participation rates in India and the role of public policies in this context (Afridi et al. 2016; Klasen and Pieters 2015; Sarkar et al. 2019).

13.2 Theoretical Framework

In this section, we discuss the theoretical framework for dealing with sample selection bias in cross-sectional and panel data settings.

13.2.1 Overview of Sample Selection Bias and Its Correction

There are several causes of non-random sample selection. Often the sample selection is non-random due to truncated sample which results from survey design. Occasional non-response to specific questions results in missing data for the dependent and independent variables. This leads to non-random sample selection as we cannot use these observations and dropping them may result in biased estimators.

Another major cause of non-random sample selection is incidental truncation. Think about how labor economics estimates the so-called wage offer function. We consider the pay offer to be the current wage for those who are working. We do not, however, observe the wage offer for those who are not currently employed. Therefore, wage offer is observable for an individual only if he/she decides to participate in the labor market. It is possible that the choice to work or to engage in the labor market is systematically connected with unobservable factors that influence the pay offer. Therefore, excluding those who are not employed could result in inaccurate parameter estimations for the wage offer equation.

To explain the non-random sample selection more formally, we write down the following population regression model:

$$y = \beta_0 + \beta_1 x_1 + \beta_2 x_2 + \cdots + \beta_k x_k + u,\ E(u|x_1, x_2, \ldots, x_k) = 0$$

The population model for a random draw can be written as

$$y_i = \boldsymbol{X}_i \boldsymbol{\beta} + u_i \tag{13.1}$$

where we use $\boldsymbol{X}_i \boldsymbol{\beta}$ as shorthand for $\beta_1 x_{i1} + \beta_2 x_{i2} + \cdots + \beta_k x_{ik}$ (the subscript i stands for 'i'th observation). Let n be the size of a sample drawn at random from the population. We would only apply Ordinary Least Squares (OLS) if we could witness y_i and each x_{ij} for all i. However, for some members of the sample, dependent or independent variables might not be present. We define a selection indicator d_i for each i. This selection indicator d_i takes the value 1 if we observe all of $(y_i, \boldsymbol{X}_i)$. Otherwise, it takes the value zero. Any observation is used in the analysis only if d_i =1. Therefore, in a selected sample, number of observations is fewer than the original sample.

In reality, we are only capable of estimating the equation:

$$d_i y_i = d_i \boldsymbol{X}_i \boldsymbol{\beta} + d_i u_i \tag{13.2}$$

The OLS estimators from Eq. (13.2) are consistent if:

$$E(du) = 0\, and\; E\big[(dx_j)(du)\big] = E\big[dx_j u\big] = 0$$

where d, x_j and u are random variables that represent the population. Since d_i is a binary variable, we have exploited the knowledge that $d^2 = d$.

The main statistical condition required for unbiased estimation of parameters is:

$$E(du|dx_1, dx_2, \ldots, dx_k) = 0$$

The above condition says that the conditional expectation of u given dx_j $(j =$ 1,2,...,$k)$ must be zero. This is a stronger restriction as the consistency of $\boldsymbol{\beta}s$ under OLS requires u to be uncorrelated with dx_j.

dx_j is a function of the explanatory variables if the binary variable d depends only on them. Therefore, the exogeneity of the independent variables implies that the variables $dx_1, dx_2, \ldots, dx_k$ are all uncorrelated with the error term u. This is an instance of exogenous sample selection where the exogenous explanatory variables alone control $d_i = 1$. Exogenous sample selection ensures consistent estimators under OLS. If the sample selection is entirely random i.e., d_i is independent of $(\boldsymbol{X}_i, u_i)$, then $E(dx_j u) = E(d)E(x_j u) = 0 \;\; (\forall j = 1, 2, \ldots, k)$. OLS is still consistent in this case.

The consistent estimation under OLS for the selected sample can be extended to instrumental variable estimation. Suppose one or more variables in the vector $\boldsymbol{X}$ are endogenous (i.e., correlated with the error term u). Assume that $\mathbf{Z}$ is a vector of exogenous variables that can be used as instruments for the endogenous variables. If the binary indicator d is determined entirely by the instrumental variables $\mathbf{Z}$ or determined by some other factors which are independent of u and $\mathbf{Z}$**,** then we can consistently estimate the parameters (i.e., $\boldsymbol{\beta}s$) using 2SLS method.

The estimation of the parameters under OLS becomes inconsistent when the correlation between the binary variable d and the error term is non-zero. Then the selected sample no longer remains exogenous. Consider a sample that has been reduced by the truncation from above. Suppose d_i =1 if $y_i \leq c_i$, where c_i represents the truncation threshold. Therefore, from Eq. (13.1) we can say that $y_i \leq c_i$ implies $u_i \leq c_i - \boldsymbol{X}_i\boldsymbol{\beta}$. As d_i depends on u_i, they will be correlated.

We already mentioned the concept of incidental truncation. It is a common form of sample selection problem which leads to inconsistent estimates of the parameters. Let us focus on incidental truncation in detail. As mentioned in the example at the beginning, wage offer is observed when the person is actually working at the time of the survey. We cannot, however, observe the wage for those who are not employed. As a result, the wage offer's truncation is incidental because it depends on another factor, specifically, labor force participation. The information on all explanatory variables are observed. The incidental truncation model can be represented in the following way:

$$y = \boldsymbol{x\beta} + u,\ E(u|x) = 0 \tag{13.3}$$

$$d = 1\left[\boldsymbol{z\gamma} + v \geq 0\right] \tag{13.4}$$

where d is 1 when we observe y, and 0 when we don't.

Assuming that the components of $\boldsymbol{x}$ and z are consistently observed, we write $\boldsymbol{x\beta} = \beta_0 + \beta_1 x_1 + \beta_2 x_2 + \cdots + \beta_k x_k$ and $\boldsymbol{z\gamma} = \gamma_0 + \gamma_1 z_1 + \gamma_2 z_2 + \cdots + \gamma_m z_m$.

Equation (13.3) is the relevant equation. We call this the main/response equation. Equation (13.4) is called the selection equation. The selection equation is dependent on the observable vector z and unobserved error term v. We assume that there is no correlation between z and the disturbance term of the main/response equation. The statistical condition for this assumption is written as $E(u|\boldsymbol{x}, z) = 0$. The sample selection equation also assumes that the error factor v is independent of z and $\boldsymbol{x}$. Additionally, we presume that v has a standard normal distribution. It is assumed that the error terms of the main and selection equations, u and v, are correlated and have a joint normal distribution. We can demonstrate the issue with sample selection caused by the correlation between u and v.

In order to show that, we take the expectation of Eq. (13.3) conditional on z and v by assuming that the error terms u and v are independent of z and also that $\boldsymbol{x}$ is a subset of z.

$$E(y|z, v) = \boldsymbol{x\beta} + E(u|z, v) = \boldsymbol{x\beta} + E(u|v)$$

Here u and v are independent of, therefore$E(u|z, v) = E(u|v)$. The assumption is that the error terms u and v have a joint normal distribution with a mean of zero. The dependency between u and v is written as $E(u|v) = \rho v$ for some parameter ρ that reflects the correlation between u and$v$. Therefore,

$$E(y|z, v) = \boldsymbol{x\beta} + \rho v \tag{13.5}$$

Although we cannot observe v, we can compute $E(y|z, d)$ by using Eq. (13.5).

$$E(y|z, d) = \boldsymbol{x\beta} + \rho E(v|z, d) \tag{13.6}$$

When $d = 1$, Eq. (13.6) is written as

$$E(y|z, d = 1) = \boldsymbol{x\beta} + \rho E(v|z, d = 1) \tag{13.7}$$

Now,

$$E(v|z, d = 1) = E(v|\boldsymbol{z\gamma} + v \geq 0) = E(v|v \geq -\boldsymbol{z\gamma})$$

If any random variable A follows standard normal distribution, the following well-known statistical result holds:

$$E(A|A \geq c) = \frac{\theta(c)}{1 - \varphi(c)}$$

where c is a constant, θ and φ represent standard normal probability density function (pdf) and standard normal cumulative distribution function (cdf) respectively.

As v follows the standard normal distribution, we can directly apply the above result and write down Eq. (13.7) as

$$E(y|z, d = 1) = \boldsymbol{x\beta} + \rho E(v|z, d = 1)$$

$$= \boldsymbol{x\beta} + \rho E(v|v \geq -\boldsymbol{z\gamma}) = \boldsymbol{x\beta} + \rho \frac{\theta(-\boldsymbol{z\gamma})}{1 - \varphi(-\boldsymbol{z\gamma})} \quad (13.8)$$

Using the symmetry of the standard normal distribution, we can write $\theta(-\boldsymbol{z\gamma}) = \theta(\boldsymbol{z\gamma})$ and $1 - \varphi(-\boldsymbol{z\gamma}) = \varphi(\boldsymbol{z\gamma})$.

Therefore, Eq. (13.8) can be re-written as

$$E(y|z, d = 1) = \boldsymbol{x\beta} + \rho \frac{\theta(\boldsymbol{z\gamma})}{\varphi(\boldsymbol{z\gamma})} = \boldsymbol{x\beta} + \rho\tau(\boldsymbol{z\gamma}) \quad (13.9)$$

τ is the ratio of pdf to cdf and it is called the Inverse Mills Ratio (IMR). The expected value of y, given z and observability of y, equals $\boldsymbol{x\beta}$, plus an additional term that depends on the Inverse Mills Ratio, according to Eq. (13.9). Therefore, in order to estimate $\boldsymbol{\beta}$ consistently, we need to include the term $\tau(\boldsymbol{z\gamma})$ as an additional regressor in the main equation i.e., Eq. (13.3).

When $= 0$, i.e., u and v are uncorrelated, the Inverse Mills Ratio $\tau(\boldsymbol{z\gamma})$ does not appear. Then we can consistently estimate $\boldsymbol{\beta}$ by running an OLS regression of y on $\boldsymbol{x}$ on the selected sample. Otherwise $\tau(\boldsymbol{z\gamma})$ is just like an omitted factor and it is usually associated with$\boldsymbol{x}$. As $\boldsymbol{\gamma}$ is unknown, we are unable to compute $\tau(z_i\boldsymbol{\gamma})$ for every observation$i$. However, given our assumptions (i.e., d is a binary variable, and the error term v follows standard normal distribution), d given z follows a probit model:

$$P(d = 1|z) = \varphi(\boldsymbol{z\gamma})$$

where P stands for probability and φ represents the standard normal distribution's cumulative distribution function (CDF).

Therefore, using the entire sample and running a probit regression of d_i on z_i, we can estimate $\boldsymbol{\gamma}$. Using the estimate of $\boldsymbol{\gamma}$, we can calculate the Inverse Mills Ratio for every observation i and use it as another regressor in the main equation to estimate $\boldsymbol{\beta}$ consistently. Heckman (1976) proposed this two-stage estimation process.

We can summarize this two-stage method more formally below:

(1) Using all the observations (say the entire sample size is n), we estimate a probit model of d_i on z_i. We derive the estimates of $\widehat{\gamma_k}$ ($\forall \gamma_k s\prime$ belongs to the vector

$\boldsymbol{\gamma}$). Then we obtain the Inverse Mills Ratio $\widehat{\tau_i} = \tau\left(z_i\widehat{\boldsymbol{\gamma}}\right)$ for each observation i by using the estimated vector $\widehat{\boldsymbol{\gamma}}$.

(ii) Suppose there are n_1 ($n_1 < n$) observations for which $d_i = 1$. We run the following regression on the chosen sample:

$$y_i \text{ on } \boldsymbol{x}_i, \quad \widehat{\tau_i}$$

The estimated $\widehat{\beta_j}s$ from the second step are consistent.

From the estimated coefficients in the second stage, we can test the sample selection bias by conducting a t test of the coefficient of $\widehat{\tau_i}$. The null hypothesis is $H_0 : \rho = 0$. We can rule out sample selection bias if null hypothesis can't be rejected.

When $\neq 0$, the usual OLS standard errors reported from second stage are not accurate. This is because they do not use the estimation of $\boldsymbol{\gamma}$. Modern econometric packages compute corrected standard errors.

Two consequences follow from the presumption that $\boldsymbol{x}$ must be a strict subset of z. First of all, the selection equation should include all factors that appear as an independent variable in the main equation. Second, at least one element in z does not appear in $\boldsymbol{x}$. The second implication is very crucial as the Inverse Mills Ratio is very often linearly related to $\boldsymbol{x}$. If $\boldsymbol{x} = z$, our estimate of $\boldsymbol{\beta}$ will suffer from multicollinearity and we will likely have very large standard errors of the coefficients. Therefore if $\boldsymbol{x} = z$, the attempt to correct the sample selection bias may well lead to a misspecified empirical model. If the set of covariates are same for the main/response equation and the selection equation, then we need sufficient/enough observations at the tail of the distribution of the covariates as the Inverse Mills Ratio is usually non-linearly related to the covariates for the extreme values. If we do not have enough observations at the tail, credible estimates are only ensured through exclusion restriction i.e., the vector z should contain all elements of $\boldsymbol{x}$ and there must be one element in z which is not included in the vector $\boldsymbol{x}$.

The Heckman sample selection model also deals with endogenous explanatory variable in the main/response equation. Then the sample selection bias and the endogeneity issue need to be tackled simultaneously. By estimating the selection equation, one can compute the Inverse Mills Ratio. Including the Inverse Mills Ratio in the main/response equation, we can run a 2SLS regression. We require two exogenous variables that are not part of the main equation in order to be convincing. The selection decision should be influenced by one, and the endogenous explanatory variable should be associated with the other.

13.2.2 Panel Data Sample Selection

A major advantage of using panel data when carrying out econometric analysis is that it takes account of unobservable heterogeneity. This suggests that selection bias as well as unobserved heterogeneity need to be dealt with in parallel when we're discussing the issue of sampling on a panel data set. The panel estimators can resolve both problems if the selection procedure does not change over time. For instance, if the unobservable factors that affect whether someone chooses to participate in the labor market remain constant over time, the time-demeaned or time-differenced panel estimator will account for selection bias. But there are a lot of cases where it does not happen. Lately, a number of estimators have been suggested to address both sources of estimation bias.

It is easy to extend the sample selection model to panel data. Following Wooldridge (1995), we can represent it in the following way:

$$y_{it} = \boldsymbol{x}_{it}\boldsymbol{\beta} + \alpha_i + u_{it}; i = 1, 2, \ldots, N \& t = 1, 2, \ldots, T \tag{13.10}$$

$$d_{it} = 1\left[z_{it}\boldsymbol{\gamma} + \delta_i + v_{it} \geq 0\right] \tag{13.11}$$

An individual/unit of observation is represented by the subscript i, while a time period is represented by the subscript t. $1[.]$ stands for the indicator function. It takes the value one when the argument is true, and zero otherwise. In addition, $\boldsymbol{\beta}$ and $\boldsymbol{\gamma}$ are unknown parameter vectors, and $\boldsymbol{x}_{it}$, and z_{it} include both time variant and time invariant explanatory variables, as well as time effects. Individual-specific effects such as α_i and δ_i are unobservable and time-invariant and may be related to $\boldsymbol{x}_{it}$ and z_{it}. Unobserved disturbances are u_{it} and v_{it}. If $d_{it} = 1$, then the variable is observed. Estimating the parameter vector $\boldsymbol{\beta}$ is our goal.

When panel data is available, we can estimate Eq. (13.10) in levels by pooled ordinary least squares. This results in consistent estimates of $\boldsymbol{\beta}$ if the unobserved time invariant individual heterogeneity term as well as the time varying error term is uncorrelated to the set of explanatory variables and the sample selection is random. This is explained by the following statistical condition:

$$E(\alpha_i + u_{it}|\boldsymbol{x}_{it}, d_{it} = 1) = E(\alpha_i|\boldsymbol{x}_{it}, d_{it} = 1) + E(u_{it}|\boldsymbol{x}_{it}, d_{it} = 1) = 0\forall t \tag{13.12}$$

Condition (13.12) gets violated if the selection is not random i.e., $E(u_{it}|\boldsymbol{x}_{it}, d_{it} = 1) \neq 0$ and/or there is associated individual heterogeneity, i.e., $E(\alpha_i|\boldsymbol{x}_{it}, d_{it} = 1) \neq 0$. The conditional expectation in (13.12) is not equal to zero if either of these two scenarios is true and that leads to inconsistent OLS estimate on the chosen subsample.

One method of eliminating the fixed effect α_i is to use some kind of demeaned/ differenced estimator. The time differenced equation corresponding to equation of interest (13.10) can be written as

$$y_{it} - y_{is} = \boldsymbol{x}_{it}\boldsymbol{\beta} - \boldsymbol{x}_{is}\boldsymbol{\beta} + u_{it} - u_{is}, s \neq t \tag{13.13}$$

where s and t denote the time periods.

The following statement represents the consistency requirement for an estimator using differences across time as opposed to level equations.

$$E(u_{it} - u_{is}|\boldsymbol{x}_{it}, \boldsymbol{x}_{is}, d_{it} = d_{is} = 1) = 0; s \neq t \tag{13.14}$$

Since condition (13.14) puts no restriction on how the selection mechanism or the regressors relate to α_i, differencing Eq. (13.10) across time (which leads to Eq. (13.13)) eliminates not only any potential selection issue that operates through α_i, but also the issue of correlated individual heterogeneity.

The OLS estimator or the differenced estimator, respectively, leads to consistent estimates if condition (13.12) or condition (13.14) are met. If these conditions are violated, we need to consider the selection process for consistent estimation in the panel data framework. An expression for (13.12) is derived by Wooldridge (1995) and added to the relevant equation, which is (13.10). The Rochina-Barrachina (1999) estimator creates an expression for the expected value in (13.14) by adding a second regressor to the differenced Eq. (13.13).

Following the steps below, we can derive the expression by Wooldridge (1995).

1. As suggested by Mundlak (1978) and Chamberlain (1980), observation-specific (individual/household/firm/any other unit) fixed effects in the selection equation are expressed as a linear function of the unit/observation-specific average values of the observed explanatory variables.

$$\delta_i = \eta_0 + \overline{z}_i\boldsymbol{\eta} + e_i \; i = 1, 2, \ldots, N \tag{13.15}$$

where e_i is the stochastic variable which is uncorrelated to any other factors and $\overline{z}_i$ represents the average of the explanatory variables (averaged over time) in the selection equation.

2. The selection equation is reduced to the following form:

$$d_{it} = 1\left[\eta_0 + \overline{z}_i\boldsymbol{\eta} + z_{it}\boldsymbol{\gamma} + \varepsilon_{it} \geq 0\right] \tag{13.16}$$

where $\varepsilon_{it} = e_i + v_{it}$.

3. We assume that ε_{it} is independent of $\tilde{z}_i$ and $\varepsilon_{it} \sim Normal(0, \sigma_t^2)$, where $\tilde{z}_i = (\boldsymbol{x}_i, z_i)$ with $\boldsymbol{x}_i = (x_{i1}, x_{i2}, \ldots, x_{iT})$ and $z_i = (z_{i1}, z_{i2}, \ldots, z_{iT})$. The vectors $\boldsymbol{x}_i$ and z_i represent the leads and lags of the explanatory variables.
4. The conditional expectation of α_i (i.e., the fixed effects in the main equation) given $\boldsymbol{x}_i$ and ε_{it}, is written in the following linear form (following Mundlak 1978; Nijman and Veerbek 1992; Zabel 1992):

$$E\left(\alpha_i | \tilde{z}_i, \varepsilon_{it}\right) = \psi_0 + \overline{\boldsymbol{x}}_i\boldsymbol{\psi} + \pi_t\varepsilon_{it} \tag{13.17}$$

where $\overline{\boldsymbol{x}}_i$ is the average of the explanatory variables (averaged over time) in the main/response equation. We do not observe ε_{it}, however, but only the binary selection indicator d_{it}. We can use Eq. (13.17) to compute $E\left(\alpha_i|\,\widetilde{z}_i, d_{it}\right)$.

$$E\left(\alpha_i|\,\widetilde{z}_i, d_{it}\right) = \psi_0 + \overline{\boldsymbol{x}}_i\boldsymbol{\psi} + \pi_t E\left(\varepsilon_{it}\middle|\widetilde{z}_i, d_{it}\right) \tag{13.18}$$

When $d_{it} = 1$, Eq. (13.18) is written as

$$E(\alpha_i|\widetilde{z}_i, d_{it} = 1) = \psi_0 + \overline{\boldsymbol{x}}_i\boldsymbol{\psi} + \pi_t E(\varepsilon_{it}|\widetilde{z}_i, d_{it} = 1) \tag{13.19}$$

5. Finally, we also assume that

$$E\left(u_{it}|\,\widetilde{z}_i, \varepsilon_{it}\right) = E(u_{it}|\varepsilon_{it}) = \rho_t\varepsilon_{it} \tag{13.20}$$

Expression (13.20) implies that u_{it} is mean independent of $\widetilde{z}_i$ conditional on ε_{it} and its conditional mean is linear in ε_{it}. As ε_{it} is unknown, we combine $E\left(u_{it}|\,\widetilde{z}_i, d_{it}\right)$ with the observed binary selection indicator d_{it}. We can write down the following:

$$E\left(u_{it}|\,\widetilde{z}_i, d_{it}\right) = \rho_t E(\varepsilon_{it}|d_{it}) \tag{13.21}$$

When $d_{it} = 1$, Eq. (13.21) is written as

$$E\left(u_{it}|\,\widetilde{z}_i, d_{it} = 1\right) = \rho_t E(\varepsilon_{it}|d_{it} = 1) \tag{13.22}$$

Combining Eqs. (13.19) and (13.22) and all the assumptions explained in steps 1–5, we can derive an explicit expression for $E\left(\alpha_i + u_{it}|\,\widetilde{z}_i, d_{it} = 1\right)$ and this turns out to be

$$E\left(\alpha_i + u_{it}|\,\widetilde{z}_i, d_{it} = 1\right) = \psi_0 + \overline{\boldsymbol{x}}_i\boldsymbol{\psi} + (\pi_t + \rho_t)E\left(\varepsilon_{it}\middle|\widetilde{z}_i, d_{it} = 1\right) \tag{13.23}$$

The main/response equation is modified according to the econometric structure written above and we can write it as

$$E\left(y_{it}|\,\widetilde{z}_i, d_{it} = 1\right) = \psi_0 + \overline{\boldsymbol{x}}_i\boldsymbol{\psi} + \boldsymbol{x}_{it}\boldsymbol{\beta} + \zeta_t E\left(\varepsilon_{it}\middle|\widetilde{z}_i, d_{it} = 1\right) \tag{13.24}$$

where $\zeta_t = \pi_t + \rho_t$. When $d_{it} = 1$, from the reduced form of the selection equation in (13.16) we obtain $\varepsilon_{it} \geq -(\eta_0 + \overline{z}_i\boldsymbol{\eta} + z_{it}\boldsymbol{\gamma})$.

Therefore,

$$\begin{aligned} E(y_{it}|\widetilde{z}_i, d_{it} = 1) &= \psi_0 + \overline{\boldsymbol{X}}_i\boldsymbol{\psi} + \boldsymbol{x}_{it}\boldsymbol{\beta} + \zeta_t E(\varepsilon_{it}|\widetilde{z}_i, d_{it} = 1) \\ &= \psi_0 + \overline{\boldsymbol{X}}_i\boldsymbol{\psi} + \boldsymbol{x}_{it}\boldsymbol{\beta} + \zeta_t E(\varepsilon_{it}|\varepsilon_{it} \geq -(\eta_0 + \overline{z}_i\boldsymbol{\eta} + z_{it}\boldsymbol{\gamma})) \end{aligned} \tag{13.25}$$

Since ε_{it} has a normal distribution with mean 0 and variance σ_t^2, $\varepsilon_{it}/\sigma_t$ follows standard normal distribution (with mean 0 and variance 1).[1] Therefore, following the property of a standard normal distribution already mentioned in Sect. 2.1, we can write the following expression:

$$E[(\varepsilon_{it}/\sigma_t)|(\varepsilon_{it}/\sigma_t) \geq -((\eta_0 + \overline{z}_i\boldsymbol{\eta} + z_{it}\boldsymbol{\gamma})/\sigma_t)] = \frac{\widetilde{\theta}\ (-(\eta_0 + \overline{z}_i\boldsymbol{\eta} + z_{it}\boldsymbol{\gamma})/\sigma_t)}{1-\widetilde{\varphi}\ (-(\eta_0 + \overline{z}_i\boldsymbol{\eta} + z_{it}\boldsymbol{\gamma})/\sigma_t)}$$

As σ_t is constant, the expression above can also be re-written as

$$E(\varepsilon_{it}|\varepsilon_{it} \geq -(\eta_0 + \overline{z}_i\boldsymbol{\eta} + z_{it}\boldsymbol{\gamma})) = \sigma_t\frac{\widetilde{\theta}\ (-(\eta_0 + \overline{z}_i\boldsymbol{\eta} + z_{it}\boldsymbol{\gamma})/\sigma_t)}{1-\widetilde{\varphi}\ (-(\eta_0 + \overline{z}_i\boldsymbol{\eta} + z_{it}\boldsymbol{\gamma})/\sigma_t)}$$

As the normal distribution follows symmetry around mean, we can write $\widetilde{\theta}\ (-(\eta_0 + \overline{z}_i\boldsymbol{\eta} + z_{it}\boldsymbol{\gamma})/\sigma_t) = \widetilde{\theta}\ ((\eta_0 + \overline{z}_i\boldsymbol{\eta} + z_{it}\boldsymbol{\gamma})/\sigma_t)$ and $1-\widetilde{\varphi}\ (-(\eta_0 + \overline{z}_i\boldsymbol{\eta} + z_{it}\boldsymbol{\gamma})/\sigma_t) = \widetilde{\varphi}\ ((\eta_0 + \overline{z}_i\boldsymbol{\eta} + z_{it}\boldsymbol{\gamma})/\sigma_t)$. and $\widetilde{\varphi}$ represent standard normal pdf and standard normal cdf respectively.

As shown earlier, $\tau_t = \frac{\widetilde{\theta}((\eta_0+\overline{z}_i\boldsymbol{\eta}+z_{it}\boldsymbol{\gamma})/\sigma_t)}{\widetilde{\varphi}((\eta_0+\overline{z}_i\boldsymbol{\eta}+z_{it}\boldsymbol{\gamma})/\sigma_t)}$ is the Inverse Mills Ratio and using it we can re-write Eq. (13.25) as

$$E\left(y_{it}|\ \widetilde{z}_i, d_{it} = 1\right) = \psi_0 + \overline{\boldsymbol{X}}_i\boldsymbol{\psi} + \boldsymbol{x}_{it}\boldsymbol{\beta} + \mu_t\tau_{it}\left(\frac{\eta_0 + \overline{z}_i\boldsymbol{\eta} + z_{it}\boldsymbol{\gamma}}{\sigma_t}\right) \tag{13.26}$$

where $\mu_t = \sigma_t\tau_t$.

A consistent estimate of $\boldsymbol{\beta}$ is obtained from Eq. 13.26 following a few steps. The procedure is fairly similar to those that were described in Sect. 2.1 when discussing the sample selection problem in cross sectional data. First, the reduced form sample selection equation (Eq. 13.16) is estimated using standard probit model for each time period t, and the Inverse Mills ratio i.e. τ_{it} is estimated from the estimated $\widehat{\boldsymbol{\gamma}}$, $\widehat{\boldsymbol{\eta}}$ and $\widehat{\eta_0}$. These Inverse Mills Ratios are then added as extra regressors to Eq. (13.26) in the following phase. Wooldridge (1995) proposes to estimate Eq. (13.26) using either pooled OLS regression or minimum distance regression. The selection equation should have an additional variable in z that is legitimately removed from $\boldsymbol{x}$ in the main/outcome equation. This will make it easier to identify the selection equation.

The fixed effects in the selection equation (i.e., δ_i) and main/response equation (i.e., α_i) are so far assumed to be a linear function of the time average of the z and $\boldsymbol{x}$ variables respectively. Alternatively, following Chamberlain (1984), Wooldridge (1995), one can write down δ_i as a linear function in the leads and lags of the observable variables:

[1] If a random variable X $\sim$ $Normal(0, \sigma^2)$, then X/σ follows standard normal distribution with mean 0 and variance 1.

$$\delta_i = \eta_0 + \boldsymbol{Z}_{i1}\boldsymbol{\eta}_1 + \boldsymbol{Z}_{i2}\boldsymbol{\eta}_2 + \cdots + \boldsymbol{Z}_{iT}\boldsymbol{\eta}_T + e_i \tag{13.15A}$$

Similarly, the conditional mean of α_i given $\boldsymbol{x}_i$ and ε_{it} is written as the leads and lags of the $\boldsymbol{x}$ variables:

$$E\left(\alpha_i \middle| \tilde{z}_i, \varepsilon_{it}\right) = \psi_0 + \boldsymbol{x}_{i1}\boldsymbol{\psi}_1 + \boldsymbol{x}_{i2}\boldsymbol{\psi}_2 + \cdots + \boldsymbol{x}_{iT}\boldsymbol{\psi}_T + \pi_t\varepsilon_{it} \tag{13.17A}$$

Based on the assumptions written in (13.15A) and (13.17A), we can write down the main/response equation as:

$$E\left(y_{it} \middle| \tilde{z}_i, d_{it} = 1\right) = \psi_0 + \overline{\boldsymbol{X}}_i\boldsymbol{\psi} + \boldsymbol{x}_{it}\boldsymbol{\beta} + \mu_t\tau_{it}\left(\frac{H_{it}}{\sigma_t}\right) \tag{13.26A}$$

where in the selection equation for period t, $H_{it} = \eta_0 + \boldsymbol{Z}_{i1}\boldsymbol{\eta}_{t1} + \boldsymbol{Z}_{i2}\boldsymbol{\eta}_{t2} + \cdots + \boldsymbol{Z}_{iT}\boldsymbol{\eta}_{tT}$ is the reduced form index and $\tau_{it}\left(\frac{H_{it}}{\sigma_t}\right) = E\left(\varepsilon_{it} \middle| \tilde{z}_i, d_{it} = 1\right)$ is the inverse Mills Ratio. By taking the same processes outlined in expressions (13.15)–(13.23), one can get to expression (13.26A). The estimation is also done in a similar way.

As a first step, a probit on $H_{it} = \eta_0 + \boldsymbol{Z}_{i1}\boldsymbol{\eta}_{t1} + \boldsymbol{Z}_{i2}\boldsymbol{\eta}_{t2} + \cdots + \boldsymbol{Z}_{iT}\boldsymbol{\eta}_{tT}$ is estimated for each t in order to obtain estimates for $\tau(.)$. Next, we estimate Eq. (13.26A) either by minimum distance or by pooled OLS regression.

The outcome variable in the outcome/main equation can be a binary variable. After adding the Inverse Mills Ratio, we can then estimate the outcome equation using a linear probability model. When the outcome equation is also estimated as a probit model (along with the selection equation), we call it bivariate probit with sample selection. As an example of this model, Berinsky (2004) investigates attitudes toward race in his book. He claims that because he only monitors racial sentiments among people who are willing to respond to the inquiry, he has a selected sample. In this manner, the first probit model is whether respondents agreed to respond on racial discrimination, and the second probit model is the respondent's binary position on racial issues.

For individuals meeting $d_{it} = d_{is} = 1, t \neq s$, the estimator developed by Rochina-Barrachina (1999) is based on Eq. (13.10) for pairwise differencing. The conditional expectation in (13.14), which was parameterized, is the foundation of Rochina-Barrachina's (1999) estimator. The following assumptions are used in the estimator's implementation:

1. The selection equation's fixed effect, δ_i has a linear regression function on z_i that is linear in both the leads and lags of the observable variables as illustrated in (13.15A).
2. The errors in the selection equation is $\varepsilon_{it} = e_i + v_{it}$. The error term follows normal distribution with mean 0 and variance σ_t^2 conditional on $\tilde{z}_i$.
3. The error terms $[(u_{it} - u_{is}), \varepsilon_{it}, \varepsilon_{is}]$ are trivariate normally distributed conditional on $\tilde{z}_i$.

The first two assumptions, which deal with the selection equation, are comparable to those used to derive the Wooldridge estimator (1995). The joint conditional distribution of the error terms in the two equations is constrained by the third assumption.

Under the three assumptions mentioned above, the resulting estimation equation is given by (details of the derivation is shown in Rochina-Barrachina 1999):

$$y_{it} - y_{is} = (\boldsymbol{x}_{it} - \boldsymbol{x}_{is})\boldsymbol{\beta} + \mu_{ts}\tau(\frac{H_{it}}{\sigma_t}, \frac{H_{is}}{\sigma_s}, \omega_{ts}) + \mu_{st}\tau(\frac{H_{is}}{\sigma_s}, \frac{H_{it}}{\sigma_t}, \omega_{ts}) \quad (13.27)$$

where $H_{iS} = \eta_0 + \boldsymbol{Z}_{i1}\boldsymbol{\eta}_{S1} + \boldsymbol{Z}_{i2}\boldsymbol{\eta}_{S2} + \cdots + \boldsymbol{Z}_{iT}\boldsymbol{\eta}_{ST}, S = t, s$ are the resulting reduced form indices in the selection equation for periods t and s, and $\omega_{ts} = \omega_{(\frac{\varepsilon_t}{\sigma_t})(\frac{\varepsilon_s}{\sigma_s})}$ is the correlation coefficient between the errors in the selection equation. In addition, $\mu_{ts}\tau(\frac{H_{it}}{\sigma_t}, \frac{H_{is}}{\sigma_s}, \omega_{ts}) + \mu_{st}\tau(\frac{H_{is}}{\sigma_s}, \frac{H_{it}}{\sigma_t}, \omega_{ts})$ is the conditional mean $E\left(u_{it} - u_{is} | \tilde{z}_i, d_{it} = d_{is} = 1\right)$ derived from the three-dimensional normal distribution assumption.[2]

In particular, $\tau\left(\frac{H_{it}}{\sigma_t}, \frac{H_{is}}{\sigma_s}, \omega_{ts}\right) = \frac{\theta(\frac{H_{it}}{\sigma_t})\varphi(M^*_{its})}{\varphi_2(\frac{H_{it}}{\sigma_t}, -\frac{H_{is}}{\sigma_t}, \omega_{ts})}$ and $\tau\left(\frac{H_{is}}{\sigma_s}, \frac{H_{it}}{\sigma_t}, \omega_{ts}\right) = \frac{\theta(\frac{H_{is}}{\sigma_s})\varphi(M^*_{ist})}{\varphi_2(\frac{H_{it}}{\sigma_t}, \frac{H_{is}}{\sigma_t}, \omega_{ts})}$, where $M^*_{its} = \frac{(H_{is} - \omega_{ts}H_{it})}{(1-\omega^2_{ts})^{(\frac{1}{2})}}$ and $M^*_{ist} = \frac{(H_{it} - \omega_{ts}H_{is})}{(1-\omega^2_{ts})^{(\frac{1}{2})}}$, $\theta(.)$. is the standard normal density and $\varphi(.)$ and $\varphi_2(.)$ are standard univariate and bivariate standard normal cumulative distribution function. The conditional expectation associated with the new error term $u^*_{its} = (u_{it} - u_{is}) - [\mu_{ts}\tau_{its} + \mu_{st}\tau_{ist}]$ turns out to be $E(u^*_{its} | \tilde{z}_i, \varepsilon_{it} \le H_{it}, \varepsilon_{is} \le H_{is}) = 0$. Estimates of the $\tau(.)$ terms i.e., the Inverse Mills Ratio will be constructed utilizing the reduced form coefficients $(\boldsymbol{\eta}_t, \boldsymbol{\eta}_s)$, which will be determined with ω_{ts}, using a bivariate probit model for each combination of time periods. Equation (13.27) is then estimated using OLS. Therefore, Rochina-Barrachina (1999) adds the Inverse Mills Ratio as an additional regressor to the differenced Eq. (13.13) rather than the level form Eq. (13.10) as Wooldridge (1995) did. In this way, the two estimators are different.

The estimator proposed by Rochina-Barrachina (1999) and Wooldridge (1995) assumes that regressors in the main equation are strictly exogenous. The strict exogeneity condition often fails to hold in empirical applications (once individual heterogeneity and sample selection have been considered). But the estimation method proposed by Rochina-Barrachina (1999) and Wooldridge (1995) can be extended in order to incorporate endogenous regressors into the main equation. A way to do that is to use generalized method of moments IV estimator. Strict exogeneity is also violated in the presence of measurement error and this issue can be addressed too.

The panel data sample selection models can also be extended to dynamic panel data models. In a dynamic panel data model with sample selection, we typically assume a lagged dependent variable in the main equation/equation of interest. In their work, Bernard and Jensen (1999) specify the first stage as a dynamic linear

[2] For details, see Rochina-Barrachina (1999).

probability model. Semykina and Wooldridge (2013) consider dynamic panel data models, where estimation of the equation of interest may be subject to selection bias. They propose a new method for estimating such models, as well as a simple test for selection bias. The test is based on the inclusion of a selection term to the first differenced equation, followed by a test of the selection term's significance. The lagged dependent variable is substituted backwards to provide an estimating equation that only needs to be corrected for selection in one period. Other notable works on the estimation of the dynamic panel data sample selection model include Gayle and Viauroux (2007) and Raymond et al. (2010), Sasaki (2015), and Lai and Tsay (2012).

13.3 Empirical Application

In this section, we discuss an application of the empirical approach to tackle sample selection issue in panel data framework.

a. Background and Hypothesis

The impact of rural workfare programs on the economy, especially on the livelihoods of people, is an important question in development economics. We test the hypothesis that such a program initiated by the Indian government would impact the wage rates of female workers in the rural areas of India. Specifically, we investigate this question in the context of the Mahatma Gandhi National Rural Employment Guarantee Scheme (MGNREGS) initiated by the Indian government in 2006.[3] This scheme was implemented following an Act of the Indian parliament and it was devised as a right to work program. Every rural household would be granted the right to 100 days of manual labor employment at a predetermined minimum pay. The program offered equal wage rate to men and women for the same type of work and targeted at least one-third of the beneficiaries to be women. This aspect of the scheme makes it especially relevant to investigate whether it impacted the wage rate of rural women.

MGNREGS can affect the wage rate of workers through multiple channels. First, the policy of offering wage rate at least at the level prescribed by the statutory minimum wage rate law is better enforced in this program than in the private labor market. Thus, workers engaged in this public scheme may get a higher wage rate than elsewhere. Apart from this direct effect, the program can have general equilibrium effects on the rural labor market. For instance, availability of public works and better wages through MGNREGS may crowd out private sector employment and increase private sector wages (Imbert and Papp 2015). Therefore, the program can affect an individuals' likelihood of being employed as well as the wage rates.

The inception of the scheme coincides with a period marked by low and declining female labor force participation rate (FLFPR) in rural India (Klasen and Pieters 2015).

[3] The scheme was implemented in a phased manner across the districts, starting in 2006 and covering all the districts by 2008.

The existing literature has delved into understanding the potential explanations for the low labor market attachment of women during a period of high economic growth, falling fertility rate, and rising education levels of women in India (Sarkar et al. 2019). Against this backdrop, some studies have also shown that MGNREGS increased FLFPR due to its emphasis target on having women as beneficiaries of the public works program (Afridi et al. 2016). The existing literature has also shown that the scheme had a general equilibrium effect by not only increasing the income of the poor but also raising aggregate economic output (Berg et al. 2018; Cook and Shah 2022).

b. Data Description

Given this background motivation, we intend to test if the intensity of implementation of MGNREGS had any impact on rural women's wage rates. We utilize the nationally representative panel data from the India Human Development Survey (IHDS). IHDS collected information from the same set of households twice, first in 2004–05 and second in 2011–12. Since the same households and individuals living in the households were tracked, we construct a balanced panel of 22,352 women who were aged 25–55 years in the baseline; since we have two time periods, our sample consists of 44,704 observations. The main outcome variables we are interested in is the hourly wage rate received by these women. The main treatment variable is the district-level average amount of funds sanctioned for MGNREGS since its inception until 2011, i.e., before the survey. This variable reflects the intensity of the program implementation in the district. We present the summary statistics of these variables along with other covariates in Table 13.1. Figure 13.1 shows the bivariate relationship of average MGNREGS funds with the changes in employment participation rate and average earnings at the district level. We find that there is a weak positive correlation of funds with both these outcome variables.

c. Empirical Strategy

The straightforward approach to estimating the average impact of the program on women's wage rate would be to estimate a linear regression using the OLS method. There are two challenges to this approach in our context. First, the outcome variable, i.e., wage rate, is available for only women engaged in casual wage labor (agriculture or non-agriculture) and salaried employment. Over the two time periods, around 31% of the women in our sample are employed in such activities. These employed women may be systematically different in unobservable characteristics from women not employed in these occupations. This leads to the possibility of sample selection bias if we estimate the regression on the selected sample of employed women for whom we have information on hourly wage rate.

The second empirical challenge is the potential omitted variable bias due to unobserved district level heterogeneity being correlated with both the intensity of MGNREGS implementation and women's labor market outcomes. This possibility arises because, among other reasons, the workfare program was envisaged as a demand-driven program. Thus, pre-existing variation in women's engagement in the labor market may drive program intensity. For instance, in districts where workers

Table 13.1 Summary statistics

	(1)	(2)	(3)
Variables	N	Mean	sd
Log of hourly income	13,996	2.080	0.754
Participation in salaried/casual wage employment	44,704	0.313	0.464
Household size	44,704	5.882	3.023
Primary educated	44,704	0.112	0.315
Secondary educated	44,704	0.186	0.389
Tertiary educated	44,704	0.0130	0.113
Age	44,704	41.65	9.495
Square of age	44,704	1.825	817.2
Caste: OBC	44,704	0.409	0.492
Caste: SC	44,704	0.216	0.411
Caste: ST	44,704	0.0999	0.300
Religion: Muslim	44,704	0.0928	0.290
Religion: Others	44,704	0.0772	0.267
Average MGNREGS funds in district	44,704	3.450	5.880
Average rainfall in district (standardized)	44,704	−0.0601	0.958
Average nightlights in district (standardized)	44,704	−0.209	0.454
Year dummy	44,704	0.500	0.500

Source IHDS 2004–05 and 2011–12 data. Information on MGNREGS funds is obtained from the official website of Ministry of Rural Development, Government of India. Rainfall and nightlights data are obtained from the India Meteorological Department and the National Oceanic and Atmospheric Administration of the US Government. The nightlights data are processed using Indian district level shape files to generate district level estimates

are more empowered historically, they may earn higher wages and demand more employment as part of the workfare program. Insofar as these unobserved factors are time-invariant, we can control for them using fixed effects.

We implement the model prescribed by Wooldridge (1995) and discussed in Sect. 2.2 to tackle the dual problem of sample selection and unobserved heterogeneity in this context. In particular, we estimate the sample selection model including the Mundlak or the Chamberlain version of individual fixed effects. The selection equation denotes the binary choice of employment participation given below:

$$\begin{aligned} &P\left(Participation_{idt} = 1 | X_{idt}, W_{id}, Z_{idt}, \overline{X}_{id}, \overline{Z}_{id}\right) \\ &= \Phi\left(\alpha_0 + \alpha_1 X_{idt} + \alpha_2 W_{id} + \alpha_3 Z_{idt} + \gamma_1 \overline{X}_{id} + \gamma_2 \overline{Z}_{id}\right) \end{aligned} \tag{13.28}$$

The outcome variable $Participation_{idt}$ is a binary indicator of whether woman i from district d in time period t participated in employment. The time varying explanatory variables are denoted by X_{idt} and include the main treatment variable,

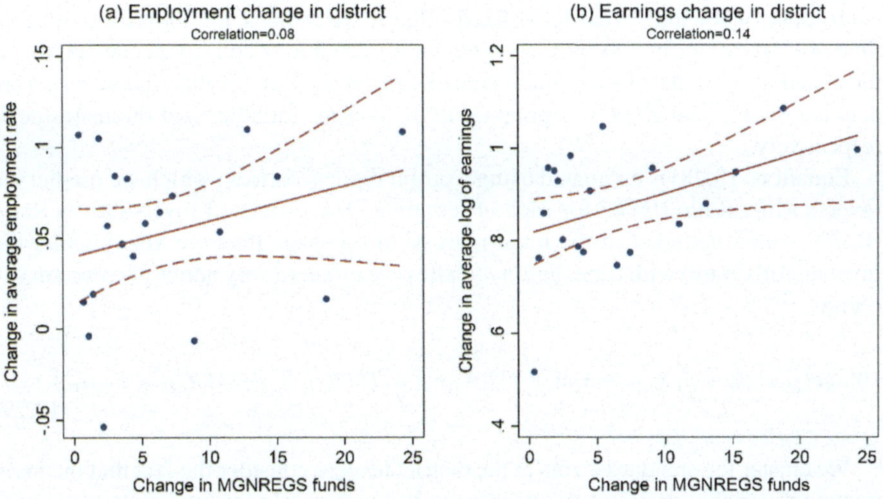

Fig. 13.1 Bivariate relationship of changes in women's employment participation and earnings with MGNREGS funds sanctioned in the district. *Note* This graph shows the binned scatter plot of the bivariate relationship between change in women's average employment participation and average MGNREGS funds sanctioned (panel a) and women's average log of earnings and average MGNREGS funds sanctioned (panel b) at the district level. The linear fit with 95% confidence interval is shown along with the scatter plot for each graph. The bivariate correlation coefficients are also indicated

i.e., average MGNREGS funds sanctioned prior to the respective round of the survey.[4] Other time varying individual controls include the woman's age, age squared, and education level.[5] We also include the following time varying controls at the district level that can affect demand for labor and wages: average rainfall and average night-time luminosity representing overall development of the region in the year preceding to the survey. W_{id} includes time-invariant controls such as caste and religion of the individual. Further, the selection equation should include a variable (instrument) that is likely to affect employment participation but not wage rate directly. We posit that household size is likely to affect women's participation, but it is unlikely to affect the hourly wage rate she receives once she participates in the labor market.

---

[4] Since MGNREGS did not exist before the first round of IHDS survey, the treatment variable takes the value 0 for every observation in the baseline. In an individual fixed effects estimation framework, therefore, the entire variation in the treatment variable is driven by the variation in the values across districts in the endline. In other words, if we were to estimate the model using first difference, the change in the treatment variable would be measured by: $\Delta Treatment_d = Treatment_{d2} - Treatment_{d1} = Treatment_{d2}$, since $Treatment_{d1} = 0 \forall d$. This is a special feature of the program we evaluate here, and it does not have any implication for the overall applicability of the model we estimate.

[5] The linear term for age changes by 7 years between the rounds for every individual; thus, it is perfectly collinear with time fixed effects. Therefore, we do not explicitly include time fixed effects in the regression although it is subsumed in age and is controlled for.

To control for individual level fixed effects, we include the individual-specific time averages of each time-varying explanatory variable as additional control; this is the Mundlak versions of individual fixed effects (Wooldridge 1995). These terms are denoted by $\overline{X}_{id}$ and $\overline{Z}_{id}$ corresponding to the control variables and the instrument, respectively.

Equation (13.28) is estimated using a probit regression from which we predict the Inverse Mills Ratio (IMR) for each observation. The estimated Inverse Mills Ratio (IMR) is then included in the main regression for wage rate; we also interact the Inverse Mills Ratio with time dummy to allow its effect to vary across the two survey rounds.

$$Wage_{idt} = \beta_0 + \beta_1 X_{idt} + \beta_2 W_{id} + \delta_1 \overline{X}_{id} + \psi_1 IMR_{idt} + \psi_2 IMR_{idt} \times Year_t + \varepsilon_{idt} \tag{13.29}$$

We cluster the standard errors at the district level to consider the fact that the main treatment variable varies at the district level. Further, to account for the generated regressors in Eq. (13.29), we estimate the standard errors using non-parametric block bootstrapping method for the wage equation.

Instead of using the Mundlak version of the fixed effects, we can also use the Chamberlain version where the fixed effects are expressed as linear additive function of the values of the time-varying explanatory variables at each time point. This model is presented below:

$$\begin{aligned} P(Participation_{idt} &= 1 | X_{idt}, W_{id}, Z_{idt}, X_{id1}, X_{id2}, Z_{id1}, Z_{id2}) \\ &= \Phi(\alpha_0 + \alpha_1 X_{idt} + \alpha_2 W_{id} + \alpha_3 Z_{idt} + \gamma_1 X_{id1} + \gamma_2 X_{id2} + \gamma_3 Z_{id1} + \gamma_4 Z_{id2}) \end{aligned} \tag{13.30}$$

$$\begin{aligned} Wage_{idt} = & \beta_0 + \beta_1 X_{idt} + \beta_2 W_{id} + \delta_1 X_{id1} + \delta_2 X_{id2} \\ & + \psi_1 IMR_{idt} + \psi_2 IMR_{idt} \times Year_t + \varepsilon_{idt} \end{aligned} \tag{13.31}$$

d. Results

The results of estimation are presented in Table 13.2. Columns 1–2 show the estimates from the selection correction model using Mundlak fixed effects. Columns 3–4 show the estimates using Chamberlain fixed effects. We find that the estimates are very similar across these two types of specifications. Let us focus on the main variables of interest. We find that the instrument is a strong predictor of employment participation, with a significant negative effect. This implies that women are less likely to participate in wage/salaried employment when household size is large; this is potentially due to the fact that large families may also be joint families where women are more likely to engage in domestic activities than participating in labor market.

Turning to the estimates for the wage regression, the selection correction term (i.e., estimated IMR) and its interaction with the year dummy are both statistically significant, implying that sample selection bias would indeed be a potential concern

Table 13.2 Regression results with selection correction

	Mundlak fixed effects		Chamberlain fixed effects	
	(1)	(2)	(3)	(4)
Variables	Participation	Log of hourly earning	Participation	Log of hourly earning
Age (years)	0.114***	0.174***	0.115***	0.173***
	(0.012)	(0.010)	(0.012)	(0.010)
Square of age	−0.001***	-0.000	−0.001***	−0.000*
	(0.000)	(0.000)	(0.000)	(0.000)
Primary educated	0.072*	0.033	0.078*	0.041
	(0.042)	(0.034)	(0.042)	(0.034)
Secondary educated	0.019	0.077*	0.011	0.107**
	(0.048)	(0.042)	(0.048)	(0.042)
Tertiary educated	0.122	0.329*	0.111	0.255
	(0.130)	(0.174)	(0.130)	(0.180)
Caste: OBC	0.391***	−0.041	0.389***	−0.039
	(0.044)	(0.032)	(0.043)	(0.031)
Caste: SC	0.718***	0.023	0.717***	0.025
	(0.048)	(0.033)	(0.048)	(0.033)
Caste: ST	0.893***	−0.033	0.909***	−0.035
	(0.071)	(0.040)	(0.071)	(0.040)
Religion: Muslim	−0.277***	−0.044	−0.270***	−0.051
	(0.065)	(0.037)	(0.066)	(0.036)
Religion: Others	−0.139*	0.106**	−0.126	0.098*
	(0.078)	(0.053)	(0.082)	(0.051)
Average rainfall in district (standardized)	−0.054	−0.084**	−0.062	−0.075*
	(0.039)	(0.041)	(0.043)	(0.041)
Average nightlights in district (standardized)	0.343*	0.200	0.345*	0.211
	(0.177)	(0.127)	(0.182)	(0.130)
Average MGNREGS funds in district	0.008*	0.004	0.008*	0.004
	(0.005)	(0.003)	(0.005)	(0.003)
Household size	−0.029***		−0.028***	
	(0.005)		(0.005)	
Inverse Mills Ratio		0.189***		0.191***
		(0.046)		(0.045)
Year X Inverse Mills Ratio		−0.147***		−0.144***
		(0.041)		(0.041)
Constant	−1.478***	1.578***	−1.566***	1.015***
	(0.244)	(0.141)	(0.228)	(0.146)

(continued)

Table 13.2 (continued)

	Mundlak fixed effects		Chamberlain fixed effects	
	(1)	(2)	(3)	(4)
Variables	Participation	Log of hourly earning	Participation	Log of hourly earning
Observations	44,704	13,996	44,704	13,996
R-squared		0.573		0.575
Individual fixed effects	Mundlak	Mundlak	Chamberlain	Chamberlain

Robust standard errors clustered at the district level (bootstrapped in columns 2 and 4) are given in parentheses. *** $p < 0.01$, ** $p < 0.05$, * $p < 0.1$

if it was not addressed in the model. We find that the variable capturing the intensity of MGNREGS implementation does not have significant impact on wages once selection is corrected for. On the other hand, it has a significant and positive impact on employment participation of women.

We contrast these results with models that do not correct for sample selection correction. These estimates are presented in Table 13.3 where columns 1, 2, and 3 show specifications that include Mundlak, Chamberlain, and the usual non-parametric versions of the individual fixed effects. The magnitude of the estimate of the MGNREGS variable is very similar across specifications, although it is statistically significant at 10% level in the first two columns.

Overall, the findings indicate that MGNREGS does not have any significant effect on wage rate, although it is likely to impact women's earnings through improving their likelihood of participating in employment.

13.4 Concluding Remarks

In this chapter, we discussed different approaches to addressing sample selection bias in a panel data framework. We surveyed the existing literature and discussed the theoretical framework in the first part. In the second part, we applied the relevant models using Indian data to examine if a rural workfare program affected women's wage rate. In the application, we relied on the use of individual fixed effects to tackle the potential endogeneity of the main treatment variable, while applying the sample selection model to account for non-random employment participation.

Table 13.3 Regression results without selection correction

	(1)	(2)	(3)
Variables	Log of hourly earning		
Age (years)	0.151***	0.150***	0.159***
	(0.008)	(0.008)	(0.009)
Square of age	−0.000**	−0.000**	−0.000***
	(0.000)	(0.000)	(0.000)
Primary educated	0.035	0.036	0.010
	(0.034)	(0.034)	(0.040)
Secondary educated	0.045	0.080*	−0.038
	(0.044)	(0.044)	(0.056)
Tertiary educated	0.292*	0.222	−0.023
	(0.174)	(0.184)	(0.170)
Caste: OBC	−0.071**	−0.070**	
	(0.028)	(0.027)	
Caste: SC	−0.031	−0.032	
	(0.025)	(0.025)	
Caste: ST	−0.097***	−0.104***	
	(0.033)	(0.032)	
Religion: Muslim	−0.017	−0.023	
	(0.034)	(0.034)	
Religion: Others	0.114**	0.106**	
	(0.050)	(0.049)	
Average rainfall in district (standardized)	−0.083**	−0.066	−0.023
	(0.041)	(0.041)	(0.051)
Average nightlights in district (standardized)	0.134	0.141	0.206
	(0.125)	(0.127)	(0.132)
Average MGNREGS funds in district	0.005*	0.005*	0.004
	(0.003)	(0.003)	(0.003)
Constant	1.855***	1.846***	−3.968***
	(0.124)	(0.138)	(0.294)
Observations	13,996	13,996	13,996
R-squared	0.571	0.573	0.769
Individual fixed effects	Mundlak	Chamberlain	Non-parametric

Robust standard errors clustered at the district level are given in parentheses. *** $p < 0.01$, ** $p < 0.05$, * $p < 0.1$

Acknowledgement We thank Cathrine Varghese for helpful comments on the draft.

References

Afridi F, Mukhopadhyay A, Sahoo S (2016) Female labor force participation and child education in India: evidence from the National Rural Employment Guarantee Scheme. IZA J Labor Dev 5(1):1–27

Ahn J (2004) Panel data sample selection model: an application to employee choice of health plan type and medical cost estimation. In: Econometric society 2004 Far Eastern Meetings

Berg E, Bhattacharyya S, Rajasekhar D, Manjula R (2018) Can public works increase equilibrium wages? Evidence from India's National Rural Employment Guarantee. World Dev 103:239–254

Berinsky AJ (2004) Silent voices: opinion polls and political representation in America. Princeton University Press, Princeton, NJ

Bernard AB, Jensen JB (1999) Exceptional exporter performance: cause, effect, or both? J Int Econ 47(1):1–25

Chamberlain G (1980) Analysis of covariance with qualitative data. Rev Econ Stud 47(1):225–238

Chamberlain G (1984) Panel data. In: Griliches Z, Intriligator MD (eds) Handbook of econometrics, vol II, Ch. 22. Amsterdam, North-Holland, pp 1247–1317

Chinnakum W, Sriboonchitta S, Pastpipatkul P (2013) Factors affecting economic output in developed countries: a copula approach to sample selection with panel data. Int J Approx Reason 54(6):809–824

Cook CJ, Shah M (2022) Aggregate effects from public works: evidence from India. Rev Econ Stat 104(4):797–806

d'Addio AC, De Greef I, Rosholm M (2002) Assessing unemployment traps in Belgium using panel data sample selection models. IZA discussion Paper

Dustmann C, Rochina-Barrachina ME (2007) Selection correction in panel data models: an application to the estimation of females' wage equations. Economet J 10(2):263–293

Gayle GL, Viauroux C (2007) Root-N consistent semiparametric estimators of a dynamic panel-sample-selection model. J Econom 141(1):179–212

Heckman JJ (1976) The common structure of statistical models of truncation, sample selection, and limited dependent variables and a simple estimator for such models. Ann Econ Soc Meas 5:475–492

Imbert C, Papp J (2015) Labor market effects of social programs: evidence from India's employment guarantee. Am Econ J Appl Econ 7(2):233–263

Klasen S, Pieters J (2015) What explains the stagnation of female labor force participation in urban India? World Bank Econ Rev 29(3):449–478

Knoef M, Been J (2015) Estimating a panel data sample selection model with part-time employment: selection issues in wages over the life-cycle. University of Leiden, WP

Lai HP, Tsay WJ (2012) Maximum likelihood estimation of the panel sample selection model (No. 12-A006). Institute of Economics, Academia Sinica, Taipei, Taiwan

Mundlak Y (1978) On the pooling of time series and cross section data. Econom J Econom Soc 69–85

Nijman T, Verbeek M (1992) Nonresponse in panel data: the impact on estimates of a life cycle consumption function. J Appl Economet 7(3):243–257

Oaxaca RL, Choe C (2016) Wage decompositions using panel data sample selection correction. IZA Discussion Paper No. 10157, Institute of Labor Economics (IZA)

Raymond W, Mohnen P, Palm F, Van Der Loeff SS (2010) Persistence of innovation in Dutch manufacturing: is it spurious? Rev Econ Stat 92(3):495–504

Rochina-Barrachina ME (1999) A new estimator for panel data sample selection models. Annales d'Economie et de Statistique 153–181

Sarkar S, Sahoo S, Klasen S (2019) Employment transitions of women in India: a panel analysis. World Dev 115:291–309

Sasaki Y (2015) Heterogeneity and selection in dynamic panel data. J Econom 188(1):236–249

Semykina A, Wooldridge JM (2013) Estimation of dynamic panel data models with sample selection. J Appl Economet 28(1):47–61

Semykina A, Wooldridge JM (2018) Binary response panel data models with sample selection and selfselection. J Appl Economet 33(2):179–197

Wooldridge JM (1995) Selection corrections for panel data models under conditional mean independence assumptions. J Econom 68(1):115–132

Zabel JE (1992) Estimating fixed and random effects models with selectivity. Econ Lett 40(3):269–272

Chapter 14
Linear Dynamic Panel Data Models: Exploring the Patent-R&D Relationship in Europe

Laura Magazzini

Abstract This chapter discusses the econometric tools for the empirical analysis of linear dynamic panel data (DPD) models. Many economic relationships are dynamic in nature, and, as a major advantage, panel data allow modeling the evolution of economic phenomena at the microeconomic level. Operationally, this is accomplished by including the lag(s) of the dependent variable on the right-hand side of the estimated equation. As a result, ordinary least squares, and panel fixed effect methods are inconsistent. Even though biased, the estimators are a useful benchmark for assessing the small sample properties of available estimation procedures. Among these, empirical analysis largely relies on the generalized method of moments (GMM). Estimation procedures for DPD models other than GMM, including maximum likelihood and bias-corrected estimation, are also discussed. Theoretical developments are complemented by the empirical analysis of a simplified regional knowledge production function in Europe, aimed at helping students in understanding the proposed estimators. The example is developed using Stata and R.

Keywords Linear panel data · Dynamic modeling · GMM · Maximum likelihood · Bias-corrected methods

14.1 Introduction and Notation

Panel (or longitudinal) data are composed of repeated observations over time (e.g., on a yearly or monthly basis) on the same cross-sectional units (individuals, households, firms, regions, etc.). Observations are therefore uniquely identified by the double

Supplementary Information The online version contains supplementary material available at https://doi.org/10.1007/978-981-99-4902-1_14.

L. Magazzini (✉)
Sant' Anna School of Advanced Studies, Pisa, Italy
e-mail: laura.magazzini@santannapisa.it

D. Mukherjee (ed.), *Applied Econometric Analysis Using Cross Section and Panel Data*, Contributions to Economics, https://doi.org/10.1007/978-981-99-4902-1_14

index it: subscript i refers to the unit ($i = 1, \ldots, N$), and subscript t refers to the time period ($t = 1, \ldots, T$).[1] Typically, in microeconometric applications, the number of units N is "large", and the time dimension T is small. Discussion of the asymptotic properties of the estimators described in this chapter is based on the case in which N "grows large" (i.e., $N \to \infty$) and T is fixed.

Many economic relationships are dynamic in nature, and availability of panel data allow modeling dynamic in behavior to understand whether and how current realizations of the dependent variable are affected by its past values. The model is specified as ($i = 1, \ldots, N$; $t = 1, \ldots, T$):

$$y_{it} = \rho y_{it-1} + \boldsymbol{x}_{it}'\beta + u_i + d_t + e_{it} \tag{14.1}$$

with y_{it} the observation on the dependent variable ($y_{it\text{-}1}$ representing its first lag) and $\boldsymbol{x}_{it}$ a vector of regressors, $\boldsymbol{x}_{it}' = (x_{1it}, x_{2it}, \ldots x_{kit})'$, eventually also including lags of the regressors (a constant term is usually included); ρ and β are, respectively, a scalar and a vector of parameters to be estimated; u_i is a unit/individual effect varying across units but invariant over time, d_t captures the effect of economy-wide variables that are changing over time but are constant across all the units, and e_{it} represents an idiosyncratic component. In the current set up, in which the number of time periods T is held fixed, the time effects d_t can be accounted for by including time dummies in the equation (included in $\boldsymbol{x}_{it}$). The individual effect u_i is generally allowed to be correlated with the vector of regressors $\boldsymbol{x}_{it}$, and it is, by construction, related to $y_{it\text{-}1}$.[2] It is assumed $|\rho| < 1$.

From a policy perspective, it is of interest to distinguish among the two explanations for the correlation of the dependent variable over time: (i) true state dependence when $y_{it\text{-}1}$ has a causal effect on y_{it} ($\rho \neq 0$; i.e., y_{it} is determined by $y_{it\text{-}1}$; changes in x also have a long-lasting effect); (ii) unobserved heterogeneity, as correlation can arise even when there is no causal relation ($\rho = 0$) driven by unobserved characteristics at the unit level, i.e., the cross-sectional effect u_i (Hsiao 1986; Cameron Trivedi 2005).

In this framework, the strict exogeneity assumption invoked in a static context is not satisfied because of the presence of $y_{it\text{-}1}$ on the right-hand side. Rather, *sequential exogeneity* is assumed (Wooldridge 2010):

$$E(e_{it}|y_{it-1}, y_{it-2}, \ldots, y_{i1}, \boldsymbol{x}_{it}, \boldsymbol{x}_{it-1}, \boldsymbol{x}_{it-2}, \ldots, \boldsymbol{x}_{i1}, u_i) = 0$$

As a result, u_i and e_{it} are uncorrelated, $E(u_i\, e_{it}) = 0$, and the idiosyncratic component e_{it} is uncorrelated over time: $E(e_{it}\, e_{is}) = 0$ for all t and all $s < t$. Proof of the latter result exploits the law of iterated expectations:

[1] The notation refers to a balanced panel dataset in which T time periods are available for each cross-sectional unit, so that the sample is composed of NT observations. The methods reviewed in this chapter can be applied in the case of unbalanced panel datasets in which a different number of observations T_i is available for each cross-sectional unit i.

[2] Indeed, $y_{it\text{-}1} = \rho\, y_{it\text{-}2} + \boldsymbol{x}_{it\text{-}1}'\, \beta + d_{t\text{-}1} + u_i + e_{it\text{-}1}$.

$$E(e_{it}e_{is}) = E\big[E(e_{it}e_{is}|y_{it-1}, y_{it-2}, \ldots, y_{i1}, \boldsymbol{x}_{it}, \boldsymbol{x}_{it-1}, \boldsymbol{x}_{it-2}, \ldots, \boldsymbol{x}_{i1}, u_i)\big]$$

and, as e_{is} is a function of the variables in the conditioning set, we can write:

$$E(e_{it}e_{is}) = E\big[e_{is}E(e_{it}|y_{it-1}, y_{it-2}, \ldots, y_{i1}, \boldsymbol{x}_{it}, \boldsymbol{x}_{it-1}, \boldsymbol{x}_{it-2}, \ldots, \boldsymbol{x}_{i1}, u_i)\big] = 0$$

This property is the key for identification of the model parameters in a dynamic specification.

Furthermore, the correlation between the initial observation, y_{i1}, and the composite error term $(e_{it} + u_i)$ in subsequent time period is constant over time, as it is only driven by the presence of u_i.[3]

Summing up, the following "standard assumptions" are imposed on the model (Ahn and Schmidt 1995):

- $E(e_{it}\ e_{is}) = 0$ for all t and all $s \neq t$,
- $E(u_i\ e_{it}) = 0$,
- the correlation between the initial observation, y_{i1}, and the composite error term $(e_{it} + u_i)$ in subsequent time period is constant over time.

Throughout the chapter, discussion of the theoretical concepts is complemented by an empirical example, presented in the next Section.

To keep the exposition simple, the theoretical discussion first focuses on the estimation of ρ, with only the lagged dependent variable included in the equation. Section 14.3 discusses the distortion in ordinary least squares (OLS) estimation and in the fixed effect (FE) framework arising from the inclusion of the lagged dependent variable in the model. Endogeneity is present, due to the correlation between the lagged dependent variable and the error term in the estimating equation. Even though biased, these estimators can provide guidance about the small sample properties of available estimation procedures.

Section 14.4 shows how the lack of correlation in the idiosyncratic component can be exploited to define "internal" instrument(s) that can be successfully exploited in the estimation process. An early solution to the inconsistency of OLS and FE estimation was based on instrumental variable (IV) estimation (Anderson and Hsiao 1981, 1982). Next, the generalized method of moments (GMM; Hansen 1982; White 1982) framework has been adopted. Different methods have been proposed in the literature exploiting different sets of assumptions, that are reviewed in Sect. 14.5 (e.g. Arellano and Bond 1991; Ahn and Schmidt 1995; Blundell and Bond 1998). Software implementation of GMM DPD procedures is discussed in Sect. 14.6, focusing on Stata and R.

Diagnostic procedures for assessing the validity of the GMM procedure are presented in Sect. 14.7.

---

[3] No assumption is made on the variance of the two error components: the focus is on methods that are robust to the presence of heteroskedasticity, that is typically encountered in microeconomic studies. Homoskedasticity is discussed as a particular case.

Model with additional regressors (i.e., estimation of β) and the possibility of correlation between $\boldsymbol{x}_{it}$ and e_{is} ($s = 1,\ldots, T$) is discussed in Sect. 14.8. Finite sample issues with GMM estimation are also discussed in the context of the empirical example. Maximum likelihood estimation and methods based on bias correction are presented in Sect. 14.9. Section 14.10 concludes.

14.2 Empirical Example: The Patent-R&D Relationship in Europe

Innovation is an important driver of economic growth. The empirical literature has studied the relationship between innovation inputs and output. The focus is on the role of R&D expenditures in generating new knowledge (often measured by patents) at different levels of aggregation.

The empirical example relies on Eurostat data about patent and R&D expenditures in the European regions. Data are extracted from the Eurostat database,[4] and the analysis is based on a combination of 171 NUTS1 and NUTS2 regions (Charlot et al. 2015) over the period 2001–2011. A simplified knowledge production function (KPF; Griliches 1979) is considered to estimate the relationship between the (log) number of patents *at* the regional level, *pt*, and (log) knowledge stock (measured using R&D expenditures, *rd*, computed on the basis of the perpetual inventory method; see, e.g., Peri 2005). The log-transformed variables are denoted, respectively, *lpt* and *lrd*.

A dynamic model can be specified in a partial adjustment framework (Falk 2004; Cave et al. 2023). Let *lpt** denote the (unobservable) desired output of the KPF of region *i* at time *t*. The adjustment process is defined as

$$lpt_{it} - lpt_{it-1} = \theta\left(lpt^*_{it} - lpt_{it-1}\right) + u_i + e_{it} \tag{14.2}$$

with θ the coefficient of adjustment, that is the proportion of the gap between the observed and desired innovation output that is closed over the period.

The desired output is then specified as a function of R&D expenditures: $lpt^*_{it} = \delta lrd_{it} + \tau_t$. By substituting in (14.2), the dynamic specification is obtained as

$$lpt_{it} = \rho lpt_{it-1} + \beta lrd_{it} + u_i + d_t + e_{it} \tag{14.3}$$

with $\rho = 1 - \theta$, $\beta = \theta\ \delta$, $d_t = \theta\ \tau_t$.

In the first part of the chapter, estimation of the autoregressive model without additional regressors is considered. Inclusion of *lrd* on the right-hand side is discussed in Sect. 14.8.

[4] https://ec.europa.eu/eurostat/data/database.

14.3 Bias of OLS and FE Estimation

In order to simplify the discussion, this Section considers an autoregressive model with no additional regressors, i.e.:

$$y_{it} = \rho y_{it-1} + u_i + e_{it} = \rho y_{it-1} + v_{it} \tag{14.4}$$

where $v_{it} = u_i + e_{it}$.

Parameter estimates with OLS and FE are inconsistent.

The OLS estimator of Eq. (14.4) can be computed as:

$$\hat{\rho}^{OLS} = \left(\sum_i \sum_t y_{it-1}^2\right)^{-1} \left(\sum_i \sum_t y_{it-1} y_{it}\right)$$

By substituting (14.4):

$$\begin{aligned} \hat{\rho}^{OLS} &= \left(\sum_i \sum_t y_{it-1}^2\right)^{-1} \left(\sum_i \sum_t y_{it-1}(\rho y_{it-1} + u_i + e_{it})\right) \\ &= \left(\sum_i \sum_t y_{it-1}^2\right)^{-1} \left(\sum_i \sum_t \rho y_{it-1}^2 + y_{it-1}(u_i + e_{it})\right) \\ &= \rho + \left(\sum_i \sum_t y_{it-1}^2\right)^{-1} \left(\sum_i \sum_t y_{it-1}(u_i + e_{it})\right) \end{aligned}$$

The asymptotic properties of the OLS estimator can be derived by studying $E\left[y_{it-1}(u_i + e_{it})\right]$:

$$E\left[y_{it-1}(u_i + e_{it})\right] = E(y_{it-1}u_i) + E(y_{it-1}e_{it})$$

that is generally different from zero due to the correlation between $y_{it\text{-}1}$ and u_i (recall that under sequential exogeneity e_{it} is uncorrelated over time, so that $y_{it\text{-}1}$ and e_{it} are uncorrelated). It is also possible to claim that $E\left[y_{it-1}u_i\right] > 0$, so that the OLS estimator is biased upward, i.e., the probability limit ($N \to \infty$) of the OLS bias is positive (see Hsiao 1989 for details).

A FE approach might be considered to solve the issue of the correlation between the lagged dependent variable $y_{it\text{-}1}$ and the unobserved heterogeneity. However, this would induce correlation between the lagged dependent variable and the error term in the estimating equation.

Consider first the within-group (WG) transformation. The regression on the unit average can be written as:

$$\overline{y}_i = \rho \overline{y}_{i(-1)} + u_i + \overline{e}_i$$

with $\overline{y}_i = \sum_{t=2}^{T} y_{it}/(T-1)$, $\overline{y}_{i(-1)} = \sum_{t=1}^{T-1} y_{it}/(T-1)$ and $\overline{e}_i = \sum_{t=2}^{T} e_{it}/(T-1)$
Therefore, the WG transformation removes u_i from the estimating equation:

$$y_{it} - \overline{y}_i = \rho\big(y_{it-1} - \overline{y}_{i(-1)}\big) + e_{it} - \overline{e}_i$$

By defining $\ddot{y}_{it} = y_{it} - \overline{y}_i$, $\ddot{y}_{it-1} = y_{it-1} - \overline{y}_{i(-1)}$, and $e_{it} = e_{it} - \overline{e_i}$, the FE estimator can be obtained as an OLS estimator on the WG transformed regression:

$$\ddot{y}_{it} = \rho\ddot{y}_{it-1} + \ddot{e}_{it}$$

The estimator can be written as:

$$\begin{aligned}
\widehat{\rho}^{FE} &= \left(\sum_i\sum_t \ddot{y}_{it-1}^2\right)^{-1}\left(\sum_i\sum_t \ddot{y}_{it-1}\ddot{y}_{it}\right) \\
&= \left(\sum_i\sum_t \ddot{y}_{it-1}^2\right)^{-1}\left(\sum_i\sum_t \ddot{y}_{it-1}(\rho\ddot{y}_{it-1} + \ddot{e}_{it})\right) \\
&= \left(\sum_i\sum_t \ddot{y}_{it-1}^2\right)^{-1}\left(\sum_i\sum_t (\rho\ddot{y}_{it-1}^2 + \ddot{y}_{it-1}\ddot{e}_{it})\right) \\
&= \rho + \left(\sum_i\sum_t \ddot{y}_{it-1}^2\right)^{-1}\left(\sum_i\sum_t \ddot{y}_{it-1}\ddot{e}_{it}\right)
\end{aligned}$$

The magnitude and direction of the bias depends on $E(\ddot{y}_{it-1}\ddot{e}_{it})$, that is different from zero: correlation of the order 1/*T* is introduced between the regressor and the error term in the transformed model (Hsiao 1989). Nickel (1981) derived the formula for the bias of the FE estimator, that, for relatively large *T*, can be approximated as:

$$\underset{N\to\infty}{\text{plim}}\,\widehat{\rho}^{FE} = \rho + \frac{-(1+\rho)}{T-1}$$

In the case of $\rho > 0$ (most common in economic applications), the bias of the FE estimator is negative. The bias vanishes if *T* "grows large"; however, it cannot be ignored for finite *T*. As an example, with $\rho = 0.5$ and T = 10, the asymptotic bias is –0.17 (Nickel 1981).

Derivation for the FD transformation is analogous. OLS regression based on the FD transformation of the Eq. (14.4) produces a biased result, because affected by the correlation between $\Delta y_{it\text{-}1}$ $(= y_{it\text{-}1} - y_{it\text{-}2})$ and Δe_{it} $(= e_{it} - e_{it\text{-}1})$. In this case the bias does not depend on *T*, so it won't disappear as *T* grows large.

Summing up, in the case $\rho > 0$:

- the OLS estimator is upward biased,
- the FE estimator is downward biased.

Table 14.1 OLS and FE estimation of the dynamic relationship (4); dependent variable lpt_{it} (*Source* authors' computation on Eurostat data)

	OLS	OLS	FE	FE
lpt_{it-1}	0.9577 (0.0052)	0.9585 (0.0051)	0.3429 (0.0609)	0.2272 (0.0661)
Region FE	No	No	Yes	Yes
Time FE	No	Yes	No	Yes

Note *Robust (clustered) standard errors in parenthesis*

The two information, combined, are nonetheless useful, as any consistent estimator needs to lie in the interval defined by the FE and the OLS estimator (Bond 2002).

In the case of the data employed in this chapter, the OLS and FE estimates of the dynamic model (14.4) are reported in Table 14.1. The model is estimated both with and without time dummies (time FE).

14.4 The Idea of Internal Instruments

OLS and FE bias emerge because of an endogeneity issue. Following the standard theory of regression analysis, in the case of correlation between the regressor(s) and the error term, consistent estimation can be obtained by an IV approach. With cross-sectional data, the difficulty is in finding legitimate instruments. However, in the context of panel data, under the "standard assumptions," it is possible to rely on "internal" instruments, i.e., instruments based on appropriate transformation(s) of the available observations.[5]

A way of consistently estimating the parameters of a DPD model (14.4) was first proposed by Anderson and Hsiao (1981, 1982). First, to solve the issue of correlation between $y_{it\text{-}1}$ and u_i, use the FD transformation: rather than estimate the model in (14.4), consider the following transformation

$$y_{it} - y_{it-1} = \rho(y_{it-1} - y_{it-2}) + (e_{it} - e_{it-1})$$

or, using the first difference operator, Δ[6]

$$\Delta y_{it} = \rho \Delta y_{it-1} + \Delta e_{it} \tag{14.5}$$

[5] If also "external" instruments are available, they can be included in the analysis.

[6] Alternative transformations to remove u_i have been proposed in the literature, e.g., the "forward orthogonal deviations" or "orthogonal deviations" (Arellano and Bover 1995) that remove the individual effect u_i by subtracting the average of all future available observations of a variable. See also Han and Phillips (2010).

The transformed estimating equation does not include u_i, so that the correlation between u_i and $y_{it\text{-}1}$ is unrestricted. However, as discussed in Sect. 14.3, OLS estimation of (14.5) does not produce consistent estimates because of the correlation between the differenced regressor, $\Delta y_{it\text{-}1}$, and the differenced error term Δe_{it}.

Key to identification of the model parameter is the assumption of lack of autocorrelation in e_{it}. When this is satisfied, it is possible to claim that $y_{it\text{-}2}$ can be used as a legitimate instrument for the endogenous variable $\Delta y_{it\text{-}1}$ in Eq. (14.5):

- the chosen instrument is relevant, as $y_{it\text{-}2}$ is correlated with $\Delta y_{it\text{-}1}$;
- the chosen instrument is exogenous, because $y_{it\text{-}2}$ is a function of $e_{it\text{-}2}$ and its past values: under the condition of lack of autocorrelation in e_{it}, it holds that $e_{it\text{-}2}$ (and its past occurrences $e_{it\text{-}3}, \ldots$) are uncorrelated with Δe_{it} (equal to $e_{it} - e_{it\text{-}1}$).

Based on this intuition, Anderson and Hsiao (1981, 1982) propose to estimate the model in (14.5) using an IV approach (two-stage least squares, 2SLS) selecting $y_{it\text{-}2}$ as instrumental variable for the endogenous variable $\Delta y_{it\text{-}1}$, to produce a consistent estimate of the model parameters.[7]

Need it here to mention the fact that, even if IV allows consistent estimation of the model parameter, a proper formula for inference has to be applied because (under the assumption of lack of autocorrelation in e_{it}) the error term in (14.5) is autocorrelated of order one:

- $\mathrm{E}(\Delta e_{it}\ \Delta e_{it\text{-}1}) = E[(e_{it} - e_{it\text{-}1})\ (e_{it\text{-}1} - e_{it\text{-}2})] = -\sigma_{t-1}^2$, with $\sigma_{t-1}^2 = E(e_{it-1}^2) \neq 0$;
- $\mathrm{E}(\Delta e_{it}\ \Delta e_{it\text{-}2}) = E[(e_{it} - e_{it\text{-}1})\ (e_{it\text{-}2} - e_{it\text{-}3})] = 0$, or more generally, $\mathrm{E}(\Delta e_{it}\ \Delta e_{it\text{-}j})$ $= E[(e_{it} - e_{it\text{-}1})\ (e_{it\text{-}j} - e_{it\text{-}j\text{-}1})] = 0$ for any $j > 1$.

As a result, the formula of the standard errors that adjust for clustering at the unit level should be applied for valid inference.

To apply this estimator to the regional KPF, the IV regression can be specified in Stata as:

```
. ivregress 2sls D.lpt (DL.lpt=L2.lpt), cluster(id)
```

or, using the *plm* package in R (Croissant and Millo 2008, assume the panel dataset is stored in memory in *dpddata*):

```
>> ah1 <- plm(diff(lpt) ~ lag(diff(lpt)) | lag(lpt,2) , data =
dpddata, model = "pooling")
```

The dependent variable is the FD transformation of the variable *lpt* ($\Delta\ lpt_{it}$), written as a function of its first lag ($\Delta\ lpt_{it\text{-}1}$), and the instrumental variable is the second lag of *lpt* ($lpt_{it\text{-}2}$). The estimated value of the coefficient is 0.470 with a standard error (s.e.) equal to 0.096 (statistically different from zero). When time

[7] Analogous reasoning leads to identify also $\Delta y_{it\text{-}2}$ as a legitimate instrument; however, this approach would not be recommended (Arellano 1989).

dummies are included in the equation, the estimated value of ρ equals 0.458 (s.e. 0.096).[8]

14.5 GMM Estimation of DPD Models

The procedure based on the IV approach described in the previous section is not efficient for at least two reasons (Baltagi 2005). First, without introducing further assumptions on the data generating process, it is possible to find additional valid instruments in the FD equation. The assumption of uncorrelated e_{it} implies that lag 2 *and older values* of the dependent variable can be used as legitimate instruments for $\Delta\, y_{it\text{-}1}$ (Holtz-Eakin et al. 1988; Arellano and Bond 1991). This enlarged instrument set can be used to increase the efficiency of the estimator. Second, the instrumental variable approach (in the form of 2SLS) is efficient in the case of homoskedasticity and uncorrelation in the error term. However, by taking the FD transformation, autocorrelation in the error term is introduced. Therefore, a GMM approach may allow further improvements in estimation efficiency.

14.5.1 A (Brief) Introduction to GMM Estimation

With the IV approach of Anderson and Hsiao (1981, 1982) $y_{it\text{-}2}$ is selected to serve as instrumental variable for the endogenous variable $\Delta\, y_{it\text{-}1}$ in (14.5); the model is exactly identified (the number of instruments equals the number of endogenous variables in the model). The 2SLS estimator can also be obtained as a method of moment estimator. The invoked exogeneity of the instrumental variable can be written in terms of an orthogonality condition that holds in the population: $\mathrm{E}(y_{it\text{-}2}\ \Delta\ e_{it}) = 0$. Exploiting this moment condition, the parameter ρ in (14.5) can be identified, i.e., written in terms of observable variables:

$$0 = E(y_{it-2}\Delta e_{it}) = E[y_{it-2}(\Delta y_{it} - \rho \Delta y_{it-1})] = E(y_{it-2}\Delta y_{it}) - \rho E(y_{it-2}\Delta y_{it-1})$$

and therefore:

$$E(y_{it-2}\Delta y_{it}) = \rho E(y_{it-2}\Delta y_{it-1})$$

The system of 1 equation in 1 parameter can be solved as:

$$\rho = E(y_{it-2}\Delta y_{it})/E(y_{it-2}\Delta y_{it-1})$$

[8] Time dummies can enter in first difference or levels. The choice changes the interpretation of their coefficients but does not affect the estimation of ρ in (14.5). It is recommended to include time dummies in dynamic specifications.

(note how the condition of relevance of $y_{it\text{-}2}$ is needed to avoid dividing by zero).

The estimator is obtained by replacing the population moment conditions with their sample analogue, and in this case, it equals the 2SLS estimator.

However, a larger set of instrumental variables is available ($y_{it\text{-}2}$ and older values of the dependent variable: $y_{it\text{-}3}, \ldots, y_{i1}$). As a result, the number of instruments grows and is larger than the number of endogenous variables in the model (one in the current framework), i.e., the model is overidentified.

In the context of IV regression with 2SLS approach, in the overidentified case, a linear combination of the instruments is considered in order to estimate the model parameters. In the first stage the endogenous variable is written as a function of the exogenous variables, and OLS-fitted values from the first stage are then used (in a second stage) to get a consistent estimator.

The GMM solution slightly differs, but 2SLS can be obtained as a special case of GMM estimation.

The starting point is, again, the orthogonality (moment) conditions spanning from the assumption of exogeneity of the instrumental variables. When R instrumental variables are available, R orthogonality (moment) conditions can be defined, thus forming a system of R equations in one unknown parameter ρ. In this context, it is not possible to find a single value that jointly satisfies all the equations. How to find a solution? The GMM searches for the value of ρ that makes the moment conditions in the population "as close as possible" to their theoretical value (zero in this case). The estimator is then obtained by replacing the population moment conditions with their sample analogue. Further details will be provided in the next Sections in the context of DPD models' estimation. For a general treatment of GMM, please refer to, among others, Verbeek (2008, Chap. 5), Cameron and Trivedi (2005, Chap. 6), and Wooldridge (2010, Chap. 8). Under suitable assumptions, it can be shown that the GMM estimator is consistent, and asymptotically normal distributed; it can also be made efficient.

14.5.2 The "Difference" GMM Estimator

When the "standard assumptions" are satisfied (see Sect. 14.1), the use of lag 2 and older values of the dependent variable as instrument defines $R = (T\text{-}1)(T\text{-}2)/2$ exogenous variables. The corresponding R moment conditions that hold in the population are specified as ($t \geq 3, j \geq 2$):

$$E\left(y_{it-j}\Delta e_{it}\right) = E\left(y_{it-j}(\Delta y_{it} - \rho\Delta y_{it-1})\right) = 0 \tag{14.6}$$

More explicitly:

- starting at time $t = 3$, y_{i1} can be used as instrument to form the moment condition $E(y_{i1}\ \Delta\ e_{i3}) = 0$;

- at time $t = 4$, two instruments are available, namely y_{i2} and y_{i1}, to form the moment conditions $E(y_{i2}\ \Delta\ e_{i4}) = 0$ and $E(y_{i1}\ \Delta\ e_{i4}) = 0$;
- at time $t = 5$, the available instruments are y_{i3}, y_{i2}, and y_{i1} and the moment conditions $E(y_{i3}\ \Delta\ e_{i5}) = 0$, $E(y_{i2}\ \Delta\ e_{i5}) = 0$ and $E(y_{i1}\ \Delta\ e_{i5}) = 0$; and so on.

The GMM estimator based on these moment conditions is termed in the literature as difference GMM estimator.

The set of moment conditions can be written in compact form by introducing the $(T\text{-}2) \times R$ matrix of instruments Z_i:

$$Z_i = \begin{pmatrix} y_{i1} & 0\ 0 \ldots & 0\ 0 \ldots 0 \\ 0 & y_{i1}\ y_{i2} \ldots & 0\ 0 \ldots 0 \\ \vdots & \vdots\ \vdots\ \ddots & \vdots\ \vdots\ \ddots\ \vdots \\ 0 & 0\ 0 \ldots & y_{i1}\ y_{i2} \ldots y_{iT-2} \end{pmatrix} \tag{14.7}$$

and the $(T\text{-}2) \times 1$ vector of differenced residuals $\Delta\ e_i$:

$$\Delta e_i = \begin{pmatrix} \Delta e_{i3} \\ \Delta e_{i4} \\ \vdots \\ \Delta e_{iT} \end{pmatrix}$$

The moment conditions in (14.6) can be therefore written as:

$$E(Z_i\prime \Delta e_i) = 0 \tag{14.8}$$

Let $\Delta\ y_i$ and $\Delta\ y_{i,\text{-}1}$ be defined such that $\Delta\ e_i = \Delta\ y_i - \rho\ \Delta\ y_{i,\text{-}1}$, that is:

$$\Delta y_i = \begin{pmatrix} \Delta y_{i3} \\ \Delta y_{i4} \\ \vdots \\ \Delta y_{iT} \end{pmatrix} \text{ and } \Delta y_{i,-1} = \begin{pmatrix} \Delta y_{i2} \\ \Delta y_{i3} \\ \vdots \\ \Delta y_{iT-1} \end{pmatrix}$$

so that (14.8) can be written as a function of the parameter and the observable variables as:

$$E[Z_i\prime(\Delta y_i - \rho \Delta y_{i,-1})] = 0$$

This is a system of R equations in the unknown parameter ρ.

Denote $m(\rho) = E\left[Z_i\prime\left(\Delta y_i - \rho \Delta y_{i,-1}\right)\right]$. Its sample analogue can be specified as:

$$m_N(\rho) = \frac{1}{N}\sum\nolimits_{i=1}^{N} Z_i{}'(\Delta y_i - \rho \Delta y_{i,-1})$$

The GMM estimate is obtained by choosing the value of the parameter that minimizes the distance between the empirical counterpart of the moment conditions and their theoretical value (in this case, 0). In the exactly identified case (i.e., when the number of moment conditions equal the number of parameters, as it would be the case with $T = 3$) a unique solution can be found, corresponding to the 2SLS estimator. On the contrary, when the model is overidentified, i.e., there are more moment conditions than parameters, it is not possible to find a unique solution satisfying all the moment conditions at once. Rather, the estimation process will set the moment conditions as close as possible to zero. This can be accomplished by considering the following quadratic form:

$$Q(\rho, W) = m_N(\rho)\prime W m_N(\rho) = \left(\frac{1}{N}\sum\nolimits_{i=1}^{N} Z_i{}'(\Delta y_i - \rho \Delta y_{i,-1})\right)' \\ W\left(\frac{1}{N}\sum\nolimits_{i=1}^{N} Z_i{}'(\Delta y_i - \rho \Delta y_{i,-1})\right) \tag{14.9}$$

with W a $R \times R$ (positive-definite and symmetric) weighting matrix. In order to establish the properties of GMM, it is required that plim $W = W_O$ exists and is a symmetric and positive definite matrix.[9]

In the case of the difference GMM estimator, moment conditions (14.8) are linear in the parameters and a closed-form solution exists for the minimization problem (14.8), that can be found by taking first derivative with respect to ρ and equating it to zero:

$$\widehat{\rho}^{GMM} = \left[\left(\sum\nolimits_i Z_i{}'\Delta y_{i,-1}\right)\prime W\left(\sum\nolimits_i Z_i{}'\Delta y_{i,-1}\right)\right]^{-1}\left(\sum\nolimits_i Z_i{}'\Delta y_{i,-1}\right)\prime W\sum\nolimits_i Z_i{}'\Delta y_i \tag{14.10}$$

For any choice of W, the GMM estimator is consistent. The asymptotic variance depends on the chosen W employed in estimation.[10] Also, the central limit theorem can be applied to show that the estimator is asymptotically normally distributed:

$$\sqrt{N}\left(\widehat{\rho}^{GMM} - \rho\right) \to_d N(0, V)$$

With

$$V = (\Gamma W \Gamma')^{-1} \Gamma W \Sigma W \Gamma' (\Gamma W \Gamma')^{-1} \tag{14.11}$$

---

[9] As an example, set W equal to the identity matrix. The solution would be the value of the parameter that minimizes the sum of squared value of the moment conditions. However, it will be clear that W = I is not the optimal choice in this context.

[10] The 2SLS estimator is obtained by setting $W = \left(\sum_i Z_i{}'Z_i\right)^{-1}$.

where Σ is the variance–covariance matrix of the moment conditions, and $\Gamma = \mathrm{E}(Z_i\prime\Delta y_{i,-1})$ (see, e.g. Cameron and Trivedi 2005; Wooldridge 2010).

It is appropriate to ask what is the choice of W that makes the estimator "efficient" in the sense of having the minimum variance. It can be shown that, the optimal choice of W is the inverse of the variance covariance matrix of the moment conditions:

$$W^{opt} = [E(Z_i\prime\Delta e_i\Delta e_i\prime Z_i)]^{-1} = \Sigma^{-1} \tag{14.12}$$

so that, when W is chosen optimally (i.e., $W = W^{opt}$)

$$V = (\Gamma W^{opt}\Gamma\prime)^{-1} \tag{14.13}$$

In the general case, the matrix W^{opt} is a function of model parameters, so estimation proceeds in two steps[11]:

1. for any choice of W, a consistent estimator of ρ is obtained; the estimate is labeled one-step GMM estimator, $\widehat{\rho}_1$;
2. the estimate obtained in the first step is used to obtain a consistent estimator of the matrix W^{opt}, that is used in the formula (14.10) to get an efficient estimator ofρ, labeled two-step GMM estimator $\widehat{\rho}_2$.

In the context of DPD modeling, the matrix W^{opt} can be estimated as:

$$W(\widehat{\rho}_1) = \left(\frac{1}{N}\sum\nolimits_{i=1}^{N} Z_i\prime\Delta\widehat{e}_i\Delta\widehat{e}_i\prime Z_i\right)^{-1}$$

with $\widehat{\rho}_1$ a consistent estimator of ρ, based on the first stage regression, used to compute the first-step (differenced) residuals $\Delta\widehat{e}_i$.

In the special case of conditional homoskedastic e_{it}, $\mathrm{E}(e_{it} \mid Z_i) = \sigma_e^2$, the optimal matrix is proportional to a known matrix as $E(Z_i\prime\Delta e_i\Delta e_i\prime Z_i) = E(Z_i\prime \mathrm{D} Z_i)$ where

$$D = \sigma_e^2 \begin{pmatrix} 2 & -1 & 0 \cdots 0 \\ -1 & 2 & -1 \cdots 0 \\ 0 & -1 & 2 \cdots 0 \\ \vdots & \vdots & \vdots \ddots \vdots \\ 0 & 0 & 0 \cdots 2 \end{pmatrix} \tag{14.14}$$

As a result, the first-step estimator can be computed in an efficient way (the term $\sigma_e{}^2$ cancels out in Eq. 14.10). In the general case, both steps would be required for efficiency.

Simulation studies on the small sample performance of the difference GMM estimator show that it has large finite sample bias and poor performance especially

[11] The two-step estimator is generally applied in empirical work. The GMM estimator can alternatively be obtained using an iterative or a continuously update procedure (Hansen et al. 1996).

when ρ approaches 1 or the variance of the individual component is larger than the variance of the idiosyncratic error term (Arellano and Bover 1995; Blundell and Bond 1998). When the process is close to a random walk, past levels of y convey little information about future changes, so that they are "weak instruments" for transformed variables (Roodman, 2009b).

14.5.3 A Nonlinear GMM Estimator

Ahn and Schmidt (1995) noticed that additional moment conditions can be derived as a result of the standard assumptions.

Let $v_{it} = u_i + e_{it}$. Standard assumptions also imply the following moment conditions that can be additionally exploited in the estimation process ($t = 3, \ldots, T\text{-}1$):

$$E(\Delta v_{it} v_{iT}) = 0 \tag{14.15}$$

Ahn and Schmidt (1995) show that, by adding the T-3 moment conditions (14.15) to the moment conditions (14.6) characterizing the difference GMM estimator, gains in asymptotic efficiency are achieved. The estimator makes efficient use of second moment information.[12] Gains in performance are larger when ρ approaches 1 or the variance of the individual component is larger than the variance of the idiosyncratic error term. The estimator is nonlinear in the parameters, so that no closed form solution exists for the estimator (see also Ahn and Schmidt 1997). However, the solution to the minimization problem (14.9) can be obtained by using standard optimization techniques.

14.5.4 "System" GMM Estimation

Few years later, Arellano and Bover (1995) and Blundell and Bond (1998) identified the assumption needed to use the lagged difference of the dependent variable as instrument in the equation in level.

This is accomplished by exploiting the following moment conditions ($t \geq 3$):

$$E(\Delta y_{it-1} v_{it}) = E(\Delta y_{it-1}(u_i + e_{it})) = 0 \tag{14.16}$$

Blundell and Bond (1998) show that these instruments remain informative even with persistent processes (i.e., when ρ approaches 1 or the variance of the individual component is larger than the variance of the idiosyncratic error term).

[12] Calzolari and Magazzini (2019) shows that further efficiency gains can be obtained by exploiting third moments, with asymmetric distribution of the error terms.

It is important to understand that when using (14.16), additional assumptions are imposed on the data generating process. In particular, an additional assumption on the initial observation is needed for the validity of (14.16), labeled "mean stationarity assumption." To see how, it is useful to rewrite the moment conditions as in Roodman (2009a):

$$\begin{aligned} E(\Delta y_{it-1} v_{it}) &= E\big[(y_{it-1} - y_{it-2})(u_i + e_{it})\big] \\ &= E\big[(\rho y_{it-2} + u_i + e_{it-1} - y_{it-2})(u_i + e_{it})\big] \\ &= E\big[((\rho - 1) y_{it-2} + u_i + e_{it-1})(u_i + e_{it})\big] \end{aligned}$$

Because of the assumption of lack of serial correlation in e_{it}, and uncorrelation between u_i and e_{it}, it is possible to write ($t \geq 3$)

$$E(\Delta y_{it-1} v_{it}) = E\big[((\rho - 1) y_{it-2} + u_i) u_i\big]$$

The moment condition can be rewritten as ($t \geq 1$)

$$E[((\rho - 1) y_{it} + u_i) u_i] = 0$$

or, by dividing both side by (1-ρ):

$$E\left(\left(y_{it} - \frac{u_i}{1 - \rho}\right) u_i\right) = 0$$

stating that, at each point in time, deviations from the long-run mean of the process, $u_i / (1 - \rho)$, must not be correlated with the FE u_i (Blundell and Bond 1998; Roodman 2009a).[13] Roodman (2009a) shows that, if this condition holds at time t, it also holds at subsequent time periods, so that the mean stationarity assumption is effectively an assumption on the initial observation, y_{i1}, excluding correlation between deviation of y_{i1} from its long run mean and the individual effect u_i. Accordingly, in the simplified framework of model (14.4), Magazzini and Calzolari (2020) show that the system GMM estimator can be obtained by adding the single moment condition $E(\Delta y_{i2} v_{i3}) = 0$ to the nonlinear GMM estimator proposed by Ahn and Schmidt (1995), i.e., to the set of moments conditions (14.6) and (14.15).

When the mean stationarity assumption is satisfied, Blundell and Bond (1998) propose to build a system of equations that include the moment condition related to the equation in first difference (14.6) and the T-2 moment conditions in (14.16).[14]

---

[13] On the basis of the standard assumptions, $E(y_{it} \mid u_i) = \rho\, y_{it-1} + u_i$. At steady-state $E(y_{it} \mid u_i) = E(y_{it+1} \mid u_i)$, so that it is possible to write $y_{it} = \rho\, y_{it} + u_i$, implying that $y_{it} = u_i / (1 - \rho)$. See Roodman (2009a).

[14] Moment conditions including longer lags could also be specified, but these are redundant when the moment conditions (14.6) are included for estimation (Arellano and Bover 1995; Blundell and Bond 1998).

The system GMM estimator is obtained as the solution to the following "system" of moment conditions, stacking the equation in first differences and in levels:

- from the first-difference equation: $E(y_{it\text{-}j}\ \Delta e_{it}) = 0$ for $j \geq 2$, $t \geq 3$;
- from the equation in levels: $E(\Delta y_{it\text{-}1}\ v_{it}) = 0$ for $t \geq 2$.

The matrix of instruments can be written as:

$$Z_i^s = \begin{pmatrix} Z_i^d & 0 \\ 0 & Z_i^l \end{pmatrix} \tag{14.17}$$

with $Z_i{}^d$ defined in (14.7) and

$$Z_i^l = \begin{pmatrix} \Delta y_{i2} & 0 & \dots & 0 \\ 0 & \Delta y_{i3} & \dots & 0 \\ \vdots & \vdots & \ddots & \vdots \\ 0 & 0 & \dots & \Delta y_{iT-1} \end{pmatrix} \tag{14.18}$$

The moment conditions can therefore be written, in compact form, as:

$$E\left(Z_i^s{}'\varepsilon_i\right) = 0$$

with

$$\varepsilon_i = \begin{pmatrix} \Delta e_{i3} \\ \vdots \\ \Delta e_{iT} \\ v_{i3} \\ \vdots \\ v_{iT} \end{pmatrix}$$

The vector containing the observations on the dependent variables and the regressors (the lagged dependent variable in this case) also needs to be adjusted to include both first differences and levels of the variables.

Note that, in the context of system GMM, the form of the optimal weighting matrix generally depends on the (conditional) variance–covariance matrix of ε_i and is therefore a function of the variance of the two error components, u_i and e_{it}. An "optimal" weighting matrix can be derived under the assumption that the variance of the unobserved heterogeneity u_i is equal to zero (Windmeijer 2000; use of "robust" standard errors is therefore recommended with first-step system GMM estimates).

The system GMM estimator allows substantial gains in performance both with respect to the difference GMM estimator and to the estimator proposed by Ahn and Schmidt (1995). Differenced instruments for the equation in levels are indeed more relevant especially in cases in which the process is highly persistent or when the variance of the individual effect is higher with respect to the idiosyncratic component (Blundell and Bond 1998; Hayakawa 2007; Roodman 2009b).

14.5.5 Estimating the Variance of the GMM Estimator

For a general W, in a finite sample, the variance–covariance matrix of the estimator can be consistently estimated as (Cameron and Trivedi 2005)[15]:

$$\widehat{V}_N(\widehat{\rho}, W) = (B\prime WB)^{-1} B\prime W\widehat{S}WB(B\prime WB)^{-1} \tag{14.19}$$

with

$$B = \frac{1}{N}\sum\nolimits_i Z_i\prime \Delta y_{i,-1}$$

and

$$\widehat{S} = \frac{1}{N}\sum Z_i\prime \Delta\widehat{e}_i \Delta\widehat{e}_i\prime Z_i$$

This estimate of the variance of the GMM estimator can be generally employed to compute robust standard errors in context in which the matrix the weighting matrix W is not chosen optimally (e.g., first-stage estimates). When W is chosen optimally ($W^{opt} = \widehat{S}^{-1}$), the formula reduces to:

$$\widehat{V}_N(\widehat{\rho}, W^{opt}) = \left(B\prime W^{opt} B\right)^{-1} \tag{14.20}$$

The formula (14.20) is valid asymptotically, however it can lead to substantial downward bias in estimated standard errors in finite samples (and, correspondingly, over-rejections in t-statistics to assess coefficients' significance). The issue was already highlighted in the Monte Carlo experiments of Arellano and Bond (1991), with estimated second-step standard errors being about 20% lower than expected.

When estimated according to (14.20), the formula that estimates second-step standard errors does not account for the variation due to the presence of estimated parameters in W. A solution has been proposed by Windmiejer (2005) that noticed that this extra variation can be estimated, resulting in a finite sample correction of the estimated variance. The correction is customarily included in software implementation of DPD GMM estimators.

---

[15] Formulas refer to the difference GMM estimator, but can be adjusted to consider non-linear and system GMM.

14.6 Software Implementation of GMM Procedures

GMM estimation of DPD model is available with most econometric software.

In Stata there are various commands that can be used to perform GMM estimation of the parameters of a DPD model. The Stata-developed commands for this purpose are:

- *xtabond* computes the difference GMM estimator;
- *xtdpdsys* computes the system GMM estimator;
- *xtdpd* allows more general modeling than *xtabond* and *xtdpdsys*.

For example, by typing the Stata command.

```
. xtabond lpt dy3-dy11, robust
```

the one-step difference GMM estimation (Arellano and Bond 1991) of the autoregressive model for (log) patents is computed including only time dummies as additional regression. Robust standard errors are considered as in (14.19). To produce two-step results the option *twostep* has to be specified. By combining the *twostep* option with *robust*, computation of the standard error relies on the Windmejer's corrected formula (Windmeiejer 2005).[16]

It is also worth mentioning two user-developed Stata commands. First, *xtabond2* has been developed by Roodman (2009b) and offers the possibility of estimating both the difference and system GMM estimators. A recently developed command, *xtdpdgmm* (Kripfganz 2017, 2019), additionally offers the possibility of estimating the model parameters via the nonlinear Ahn and Schmidt (1995) estimator.

Contrary to the Stata official commands *xtabond* and *xtdpdsys*, the user-developed commands *xtabond2* and *xtdpdgmm* require to separately specify the equation of interest and the variables in the instrument set, dividing GMM-type instruments built on the basis of lags of selected variables and IV-type variables that are to be treated as exogenous in the FD equation.[17]

Packages dedicated to estimation of DPD are also available in R (www.r-projec t.org). The package *plm* (Croissant and Millo 2008) includes the command *pgmm* for computation of the difference and system GMM estimators; whereas the command/ package *pdynmc* also includes the possibility of estimating nonlinear GMM (Fritsch et al. 2021).

---

[16] Absent the *robust* option, the (unreliable in finite samples) asymptotic formula (14.20) is considered in computation.

[17] Please refer to the command help, Kripfganz (2017, 2019) and Roodman (2009b) for details on the commands' syntax. Note that the two commands need to be installed (you can use "*net install*" for this purpose).

Results of the estimation of the autoregressive model for *lpt* are reported in Table 14.2. The estimated model includes the lagged dependent variable and the time dummies. The instrument count is reported at the bottom of the Table.[18]

When the difference GMM estimator is considered, the estimated value of ρ is about 0.2 (both one-step and two-step results), statistically different from zero at the 5% level. The model is first differenced and 55 moment conditions (number of instruments) are exploited for estimation:

- for the differenced equation, instruments based on lag 2 and older of lpt_{it} are (11–2)(11–1)/2 = 45 moment conditions $E(lpt_{it\text{-}2}\ \Delta e_{it}) = E(lpt_{it\text{-}3}\ \Delta e_{it}) = \ldots = E(lpt_{i1}\ \Delta e_{it}) = 0$ $(t = 3, \ldots, 11)$;
- for the differenced equation, the first difference of the time dummies is treated as strictly exogenous, corresponding to nine moment condition $E(\Sigma_t\ \Delta d_t\ \Delta e_{it}) = 0$ $(t = 3, \ldots, 11)$;
- finally, to estimate the constant term, the following moment condition is considered: $E(\Sigma_t\ v_{it}) = 0$.

When the nonlinear moment estimator proposed by Ahn and Schmit (1995) is computed, additional 8 nonlinear moment conditions are available. The estimated value of ρ is 0.36 (one-step)-0.38 (two-step), statistically different from zero at the 5% level.

The estimated value of ρ obtained with system GMM estimation is quite different, being equal to about 0.6 (statistically significant at the 5% level).

The difference between the three versions of the estimator may be ascribed to two competing explanations. On the one side, difference GMM estimator may suffer of substantial bias with persistence data (note also that the difference GMM estimates are quite close to FE estimates), whereas system GMM estimate is apt at solving this issue. On the contrary, the system GMM estimator additionally requires the validity of the mean stationarity (initial condition) assumption. The number of instruments (moment conditions) is 64: 55 moment conditions in the differenced equation and 9 additional moment conditions in the level equation spanning from the mean stationarity assumption (build on the basis of $\Delta lpt_{it\text{-}1}$ in the level equation), so that validity of system GMM also relies on this assumption. Diagnostic testing procedures that might help discriminate among the two explanations are discussed in the next Section.

14.7 GMM Estimation: Diagnostic Procedures

According to general GMM theory, the consistency of the estimation procedure relies on the validity of the moment conditions in the population.

[18] In the context of this simplified model, a set of issues are omitted, that will be discussed in Sect. 14.8 when *lrd* is also included in the equation. These refer to computation of the initial weighting matrix with system GMM and the treatment of time dummies.

When there are more moment conditions (R) than parameters to be estimated (K), as it is typically the case with GMM estimates of DPD models, the validity of the $R - K$ overidentification conditions can be verified using the Hansen J statistics (Hansen 1982). This is computed on the basis of the value of the minimized GMM criterion function as:

$$J = NQ(\widehat{\rho}^{GMM}) \tag{14.21}$$

when the estimator is computed using the optimal weighting matrix (optimal first-step matrix if available, or second-step results). Under the null hypothesis that the overidentifying moment conditions are satisfied in the population, the test statistics is asymptotically chi-squared distributed with R-K degrees of freedom. In the case of homoskedastic error terms, the optimal weighting matrix of the difference GMM estimator is given by (14.14) and the efficient first-step estimator can be computed. In this context the test is referred to as the Sargan statistic (in some cases the two terms are used interchangeably).

In finite samples, the Hansen test can behave poorly with large size distortion and low power with a "large" number of instruments (Bowsher 2002; Roodman 2009a; Hayakawa 2016). The test of overidentifying restrictions computed under the assumption of homoskedasticity (i.e. the Sargan test) would not be weakened with instrument proliferation, as it does not require estimating the optimal weighting matrix (see Eq. 14.14). However, it is only valid with homoskedastic disturbances, rarely assumed in microeconometric studies (Roodman 2009a).

In the context of DPD model, ad-hoc test procedures have also been developed. The moment conditions (14.6)—as well as (14.15)—span from the assumption of lack of serial correlation in e_{it}. As discussed in Sect. 14.3, this assumption has implications on the autocorrelation structure of first differenced residuals: (i) presence of autocorrelation of order 1; (ii) no autocorrelation of order 2 (and higher). Accordingly, Arellano and Bond (1991) developed a test that verifies the validity of the difference GMM estimator on the basis of the correlation structure in first-differenced residuals. The test can also be used in the context of the nonlinear GMM. In particular, it is possible to claim that moment conditions of the difference (and non-linear GMM) are satisfied in the population when

- the null hypothesis of zero serial correlation of order one in the first difference residuals is *rejected*;
- the null hypothesis of zero serial correlation of order two in the first difference residuals is *not rejected*.

In Monte Carlo experiments, Arellano and Bond (1991) show that the test for serial correlation of first difference residuals has larger power (i.e., it is better able to detect violation of the null hypothesis) than the Sargan/Hansen test.

Finally, in assessing the validity of the system GMM estimation, attention also needs to be devoted to the initial condition assumption (mean stationarity). For this purpose, a difference-in-Hansen test can be employed, based on the difference between the value of the minimized GMM criterion of the system GMM estimator and the difference GMM estimator (Blundell et al. 2001). The two estimators are computed: (i) the system GMM estimator based on both (14.6) and (14.16), and (ii) the difference GMM estimator based on (14.6) only. If the initial moment condition is satisfied, then adding the level moment condition (14.16) should not deteriorate the value of the GMM criterion. The test is chi-squared distributed with a number of degrees of freedom equal to the number of "level" moment conditions that are added.

Magazzini and Calzolari (2020) propose a different testing strategy, based on a Lagrange multiplier approach, that, in the context of dynamic models with no additional regressors (14.4), is better able to detect departure from the initial condition assumption. This is asymptotically equivalent to the difference-in-Hansen test that compares the system GMM estimator and the non-linear GMM estimator by Ahn and Schmidt (1995). In Stata, the command *xttestms* is available to compute the test (Magazzini and Calzolari 2023).

14.7.1 Assessing the Validity of GMM Estimates of the Regional KPF

In Stata, the output of the command *xtabond2* reports the Arellano and Bond test of autocorrelation in first differenced residuals and the Sargan and Hansen test of overidentifying restrictions. When the model is estimated using *xtabond* and *xtdpdsys*, the post estimation commands *estat abond* and *estat sargan* produce, respectively the Arellano and Bond test of autocorrelation in first differenced residuals and the Sargan test of overidentifying restrictions. Finally, when the model is estimated using *xtdpdgmm*, the post estimation commands *estat serial* and *estat overid* are available to compute the relevant diagnostic statistics.

When using R, testing procedures have been developed within the packages described in Sect. 14.6 (*mtest* and *sargan*).

Table 14.3 reports diagnostics for the models estimated in Table 14.2. Second-step estimates are considered.

Coherently with the lack of serial correlation in the error term, lack of autocorrelation of order one in FD residuals (AB1) is rejected, whereas it is not possible to reject the null hypothesis of lack of autocorrelation of order two (AB2, generally at the 1% level of statistical significance; at the 5% only for the difference GMM estimator). However, the Hansen-J statistics is rejected posing concerns about the validity of the selected overidentifying restrictions.

Table 14.2 First-step and two-step GMM estimated coefficients ("robust" s.e. in parenthesis) of the dynamic KPF with no additional regressors (time dummies included in all specifications). Dependent variable: lpt_{it} (*Source* authors' computation on Eurostat data)

	Difference GMM		Nonlinear GMM		System GMM	
	One-step	Two-step	One-step	Two-step	One-step	Two-step
$lpt_{it\text{-}1}$	0.211 (0.093)**	0.227 (0.093)**	0.357 (0.095)***	0.376 (0.101)***	0.650 (0.067)***	0.639 (0.067)***
Time FE	Yes	Yes	Yes	Yes	Yes	Yes
No. instruments	55		63		64	

Note *robust standard errors in parenthesis*
Statistical significance of coefficients: *** 1%, ** 5%, * 1%

Table 14.3 Two-step GMM estimated coefficients (standard errors in parenthesis) and p-value of diagnostic statistics of the dynamic KPF with no additional regressors (time dummies included in all specifications). Dependent variable: lpt_{it} (*Source* authors' computation on Eurostat data)

	Difference GMM	Non-linear GMM	System GMM
$lpt_{it\text{-}1}$	0.227 (0.093)**	0.376 (0.101)***	0.639 (0.067)***
Time FE	Yes	Yes	Yes
p-value of diagnostic statistics			
AB1	*< 0.001*	*< 0.001*	*< 0.001*
AB2	*0.085*	*0.028*	*0.037*
Hansen-J	*0.003*	*0.002*	*< 0.001*
Diff-in-Hansen: diff. *versus* system GMM	–	–	*< 0.001*
LM test for mean stationarity			*< 0.010*

*Note statistical significance of coefficients: *** 1%, ** 5%, * 1%*

14.8 Models with Additional Regressors

Additional regressors can be included on the right-hand side, as in (14.1). Correlation is allowed between the individual effect and the regressors, as the first difference transformation is still considered to remove u_i[19]:

$$\Delta y_{it} = \rho \Delta y_{it-1} + \Delta \boldsymbol{x}_{it}{}'\beta + \Delta e_{it}$$

The way in which the moment conditions for the variables in $\boldsymbol{x}_{it}$ are defined depends on the assumptions about the correlation between $\boldsymbol{x}_{it}$ and e_{is} ($t, s = 1, \ldots, T$; conditional on u_i). Three cases can be considered: strictly exogenous, predetermined, and simultaneously determined variables (Blundell et al 2001).

[19] The case of time-varying regressors is considered. Time dummies can be included in x_{it}.

14.8.1 Strictly Exogenous Regressors

First consider the case of strictly exogeneous regressors (as it is the case with FE estimation in a static framework): correlation is ruled out between the regressors and the error terms at any time period, i.e. between $\boldsymbol{x}_{it}$ and e_{is} for any $s, t = 1, \ldots, T$. In this case, $\Delta\boldsymbol{x}_{it}$ is exogenous in the first differenced equation, so that the following moment conditions can be specified $\mathrm{E}(\Delta\boldsymbol{x}_{it}\ \Delta e_{it}) = 0$.[20]

When correlation between $\boldsymbol{x}_{it}$ and u_i is allowed, no additional moment conditions can be specified within system GMM and nonlinear GMM estimation (Blundell et al. 2001).

The strict exogeneity assumption is perceived as too restrictive in some cases, as it does not allow for feedback effects and simultaneity.

Time dummies are usually treated as strictly exogenous variables. In the context of the differenced equations, first differenced time dummies are included in the instrument set. However, in the context of system GMM the level of time dummies may also be used as legitimate instrument in the level equation so that the following moment conditions also hold $\mathrm{E}(d_t\ (u_i + e_{it})) = 0\ (t = 2, \ldots, T)$. On this issue, Bond (2002) suggests using the time dummies as instruments for the equations in levels only. This treatment is specific to time dummies, and it is generally not allowed for other variables, unless a random effect structure is assumed (i.e. the variable is assumed to be uncorrelated with u_i).

14.8.2 Predetermined Variables

A weaker assumption, directly spanning from sequential exogeneity, rules out correlation between e_{it} and past and present values of $\boldsymbol{x}_{it}$ but allows feedback effects, i.e., future values of the regressors can be correlated with e_{it} (as it would be the case with $y_{it\text{-}1}$). In this case, $\Delta\boldsymbol{x}_{it}$ is endogenous in the first differenced equation due to the correlation between $\boldsymbol{x}_{it}$ and $e_{it\text{-}1}$. By exploiting lack of serial correlation in e_{it}, it is possible to claim that $\boldsymbol{x}_{it\text{-}1}$ and its further lags can be used as instruments in the first differenced equation.

The following moment condition holds $E[\boldsymbol{x}_{it\text{-}1}\ (e_{it} - e_{it\text{-}1})] = 0$; and, more generally, it is possible to write

$$E[x_{it-j}\Delta e_{it}] = 0 \text{ for any } j \geq 1 \tag{14.22}$$

[20] The strict exogeneity assumption generally implies $\mathrm{E}(\Delta\boldsymbol{x}_{it}\ \Delta e_{is}) = 0$ or any t and s (Ahn and Schmidt 1995), so that additional moment conditions would also be available. However, these are not used in estimation. Note that this is the treatment of the time dummies that has been adopted in Sect. 14.4.

If a mean stationarity condition is additionally imposed on the regressors, so that $E(\Delta \boldsymbol{x}_{it}\, u_i) = 0$ for any t, additional moment conditions can be written for the level equations as:

$$E[\Delta x_{it} v_{it}] = 0. \tag{14.23}$$

14.8.3 Simultaneously Determined Regressors

Finally, consider the case of simultaneously determined regressors, in which also correlation between e_{it} and $\boldsymbol{x}_{it}$ is allowed (still ruling out correlation between e_{it} and past values of $\boldsymbol{x}_{it}$, whereas correlation is allowed between e_{it} and present and future values of $\boldsymbol{x}_{it}$). Again, $\Delta \boldsymbol{x}_{it}$ is endogenous in the first differenced equation (correlated with Δe_{it}) and conditions (14.22) and (14.23) do not hold. On the basis of the assumption of lack of serial correlation in e_{it}, it is possible to claim that $\boldsymbol{x}_{it\text{-}2}$ and its further lags are legitimate instruments in the first differenced equation. The following moment conditions hold:

$$E[x_{it-j} \Delta e_{it}] = 0 \text{ for any } j \geq 2 \tag{14.24}$$

If mean stationarity is further assumed, it is also possible to exploit the following moment conditions:

$$E[\Delta x_{it-1} v_{it}] = 0 \tag{14.25}$$

Estimation can proceed as discussed in Sect. 14.5, after having included additional columns in the matrix of instruments Z_i.

14.8.4 The Dynamic Patent-R&D Relationship in Europe

Table 14.4 reports difference, nonlinear, and system two-step GMM estimates of the regional KPF that also includes *lrd* among the regressors, treated both as strictly exogenous and predetermined regressor.[21] Time dummies are included in all the specifications.

Three different versions of the system GMM estimator are computed, differencing for the treatment of time dummies and the initial (first-step) weighting matrix:

[21] In the Stata and R files accompanying this chapter, the model is also estimated treating *lrd* as a simultaneously determined regressor.

Table 14.4 Two-step GMM estimated coefficients (standard error in parenthesis) and p-value of diagnostic statistics of the dynamic KPF including R&D stock (time dummies included in all specifications). Dependent variable: lpt_{it} (*Source* author's computation on Eurostat data)

	Difference GMM	Nonlinear GMM	System GMM.1	System GMM.2	System GMM.3
Strictly exogenous *lrd*					
$lpt_{it\text{-}1}$	0.171 (0.074)**	0.172 (0.079)**	0.231 (0.089)***	0.598 (0.105)***	0.588 (0.115)***
lrd_{it}	0.605 (0.245)**	0.745 (0.119)***	1.020 (0.151)***	0.508 (0.146)***	0.505 (0.143)***
No. instruments	*56*	*64*	*65*	*65*	*65*
AB1	*< 0.001*	*< 0.001*	*< 0.001*	*< 0.001*	*< 0.001*
AB2	*0.203*	*0.154*	*0.161*	*0.059*	*0.065*
Hansen-J	*0.012*	*0.040*	*0.095*	*0.080*	*0.067*
Diff-in-Hansen: diff. *vs.* system GMM	–	–	*0.413*	*0.818*	*0.507*
LM test for mean stationarity	–	–	*0.206*	*0.948*	*0.485*
Diff-in-Hansen: *lrd* as strictly exogenous	*0.074*	–	*0.002*	*0.009*	*0.013*
Predetermined *lrd*					
$lpt_{it\text{-}1}$	0.212 (0.068)***	0.226 (0.071)***	0.290 (0.076)***	0.668 (0.068)***	0.674 (0.064)
lrd_{it}	0.583 (0.202)***	0.691 (0.136)***	0.821 (0.122)***	0.393 (0.100)***	0.387 (0.094)***
No. instruments	109	117	128	128	128
AB1	*< 0.001*	*< 0.001*	*< 0.001*	*< 0.001*	*< 0.001*
AB2	*0.164*	*0.112*	*0.123*	*0.047*	*0.046*
Hansen-J	*0.072*	*0.085*	*0.081*	*0.131*	*0.143*
Diff-in-Hansen: diff. *vs.* system GMM	–	–	*0.924*	*0.366*	*0.827*
LM test for mean stationarity	–	–	*0.874*	*0.465*	*0.885*

*Note Statistical significance of coefficients: *** 1%, ** 5%, * 1%*

- System GMM.1: The weighting matrix in the first step imposes zero correlation between the error term in the two equation – even if the assumption is not satisfied, this version of the matrix is sometimes used;

- System GMM.2: The weighting matrix in the first step is the one that would be optimal in the case of homoskedasticity when zero variance is also assumed for u_i;
- System GMM.3: The weighing matrix as in System GMM.2, but time dummies are included as instruments in the level equation only (Bond 2002).

Consider first the results of the model estimation that treats *lrd* as a strictly exogenous variables, therefore ruling out feedback effects and simultaneity.

AB1 and AB2 tests have generally the expected statistical significance (at the 5% level) and do not allow rejecting the null hypothesis of lack of serial correlation in e_{it}. The R&D stock, *lrd*, is positive and statistically significant. Note that the Hansen-*J* statistics allows rejecting the validity of the strict exogeneity assumption (see the *p*-value associated to "Diff-in-Hansen: *lrd* as strictly exogenous"), raising concerns about the validity of this assumption.

Focusing on the result related to predetermined *lrd*, it is not possible to reject the Hansen-J statistics (at 5% level of statistical significance), providing support to the validity of the chosen (overidentifying) moment conditions. However, the hypothesis of lack of autocorrelation in the idiosyncratic component has to be rejected at the 5% level of statistical significance in the case of system GMM.2 and GMM.3, posing concerns for the validity of the results. In this case further lags may be considered and inclusion of additional lags of the dependent variable may solve the issue. Looking at the difference-in-Hansen and LM test that assess the validity of the mean stationarity assumption, the hypothesis cannot be rejected at 5% level of statistical significance. Kiviet (2007) shows that the quality of system GMM may depend on the initial weighting matrix.

An essential step in empirical analysis using GMM includes the assessment of the sensitivity of the results to different choices of the instrument set. The difference GMM generates moment conditions prolifically (Roodman 2009a): in the case of predetermined R&D expenditures, the number of moment condition considered exceeds 100. Instrument proliferation can be problematic, and finite sample issues may emerge with GMM estimation as the number of instruments increases (Ziliak 1997; Bun and Kiviet 2006; Roodman 2009a).

First, as it is also the case with 2SLS estimation, overfitting in the first stage can lead to substantial bias. In the limiting case when the number of instruments equals the number of observations, the endogenous variable is perfectly predicted in the first stage regression, so that the predicted values equal the observed ones, and the 2SLS estimator equals OLS (Roodman 2009a; Wooldridge 2010). This issue extends to estimation of DPD models (Arellano 2003).

With the two-step estimator, the number of elements in the (estimated) "optimal" $R \times R$ weighting matrix is quadratic in the instrument count (R) and therefore quartic in T. A "small" finite sample might lack adequate information for providing a good approximation, making the matrix far from the (asymptotically) theoretically optimal one (Roodman 2009a).

Finally, the Hansen test can behave poorly with large size distortion and low power with a "large" number of instruments (see Sect. 14.7).

Unfortunately, there is no clear guidance in the literature about this issue. In applied work, it is good practice to report the instrument count and assess the robustness of results to changes in the instrument set. One simple strategy is to limit the number of lags and only include less distant lags as instruments. Alternatively, the number of instruments can be "collapsed" (see Roodman, 2009a, 2009b).

14.9 Alternative Estimation Procedures

Estimation procedures based on different methods have been proposed in the literature.

Starting from Balestra and Nerlove (1966), there is a long tradition of maximum likelihood (ML) estimation in DPD models with normally distributed errors. However, ML estimation in a FE framework is complicated by the incidental parameter problem and reliance on initial condition assumptions (Hsiao 1986). Against this background, Hsiao et al. (2002) propose a transformed likelihood and a minimum distance approach to DPD data models in a FE framework. The estimating procedure is developed by first taking differences of model (1) in order to remove u_i. Monte Carlo simulation by Hsiao et al. (2002) shows that these methods dominate the GMM approach both in terms of the bias and root mean square error of the estimators and the size and power of the test statistics. The estimation procedure has been extended to incorporate cross-sectional heteroskedasticity by Hayakawa and Pesaran (2015). The estimator is available in Stata with the command *xtdpdqml* (Kripfganz, 2016).

A different strategy for estimating DPD models aims at correcting the bias of the FE estimator (see Sect. 14.3). In this context, a formula for the bias of the FE estimator can be developed and then used to correct FE estimates (Kiviet 1995; Bun and Carree 2006, 2012). Breitung et al. (2022) show that bias-corrected estimator can be obtained as a method of moments estimator.

Bootstrap procedure and indirect inference (Gouriéroux et al. 1993) have also been applied in this context as a bias-correction strategy (Gouriéroux et al. 2010; Bao 2021; Everaert and Pozzi, 2007).

14.10 Concluding Remarks

The Chapter has presented estimation of DPD models. Inclusion of the lagged dependent variable on the right-hand side of the equation along with time-invariant fixed effects leads to a number of econometric issues. Various estimators have been proposed with GMM most often applied in empirical studies.

A recent comparison of available procedures is presented in Cave et al. (2023). The key challenge to estimators' performance is the degree of dynamic persistence in the dependent variable, and problems are common with highly persistent data. In this setting difference GMM estimator is known to have poor finite sample performance that may be mitigated using nonlinear and system GMM estimators (the latter with additional assumptions). When the mean stationarity assumption fails, Hayakawa (2009) and Hayakawa and Nagata (2016) show that the difference GMM estimator exhibits better properties, even with strong persistency. In addition, the possibility of weak instruments has also been detected in the context of system GMM estimation (Bun and Windmeijer 2010). In empirical analysis, it is therefore essential to assess robustness of employed methodologies in order to avoid spurious economic conclusions and misleading policy recommendations (Cave et al. 2023).

When discussing the inclusion of additional regressors, this Chapter considers the case of time-varying regressors. Recent literature considers the estimation of the effect of time-invariant variables (e.g., gender of individuals or firm sector). Using the FD transformation, the effect of these variables is not identified, whereas estimation may be feasible when information from the equation in levels is used in the estimation process (Kripfganz and Schwarz 2019).

Acknowledgements I thank Giorgio Calzolari for his precious support and invaluable discussions. This chapter is dedicated to the memory of Alessandro Sembenelli, who introduced me to DPD modeling.

References

Ahn SC, Schmidt P (1995) Efficient estimation of models for dynamic panel data. J Econometrics 68(1):5–27

Ahn SC, Schmidt P (1997) Efficient estimation of dynamic panel data models: alternative assumptions and simplified estimation. J Econ 76(1–2):309–321

Anderson TW, Hsiao C (1981) Estimation of dynamic models with error components. J Am Stat Assoc 76(375):598–606

Anderson TW, Hsiao C (1982) Formulation and estimation of dynamic models using panel data. J Econ 18:47–82

Arellano M (1989) A note on the Anderson-Hsiao estimator for panel data. Econ Lett 31:337–341

Arellano M (2003) Panel data econometrics. Oxford University Press

Arellano M, Bond S (1991) Some tests of specification for panel data: Monte Carlo evidence and an application to employment equations. Rev Econ Stud 58(2):277–297

Arellano M, Bover O (1995) Another look at the instrumental variable estimation of error-components models. J Econ 68(1):29–51

Balestra P, Nerlove M (1966) Pooling cross section and time series data in the estimation of a dynamic model: the demand for natural gas. Econometrica 34(3):585–612

Baltagi BH (2005) Econometric analysis of panel data. Wiley

Bao Y (2021) Indirect inference estimation of a first-order dynamic panel data model. J Quant Econ 19:79–98

Blundell R, Bond S (1998) Initial conditions and moment restrictions in dynamic panel data models. J Econ 87(1):115–143

Blundell R, Bond S, Windmeijer F (2001) Estimation in dynamic panel data models: improving on the performance of the standard GMM estimator, vol. 15. Emerald Group Publishing Limited

Bond S (2002) Dynamic panel data models: a guide to micro data methods and practice. Port Econ J 1:141–162

Bowsher CG (2002) On testing overidentifying restrictions in dynamic panel data models. Econ Lett 77:211–220
Breitung J, Kripfganz S, Hayakawa K (2022) Bias-corrected method of moments estimators for dynamic panel data models. Econ Stat 24:116–132
Bun MJG, Carree MA (2006) Bias-corrected estimation in dynamic panel data models with heteroscedasticity. Econ Lett 92(2):220–227
Bun MJG, Carree MA (2012) Bias-corrected estimation in dynamic panel data models. J Bus Econ Stat 23(2):200–210
Bun MJG, Kiviet JF (2006) The effects of dynamic feedbacks on LS and MM estimator accuracy in panel data models. J Econometrics 132(2):409–444
Bun MJ, Windmeijer F (2010) The weak instrument problem of the system GMM estimator in dynamic panel data models. Economet J 13(1):95–126
Calzolari G, Magazzini L (2019) Improving GMM efficiency in dynamic models for panel data with mean stationarity. In: Ickstadt K, Lübke K, Szepannek G, Trautmann H, Vichi M (eds) Bauer N. Applications in statistical computing - from music data analysis to industrial quality improvement, Springer, pp 201–216
Cameron AC, Trivedi PK (2005) Microeconometrics: methods and applications. Cambridge University Press
Cave J, Chaudhuri K, Kumbhakar SC (2023) Dynamic firm performance and estimator choice: a comparison of dynamic panel data estimators. Eur J Oper Res 307:447–467
Charlot S, Crescenzi R, Musolesi A (2015) Econometric modelling of the regional knowledge production function in Europe. J Econ Geogr 15(6):1227–1259
Croissant Y, Millo G (2008) Panel data econometrics in R: the plm package. J Stat Softw 27(2):1–43
Everaert G, Pozzi L (2007) Bootstrap-based bias correction for dynamic panels. J Econ Dyn Control 31(4):1160–1184
Falk M (2004) What determines patents per capita in OECD countries? WIFO Working Papers No. 242, Austrian Institute of Economic Research (WIFO), Vienna
Fritsch M, Pua AAY, Schnurbus J (2021) Pdynmc: a package for estimating linear dynamic panel data models based on nonlinear moment conditions. R J 13(1):218–231
Gouriéroux C, Monfort A, Renault E (1993) Indirect inference. J Appl Econ 8(S1):S85-S118
Gouriéroux C, Phillips PCB, Yu J (2010) Indirect inference for dynamic panel models. J Econ 157(1):68–77
Griliches Z (1979) Issues in assessing the contribution of R&D to productivity growth. Bell J Econ 10:92–116
Han C, Phillips PCB (2010) GMM estimation for dynamic panels with fixed effects and strong instruments at unity. Econ Theor 26(1):119–151
Hansen LP (1982) Large sample properties of generalized method of moments estimators. Econometrica 50(4):1029–1054
Hansen LP, Heaton J, Yaron A (1996) Finite-sample properties of some alternative GMM estimators. J Bus Econ Stat 14(3):262–280
Hayakawa K (2007) Small sample bias properties of the system GMM estimator in dynamic panel data models. Econ Lett 95:32–38
Hayakawa K (2009) On the effect of mean-nonstationarity in dynamic panel data models. J Econ 153(2):133–135
Hayakawa K (2016) On the effect of weighting matrix in GMM specification test. J Stat Plan Infer 178:84–98
Hayakawa K, Nagata S (2016) On the behaviour of the GMM estimator in persistent dynamic panel data models with unrestricted initial conditions. Comput Stat Data an 100:265–303
Hayakawa K, Pesaran MH (2015) Robust standard errors in transformed likelihood estimation of dynamic panel data models with cross-sectional heteroskedasticity. J Econ 188(1):111–134
Holtz-Eakin D, Newey W, Rosen HS (1988) Estimating vector autoregressions with panel data. Econometrica 56(6):1371–1395
Hsiao C (1986) Analysis of panel data. Cambridge University Press

Hsiao C (2007) Panel data analysis – advantages and challenges. TEST 16(1):1–22
Hsiao C, Pesaran MH, Tahmiscioglu AK (2002) Maximum likelihood estimation of fixed effects dynamic panel data models covering short time periods. J Econ 109(1):107–150
Kiviet JF (1995) On bias, inconsistency, and efficiency of various estimators in dynamic panel data models. J Econ 68(1):53–78
Kiviet JF (2007) Judging contending estimators by simulation: tournaments in dynamic panel data models. In Phillips GDA, Tzavalis E (eds) The refinement of econometric estimation and test procedures. Cambridge University Press
Kripfganz S (2016) Quasi–maximum likelihood estimation of linear dynamic short-T panel-data models. Stata J 16(4):1013–1038
Kripfganz S (2017) XTDPDGMM: Stata module to perform generalized method of moments estimation of linear dynamic panel data models. https://econpapers.repec.org/software/bocbocode/s458395.htm
Kripfganz S (2019) Generalized method of moments estimation of linear dynamic panel data models. Proceedings of the 2019 London stata conference
Kripfganz S, Schwarz C (2019) Estimation of linear dynamic panel data models with time-invariant regressors. J Appl Econ 34(4):526–546
Magazzini L, Calzolari G (2020) Testing initial conditions in dynamic panel data models. Econ Rev 39(2):115–134
Magazzini L, Calzolari G (2023) A Lagrange multiplier test for the mean stationarity assumption in dynamic panel-data models. Stata J 23(2):418–437
Nickell S (1981) Biases in dynamic models with fixed effects. Econometrica 49(6):1417–1426
Peri G (2005) Determinants of knowledge flows and their effect on innovation. Rev Econ Statistics 87(2):308–322
Roodman D (2009a) A note on the theme of too many instruments. Oxford B Econ Stat 71(1):135–158
Roodman D (2009b) How to do xtabond2: An introduction to difference and system GMM in Stata. Stata J 9(1):86–136
Verbeek M (2008) A guide to modern econometrics. Wiley
White H (1982) Instrumental variable regression with independent observations. Econometrica 50(2):483–499
Windmeijer F (2000) Efficiency comparisons for a system GMM estimator in dynamic panel data models. IFS working papers no. W98/01
Windmeijer F (2005) A finite sample correction for the variance of linear efficient two-step GMM estimators. J Econ 126(1):25–51
Wooldridge JM (2010) Econometric analysis of cross section and panel data. The MIT Press
Ziliak JP (1997) Efficient estimation with panel data when instruments are predetermined: an empirical comparison of moment-condition estimators. J Bus Econ Stat 15(4):419–431

Chapter 15
Spatial Dynamic Panel Model: An Application to Environmental Violations in Brazil

André Luis Squarize Chagas

Abstract This chapter presents a review of the Spatial Econometrics literature, which deals with interactions of economic units in space, traditionally using cross-sectional data. In recent years, a great deal of theoretical effort has been made to deal with data from spatial observations that are repeated throughout time, named panel data models. These models take advantage of the more information available, which helps to fix some selection problems existing in the cross-sectional models, less collinearity, and higher variation in the data. The spatial panel data model can include dynamic effects to investigate the spatial dependence and serial correlations simultaneously. This kind of model considers variation in space and time and treats the serial dependence among spatial units; the spatial dependence over time; specific non-observable space–time effects; and the endogeneity in one or more regressors other than the spatial or time lag in the dependent variable This chapter presents a new method to estimate this kind of model, called Spatial Dynamic Limited Information Maximum Likelihood (SDLIML), when some exploratory variables are endogenous. A Monte Carlo simulation shows that this estimator performs better than the alternative Generalized Method of Moments (GMM) in all situations. We include an illustration section, showing how to perform a small version of the Monte Carlo experiment. In the end, an application using Brazilian data on environmental violations is also presented. Evidence of a pedagogical deterrent effect associated with the value of fines is also found.

Keywords Spatial econometrics · Spatial dynamic model · Limited information maximum likelihood · Environmental violations

Supplementary Information The online version contains supplementary material available at https://doi.org/10.1007/978-981-99-4902-1_15.

A. L. S. Chagas (✉)
Department of Economics, NEREUS, University of Sao Paulo, Sao Paulo, Brazil
e-mail: achagas@usp.br

D. Mukherjee (ed.), *Applied Econometric Analysis Using Cross Section and Panel Data*, Contributions to Economics, https://doi.org/10.1007/978-981-99-4902-1_15

15.1 Introduction

Spatial econometrics consists of techniques that deal with interactions of economic units in space. It is a combination of the spatial analysis approach with economic techniques. Spatial analysis is a set of mathematical techniques that study space's influence on natural or social phenomena' behavior. Econometrics, on this side, are statistical and mathematical analysis methods that analyze the relationship between economic variables. The term "spatial econometrics" was first used by Jean Paelinck and Leo Klassen in a 1979 book (Paelinck and Klaassen 1979).

A modern view on the topic defines spatial econometrics as a subarea of econometrics that deals with spatial interactions, comprising interdependence, spillovers (spillovers), and heterogeneity in regression models in the cross section or data panel (Anselin 2001). However, the notion of space involves not only geographic space, typical of Regional Science or Urban Economics models, but also the interaction may involve other forms of measurement common to other areas, such as Political Science, Commerce, Industrial Organization, etc. (Anselin 2010).

In this chapter, a review is done of the estimators of spatial models of dynamic panel data. This approach aims to consider how the interaction between effects lagged in time, space, and time-space can contribute to understanding the dynamics of the analyzed process. A new approach is proposed for dynamic models with panel data and spatial dependence to address both the endogeneities induced by spatial simultaneity and the relationship between fines and contemporaneous values of infractions. As an alternative to adapting the Generalized Method of Moments (GMM) by Kapoor et al. (2007), we propose an approach exploring the likelihood of the data with a *Limited Information* estimator called Spatial Dynamic Limited Information Maximum Likelihood (SDLIML). The Monte Carlo simulation shows that this estimator performs better than the GMM. Employing a spatial Cochrane-Orcutt decomposition also achieves good performance in terms of computational time.

The chapter is organized as follows. The next session presents an overview of the literature in the Spatial Econometrics field, both in the cross section and panel data approach. The following section discusses the dynamic models and presents a new estimator, named the limited information maximum likelihood. A Monte Carlo experiment compare the performance of this estimator and the alternative GMM estimator, and an application is also presented. The last section presents the conclusion.

15.2 Spatial Econometrics: A Definition

The definition of space can be general. Usually, it is geographic, but economic or social interaction spaces are also possible. Ideally, a spatial model should deal with: the importance of interdependence between variables; potentially asymmetrical spatial relationships; the interrelation between explanatory variables from other regions in the result of a specific region (space-distant explanatory factors); differentiation

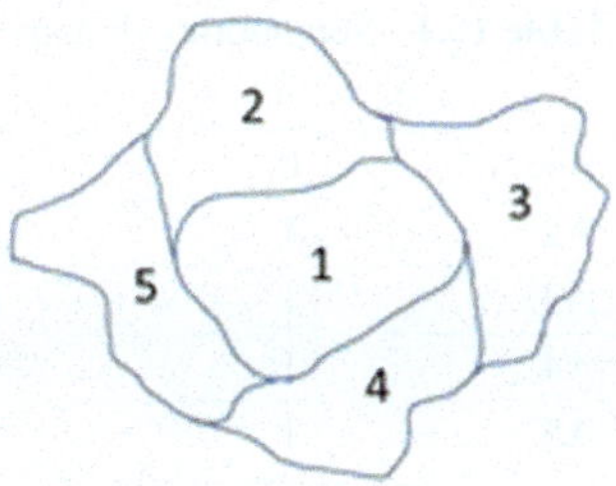

Fig. 15.1 Hypothetical regions

between ex ante interaction (identifiable in the data before intervention) and ex post (obtained through simulations and specific modeling); and the explicit consideration of space in modeling.

A modern view on the topic defines spatial econometrics as a sub-area of econometrics that deals with spatial interactions, comprising interdependence, spillovers (spillovers between regions), and heterogeneity (like heteroscedasticity and spatial stability of coefficients) in cross-sectional regression models or panel data. However, the notion of space involves not only geographic space but also typical of Regional Science or Urban Economics models. The interaction may involve other forms of measurement common to other areas, such as Political Science, Commerce, and Industrial Organization. In this broader view, spatial interaction is seen as a special case of dependence between observations. The structure of correlation (or covariance) between variables in different locations is given by a specific ordering, determined by the relative position of the unit in the space. Although there is some similarity with correlation in the time domain, the nature of spatial dependence requires a specialized set of techniques.

When looking at data in space, it is common to see that a given location exhibits a pattern more similar to that of its closest neighbors than to more distant locations. This characteristic follows the first law of geography statement, which postulates that "everything is related to everything, but the closest things are related more intensely" (Tobler 1970). Geographic neighborhood criterion incorporates this postulate in the form of distance or contiguity. Contiguity refers to the adjacency position of a unit in space concerning the others and considers the size and position of the border between two different locations, for example. Neighboring locations are those that meet the chosen criterion, and non-neighbors are those that do not (by definition, a region is not a neighbor of itself).

In the figure below, for example, region 1 is a neighbor of all the others by the contiguity criterion, as it has a common border and vertices with all the other regions. The other regions have three contiguous neighbors. Region 2, for instance, has regions 1, 3, and 5 as neighbors. Region 3 has neighbors 1, 2, 4, and so on.

This information can be stored in a matrix (neighborhood matrix), where the regions are organized in rows and columns, and the value 1 (or any other positive value) is assigned to neighboring regions and zero to non-neighboring ones (see Table 15.1).

Table 15.1 Neighborhood matrix of hypothetic regions of Fig. 15.1

	A1	A2	A3	A4	A5
A1	0	1	1	1	1
A2	1	0	1	0	1
A3	1	1	0	1	0
A4	1	0	1	0	1
A5	1	1	0	1	0

Table 15.2 Weighted spatial matrix of hypothetic regions of Fig. 15.1

	A1	A2	A3	A4	A5
A1	0	1/4	1/4	1/4	1/4
A2	1/3	0	1/3	0	1/3
A3	1/3	1/3	0	1/3	0
A4	1/3	0	1/3	0	1/3
A5	1/3	1/3	0	1/3	0

In the distance criterion, those locations at a pre-established maximum distance are considered neighbors. One can also consider the inverse of the distance and assign "neighborhood weights" proportional to the inverse distance. By this criterion, greater weights can be attributed to closer regions, for example, and smaller weights to distant regions. In this case, the neighborhood matrix would have positive values different from zero for neighboring regions and values equal to zero for non-neighboring ones.

It is usual in spatial econometrics models to standardize the neighborhood matrix according to some criterion that guarantees the existence and stationarity of the model. The most used is the standardization by the sum of the lines (standardized line). The standardized matrix defines the weighted spatial matrix. When the matrix is row-standard, the sum of the weights of the neighbors is equal to 1.

In the previous example, the standardized matrix would look like Table 15.2. Region 1 has four neighbors, each being assigned a weight of 1/4. The remaining regions all have three neighbors, which are assigned equal weights.

Table 15.2 defines a matrix mathematically expressed as

$$\mathbf{W} = w_{ij}$$

where w_{ij} represents the weight assigned to the j-th neighbor of i region. By definition, $w_{ii} = 0$.

15.2.1 Spatial Models Taxonomy

The simplest spatial model is the Ordinary Least Square (OLS) or the classical linear model. It is also the most constrained model because it assumes no spatial relationship among the observations. The models most studied and used in empirical applications are the models: SAR (Spatial Autoregressive Model), SEM (Spatial Error Model), and SLX (Spatial model with spatial lag in the explanatory variables). Combining these models leads to higher order spatial models with more complex spatial process controls.

The concept of spatial lag is borrowed from the time series literature. Here, lags are defined in terms of distance in time. In spatial econometrics, the lag is defined in terms of the spatial relationship. The matrix of spatial weights measures distance in space. The pre-multiplication of any model variable by the spatial weights matrix results in spatial lags of the variable (spatial lag).

Figure 15.2 shows an overview of the various possibilities of existing spatial relationships in the data generation process. Starting with the most general model (General Spatial Model), which includes interdependence, spillover, and heterogeneity of the autoregressive and moving average type, and can be represented by the equations:

$$
\begin{aligned}
y &= \rho \mathbf{W} y + \mathbf{X}\beta + \mathbf{W}\mathbf{X}\theta + u \\
u &= \lambda \mathbf{W} u + \gamma \mathbf{W}\varepsilon + \varepsilon
\end{aligned}
\tag{15.1}
$$

where y is a vector $n \times 1$ of the dependent variable, $\mathbf{X}$ is matrix $n \times k$ of explanatory variables, $\mathbf{W}$ is a $n \times n$ spatial weights matrix, u is an error term spatially related in the autoregressive (captured by $\lambda \mathbf{W} u$) and moving average ways (captured by $\mathbf{w}\varepsilon$), and ε is an error term with zero means. The parameters of interest in this model are β, of course, and also the spatial parameter ρ, θ, λ, and γ. Different restrictions on one or some of these parameters result in different spatial models. For instance,

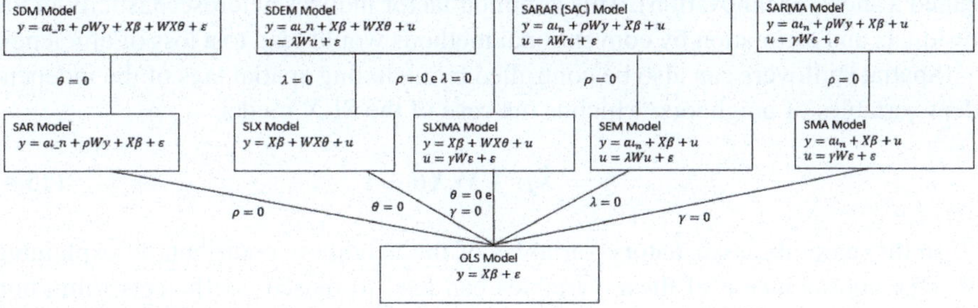

Fig. 15.2 Spatial models taxonomy

if we assume $\theta = \lambda = \gamma = 0$, then the remained parameters of interest are β and ρ (the latter captures how the interaction with the dependent variable impacts the dependent variable of the neighbors). This would be the case, for example, where the generation of transport trips was interdependent, that is, the generation of trips in one region explains the generation of trips in other regions. In this example, the dependent variable, y appears on the right side of the spatially lagged equation ($\mathbf{W}y$). For example, in the SAR model, the spatial lag occurs in the dependent variable, that is

$$y = \rho \mathbf{W} y + \mathbf{X}\beta + \varepsilon \tag{15.2}$$

The parameters of interest in this model are β and ρ (the latter captures how the interaction with the dependent variable impacts the dependent variable of the neighbors). This would be the case, for example, where the generation of transport trips was interdependent, that is, the generation of trips in one region explains the generation of trips in other regions. In this example, the dependent variable, y appears on the right side of the spatially lagged equation ($\mathbf{W}y$). In the case where the matrix $\mathbf{W}$ is a matrix standardized by the row, this pre-multiplication of y by $\mathbf{W}$ is equivalent to calculating, for each region, the weighted average of the variable y of the neighbors, where the spatial weights give the weights. As in the case of the classical model, the estimated coefficient (ρ) controls the correlation of $\mathbf{W}y$ over y. As it deals with the correlation of the variable with a linear combination of the variable itself, it is called autocorrelation.

Spatial models deal with these issues in different ways. Including spatial controls in a regression model helps to control spatial heterogeneity and, thus, produces better estimators for the standard errors of the regression model parameters. Including the spatial lag in the residuals is a simple way to do this, as in the SEM model:

$$\begin{aligned} y &= \mathbf{X}\beta + u \\ u &= \lambda \mathbf{W} u + \varepsilon \end{aligned} \tag{15.3}$$

In this case, the regions share a common shock, as the spatial lags of the residuals impact the dependent variable, which can happen if some unobserved common factor is not correlated with the other independent variables (a factor of this type is also called a shock or innovation). This common factor induces heteroscedasticity in the residuals and estimation by conventional methods would lead to a loss of efficiency.

Spatial spillovers can also be controlled by including spatial lags of the independent variables of neighbors, which is the case of the SLX model:

$$y = \mathbf{X}\beta + \mathbf{W}X\theta + \varepsilon \tag{15.4}$$

In this case, the explanatory variables of the neighbors contribute to explaining y. This non-inclusion of these variables can lead to biased coefficients (omission of relevant variables). In this case, neighboring regions' characteristics explain the dependent variable.

Interdependence, on the other hand, requires treating the simultaneity of the dependent variable, as in the SAR model seen earlier. As the dependent variable's spatial lag is endogenous, the estimation process requires more advanced techniques than ordinary least squares models and their derivations.

Among the estimation methods usually employed are the maximum likelihood method, with adequate treatment for spatial dependence in the likelihood function; the generalized method of moments, with the use of higher order spatial lags as instruments; and Bayesian methods, adopting distribution functions for the model parameters and uninformative priors at the beginning of the iterative estimation process.

Unlike the descriptive approach of spatial statistics, using the correct spatial matrix is very important for econometric models. Selection criteria such as Akaike or Schwartz can be used to decide between matrices of different criteria. The choice between spatial models (SAR, SEM, SLX, etc.) can be made using spatial correlation tests for residuals (Moran's I) and Lagrange multiplier or likelihood ratio tests.

For the autoregressive model (SAR) and its derivations, the marginal effect is not directly calculated because of the implicit non-linearity in the model. The marginal effects must consider the direct and indirect effects induced by the autoregressive process, which requires an additional calculation based on the parameters estimated in the regression model (see LeSage and Pace 2009).

15.2.2 Spatial Panel Data

In recent years, a great deal of theoretical effort has been made to deal with data from spatial observations that are repeated throughout time, named panel data models. The use of these types of models is interesting due to the more information available, which help to fix some selection problems existing in the cross-sectional models, less collinearity, and higher variation in the data.

The extent of a cross-sectional spatial model, with N observations for a spatio-temporal panel data model data, with N observations in the cross-section and T periods, can be seen as

$$\begin{aligned} y_t &= \rho \mathbf{W} y_t + \alpha \iota_N + X_t \beta + \mathbf{W} X_t \gamma + u_t \\ u_t &= \lambda \mathbf{W} u_t + \epsilon_t \end{aligned} \tag{15.5}$$

This model is several cross-sections stacked and, with some adjustments, can be estimated by the same methods and algorithms used to estimate the models in the cross section.

The main objection to this pooling of data is that it does not consider spatial or temporal heterogeneities. Spatial units can have specific attributes, usually not time-varying but difficult to measure (observe). Some space units are on the coast, others on the edge or inland, others had different colonization, etc. Failure to measure these variables increases the risk of getting biased estimators. One way to remedy this situation is to include an intercept variable, μ_i, representing the locale-specific omitted effects. That is

$$
\begin{aligned}
y_t &= \rho \mathbf{W} y_t + \alpha \iota_N + X_t \beta + \mathbf{W} X_t \gamma + \mu + u_t \\
u_t &= \lambda \mathbf{W} u_t + \epsilon_t
\end{aligned}
$$

where $\mu = (\mu_1, \ldots, \mu_N)'$. Similarly, one can add a time-specific effect to control for space-invariant effects but specific to a given moment. The absence of such a variable can lead to biased estimates, as widely studied in time series models (Arellano 2003; Hsiao 2003; Baltagi and Baltagi 2005). Specific market conditions include booms or recessions, economic plans, or currency devaluations.

$$
\begin{aligned}
y_t &= \rho \mathbf{W} y_t + \alpha \iota_N + X_t \beta + \mathbf{W} X_t \gamma + \varepsilon_t \iota_N + u_t \\
u_t &= \lambda \mathbf{W} u_t + \epsilon_t
\end{aligned} \tag{15.6}
$$

A model including both space and time-specific effects can be written as

$$
\begin{aligned}
y_t &= \rho \mathbf{W} Y_t + \alpha \iota_N + X_t \beta + W X_t \gamma + \mu + \varepsilon_t \iota_N + u_t \\
u_t &= \lambda \mathbf{W} u_t + \epsilon_t
\end{aligned} \tag{15.7}
$$

This model can be estimated considering μ and ε as fixed or random effects.

In the case of random effects, μ and ε are treated as iid variables, with zero mean and constant variances, not necessarily equal.

Let us consider the necessary changes in the non-spatial panel data model to include spatial interaction terms. As before, the interaction can be spatial lag type (SAR/SDM) or spatial error type (SEM/SDEM). The matrix **W** is assumed to be constant over time, and the panel is balanced, with means that the database includes full information for all spatial units over time.

One can modify the estimator to include **W** matrices varying over time due to environmental changes. A quasi-maximum likelihood estimator with time-varying matrices is consistent and asymptotically normal (Yu et al. 2012). Considering an unbalanced panel is more problematic, mainly if the reason for missing data is unknown (Pfaffermayr 2009; Wang and Lee 2013).

The spatial lag model can be specified as

$$
y_{it} = \rho \sum_{j=1}^{N} w_{ij} y_{it} + x_{it} \beta + \mu_i + \varepsilon_{it} \tag{15.8}
$$

where w_{ij} is an element of the spatial weights matrix, W.

According to Anselin et al. (2008a), this model is the result of the equilibrium of a spatial process in which the values of the variables of neighboring agents jointly determine the value of the dependent variable of an agent.

The spatial error model is

$$y_{it} = x_{it}\beta + \mu_i + u_{it} \tag{15.9}$$
$$u_{it} = \lambda \sum_{j=1}^{N} w_{ij} u_{it} + \varepsilon_{it}$$

There are two main approaches to the estimation of spatial panel data models:

i. maximum likelihood (ML) as the proposal for Elhorst (2003), and
ii. Instrument variables (IV)/GMM model, as in Kapoor et al. (2007).

The maximum likelihood estimators assume residual normality and can use a normality test to verify this assumption. However, even in the non-normal case, the quasi-maximum likelihood estimator can be used if the model is rightly specified (Lee 2004). On the other hand, the GMM estimator has the disadvantage of the values for the spatial coefficients can be outside the parameter space $(1/\omega_{min}, 1/\omega_{max})$.

Franzese and Hays (2007) compare the performance of ML and IV estimators for spatial lagged panel data models, but they do not consider the presence of fixed or random effects. They find that the ML estimator weakly dominates the IV estimator in terms of efficiency and bias but sometimes lags behind the IV estimator for small values in the spatial parameter.

15.3 Dynamic Spatial Panel Data Models

The spatial panel data model can include dynamic effects to investigate the spatial dependence and serial correlations simultaneously. Sometimes, spatial dynamic models are called space–time models (Anselin et al. 2008b). This kind of model considers variation in space and time and needs to be able to treat:

- The serial dependence among spatial units observations in the time, a typical topic of time series econometric models (Enders 2008; Hamilton 2020);
- spatial dependence among the units over time (Anselin 1988; LeSage and Pace 2009; Arbia 2014; Kelejian and Piras 2017);
- specific non-observables space–time effects (Hsiao 2014; Baltagi 2008; Wooldridge 2010); and
- the endogeneity in one or more regressors other than the spatial or time lag in the dependent variable

The dynamic panel data model has become important in applied works after the seminal paper of Arellano and Bond (1991), which presents a GMM method exploring linear moment restrictions to estimate spatial fixed effects in a dynamic model. The paper was cited more than 33,000 until this chapter was written. In the spatial context, the development is more recent. The first works are Elhorst (2005) and Mutl (2006). Lee and Yu (2010b) did a good overview of this literature.

Anselin et al. (2008b) classified the dynamic spatial models into four categories:

1. Pure space recursive, if only the space–time is present;
2. Space–time recursive, if only the space–time lag is present;
3. Space–time simultaneous, if spatial and time lags are present;
4. Space–time dynamic, if all space and time are present.

Lee and Yu (2010b) called the last one as Spatial Dynamic Panel Data Model (SDPD) and linked it to the panel data literature. The dynamic space–time model, or dynamic spatial panel data model, includes all the forms of lag: the time lag, the contemporary spatial lag, and the space–time lag:

$$y_t = \phi y_{t-1} + \rho \mathbf{W} y_t + \gamma \mathbf{W} y_{t-1} + X_t \beta + \varepsilon_t \tag{15.10}$$

The models resulted in complex non-linear relationships. Considering only the serial lag terms, and substituting the expression to $t-1$, then:

$$\begin{aligned} y_t &= \phi \left[\phi y_{t-2} + \rho \mathbf{W} y_{t-1} + \gamma \mathbf{W} y_{t-2} + X_{t-1}\beta + \varepsilon_{t-1}\right] + \\ &\gamma \mathbf{W} \left[\phi y_{t-2} + \rho \mathbf{W} y_{t-1} + \gamma \mathbf{W} y_{t-2} + X_{t-1}\beta + \varepsilon_{t-1}\right] + \\ &\rho \mathbf{W} y_t + X_t \beta + \varepsilon_t \\ &= \rho \mathbf{W} y_t + X_t \beta + \varepsilon_t + \phi \rho \mathbf{W} y_t + \gamma \rho \mathbf{W}^2 y_{t-1} \\ &+ \phi X_{t-1}\beta + \gamma \mathbf{W} X_{t-1}\beta + \phi \varepsilon_{t-1} + \gamma \mathbf{W} \varepsilon_{t-1} \\ &+ \phi^2 y_{t-2} + \gamma \phi \mathbf{W} y_{t-2} + \gamma^2 \mathbf{W}^2 y_{t-2} \end{aligned}$$

Korniotis (2010) employs a recursive space–time model with fixed effects applied to consumption growth in each state in the United States. He proposes a *Least Square Dummy Variable* (LSDV) estimator with adjustment for the bias arising from the model's dynamics, extending the work of Hahn and Kuersteiner (2002) to the non-spatial case. For a dynamic panel data model with spatial error, Elhorst (2005) estimates the model with the unconditional maximum likelihood method, and (Mutl 2006) investigates the model using a generalized method of moments (GMM) in three steps. Su and Yang (2015) derive quasi-maximum likelihood estimators from the same model with fixed and random effects specifications. Lee and Yu (2010b), following previous works by the authors Lee (2007), Yu et al. (2008), Lee and Yu (2010a), derive the stability, cointegration, and unit root cases for the SDPD model. The dynamic spatial model can be applied to the convergence and growth analysis of countries and regions (Baltagi et al. 2007; Ertur and Koch 2007), regional markets (Keller and Shiue 2007), labor economics (Foote 2007), public sector economics (Revelli 2001; Franzese and Hays 2007), and other fields.

In a dynamic panel data model with fixed individual effects, the autoregressive coefficient is skewed and inconsistent when n tends to infinity and T is fixed (Nickell 1981; Hsiao 2014). Taking first differences to eliminate fixed effects in the dynamic equation and constructing instrumental variables (IVs), Anderson and Hsiao (1981) shows that IV methods can provide consistent estimates. When T is finite, additional

IVs can improve the efficiency of estimation. However, if the number of IVs is too large, the problem of too many IVs will arise, as the asymptotic bias would increase in this situation.

When n and T go to infinity, the incidental parameter problem becomes less severe because each fixed effect can be consistently estimated. However, Hahn and Kuersteiner (2002) and Alvarez and Arellano (2003) showed an asymptotic bias of order $O(1/T)$ in the Maximum Likelihood (ML) estimator of the autoregressive parameter when n and T tend to infinity at the same rate. In addition to the ML estimator, Alvarez and Arellano (2003) also investigated the asymptotic properties of the IV estimators of Arellano and Bond (1991). They found an asymptotic bias of the same order as ML due to the use of many-moment conditions.

As asymptotic bias is an undesirable feature of these estimates, Hahn and Kuersteiner (2002) built estimators that correct the bias for the dynamic panel data model, analytically modifying the internal estimator. They further provided a rigorous asymptotic theory for the *within* estimator and the bias-corrected estimator when n and T go to infinity at the same rate. As an alternative to analytical bias correction, Hahn and Newey (2004) also considered the bias reduction approach by *Jackknife*.

15.3.1 A Limited Information Maximum Likelihood Approach for the Dynamic Spatial Panel Case

The standard dynamic spatial panel methodology does not cope with spatial dependence. However, models can be extended to incorporate these effects. One advantage of the panel approach is that it deals with many aspects of spatial heterogeneity Anselin et al. (2008b). A further problem arises as a result of the factor of endogeneity of one of the regressors. In this situation, the usual maximum likelihood methods no longer apply because the error term has a variance and covariance matrix that is no longer diagonal. The most used method in this situation is the GMM. But here we propose an approach that uses maximum likelihood and explicitly models the error variance and covariance matrix. The suggestion is to use a Spatial Dynamic Panel Data model (SDPD) Lee and Yu (2010b), including spatial, temporal, and spatial time lag effects with endogenous explanatory variables. To do that with maximun likelihood, I used a limited information maximun likelihood approach (Anderson and Rubin 1949; Anderson and Hsiao 1981; Davidson et al. 1993).

Consider the model

$$y_{nt} = \rho W_n y_{nt} + \tau y_{nt-1} + \eta W_n y_{nt-1} + Y_{1nt}\gamma + X_{2nt}\beta + \epsilon_{nt} \tag{15.11}$$

With

$$Y_{1nt} = X_{1nt}\Pi + U_{nt} \tag{15.12}$$

where y_{nt} is a $nt \times 1$ vector of the dependent variable, W_n is a $n \times n$ spatial weights matrix of known constants with a zero diagonal and row or columns sum less than 1. Consider that Y_{1nt} is a $n \times k$ matrix of endogenous explanatory variables, then Y_{1nt} are potentially correlated with ϵ_{nt}, X_{1nt} is a $n \times k_1$ set of instrumental variables that directly affect Y_{1nt} and X_{2nt} is a $n \times k_2$ set of regressors impacting the endogenous variables y_{nt}. ρ, τ, and η are autoregressive parameters associated with spatial, time-lag, and spatial-time lag dependencies. γ is the parameter of the endogenous independent variable, and β, and Π are parameters of exogenous independent variables in the first and second equations. It is assumed that $E(U_nt) = 0$ and $E(U_nt'U_nt) = \Sigma_u$. The correlation between Y_{1nt} and ϵ_{nt} is captured by $E(U'_{nt}\epsilon_{nt}) = \sigma'_{u\epsilon}$.

Note that in Eq. (15.11) there are many terms referring to y_{nt} or your lags (spatial or time). Let us define a term, $S(\rho)$ grouping all of them, like

$$S(\rho) = I_{nt} - \rho W_{nt} - \tau I_{-1,nt} - \eta W_{-1n}, Y_{nt}(\rho) = [S(\rho)y_{nt}, Y_{1nt}]$$

where

$$W_{nt} = \begin{bmatrix} W_n & \mathbf{0} & \cdots & \mathbf{0} \\ \mathbf{0} & W_n & \cdots & \mathbf{0} \\ \vdots & \vdots & \ddots & \vdots \\ \mathbf{0} & \mathbf{0} & \cdots & W_n \end{bmatrix}$$

$$I_{nt} = \begin{bmatrix} I_n & \mathbf{0} & \cdots & \mathbf{0} \\ \mathbf{0} & I_n & \cdots & \mathbf{0} \\ \vdots & \vdots & \ddots & \vdots \\ \mathbf{0} & \mathbf{0} & \cdots & I_n \end{bmatrix}$$

$$I_{-1,nt} = \begin{bmatrix} \mathbf{0} & \mathbf{0} & \cdots & \mathbf{0} \\ I_n & \mathbf{0} & \cdots & \mathbf{0} \\ \vdots & \vdots & \ddots & \vdots \\ \mathbf{0} & \cdots & I_n & \mathbf{0} \end{bmatrix}$$

$$W_{-1,nt} = \begin{bmatrix} \mathbf{0} & \mathbf{0} & \cdots & \mathbf{0} \\ W_n & \mathbf{0} & \cdots & \mathbf{0} \\ \vdots & \vdots & \ddots & \vdots \\ \mathbf{0} & \cdots & W_n & \mathbf{0} \end{bmatrix}$$

Now, let us define a matrix relating both Eqs. (15.11) and (15.12), in a system of equations. As there are two equations, the matrix will be a 2×2 matrix of vector parameters,

$$\Gamma = \begin{bmatrix} 1 & 0 \\ -\gamma & I_g \end{bmatrix},$$

where I_g is the identity matrix $g \times g$.

With both definitions, the model can be written in its short form as

$$Y_{nt}(\rho)\Gamma = Z_{nt}B + \mathcal{H}_{n0} + V_{nt},$$

where

$$\begin{aligned}
Y_{nt} &= [S(\rho)y_{nt}, Y_{1nt}] \\
Z_{nt} &= [X_{1nt}, X_{2nt}] \\
B &= \begin{bmatrix} 0 & \Pi \\ \beta & 0 \end{bmatrix} \\
\mathcal{H}_{n0} &= \begin{bmatrix} \tau y_{n0} & \eta W_n y_{n0} \\ \mathbf{0} & \mathbf{0} \\ \vdots & \vdots \\ \mathbf{0} & \mathbf{0} \end{bmatrix} \\
V_{nt} &= [\epsilon_{nt}, U_{nt}]
\end{aligned}$$

Assuming a normal multivariate distribution to the errors, the density of $V_{nt,i}$ is given by

$$(2\pi)^{-(g+1)/2}|\Sigma|^{-1/2}\exp\left(-\frac{1}{2}V_{nt,i}\Sigma^{-1}V_{nt,i}\right)$$

where

$$\Sigma = \begin{bmatrix} \sigma_\epsilon^2 & * \\ \sigma_{u\epsilon} & \Sigma_u \end{bmatrix}.$$

As $V_{nt,i}$ is non-observable, the dependent and independent variables are used to estimate it. Specifically, we need to use the random variables transformation propriety, that is

$$f(y) = \left|\frac{\partial e}{\partial y}\right| f(e),$$

where $f(\cdot)$ is the density of the generic random variables e and y. The term $\left|\frac{\partial y}{\partial e}\right|$ is named Jacobian determinant and consists of the determinant of the matrix of all its first-order partial derivatives. In our case, the determinant of the Jacobian transformation of V_{nt} into $[y_{nt}, Y_{1nt}]$ is

$$\begin{vmatrix} S'_{nt}(\rho) & \gamma' \otimes I_{nt} \\ 0_{ntg\times nt} & I_{ntg} \end{vmatrix} = |S_{nt}(\rho)| \tag{15.13}$$

Therefore, the feasible density is

$$(2\pi)^{-(g+1)/2}|S_{nt}(\rho)||\Sigma|^{-1/2}e^{\left(-\frac{1}{2}[Y_{nt,i}\Gamma - Z_{nt,i}B - \mathcal{H}_{n0}]\Sigma^{-1}[Y_{nt,i}\Gamma - Z_{nt,i}B - \mathcal{H}_{n0}]'\right)}$$

the log-likelihood function of this model can be written as

$$\mathcal{L}(\theta, \Pi, \Sigma) = -\frac{nt(g+1)}{2}\ln(2\pi) + t\ln|S_{nt}(\rho)| - \frac{nt}{2}\ln|\Sigma|$$
$$-\frac{1}{2}\sum_i [Y_{nt,i}\Gamma - Z_{nt,i}B - \mathcal{H}_{n0}]\Sigma^{-1}[Y_{nt,i}\Gamma - Z_{nt,i}B - \mathcal{H}_{n0}]' \tag{15.14}$$

where $\theta = [\rho, \tau, \eta, \beta]$. It is convenient to concentrate the log-likelihood function concerning Σ^{-1}, as suggested by (Davidson et al. 1993). As

$$\frac{\delta \mathcal{L}}{\delta \Sigma^{-1}} = \frac{nt}{2}\Sigma - \frac{1}{2}[Y_{nt}\Gamma - Z_{nt}B]'[Y_{nt}\Gamma - Z_{nt}B],$$

we have

$$\Sigma = \frac{1}{nt}[Y_{nt}\Gamma - Z_{nt}B]'[Y_{nt}\Gamma - Z_{nt}B].$$

Substituting in (15.14), the concentrate log-likelihood function becomes

$$\mathcal{L}(\theta, \Pi) = c + t\ln|S_{nt}(\rho)| -$$
$$\frac{nt}{2}\ln\left[\frac{1}{nt}[Y_{nt,i}\Gamma - Z_{nt,i}B - \mathcal{H}_{n0}][Y_{nt,i}\Gamma - Z_{nt,i}B - \mathcal{H}_{n0}]'\right]$$
$$= c + t\ln|S_{nt}(\rho)| - \frac{nt}{2}\ln|V_{nt}'V_{nt}| \tag{15.15}$$

where c is a constant. The $|V_{nt}'V_{nt}|$ term is the unobservable variance–covariance of the error terms.

Consider now an alternative representation of Eq. (15.11)

$$y_{nt} - \rho W_n y_{nt} = \tau y_{nt-1} + \eta W_n y_{nt-1} + Y_{1nt}\gamma + X_{2nt}\beta + \epsilon_{nt}$$
$$= z_{nt}b' + \epsilon_{nt} \tag{15.16}$$

where $z_{nt} = [y_{nt-1}, Wy_{nt-1}, X_{2nt}, Y_{1nt}]$ and $b = [\tau, \eta\beta, \gamma]'$. Applying a Cochrane–Orcutt transformation to this equation, we obtain

$$y_{nt} - \rho W_n y_{nt} = z_{nt}(z_{nt}'z_{nt})^{-1}z_{nt}'(y_{nt} - \rho W_n y_{nt}) + \epsilon_{nt} \tag{15.17}$$

Equation (15.17) shows that the spatial transformation in the dependent variable could be represented as a projection of this transformed variable on the regression plus the error term. Due to the endogeneity in Y_{1nt}, the projection of y_{nt} and Wy_{nt} in z_{nt} are potentially biased. Then we suggest applying an intravenous correction using all exogenous variables as instruments. Consider h_{nt} formed by all exogenous variables; then $h_{nt} = [y_{nt-1}, Wy_{nt-1}, X_{1nt}, X_{2nt}, W_nX_{1nt}, W_nX_{2nt}, W_n^2X_{1nt}, W_n^2X_{2nt}]_{LI}$,where LI stressed that only linear independent columns of h are considered. Then, we can consider a correction in (15.17), as

$$y_{nt} - \rho W_n y_{nt} = \hat{z}_{nt}(\hat{z}'_{nt}\hat{z}_{nt})^{-1}\hat{z}'_{nt}(y_{nt} - \rho W_n y_{nt}) + \epsilon_{nt} \tag{15.17$'$}$$

where $\hat{z}_{nt} = h_{nt}(h'_{nt}h_{nt})^{-1}h'_{nt}z_{nt}$. Then, we can express ϵ_{nt} as the sum of the two terms,

$$\epsilon_{nt} = \epsilon^0_{nt} - \rho\epsilon^L_{nt} \tag{15.18}$$

where

$$\epsilon^0_{nt} = y_{nt} - \hat{z}_{nt}(\hat{z}'_{nt}\hat{z}_{nt})^{-1}\hat{z}'_{nt}y_{nt}$$

and

$$\epsilon^L_{nt} = W_n y_{nt} - \hat{z}_n t(\hat{z}'_{nt}\hat{z}_{nt})^{-1}\hat{z}'_{nt}W_n y_{nt}.$$

Substituting (15.18) in V_{nt}, we have

$$E|V'_{nt}V_{nt}| = \left(\frac{1}{n}\right)^{k+1} \begin{vmatrix} \epsilon^{0'}_{nt}\epsilon^0_{nt} - \rho\epsilon^{0'}_{nt}\epsilon^L_{nt} - \rho\epsilon^0_{nt}\epsilon^{L'}_{nt} + \rho^2\epsilon^{L'}_{nt}\epsilon^L_{nt} & (\epsilon^0_{nt} - \rho\epsilon^L_{nt})'U_{nt} \\ U'_{nt}(\epsilon^0_{nt} - \rho\epsilon^L_{nt}) & U'_{nt}U_{nt} \end{vmatrix} \tag{15.19}$$

Finally, we can rewrite the log-likelihood (15.15), using (15.19) as

$$\mathcal{L}(\rho) = c + t\ln|S_{nt}(\rho)| - \frac{nt}{2}\ln|e(\rho)| - \frac{nt}{2}\ln|\mathcal{U}(\rho)| \tag{15.20}$$

where $\ln|S_{nt}(\rho)| = \ln|I_n - \rho W_n|$, due to the proprieties of the determinant of diagonal block matrices,

$$e(\rho) = \frac{1}{n}(\epsilon^{0'}_{nt}\epsilon^0_{nt} - 2\rho\epsilon^{0'}_{nt}\epsilon^L_{nt} + \rho^2\epsilon^{L'}_{nt}\epsilon^L_{nt}),$$

and

$$\mathcal{U}(\rho) = \frac{1}{n}[U'_{nt}U_{nt} - U'_{nt}(\epsilon^0_{nt} - \rho\epsilon^L_{nt})e(\rho)^{-1}(\epsilon^0_{nt} - \rho\epsilon^L_{nt})'U_nt].$$

This function can be maximized adopting usual techniques to maximum likelihood and using as initial value to the maximization process that ones given by a GMM regression on (15.17$'$).

15.3.2 Monte Carlo Simulation

We run a Monte Carlo evaluation of the Spatial Dynamic LIML (SD-LIML) estimator performance compared to the results with a GMM-IV estimator, similar to (Kelejian and Prucha 1998) and (Kapoor et al. 2007) approaches, in which the endogeneity of $W_n y_{nt}$ is treated considering the spatial lag of the exogenous variable as an instrumental variable. Specifically, we consider $W_n X_{2nt}$, $W_n X_{1nt}$ and $X_{1nt} X_{2nt}$ as instrumental variables. We change the panel sample size in each simulation by considering $n = (20, 100)$ and $t = (10, 25, 50)$. We also change the correlation between U_{nt} and ϵ_{nt}, considering three situations: small (0.1), median (0.5), and strong correlation (0.9). For each simulation, we change the spatial parameters (ρ, τ and η) in a set of values (–0.9, –0.5, –0.2, 0, 0.2, 0.5, 0.9).

The spatial matrix was defined as a circular world in the following sense: for the first and last one-third of the regions, we consider one neighbor at the right and one at the left; for the remaining one-third of the regions, we consider five neighbors at right and five neighbors at left. To avoid nonstationarity, we limit the simulations to that combination of parameters in that $\left|\frac{\tau+\eta}{1-\rho}\right| < 1$, and $\left|\frac{1}{1-\rho-\tau-\eta}\right| < 1$. These inequalities assure the short- and long-run stationarity, respectively Lee and Yu (2010b).

Then, we considered 1,032 different parameter combinations, and 500 simulations were run for each. We presented the graphs with bias and the root mean square error (RMSE), resuming the results by the level of the spatial and temporal parameters (Fig. 15.3). For the spatial parameter (ρ), both estimators (SD-LIML and GMM-IV) have good results in terms of bias, but spatial dynamic LIML has RMSE lower than the GMM-IV estimator. For the two other parameters, the temporal (τ) and spatial–temporal (η) lags of the spatial dynamic LIML overcome the GMM estimator in terms of bias and RMSE statistic. These results give us certainty about the use of SD-LIML in empirical work.

15.4 Illustration of Monte Carlo Simulation

An MC application example is provided on my website or under request. I consider a small version where $\rho = 0.5$, $\tau = 0.2$, and $\eta = -0.2$. Additionally, $n = 100$ and $t = 50$, the panel data has 5,000 observations. As in the main Monte Carlo Simulation, all other parameters equal 1. The endogeneity is attained by generating random numbers from a multivariate normal, with zero mean, variance equal to 1, and covariance equal to 0.9. The screen in Fig. 15.4 shows how these parameters are fixed in the demo file.

We use an auxiliary function named `gen_variables` to generate the simulation variables. This function generate all exogenous variables (X_1 and X_2) and the endogenous ones (Y_1 and Y). The model equations are

$$Y_t = \tau Y_{t-1} + \rho W Y_t + \eta W Y_{t-1} + \gamma Y_{1t} + \beta X_{2t} + \mu + \delta_t + \epsilon_t,$$

and

$$Y_{1t} - \pi X_{1t} + \mu_{y_1} + \delta_{t_{y_1}} + \varepsilon_t.$$

Then, we run 500 draws. In the model, IV variables include X_1, $W X_1$, $W X_2$, and $W X_1 X_2$. Figure 15.5 presents that part of the simulation in the Demo code.

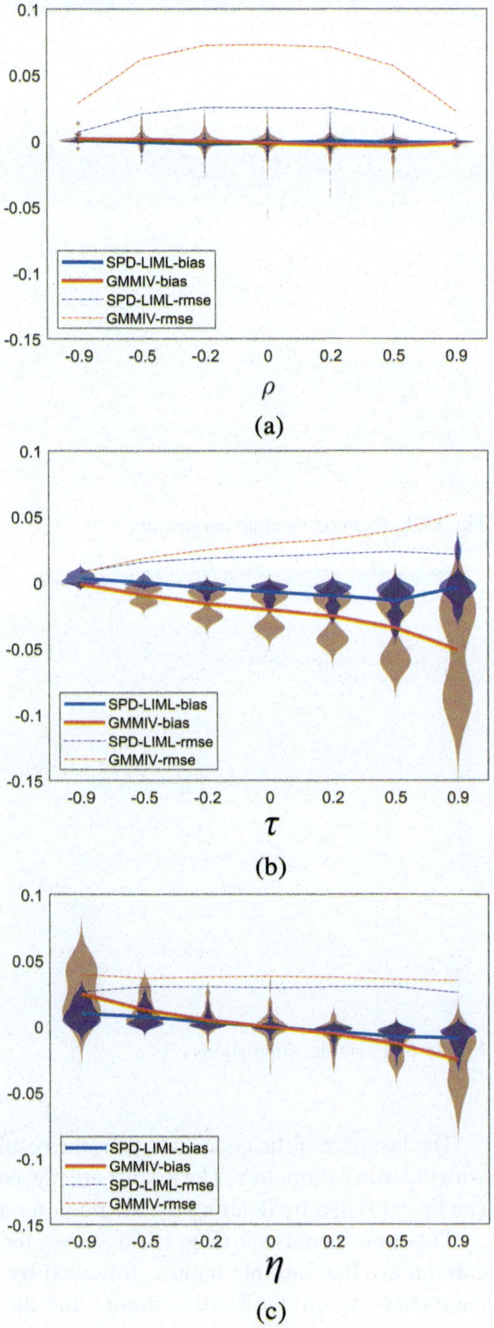

Fig. 15.3 Monte Carlo simulation results for autoregressive parameters

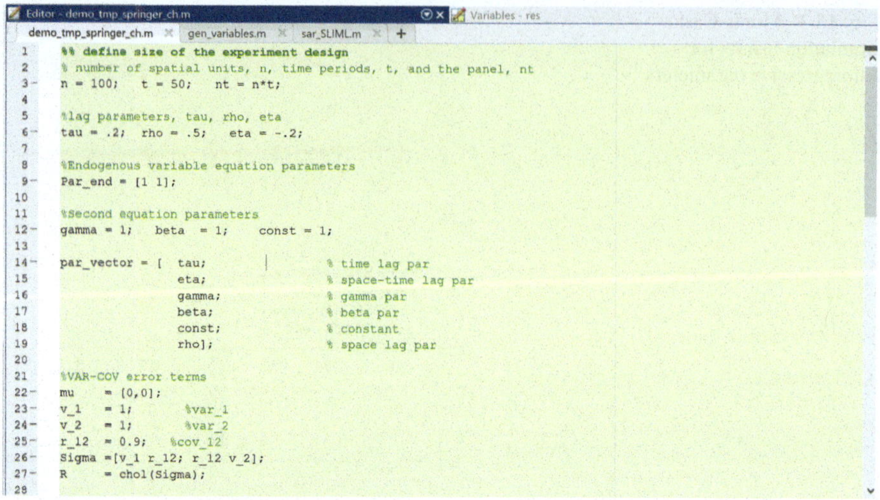


```
%% define size of the experiment design
% number of spatial units, n, time periods, t, and the panel, nt
n = 100;    t = 50;    nt = n*t;

%lag parameters, tau, rho, eta
tau = .2;  rho = .5;    eta = -.2;

%Endogenous variable equation parameters
Par_end = [1 1];

%Second equation parameters
gamma = 1;    beta  = 1;    const = 1;

par_vector = [  tau;                  % time lag par
                eta;                  % space-time lag par
                gamma;                % gamma par
                beta;                 % beta par
                const;                % constant
                rho];                 % space lag par

%VAR-COV error terms
mu     = [0,0];
v_1    = 1;        %var_1
v_2    = 1;        %var_2
r_12   = 0.9;   %cov_12
Sigma =[v_1 r_12; r_12 v_2];
R      = chol(Sigma);
```

Fig. 15.4 Example: setting parameters

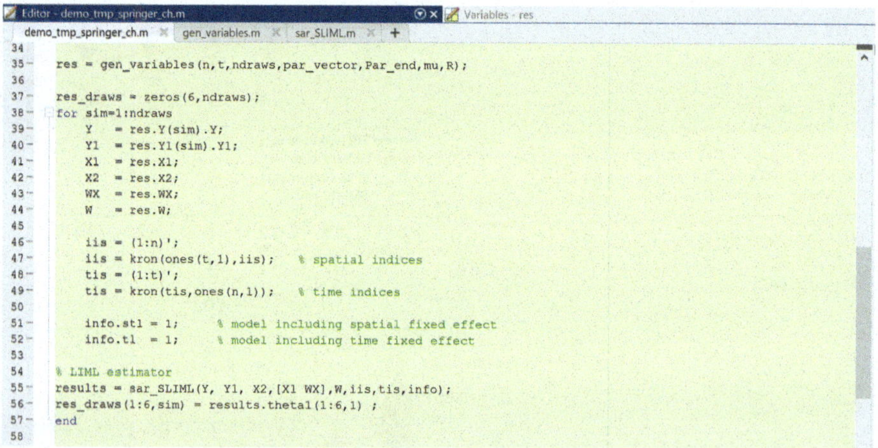


```

res = gen_variables(n,t,ndraws,par_vector,Par_end,mu,R);

res_draws = zeros(6,ndraws);
for sim=1:ndraws
    Y   = res.Y(sim).Y;
    Y1  = res.Y1(sim).Y1;
    X1  = res.X1;
    X2  = res.X2;
    WX  = res.WX;
    W   = res.W;

    iis = (1:n)';
    iis = kron(ones(t,1),iis);   % spatial indices
    tis = (1:t)';
    tis = kron(tis,ones(n,1));   % time indices

    info.stl = 1;      % model including spatial fixed effect
    info.tl  = 1;      % model including time fixed effect

% LIML estimator
results = sar_SLIML(Y, Y1, X2,[X1 WX],W,iis,tis,info);
res_draws(1:6,sim) = results.theta1(1:6,1) ;
end
```

Fig. 15.5 Example: simulations

The last part of the code computes the results of the simulations, comparing them with the true parameters. The results are presented in an object named `TABLE`, which can be exhibited by deleting the semicolon on line 73 (see Fig. 15.6).

The table generated (Fig. 15.7) shows the basic simulation results. In the first column are the variable names, followed by the sample size (N and T). The true parameters are in the fourth column, and the others present the simulation results. The average of the simulated parameters in the 500 draws is in the fifth column. The sixth column shows the bias, the difference between the true and the estimated parameter. The RMSE is in the last column, a statistic important to compare different

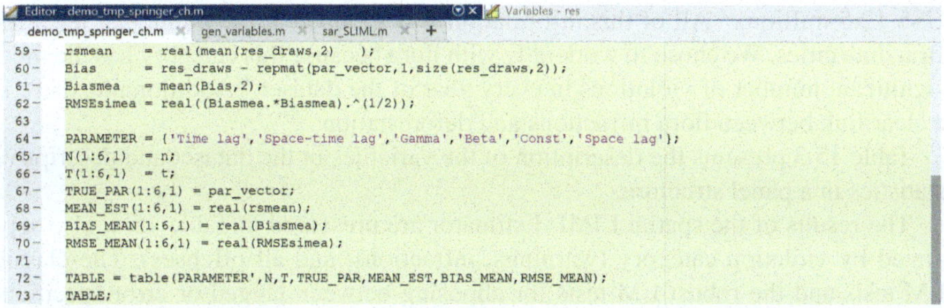

```
rsmean      = real(mean(res_draws,2)   );
Bias        = res_draws - repmat(par_vector,1,size(res_draws,2));
Biasmea     = mean(Bias,2);
RMSEsimea = real((Biasmea.*Biasmea).^(1/2));

PARAMETER = {'Time lag','Space-time lag','Gamma','Beta','Const','Space lag'};
N(1:6,1)    = n;
T(1:6,1)    = t;
TRUE_PAR(1:6,1) = par_vector;
MEAN_EST(1:6,1) = real(rsmean);
BIAS_MEAN(1:6,1) = real(Biasmea);
RMSE_MEAN(1:6,1) = real(RMSEsimea);

TABLE = table(PARAMETER',N,T,TRUE_PAR,MEAN_EST,BIAS_MEAN,RMSE_MEAN);
TABLE;
```

Fig. 15.6 Example: results

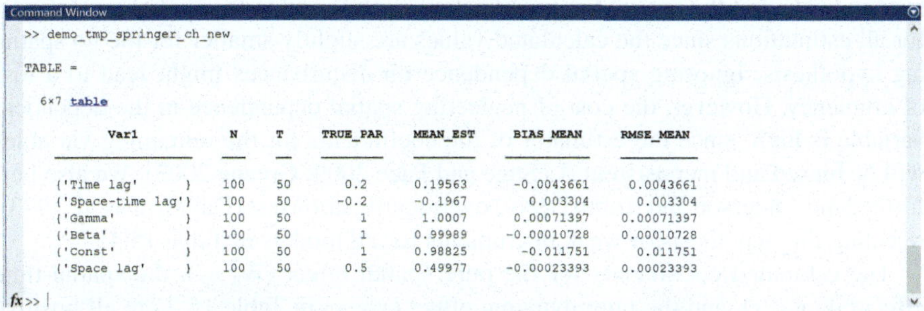

```
>> demo_tmp_springer_ch_new

TABLE =

  6×7 table
```

Var1	N	T	TRUE_PAR	MEAN_EST	BIAS_MEAN	RMSE_MEAN
{'Time lag' }	100	50	0.2	0.19563	-0.0043661	0.0043661
{'Space-time lag'}	100	50	-0.2	-0.1967	0.003304	0.003304
{'Gamma' }	100	50	1	1.0007	0.00071397	0.00071397
{'Beta' }	100	50	1	0.99989	-0.00010728	0.00010728
{'Const' }	100	50	1	0.98825	-0.011751	0.011751
{'Space lag' }	100	50	0.5	0.49977	-0.00023393	0.00023393

Fig. 15.7 Example: results table

simulations, but it has the same information as the bias here. The difference between the true and the estimate parameters is very small for all parameters, as in the main MC results.

15.4.1 Application

As an example of applying the proposed method, we used data on Brazilian environmental policy.[1] The database contains environmental crimes with fines varying between BRL 50 (US$12.5) and BRL 50 million (US$12.5 million), which are the minimum and maximum values as defined by law. The offenses were classified into three categories (warnings, infractions, and outliers) to separate the milder cases from those of more significant environmental harm. The law defines as "warning" the infractions less harmful to the environment, with a maximum fine not exceeding BRL 1,000 (about US$ 250). Infractions are considered those cases with penalties varying between more than BRL 1,000 and less than or equal to BRL 2.5 million (US$ 625 000). Outliers are the remaining violations (fines up to BRL 50 million or

[1] A more extensive application can be found on Uhr et al. (2021).

US$ 12.5 million).[2] All of this information was grouped at the municipal level for Brazilian cities. We chose to work only with flora because this category has the most significant number of violations in every year of the dataset.[3] Additionally, there is a clear link between flora infractions and deforestation.

Table 15.3 presents the description of the variables in the dataset and descriptive statistics in a panel structure.

The results of the spatial LIML Estimator are presented in Table 15.4, also separated by violation category (warnings, infractions, and all offenses). The classic LM tests and the robust LM tests for choosing between lagged or error specifications point out that the hypotheses of no spatially lagged dependent variable and no spatially autocorrelated error terms are both rejected. However, the Robust LM tests indicate that the spatial lag specification is preferred to the spatial error model for all estimations since the calculated values are slightly smaller for the no spatial lag hypothesis. Ignoring spatial dependence on disturbances might lead to a loss of efficiency. However, the cost of neglecting spatial dependence in the dependent variable is high, since the estimator of the coefficients for the remaining variables will be biased and inconsistent (LeSage and Pace 2009; Greene 2003). We also performed the Anderson and Rubin (1949) overidentification test (Davidson et al. 1993), rejecting the hypothesis of weak instruments for all models in Table 15.4.

The estimated coefficients for the pure spatial effect ($W_n y_{nt}$), the spatial-time effect ($W_n y_{nt-1}$), and the pure dynamic effect (y_{nt-1}) in Table 15.2 are all positive and significant between specifications, with combined values of less than one (not explosive). They indicate the existence of a time- and space-dependence for violations in all categories. Municipalities with more infractions in the past or surrounded by other municipalities with a high number of infringements tend to present a higher number of assessments. That might indicate that some regions are more promising for environmental offenses than others.

The coefficient for Fines is also positive and significant for all models in both estimation procedures, but the quadratic term is negative, indicating the existence of an inflection point. As pointed out, we included a quadratic term due to the expressive number of municipalities without registered violations in each period. In linear regression, this large number of zeros can pull the regression line down towards it, mixing up the interpretation of the effectiveness of sanction charges. With the quadratic term, we still consider those cases with zero offenses, but we can capture fine impacts more clearly. Conversely, fines applied in neighboring municipalities have a negative signal with a positive quadratic effect. However, these coefficients cannot be interpreted directly because they do not represent the partial derivatives (LeSage and Pace 2009). To do that, we must calculate the direct and indirect effects (spillovers). Direct, indirect, and total effects are also presented in Table 15.2 for

[2] We apply these definitions for the entire period. We deflate fine values for 2015 and then use the listed criteria to classify offenses in warnings, infractions, or outliers for each year of the dataset. Warnings represent 27% of the cases, infractions 72,2%, and outliers 0,8%.

[3] There are 190,921 reported cases up to 2012, against 78,432 fauna infractions, the second major category of violations.

Table 15.3 Descriptive statistics

Variable	Description	Mean	Std.	Max.	Min.
Dependent variables					
Warning[a]	Number of notices lower than BRL 1,000	0.288	2.45	252	0
Infractions[a]	Number of notices between BRL 1.000 and BRL 2.5 millions	1.813	9.892	763	0
Outliers[a]	Number of notices higher than BRL 2.5 millions	0.025	0.402	38	0
Total infractions	Number of fines	2.127	11.107	945	0
Independent variables					
Warning values[a]	Fine per notices	162.99	1,267	147,696	0
Infraction values[a]	Fine per notices	151,234	1.6 mi	125 mi	0
Outliers values[a]	Fine per notices	237,855	5.2 mi	560 mi	0
Total values[a]	Fine per notices	389,251	6 mi	567 mi	0
Population	Total resident population	33,732	200,164	12 mi	724
Rice	Rice area in ha.	554.20	2,885	91,229	0
Sugarcane	Sugarcane area in ha.	1,336	4,965	114,000	0
Livestock	Number of head cattle	35,996	83,119	2.3 mi	0
Coal mining	Toneladas	312,13	3.924	506.888	0
Agriculture GDP[a,b]	Valor adicionado bruto	24.787	47.492	1,7 mi	0
Industrial GDP[a,b]	Valor adicionado bruto	120,99 mil	1 mi	67 mi	–2,9 mi
Services GDP[a,b]	Valor adicionado bruto	268,29 mil	3,8 mi	411 mi	1.194
Lower income	Workers earning up to 2 Minimum Wage (%) SM	69.854	17.98	100	0
Lover educational level	Workers up to elementary school (%)	21.83	15.35	100	0

[a] In 2015 values

[b] Values per BRL 1,000

Data represent city-level statistics over the entire panel period

Table 15.4 Results of the spatial dynamic model with endogeneity (SD-LIML estimator)

	Warning	Infraction	Total
Spatial lag ($W_n y_{nt}$)	0.349831***	0.294758***	0.353774***
Temporal lag (y_{nt-1})	0.027987***	0.034461***	0.041713***
Space–time lag ($W_n y_{nt-1}$)	0.004653*	0.016672***	0.004643*
Fines (F_{nt})	0.795785***	0.464668***	0.548639***
Fines squared (F_{nt}^2)	–0.062872***	–0.019403***	–0.026240***
Neighbor fines ($W_n F_{nt}$)	–0.103943***	–0.092236***	–0.105661***
Neighbor fines squared ($W_n F_{nt}^2$)	0.003220*	0.004229***	0.004149***
R^2 (total)	0.7371	0.8002	0.7808
Log-verossimilhança	2083745.8	1695662.9	1595747.3
Akaike	–7592350	–6176506	–5811983
LM-(*lag*) test	109.3325***	20897.43***	40666.20***
Robust LM-(*lag*) test	2618040.5***	2147774.83***	4910717.01***
LM-(*error*) test	103430.38***	85855.17***	134076.47***
Robust LM-(*error*) test	2721361.5***	2212732.58***	5004127.28***
Anderson-Rubin[a] test	0.2655(0.876)	0.0031(0.998)	0.1993(0.905)
N, obs,	87,712	87,712	87,712
Direct, indirect and total effects[b]			
	Short term effects		
	Direct		
Fines	0.807837	0.467169	0.554836
Fines squared	–0.06417	–0.01949	–0.0266
	Indirect		
Fines	0.25626	0.06092	0.13065
Fines squared	–0.0276	–0.002	–0.0076
	Total		
Fines	1.0641	0.52809	0.68549
Fines squared	–0.0918	–0.002	–0.0342
	Long term effects		
	Direct		
Fines	0.83266	0.48498	0.580341
Fines squared	–0.06616	–0.02023	–0.02783
	Indirect		
Fines	0.28768	0.08439	0.15812
Fines squared	–0.03044	–0.00297	–0.0081
	Total		
Fines	1.12034	0.56937	0.73846
Fines squared	–0.0965	–0.02311	–0.03683

Notes Control variables are Population, Rice Area, Sugarcane Area, livestock, coal extraction, Agro. GDP, Ind. GDP, Serv. GDP, and their spatial lags
Regressions include constant, time, and space-fixed effects
Instruments: Lower income, Lover educ. level, and spatial lag of those variables
Significant levels: ***1%. **5%. *10%
[a] p-value in parentheses.
[b] The effects are the respective elasticities for the Spatial Dynamic Model with Endogeneity (SLIML Estimator) (LeSage and Pace 2009, See details in). Results are significant at 1%

the short- and long-run (Elhorst 2012) and were calculated for the Spatial Dynamic Model with Endogeneity only.

The calculated direct, indirect, and total effects have different magnitudes depending on the offense category. For fines, all three effects are positive and significant for all categories of violation in the short and long run. For the quadratic term, all three effects are negative and significant. So, specific deterrence (direct effect), spillovers (indirect effect), and general deterrence (total effect) all obey an inverted U pattern, indicating the existence of an inflection point after which increases in sanction charges have a negative impact on violations at the same municipality and neighboring locations.

15.5 Conclusion

Dynamic panel data models represent a great and reasonable theoretical and empirical advance in understanding how certain processes propagate in time and space. Following the traditional econometric literature, spatial econometric models have advanced towards including instruments to correct the bias induced by the fixed effect estimator, especially for short panels. This makes the GMM estimators the most used. However, the non-linearity caused by spatial, temporal, and spatiotemporal correlation may not be fully controlled with the normally employed moment conditions. The maximum likelihood estimator gains importance under these conditions. This work developed a new estimator for dynamic spatial panels, controlling the endogeneity in the dependent variable and the possible endogeneity in an explanatory variable. The proposed *Spatial Dynamic Limited Information Maximum Likelihood* (SD-LIML) estimator performs better than the alternative GMM estimator in all situations.

Using this new estimator in a specific problem related to environmental policy in Brazil, there is evidence of temporal and spatial dependence for environmental violations in all categories studied. Municipalities with more crimes in the past, or which are surrounded by other cities with a large number of crimes, tend to have higher assessments. A possible explanation for this result is *Targeting of the regulator*. Evidence of a pedagogical deterrent effect associated with the value of fines was also found. Fees imposed on a municipality and its neighbors are important in deterring new offenses. Low fine values encourage further violations, but the sanction's quadratic effect shows that crimes decrease above a certain value. This result can open the discussion and support future public policies on changes in the minimum amount of fines.

References

Alvarez J, Arellano M (2003) The time series and cross-section asymptotics of dynamic panel data estimators. Econ 71:1121–1159

Anderson TW, Hsiao C (1981) Estimation of dynamic models with error components. J Am Stat Assoc 76:598–606

Anderson TW, Rubin H (1949) Estimation of the parameters of a single equation in a complete system of stochastic equations. Ann Math Stat 20:46–63

Anselin L (1988) Spatial econometrics: methods and models. Kluwer Academic Publishers, Dordecht

Anselin L (2001) Spatial econometrics. In: Baltagi BH (ed) A companion to theoretical econometrics, chapter 14. Wiley Online Library, pp 310–330

Anselin L (2010) Thirty years of spatial econometrics. Pap Reg Sci 89:3–25

Anselin L, Gallo JL, Jayet H (2008) Spatial panel econometrics. The econometrics of panel data: fundamentals and recent developments in theory and practice, pp 625–660

Anselin L, Gallo JL, Jayet H (2008b) Spatial panel econometrics. In: Baltagi BH, Hong Y, Koop G, Krämer W (eds) Advanced studies in theoretical and applied econometrics, vol 46. Springer

Arbia G (2014) A primer for spatial econometrics: with applications in R. Springer

Arellano M (2003) Panel data econometrics. OUP Oxford

Arellano M, Bond S (1991) Some tests of specification for panel data: Monte Carlo evidence and an application to employment equations. Rev Econ Stud 58:277–297

Baltagi B (2008) Econometric analysis of panel data. John Wiley & Sons

Baltagi BH, Baltagi BH (2005) Econometric analysis of panel data. Springer

Baltagi BH, Bresson G, Pirotte A (2007) Panel unit root tests and spatial dependence. J Appl Econ 22:339–360

Davidson R, MacKinnon JG et al (1993) Estimation and inference in econometrics. OUP Catalogue

Elhorst JP (2003) Specification and estimation of spatial panel data models. Int Reg Sci Rev 26:244–268

Elhorst JP (2005) Unconditional maximum likelihood estimation of linear and log-linear dynamic models for spatial panels. Geogr Anal 37

Elhorst JP (2012) Dynamic spatial panels: models, methods, and inferences. J Geogr Syst 14:5–28

Enders W (2008) Applied econometric time series. John Wiley & Sons

Ertur C, Koch W (2007) Growth, technological interdependence and spatial externalities: theory and evidence. J Appl Econ 22:1033–1062

Foote CL (2007) Space and time in macroeconomic panel data: young workers and state-level unemployment revisited. Technical report, Working Papers

Franzese Jr RJ, Hays JC (2007) Spatial econometric models of cross-sectional interdependence in political science panel and time-series-cross-section data. Polit Anal :140–164

Greene W (2003) Econometric analysis. Prentice Hall

Hahn J, Kuersteiner G (2002) Asymptotically unbiased inference for a dynamic panel model with fixed effects when both n and t are large. Econ 70:1639–1657

Hahn J, Newey W (2004) Jackknife and analytical bias reduction for nonlinear panel models. Econ 72:1295–1319

Hamilton JD (2020) Time series analysis. Princeton University Press

Hsiao C (2003) Analysis of panel data. Cambridge University Press

Hsiao C (2014) Analysis of panel data, vol 54. Cambridge University Press

Kapoor M, Kelejian HH, Prucha I (2007) Panel data models with spatially correlated error components. J Econ 140:97–130

Kelejian HH, Piras G (2017) Spatial econometrics. Academic Press

Kelejian HH, Prucha IR (1998) A generalized spatial two stage least square procedure for estimating a spatial autoregressive model with autoregressive disturbance. J R State Financ Econ 17:99–121

Keller W, Shiue CH (2007) The origin of spatial interaction. J Econ 140:304–332

Korniotis GM (2010) Estimating panel models with internal and external habit formation. J Bus & Econ Stat 28:145–158

Lee L-F (2004) Asymptotic distributions of quasi-maximum likelihood estimators for spatial autoregressive models. Econ 72:1899–1925

Lee L-F (2007) Identification and estimation of econometric models with group interactions, contextual factors and fixed effects. J Econ 140:333–374

Lee L-F, Yu J (2010) Estimation of spatial autoregressive panel data models with fixed effects. J Econ 154:165–185

Lee L-F, Yu J (2010) Some recent developments in spatial panel data models. Reg Sci Urban Econ 40:255–271

LeSage J, Pace RK (2009) Introduction to spatial econometrics. CRC Press, Boca Raton

Mutl J (2006) Dynamic panel data models with spatially correlated disturbances. PhD thesis, University of Maryland

Nickell S (1981) Biases in dynamic models with fixed effects. Econ J Econ Soc :1417–1426

Paelinck JHP, Klaassen LLH (1979) Spatial econometrics, vol 1. Saxon House

Pfaffermayr M (2009) Maximum likelihood estimation of a general unbalanced spatial random effects model: a Monte Carlo study. Spat Econ Anal 4:467–483

Revelli F (2001) Spatial patterns in local taxation: tax mimicking or error mimicking? Appl Econ 33:1101–1107

Su L, Yang Z (2015) QML estimation of dynamic panel data models with spatial errors. J Econ 185:230–258

Tobler WR (1970) A computer movie simulating urban growth in the Detroit region. Econ Geogr 46:234–240

Uhr JG, Chagas AS, Uhr DAP, Peres RP (2021) A study on environmental violations for Brazilian municipalities: a limited information maximum likelihood approach to a spatial dynamic panel data. Econ Anal Law Rev 12:176–199

Wang W, Lee L-F (2013) Estimation of spatial panel data models with randomly missing data in the dependent variable. Reg Sci Urban Econ 43:521–538

Wooldridge JM (2010) Econometric analysis of cross section and panel data. MIT press

Yu J, De Jong R, Lee L-F (2008) Quasi-maximum likelihood estimators for spatial dynamic panel data with fixed effects when both n and t are large. J Econ 146:118–134

Yu J, de Jong R, Lee L-F (2012) Estimation for spatial dynamic panel data with fixed effects: the case of spatial cointegration. J Econ 167:16–37

Chapter 16
Panel ARDL and NARDL Models: Role of Agriculture in Economic Growth in Selected Asian Countries

Siok Kun Sek, Khang Yi Sim, and Deep Mukherjee

Abstract In recent macroeconometric literature, the nonstationary panel models have attracted more attention. Conventional panel data approaches assume all parameters share the common value across homogeneous cross-section units and the regressor has the symmetric effect on the dependent variable. Conventional panel models might not be applicable to macro-level panel data that characterize nonstationary and heterogeneous effects. Besides, the asymmetric effect could also be present in the relationship in which the increases of a regressor might have a different magnitude of effect on the dependent variable as compared to its decreases. Taking into these issues, this chapter will introduce the panel autoregressive distributed lags model (ARDL) and its nonlinear form (NARDL) using the three estimators, namely, mean group (MG), pooled mean group (PMG), and dynamic fixed effect (DFE) to handle the heterogeneous and asymmetric effect in modeling the long panel data. The chapter will then demonstrate the application using country-level data from Southeast and South Asia. ARDL and NARDL models are estimated using EViews and Stata to examine how the global commodity prices and each sub-agriculture productivity might contribute to economic growth, and if such effects are symmetric or asymmetric. We find that the model based on PMG estimator (Pesaran et al., J Am Stat Assoc 94:621–634, 1999) outperforms other models.

Keywords Autoregressive distributed lags model · Nonstationary panels · Mean group estimator · Pooled mean group estimator

Supplementary Information The online version contains supplementary material available at https://doi.org/10.1007/978-981-99-4902-1_16.

S. K. Sek (✉) · K. Y. Sim
School of Mathematical Sciences, Universiti Sains Malaysia, Gelugor, Malaysia
e-mail: sksek@usm.my

D. Mukherjee
Department of Economic Sciences, Indian Institute of Technology Kanpur, Kanpur, India

D. Mukherjee (ed.), *Applied Econometric Analysis Using Cross Section and Panel Data*, Contributions to Economics, https://doi.org/10.1007/978-981-99-4902-1_16

16.1 Introduction

Panel data refers to the pooling of observations on both cross-sectional units and time periods. In recent years, panel data has gained popularity with growing researches and applications. Hsiao (2003) and Baltagi (2005) discussed the advantages of panel data. One of the benefits is panel data that helps to control for individual heterogeneity. Heterogeneity might exist as countries may exhibit different country-specific effects or characteristics, hence restricting all countries to be homogeneous might lead to misspecification. Besides, panel data also provide more information and variability, but less collinearity, and more degrees of freedom, hence providing more efficient estimates due to its two-dimensional data. Panel data also provides better dynamics of adjustment of estimates, i.e., based on the speed of adjustments on how economic policy changes. Besides, it also enables estimates that are not detectable in the pure cross-section or pure time-series data by combining both dimensional data. In addition, panel data models also enable more complicated tests and behavioral models. As indicated, panel data is a better choice for studying technical efficiency (Baltagi and Griffin 1988; Koop and Steel 2001). Finally, micro (short panel data) provides more accurate measures on micro variables while macro (long panel data) has asymptotic distributions and provides efficient estimates.

In general, panel data can be classified as micro data and macro data. Micro panel refers to data with cross-section units indicated in micro-units, normally with cross-sectional unit $N > T$ (time or period). They are called cross-section panels or short panels. Macro data are cross-section units measured in macro units, they are called macro panels or long panels with $T > N$. Some data might have similar N and T. The main concern is, however, on the nature of variations that exist in the data, but not the size of T (Arellano 2004). Recently, more concerns are shifted to study the asymptotic property of macro panels with large sizes in both N and T rather than the usual panel with large N and small T. By allowing T to increase to infinity, this leads to the growth of two strands of studies. First, the rejection of homogeneity regression in favor of heterogeneous regression. Second, the growth of nonstationary panel models to handle data with nonstationarity and heterogeneous effect (Baltagi and Kao 2000).

The assumption of homogeneity that is applied to short panels is no longer valid when using the long panels. When time period T is long, the cross-section units, for example, countries might exhibit different structures and characteristics, leading to different slopes of estimates from one to another. The first strand of studies claimed that the application of homogeneous regression such as pooled FE estimator to estimate the dynamic panel model might lead to biases due to the existence of heterogeneous effect across countries and serially correlation issues. The second strand of studies is concerned about nonstationarity, spurious regression, and cointegration in the long panels. Panel data spurious regressions provide a consistent estimate when both N and T approach infinity. As indicated in Baltagi and Kao (2000), the reason for such a consistent estimate is because panel data estimators take the averages of individual countries and consider the information of the independent cross-section data in regression, hence leading to a stronger signal than the case of pure time-series.

Besides the heterogeneity issue on long panel data, nonlinear regression in panel data is also a hot research topic. In the real economic situation, the relationship between two or more economic variables could be nonlinear but might vary over time, due to influences of the change in economic structure, the change in the environment and policy decision, sudden shocks, or crises. Hence, a nonlinear regression might provide a better estimate to capture the real-world situation than the static or linear models. This chapter will introduce one of the nonstationary panel models, the ARDL model to tackle heterogeneous effects. This is followed by the introduction to its extended version to the nonlinear format (NARDL model). Both ARDL and NARDL models will be estimated using three estimators of the mean group (MG), pooled mean group (PMG), and dynamic fixed effect (DFE). The discussion will also cover the application of the models using a real data analysis.

The chapter is organized as follows: Sect. 16.1 is the introduction; Sect. 16.2 explains few concepts and issues in nonstationary panels; Sect. 16.3 explains the models and estimators as well as the estimation procedures; Sect. 16.4 explains the data and the illustration of analysis, the procedure/codes using EViews and Stata and the interpretation of results.

16.2 Panel Data and Related Concepts

16.2.1 Long Panels and Heterogeneous Models

Panel data can be divided into two main groups, microdata (short panels) versus macro data (long panels). In general, the short panel data refers to the panel data with $N > T$ while long panels refer to the panel data with $T > N$. Based on the different data formats, panel data models can be classified into two main groups, homogeneous models versus heterogeneous models. Homogeneous models assume model parameters to be invariant across cross-section units which are applicable for data with very large N and very small T. However, when T increases, such homogeneous assumption is no more valid as panel data might exhibit heterogeneous effect in which model parameters vary across cross-section units. This condition is very common in macro data with large T and N.

A number of researchers agreed that heterogeneous models as a better option as it is very common panel data to exhibit variations and heterogeneous effects. Robertson and Symons (1992) found that the homogeneous (static) model leads to severe biases in dynamic estimations when heterogeneous exists in the data. On the other hand, Pesaran and Smith (1995) illustrated that when T is small, the four estimation procedures (taking group averaging on time-series regressions, averaging cross-section regressions over time, pooled regression, separating group regression with average coefficient estimates) yielded inconsistent estimates. On top of these studies, Baltagi and Griffin (1997) pointed out that the pooling data approach might encounter several problems. They argued that pure cross-section analysis might not be able to manage the unobservable country effects while pure time-series specification fails to control for unobservable effects such as oil shocks or behavioral changes over time. Such findings and arguments highlight the importance to consider the heterogeneous effect in panel estimations.

16.2.2 Nonstationary Panels and the Notion of Cointegration

More recently, there has been increasing interest to study the macro panel data with large N and large T. One main feature that distinguishes the new macro panel data from the traditional panels is that they are used for regression with nonstationary regressors while the traditional panels are dealing with stationary regressors. Such a feature as indicated in Nelson and Plosser (1982), can be explained by the nonstationary macroeconomic time-series data in panels. This further leads to the nonstationary in the new macro panels. Hence, panel unit-root and panel cointegration tests should be applied in examining the property of macro panels. Panel cointegration tests are crucial to identify the existence of the long-run relationships in the panel data.

Panel unit-root and panel cointegration share a similar notion and concept as in time-series data. A series of data is said to be statistically stationary if its statistical properties (such as mean, variance, etc.) are constant over time. In real application, economic data are far from stationary. Differencing is one way to transform the nonstationary data into the stationary form. A series of data is integrated of order one, $I(1)$ if it gets stationary after first differencing. If a series of data is stationary at its original form without any differencing process, it is denoted as $I(0)$. On the other hand, cointegration is the long-run equilibrium in which several series of data or variables are moving together and fluctuating around this long-run equilibrium. It is defined to be the condition when a linear combination of several nonstationary $I(1)$ series leads to a stationary regression, implying that these series share the common stochastic trend or behavior. Such property can be tested using the residual-based cointegration tests. If U is residual of the linear regression between X and Y, where both X and Y are $I(1)$, and U is $I(0)$, then there exists a cointegration relationship between X and Y.

An accumulated studies questioned the validity of conventional models, for instance, pooled time-series cross-section (PTCS) in dealing with data exhibiting stochastic trends and nonstationarity. Birkel (2014) provided a review on the consequences of nonstationary panels using conventional models. According to the review, the cointegration properties and the degree of homogeneity of the cointegrating relationship in nonstationary panels are crucial in determining the behavior of panel estimators. They discussed the results of the no cointegration versus cointegration case. In the absence of cointegration in panel data, the PTCS still applicable to estimate long-run relationships based on the pooling approach which leads to consistency of standard estimators. Hence, even no cointegration exists, the panel estimators will converge to zero for large T and N panels. Such consistency property also holds for detrended data. In addition, the fixed effect (FE) estimator also pertains to this property when applied to pure random walks with the exception of cross-section dependencies in the regression.

Next, if cointegration exists, OLS and FE remain to be consistent estimators of the cointegrating relationship in the panels which are cross-section independence, but subject to some circumstances. These estimators might produce biased estimates on small sample due to exogeneity problem and serial correlation in residuals. If there exists cross-section dependence with common stationary or nonstationary factors detected in the residuals, FE might lead to bias estimates on the homogeneous cointegration parameters. But both estimators provide consistent estimates if cross-section dependency is causing by the common nonstationary factors in both dependent and independent variables (see Birkel 2014 for detailed discussions).

Based on the above views, the conventional estimators (such as OLS and FE) might produce consistent estimates but are subject to specified circumstances. Besides, the behavior of these estimators is determined by the cointegration properties in panel data. Hence, it is very important to examine the unit-root and cointegration tests, especially for nonstationary panels. These preliminary tests are crucial in deciding on the appropriate models or estimators for nonstationary panels.

16.3 Econometric Methods for Nonstationary Heterogeneous Panels

When N and T are large in panel data, there are two things to be concerned about, i.e., nonstationary and heterogeneous parameters. According to the literature studies in the panel data, when both N and T are large, it is no more valid to assume homogeneity of slope across cross-sectional units due to the variation and specific characteristics that exist in each cross-section unit. In this section, we will discuss the three estimators namely mean group (MG), pooled mean group (PMG), and dynamic fixed effect (DFE) to estimate nonstationary dynamic panels with heterogeneous effect across groups. The estimation is based on the autoregressive distributed lags (ARDL) and its extended version nonlinear ARDL or NARDL.

One difficulty faced by researchers for nonstationary panels is the selection of models when variables are integrated with different orders. The ARDL and NARDL models are a better option as it does not require all variables in the regression to be integrated with the same order one, but it allows the combination of regressors to be $I(0)$ and $I(1)$. With the advancement in technology skills and the growth of estimation techniques, the application of nonlinear models is getting broader. In terms of interpretation, nonlinear models provide more information and approximation on the relationships to represent the real economic situation. In the real economic situation, the relationship between two variables might not be constant over time, but may vary in response to sudden shocks, the change in economic policy and structure, etc. Nonlinear models are capable to capture the change in the relationship which could be nonlinear. Restricting the relationship to be linear in the existence of nonlinearity might lead to misleading results.

The NARDL model is the extended version of ARDL initialized by Shin et al. (2011) using the time-series data. After that, there are attempts to formulate the model to the panel data settings by Sek (2017). The NARDL model is applied broadly to examine the asymmetric effects of oil price changes either in time-series or panel data setting. These studies reported asymmetric effects of oil price changes in which the effects may vary across sectors and countries. For instance, Ibrahim (2015) examined the effects of oil price changes on sectoral CPI inflation using time-series data of Malaysia. The results captured asymmetric effect in the food sector in which oil price increases cause higher CPI food price while decreases in oil price do not signify any effect. Filis and Chatziantoniou (2014) found that oil-importing countries tend to experience the larger negative effects from oil price increases than their decreases. These findings reveal evidence on the existence of asymmetric (nonlinear) relationships in economic variables which could be neglected if linear regression is used.

16.3.1 Preliminary Tests

ARDL and NARDL models require all variables to have integration levels less than two, and allow combination of variables with integration orders between zero and one. This can be examined through panel unit-root tests. If a series is stationary at level, it is integrated of order zero, I(0). The series is integrated of order one or I(1) if it is stationary at first differenced. Both ARDL and NARDL models are applicable if the data contain cointegrating or long-run relationship. The long-run relationship can be tested through panel cointegration tests. Alternatively, the speed of adjustment in the ARDL and NARDL models should be in negative value, below -1 and is significant. This section will explain the panel unit-root and panel cointegration tests.

16.3.1.1 Panel Unit-Root Tests

Panel unit-root and panel cointegration tests are performed before applying the estimation. The purpose of unit root tests is to check and confirm the integration level of the variables is not higher than order two, which is the requirement of the following applied model estimations, whereas the cointegration tests are to detect the presence of a long-run relationship between the dependent variable and the regressors. Here we discuss the three tests: Levin et al. (2002), Im et al. (2003), and Fisher-type ADF test (Maddala and Wu 1999; Choi 2001) panel unit-root tests. The first two tests are also known as the Levin, Lin, and Chu (LLC) test, and the Im, Pesaran, and Shin (IPS) test, respectively.

Suppose that a sample of N countries and T periods are studied. The dependent variable y_{it} follows the first order autoregressive AR(1) process,

$$y_{it} = \rho_i y_{i,t-1} + \gamma_i d_t + \varepsilon_{it},\ i = 1, 2, ..., N,\ t = 1, 2, ..., T,$$

where $y_{i,t-1}$ is the lag term of y_{it}, ρ_i is the autoregressive coefficient, d_t is the optional deterministic component with its coefficient γ_i, and ε_{it} is the disturbance or error term. d_t could be zero or one. If $d_t = 0$, then there is no deterministic term in the equation. There are two cases when d_t is one. The first case, the equation contains a constant ($d_t = 1$); the second case, the equation includes both constant and trend ($d_t = (1, t)$). The ρ_i is the term to be focused in testing the null hypothesis of unit-root, $H_0 : \rho_i = 1$ for all i. This general testing framework can be expressed as

$$\Delta y_{it} = \alpha_i y_{i,t-1} + \gamma_i d_t + \varepsilon_{it},$$

where $\alpha_i = -(1 - \rho_i)$ and $\Delta y_{it} = y_{it} - y_{i,t-1}$. Then, the null hypothesis of unit-root becomes

$$H_0 : \alpha_i = 0 \text{ for all } i.$$

The hypothesis testing of the LLC and IPS tests are based on the augmented Dickey-Fuller (ADF) regression,

$$\Delta y_{it} = \alpha_i y_{i,t-1} + \sum_{j=1}^{p_i} \beta_{ij} \Delta y_{i,t-j} + \gamma_i d_t + \varepsilon_{it},$$

where the lag order p_i is allowed to vary across i. The difference between the LLC test and IPS test is the homogeneous assumption of the autoregressive parameter across i.

The null hypothesis of the LLC test assumes a common unit-root across all countries i in which the homogeneous assumption holds, i.e.,

$$H_0 : \alpha_i = \alpha = 0 \text{ against } H_1 : \alpha_i = \alpha < 0,$$

and the adjusted t-statistic is

$$t_\alpha^* = \frac{t_\alpha - N\tilde{T}\hat{S}_N\hat{\sigma}^{-2}se(\hat{\alpha})\mu_{\tilde{T}}^*}{\sigma_{\tilde{T}}^*},$$

where t_α is the conventional regression t-statistic, $\tilde{T}$ is the average observations per individual, i.e., $\tilde{T} = T - \frac{1}{N}\sum_{i=1}^{N} p_i - 1$, $\hat{S}_N$ is the estimator for the average standard deviation ratio, $\hat{\sigma}^2$ is the estimated variance, $se(\hat{\alpha})$ is the standard error, and $\mu_{\tilde{T}}^*$ and $\sigma_{\tilde{T}}^*$ are the mean and standard deviation adjustment, respectively.

By contrast, the IPS test assumes the null of the individual unit-root process, $H_0 : \alpha_i = 0$ for all i, is tested against the heterogeneous alternatives,

$$H_1 : \begin{cases} \alpha_i < 0 \text{ for } i = 1, 2, ..., N_1 \\ \alpha_i = 0 \text{ for } i = N_1 + 1, N_2 + 1, ..., N \end{cases},$$

with $0 < N_1 \leq N$. The average statistic considered by the IPS test is

$$\tilde{t}\text{ - bar}_{NT} = \frac{1}{N} \sum_{i=1}^{N} \tilde{t}_{iT}.$$

Maddala and Wu (1999) and Choi (2001) suggested the non-parametric Fisher-type test and claimed that there are several advantages over the LLC and IPS tests. The advantages of the Fisher test include the panel does not necessarily need to be balanced as required by the IPS test, different lag lengths are possible in performing the individual ADF regression, and applicable to any unit-root test derived. However, Monte Carlo simulation is required to derive the p-values of the Fisher test. Similar to the IPS test, the Fisher test is also based on the heterogeneity of the autoregressive parameter. However, the Fisher test with the bootstrap approach performs better than the IPS test. The proposed Fisher test is

$$P = -2 \sum_{i=1}^{N} \ln \pi_i,$$

where π_i is the p-value of a unit-root test for country i (Maddala and Wu 1999).

16.3.1.2 Panel Cointegration Tests

The Kao (1999) and Pedroni (1999, 2004) panel cointegration tests are applied in this study. Both tests are residual-based, and they assume the null hypothesis of no cointegration. However, Kao (1999) assumes slope homogeneity while Pedroni (1999, 2004) assumes slope heterogeneity in the panel cointegration tests.

Kao (1999) studied the following panel regression model,

$$y_{it} = \alpha_i + \beta x_{it} + e_{it},\ i = 1, 2, ..., N,\ t = 1, 2, ..., T,$$

where y_{it}, x_{it} and e_{it} are $I(1)$. The estimate of e_{it} is

$$\hat{e}_{it} = \rho \hat{e}_{i,t-1} + v_{it}.$$

By including the lagged changes in the residuals, the ADF test statistic can be obtained from the equation as follows,

$$\hat{e}_{it} = \rho \hat{e}_{i,t-1} + \sum_{j=1}^{p} \varphi_j \Delta \hat{e}_{i,t-j} + v_{it},$$

where p is selected so that v_{it} is serially uncorrelated. The null hypothesis of no cointegration, $H_0 : \rho = 1$, is tested against its alternative, $H_1 : \rho < 1$.

Pedroni (1999, 2004) proposed four within-dimension tests (pooled approach) and three between-dimension tests (group mean approach) in considering the heterogeneity of the slope parameter. Consider the following heterogeneous panel model,

$$y_{it} = \alpha_i + \beta_i x_{it} + e_{it},\ i = 1, 2, ..., N,\ t = 1, 2, ..., T,$$

where both y_{it} and x_{it} are $I(1)$, β_i is allowed to vary across i. Under the null of no cointegration, e_{it} is $I(1)$.

The four within-dimension tests are panel v-statistic, panel ρ-statistic, nonparametric panel t-statistic, and parametric panel t-statistic. On the other hand, the three between-dimension tests include group ρ-statistic, nonparametric group t-statistic, and parametric group t-statistic. The nonparametric test statistics (all except the mentioned parametric t-statistics) can be obtained by estimating the following equation,

$$\hat{e}_{it} = \rho_i \hat{e}_{i,t-1} + v_{it},$$

whereas for parametric test statistics, the equation is

$$\hat{e}_{it} = \rho_i \hat{e}_{i,t-1} + \sum_{j=1}^{p} \varphi_{ij} \Delta \hat{e}_{i,t-j} + v_{it},$$

where ρ_i and φ_{ij} are permitted to vary across i. For the within-dimension statistics, the null hypothesis $H_0 : \rho_i = 1$ is tested against the alternative hypothesis $H_1 : \rho_i = \rho < 1$. By contrast, $H_0 : \rho_i = 1$ is tested against $H_1 : \rho_i < 1$ for the between-dimension statistics.

16.3.2 The Model

Suppose that the panel data has the cross-section unit denoted by $i = 1, 2, \ldots, N$ and the time-series dimension, $t = 1, 2, \ldots, T$. Then, ARDL ($p, q, \ldots, q$) model with p lags of dependent variable and q lags of regressors can be written as follows (Pesaran et al. 1999):

$$y_{it} = \sum_{j=1}^{p} \lambda_{ij} y_{i,t-j} + \sum_{j=0}^{q} \delta_{ij}{}' x_{i,t-j} + \varepsilon_{it}, \tag{16.1}$$

where y_{it} is the dependent variable, λ_{ij} is the coefficient of the lagged dependent variable, x_{it} is the $(k \times 1)$ vector of regressors with its $(k \times 1)$ coefficient vector denoted as δ_{ij}, and the disturbances ε_{it} are independently distributed across i and t. The ARDL model in Eq. (16.1) can be re-parameterized as

$$\Delta y_{it} = \phi_i y_{i,t-1} + \beta_i{}' x_{it} + \sum_{j=1}^{p-1} \lambda_{ij}^{*} \Delta y_{i,t-j} + \sum_{j=0}^{q-1} \delta_{ij}^{*}{}' \Delta x_{i,t-j} + \varepsilon_{it}, \tag{16.2}$$

where $\phi_i = -\left(1 - \sum_{j=1}^{p} \lambda_{ij}\right)$, $\beta_i = \sum_{j=0}^{q} \delta_{ij}$,

$$\lambda_{ij}^{*} = - \sum_{m=j+1}^{p} \lambda_{im},\ j = 1, 2, \ldots, p - 1,$$

and

$$\delta_{ij}^{*} = - \sum_{(m=j+1)}^{q} \delta_{im},\quad j = 1, 2, \ldots, q - 1.$$

It is assumed that there is a long-run connection between the dependent and independent variables. Moreover, assume that the long-run factors are the same across cross-section units. Equation (16.2) can also be written in an error correction form as follows,

$$\Delta y_{it} = \phi_i \left(y_{i,t-1} - \theta_i{}' x_{it}\right) + \sum_{j=1}^{p-1} \lambda_{ij} \Delta y_{i,t-j} + \sum_{j=0}^{q-1} \delta_{ij}^{*}{}' x_{i,t-j} + \varepsilon_{it}, \tag{16.3}$$

where $\theta_i = -\beta_i / \phi_i$ is the long-run coefficient on x_{it}, and ϕ_i is the error correction coefficient which captures the speed of adjustment of the dependent variable in converging to the long-run equilibrium level in reacting to the regressors. Hence, ϕ_i should be in negative value and not exceed $|-1|$ to signify the convergence and stability of the model. The fulfillment of this condition $\phi_i < 0$ also implies the existence of the long-run relationship between y_{it} and x_{it} (Pesaran et al. 1999). If $\phi_i = 0$, then the long-run relationship in the model (the term in the bracket) will be cancelled out.

The ARDL model is used to examine the symmetric (linear) relationship. This model is extended to include the asymmetric variables and is termed as nonlinear ARDL or NARDL model. The NARDL (time-series) model was first developed by Shin et al. (2014) to be applied using time-series data. The NARDL model shares the same model setting and interpretation as in the ARDL model. The only difference is to replace x_{it} in Eq. (16.1) in ARDL model with the asymmetric parameters x_{it}^{+} and x_{it}^{-}. Both x_{it}^{+} and x_{it}^{-} are the products of decomposition from x_{it}, where $x_{it} = x_0 + x_{it}^{+} + x_{it}^{-}$. Both x_{it}^{+} and x_{it}^{-} are interpreted as the partial sum process of positive and negative changes in x_{it}, i.e.,

$$\chi_{it}^{+} = \sum_{j=1}^{t} \Delta x_{ij}^{+} = \sum_{j=1}^{t} \max(\Delta x_{ij}, 0),\ x_{it}^{-} = \sum_{j=1}^{t} \Delta x_{ij}^{-} = \sum_{j=1}^{t} \min(\Delta x_{ij}, 0).$$

The asymmetric long-run regression is as follows,

$$y_{it} = \beta^{+} x_{it}^{+} + \beta^{-} x_{it}^{-} + u_{it},\ \Delta x_{it} = \mathrm{v}_{it},$$

Therefore, the NARDL(*p, q, …, q*) model can be written in the same form as ARDL model in Eq. (16.3) but replacing x_{it} with x_{it}^{+} and x_{it}^{-}:

$$\Delta y_{it} = \phi_i\left(y_{i,t-1} - \theta_i^{+\prime} x_{it}^{+} - \theta_i^{-\prime} x_{it}^{-}\right) + \sum_{j=1}^{p-1} \lambda_{ij}^{*} \Delta y_{i,t-j} + \sum_{j=0}^{q-1} \delta_{ij}^{+*\prime} \Delta x_{i,t-j}^{+} + \sum_{j=0}^{q-1} \delta_{ij}^{-*\prime} \Delta x_{i,t-j}^{-} + \varepsilon_{it}, \tag{16.4}$$

where all parameters are as explained in Eq. (16.3), $\theta_i^{+'}$ and $\theta_i^{-'}$ denote the long-run coefficients for the positive series and negative series while $\delta_{ij}^{+*'}$ and $\delta_{ij}^{-*'}$ are the short-run coefficients for the positive and negative changes in x_{it}.

16.3.3 The Estimators and Model Selection

In this section, we consider three estimation approaches to estimate the ARDL and NARDL models. The first approach is the DFE estimator which is applied based on the fixed-effects estimation approach. This is the most restricted estimator. This approach is to apply pooling on the time-series data for each cross-section unit, i.e., to restrict the same parameter estimate across each unit. DFE assumes common slope coefficients and error variances. The only variation is the intercept which can differ across each group or cross-section unit. The second approach takes the other extreme with the least restriction which is the MG estimator (Pesaran and Smith 1995). This estimator does not impose any restriction on the parameters. The coefficients are calculated by a simple arithmetic average across groups. This estimator allows the intercepts, slope, and error of variances to vary across groups.

The MG estimator operates by conducting separate ordinary least squares (16.3) regressions for each panel unit, thereby allowing for the parameters to differ across panel units and finally averaging them. Thus, estimated model parameters are the average of *N* unit-specific slope estimates $\widehat{\beta}_{OLS,i}$ and these indicate the average relationship across cross-sectional units. Mathematically, one can summarize the MG estimator as

$$\hat{\beta}_{MG} = \frac{1}{N}\sum_{i=1}^{N}\hat{\beta}_{OLS,i} \tag{16.5}$$

and the variance of the MG estimator is given by

$$V\left(\hat{\beta}_{MG}\right) = \frac{1}{N(N-1)}\sum_{i=1}^{N}\left(\hat{\beta}_{OLS,i} - \hat{\beta}_{MG}\right)\left(\hat{\beta}_{OLS,i} - \hat{\beta}_{MG}\right)^{/}. \tag{16.6}$$

According to Pesaran and Smith (1995), both unweighted averages and the generalized least squares weighted averages would yield consistent estimates for the parameter of interest.

Let us briefly go through the PMG estimator which takes the intermediate position between MG and DFE. It is the combination of both pooling and averaging approaches. According to Pesaran et al. (1999), there exists a long-run relationship between y_{it} and x_{it} which is defined by

$$y_{it} = \theta' x_{it} + \eta_{it}\ i = 1, 2, \ldots\ldots N; t = 1, 2, \ldots\ldots.T \tag{16.7}$$

where, θ_i is the k × 1 vector of the long-run coefficients and η_{it}'s are stationary with possibly non-zero means (including the fixed effects). Hence, Eq. (16.3) can be re-written with fixed effects

$$\Delta y_{it} = \phi_i \eta_{i,t-1} + \sum_{j=1}^{p-1}\lambda_{ij}\Delta y_{i,t-j} + \sum_{j=0}^{q-1}\delta_{ij'}\Delta x_{i,t-j} + \mu_i + \varepsilon_{it} \tag{16.8}$$

where $\eta_{i,t-1}$ is the error correction term and ϕ_i is the error correction term coefficient. This parameter is anticipated to be negative, implying that variables return to a long-run equilibrium. PMG constraints the long-run coefficient to be common or similar across cross-section units i.e. $\theta_i = 0$ for all's, but no restriction on the intercept, short-run coefficients, and error variances. These parameters are allowed to vary across groups. For estimation of short-run coefficients and the common long-run coefficients, the pooled maximum likelihood estimation method is implemented by assuming that the error terms or stochastic disturbances are normally distributed.

One advantage of PMG estimator is that it can be applied to stationary as well as nonstationary variables (Zare et al. 2014). According to Pesaran et al. (1999), the MG estimator gives consistent estimates. However, under the circumstance when the slope is homogeneous, the MG estimator is inefficient, but the PMG estimator is consistent and efficient. Hence, the Hausman test is applicable to examine the difference between these two estimators (MG and PMG) or the DFE estimator. Hausman's (1978) specification test is applied to the estimated models so that the best estimator is selected with the proper restrictions imposed. The algorithm of the Hausman test is to test the difference between two estimators. The test statistic is given by the expression

$$H = \left(\hat{\beta}^{I} - \hat{\beta}^{II}\right)' \left[Var\left(\hat{\beta}^{I}\right) - Var\left(\hat{\beta}^{II}\right)\right]^{-1} \left(\hat{\beta}^{I} - \hat{\beta}^{II}\right), \quad (16.9)$$

where $\hat{\beta}^{I}$ and $\hat{\beta}^{II}$ are the estimates of Model I and Model II, respectively. $Var\left(\hat{\beta}^{I}\right)$ and $Var\left(\hat{\beta}^{II}\right)$ are the variances of the respective estimates. The test statistic follows a χ^2-distribution under the null hypothesis. Hausman (1978) claims that there is a consistent and efficient estimator under the null hypothesis of no model misspecification. Nevertheless, this estimator is biased and inconsistent under the alternative hypothesis of model misspecification. By contrast, there is an estimator that is not efficient under the null hypothesis, but it is consistent regardless of whether the hypothesis is true.

16.3.4 Estimation of Models

The estimation procedures are as described in Fig. 16.1. The analysis starts with the preliminary tests, specifically, panel unit-root tests and panel cointegration tests. ARDL and NARDL models allow variables with a mix of $I(0)$ and $I(1)$, but no variable with higher-order integration than two. Conducting panel unit-root tests is a crucial step to determine the order of integration of each variable in fulfilling the pre-conditions mentioned. On the other hand, panel cointegration tests are executed to detect the presence of a long-run relationship between the dependent variable and the regressors.

The rejection of the null hypothesis of unit-root implies the variable tested does not contain unit-root, it is stationary, $I(0)$. On the other hand, if the variable tested fails to reject the null hypothesis, implying it is not stationary. Then, this variable should be differenced once and the panel unit-root tests are repeated to test the differenced series. In most cases, all variables are stationary after first differencing, termed as $I(1)$. The nonstationary variables should further be examined to detect the existence of the long-run relationship via cointegration tests. In general, cointegration exists when the linear combination of $I(1)$ variables is stationary or $I(0)$. The more specific definition is as discussed in Brooks (2008), in which under most circumstances, the linear combination of $I(1)$ variables will also be $I(1)$, and the combination of variables with different integrated orders will be equal to the highest order of integration. Thus, the panel cointegration test is the succeeding procedure to test for the linear combination of the variables, or termed as the residuals, if the variables are not $I(0)$. The rejection of the null hypothesis of no cointegration will be evident in the existence of the long-run relationship in the regression. However, panel cointegration tests are not the only option to evidence the long-run relationship. The speed of adjustment

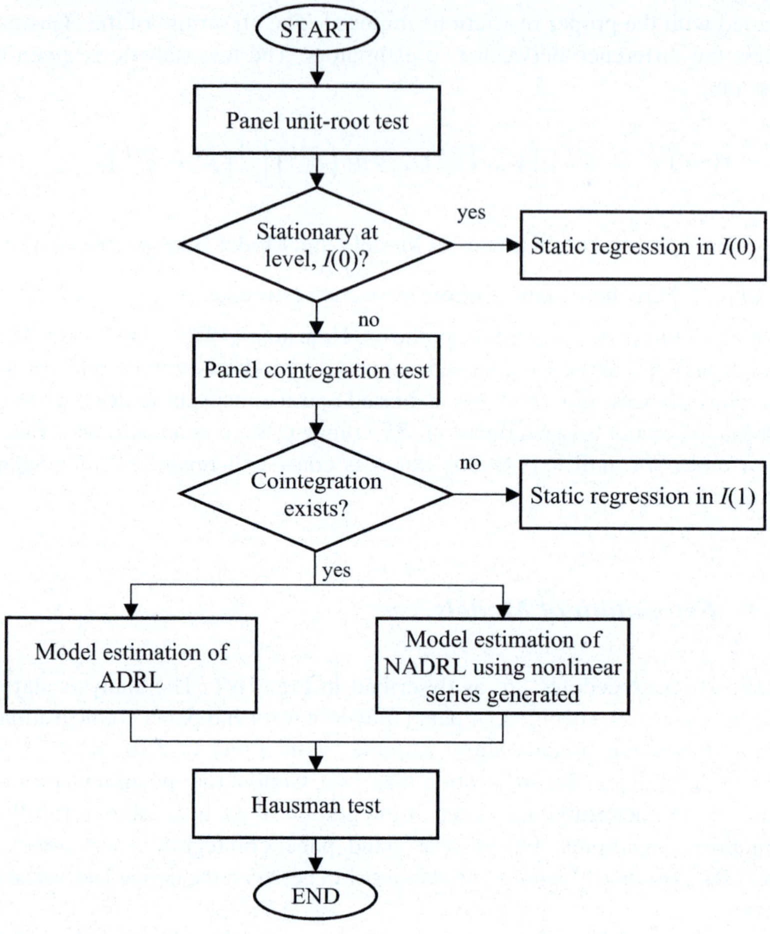

Fig. 16.1 The flowchart of the analysis

parameters in both ARDL and NARDL models should be checked to confirm the existence of the long-run relationship as well.

If no cointegration is present in the model, the static regression is carried out using the first differenced variables. If there is cointegration, we can proceed to the model estimation of ARDL using the MG, PMG, and DFE estimators, followed by the Hausman specification test. In the estimation of the ARDL model, the speed of adjustment is not significant, the model estimation should be repeated by changing the specification of the model, such as adding the deterministic trend or the dummy. For the model estimation of NARDL, the process is initiated with generating the nonlinear series at the very beginning, which is before performing the panel unit-root test. Then, subsequence processes are similar to the procedures in developing the ARDL model.

16.4 Illustration with Case Study

For illustration purpose, we empirically investigate the role of agriculture on economic growth in selected nations of Asia by adopting DFE, MG, and PMG estimators. There exists literature on the application of these techniques on the agriculture and economic growth in Asian countries (e.g. Ozdemir 2022; Sinha and Sengupta 2022; Salim et al. 2020). In particular, we chose eight countries from Southeast Asia and South Asia. Specifically, the countries for South Asia are India, Nepal, Pakistan, and Sri Lanka, while for Southeast Asia, the countries involved are Indonesia, Malaysia, the Philippines, and Thailand. Agriculture is an important sector in these countries and might play an essential role in their economic development. Accordingly, gross domestic product (GDP) is the dependent variable in the analysis. The regressors include three agricultural production indices (crop, food, and livestock) and two commodity price indices (energy and non-energy commodities). All data are collected from the databank of the World Bank. The GDP series and agricultural production indices are data by country, while the commodity price data are the averaged world data. To study the nonlinear relationship of commodity price indices on GDP, the energy and non-energy commodities data are decomposed into their positive and negative series. To note, one may decompose more than one variable to nonlinear series, but rarely decompose all regressors to nonlinear series. This is because, including too many regressors in the model and the inclusion of lag terms specification may shorten the degree of freedom, yet leads to the waste of information. All data are transformed into natural logarithm form for consistency as the original data are given in different units of measurements. Table 16.1 provides the descriptions of variables applied in the analysis. This study uses yearly data from 1961 to 2018, which comprises 58 years.

In this example, the energy and non-energy commodity price indices (*LENER* and *LNONE*) are decomposed into their respective positive and negative series, i.e., *LENER+*, *LENER–*, *LNONE +*, and *LNONE–*. The dependent variable is the *LGDP*, while the other regressors are *LCROP*, *LFOOD*, and *LLIVE*. Generally, the estimated models are as follows. Model 1 is the linear model estimated using the ARDL approach. The model estimations of NARDL are based on Models 2 and 3, where a pair of nonlinear *LENER* are included in Model 2 while Model 3 comprises a pair of nonlinear *LNONE*.

Model 1: *LGDP* = *F*(*LCROP, LFOOD, LLIVE, LENER, LNONE*).
Model 2: *LGDP* = *F*(*LCROP, LFOOD, LLIVE, LENER+, LENER–, LNONE*).
Model 3: *LGDP* = *F*(*LCROP, LFOOD, LLIVE, LENER, LNONE+, LNONE–*).

Table 16.1 A summary of variables

Variable	Description	Remark/unit of measurement
LGDP	Natural log of GDP per capita	Constant 2010 US$
LCROP	Natural log of crop production index. It shows agricultural production which includes all crops, but except fodder crops	Base period 2014–2016 = 100
LFOOD	Natural log of food production index which covers food crops that are considered edible and that contain nutrients. Coffee and tea are excluded because, although edible, they have no nutritive value	Base period 2014–2016 = 100
LLIVE	Natural log of livestock production index. It includes meat and milk from all sources, dairy products such as cheese, and eggs, honey, raw silk, wool, and hides and skins	Base period 2014–2016 = 100
LENER	Natural log of energy commodity real annual index, which includes coal, crude oil and natural gas. It is the world data	Base year 2010 = 100
LENER +	Natural log of energy commodity real annual index increases	Generated from *LENER* by data decomposition
LENER-	Natural log of energy commodity real annual index decreases	Generated from *LENER* by data decomposition
LNONE	Natural log of non-energy commodity real annual index, which includes agriculture, fertilizers, and metals and minerals. It is the world data	Base year 2010 = 100
LNONE +	Natural log of non-energy commodity real annual index increases	Generated from *LNONE* by data decomposition
LNONE-	Natural log of non-energy commodity real annual index decreases	Generated from *LNONE* by data decomposition

16.4.1 Data Organization and Decomposition

The analyses are conducted via two software packages, namely Stata software and EViews software. After importing the data into Stata, declare the cross-section and time-series dimensions using the **xtset CODE YEAR** command (in the mentioned order), where **xtset** is meant for panel data, **CODE** is the variable name that contains the number designated for the cross-sectional units, and **YEAR** is the name of the time variable. Save it after declaring the panel data so that the declaration process only has to do it once with the same dataset. The details of analysis processes are as presented in the following subsections with the empirical example.

As discussed in the methodology section for the NARDL model estimation, the positive and negative series of the explanatory variables are obtained via the partial sum decomposition method. The following demonstrates two possible ways to generate asymmetric series using Stata software.

Option 1:

This option requires a few steps to generate a pair asymmetric series. First, take the first difference of the series (*LENER* is used as an example), i.e.,

gen DLENER = d.LENER

Next, the positive and negative series (*DLENER_POS* and *DLENER_NEG*) are generated using the first differenced variable (*DLENER*), i.e.,

gen DLENER_POS = DLENER if DLENER > = 0
gen DLENER_NEG = DLENER if DLENER < = 0

Otherwise, it is zero, which means that the missing values in the series generated above are replaced with zero, i.e.,

replace DLENER_POS = 0 if DLENER < 0
replace DLENER_NEG = 0 if DLENER > 0

It is followed by generating the positive and negative series in its level form (*LENER_POS* and *LENER_NEG*) with cumulative sums, i.e.,

bysort CODE (YEAR): Gen LENER_POS = sum(DLENER_POS)
bysort CODE (YEAR): Gen LENER_NEG = sum(DLENER_NEG)

Then, the first-year observation is dropped for each country in the panel group, i.e.,

drop if YEAR < 1962

Finally, remove the unnecessary variables, i.e.,

drop DLENER DLENER_POS DLENER_NEG

Option 2:

Alternatively, the following commands can be used as another option. This is a set of commands that can be performed in one go.

```
foreach V in LENER {
 generate 'V'_POS = 0
 generate 'V'_NEG = 0
 generate d'V'_POS = max(0,D.'V')
 generate d'V'_NEG = min(0,D.'V')
 replace 'V'_POS = L.'V'_POS + d'V'_POS if YEAR > 1961
 replace 'V'_NEG = L.'V'_NEG + d'V'_NEG if YEAR > 1961
}"
```

The commands above are to generate *LENER_POS* and *LENER_NEG* from the linear series *LENER*. **YEAR** and **1961** represent the time variable and the first period, respectively. Hence, they can be replaced according to the name of the time variable and the period of data imported. The same commands are repeated to generate the other pair of nonlinear series by substituting **LENER** (in the first line of commands) with another variable.

Since the process of data decomposition involves differencing the series, use the following command to drop the first-year observation (the observation for 1961) for each country.

drop if YEAR < 1962

Four observations are deleted because there are only four countries in a group for the analysis. Hence, the range of data for nonlinear models is from 1962 to 2018 that is 57 years. The linear model uses the data from 1961 to 2018.

16.4.2 Software Procedures

Blackburne and Frank (2007) introduced the Stata syntax **xtpmg** to execute the estimation on panel ARDL model based on three estimates discussed above. The estimation is based on nonstationary heterogeneous panels with large T and large N. Further details about the syntax can refer to Blackburne and Frank (2007) or typing the command "**help xtpmg**" using the Stata program. On the other hand, EViews also provides the option to perform the panel ARDL model using the PMG estimator, but not for the other estimators (DFE and MG). The panel NARDL model can be executed using the Stata and EViews options for the panel ARDL model, but before the estimation, the asymmetric variables (positive_x and negative_x) should be generated by running some commands either using EViews or Stata.

For illustration, we apply the combination of both EViews and Stata software. The good feature of EViews is the availability of the optimal lag length search option in panel unit-root tests and panel ARDL(PMG) model which is not available in Stata. But EViews does not have the option to perform DFE and MG estimations and the Hausman test. Hence, it is more convenient to perform the panel unit-root and panel cointegration tests and PMG estimation using EViews and then continue the remaining estimation steps and Hausman test in Stata. The following explanations assume readers have the basic knowledge to use both software and hence we do not show the process how to get started with new workfile creation, importing, plotting, and describing data.

16.4.2.1 Phase 1: Preliminary Tests

Panel Unit-Root Tests

The preliminary tests (panel unit-root and panel cointegration) are performed in EViews. The illustration is based on EViews version 12. First, double click to open the single variable to be tested for the presence of unit-root. Then, a Series Window will appear. From the Series View Menu, click on Unit Root Tests > > Cross-Sectionally Independent. The following will provide a summary of test results for testing the selected variable in level with individual intercept included. One may start with the variable indicated in the level. If the result of unit-root is not significant, repeat the unit-root test in first difference. One may also change the test specification options, e.g., individual intercept or intercept with the trend. Repeat this step for all variables. Alternatively, panel unit root tests can be conducted using the Stata software. The command to get the test statistic of the LLC test is as follows.

xtunitroot llc LGDP, lags(aic)

The **xtunitroot** is the Stata syntax to conduct the panel unit root tests. To obtain other panel unit root test results, for example, the IPS test, the **llc** in the command can be replaced by **ips**. Then, it is followed by the variable to be tested. Finally, a few options can be added. The command stated above specifies that the number of lags is selected using the AIC. One may type the command **help xtunitroot** at the command window to get further explanations about the options under this syntax. To note, the results reported in this empirical example follow the results generated from the EViews software. The test statistics might show slightly different values depending on the default specifications, such as the lag length and the spectral estimation (the kernel), set by both software.

Panel Cointegration Test

To conduct a panel cointegration test, one may refer to the model function mentioned above. For example, we wish to examine the relationship in Model 1: $LGDP = F(LCROP, LFOOD, LLIVE, LENER, LNONE)$. First, click to select the dependent variable (*LGDP*), then click "ctrl" button to continue to select the independent variables in Model 1. Right-click to open the selected variables as a group. Make sure the dependent variable is selected first. Once the selected variables workfile opens, at the Workfile Window Toolbars, click on View > > Cointegration Test > > Panel Cointegration Test. There are three types of tests available, you may select one of the tests and click OK and repeat the same step to perform the other tests. Again, you may select different options of specifications available under each test. Similarly, panel cointegration tests can be conducted using the Stata software with the syntax **xtcointtest**. For example,

xtcointtest Kao LGDP LCROP LFOOD LLIVE LENER LNONE

The command shown above is conducted for the Kao test. The **kao** from the command can be substituted by **pedroni** to obtain the test statistics of the Pedroni test. Then, the dependent variable is first stated, followed by a list of the explanatory variables. For detailed explanations of the syntax, please refer to the note from Stata (**help xtcointtest**). Again, the EViews results are reported, and the outcomes might be different from the results obtained from the Stata software because of different default specifications.

16.4.2.2 Phase 2: Model Estimation and Selection

EViews software and Stata software are utilized to estimate the panel ARDL and NARDL models with different model restrictions (MG, PMG, and DFE estimators). These models provide both short-run and long-run estimates, in which the models are generated with lag terms for the dependent variable and regressors. The EViews provides the lag selection criterion in determining the optimal lags while Stata does not have such an option.

However, EViews only provides the PMG option while Stata syntax covers the estimation for MG, PMG, and DFE. Hence, one may first perform the PMG estimation using EViews. After determining the optimal lags, one may apply the same lag specification to continue the estimation in Stata for these three estimators. The procedure of estimation is similar for both ARDL and NARDL models. The only difference is to replace the decomposed positive and negative series with the intended original regressor. The following subsections demonstrate the procedures to estimate the nonlinear ARDL (NARDL) model using EViews and Stata.

Panel Nonlinear ARDL Model Estimation in EViews – PMG Model

From the Main Menu, click on Quick >> Estimate Equation. Then, from the "Method" drop-down menu under the "Estimation settings," select the "PMG/ARDL—Pooled Mean Group/AR Distributed Lag Models." Key in the variable names (dependent variable followed by regressors) under the "Dynamic Specification." The maximum lags for the dependent variable and regressors are set at one. The linear trend can be added from the "Trend specification" drop-down menu. The "Model selection criterion" is available in the "Options" page tab. An example of the PMG result is shown in Fig. 16.2.

In this example, the dependent variable is DLGDP and there are six regressors (*LCROP*, *LFOOD*, *LLIVE*, *LENER_POS*, *LENER_NEG*, *LNONE*). The selected model is NARDL(1,1,1,1,1,1,1) with the constant and linear trend included. This model will be re-run in Stata. NARDL(1,1,1,1,1,1,1) signifies one lag for each variable. However, the short-run variables are in the first difference form. Hence, this reduces one lag. On the other hand, the long-run estimates are in the log-level form. "COINTEQ01" is the speed of adjustment that must be negative and significant so that the estimated model is valid (the long-run relationship is present).

Panel Nonlinear ARDL Model Estimation in Stata—PMG Model

Since the nonlinear model selected in EViews is estimated with the constant and trend terms included (obtained after comparing the R-squared, AIC, RMSE, and MAE), it is necessary to generate the trend term in Stata. The command is as follows.

egen t = group(YEAR)

The **egen** command is the extension to the **generate** command. The **t** is the variable name created for the trend term. The **group** is the function that forms a variable with natural numbers (1, 2, …) for the groups formed by **YEAR**.

Next, the nonlinear ARDL model is estimated by using the **xtpmg** syntax. Installation of this command (**ssc install xtpmg**) is necessary for the first-time user. The syntax takes the following form:

xtpmg depvar [indepvars] [if] [in] [, options]

Equation: UNTITLED Workfile: SOUTH ASIA::SA_nonline...

View | Proc | Object | Print | Name | Freeze | Estimate | Forecast | Stats | Resids

Dependent Variable: D(LGDP)
Method: ARDL
Date: 12/05/21 Time: 20:55
Sample: 1963 2018
Included observations: 224
Maximum dependent lags: 1 (Automatic selection)
Model selection method: Akaike info criterion (AIC)
Dynamic regressors (1 lag, automatic): LCROP LFOOD LLIVE
LENER_POS LENER_NEG LNONE
Fixed regressors: C
Number of models evalulated: 1
Selected Model: ARDL(1, 1, 1, 1, 1, 1, 1)
Note: final equation sample is larger than selection sample

Variable	Coefficient	Std. Error	t-Statistic	Prob.*
		Long Run Equation		
LCROP	1.607899	0.454642	3.536628	0.0005
LFOOD	-1.288104	0.441674	-2.916413	0.0040
LLIVE	0.262282	0.135407	1.936991	0.0543
LENER_POS	0.031571	0.039829	0.792655	0.4290
LENER_NEG	-0.104879	0.053127	-1.974124	0.0498
LNONE	0.259531	0.057717	4.496613	0.0000
		Short Run Equation		
COINTEQ01	-0.122262	0.057591	-2.122920	0.0351
D(LCROP)	-0.332898	0.288710	-1.153051	0.2504
D(LFOOD)	0.547675	0.326846	1.675636	0.0955
D(LLIVE)	-0.242592	0.173708	-1.396551	0.1642
D(LENER_POS)	-0.019035	0.005665	-3.360221	0.0009
D(LENER_NEG)	-0.001835	0.007692	-0.238544	0.8117
D(LNONE)	-0.008201	0.011702	-0.700825	0.4843
C	0.342075	0.156050	2.192085	0.0296
@TREND	0.001349	0.001474	0.915466	0.3611

Root MSE	0.018273	Mean dependent var	0.027522
S.D. dependent var	0.026337	S.E. of regression	0.020231
Akaike info criterion	-4.719082	Sum squared resid	0.076130
Schwarz criterion	-4.087360	Log likelihood	579.9753
Hannan-Quinn criter.	-4.464201		

*Note: p-values and any subsequent tests do not account for model selection.

Fig. 16.2 EViews screenshot of PMG estimation

One may type the command **help xtpmg** at the command window to get further explanation about the options under this syntax. One should start the estimation by the syntax **xtpmg** followed by the dependent variable and then dependent variables. In this example, NARDL(1,1,1,1,1,1,1) model with lag 1 (in level) is with zero lag when it is specified in differenced term in Stata. This can be written in Stata as:

xtpmg d.LGDP d.LCROP d.LFOOD d.LLIVE d.LENER_POS d.LENER_NEG d.LNONE t, lr(l.LGDP LCROP LFOOD LLIVE LENER_POS LENER_NEG LNONE) ec(ect) replace pmg

From the command above, the **d.LGDP** indicates the first difference of *LGDP*, where *LGDP* is the dependent variable. Then, it is followed by the list of independent variables (with the lags if needed), in which the trend term generated should appear. The **lr**(*varlist*) option is for the long-run cointegrating vector, which should be the same for all specifications. The **l.LGDP** specified in the **lr**(*varlist*) represents the lag of *LGDP*. The **ec(ect)** specifies the error correction term with a name "ect." The **replace** option will substitute the previous error correction term. The **pmg** option estimates the pooled mean group approach. We can replace **pmg** with **mg** or **dfe** if we wish to run the model using MG or DFE estimator later. Typically, PMG results in EViews should be similar to PMG results in Stata, but sometimes in strange situations, the results may be slightly different. Then, the **difficult** option, which will employ a different stepping algorithm in non-concave regions of the log likelihood, would be useful.

In the other example, if the model is ARDL(1, 2, 3) with dependent variable y, and the regressor x_1 and x_2. Then, the Stata syntax is:

xtpmg d.y d. x 1 dl. x 1 dl(1/2). x 2, lr(l.y x 1 x 2) ec(ect) replace mg

This syntax runs the MG estimation. The term dl(1/2). x 2 means the lag difference term takes the lag term from one to two. In order to perform the Hausman test to decide on a better estimator, one should run the xtpmg syntax for two different estimators. Next, run the Hausman specification test with the syntax **hausman mg pmg, sigmamore.** The details are as below:

xtpmg d.y d. x 1 dl. x 1 dl(1/2). x 2, lr(l.y x 1 x 2) ec(ect) replace mg
xtpmg d.y d. x 1 dl. x 1 dl(1/2). x 2, lr(l.y x 1 x 2) ec(ect) replace pmg
hausman mg pmg, sigmamore

The sequence in which we specify the model estimations does not matter, i.e., we can switch the order of **mg** and **pmg** in the command. Example of the Hausman test result (PMG versus MG) is shown in Fig. 16.3. Under the null hypothesis, there is no significant difference between MG and PMG, and the PMG is more efficient. Since the probability as shown in the Hausman test is greater than the 5% significance level, the null hypothesis of the PMG is more efficient and could not be rejected. Hence, the analysis ends.

However, if the null hypothesis is rejected, it implies that the MG model is preferred. Then, it is necessary to run the DFE model followed by the Hausman test to compare the MG and DFE models. The following command executes the Hausman specification test to obtain the efficient estimator by comparing the estimation results of MG and DFE models.

```
. hausman mg pmg, sigmamore

                 ---- Coefficients ----
             |      (b)          (B)            (b-B)     sqrt(diag(V_b-V_B))
             |      mg           pmg         Difference          S.E.
-------------+----------------------------------------------------------------
       LCROP |   1.188957     1.607897       -.4189398        5.076545
       LFOOD |  -2.078237    -1.288101       -.7901354        6.178168
       LLIVE |   1.841983     .2622815        1.579701        1.898113
  LENER_POS  |  -.0043059     .0315705       -.0358765         .027656
  LENER_NEG  |  -.1274366    -.1048788       -.0225579               .
       LNONE |   .2048699     .2595314       -.0546615        .1425542
------------------------------------------------------------------------------
                         b = consistent under Ho and Ha; obtained from xtpmg
          B = inconsistent under Ha, efficient under Ho; obtained from xtpmg

    Test:  Ho:  difference in coefficients not systematic

                  chi2(6) = (b-B)'[(V_b-V_B)^(-1)](b-B)
                          =        2.07
                Prob>chi2 =      0.9134
                (V_b-V_B is not positive definite)
```

Fig. 16.3 Stata screenshot of Hausman test

Full Option on Panel ARDL (or NARDL) Model Estimation in Stata

Adding the **full** option to the PMG model will display the result of short-run estimates for all countries individually.

xtpmg d.LGDP d.LCROP d.LFOOD d.LLIVE d.LENER_POS d.LENER_NEG d.LNONE t, lr(l.LGDP LCROP LFOOD LLIVE LENER_POS LENER_NEG LNONE) ec(ect) replace pmg full

For the MG model, if the **full** option is added, it will display the result of short-run and long-run estimates for all countries separately. However, the **full** option is meaningless with the DFE model since this model assumes common short-run and long-run slope parameters. Hence, Stata will ignore the option and continue the model estimation.

Some Other Information—Dummy Variable

In certain estimations, the long-run coefficients might not be significant although the speed of adjustment is negatively significant. To further improve the results, one might modify the model specification by adding dummies as regressors to consider for the structure breaks. In general, the procedures for generating a dummy are as follows. First, try to check which year decreases or increases sharply from the plots of variables. Then, allocate a dummy for that particular year, i.e., assign one to the year with a break, and zero for the other years. Repeat for all counties examined in the dataset.

Next, we show how to generate a Dummy in EViews. From the Workfile Window Toolbars, click on "Genr." A "Generate Series by Equation" window will appear. In the text box under the "Enter equation," key in the following command.

dummy_1998 = @year = 1998

From the command, the term before the first equal sign, **dummy_1998**, is the dummy's name and can be replaced with another name. The word **year** is the time variable. The last term, **1998**, is the year to assign a dummy. In other words, the command generates a dummy on the year 1998 with the name dummy_1998.

The following command will generate a dummy in Stata. Applying the **egen** command with the **anymatch** function, it is one if the time variable (the year) equals 1998 and zero otherwise.

egen dummy_1998 = anymatch(YEAR), values(1998)

To proceed with the estimation, one may write in the following examples using Stata syntax:

xtpmg d.y d. x 1 dl. x 1 dl(1/2). x 2 dummy_1998, lr(l.y x 1 x 2) ec(ect) replace mg

xtpmg d.y d. x 1 dl. x 1 dl(1/2). x 2 dummy_1998, lr(l.y x 1 x 2 dummy_1998) ec(ect) replace mg

16.4.2.3 Phase 3: Interpretations of Results

Table 16.2 summarizes the results of panel unit-root tests of Lin, Levin, and Chu (LLC), Im, Pesaran, and Shin (IPS) and augmented Dicky-Fuller (ADF). The world commodity price indices (*LENER* and *LNONE*) and their decomposition series are listed in the first panel in Table 16.2 while the country-based variables are listed in the following panels under South Asia and Southeast Asia. In general, all tests show very consistent results, i.e., reject unit-root after first differencing, suggesting that all variables are $I(1)$. This fulfills the notion to conduct a panel cointegration test.

Table reports the results of panel cointegration tests of Kao's and Pedroni. The rejection of the null hypothesis implies the existence of the cointegrating relationship. Kao's test is rejected in almost all models. On the other hand, the results from the Pedroni test are different between South Asia and Southeast Asia with more significant results reported in South Asia but no significant results found in Southeast Asia. Since both tests report inconsistent results, one might examine the ECT term or speed of adjustment in the estimation output to further judge the existence of the long-run relationship which will be discussed in the following tables.

Both ARDL and NARDL models are estimated using MG, PMG, and DFE estimators. Hausman test is executed to decide on a more efficient estimator by comparing MG and PMG estimators. The results of the Hausman test are reported in Table 16.3. Since the test is not significant, suggesting PMG as the more efficient estimator, we no need to further compare MG and DFE. The results of PMG are reported in Table 16.3. Since the ECT coefficient (speed of adjustment) is negatively significant in all models, this signifies the existence of the long-run relationship in each model.

Table 16.2 The results of panel unit-root tests

Variable	Constant			Constant + trend		
	LLC	IPS	ADF	LLC	IPS	ADF
LENER	–0.4902	0.3850	4.1120	0.9932	0.7991	3.2930
D(LENER)	–12.3308***	–12.9107***	130.7210***	–11.8831***	–12.3990***	112.0830***
LENER +	0.4449	2.9645	0.6047	–1.0851	–2.3655***	17.1004**
D(LENER +)	–12.8124***	–12.1583***	121.5460***	–12.4965***	–11.5283***	102.5850***
LENER-	2.3364	4.6244	0.1230	–1.0146	–0.7540	8.6342
D(LENER-)	–16.0260***	–14.3911***	146.5740***	–16.2479***	–14.2960***	130.7900***
LNONE	–0.1591	–0.3185	6.2137	1.9003	2.4370	0.7534
D(LNONE)	–15.8342***	–13.8394***	142.6570***	–15.9288***	–13.5618***	125.8230***
LNONE +	0.6848	3.2804	0.4592	0.6768	0.1822	5.0347
D(LNONE +)	–12.8539***	–11.1859***	110.0950***	–12.7478***	–10.5169***	91.9335***
LNONE-	–1.6671**	1.1084	2.3238	2.8467	3.2504	0.3516
D(LNONE-)	–14.8900***	–12.5332***	127.3370***	–15.2691***	–12.1413***	110.7140***
South Asia						
LGDP	4.8983	8.7915	2.8260	0.1821	2.5739	4.5747
D(LGDP)	–2.3041**	–3.4290***	44.0400***	–4.4457***	–9.2554***	82.8365***
LCROP	–0.9139	2.0375	4.1894	–2.8413***	–2.7307***	22.7430***
D(LCROP)	–18.7943***	–16.3033***	154.0030***	–19.3111***	–16.5109***	142.4800***
LFOOD	–0.3535	3.1313	1.4005	–0.5810	–1.5590	17.4325
D(LFOOD)	–22.0488***	–20.3961***	194.6520***	–22.5067***	–20.7826***	180.1330***

(continued)

Table 16.2 (continued)

Variable	Constant			Constant + trend		
	LLC	IPS	ADF	LLC	IPS	ADF
LLIVE	1.2352	4.1468	0.3115	–0.5087	–0.4717	7.7882
D(LLIVE)	–7.8698***	–7.8362***	75.2232***	–8.2981***	–7.3180***	65.3622***
Southeast Asia						
LGDP	–0.7367	2.5854	1.6326	1.0931	0.8970	5.4188
D(LGDP)	–8.4191***	–8.2177***	75.7682***	–8.4607***	–7.5713***	62.5692***
LCROP	–3.0093***	–1.2032	12.4622	–0.4522	1.2907	2.7837
D(LCROP)	–14.7049***	–13.4210***	132.3630***	–9.7750***	–10.3696***	94.2867***
LFOOD	–4.0965***	–1.4725*	14.8936*	1.0047	1.6303	1.8353
D(LFOOD)	–14.3700***	–12.9166***	126.7090***	–8.4750***	–9.4031***	83.9963***
LLIVE	–1.9214**	1.1637	2.7374	0.0381	0.2533	6.7917
D(LLIVE)	–10.9804***	–10.3306***	100.7660***	–11.0001***	–9.7532***	84.9305***

Hence, the results of the estimation are valid. The negative value of the ECT coefficient indicates the convergence of the dependent variable to the long-run equilibrium with a gradual speed of adjustment (as the absolute of ECT is around 10%).

The upper panel of Table 16.3 is the long-run estimates while the lower panel is the short-run estimates. Model 1 is the ARDL model while Model 2 and Model 3 are the NARDL models. As observed, the NARDL models capture the asymmetric effect of world commodity variables on GDP growth while the ARDL model only captures the symmetric net effect of commodity variables. For instance, the energy commodity (*LENER*) does not have a significant (net) effect on GDP growth in South Asia under Model 1 (ARDL model). But Model 2 (NARDL model) captures the asymmetric effect, in which the increases of *LENER* lead to no significant effect while its decreases cause the drop in GDP growth in South Asia in the long run. Hence, the effect of *LENER* is more impactful. But the result is different for Southeast Asia in which increases in *LENER* have larger influences on GDP growth in the long run. Also, the impact is much larger in the long-run than its short-run counterpart. On the other hand, Model 3 captures the asymmetric of none energy commodity prices (*LNONE*) which includes agriculture, fertilizers, and metals and minerals. As observed, increases in *LNONE* lead to higher GDP growth in South Asia while its decreases have no significant effect. A different result is observed in Southeast Asia as both increases and decreases in *LNONE* do not affect GDP growth as reported by Model 3. The result is consistent in that Model 1 also reports no significant effect from the symmetric counterpart. Based on these findings, we can say that increases in none energy commodity prices contribute to GDP growth in South Asia as they are none energy producers while increases in energy commodity price benefit Southeast Asia. This is because some Southeast Asia countries are energy producers, hence higher energy prices contribute to higher income. At the same time, they are also energy-intensive as these economies are manufacturing-based. Hence, decreases in energy prices might reduce the cost of production and contribute to output growth.

Next, comparing the impacts of production indices, the results reveal that crop production is the main factor that contributes to GDP growth while food production is the main factor that causes the decline in GDP growth in South Asia in the long run. The negative effect of the food production index might be due to the higher consumption than its production. On the other hand, the food production index contributes to higher GDP growth in Southeast Asia in the long run.

According to The World Bank Group (2021), South Asia is the most vulnerable regions to climate change and badly affected in terms of food insecurity and poverty. Besides, this region is also disaster-prone. Production and food security are threatened by natural disasters such as cyclones, floods, and droughts. A huge amount of resources has to be devoted to coping with frequent natural disasters (Tables 16.4 and 16.5).

Table 16.3 The results of panel cointegration tests

Model		Kao	Pedroni panel statistics				Pedroni group statistics		
		ADF	v	rho	PP	ADF	rho	PP	ADF
South Asia									
Model 1	C	–0.7749	0.4448	–1.5680*	–3.3622***	–3.3927***	–0.2877	–1.8528**	–1.9135**
	C + trend	–	2.8082***	0.1370	–1.3296*	–1.3315*	0.9085	–0.9092	–0.9233
Model 2	C	–2.8616***	1.1220	–0.6261	–1.9585**	–1.1758	0.0693	–1.6965**	–0.7890
	C + trend	–	0.2095	0.0901	–1.4806*	–0.2958	0.8882	–0.9901	0.1112
Model 3	C	–1.8246**	0.9438	–1.0330	–2.6600***	–2.1309**	–0.2321	–2.2099**	–1.5574*
	C + trend	–	0.3251	–0.0476	–2.0012**	–1.4374*	0.6912	–1.6622**	–1.0977
Southeast Asia									
Model 1	C	–1.8532**	1.9097**	0.2184	–0.4362	–0.4918	0.7041	–0.2639	–1.2563
	C + trend	–	1.5145*	1.0535	0.3870	0.7269	1.6182	0.6657	–0.1331
Model 2	C	–2.0476**	0.7886	0.8442	0.2657	0.3342	1.4407	0.6032	–0.6906
	C + trend	–	0.4508	1.4382	0.8708	0.9171	1.8863	1.0272	–0.3308
Model 3	C	–1.7378**	1.0367	0.3993	–0.3057	–0.4325	1.0322	0.0819	–1.1519
	C + trend	–	0.8546	1.3898	0.7600	0.7521	1.7769	0.8055	–0.3875

Table 16.4 The results of Hausman test statistics

Model	South Asia			Southeast Asia		
	PMG versus MG	DFE versus MG	Best	PMG versus MG	DFE versus MG	Best
Model 1	5.87	–	PMG	0.07	–	PMG
Model 2	2.07	–	PMG	10.73*		PMG
Model 3	0.93	–	PMG	7.19	–	PMG

16.5 Concluding Remarks

This chapter introduces the nonstationary heterogeneous panels, i.e., the panel ARDL model and its nonlinear form (NARDL) using the three estimators, namely MG, PMG, and DFE, to handle the heterogeneous and asymmetric effect in modeling the long panel data. PMG is a superior estimator among these options. In traditional panel models, short-run relationships are modeled with stationary variables, such as static fixed effects and random effects regression models and long-run relationships are modeled with nonstationary variables, such as panel cointegration. However, at times researchers face a problem of modeling the relationship between variables which may not be integrated at the same level. In such situations above approaches are not suitable for data in hand. PMG estimator is free from such restriction.

The empirical example utilizes both ARDL and NARDL models to examine how the global commodity prices and each sub-agriculture productivity (food, crops, and livestock) might contribute to economic growth, and if such effects are symmetric or asymmetric. The datasets of Southeast and South Asia are used in the demonstrations. The empirical findings show that the PMG (i.e., the intermediate estimator between MG and DFE) is the best or preferred estimator among the three estimators for all cases in this study. As observed, the NARDL models (i.e., the PMG estimator for this study) capture the asymmetric effect of world commodity variables on GDP growth while the ARDL model (i.e., the PMG) only captures the symmetric net effect of commodity variables. The inclusion of asymmetric estimates in the NARDL models makes the difference between the ARDL and NARDL models.

Table 16.5 The results of panel ARDL and NARDL models

Variable	South Asia			Southeast Asia		
	Model 1	Model 2	Model 3	Model 1	Model 2	Model 3
Long-run coefficients						
LCROP	1.9084***	1.6079***	2.1391***	–0.0861	–0.0666	0.0169
LFOOD	–1.5757**	–1.2881***	–1.8453***	0.8607***	0.8361***	1.1909**
LLIVE	0.2082	0.2623*	0.3771**	0.1743	0.1649	0.5303**
LENER	–0.0062	–	–0.0157	0.0904***	–	0.0443
LENER +	–	0.0316	–	–	0.0985***	–
LENER-	–	–0.1049**	–	–	0.0832*	–
LNONE	0.2835***	0.2595***	–	–0.0172	–0.0304	–
LNONE +	–	–	0.4101***	–	–	0.0953
LNONE-	–	–	0.1011	–	–	0.2890
DUM_98	–	–	–	–	–	–1.3535***
Short-run coefficients						
ECT	–0.0842*	–0.1223**	–0.1049*	–0.1264*	–0.1194*	–0.0719***
D(LCROP)	–0.3076	–0.3329	–0.3353	–0.0808	–0.1230	0.0955
D(LFOOD)	0.5346	0.5477*	0.5481*	0.0972	0.1746	–0.0680
D(LLIVE)	–0.2661	–0.2426	–0.2469*	0.0733	0.0606	0.0474
D(LENER)	–0.0134***	–	–0.0115**	0.0124	–	0.0054
D(LENER +)	–	–0.0190***	–	–	–0.0023	–
D(LENER–)	–	–0.0018	–	–	0.0401**	–
D(LNONE)	–0.0042	–0.0082	–	0.0700***	0.0610***	–
D(LNONE +)	–	–	–0.0218	–	–	0.0191

(continued)

Table 16.5 (continued)

Variable	South Asia			Southeast Asia		
	Model 1	Model 2	Model 3	Model 1	Model 2	Model 3
D(LNONE−)	–	–	0.0143	–	–	0.0837***
D(DUM_98)	–	–	–	–	–	0.0022
C	0.2357*	0.3407**	0.3854*	0.5545*	0.5658*	0.1545**
trend	0.0019	0.0013	0.0009	–	–	−0.0010*
Model specification	ARDL (1,1,1,1,1,1)	NARDL (1,1,1,1,1,1,1)	NARDL (1,1,1,1,1,1,1)	ARDL (1,1,1,1,1,1)	NARDL (1,1,1,1,1,1,1)	NARDL (1,1,1,1,1,1,1)
Estimator	PMG	PMG	PMG	PMG	PMG	PMG

References

Arellano M (2004) Panel data econometrics. Oxford University Press, Oxford

Baltagi BH (2005) Econometric analysis of panel data, 3rd edn. Wiley Inc., New York

Baltagi BH, Griffin JM (1988) A generalized error component model with heteroscedastic disturbances. Int Econ Rev 29:745–753

Baltagi BH, Griffin JM (1997) Pooled estimators vs. their heterogeneous counterparts in the context of dynamic demand for gasoline. J Econom 77(2):303–327

Baltagi BH, Kao C (2000) Nonstationary panels, cointegration in panels and dynamic panels: a survey. Adv Econom 15:7–51

Birkel C (2014) The analysis of non-stationary pooled time series cross-section data. Int J Confl Violence 8(2):222–242

Blackburne EF, Frank MW (2007) Estimation of nonstationary heterogeneous panels. Stata J 7:197–208

Brooks C (2008) Introductory econometrics for finance, 2nd edn. Cambridge University Press, New York

Choi I (2001) Unit root tests for panel data. J Int Money Finance 20(2):249–272

Filis G, Chatziantoniou I (2014) Financial and monetary policy responses to oil price shocks: evidence from oil-importing and oil-exporting countries. Rev Quant Finance Account 42(4):709–729

Hausman JA (1978) Specification tests in econometrics. Econometrica 46(6):1251–1271

Hsiao C (2003) Analysis of panel data. Cambridge University Press, Cambridge

Ibrahim MH (2015) Oil and food prices in Malaysia: a nonlinear ARDL analysis. Agric Food Econ 3(2):1–14

Im KS, Pesaran MH, Shin Y (2003) Testing for unit roots in heterogeneous panels. J Econom 115(1):53–74

Kao C (1999) Spurious regression and residual-based tests for cointegration in panel data. J Econom 90(1):1–44

Koop G, Steel MFJ (2001) Bayesian analysis of stochastic frontier models. In: Baltagi BH (ed) A Companion to theoretical econometrics. Blackwell Publishers, Massachusetts, pp 520–537

Levin A, Lin CF, Chu CSJ (2002) Unit root tests in panel data: asymptotic and finite-sample properties. J Econ 108(1):1–24

Maddala GS, Wu S (1999) A comparative study of unit root tests with panel data and a new simple test. Oxf Bull Econ Stat 61(S1):631–652

Nelson C, Plosser C (1982) Trends and random walks in macroeconomics time series, some evidence and implications. J Monet Econ 10:139–162

Ozdemir D (2022) The impact of climate change on agricultural productivity in Asian countries: a heterogeneous panel data approach. Environ Sci Pollut Res 1–13

Pedroni P (1999) Critical values for cointegration tests in heterogeneous panels with multiple regressors. Oxf Bull Econ Stat 61(S1):653–670

Pedroni P (2004) Panel cointegration: asymptotic and finite sample properties of pooled time-series tests with an application to the PPP hypothesis. Econ Theory 20(3):597–625

Pesaran MH, Smith R (1995) Estimating long-run relationships from dynamic heterogeneous panels. J. Econom. 68(1):79–113

Pesaran MH, Shin Y, Smith RP (1999) Pooled mean group estimation of dynamic heterogeneous panels. J Am Stat Assoc 94(446):621–634

Robertson D, Symons J (1992) Some strange properties of panel data estimators. J Appl Econom 7:175–189

Salim R, Hassan K, Rahman S (2020) Impact of R&D expenditures, rainfall and temperature variations in agricultural productivity: empirical evidence from Bangladesh. Appl Econ 52(27):2977–2990

Sek SK (2017) Impact of oil price changes on domestic price inflation at disaggregated levels: evidence from linear and nonlinear ARDL modeling. Energy 130(C):204–217

Shin Y, Yu B, Greenwood-Nimmo M (2014) Modelling asymmetric cointegration and dynamic multipliers in a nonlinear ARDL framework. Festschrift in honor of Peter Schmidt. Springer, New York, pp 281–314

Sinha M, Sengupta PP (2022) FDI inflow, ICT expansion and economic growth: an empirical study on Asia-pacific developing countries. Glob Bus Rev 23(3):804–821

Wooldridge JM (2013) Introductory econometrics: a modern approach, 5th ed. South-Western Cengage Learning, Mason OH

The World Bank Group (2021) Climate change action plan 2021–2025 South Asia roadmap

Zare R, Azali M, Habibullah MS, Azman-Saini WNW (2014) Monetary policy effectiveness and stock market cycles in ASEAN-5. Appl Econ 46:2362–2374

Chapter 17
Threshold Regression Model with Panel Data: Investigating Inflation-Growth Relationship in Europe

Panchanan Das

Abstract The classical fixed effect or random effect model captures the heterogeneity in intercepts only. The threshold regression model allows heterogeneity of the slope parameters. Threshold regression model was extended for panel data first by (Hansen, J Econ 93:345–368, 1999) in estimating firms' investment function under financial constraints. (Hansen, J Econ 93:345–368, 1999) model is fixed effect static model which requires covariates to be strongly exogenous for the estimator to be consistent. Later on, the model was used in many areas like relationship between fiscal deficit and economic growth, inflation and economic growth etc. The Stata command ***xthreg*** developed by (Wang, Stata J 15:121–134, 2015) computes the Hansen's fixed effect estimator. (Seo and Shin, J Econ 195:169–186, 2016) extended (Hansen, J Econ 93:345–368, 1999) model to the dynamic panel model with a potentially endogenous threshold variable to allow endogenous covariates. This model captures nonlinear asymmetric dynamics and cross-sectional heterogeneity simultaneously. This Chapter presents the basic threshold regression model with panel data in one-way error component fixed effect framework as developed in (Hansen, J Econ 93:345–368, 1999) and its further development. To illustrate the application of these models, the inflation threshold in growth is estimated with data from 20 European countries by using Stata 17 software.

Keywords Threshold regression · Panel data · Endogeneity

JEL Classification C21 · C24 · C26

Supplementary Information The online version contains supplementary material available at https://doi.org/10.1007/978-981-99-4902-1_17.

P. Das (✉)
University of Calcutta, Kolkata, India
e-mail: pdeco@caluniv.ac.in

D. Mukherjee (ed.), *Applied Econometric Analysis Using Cross Section and Panel Data*, Contributions to Economics, https://doi.org/10.1007/978-981-99-4902-1_17

17.1 Introduction

The conventional regression model is based on homogeneity assumption. But, there may be differential effects of explanatory variables on response variable in the sample among different groups, or different individuals, or different regimes, or over different phases of a business cycle. For example, demand function for refrigerator, is different in different income groups (high income and low income), inflationary effect on economic growth depends on the inflation level. High level of inflation is harmful to economic growth, while low level of inflation is beneficial to it. Similarly, the relationship between finance and growth depends on inflation threshold—when inflation exceeds the threshold, finance ceases to increase economic growth (Rousseau and Wachtel 2009). The productivity benefit from FDI increases with absorptive capacity until some threshold level, at which point it becomes less pronounced (Girma 2005).

Furthermore, the classical regression model assumes that relationships are linear. But, economic theory plays a very passive role on linearity assumption. In many cases, for example, the data generating process of trending behavior of stock return, exchange rate, and many macroeconomic variables is nonlinear and linear specifications may not be a realistic representation of econometric model to analyze those behavior. In the early literature, regime switching and threshold autoregressive (TAR) models have been introduced to accommodate nonlinear dynamic behavior of macroeconomic mechanisms (Priestley 1980, 1988; Granger and Terasvirta 1993). Threshold regression model is nonlinear describing piecewise linear specifications on the basis of regime switching.

The threshold model splits the sample into different parts on the basis of some thresholds and describes the differential effects on the relationship between variables. The threshold variable is determined on the basis of the economic model. For instance, in estimating investment function firm size may be considered as a threshold variable. In most of the cases threshold is unknown and it needs to be estimated. Threshold regression model is used to find out differential effects of explanatory variables on the response variable among different groups of observations in a sample. It allows regression coefficients to differ among different groups, or captures the asymmetric effect of the exogenous variables on the response variable over different phases of a business cycle. One of the major applications of threshold regression model has been to the business cycle (Beaudry and Koop 1993; Pesaran and Potter 1997; Koop, Pesaran and Potter 1996; Altissimo and Violante 2001). Another application of threshold autoregressive models is the forecasting of economic variables (Rothman 1998; Clements and Smith 1997). Multivariate threshold autoregressive models are used to analyze the term structure of interest rates (Anderson 1997; Hansen and Seo 2002; Gospodinov 2005). Rabemananjara and Zakoian (1993) introduced a threshold effect into the ARCH equation, allowing nonlinearity in the volatility process. A large number of studies apply threshold models to analyze exchange rates (Krager and Kugler 1993; Balke and Wohar 1998; Peel and Taylor 2002; Gouveia and Rodrigues 2004).

Section 17.2 of this Chapter discusses the basic structure of threshold regression model with panel data as developed in Hansen (1999) by considering single threshold as well as multiple threshold. Section 17.3 deals with the methodological steps in threshold regression when some of the regressors are endogenous. Testing for threshold effect is displayed in Sect. 17.4. Section 17.5 discusses dynamic threshold regression model with panel data. A brief analysis of nonstationarity in threshold regression is placed in Sect. 17.6. Section 17.7 is the application of threshold regression model with panel data of 20 European countries from 1995 to 2022 taken from the World Economic Outlook by using Stata. Section 17.8 concludes by providing further scope of studies of threshold regression model.

17.2 Threshold Regression in Panel Data

Threshold regression model is popular in time series econometrics since the pioneering work by Tong (1983). If the regressors contain only the lagged values of the dependent variable, the model will be called threshold autoregressive (TAR) model. In a TAR model, when the threshold is the *d*th lagged value of the dependent variable, it will be a self-exciting threshold autoregressive (SETAR) model with delay *d*. The threshold regression model is similar to regime switching model where regime is observable, contrary to the Markov switching model. Here, the regime switching mechanism depends on a threshold variable.

The classical fixed effect or random effect model captures the heterogeneity in intercepts only. The threshold regression model allows heterogeneity of the slope parameters. Threshold regression model was extended for panel data first by Hansen (1999) in estimating firms' investment function under financial constraints. Hansen's (1999) model is fixed effect static model which requires covariates to be strongly exogenous for the estimator to be consistent. Later on, the model was used in many areas like relationship between fiscal deficit and economic growth, inflation, and economic growth (Adam and Bevan 2005; Khan and Senhadji 2001). The Stata command ***xthreg*** developed by Wang (2015) computes the Hansen's fixed effect estimator.

17.2.1 Single Threshold Model

A single threshold splits the whole sample into two parts and the regression model is expressed as

$$y_{it} = \beta_0 + \beta_1' x_{it} + \beta_2' x_{it} h(q_{it}, \tau) + u_{it} \tag{17.1}$$

where $h(q_{it}, \tau)$ is a transition function, q_{it} is a threshold variable, τ is a location parameter.

$$0 \leq h(q_{it}, \tau) \leq 1$$

The threshold variable is assumed to be exogenous or predetermined. While in classical threshold regression model the threshold variable is determined parametrically, Lee and Wang (2023) developed a nonparametric method of determining the threshold variable. In their framework, the threshold is heterogenous and cross section specific, and is determined by the direction of a prediction error following some moment conditions.

Suppose that

$$u_{it} = \mu_i + \varepsilon_{it} \tag{17.2}$$

If the cross section specific character, μ_i, is non-stochastic, Eq. (17.1) will be the structural form of one-way error component fixed effect model with single threshold.

The random error ε_{it} is assumed to be *iid* with zero mean and constant variance,

$$\varepsilon_{it} \overset{iid}{\rightarrow} (0, \sigma^2)$$

If the transition function is binary defined on the basis of location parameter, it takes the form of an indicator function:

$$h(q_{it}, \tau) = \begin{cases} 1\ if q_{it} \leq \tau \\ 0\ if q_{it} > \tau \end{cases} \tag{17.3}$$

The location parameter τ is selected by restricting the following:

$$\tau = \left[quantile\left((q_{it})_{i=1,t=1}^{N,T}, 0.05\right), quantile\left((q_{it})_{i=1,t=1}^{N,T}, 0.95\right)\right]$$

This restriction implies that the valuesof τ are selected such that they do not lie at the terminal 5% of the observations in each regime.

The structural form of one-way error component fixed effect threshold model with indicator function as defined in (17.3) is

$$y_{it} = \beta_0 + \beta_1{\prime} x_{it} + \beta_2{\prime} x_{it} I(q_{it} \leq \tau) + \mu_i + \varepsilon_{it} \tag{17.4}$$

The dependent variable y_{it} is a scalar, the regressor x_{it} is a vector of order $k \times 1$, the threshold variable q_{it} is a scalar, I() is an indicator function, μ_i is cross section specific heterogeneity. Here, i = 1,2,….,N; t = 1, 2, ……, T; total observation $= N \times T$.

The threshold model shown in Eq. (17.4) provides a regime switching mechanism for the slope parameters that depends on the threshold variable and a location parameter :

$$y_{it} = \begin{cases} \beta_0 + (\beta_1\prime + \beta_2\prime)x_{it} + \mu_i + \varepsilon_{it} \; if q_{it} \le \tau \\ \beta_0 + \beta_1\prime x_{it} + \mu_i + \varepsilon_{it} \quad if q_{it} > \tau \end{cases} \tag{17.5}$$

In this model, there are two regimes for the slope parameter, $(\beta_1 + \beta_2)$ and β_1 Another way to specify a single threshold model is

$$y_{it} = \beta_1\prime x_{it} I(q_{it} \le \tau) + \beta_2\prime x_{it} I(q_{it} > \tau) + \mu_i + \varepsilon_{it} \tag{17.6}$$

or,

$$\begin{aligned} y_{it} &= \mu_i + \beta_1\prime x_{it} + \varepsilon_{it}, \quad \text{if}(q_{it} \le \tau) \\ y_{it} &= \mu_i + \beta_2\prime x_{it} + \varepsilon_{it}, \quad \text{if } (q_{it} > \tau) \end{aligned} \tag{17.7}$$

or, in more compact form as

$$y_{it} = \mu_i + \beta\prime x_{it}(\tau) + \varepsilon_{it} \tag{17.8}$$

$$x_{it}(\tau) = \begin{cases} x_{it} I(q_{it} \le \tau) \\ x_{it} I(q_{it} > \tau) \end{cases}$$

Another formulation of single threshold model is the following:

$$y_{it} = \delta\prime y_{i,-t} + \beta_1\prime x_{it} I(q_{it} \le \tau) + \beta_2\prime x_{it} I(q_{it} > \tau) + \mu_i + \varepsilon_{it} \tag{17.6$'$}$$

Here, $y_{i,-t}$ is $1 \times p$ vector of lagged dependent variable and δ is the corresponding vector of regime invariant parameters. When lagged dependent variable is used as a regressor, the model becomes dynamic which will be discussed later on.

In a single threshold model, the observations are divided into two segments depending on whether the threshold variable q_{it} smaller or larger than τ. The threshold variable may be one of the variables in x_{it}, or any past value of y_{it}. The indicator function may be derived by Markov chain. When the Markov chain is unobserved, it becomes a Markov switching model which is the switching autoregressive model (Hamilton 1989).

In (17.6), the regimes are differentiated by the slope coefficients, $\beta_j, j = 1, 2$.

The magnitude of the threshold effect is the difference between the slope parameter:

$\delta_n = \beta_2\prime$, in Eq. (17.4)

$\delta_n = \beta_2\prime - \beta_1\prime$, in Eq. (17.6).

The parameters of a panel threshold regression model are heterogenous and time varying

$$y_{it} = \mu_i + \beta_{it}\prime x_{it} + \varepsilon_{it} = \begin{cases} \mu_i + \beta_1\prime x_{it} + \varepsilon_{it} \; if q_{it} \le \tau \\ \mu_i + \beta_2\prime x_{it} + \varepsilon_{it} \; if q_{it} > \tau \end{cases} \tag{17.9}$$

Therefore,

$$\frac{\partial y_{it}}{\partial x_{it}} = \beta_{it} = \begin{cases} \beta_1 \; if q_{it} \leq \tau \\ \beta_2 \; if q_{it} > \tau \end{cases} \tag{17.10}$$

In this model, at a given time t, two cross section units i and j may have two different slope parameters

$$\frac{\partial y_{it}}{\partial x_{it}} = \beta_1 \neq \frac{\partial y_{jt}}{\partial x_{jt}} = \beta_2, \text{ if } q_{it} \leq \gamma \text{ and } q_{jt} \leq \tau \tag{17.11}$$

Similarly, a given cross section unit i may have different slope parameters at different time points t and s:

$$\frac{\partial y_{it}}{\partial x_{it}} = \beta_1 \neq \frac{\partial y_{is}}{\partial x_{is}} = \beta_2, \text{ if } q_{it} \leq \gamma \text{ and } q_{is} > \gamma \tag{17.12}$$

Regression model shown in Eq. (17.1) or its variants is nonlinear. While in a linear regression framework we can eliminate cross section specific unobserved heterogeneity μ_i by using within group means, this trick cannot be used in a straight forward manner for Eq. (17.1) which is nonlinear.

By taking within entity mean, Eq. (17.8) becomes

$$\overline{y}_i = \mu_i + \beta\prime\overline{x}_i(\tau) + \overline{\varepsilon}_i \tag{17.13}$$

where

$$\overline{y}_i = \frac{\sum_{t=1}^{T} y_{it}}{T},$$

$$\overline{\varepsilon}_i = \frac{\sum_{t=1}^{T} \varepsilon_{it}}{T}$$

$$\overline{x}_i(\tau) = \frac{\sum_{t=1}^{T} x_{it}(\tau)}{T}$$

Therefore, the model in mean corrected form

$$\tilde{y}_{it} = \beta\prime\tilde{x}_{it}(\tau) + \widetilde{\varepsilon}_{it} \tag{17.14}$$

where

$$\tilde{y}_{it} = y_{it} - \overline{y}_i$$

$$\tilde{x}_{it}(\tau) = x_{it}(\tau) - \overline{x}_i(\tau)$$

$$\widetilde{\varepsilon}_{it} = \varepsilon_{it} - \overline{\varepsilon}_i$$

In stacked form for entity i,

$$\tilde{y}_i = \beta\prime\tilde{x}_i(\tau) + \widetilde{\varepsilon}_i$$

where

$$\tilde{y}_i = \begin{bmatrix} \tilde{y}_{i1} \\ \dots \\ \tilde{y}_{iT} \end{bmatrix},\ \tilde{x}_i(\tau) = \begin{bmatrix} \tilde{x}_{i1}(\tau)\prime \\ \dots \\ \tilde{x}_{iT}(\tau)\prime \end{bmatrix},\ \tilde{\varepsilon}_i = \begin{bmatrix} \tilde{\varepsilon}_{i1} \\ \dots \\ \tilde{\varepsilon}_{iT} \end{bmatrix}$$

In stacked form for all entities,

$$\tilde{Y} = \tilde{X}(\tau)\beta + \widetilde{\varepsilon} \tag{17.15}$$

Here,

$$\tilde{Y} = \begin{bmatrix} \tilde{y}_1 \\ \dots \\ \tilde{y}_N \end{bmatrix},\ \tilde{X}(\tau) = \begin{bmatrix} \tilde{x}_1(\tau) \\ \dots \\ \tilde{x}_N(\tau) \end{bmatrix},\ \tilde{\varepsilon} = \begin{bmatrix} \tilde{\varepsilon}_1 \\ \dots \\ \tilde{\varepsilon}_N \end{bmatrix}$$

The OLS estimate of β, conditional on τ is obtained as

$$\widehat{\beta}(\tau) = \left(\tilde{X}(\tau)\prime\tilde{X}(\tau)\right)^{-1}\tilde{X}(\tau)\prime\tilde{Y} \tag{17.16}$$

The OLS residual, $\widehat{\widetilde{\varepsilon}}(\tau) = \tilde{Y} - \tilde{X}(\tau)\widehat{\beta}(\tau)$
Sum of squared residual (SSR) is

$$\begin{aligned}
S(\tau) &= \hat{\tilde{\varepsilon}}(\tau)\prime\hat{\tilde{\varepsilon}}(\tau) = \left(\tilde{Y} - \tilde{X}(\tau)\hat{\beta}(\tau)\right)\prime\left(\tilde{Y} - \tilde{X}(\tau)\hat{\beta}(\tau)\right) \\
&= \left(\tilde{Y}\prime - \hat{\beta}(\tau)\prime\tilde{X}(\tau)\prime\right)\left(\tilde{Y} - \tilde{X}(\tau)\hat{\beta}(\tau)\right) \\
&= \tilde{Y}\prime\tilde{Y} - \tilde{Y}\prime\tilde{X}(\tau)\hat{\beta}(\tau) - \hat{\beta}(\tau)\prime\tilde{X}(\tau)\prime\tilde{Y} + \hat{\beta}(\tau)\prime\tilde{X}(\tau)\prime\tilde{X}(\tau)\hat{\beta}(\tau) \\
&= \tilde{Y}\prime\tilde{Y} - 2\tilde{Y}\prime\tilde{X}(\tau)\left(\tilde{X}(\tau)\prime\tilde{X}(\tau)\right)^{-1}\tilde{X}(\tau)\prime\tilde{Y} + \tilde{Y}\prime\tilde{X}(\tau)\left(\tilde{X}(\tau)\prime\tilde{X}(\tau)\right)^{-1} \\
&\quad \times \tilde{X}(\tau)\prime\tilde{X}(\tau)\left(\tilde{X}(\tau)\prime\tilde{X}(\tau)\right)^{-1}\tilde{X}(\tau)\prime\tilde{Y} = \tilde{Y}\prime\tilde{Y} - \tilde{Y}\prime\tilde{X}(\tau)\left(\tilde{X}(\tau)\prime\tilde{X}(\tau)\right)^{-1}\tilde{X}(\tau)\prime\tilde{Y} \\
&= \tilde{Y}\prime\left(I - \tilde{X}(\tau)\left(\tilde{X}(\tau)\prime\tilde{X}(\tau)\right)^{-1}\tilde{X}(\tau)\prime\right)\tilde{Y}
\end{aligned} \tag{17.17}$$

The least squares estimator of τ is obtained as

$$\widehat{\tau} = argminS(\tau)$$

The estimation of the threshold is done by minimizing the sum of squared residual function with respect to τ through the indicator function, $I(q_{it} \le \tau)$. To implement the minimization rule we need to sort the distinct values of the observations on the threshold variable q_{it} after eliminating some values at the terminal ends. Then estimate Eq. (17.15) corresponding to each distinct value τ of q_{it} to find out squared residual. The smallest value of squared residual yields $\hat{\tau}$.

The OLS estimates of the slope coefficients after finding out $\hat{\tau}$ is

$$\hat{\beta}(\hat{\tau}) = \left(\tilde{X}(\hat{\tau})\prime\tilde{X}(\hat{\tau})\right)^{-1}\tilde{X}(\hat{\tau})\prime\tilde{Y} \tag{17.18}$$

17.2.2 *Multiple Threshold Model*

Threshold regression model may contain more than 1 threshold. A regression model with m thresholds and $m + 1$ regime is specified as.

$$\begin{aligned} y_{it} &= \mu_i + \beta_1\prime x_{it} I(q_{it} \le \tau_1) \\ &\quad + \beta_2\prime x_{it} I(\tau_1 \le q_{it} < \tau_2) + \ldots. + \beta_{m+1}\prime x_{it} I(q_{it} > \tau_m) + \varepsilon_{it} \end{aligned} \tag{17.19}$$

Or, alternatively,

$$y_{it} = \mu_i + x_{it}\prime\beta(\tau) + \varepsilon_{it} \tag{17.20}$$

Suppose that the threshold variable, q_{it}, is observable with increasing threshold values $\tau_1 < \tau_2 < \ldots.. < \tau_m$ such that the regime j is defined as $\tau_j \le q_{it} < \tau_{j+1}$,

We can combine $m + 1$ regime as

$$y_{it} = \mu_i + x_{1it}\prime\beta + \sum_{j=1}^{m+1} I_j(q_{it}, \tau)x_{2it}\prime\gamma_j + \varepsilon_{it} \tag{17.21}$$

The optimal number of thresholds is determined by using AIC, SBIC, or HQIC rule.

In a multiple threshold regression model, the threshold values are estimated sequentially. The first threshold is estimated by assuming that the sample is divided into 2 regimes as described in the previous section. The conditional estimation of second threshold is obtained given the first threshold by minimizing the sum of squared errors over all observations in q_{it} excluding the first threshold. In other words, the estimator of the second threshold, $\hat{\tau}_2$, is obtained by minimizing the least square residuals of a regression with three regimes conditional on the first regime:

$$\hat{\tau}_2 = argminS(\tau_2|\hat{\tau}_1)$$

In this way, the *m*th threshold is obtained by minimizing the least square residuals conditional on the *m*–1 estimated thresholds:

$$\hat{\tau}_m = argminS(\tau_m|\hat{\tau}_1, \hat{\tau}_2, \ldots.., \hat{\tau}_{m-1})$$

Consider the following model with two thresholds:

$$y_{it} = \mu_i + \beta_1{\prime}x_{it}I(q_{it} \leq \tau_1) + \beta_2{\prime}x_{it}I(\tau_1 \leq q_{it} < \tau_2) + \beta_3{\prime}x_{it}I(q_{it} > \tau_2) + \varepsilon_{it} \quad (17.22)$$

Here, τ_1 and τ_2 are the thresholds that divide the structural equation into three regimes with coefficients β_1, β_2, and β_3.

Bai and Perron (1998) suggested the following sequential method to estimate the thresholds:

Step 1: Estimate the single-threshold model to obtain the estimated value for τ_1 and the SSR, $S_1(\hat{\tau}_1)$.

Step 2: The second threshold and the corresponding confidence interval are obtained after estimating the first threshold as

$$\hat{\tau}_2^r = argminS_2^r(\tau_2)$$

where

$$S_2^r(\tau_2) = S\{min(\hat{\tau}_1, \tau_2)max(\hat{\tau}_1, \tau_2)\}$$

The likelihood ratio,

$$LR_2^r(\tau_2) = \frac{\{S_2^r(\tau_2) - S_2^r(\hat{\tau}_2)\}}{\hat{\sigma}_{22}^2} \quad (17.23)$$

Step 3: Re-estimate the first threshold as

$$\hat{\tau}_1^r = argminS_1^r(\tau_1)$$

where

$$S_1^r(\tau_1) = S\{min(\tau_1, \hat{\tau}_2)max(\tau_1, \hat{\tau}_2)\}$$

And

$$LR_1^r(\tau_1) = \frac{\{S_2^r(\tau_1) - S_2^r(\hat{\tau}_1)\}}{\hat{\sigma}_{21}^2} \quad (17.24)$$

17.3 Threshold Model with Endogenous Variable

Hansen's (1999) model is static and the fixed effect estimator requires the covariates to be strongly exogenous for the estimator to be consistent. However, the strong exogeneity can be restrictive in many real applications. Consider linear models with endogenous variables and an exogenous threshold variable. In this case, reduced form regression for the endogenous variables (a function of exogenous instruments on the basis of large sample distribution theory) is used for the parameter estimates and test statistics. Predicted values for the endogenous variables are to be substituted into the structural equation of interest. The threshold is estimated by using least squares, and the slope parameters are estimated by using two-stage least squares (2SLS) or generalized method of moments (GMM).

In a single threshold, let the structural form of the model be

$$y_{it} = \mu_i + \beta_1{}' x_{it} I(q_{it} \leq \tau) + \beta_2{}' x_{it} I(q_{it} > \tau) + \varepsilon_{it} \tag{17.25}$$

Let,

$x_{it} = \left(x_{1it}\ x_{2it}\right)$, x_{1it} is $k_1 \times 1$ vector of endogenous variables and x_{2it} is $k_2 \times 1$ vector of exogenous variables, $k_1 + k_2 = k$.

Let $z_{it} = \left(z_{1it}\ x_{2it}\right)$ be a vector of instruments, where x_{2it} is a vector of included exogenous variable, while z_{1it} is a vector of excluded exogenous variables.

In the first stage estimation, relationship between x_{it} and z_{it} is to be estimated

$$x_{it} = \pi{}' z_{it}(\rho) + u_{it} = \pi_1{}' z_{it} I(q_{it} \leq \rho) + \pi_2{}' z_{it} I(q_{it} > \rho) + u_{it} \tag{17.26}$$

Here, z_{it} is $k \times 1$ vector of instruments and π is the corresponding coefficient vector, ρ is the reduced form threshold parameter

The estimated coefficients are obtained by solving the following problem

$$\hat{\pi} = \underset{\pi}{argmindet} \left(\sum_{i=1}^{N} \sum_{t=1}^{T} (x_{it} - \pi{}' z_{it}(\rho))(x_{it} - \pi{}' z_{it}(\rho))' \right) \tag{17.27}$$

The OLS estimates

$$\hat{\pi}_1(\rho) = \left(\sum_{i=1}^{N} \sum_{t=1}^{T} z_{it} z_{it}{}' I(q_{it} \leq \rho) \right)^{-1} \sum_{i=1}^{N} \sum_{t=1}^{T} z_{it} x_{it}{}' I(q_{it} \leq \rho) \tag{17.28}$$

$$\hat{\pi}_2(\rho) = \left(\sum_{i=1}^{N} \sum_{t=1}^{T} z_{it} z_{it}{}' I(q_{it} > \rho) \right)^{-1} \sum_{i-1}^{N} \sum_{t-1}^{T} z_{it} x_{it}{}' I(q_{it} > \rho) \tag{17.29}$$

The residual,

$$\hat{u}_{it}(\rho) = x_{it} - \hat{\pi}_1(\rho)' z_{it} I(q_{it} \leq \rho) - \hat{\pi}_2(\rho)' z_{it} I(q_{it} > \rho) \tag{17.30}$$

If there is no cross-equation restriction, the reduced form parameters can be estimated by applying OLS separately for each variable in x_{it}. In the presence of cross equation restrictions we need to apply multivariate approach. As the threshold parameter is common across equations, a cross-equation restriction is applicable and the multivariate estimator is an appropriate one. The reduced form threshold parameter is obtained as

$$\widehat{\rho} = \underset{\rho}{argmindet} \left(\sum_{i=1}^{N} \sum_{t=1}^{T} \widehat{u}_{it}(\rho) \widehat{u}_{it}(\rho)\prime \right) \tag{17.31}$$

The estimated coefficients are $\widehat{\pi}_1(\widehat{\rho})$, $\widehat{\pi}_2(\widehat{\rho})$ and the predicted endogenous variables will be

$$\widehat{x}_{it} = \widehat{\pi}_1\prime z_{it} I(q_{it} \leq \widehat{\rho}) + \widehat{\pi}_2\prime z_{it} I(q_{it} > \widehat{\rho}) \tag{17.32}$$

After substituting $\widehat{x}_{it}$ into Eq. (17.25) the second stage estimation is obtained,

$$y_{it} = \mu_i + \beta_1\prime \widehat{x}_{it} I(q_{it} \leq \tau) + \beta_2\prime \widehat{x}_{it} I(q_{it} > \tau) + \varepsilon_{it} \tag{17.33}$$

Let $S_N(\tau)$ be the sum of squared residual for OLS regression of y_{it} on $\widehat{x}_{it}$. 2SLS estimator for τ is obtained from the following solution:

$$\widehat{\tau} = \underset{\tau}{argmin} \, S_N(\tau)$$

After estimating the threshold parameter, we can estimate the slope parameters β_1 and β_2 by applying 2SLS or GMM on the split samples based on the indicators $I(q_{it} \leq \widehat{\tau})$ and $I(q_{it} > \widehat{\tau})$

$$\begin{aligned} \hat{\beta}_1 = & \left(\hat{x} I(q_{it} \leq \hat{\tau})\prime z I(q_{it} \leq \hat{\tau})(z I(q_{it} \leq \hat{\tau})\prime z I(q_{it} \leq \hat{\tau}))^{-1} z I(z q_{it} \leq \hat{\tau})\prime \hat{x} I(q_{it} \leq \hat{\tau})\right)^{-1} \\ & \left(\hat{x} I(q_{it} \leq \hat{\tau})\prime z I(q_{it} \leq \hat{\tau})(z I(q_{it} \leq \hat{\tau})\prime z I(q_{it} \leq \hat{\tau}))^{-1} z I(q_{it} \leq \hat{\tau})\prime y\right) \end{aligned} \tag{17.34}$$

$$\begin{aligned} \hat{\beta}_2 = & \left(\hat{x} I(q_{it} > \hat{\tau})\prime z I(q_{it} > \hat{\tau})(z I(q_{it} > \hat{\tau})\prime z I(q_{it} > \hat{\tau}))^{-1} z I(q_{it} > \hat{\tau})\prime \hat{x} I(q_{it} > \hat{\tau})\right)^{-1} \\ & \left(\hat{x} I(q_{it} > \hat{\tau})\prime z I(q_{it} > \hat{\tau})(z I(q_{it} > \hat{\tau})\prime z I(q_{it} > \hat{\tau}))^{-1} z I(q_{it} > \hat{\tau})\prime y\right) \end{aligned} \tag{17.35}$$

The residual of the structural form

$$\widehat{\varepsilon}_{it} = y_{it} - \widehat{\beta}_1\prime x_{it} I(q_{it} \leq \widehat{\tau}) - \widehat{\beta}_2\prime x_{it} I(z q_{it} > \widehat{\tau}) \tag{17.36}$$

For GMM estimate, construct the following weight matrices

$$\widehat{\mathrm{W}}_1 = \sum_{i=1}^{n} \sum_{t=1}^{T} z_{it} z_{it}\prime \widehat{\varepsilon}_{it}^{\,2} I(q_{it} \leq \widehat{\tau}) \tag{17.37}$$

$$\widehat{W}_2 = \sum_{i=1}^{n}\sum_{t=1}^{T} z_{it} z_{it}{\prime} \hat{\varepsilon}_{it}{}^2 I(q_{it} > \hat{\tau}) \tag{17.38}$$

The GMM estimators

$$\begin{aligned}\hat{\beta}_1 =& \left(\hat{x}I(q_{it} \le \hat{\tau})\prime zI(q_{it} \le \hat{\tau})\left(\hat{W}_1\right)^{-1} zI(q_{it} \le \hat{\tau})\prime\hat{x}I(q_{it} \le \hat{\tau})\right)^{-1}\\ &\left(\hat{x}I(q_{it} \le \hat{\tau})\prime zI(q_{it} \le \hat{\tau})\left(\hat{W}_1\right)^{-1} zI(q_{it} \le \hat{\tau})\prime y\right)\end{aligned} \tag{17.39}$$

$$\begin{aligned}\hat{\beta}_2 =& \left(\hat{x}I(q_{it} > \hat{\tau})\prime zI(q_{it} > \hat{\tau})\left(\hat{W}_2\right)^{-1} zI(q_{it} > \hat{\tau})\prime\hat{x}I(q_{it} > \hat{\tau})\right)^{-1}\\ &\left(\hat{x}I(q_{it} > \hat{\tau})\prime zI(q_{it} > \hat{\tau})\left(\hat{W}_2\right)^{-1} zI(q_{it} > \hat{\tau})\prime y\right)\end{aligned} \tag{17.40}$$

The estimated covariance matrices for the GMM estimators are

$$\widehat{V}_1 = \left(\hat{x}I(q_{it} \le \hat{\tau})\prime zI(q_{it} \le \hat{\tau})\left(\widehat{W}_1\right)^{-1} zI(q_{it} \le \hat{\tau})\prime\hat{x}I(q_{it} \le \hat{\tau})\right)^{-1}$$

$$\widehat{V}_2 = \left(\hat{x}I(q_{it} > \hat{\tau})\prime zI(q_{it} > \hat{\tau})\left(\widehat{W}_2\right)^{-1} zI(q_{it} > \hat{\tau})\prime\hat{x}I(q_{it} > \hat{\tau})\right)^{-1}$$

17.4 Testing for Threshold

To test whether the threshold effect is statistically significant or not consider the following model as shown in (17.6):

$$y_{it} = \beta_1\prime x_{it} I(q_{it} \le \tau) + \beta_2\prime x_{it} I(q_{it} > \tau) + \mu_i + \varepsilon_{it}$$

Here, we have to carry out the following test:

$$H_0 : \beta_1 = \beta_2$$

$$H_1 : \beta_1 \ne \beta_2$$

Under H_0, the threshold effect is not significant and we cannot use the standard distributions to carry out this test. Hansen (1996) suggested a bootstrap to simulate asymptotic distribution of the likelihood ratio test.[1]

[1] Bootstrap, proposed first by Efron (1979), is a powerful tool for approximating the distribution of statistics under i.i.d. assumption. Bootstrap of different types has been proposed in the literature, among them the sieve bootstrap and the block bootstrap are most popular (Lahiri 2003). In bootstrapping, pseudo data can be created from initial data by resampling with replacement r times to

Under H_0, the single threshold model is

$$y_{it} = \mu_i + \beta\prime x_{it} + e_{it} \tag{17.41}$$

and its mean corrected form

$$\tilde{y}_{it} = \beta\prime \tilde{x}_{it} + \tilde{e}_{it} \tag{17.42}$$

The regression parameter β is estimated by applying OLS, and the SSR is

$$S_0 = \hat{\tilde{e}}\prime \hat{\tilde{e}}$$

The test statistic used to carry out this test is

$$F_1 = \frac{S_0 - S(\hat{\tau})}{\hat{\sigma}^2} \tag{17.43}$$

Under H_0, the threshold τ is not identified, and F_1 has nonstandard asymptotic distribution. It does not correspond to a χ^2 distribution. One solution is to use a bootstrap procedure to determine the asymptotic distribution of the statistic F_1. Hansen (1996) suggested the following bootstrap on the critical values of the F statistic to test the significance of the threshold effect:

1. Estimate the model under $H_1$to obtain the residual, $\hat{\tilde{\varepsilon}}_{it}(\tau)$
2. Make a cluster resampling $\hat{\tilde{\varepsilon}}_{it}(\tau)$ with replacement, and obtain the new residual $\tilde{v}_{it}$.
3. Generate a new series under H_1

$$\tilde{y}_{it} = \beta\prime \tilde{x}_{it}(\tau) + \tilde{v}_{it}$$

4. Estimate the model under H_0 and H_1, and compute the F statistic
5. Repeat the above steps r times (bootstrap replication number).

For multiple thresholds, first, test for a single threshold. The null hypothesis is a single-threshold, and the alternative hypothesis is two-threshold.

The F statistic used for testing is

$$F_2 = \frac{\{S_1(\hat{\tau}_1) - S_2^r(\hat{\tau}_2^r)\}}{\hat{\sigma}_{22}^2} \tag{17.44}$$

get to get r + 1 pseudo sample. Statistics are computed with these pseudo-samples for statistical inference. In the residual-based bootstrap approach, the regression coefficients are estimated and pseudo data are created by resampling the residuals. The data generating process (DGP) in bootstrap must follow the null hypothesis and it should be an estimate of the true DGP as possible (Davidson 2007).

The hypothesis of one threshold is rejected if F_2 is larger than its critical value. If the null hypothesis is rejected, then test for multiple-threshold model. We can proceed to test the hypothesis of two thresholds against the alternative of three thresholds, and so on.

17.5 Dynamic Threshold Model

Hansen's (1999) panel threshold model is static. The static and fixed effect panel data threshold model requires the covariates to be strongly exogenous for the estimator to be consistent. However, the strong exogeneity can be restrictive in many real applications. As discussed in the previous section, 2SLS or GMM can be used to estimate the model with endogenous regressors.

Gonzalez et al. (2005) extended the panel threshold model which allows the coefficients to change gradually from one regime to another and is called panel smooth transition regression model. In this model, the transition function, $h(q_{it}, \tau, \gamma)$, is a continuous function of q_{it}. Here, γ is a slope parameter. In Gonzalez et al. (2005), the transition function is a logistic one:

$$h(q_{it}, \tau, \gamma) = \frac{1}{1 + exp(-\gamma(q_{it} - \tau))}, \gamma > 0$$

If $\gamma \to \infty$, the logistic transition function tends to an indicator function and the smooth threshold model will be the conventional threshold model. If $\gamma \to 0$, the panel smooth threshold regression correspondence to a linear panel model.

17.5.1 *Basic Univariate Model*

Seo and Shin (2016) extended Hansen's (1999) model to the dynamic panel model with a potentially endogenous threshold variable to allow endogenous covariates. This model captures nonlinear asymmetric dynamics and cross-sectional heterogeneity simultaneously. They proposed two estimation methods based on the first difference (FD) transformation: FD-GMM and FD-2SLS.

A very simple form of dynamic model is autoregressive model. An autoregressive threshold model with d period lag value as a threshold is similar to SETAR model and can be specified as

$$y_{it} = \begin{cases} \phi_{01} + \phi_{11} y_{i,t-1} + \phi_{21} y_{i,t-2} + \cdots + \phi_{p1} y_{i,t-p_1} + \varepsilon_{it} \; if y_{i,t-d} \leq \tau \\ \phi_{02} + \phi_{12} y_{i,t-1} + \phi_{22} y_{i,t-2} + \cdots + \phi_{p2} y_{i,t-p_2} + \varepsilon_{it} \; if y_{i,t-d} > \tau \end{cases} \quad (17.45)$$

Here, the threshold variable, $q_{it} = y_{i,t-d}$.

The order of autoregression, p_1 and p_2, are determined by AIC or SBIC rule. The stationary SETAR model can be estimated by applying OLS under homogeneity assumption.

Now, consider the cross section specific effects. The AR(1) specification of Eq. (17.45) will be

$$y_{it} = \mu_i + \beta_1 y_{it-1} I(q_{it} \leq \tau) + \beta_2 y_{it-1} I(q_{it} > \tau) + \varepsilon_{it} \tag{17.46}$$

If q_{it} is any lagged value of y_{it}, (17.46) will be the SETAR model.

When the cross section specific effects, μ_i, are nonstochastic, the least-squared dummy variable (LSDV) estimators of the linear version of (17.46) lead to inconsistent estimates of the slope parameter (Nickell 1981). The maximum likelihood estimator (MLE) also leads to an inconsistency in estimation of the slope parameter because of the problem of incidental parameter (Lancaster 2000).

The problem of incidental parameter is resolved after taking first difference of (17.46):

$$\begin{aligned} y_{it} - y_{it-1} = &\beta_1[y_{it-1} I(q_{it} \leq \tau) - y_{it-2} I(q_{it-1} \leq \tau)] \\ &+ \beta_2[y_{it-1} I(q_{it} > \tau) - y_{it-2} I(q_{it-1} > \tau)] + \varepsilon_{it} - \varepsilon_{it-1} \end{aligned}$$

or,

$$\Delta y_{it} = \beta_1 \Delta y^{*}_{i,t-1}(\tau) + \beta_2 \Delta y^{**}_{i,t-1}(\tau) + \Delta\varepsilon_{it} \tag{17.47}$$

Here, t = 2, 3, …..T, Δy_{i1} is not defined because for t = 1, $\Delta y^{*}_{i,0}$ and $\Delta y^{**}_{i,0}$ are missing.

If the time span is short, the initial condition plays a crucial role for consistent estimates because the covariance matrix depends on the initial conditions. However, this problem will disappear when the time span is large.

In a random effect model, the marginal distribution of Δy_{i1} can be written as

$$\Delta y_{i1} = \delta_1 I(q_{i1} \leq \tau) + \delta_2 I(q_{i1} > \tau) + v_{i1} \tag{17.48}$$

As the regressors in (17.47) are correlated with $\Delta\varepsilon_{it}$, the OLS estimators are not unbiased. To resolve this endogeneity issue we need a $l \times 1$ vector of instrumental variables $z_{it}{\prime}$, t = 3,4,…..≤ T such that either

$$E(\Delta\varepsilon_{it}|z_{it}) = 0 \tag{17.49}$$

or,

$$E(z_{i3}{\prime}\Delta\varepsilon_{i3}, z_{i4}{\prime}\Delta\varepsilon_{i4}, \ldots.., z_{iT}{\prime}\Delta\varepsilon_{iT}){\prime} = 0 \tag{17.50}$$

17.5.2 Problem of Estimation

Suppose that the threshold variable q_{it} is endogenous.

Let

$$g_i(\theta) = \begin{bmatrix} z_{i3}\left(\Delta y_{i3} - \beta_1 \Delta y^{*}_{i3}(\tau) - \beta_2 \Delta y^{**}_{i3}(\tau)\right) \\ \cdots \\ z_{iT}\left(\Delta y_{iT} - \beta_1 \Delta y^{*}_{iT}(\tau) - \beta_2 \Delta y^{**}_{iT}(\tau)\right) \end{bmatrix} = \begin{bmatrix} z_{i3}\Delta\varepsilon_{i3} \\ \cdots \\ z_{iT}\Delta\varepsilon_{iT} \end{bmatrix} \quad (17.51)$$

$$\overline{g}_n(\theta) = \frac{1}{N}\sum_{i=1}^{N} g_i(\theta) \quad (17.52)$$

Let $g_i = (z_{i3}{\prime}\Delta\varepsilon_{i3}, \ldots..z_{iT}{\prime}\Delta\varepsilon_{iT}){\prime}$, $\Omega = E(g_i g_i{\prime})$ is finite and positive definite, and

$$\overline{J}_N(\theta) = \left(\overline{g}_N(\theta)\right){\prime}\Omega^{-1}\overline{g}_N(\theta) \quad (17.53)$$

The GMM estimator of θ is obtained as

$$\widehat{\theta} = argmin \overline{J}_N(\theta)$$

As Eq. (17.47) is linear for each τ and $\overline{J}_N(\theta)$ is not continuous in τ, the grid search algorithm is needed for GMM estimation.

Let

$$g_{1i} = \begin{bmatrix} z_{i3}\Delta y_{i3} \\ \cdots \\ z_{iT}\Delta y_{iT} \end{bmatrix} \quad (17.54)$$

and

$$g_{2i}(\tau) = \begin{bmatrix} z_{i3}\left(\beta_1 \Delta y^{*}_{i3}(\tau) + \beta_2 \Delta y^{**}_{i3}(\tau)\right) \\ \cdots \\ z_{iT}\left(\beta_1 \Delta y^{*}_{iT}(\tau) + \beta_2 \Delta y^{**}_{iT}(\tau)\right) \end{bmatrix} \quad (17.55)$$

Therefore,

$$\overline{g}_1 = \frac{1}{N}\sum_{i=1}^{N} g_{1i} \quad (17.56)$$

$$\overline{g}_2(\tau) = \frac{1}{N}\sum_{i=1}^{N} g_{2i}(\tau) \quad (17.57)$$

The GMM estimator of β_1 and β_2 is given by

$$\left(\widehat{\beta}(\tau)\prime\right)\prime = \left(\overline{g}_2(\tau)\prime\Omega^{-1}\overline{g}_2(\tau)\right)^{-1}\overline{g}_2(\tau)\prime\Omega^{-1}\overline{g}_1 \tag{17.58}$$

where,

$$\widehat{\tau} = argmin\overline{J}_n(\tau) \tag{17.59}$$

$$\widehat{\beta}\prime = \widehat{\beta}(\widehat{\tau})\prime \tag{17.60}$$

The FD-GMM estimator is obtained by estimating the model by minimizing

$$\overline{J}_n(\theta) = \left(\overline{g}_n(\theta)\right)\prime\Omega^{-1}\overline{g}_n(\theta) \;\; \text{with} \;\; \Omega = \frac{1}{n}\sum_{i=1}^{n}\hat{g}_i\hat{g}_i\prime - \frac{1}{n^2}\sum_{i=1}^{n}\hat{g}_i\sum_{i=1}^{n}\hat{g}_i\prime$$

where,

$$\widehat{g}_i = \left(z_{i3}\prime\Delta\widehat{\varepsilon}_{i3}, \ldots ..z_{iT}\prime\Delta\widehat{\varepsilon}_{iT}\right)\prime$$

17.6 Nonstationary Threshold Model

Statistical inference of the threshold regression model is well established with stationary regressors. But, most of the macroeconomic time series data are nonstationary. Nonstationarity of a threshold regression model leads to testing the hypothesis of a unit root against a stationary TAR and testing the hypothesis of linearity against the alternative of nonlinearity. The issue of nonstationarity in a threshold model has been addressed in a large number of studies. For example, Enders and Granger (1998) considered the problem of testing unit root null when the threshold parameter is known. Caner and Hansen (2001) developed an asymptotic test of the hypothesis of a unit root process against the alternative of a stationary TAR model. They derived the limiting distribution of Wald tests for a threshold, under the null of a nonstationary linear model. Chen and Stengos (2022) generalized the threshold model with various forms of nonstationary regressors and to obtain its limiting distribution theory.

Thus the threshold regression model accommodates nonstationary and cointegration properties of the data generating process (Hansen 1997). When the variables with unit roots are cointegrated, error correction (ECM) model is appropriate to capture the dynamics. Balke and Fomby (1997) introduced a momentum TAR or M-TAR model which is basically a threshold model with error correction.

Consider the following model with 2 unit root variables:

$$y_{it} = \beta_0 + \beta_1 x_{it} + u_{it} \tag{17.61}$$

In M-TAR model, two step approach of Engle-Granger (1987) type is used for testing cointegration between the variables.

In step 1, the above equation is to be estimated by applying OLS to find out residual, $\widehat{u}_{it}$

In step 2, estimate the following model to analyze the stochastic behavior of $\widehat{u}_t$

$$\Delta\widehat{u}_{it} = \begin{cases} \phi_1 \widehat{u}_{i,t-1} + \varepsilon_{it} \; if \Delta\widehat{u}_{i,t-1} \geq 0 \\ \phi_2 \widehat{u}_{i,t-1} + \varepsilon_{it} \; if \Delta\widehat{u}_{i,t-1} < 0 \end{cases} \tag{17.62}$$

or,

$$\Delta\widehat{u}_{it} = I_t \phi_1 \widehat{u}_{it-1} + (1 - I_t)\phi_2 \widehat{u}_{i,t-1} + \varepsilon_{it} \tag{17.63}$$

where I_t is referred to as an indicator function defined as

$$I_t = \begin{cases} 1 \; if \Delta\hat{u}_{i,t-1} \geq 0 \\ 0 \; if \Delta\hat{u}_{i,t-1} < 0 \end{cases} \tag{17.64}$$

Equations (17.63) and (17.64) are referred to as M-TAR and it accommodate asymmetric adjustment as used in Enders and Granger (1998). Engle-Granger test for cointegration has been extended by Enders and Siklos (2001) to allow for threshold adjustment. Hansen and Seo (2002) developed the estimation methods for the threshold VECM model.

17.7 Application Using Stata

Wang (2015) developed the Stata command ***xthreg*** for threshold regression with panel data which estimates fixed effect panel regression model based on Hansen (1999) using ***xtreg*** with a given threshold estimator. This estimation requires balanced panel data. To estimate a 2 threshold model, the ***xthreg*** command is used with ***thgiven***. In this case the second threshold will be searched using the previous result. The bootstrap method is used to test the null hypothesis of no threshold. The default bootstrap replication number is 300 for testing a single threshold. The basic frame of the command is shown below:

xthreg y x z xz, rx(c) qx(z) thnum(1) grid(400) trim(0.05) bs(300).

Here, y is the dependent variable, x is a vector of independent variable, z is the threshold variable.

rx(c) is the regime-dependent variable.

qx(z) is the threshold variable.

thnum(1) is the number of thresholds.

grid(400) is the number of grid points.

trim(0.05) is the trimming proportion to estimate each threshold.

bs(300) is the number of bootstrap replications.

Seo et al. (2019) developed the Stata command ***xthenreg*** for first differenced generalized method of moments (GMM) estimators:

xthenregy q x_1, endo(x_2) inst(z) kink static grid num(integer 20) trim rate(real 0.4) h 0(real 1.5) boost(real 0).

Here, *y* is the dependent variable, q is the threshold variable x_1 is the exogenous independent variable, x_2 is the endogenous independent variable, *z* is the instrumental variable.

kink sets the model kink.

static sets the model static. The default model is dynamic.

grid num(integer 20) determines the number of grid points 20 to estimate the threshold.

trim rate(real 0.4) determines the trim rate.

h 0(real 1.5) determines a parameter for Silverman's rule of thumb used to kernel estimation.

boost(real 0) denotes the number of bootstrapping for linearity test.

xthenreg command uses ***mmquantile*** function and ***moremata*** library is required.

17.7.1 Empirical Relation Between Growth and Inflation

High growth with low inflation is one of the fundamental policy objectives in any economy. However, the relationship between inflation and growth has been debated in the literature. In the early studies inflation had no effect on growth or had a positive effect on growth. Inflation is not perceived as a fundamental problem in the Keynesian approach. The Phillips Curve relationship shows that high inflation would reduce unemployment and enhance economic growth. In this approach, moderate inflation is accepted as a reasonable cost on the way to full employment. Increasing inflation increases the cost of holding money that induces households to increase capital accumulation which has positive effect on economic growth. But, the upward trend of inflation with declining growth in many countries in the 1970s and 1980s led to a change in direction in the inflation-growth debate. If output of an economy grows enough to keep up with demand, high growth can be achieved without increase in inflation. Rather, rising inflation may become a serious problem at the stage of near full employment if demand continues to increase without increasing production capacity.

Thus, the way inflation affects growth is directly related to its level. Inflation enhances economic growth, but up to a certain level of inflationary rate. There is no dearth of empirical work on growth-inflation relationship in the literature, but there is a lack of consensus on empirical findings on this issue (Fisher 1993; Bruno and Easterly 1998; Khan and Senhadji 2001); Fisher (1993) observed a nonlinear positive relationship at low inflation rates and negative relationship with high rate of inflation. Later on, Bruno and Easterly (1998) found no growth enhancing effect of inflation at low inflation rates, and negative effect for high inflation rates. Khan and Senhadji (2001) estimated inflation threshold at 11% above which inflation has negative effect of growth and no effect below this threshold by using data from developing countries.

Here, the relationship between inflation and growth is investigated by following roughly similar tradition in estimating inflation thresholds for 20 European Union countries including the United Kingdom over the period 1995–2022 from World Economic Outlook. In finding out growth-inflation relationship by applying extended form of Hansen's (1999) panel threshold model with a single threshold after accounting for the effect of regime intercept. The variables used include real GDP growth rate calculated from GDP at constant price in PPP, inflation rate calculated by using CPI, current account balance as a percentage of GDP, and unemployment rate. The countries have been selected in such a manner that it makes the panel balanced.

Given the largely common nature of the energy, food, and global supply chain among the European economies, the price shocks are surprisingly heterogeneous. Inflationary rate was more than 5% in almost all European economies by late summer 2022, and it increased at a faster rate in the less developed part of Europe than it was in advanced ones. Headline inflation reached more than 20% in the Baltic countries at that time, the rate was more than 3 times the rate in the lowest-inflation countries in the euro area. The gap in core inflation between emerging and advanced part of Europe was 12% points in the second quarter of 2022. Many hypotheses for the unusual behavior of inflation have been put forward in the literature (Chahad et al. 2022 for an overview). This exercise is a preliminary attempt to look into the issue by applying panel threshold regression model.

We estimate, first, a single-threshold model specified as

$$y_{it} = \mu_i + \beta_1 x_{it} I(x_{it} \leq \tau) + \beta_2 x_{it} I(x_{it} > \tau) + \delta_1 I(x_{it} \leq \tau) + \gamma' z_{it} + \varepsilon_{it} \tag{17.65}$$

The dependent variable (y_{it}) is the growth rate of real GDP of country i in time t,x_{it} represents inflation rate, τ is the threshold level of inflation. Current account balance denoted by z_{it} represents the overall health of an economy and is used as a control variable. The control variables are selected in accordance with the empirical growth literature. We incorporate regime intercept, δ_1 which is assumed to be the same for all cross section units. Regime dependent variable is the growth rate. This model takes into account the country-specific effect through μ_i. The effect of inflation on growth is measured by β_1 where the rate of inflation is τ or less, and β_2 where the inflation rate is more than τ.

Inflation may not be an exogenous variable and there may exist endogeneity bias in the estimated coefficient. However, seriousness of the endogeneity problem depends on the direction of causality. If causality is more likely from inflation to growth, the problem of simultaneity bias is not so severe.

Average rates of GDP growth and inflation for the whole sample by countries in European Union over time (1980 to 2022) are shown in Table 17.1. The variation of economic growth and inflation across the sample countries suggests no systematic relationship between economic growth and inflation in Europe. Luxembourg experienced the highest growth with moderate inflation, while the rate of growth in Greece was the lowest with higher inflation. Average inflation was exceptionally high with extreme variation over time in Poland, and the lowest in Switzerland exhibiting low growth in both countries.

Time span is considered from 1995 to 2022 to make the panel balanced for further estimation. Table 17.2 shows the summary statistics of the variables for 20 countries and 28 years time span. Mean values are shown for the overall sample, while standard deviations are calculated by taking overall variation, within group variation and between group variation.

Figures 17.1 and 17.2 display the pattern of relationship between growth and inflation, and between unemployment and inflation respectively by taking sample observations from 20 European countries during 1995–2022. Graphical representation of the relationships is helpful to understand the inability of the conventional linear regression model with fixed or random effect to capture the actual relationship between growth- and inflation, or unemployment and inflation.

Table 17.1 Average growth and inflation by countries

	Real GDP growth		Inflation rate	
Austria	1.82	(1.97)	2.48	(1.51)
Belgium	1.86	(1.93)	2.80	(2.18)
Finland	2.10	(3.02)	3.15	(2.93)
France	1.73	(2.15)	3.05	(3.32)
Germany	1.59	(2.11)	2.16	(1.57)
Greece	0.89	(3.85)	8.10	(8.26)
Hungary	1.65	(3.52)	9.69	(8.42)
Iceland	2.74	(3.66)	11.40	(16.71)
Italy	1.07	(2.48)	4.60	(5.03)
Luxembourg	3.83	(3.02)	2.88	(2.24)
Netherlands	2.04	(2.06)	2.22	(1.65)
NewZealand	2.59	(2.04)	4.51	(4.83)
Norway	2.43	(1.77)	3.68	(3.02)
Paraguay	3.27	(3.42)	11.80	(8.77)
Poland	2.57	(4.03)	14.16	(17.75)
Portugal	2.08	(3.06)	6.22	(7.38)
Spain	2.12	(2.99)	4.55	(4.04)
Sweden	2.33	(2.21)	3.48	(3.56)
Switzerland	1.84	(1.75)	1.59	(1.88)
United Kingdom	2.02	(2.67)	3.59	(3.16)

Note Figures in parentheses indicate standard error
Source Author's estimation using WEO data

Table 17.2 Summary statistics

Variable		Mean	Std. dev	Min	Max	Observations
GDP growth	Overall	2.12	2.83	–10.80	11.10	N = 560
	Between		0.83	0.62	4.00	n = 20
	Within		2.71	–10.67	10.29	T = 28
Inflation rate	Overall	2.71	3.09	–1.40	28.30	N = 560
	Between		1.75	0.58	7.13	n = 20
	Within		2.57	–4.62	25.25	T = 28
Unemployment rate	Overall	7.64	4.25	1.70	27.50	N = 560
	Between		3.42	3.18	16.49	n = 20
	Within		2.63	–0.66	20.44	T = 28

Source As for Table 17.1

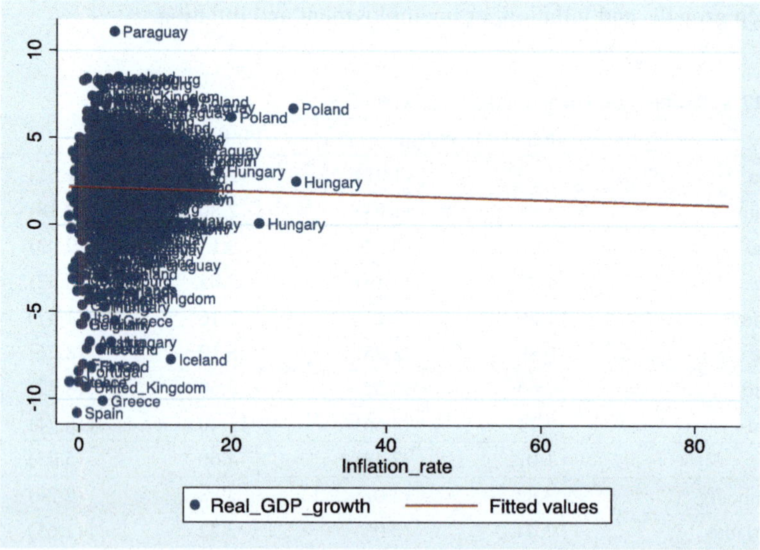

Fig. 17.1 Relation between growth and inflation. *Source* World Economic Indicators, 2022

In estimating Eq. (17.1) we use the following command

xthreg real_gdp_growth inflation_rate current_account_balance_percent_ if year > 1994, rx(real_gdp_growth) qx(inflation_rate) thnum(1) grid(400) trim(0.01) bs(300).

The threshold variable inflation rate is trimmed off 1 per cent at both sides. We use 400 grid and set 300 bootstrap replication. The Stata output is displayed in Table 17.6 in the appendix. There are four parts of the estimated results in Stata output window. The first part shows the bootstrap results. The second part is the estimation of the threshold and its confidence intervals. The third part shows the test for threshold

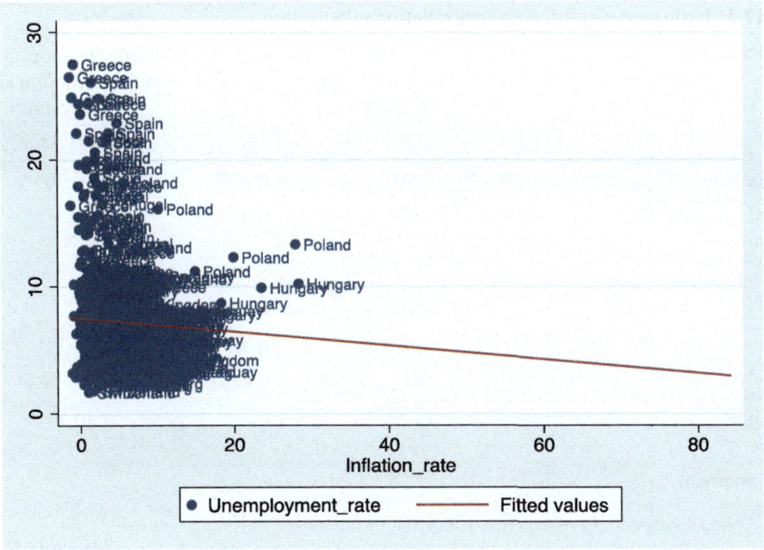

Fig. 17.2 Relation between unemployment and inflation. *Source* As for Fig. 17.1

effect in terms of the residual sum of square (RSS), the mean squared error (MSE), and the F statistic (Fstat). The fourth part is the estimation results of the fixed effect regression.

In a single-threshold model, the estimated inflation threshold is 5% with 95% confidence level (4.9 and 5.1). The F statistic is significant at 1% level and we reject the null hypothesis of no threshold linear model. Thus, inflation has differential effect on growth in low and high inflation countries. The estimated coefficients of fixed effect panel regression as shown in the fourth part of Table 17.6 or the first column of Table 17.3 suggest that inflation has negative effect on growth, although the effect is weakly significant. Current account balance has positive effect on growth as expected.

Next, we estimate the same model with 2 thresholds by using the command given below.

Xthreg real_gdp_growthinflation_ratecurrent_account_balance_percent_ if year > 1994, rx(real_gdp_growth) qx(inflation_rate) thnum(2) grid(400) trim(0.01 0.01) bs(0 300).

In the second part of the output window shown in Table 17.7, Th-1 denotes the estimator in a single-threshold model. Th-21 and Th-22 are the estimators of a 2-threshold model. The trimmings are set at 1% for the estimation of the second threshold as well. Bootstrap replication is set at 300 for the second threshold. The third panel of the output displays the testing for threshold effect in terms of residual sum of square (RSS), mean squared error (MSE), and F statistic (Fstat). The F statistic is insignificant implying that the null hypothesis of no threshold is not to be rejected

Table 17.3 Estimated results of growth-inflation relationship

Model/variables	FE	RE	Growth inflation single threshold	Growth inflation double threshold	Unemployment inflation single threshold
	(1)	(2)	(3)	(4)	(5)
Inflation rate	0.11*	0.14***	–0.03	0.007	–0.20**
Current account balance	0.02	0.02	0.03	0.01	0.13***
Growth regime					
0			(Omitted)	(Omitted)	
1			0.65***	0.48*	
2				0.64***	
Real GDP growth					–0.17***
Unemployment regime					
0					(Omitted)
1					0.33***
Intercept	1.81***	1.71***	1.95***	2.01***	8.23***
N	560	560	560	560	560

Legend: * $p < 0.05$; ** $p < 0.01$; *** $p < 0.001$
Source As for Table 17.1

against the alternative of 2 thresholds. The estimated coefficients of the fixed effects model suggest no significant relationship between growth and inflation.

We also estimate the Phillips curve relation by applying threshold regression model with the same dataset. Phillips curve suggests an inverse relationship between unemployment and inflation, but this relationship may not be the same at any inflation rate. We test this hypothesis by considering single inflation threshold as endogenous. In this model, GDP growth is taken as a control variable. The estimated results by applying the following command are shown in output Table 17.8 in the appendix.

xthregunemployment_ratereal_gdp_growthinflation_ratecurrent_account_balance_percent_, rx(unemployment_rate) qx(inflation_rate) thnum(1) grid(400) trim(0.01) bs(300).

Here, the estimated value for inflation threshold is 5.5, but the F statistic suggests that the threshold effect on Phillips curve relationship is significant at 1% level of significance. Therefore, there is a differential effect of inflation on unemployment rate. The fixed effects result shows inverse relationship between unemployment and inflation.

The estimated coefficients of the regression models are shown together in Table 17.3. Columns 1 and 2 are the estimated results of growth-inflation relationship with fixed effect and random effect models in static framework. Columns 3 and 4 display the estimated results of the similar relationship in threshold regression model with a single threshold and double threshold respectively. Column 5 shows the estimated coefficients for the Phillips curve relationship in a single threshold framework. The relationship between economic growth and inflation is observed to be positive if we do not consider the differential effects over the regimes, but the relationship becomes statistically insignificant after considering the threshold effect. In estimating this relationship we have considered the current account balance as a control variable. The estimated results suggest that there is no regime switching effect on growth-inflation relationship in Europe over the period 1995 to 2022. The Phillips curve relationship is significant at 1% level in a single threshold fixed effect model.

17.8 Concluding Remarks

The threshold regression model with panel data is able to provide meaningful analysis in finance and macroeconomics. This Chapter revisits the methodological issues of such model mainly based on Hansen (1999). This type of econometric model is widely used in the empirical research. It allows the asymmetric effect of the exogenous variables on the response variable depending on whether the threshold variable is above or below the unknown threshold. The threshold regression model developed by Hansen (1999) captures only the fixed effect. Later on, Seo and Shin (2016) extended Hansen's model in a dynamic panel framework with a potentially endogenous threshold. We have estimated the relationship between inflation and growth in 20 EU countries using threshold regression model using data between the years 1995 and 2022.

Appendix

In stacked form, the mean corrected form for all observations the structural form shown in (17.25) will be

$$\tilde{Y} = \tilde{X}(\tau)\beta + \tilde{\varepsilon}$$

Suppose that the regressors in $\tilde{X}$ are endogenous:

$$cov\left(\tilde{X}, \tilde{\varepsilon}\right) \neq 0$$

In presence of endogeneity, OLS estimator is biased and causal effect cannot be identified.

$$cov\left(\tilde{Y},\tilde{X}\right) = \beta cov\left(\tilde{X},\tilde{X}\right) + cov\left(\tilde{X},\tilde{\varepsilon}\right)$$

$$\beta = \frac{cov\left(\tilde{Y},\tilde{X}\right) - cov\left(\tilde{X},\tilde{\varepsilon}\right)}{cov\left(\tilde{X},\tilde{X}\right)} \neq \frac{cov\left(\tilde{Y},\tilde{X}\right)}{cov\left(\tilde{X},\tilde{X}\right)}$$

For estimation we need to transform it into reduced form by using valid instrumental variable (IV) or 2SLS. The valid IV is an exogenous variable which is correlated to x, but has indirect effect on y through its effect on x. The regression coefficient, β is just-identified when there is only one IV for one endogenous variable, and in this case, 2SLS is called IV estimator. The regression coefficient,β is over-identified if there are multiple IVs and under-identified if there is no excluded exogenous variable.

For IV estimator, the excluded exogenous variables $\tilde{q}$ has to satisfy the conditions $cov(\tilde{q},\tilde{\varepsilon}) = 0$, and $cov(\tilde{q},\tilde{X}) \neq 0$

Therefore,

$$cov\left(\tilde{Y},\tilde{q}\right) = cov\left(\beta\tilde{X}+\tilde{\varepsilon},\tilde{q}\right) = \beta cov\left(\tilde{X},\tilde{q}\right) + cov\left(\tilde{q},\tilde{\varepsilon}\right)$$

$$\widehat{\beta}_{IV} = \frac{cov\left(\tilde{Y},\tilde{q}\right)}{cov\left(\tilde{X},\tilde{q}\right)}$$

Or,

$$\widehat{\beta}_{IV} = \frac{cov\left(\tilde{Y},\tilde{q}\right)/var(\tilde{q})}{cov\left(\tilde{X},\tilde{q}\right)/var(\tilde{q})} = \frac{\textit{reduced form OLS estimate}}{\textit{first stage form OLS estimate}}$$

For 2SLS estimator, at the first stage we need to estimate

$$\tilde{X} = \Pi q(\rho) + U$$

The first stage estimation will be obtained by using the following projection matrix:

$$P = q(\rho)(q(\rho)\prime q(\rho))^{-1} q(\rho)\prime$$

The estimated value of first stage is $\widehat{\tilde{X}} = q(\rho)(q(\rho)\prime q(\rho))^{-1}q(\rho)\prime\tilde{X}$
The reduced form threshold parameter is obtained as

$$\widehat{\rho} = \underset{\rho}{argmindet}\left(\widehat{U}(\rho)\widehat{U}(\rho)\prime\right)$$

$$\widehat{\tilde{X}} = q(\widehat{\rho})\left(q(\widehat{\rho})\prime q(\widehat{\rho})\right)^{-1}q(\widehat{\rho})\prime\tilde{X}$$

In the second stage, $\widehat{\tilde{X}}$ is used as a regressor to estimate

$$\tilde{Y} = \widehat{\tilde{X}}(\tau)\beta + \tilde{\varepsilon}$$

$$\hat{\beta}_{2SLS} = \frac{cov\left(\tilde{Y}, \widehat{\tilde{X}}(\tau)\right)}{cov\left(X, \widehat{\tilde{X}}(\tau)\right)} = \left(\widehat{\tilde{X}}(\tau)\prime\widehat{\tilde{X}}(\tau)\right)^{-1}\widehat{\tilde{X}}(\tau)\prime\tilde{Y} = (X'PX)^{-1}X'PY$$

$$= \left(X'q(\hat{\rho})(q(\hat{\rho})\prime q(\hat{\rho}))^{-1}q(\hat{\rho})\prime X\right)^{-1}X'q(\hat{\rho})(q(\hat{\rho})\prime q(\hat{\rho}))^{-1}q(\hat{\rho})\prime Y$$

We can estimate the threshold τ from the following solution:

$$\hat{\tau} = \underset{\tau}{argmin}\ S_n(\tau)$$

The GMM estimators are efficient under the moment conditions (Tables 17.4, 17.5, 17.6, 17.7 and 17.8)

$$E(q_{it}\varepsilon_{it}I(z_{it} \leq \tau)) = 0$$

$$E(q_{it}\varepsilon_{it}I(z_{it} > \tau)) = 0$$

Table 17.4 Stata output showing fixed effect estimate

```
. xtreg real_gdp_growth inflation_rate current_account_balance_percent_ if year >1994, fe

Fixed-effects (within) regression               Number of obs     =        560
Group variable: id                              Number of groups  =         20

R-squared:                                      Obs per group:
     Within  = 0.0103                                         min =         28
     Between = 0.3409                                         avg =       28.0
     Overall = 0.0291                                         max =         28

                                                F(2,538)          =       2.80
corr(u_i, Xb) = 0.2197                          Prob > F          =     0.0617
```

real_gdp_growth	Coefficient	Std. err.	t	P>|t|	[95% conf.	interval]
inflation_rate	.1089783	.0460688	2.37	0.018	.0184816	.199475
current_account_balance_per~_	.0180903	.0349285	0.52	0.605	-.0505227	.0867034
_cons	1.806822	.177719	10.17	0.000	1.457714	2.155931
sigma_u	.73992328					
sigma_e	2.7527596					
rho	.06738152	(fraction of variance due to u_i)				

```
F test that all u_i=0: F(19, 538) = 1.92                    Prob > F = 0.0108
```

Table 17.5 Stata output showing random effect estimate

```
. xtreg real_gdp_growth inflation_rate current_account_balance_percent_ if year >1994, re

Random-effects GLS regression                   Number of obs     =        560
Group variable: id                              Number of groups  =         20

R-squared:                                      Obs per group:
     Within  = 0.0103                                         min =         28
     Between = 0.3427                                         avg =       28.0
     Overall = 0.0291                                         max =         28

                                                Wald chi2(2)      =      11.44
corr(u_i, X) = 0 (assumed)                      Prob > chi2       =     0.0033
```

real_gdp_growth	Coefficient	Std. err.	z	P>|z|	[95% conf.	interval]
inflation_rate	.1419878	.0419868	3.38	0.001	.0596952	.2242804
current_account_balance_per~_	.0206268	.0252876	0.82	0.415	-.0289361	.0701897
_cons	1.71509	.1999316	8.58	0.000	1.323231	2.106948
sigma_u	.48312755					
sigma_e	2.7527596					
rho	.02988213	(fraction of variance due to u_i)				

Table 17.6 Stata output showing estimates of growth inflation relation in a single threshold model

```
Threshold estimator (level = 95):
```

model	Threshold	Lower	Upper
Th-1	**5.0000**	**4.9000**	**5.1000**

```
Threshold effect test (bootstrap = 300):
```

Threshold	RSS	MSE	Fstat	Prob	Crit10	Crit5	Crit1
Single	**0.0000**	**0.0000**	**-529.56**	**1.0000**	**-2.4e+02**	**-1.8e+02**	**-1.1e+02**

```
Fixed-effects (within) regression               Number of obs     =       560
Group variable: id                              Number of groups  =        20

R-sq:  Within  = 0.0747                         Obs per group: min =       28
       Between = 0.3686                                        avg =     28.0
       Overall = 0.0928                                        max =       28

                                                F(3,537)          =     14.44
corr(u_i, Xb)  = 0.1117                         Prob > F          =    0.0000
```

real_gdp_growth	Coefficient	Std. err.	t	P>|t|	[95% conf.	interval]
inflation_rate	-.0279661	.0499008	-0.56	0.575	-.1259907	.0700586
current_account_balance_per~_	.0320094	.0338818	0.94	0.345	-.0345476	.0985664
_cat#c.real_gdp_growth						
0	0	(omitted)				
1	.649114	.1062098	6.11	0.000	.4404763	.8577517
_cons	1.954601	.1736943	11.25	0.000	1.613397	2.295804
sigma_u	.69857715					
sigma_e	2.6642219					
rho	.0643296	(fraction of variance due to u_i)				

```
F test that all u_i=0: F(19, 537) = 1.85                Prob > F = 0.0155
```

Table 17.7 xxxx

Threshold estimator (level = 95):

model	Threshold	Lower	Upper
Th-1	5.0000	4.9000	5.1000
Th-21	8.8000	8.1000	8.9000
Th-22	11.6000	.	.

Threshold effect test (bootstrap = 0 300):

Threshold	RSS	MSE	Fstat	Prob	Crit10	Crit5	Crit1
Single	.	.	.	.	.	.	.
Double	0.0000	0.0000	-34.90	0.9833	536.9972	639.5011	922.8372

```
Fixed-effects (within) regression               Number of obs     =        560
Group variable: id                              Number of groups  =         20

R-sq:  Within  = 0.0355                         Obs per group: min =        28
       Between = 0.3148                                        avg =      28.0
       Overall = 0.0518                                        max =        28

                                                F(4,536)          =       4.93
corr(u_i, Xb)  = 0.1297                         Prob > F          =     0.0007
```

real_gdp_growth	Coefficient	Std. err.	t	P>|t|	[95% conf.	interval]
inflation_rate	.0073849	.0532705	0.14	0.890	-.0972597	.1120295
current_account_balance_per~_	.0091734	.0346802	0.26	0.791	-.0589523	.0772991
_cat#c.real_gdp_growth						
0	0	(omitted)				
1	.4799253	.2278368	2.11	0.036	.0323629	.9274878
2	.6362861	.1864138	3.41	0.001	.2700949	1.002477
_cons	2.014988	.1855889	10.86	0.000	1.650417	2.379558
sigma_u	.73044629					
sigma_e	2.7225428					
rho	.06714898	(fraction of variance due to u_i)				

F test that all u_i=0: F(19, 536) = 1.91 Prob > F = 0.0114

Table 17.8 xxxx

Threshold estimator (level = 95):

model	Threshold	Lower	Upper
Th-1	5.5000	5.4000	5.6000

Threshold effect test (bootstrap = 300):

Threshold	RSS	MSE	Fstat	Prob	Crit10	Crit5	Crit1
Single	0.0000	0.0000	-411.96	1.0000	861.4743	974.1764	1.4e+03

```
Fixed-effects (within) regression               Number of obs     =        560
Group variable: id                              Number of groups  =         20

R-sq:  Within  = 0.0995                         Obs per group: min =        28
       Between = 0.1675                                        avg =      28.0
       Overall = 0.0016                                        max =        28

                                                F(4,536)          =      14.80
corr(u_i, Xb)  = -0.3324                        Prob > F          =     0.0000
```

unemployment_rate	Coefficient	Std. err.	t	P>|t|	[95% conf.	interval]
real_gdp_growth	-.1727906	.04027	-4.29	0.000	-.2518971	-.0936841
inflation_rate	-.2003382	.0623204	-3.21	0.001	-.3227603	-.0779161
current_account_balance_per~_	.1303799	.0323914	4.03	0.000	.0667503	.1940095
_cat#c.unemployment_rate						
0	0	(omitted)				
1	.3303287	.0839531	3.93	0.000	.1654113	.4952462
_cons	8.229437	.1901872	43.27	0.000	7.855834	8.603041
sigma_u	3.7346321					
sigma_e	2.5492407					
rho	.68215813	(fraction of variance due to u_i)				

F test that all u_i=0: F(19, 536) = 44.13   Prob > F = 0.0000

References

Adam CS, Bevan DL (2005) Fiscal deficits and growth in developing countries. J Public Econ 89:571–597

Altissimo F, Violante GL (2001) The non-linear dynamics of output and unemployment in the US. J Appl Econ 16:461–486

Anderson HM (1997) Transaction costs and nonlinear adjustment towards equilibrium in the US treasury bill market. Oxford Bull Econ Stat 59:465–484

Bai J, Perron P (1998) Estimating and testing linear models with multiple structural changes. Econometrica 66:47–78

Balke NS, Fomby TB (1997) Threshold cointegration. Int Econ Rev 38:627–645

Balke NS, Wohar ME (1998) Nonlinear dynamics and covered interest parity. Empir Econ 23:535–559

Beaudry P, Koop G (1993) Do recessions permanently change output? J Monet Econ 31:149–163

Bruno M, Easterly W (1998) Inflation crisis and long-run growth. J Monet Econ 41:3–26

Caner M, Hansen BE (2001) Threshold autoregression with a unit root. Econometrica 69:1555–1596

Chahad M, Hofmann-Drahonsky A-C, Meunier B, Page A, Tirpák M (2022) What explains recent errors in the inflation projections of eurosystem and ECB staff? ECB Economic Bulletin, Issue 3/2022

Chen C, Stengos T (2022) Estimation and inference for the threshold model with hybrid stochastic local unit root regressors. J Risk Financ Manag 15(6):242. https://www.mdpi.com/1911-8074/15/6/242

Clements MP, Smith J (1997) The performance of alternative forecasting methods for SETAR models. Int J Forecast 13:463–475

Davidson R (2007) Bootstrapping econometric models. Quantile 3:13–36

Efron B (1979) Bootstrap methods: another look at the Jackknife. Ann Stat 7(1):1–26

Enders W, Granger CWJ (1998) Unit-root tests and asymmetric adjustment with an example using the term structure of interest rates. J Business Econ Stat 16:304–311

Enders W, Siklos PL (2001) Cointegration and threshold adjustment. J Business Econ Stat 19:166–176

Engle RF, Granger CWJ (1987) Co-integration and error correction: representation, estimation, and testing. Econometrica 55:251–276

Fisher S (1993) The role of macroeconomic factors in growth. J Monet Econ 32:485–512

Girma S (2005) Absorptive capacity and productivity spillovers from FDI: a threshold regression analysis export. Oxford Bull Econ Stat 67:281–306

González A, Teräsvirta T, van Dijk D (2005) Panel smooth transitionregression model. Working paper series in economics and finance 604

Gospodinov N (2005) Testing for threshold nonlinearity in short-term interest rates. J Financ Econ 3:344–371

Gouveia P, Rodrigues P (2004) Threshold cointegration and the PPP hypothesis. J Appl Stat 31:115–127

Granger CWJ, Terasvirta T (1993) Modelling nonlinear economic relationships. Oxford University Press, Oxford

Hamilton JD (1989) A new approach to the economic analysis of nonstationary time series and the business cycle. Econometrica 57(2): 357–384

Hansen BE (1996) Inference when a nuisance parameter is not identified under the null hypothesis. Econometrica 64(2):413–430

Hansen BE (1997) Approximate asymptotic P-values for structural change tests. J Business Econ Stat 15:60–67

Hansen BE (1999) Threshold effects in non-dynamic panels: estimation, testing and inference. J Econ 93:345–368

Hansen BE, Seo B (2002) Testing for two-regime threshold cointegration in vector error-correction models. J Econ 110:293–318

Khan MS, Senhadji AS (2001) Threshold effects in the Relationship between Inflation and Growth. IMF Staff Paper 48(1):1–21

Koop G, Pesaran HM, Potter SM (1996) Impulse response analysis in nonlinear multivariate models. J Econ 74:119–147

Krager H, Kugler P (1993) Non-linearities in foreign exchange markets: a different perspective. J Int Money Financ 12:195–208

Lahiri SN (2003) Resampling methods for dependent data. Springer series in statistics. Springer, New York

Lancaster T (2000) The incidental parameter problem since 1948. J Econ 95:391–413

Lee Y, Wang Y (2023) Threshold regression with nonparametric sample splitting. J Econ 235(2):816–842

Nickell S (1981) Biases in dynamic models with fixed effects. Econometrica 49:1417–1426

Peel D, Taylor MP (2002) Covered interest rate arbitrage in the interwar period and Keynes-Einzig conjecture. J Money, Credit, Bank 34:51–75

Pesaran HM, Potter SM (1997) A floor and ceiling model of US output. J Econ Dyn Control 21:661–695

Priestley MB (1980) State-dependent models: a general approach to non-linear time series analysis. J Time Series Anal 1:47–71

Priestley MB (1988) Non-linear and non-stationary time series analysis. Academic Press, New York

Rabemananjara R, Zakoian JM (1993) Threshold arch models and asymmetries in volatility. J Appl Econ 8:31–49

Rothman P (1998) Forecasting asymmetric unemployment rates. Rev Econ Stat 80:164–168

Rousseau PL, Wachtel P (2009) What is happening to the impact of financial deepening on economic growth? Vanderbilt University Department of Economics Working Papers No. 0915, Vanderbilt University Department of Economics. http://ideas.repec.org/p/van/wpaper/0915.html

Seo M, Shin Y (2016) Dynamic panels with threshold effect and endogeneity. J Econ 195:169–186

Seo M, Kim S, Shin Y (2019) Estimation of dynamic panel threshold model using stata. Stand Genomic Sci 19(3):685–697

Tong H (1983) Threshold models in non-linear time series analysis. In: Brillinger D, Fienberg S, Gani J, Hartigan J, Krickeberg K (eds) Lecture notes in statistics, vol. 21. Springer, Berlin

Wang Q (2015) Fixed-effect panel threshold model using Stata. Stata J 15(1):121–134

Chapter 18
Granger Causality in Panel Datasets: Relationship Between Economic Growth and CO_2 Emissions

Sylvain Weber and Luciano Lopez

Abstract This chapter discusses the concept of Granger causality for panel datasets that are both wide (many individuals) and long (many time periods). Such datasets are obtained for instance when sets of countries are observed over the long run. In such settings, classical issues of time series econometrics, such as (non-)stationarity and (non-)causality, also arise. After a brief theoretical presentation of Granger causality, we provide a complete empirical application using publicly available data from the World Bank and Climate Watch. We investigate Granger causality between economic growth and CO_2 emissions for a set of 130 countries observed over 41 years. The empirical exercise is conducted with the statistical software Stata and is fully reproducible; thanks to the code that is provided. All steps of the analysis are carefully explained and the results are intuitively presented.

Keywords Panel data · Granger causality · Stationarity · Environmental Kuznets Curve · Stata

18.1 Introduction

A panel dataset is obtained when a set of individuals (N) are followed over time (T). With repeated observations on the same individuals, it becomes possible to leverage both between (inter-individuals) and within (intra-individuals) variation to

Supplementary Information The online version contains supplementary material available at https://doi.org/10.1007/978-981-99-4902-1_18.

S. Weber (✉)
University of Applied Sciences Western Switzerland (HES-SO), Haute école de gestion (HEG), Geneva, Switzerland
e-mail: sylvain.weber@hesge.ch

L. Lopez
University of Applied Sciences Western Switzerland (HES-SO), EHL Hospitality Business School, Lausanne, Switzerland
e-mail: luciano.lopez@ehl.ch

D. Mukherjee (ed.), *Applied Econometric Analysis Using Cross Section and Panel Data*, Contributions to Economics, https://doi.org/10.1007/978-981-99-4902-1_18

conduct econometric analyses. For historical reasons, panel data and time series are analyzed using different econometric models. Most panels are indeed relatively short in their temporal dimension so econometric techniques mostly rely on large-N asymptotics. However, with increasing amounts of data being collected, some panel datasets acquire a sufficiently long time dimension for techniques that take into account both large-N and large-T asymptotics to be considered (see for instance Chap. 12 in Baltagi 2005; Sect. 10.2 in Hsiao 2005). As a case in point, think about cross-country datasets such as the ones maintained by the World Bank or the OECD, in which information from dozens of countries is available over decades.

In this chapter, we discuss the concept of Granger causality, originally a concept designed for time series but now increasingly applied to panel datasets as well. We start by introducing the concept intuitively and present some theoretical aspects (Sect. 18.2). We then provide an empirical application where all steps are carefully discussed (Sect. 18.3). The empirical analysis is conducted using the software Stata, and more specifically the commands `xtgcause` (Lopez and Weber 2017), which implements the test of Granger non-causality for heterogeneous panel data models proposed by Dumitrescu and Hurlin (2012), and `xtgrangert` (Xiao et al. 2023), which implements the methodology developed by Juodis et al. (2021). A conclusion is provided in the final section (Sect. 18.4).

18.2 Theory

18.2.1 The Principle of Granger Causality

Granger (1969) introduced an operational definition of causality, which has become a standard tool in time series analysis. Extensions to this definition have been developed for panel data analysis and Granger causality is being increasingly applied to such datasets as well. According to Granger's (1969) definition, Y causes X if the following three requirements are met:

1. X and Y are stationary stochastic variables;
2. X precedes Y;
3. X significantly improves the forecast of Y, after considering all other available relevant information.

Econometrically speaking, Granger causality is usually assessed by regressing Y on its own lagged values and on the lagged values of X. If the lags of X are found to be jointly significant, it is concluded that there is Granger causality from X to Y. However, because such a test contains less information than all the information available in the universe, Granger (1988) emphasizes that any evidence of causality should be qualified as *prima facie*.

Although Granger (1980) made his definition of causality very clear and never claimed it should be considered equivalent to causality as commonly understood in economics, there is some confusion in the literature. Granger causality implies both *precedence* and *prediction*, even though it is sometimes described as being based on precedence only (see e.g., Maddala and Kim 2004, Sect. 5.9.2). A famous example used to highlight the presumed limits of the concept is the relationship between Christmas card sales and Christmas. The story goes that Christmas card sales Granger-cause Christmas, because they are purchased before Christmas. However, as discussed in detail by Atukeren (2008), this example is based on a misinterpretation of Granger causality. Indeed, the first and third requirements listed above are not met in this case, i.e., Christmas date is perfectly predictable. Therefore, Christmas date is not a stochastic event and cannot be better predicted when the Christmas card sales are taken into account than when they are not. Hence, Christmas card sales cannot and do not cause Christmas in any sense. These two variables are only related by the fact that one precedes the other, which is a necessary but not a sufficient condition for Granger causality.

When investigating relationships between variables and trying to unravel causal effects, researchers need to carefully consider the model they rely on. Indeed, the type of data will dictate which models can or cannot be used. A visual decision tree is provided by Jalil and Rao (2019). In particular, one should emphasize that Granger causality should not be used to analyze non-stationary variables. In other words, the researcher should not start analyzing the research question with the assumption that the question will be tackled using Granger causality (or any other given tool). Granger causality can only be used if the variables to be analyzed comply with the three requirements listed above.

18.2.2 Panel-Data Unit-Root and Stationarity Tests

As for the econometric analysis of time series, a necessary step with panel datasets that have a large time dimension is to check for the stationarity of the variables. With non-stationary variables, one faces the serious potential issue of spurious regressions. Moreover, some econometric approaches, in particular, Granger causality methods, cannot be implemented in the presence of non-stationary variables. In such a situation, cointegration and error correction techniques could be used instead.

Determining whether a variable is stationary or not can be done using the so-called unit-root tests or stationarity tests. The two groups of tests differ in their null hypothesis. For unit-root tests, the null hypothesis is that there is a unit-root, i.e., the variable is non-stationary, and therefore, rejecting implies stationarity. In stationarity tests, on the other hand, the null hypothesis is that the variable is stationary, so that rejecting implies non-stationarity.

Unit-root and stationarity tests have evolved over the past three decades, in particular, to be adapted to a panel context. While the first generation of tests did not allow for cross-sectional dependence, more recent tests have overcome this limitation. Whereas some tests assume a homogeneous panel, others let the model parameters vary across individuals.

Hlouskova and Wagner (2006) conduct a thorough analysis of the performance of these tests, thereby providing guidance about which one should be preferred in which context. In Stata, a wide array of tests with different null hypotheses are available from the command `xtunitroot` (in particular Breitung 2001; Hadri 2000; Harris and Tzavalis 1999; Im et al. 2003; Levin et al. 2002). Researchers may also consider second-generation panel unit-root tests such as the one proposed by Pesaran (2007) to control for cross-sectional dependence.

Although often overlooked, stationarity tests must be carefully selected and carried out before Granger causality analysis can be validly performed.

18.2.3 Panel Granger Causality Tests

Dumitrescu and Hurlin (2012) and Juodis et al. (2021) proposed tests for Granger (non-)causality in panel datasets. The equation underlying both tests is similar and written as follows:

$$Y_{i,t} = \alpha_i + \sum_{k=1}^{K} \gamma_{ik} Y_{i,t-k} + \sum_{k=1}^{K} \beta_{ik} X_{i,t-k} + \varepsilon_{i,t} \quad \text{with } i = 1, ..., N \text{ and } t = 1, ..., T \tag{18.1}$$

where $X_{i,t}$ and $Y_{i,t}$ are the observations of two stationary variables for individual i in period t. The coefficients are assumed to be time invariant, but they are allowed to differ across individuals (note the i subscripts attached to coefficients), which is why the test is adapted for heterogeneous panels. The lag order K is assumed to be identical for all individuals and the panel dataset must be balanced for these tests.

Like in Granger (1969), the procedure to determine the existence of causality is to test for significant effects of past values of X on the current value of Y. The null hypothesis is therefore defined as:

$$H_0 : \beta_{i1} = ... = \beta_{iK} = 0 \qquad \forall i = 1, ..., N \tag{18.2}$$

which corresponds to the absence of causality for all individuals in the panel.

The tests assume that there can be causality for some individuals but not necessarily for all. The alternative hypothesis thus writes:

$$\begin{aligned} H_1 : \ & \beta_{i1} = ... = \beta_{iK} = 0 & \forall i = 1, ..., N_1 \\ & \beta_{i1} \neq 0 \text{ or } ... \text{ or } \beta_{iK} \neq 0 & \forall i = N_1 + 1, ..., N \end{aligned} \tag{18.3}$$

where $N_1 \in [0, N-1]$ is unknown. If $N_1 = 0$, there is causality for all individuals in the panel. N_1 is strictly smaller than N, otherwise there is no causality for all individuals and H_1 reduces to H_0.

More concretely, Dumitrescu and Hurlin's (2012) test is implemented as follows. First, separate regressions are run for each of the N individuals in the panel (18.1).

Then, F-tests are performed for the K linear hypotheses $\beta_{i1} = ... = \beta_{iK} = 0$ and one Wald statistic W_i is obtained for each individual. Finally, an average Wald statistic $\overline{W}$ is computed[1]:

$$\overline{W} = \frac{1}{N}\sum_{i=1}^{N} W_i \tag{18.4}$$

Juodis et al.'s (2021) test differs from the previous one in that it is based on a pooled estimator. Pooling over individuals in the panel improves the convergence rate and the Wald test statistic is based on the Jackknife principle, which allows circumventing the incidental parameter problem. The authors demonstrate that their test has good power properties.

We emphasize that both tests described above are designed to detect causality at the panel level, and rejecting H_0 does not exclude non-causality for some individuals. Moreover, both tests are designed for stationary variables. Checking the stationarity of the variables is therefore a necessary preliminary step in the investigation of Granger causality.

The lag order (K) selection in (18.1) is also an empirical question for which the literature provides little guidance. One practical way to tackle this issue is to select the number of lags based on an information criterion (AIC/BIC/HQIC). In this process, note that all estimations have to be conducted on a common sample in order to be nested, and therefore, comparable. Practically, this implies that the first $K_{\max}$ time periods must be omitted during the entire lag selection process.[2]

We finally mention that there exist further alternatives to the methods developed by Dumitrescu and Hurlin (2012) and Juodis et al. (2021) to test for Granger causality in panel settings. In particular, the method proposed by Kónya (2006) is based on Seemingly Unrelated Regressions (Zellner 1962) and Wald tests with individual-specific bootstrap critical values. The main advantage of this approach is that it does not require pretesting for unit-roots and cointegration. Interested readers may find applications of Kónya's (2006) test in Chang et al. (2013), who investigate the impact of globalization on the insurance market, and in Keshavarzian and Tabatabaienasab (2021), who investigate the links between renewable or non-renewable energy consumption and economic growth.

[1] See Dumitrescu and Hurlin (2012, p. 1453) for the mathematical definition of W_i. Note however that T in Dumitrescu and Hurlin's formulas must be understood as the number of observations remaining in the estimations, that is the number of periods minus the number of lags included ($T - K$ in our notation).

[2] Where $K_{\max}$ stands for the maximum possible number of lags to be considered in the entire procedure.

18.3 Empirical Application

Kuznets (1955) hypothesized that income inequality first rises but then falls with economic development. This inverted U-shaped relationship became known as the "Kuznets curve". When Grossman and Krueger (1995) investigated the relationship between economic growth and environmental damages, they found a similar inverted U-shaped. By analogy with the original Kuznets curve, this relationship became known as the "environmental Kuznets curve" (EKC) and it is traditionally estimated using the following equation:

$$\ln\left(\frac{E}{P}\right)_{it} = \alpha_i + \gamma_t + \beta_1 \ln\left(\frac{GDP}{P}\right)_{it} + \beta_2 \left[\ln\left(\frac{GDP}{P}\right)_{it}\right]^2 + \varepsilon_{it} \quad (18.5)$$

where E are polluting emissions (for instance of CO_2), P is population, and GDP is gross domestic product.

The EKC is essentially an empirical phenomenon, and it is indeed frequently investigated using Granger causality tests (see for instance Iwata et al. 2010; Usman et al. 2019; Minlah and Zhang 2021). However, as stated by Stern (2004): "It is very easy to do bad econometrics, and the history of the EKC exemplifies what can go wrong". Researchers in this literature often pay too little attention to the statistical properties of the data, such as serial dependence and stationarity. Estimating (18.5) using traditional techniques is indeed tempting but if the variables are non-stationary and do not cointegrate, the results will be spurious.

In the following empirical application, we consider the relationship between economic growth and CO_2 emissions. Rather than trying to estimate an EKC, we conduct a simple analysis in which we test whether economic growth Granger-causes CO_2 emissions, or vice versa, in order to illustrate the concept in the context of panel data.

We use the software Stata (version 18), in which several commands are specifically tailored for our purpose. In particular, we make use of several community-contributed commands—`wbopendata`, `insheetjson`, `xtgcause`, and `xtgrangert`—, which are respectively dedicated to download indicators from World Bank databases, import data formatted in JavaScript Object Notation (JSON), and implement Dumitrescu and Hurlin's (2012) test or Juodis et al.'s (2021) test for Granger causality in panel data.[3]

Our empirical application is structured as follows. We start by loading the data from various internet sources into Stata (Sect. 18.3.1). We apply some manipulations to clean the dataset and make it more user-friendly by renaming and labeling the variables (Sect. 18.3.2), and begin our data exploration in order to select the

---

[3] Stata's programming language lets users write commands that behave just like official Stata commands. Such commands implemented by users are called *community-contributed commands* and are not installed by default. The four commands mentioned above can be installed by typing "`ssc install wbopendata`" (see Azevedo 2011), "`ssc install insheetjson`" (see Lindsley 2012), "`net install st0507.pkg`" (see Lopez and Weber 2017), and "`net install st0706.pkg`" (see Xiao et al. 2023) in Stata.

final sample (Sect. 18.3.3). The analysis is then conducted in three standard steps: visual inspection of the data (Sect. 18.3.4), unit-root tests (Sect. 18.3.5), and Granger causality tests (Sect. 18.3.6). All along this empirical exercise, we provide codes that make it straightforward to reproduce our analysis and could be easily adapted to other settings. Wherever necessary, we give explanations regarding the code itself and indicate how to interpret the results.

18.3.1 Load Data into Stata

We begin our empirical exercise by downloading some indicators from the World Bank (https://data.worldbank.org) and from Climate Watch (https://www.climatewatchdata.org/ghg-emissions). In order to investigate the EKC hypothesis in a panel data context, we need indicators related to GDP and CO_2 emissions that are comparable across countries and over a period of time as long as possible.

From World Bank databases, we extract GDP in constant US$ and population[4,5]:

- NY.GDP.MKTP.KD: GDP (constant 2015 US$)
- SP.POP.TOTL: Population, total.

A very efficient and convenient way of downloading indicators from World Bank databases into Stata is to make use of the community-contributed command `wbopendata`[6]:

```
. wbopendata, indicator(NY.GDP.MKTP.KD ; SP.POP.TOTL) long nometadata clear
. save WBdata
file WBdata.dta saved
```

With a single line of code, a dataset containing all desired indicators and all countries is loaded, and we save it under `WBdata.dta`. For GHG emissions, we

[4] Population will be used to construct per capita indicators. The description of each indicator can be obtained at https://data.worldbank.org/indicator/INDICATOR_CODE, where the last piece of the url has to be replaced by the indicator code.

[5] The World Bank provides data about CO_2 emissions (indicator EN.ATM.CO2E.KT), and we could conduct our entire analysis using data from this source only. However, CO_2 emissions are only available since 1990, which means our panel would be relatively short. Alternatively, we will use emissions from Climate Watch, which has been available since 1960, meaning that we can substantially increase the number of observations by using this alternative data source. Of course, this will cost a bit more coding, since we will have to merge separate datasets.

[6] Note that `wbopendata` uses semicolons to separate indicators, therefore, it would not be possible to use `#d;` Stata command to split this command into several lines. If the line of code is long, we could make use of `///` to split the command and present it nicely. Also, we noticed some minor issues affecting the functioning of the `wbopendata`. In particular, it is necessary to use option `clear` to avoid an error when several indicators are downloaded simultaneously and it is necessary to use option `nometadata` to avoid a mistake when the description of the indicators entails url links (as is the case for instance with indicator EN.ATM.CO2E.KT).

resort to Climate Watch, which provides various series, some of which started as early as 1960. To automate data extraction from this source, we use another community-contributed Stata command—`insheetjson`—, which allows us to query Climate Watch's API[7,8]:

```
. quietly: levelsof countrycode, local(countries)
. clear
. save CWdata, emptyok
(dataset contains 0 observations)
file CWdata.dta saved
. foreach c of local countries {
  2.         clear
  3.         local listofvars ""
  4.         local listofcols ""
  5.         local i = 0
  6.         forv y = 1960/2021 {
  7.                 gen str12 co2`y' = ""
  8.                 local listofvars `listofvars' co2`y'
  9.                 local ++i
 10.                 local listofcols `"`listofcols' "data:1:emissions:`i':value""'
 11.         }
 12.         quietly: insheetjson `listofvars' using "https://www.climatewatchdata.org/api/v1
> /data/historical_emissions?source_ids[]=194&gas_ids[]=442&sector_ids[]=2264&regions[]=`c'&s
> tart_year=1960", columns(`listofcols')
 13.         gen countrycode = "`c'"
 14.         append using CWdata
 15.         quietly: save CWdata, replace
 16. }
. reshape long co2, i(countrycode) j(year)
(j = 1960 1961 1962 1963 1964 1965 1966 1967 1968 1969 1970 1971 1972 1973 1974 1975 1976 197
> 7 1978 1979 1980 1981 1982 1983 1984 1985 1986 1987 1988 1989 1990 1991 1992 1993 1994 1995
>  1996 1997 1998 1999 2000 2001 2002 2003 2004 2005 2006 2007 2008 2009 2010 2011 2012 2013
> 2014 2015 2016 2017 2018 2019 2020 2021)
Data                               Wide   ->   Long
-----------------------------------------------------------------------------
Number of observations              266   ->   16,492
Number of variables                  63   ->   3
j variable (62 values)                    ->   year
xij variables:
           co21960 co21961 ... co22021    ->   co2
-----------------------------------------------------------------------------
. la var co2 "CO2 emissions (Mt)"
. destring co2, replace force
co2: contains nonnumeric characters; replaced as double
(4639 missing values generated)
. save CWdata, replace
file CWdata.dta saved
```

[7] In order to use `insheetjson`, packages `insheetjson.ado` and `libjson.mlib` must also be installed. Type `ssc install insheetjson` and `ssc install libjson` to do that.

[8] The query parameters for Climate Watch's API are described at: https://www.climatewatchdata.org/data-explorer/historical-emissions (below the data table).

Since the above piece of code is somewhat complicated, let us provide some explanations. We first use command `levelsof` to create a list of all countries (or more precisely ISO3 codes) present in World Bank data (which is already in Stata's memory). We then build a loop that formats and sends one request for each country to extract CO_2 emissions over 1960 to 2021 from Climate Watch's API. At each iteration, the database is expanded— by appending the observations just extracted —and saved under `CWdata.dta`.[9] At the end of the loop, the database is in wide format, which means there is a single line per country (identified by its ISO3 code in variable `countrycode`) and CO_2 emissions for each year in separate variables (named `co2yyyy`, where `yyyy` corresponds to the year). We therefore reshape the dataset from wide to long in order to have one line per country and per year, which is the format required to conduct panel data analyses in Stata.

Finally, we merge databases `WBdata.dta` and `CWdata.dta` on the ISO3 country code and the year:

```
. use WBdata

. merge 1:1 countrycode year using CWdata, nogen

    Result                      Number of obs
    -----------------------------------------
    Not matched                           266
        from master                       266
        from using                          0

    Matched                            16,492
    -----------------------------------------

. sort countrycode year
```

18.3.2 Data Manipulation

To make sense of the dataset now loaded in Stata's memory, we start by a simple description of the data:

[9] A simpler but less elegant way of obtaining the same data would be to download a CSV file from Climate Watch's data explorer and use `import delimited` to import the dataset in Stata. The interest of the above code is that it can be replicated in a fully automated way, whereas extracting the data as a CSV file requires a series of manual operations.

```
. describe

Contains data from WBdata.dta
 Observations:          16,758
    Variables:              14                  26 Jun 2023 16:00
--------------------------------------------------------------------------------
Variable         Storage   Display    Value
    name            type    format    label      Variable label
--------------------------------------------------------------------------------
countrycode      str3      %9s                   Country Code
countryname      str56     %56s                  Country Name
region           str3      %9s                   Region Code
regionname       str28     %28s                  Region Name
adminregion      str3      %9s                   Administrative Region Code
adminregionname  str52     %52s                  Administrative Region Name
incomelevel      str3      %9s                   Income Level Code
incomelevelname  str19     %19s                  Income Level Name
lendingtype      str3      %9s                   Lending Type Code
lendingtypename  str14     %14s                  Lending Type Name
year             int       %9.0g                 Year
ny_gdp_mktp_kd   double    %8.0g                 NY.GDP.MKTP.KD
sp_pop_totl      double    %8.0g                 SP.POP.TOTL
co2              double    %10.0g                CO2 emissions (Mt)
--------------------------------------------------------------------------------
Sorted by: countrycode  year
     Note: Dataset has changed since last saved.
```

We see that 14 variables and 16,758 observations are loaded. The three central variables are placed at the bottom of the list. In addition to these, the database encloses country identifiers (countrycode, countryname), the year, and some country characteristics (region and income level), which will be interesting to consider later in our analysis.

A frequency table of the region variable shows that some observations are related to groups of countries ("Aggregates") and that there are missing values in this variable. Since our objective is to work with a panel of countries, we drop these observations:

```
. tab regionname, missing

                   Region Name |      Freq.     Percent        Cum.
-------------------------------+-----------------------------------
                               |        126        0.75        0.75
                    Aggregates |      2,961       17.67       18.42
           East Asia and Pacific |      2,331       13.91       32.33
         Europe and Central Asia |      3,654       21.80       54.14
     Latin America and Caribbean |      2,646       15.79       69.92
    Middle East and North Africa |      1,323        7.89       77.82
                   North America |        189        1.13       78.95
                      South Asia |        504        3.01       81.95
              Sub-Saharan Africa |      3,024       18.05      100.00
-------------------------------+-----------------------------------
                           Total |     16,758      100.00
. drop if regionname=="Aggregates" | missing(regionname)
(3,087 observations deleted)
```

The description of the variables displayed above moreover shows that the country identifiers (both country code and country name) are saved as string variables. To work with panel data commands, we need to inform Stata about the panel structure, and therefore, transform the country identifier from a string to a numerical variable. We do so with the command `encode` and create a new variable `c` to identify countries. We additionally rename the year variable as `t` so as to have the shortest (but still meaningful) variable names:

```
. encode countrycode, gen(c) label(clab)
. ren year t
. xtset c t, yearly
Panel variable: c (strongly balanced)
 Time variable: t, 1960 to 2022
         Delta: 1 year
. xtdescribe
       c:  1, 2, ..., 217                                    n =        217
       t:  1960, 1961, ..., 2022                             T =         63
           Delta(t) = 1 year
           Span(t)  = 63 periods
           (c*t uniquely identifies each observation)
Distribution of T_i:   min      5%      25%       50%       75%     95%     max
                        63      63       63        63        63      63      63
     Freq.  Percent    Cum. |  Pattern
 ---------------------------+-----------------------------------------------------------------
      217    100.00  100.00 |  111111111111111111111111111111111111111111111111111111111111111
 ---------------------------+-----------------------------------------------------------------
      217    100.00         |  XXXXXXXXXXXXXXXXXXXXXXXXXXXXXXXXXXXXXXXXXXXXXXXXXXXXXXXXXXXXXXX
```

After having declared the panel data structure with `xtset`, we typed `xtdescribe` to obtain a description of the panel. We see that our database contains information on 217 countries over a 63-year period ranging from 1960 to 2022. The output also indicates that the panel is strongly balanced, which means that there is one observation for each country and each year. However, note that this does not guarantee the absence of missing values. In fact, we will see later that there are missing values in some variables so that the panel will not remain balanced when considering such variables. For the analyses requiring balanced panels, we will hence have to exclude some countries and/or years.

To finalize data preparation, we adjust variable names so that they are shorter and easier to manipulate than the original ones, we add variable labels, and create variables measuring GDP and CO_2 emissions per capita by dividing the original variables measured at the country level by the country population. We finally keep only the relevant information and order the variables in a logical order. Some of these steps are only cosmetic, but it is good practice to arrange the database nicely, as it will make searching for specific information easier and coding more efficient:

```
. ren ny_gdp_mktp_kd gdp
. la var gdp "GDP (constant 2015 US$)"
. ren sp_pop_totl pop
. la var pop "Population"
. gen gdpcap = gdp/pop
(3,814 missing values generated)
. la var gdpcap "GDP per capita (constant 2015 US$)"
. gen co2cap = co2/pop*1e6
(2,252 missing values generated)
. la var co2cap "CO2 emissions per capita (tons)"
. ren regionname reg
. #d ;
delimiter now ;
. gen inc =
>           1*(incomelevelname=="Low income")
>           + 2*(incomelevelname=="Lower middle income")
>           + 3*(incomelevelname=="Upper middle income")
>           + 4*(incomelevelname=="High income")
> ;
. la def inclab
>           1 "Low income"
>           2 "Lower middle income"
>           3 "Upper middle income"
>           4 "High income"
> ;
. #d cr
delimiter now cr
. la val inc inclab
. la var inc "Income level"
. keep c t reg inc gdp gdpcap co2 co2cap pop
. order c t reg inc gdp gdpcap co2 co2cap pop
. describe
Contains data from WBdata.dta
 Observations:          13,671
    Variables:               9               26 Jun 2023 16:00
----------------------------------------------------------------------------
Variable      Storage   Display    Value
    name         type    format    label      Variable label
----------------------------------------------------------------------------
c               long    %8.0g      clab       Country Code
t               int     %ty                   Year
reg             str28   %28s                  Region Name
inc             float   %19.0g     inclab     Income level
gdp             double  %8.0g                 GDP (constant 2015 US$)
gdpcap          float   %9.0g                 GDP per capita (constant 2015 US$)
co2             double  %10.0g                CO2 emissions (Mt)
co2cap          float   %9.0g                 CO2 emissions per capita (tons)
pop             double  %8.0g                 Population
----------------------------------------------------------------------------
Sorted by: c  t
     Note: Dataset has changed since last saved.
```

The final piece of the above output shows that the database is now compact with only 9 necessary variables remaining. We are thus ready to investigate our dataset in more detail.

18.3.3 Data Exploration and Sample Selection

To enhance our understanding of the data, we run a preliminary descriptive analysis. A good way to start is to compute simple summary statistics of the variables of interest (GDP and CO_2 emissions per capita) and their components[10]:

```
. sum gdp gdpcap co2 co2cap pop
```

Table 18.1 Descriptive statistics

	Mean	Std Dev.	Min	Max	N
GDP (billions of constant 2015 US$)	249.51	1,141.93	0.02	20,952.69	10,080
GDP per capita (constant 2015 US$)	11,997.66	18,954.98	144.03	204,190.97	10,080
CO_2 emissions (Mt)	121.28	565.70	0.00	11,472.37	11,419
CO_2 emissions per capita (tons)	4.49	7.09	0.00	120.31	11,419
Population (thousands)	24,886.14	104,291.74	2.65	1417173.12	13,641

Table 18.1 reveals two important features. First, there are missing values in the indicators since the number of observations differs across variables and is always smaller than $217 \times 63 = 13{,}671$, which would be obtained if data were available for all countries and all years. Second, note that CO_2 emissions are sometimes recorded as zeroes, which is unlikely to be correct.[11] We, therefore, decided to replace the zeroes with missing values. Finally, because we will use GDP per capita and CO_2 emissions per capita in our analyses, we remove observations for which any of these two variables is missing[12]:

[10] The Stata output is omitted but properly displayed in Table 18.1. Note that we have transformed GDP into billions of US$ and population into thousands for better readability.

[11] Detailed inspection of the database further reveals that zeroes generally occur several consecutive years, as in the case of Bhutan from 1970 to 1976 and the Maldives from 1971 to 1974.

[12] The Stata output from the last line (`sum ...`) is omitted but properly displayed in Table 18.2.

```
. sum co2, detail

                    CO2 emissions (Mt)
-------------------------------------------------------------
      Percentiles      Smallest
 1%          .01              0
 5%          .07              0
10%          .17              0       Obs              11,419
25%          .99              0       Sum of wgt.      11,419

50%          7.5                      Mean           121.2798
                        Largest       Std. dev.      565.6958
75%        49.44       10353.88
90%       212.48          10741       Variance       320011.7
95%       455.34       10956.21       Skewness       10.87906
99%      2129.33       11472.37       Kurtosis       150.5602

. replace co2cap = . if co2cap==0
(13 real changes made, 13 to missing)

. drop if missing(gdpcap,co2cap)
(4,593 observations deleted)

. xtdescribe

       c:  2, 3, ..., 217                                    n =        189
       t:  1960, 1961, ..., 2021                             T =         62
           Delta(t) = 1 year
           Span(t)  = 62 periods
           (c*t uniquely identifies each observation)

Distribution of T_i:   min      5%      25%       50%       75%     95%     max
                         1      22       33        54        62      62      62

     Freq.  Percent    Cum. |  Pattern
 ---------------------------+----------------------------------------------------------------
       80     42.33   42.33 |  11111111111111111111111111111111111111111111111111111111111111
       11      5.82   48.15 |  ....................111111111111111111111111111111111111111111
       10      5.29   53.44 |  ...................................111111111111111111111111111
       10      5.29   58.73 |  ..............................11111111111111111111111111111111
        7      3.70   62.43 |  ..........1111111111111111111111111111111111111111111111111111
        5      2.65   65.08 |  .................111111111111111111111111111111111111111111111
        5      2.12   67.20 |  .....................11111111111111111111111111111111111111111
        4      2.12   69.31 |  .....111111111111111111111111111111111111111111111111111111111
        4      1.59   70.90 |  ........................................1111111111111111111111
       53     29.10  100.00 | (other patterns)
 ---------------------------+----------------------------------------------------------------
      189    100.00         |  XXXXXXXXXXXXXXXXXXXXXXXXXXXXXXXXXXXXXXXXXXXXXXXXXXXXXXXXXXXXXX
. sum gdp gdpcap co2 co2cap pop
```

Table 18.2 Descriptive statistics (without missing values)

	Mean	Std Dev.	Min	Max	N
GDP (billions of constant 2015 US$)	265.39	1,165.62	0.02	20,529.46	9,078
GDP per capita (constant 2015 US$)	9,769.07	14,949.42	144.03	167,809.22	9,078
CO_2 emissions (Mt)	137.00	623.90	0.01	11,472.37	9,078
CO_2 emissions per capita (tons)	4.14	6.12	0.01	64.51	9,078
Population (thousands)	34,142.10	124,518.89	9.18	1412360.00	9,078

A substantial share of the database (4,610 observations) was concerned with missing values, and it is now reduced to 9,060 observations with complete information. Using `xtdescribe` once again allows us to visualize the resulting structure of the panel. First, 217 − 189 = 28 countries were completely discarded from the dataset: these are not covered by Climate Watch data. Second, the observation period ranges from 1960 to 2021; all observations for 2022 were removed because no data for that year are available so far from Climate Watch. Third, the observation window spans the maximum 62-year period from 1960 to 2021 for a set of 80 countries only. For all others (i.e., 189 − 80 = 109 countries), the pattern is different in most cases because the observation window starts later. This structure imposes a tradeoff for our analysis; we must choose between a dataset with more countries (but fewer time periods) or more time periods (but fewer countries).

One helpful way to decide on the best strategy to select the time frame for the analysis is to display the available data visually. We do that by sorting the countries by the year they enter into the panel and connecting the observations that do exist country by country. That yields Fig. 18.1, in which existing observations are in gray and missing values are in white:

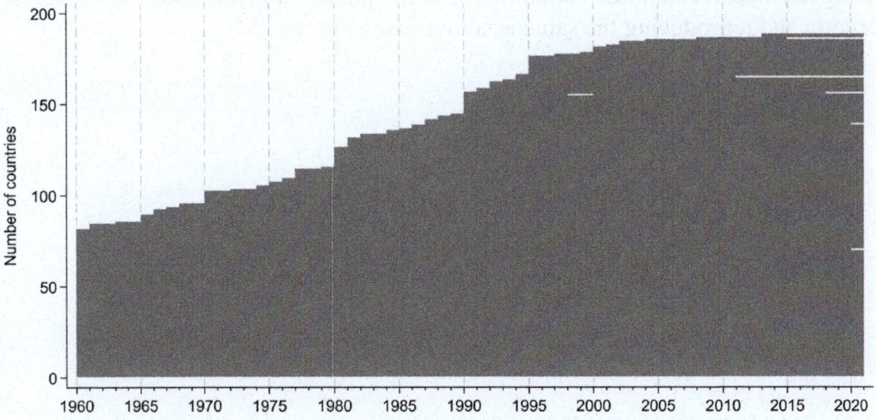

Fig. 18.1 Visual inspection of the panel structure

```
. bysort c (t): gen t1 = t[1]
. bysort t1 (c t): gen N = c!=c[_n-1]
. replace N = sum(N)
(9,077 real changes made)
. tsfill, full
. #d ;
delimiter now ;
. line N t, connect(L) lc(gs10) lw(*1.5) cmissing(n)
>           xlab(1960(5)2021) xmt(##5) xti("")
>           ylab(, nogrid) yti("Number of countries")
> ;
. #d cr
delimiter now cr
. drop N t1
. drop if missing(gdpcap,co2cap)
(2,640 observations deleted)
```

For most countries, we see that once the country enters the dataset, it remains until the end of the observation window. There are a few exceptions, for which the observation window stops before 2021 (white bars near the end of the period). Removing these 6 countries for which the most recent information is not available seems to be a wise decision, as including them would mean giving up the possibility of using the most recent information for the entire panel. Applying these data selection criteria and reproducing the same as above gives Fig. 18.2:

```
. bysort c: drop if t[_N]<2021
(151 observations deleted)
. bysort c (t): gen t1 = t[1]
. bysort t1 (c t): gen N = c!=c[_n-1]
. replace N = sum(N)
(8,926 real changes made)
. sum N if t==1960, mean
. local N1960 = r(max)
. sum N if t==1990, mean
. local N1990 = r(max)
. tsfill, full
. #d ;
delimiter now ;
. line N t, connect(L) lc(gs10) lw(*1.5) cmissing(n)
>           xlab(1960(5)2021) xmt(##5) xti("")
>           ylab(, nogrid) yti("Number of countries")
> || pci `N1960' 1960 `N1960' 2021 `N1960' 2021 0 2021 0 2021 0 1960 0 1960 `N1960' 1960, lc(
> green) lw(*2)
> || pci `N1990' 1990 `N1990' 2021 `N1990' 2021 0 2021 0 2021 0 1990 0 1990 `N1990' 1990, lc(
> red) lw(*2)
> legend(off)
> ;
. #d cr
delimiter now cr
. drop N t1
. drop if missing(gdpcap,co2cap)
(2,419 observations deleted)
```

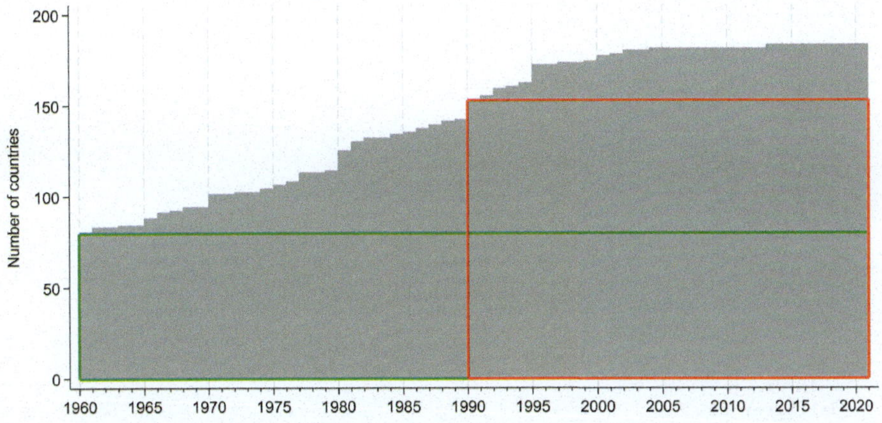

Fig. 18.2 Visual inspection of the panel structure, cleaned dataset

We are now in a position to decide which data to keep for our analysis. One way of solving the tradeoff between the number of countries and the number of years objectively might be to maximize the number of observations in the final sample, which amounts to maximize the size of the gray rectangle in Fig. 18.2. Two possible choices are represented by the green and red rectangles. Including all years from 1960 to 2021 would imply keeping only 80 countries for a total number of observations of $80 \times 62 = 4{,}960$ (green rectangle). Omitting the years before 1990 would increase the number of countries in the final sample to 153, for a total number of observations of $153 \times 32 = 4{,}896$ (red rectangle). There is no clearly dominant strategy and the choice might depend on the objective of the analysis, for instance, whether it should focus on recent data or target specific (group of) countries. Note, however, that this choice is not a trivial one; Baum et al. (2022) demonstrate that Granger causal relationships are often sensitive to the time period being considered. In real applications, robustness checks should be conducted using various samples and time windows.

In our case, where the objective is to demonstrate how to conduct Granger causality analysis, we will simply maximize the total number of observations. To this end, we search for the largest dataset by systematically counting how many observations would be included in the analysis if we were to start the observation window in each year between 1960 and 2021. The following piece of code automates these calculations within a loop and plots the results:

```
. preserve
. collapse (count) c, by(t)
. gen N = c*(2021-(t-1))
. #d ;
delimiter now ;
. tw bar N t, fc(gs10) lc(gs0)
> || bar N t if t==1960, fc(green) lc(gs0)
> || bar N t if t==1990, fc(red) lc(gs0)
> || scatter N t, ms(i) mlab(N) mlabpos(1) mlabcol(gs0) mlabangle(90)
>        xlab(1960(5)2021) xmt(##5) xti("")
>        yti("Number of observations") ysc(r(0 5500))
>        legend(off)
> ;
. #d cr
delimiter now cr
. restore
. keep if t>=1981
(2,062 observations deleted)
. bysort c (t): drop if t[1]>1981
(1,535 observations deleted)
```

In Fig. 18.3, the bars for 1960 and 1990 are highlighted, respectively, in green and red, for consistency with Fig. 18.2. We see that the number of observations is maximized if we start our analysis in 1981. Sacrificing the first 21 years of the dataset (1960–1980) allows us to include 130 countries instead of only 80 if we started in 1960, which more than offsets the loss of observations caused by the shorter observation period. Our empirical exercise is therefore based on a sample of 5,330 observations; 130 countries observed over a time frame of 41 years, from 1981 to 2021.

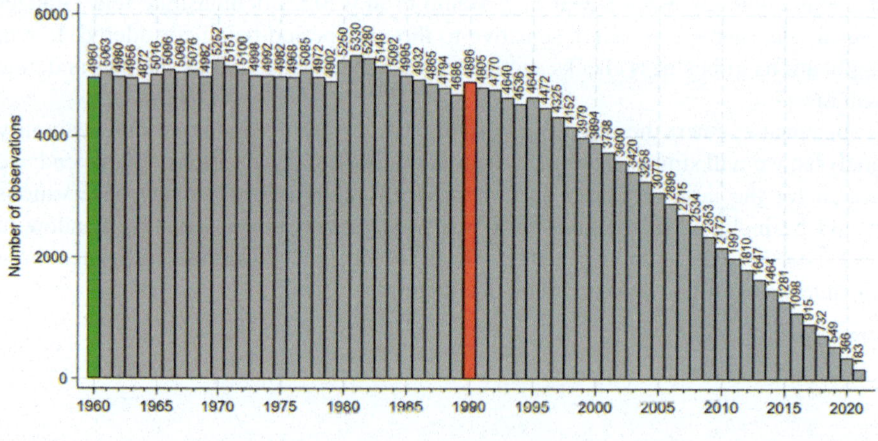

Fig. 18.3 Number of usable observations, as a function of the starting year of the observation period

18.3.4 Visual Inspection of Data

Before conducting an econometric analysis, we provide a visual inspection and look at the evolution of the variables of interest over time. We differentiate the groups of countries by income (low, lower middle, upper middle, and high) using different colors. To do that, we start by splitting the variable measuring GDP into four group-specific variables. The advantage of this approach is that colors will be automatically different across groups since they are from separate variables[13]:

```
. quietly: separate gdpcap, by(inc)
. #d ;
delimiter now ;
. line gdpcap? t, c(L ..) sort(c t)
>           ysc(log) ylab(100 1000 10000 100000, format(%10.0gc))
>           yti("GDP per capita (constant 2015 US$)")
>           xlab(1980(5)2021) xmt(##5) xti("")
>           legend(
>                   lab(1 "Low inc")
>                   lab(2 "Lower middle inc")
>                   lab(3 "Upper middle inc")
>                   lab(4 "High inc")
>                   row(1) pos(6)
>           )
> ;
. #d cr
delimiter now cr
```

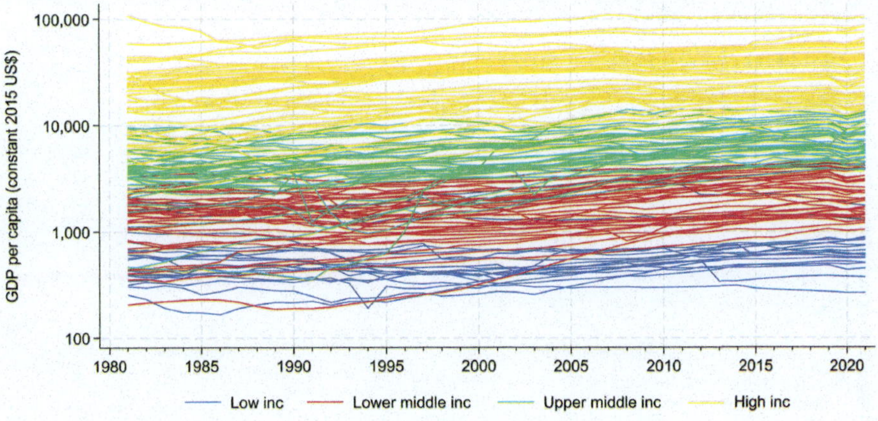

Fig. 18.4 Evolution of GDP per capita, by income group

[13] An alternative would be to use command `xtline gdpcap, over legend(off) ysc(log)`. The content of the graph would be similar, but because each country (rather than each group of countries) would be assigned a different color, the graph would be more complicated to interpret.

Note that we use a logarithmic scale to accommodate for the wide disparity across countries. With a natural scale, most countries would have been bunched at the bottom of the plot. With a logarithmic scale, even a modest slope in Fig. 18.4 corresponds to a substantial growth rate. The difference between developing and advanced countries is considerable, with GDP per capita ranging from less than US$ 300 to more than US$ 100,000 in 2021. This Figure also provides a preliminary indication regarding the characteristics of the series, which is likely non-stationary.

Variations of GDP per capita are used to measure economic growth. In Stata, the annual growth rate, defined as $\left(\frac{GDP_t}{GDP_{t-1}} - 1\right) \cdot 100$, can be computed conveniently using time series operators (see `help tsvarlist`). In particular, the lag operator `L.` refers to the lagged value of a variable and ensures that observations from different countries are not mixed. We compute the growth rate and plot the variable obtained using the same strategy as before but further adding the `by` option in command `line` to display each country group in its own panel:

```
. gen gdpcapgr = (gdpcap/L.gdpcap-1)*100
(130 missing values generated)

. la var gdpcapgr "Growth rate of GDP per capita (%)"

. quietly: separate gdpcapgr, by(inc)

. #d ;
delimiter now ;
. line gdpcapgr? t, c(L ..) sort(c t) by(inc, legend(off) note(""))
>         yti("Growth rate of GDP per capita (%)")
>         xlab(1980(5)2021, labsize(small)) xmt(##5) xti("")
> ;

. #d cr
delimiter now cr
```

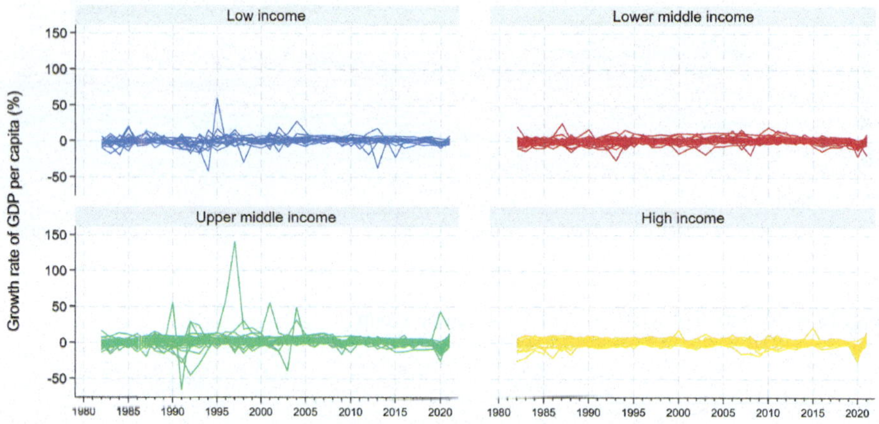

Fig. 18.5 Annual growth of GDP per capita, by income group

Figure 18.5 does not reveal any major differences across income groups regarding their growth rate, but it is possibly hidden by within-group variability. The most salient feature in this representation is in fact that there is fewer variability among high-income countries compared to other groups.

For a more compact view of the distribution of growth rates, we present the same data in box plots, excluding the extreme values using the `noout` option[14]:

```
. gr box gdpcapgr, over(inc) noout note("")
```

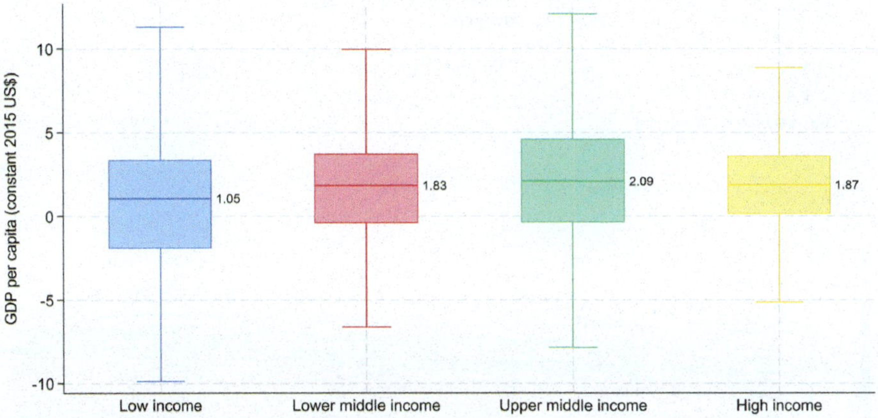

Fig. 18.6 Distribution of GDP growth, by income group

Figure 18.6 confirms our feeling. The distribution is wider for the low-income and the upper-middle-income countries. Also, we observe that the median growth rate is (much) smaller for the low income than all other groups. These results reveal divergence at the global level in GDP per capita during the period 1981–2021.

Turning to our second variable of interest, CO_2 emissions per capita, we apply the same strategy and present the evolution for each country the same using colors depending on income level. Given that emission levels are extremely different across countries, we again use a logarithmic scale:

[14] The code reproduced here does not exactly produce Fig. 18.6, but one where all boxes have the same color. Figure 18.6 in fact relies on the strategy proposed by Cox (2009), which requires substantially more coding. Here, we moreover print the median values next to each box. The exact code to build Fig. 18.6 is available in the dofile provided in the appendix.

```
. quietly: separate co2cap, by(inc)
. #d ;
delimiter now ;
. line co2cap? t, c(L ..) sort(c t)
>         ysc(log) ylab(.1 1 10 100)
>         yti("CO{sub:2} emissions per capita (tons)")
>         xlab(1980(5)2021) xmt(##5) xti("")
>         legend(
>                 lab(1 "Low inc")
>                 lab(2 "Lower middle inc")
>                 lab(3 "Upper middle inc")
>                 lab(4 "High inc")
>                 row(1) pos(6)
>         )
> ;
. #d cr
delimiter now cr
```

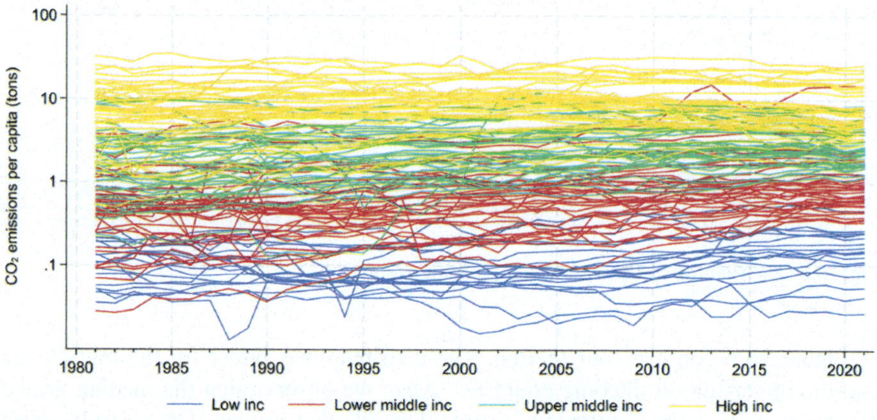

Fig. 18.7 Evolution of CO_2 emissions per capita by income group

Figure 18.7 shows that emissions have not changed much over the last 40 years. Contrarily, there is a very clear ranking of income groups: high-income countries are the ones where CO_2 emissions are the largest. Note the huge gap between countries; in 2021, the ratio between emissions at the 90th percentile and the 10th percentile is almost 40. Small variations can be observed over time within each country, but no overall trend emerges from this representation.

Since the purpose of our analysis is to investigate the relationship between GDP per capita and CO_2 emissions per capita, it is interesting to draw a scatter plot of these two variables, one against the other. We again use logarithmic scales for both variables in order to get a nice visual presentation. We also scale the markers by the total amount of CO_2 emissions in the countries and label the top 5% of emitters:

```
. quietly: sum co2 if t==2021, d
. #d ;
delimiter now ;
. scatter co2cap gdpcap if t==2021 [fw=co2], mfc(blue%25)
> || scatter co2cap gdpcap if t==2021 & co2>=`r(p95)', ms(i) mlab(c) mlabcol(gs0) mlabpos(0)
>         xsc(log) xlab(1000 10000 100000, format(%10.0gc))
>         ysc(log) ylab(.1 1 10 100) yti("CO{sub:2} emissions per capita (tons)")
>         legend(off)
> ;
. #d cr
delimiter now cr
```

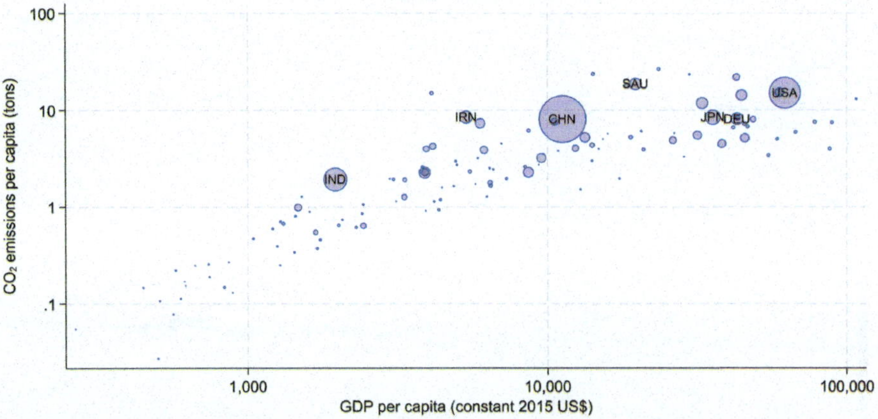

Fig. 18.8 Relationship between CO_2 emissions per capita and GDP per capita, in 2021

As expected, Fig. 18.8 shows that there is a clear and positive relationship between GDP per capita and CO_2 emissions per capita. The size of the markers also allows to spot the largest emitters, China, the USA, and India being by far the first three in this ranking.

Finally, to get an idea of the co-evolution between the two variables of interest, we plot a similar graph, but for all years and retaining only the top 5% of emitters (in the 2021 distribution). The country identifier is placed at the end of each series (i.e., in 2021):

```
. quietly: sum co2 if t==2021, d
. bys c (t): gen large = co2[_N]>=`r(p95)'
. levelsof c if large, local(largecountries)
37 51 90 92 99 168 204
. local scatters
. foreach i of local largecountries {
  2.         local scatters `scatters' scatter co2cap gdpcap if c==`i', ms(o) ||
  3. }
. #d ;
delimiter now ;
. `scatters'
> scatter co2cap gdpcap if large & t==2021, ms(i) mlab(c) mlabcol(gs0) mlabpos(3)
>         xsc(log) xlab(1000 10000 100000, format(%10.0gc))
>         ysc(log r(.1 100)) ylab(.1 1 10 100) yti("CO{sub:2} emissions per capita (tons)")
>         legend(off)
> ;
. #d cr
delimiter now cr
. drop large
```

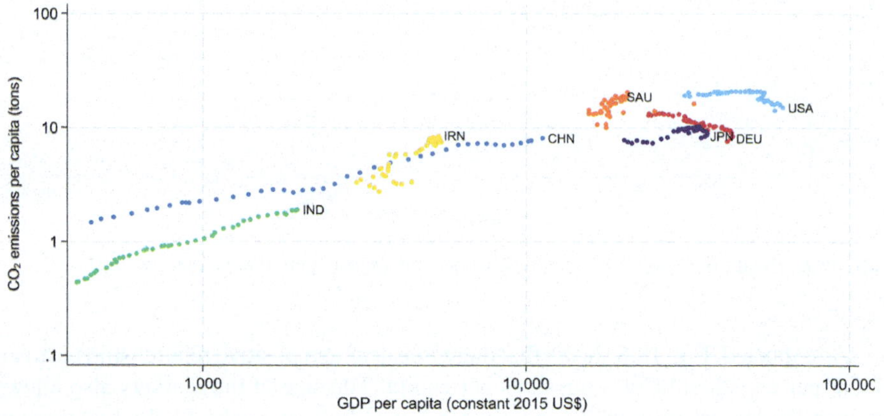

Fig. 18.9 Relationship between CO_2 emissions per capita and GDP per capita for the largest emitters, from 1981 to 2021

Figure 18.9 shows that GDP per capita increases throughout the whole period for all large emitters except Iran and Saudi Arabia, who faced severe drops during the 80s. The growth of GDP is stronger in the two least-developed countries (China and India), especially compared to the most-developed ones (Japan, Germany, and USA). Interestingly, the evolution of CO_2 emissions is very different across countries. For the least-developed ones, emissions increase substantially during the observation period. Contrarily, there is almost no change in CO_2 emissions per capita in Japan or even a decrease in Germany and the USA.

Finally, we draw a similar scatter plot for all countries and all years by income groups:

```
. #d ;
delimiter now ;
. scatter co2cap? gdpcap,
>         by(inc, rescale legend(off) note(""))
>         yti("CO{sub:2} emissions per capita (tons)")
>         msize(*.2 ..) ysc(log)
> ;
. #d cr
delimiter now cr
```

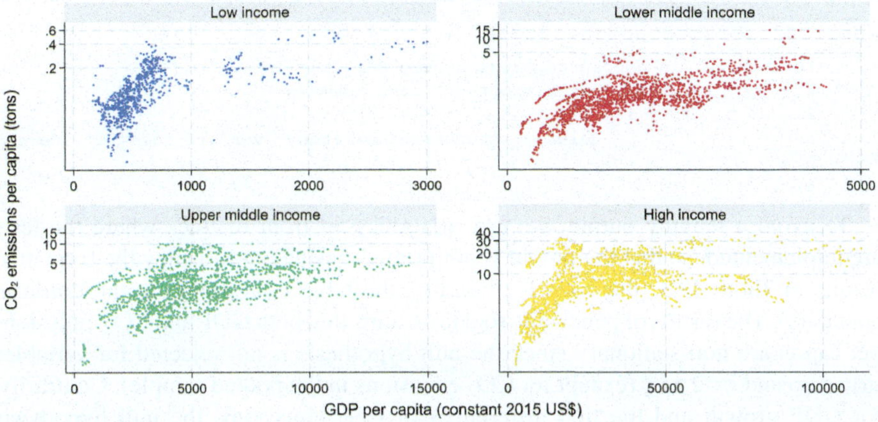

Fig. 18.10 Relationship between CO_2 emissions per capita and GDP per capita by income group from 1981 to 2021

Figure 18.10 is consistent with previous findings and looks globally consistent with the EKC hypothesis: for the least-developed countries, there seems to be a positive relationship between GDP and emissions, while the relationship flattens or even reverses for the most-developed ones.

We now turn to the econometric analysis for a formal assessment of these relationships.

18.3.5 Panel Unit-Root Tests

In order to investigate panel data stationarity, several panel unit-root tests exist, most of which are implemented in Stata command `xtunitroot`. Hlouskova and Wagner (2006) provide practical guidance about which one should be preferred in which context. In our case, with a relatively large number of panels (countries) compared to the number of time periods, we use Harris and Tzavalis (1999) test (thereafter HT), which assumes that T is fixed, whereas N goes to infinity and has favorable size and power properties for N greater than 25. When decomposing the dataset into income groups, the number of panels in each subsample, however, becomes smaller than the number of periods, except for the high-income group. For the income groups, we therefore implement Breitung's (2001) test (thereafter Br), which has good power, even with small datasets.

Both HT and Br tests are unit-root tests (as opposed to stationarity tests), in the sense that their null hypothesis is that panels contain a unit root (i.e., they are non-stationary) and their alternative hypothesis is that panels are stationary.

We apply the unit-root tests systematically to GDP per capita, GDP growth, CO_2 emissions, and the first differences of CO_2 emissions per capita. All tests are run within a double loop, over the variables and the income groups[15]:

```
. foreach var in gdpcap gdpcapgr co2cap D.co2cap {
  2.         quietly: xtunitroot ht `var', demean
  3.         forv i = 1/4 {
  4.                 quietly: xtunitroot breitung `var' if inc==`i', demean
  5.         }
  6. }
```

To avoid a lengthy output, we use `quietly` in front of lines where the tests are implemented, so that the output is not printed. Instead, we display the formatted results in Table 18.3 (the code for building the table is available in the dofile in appendix). The results of panel unit-root tests show that both GDP and CO_2 emissions per capita are non-stationary since the null hypothesis is not rejected for variables `gdpcap` and `co2cap` (except for CO_2 emissions in the pooled sample). Contrarily, for GDP growth and the first differences of CO_2 emissions, the null hypothesis is strongly rejected for all income groups. We therefore proceed with the Granger causality analysis using these two stationary variables.

18.3.6 Granger Causality Tests

We investigate the causal relationships (in the sense of Granger) between the annual growth rate of GDP per capita (`gdpcapgr`) and the yearly changes in CO_2 emissions per capita (`D.co2cap`). Ex-ante, the direction of causality between these two variables is not obvious (see for instance Payne and Taylor 2010). It is possible that greater economic growth leads to an increase or, on the contrary, to a decrease of CO_2 emissions. Conversely, more CO_2 emissions may cause greater economic growth as energy consumption is used in the production processes as a complement to capital and labor. Bidirectional causality between the two variables (called feedback) or absence of causal relationships (called neutrality) is also possible.

To unravel which of these relationships prevail, we implement a series of Granger causality tests from GDP to CO_2 emissions and in the opposite direction. We make use of Stata community-contributed commands `xtgcause` (Lopez and Weber 2017), which implements Dumitrescu and Hurlin's (2012) test, and `xtgrangert` (Xiao

---

[15] We use the `demean` option, which implements a procedure suggested by Levin et al. (2002) to mitigate the impact of cross-sectional dependence.

Table 18.3 Unit-root tests

Variable	Test	Income group	*N*	*T*	Statistic	P-value
gdpcap	*HT*	Pooled sample	130	41	0.965	1.000
gdpcap	*Br*	Low income	18	41	4.364	1.000
gdpcap	*Br*	Lower middle income	35	41	8.513	1.000
gdpcap	*Br*	Upper middle income	36	41	7.153	1.000
gdpcap	*Br*	High income	41	41	9.373	1.000
gdpcapgr	*HT*	Pooled sample	130	40	0.208	0.000
gdpcapgr	*Br*	Low income	18	40	−11.951	0.000
gdpcapgr	*Br*	Lower middle income	35	40	−9.429	0.000
gdpcapgr	*Br*	Upper middle income	36	40	−12.552	0.000
gdpcapgr	*Br*	High income	41	40	−10.459	0.000
co2cap	*HT*	Pooled sample	130	41	0.912	0.007
co2cap	*Br*	Low income	18	41	0.161	0.564
co2cap	*Br*	Lower middle income	35	41	2.478	0.993
co2cap	*Br*	Upper middle income	36	41	2.377	0.991
co2cap	*Br*	High income	41	41	2.286	0.989
D.co2cap	*HT*	Pooled sample	130	40	−0.073	0.000
D.co2cap	*Br*	Low income	18	40	−14.947	0.000
D.co2cap	*Br*	Lower middle income	35	40	−19.506	0.000
D.co2cap	*Br*	Upper middle income	36	40	−19.094	0.000
D.co2cap	*Br*	High income	41	40	−16.469	0.000

et al. 2023), which implements Juodis et al.'s (2021) test. The null hypothesis of both tests is that there is no Granger causality from the independent variable (thereafter the X variable) toward the dependent variable (thereafter the Y variable). If the null hypothesis is rejected, then X is said to Granger-cause Y.

We investigate Granger causality systematically for the pooled sample and each income group:

```
. xtgcause gdpcapgr D.co2cap if t>=1982, lag(bic 4)

Dumitrescu & Hurlin (2012) Granger non-causality test results:
--------------------------------------------------------------
Optimal number of lags (BIC): 1 (lags tested: 1 to 4).
W-bar =           1.3957
Z-bar =           3.1781    (p-value = 0.0015)
Z-bar tilde =     2.4434    (p-value = 0.0145)
--------------------------------------------------------------
H0: D.co2cap does not Granger-cause gdpcapgr.
H1: D.co2cap does Granger-cause gdpcapgr for at least one panel (c).

. xtgrangert gdpcapgr D.co2cap, maxlags(4)

Juodis, Karavias and Sarafidis (2021) Granger non-causality Test
-------------------------------------------------------------------------------
Number of units= 129                          Obs. per unit (T) = 36
Number of lags = 4                            BIC               = 12690.67
-------------------------------------------------------------------------------
JKS non-causality test

H0: D.co2cap does not Granger-cause gdpcapgr.
H1: D.co2cap does Granger-cause gdpcapgr for at least one panelvar.

HPJ Wald test   : 1.1083
p-value         : 0.8930
-------------------------------------------------------------------------------
BIC selection:
    lags = 1, BIC = 15343.65
    lags = 2, BIC = 14468.311
    lags = 3, BIC = 13596.073
    lags = 4, BIC = 12690.671*
-------------------------------------------------------------------------------
                Results for the Half-Panel Jackknife estimator

--------------------------------------------------------------------------------
             | Coefficient  Std. err.      z    P>|z|     [95% conf. interval]
-------------+------------------------------------------------------------------
      co2cap |
         LD. |  -.0479282   .1297778    -0.37   0.712     -.302288    .2064317
        L2D. |  -.0602669   .1291813    -0.47   0.641    -.3134575    .1929237
        L3D. |   .0985244   .1247556     0.79   0.430    -.1459921    .3430409
        L4D. |   .0224909   .1231571     0.18   0.855    -.2188927    .2638744
--------------------------------------------------------------------------------

. quietly: xtgcause D.co2cap gdpcapgr if t>=1982, lag(bic 4)

. quietly: xtgrangert D.co2cap gdpcapgr, maxlags(4)

. forvalues i = 1/4 {
  2.         quietly: xtgcause gdpcapgr D.co2cap if t>=1982 & inc==`i´, lag(bic 4)
  3.         quietly: xtgrangert gdpcapgr D.co2cap if inc==`i´, maxlags(4)
  4.         quietly: xtgcause D.co2cap gdpcapgr if t>=1982 & inc==`i´, lag(bic 4)
  5.         quietly: xtgrangert D.co2cap gdpcapgr if inc==`i´, maxlags(4)
  6. }
```

We use option `lags(bic 4)` in `xtgcause` and `maxlags(4)` in `xtgrangert` to request that the number of lags introduced in regressions (18.1)

Table 18.4 Granger causality tests (Dumitrescu and Hurlin 2012)

Y variable	X variable	Income group	Lags	$\overline{W}$	$\bar{Z}$	P-value ($\bar{Z}$)	$\widetilde{Z}$	P-value ($\widetilde{Z}$)
D.co2cap	gdpcapgr	Pooled sample	1	1.484	3.900	0.000	3.093	0.002
D.co2cap	gdpcapgr	Low income	1	1.573	1.719	0.086	1.393	0.164
D.co2cap	gdpcapgr	Lower middle income	1	1.415	1.735	0.083	1.345	0.179
D.co2cap	gdpcapgr	Upper middle income	1	1.814	3.453	0.001	2.893	0.004
D.co2cap	gdpcapgr	High income	1	1.214	0.967	0.334	0.633	0.527
gdpcapgr	D.co2cap	Pooled sample	1	1.380	3.067	0.002	2.342	0.019
gdpcapgr	D.co2cap	Low income	1	1.221	0.663	0.507	0.439	0.660
gdpcapgr	D.co2cap	Lower middle income	1	1.403	1.684	0.092	1.299	0.194
gdpcapgr	D.co2cap	Upper middle income	1	1.323	1.369	0.171	1.011	0.312
gdpcapgr	D.co2cap	High income	1	1.482	2.183	0.029	1.731	0.083

be chosen such that the average Bayesian information criterion is minimized among all models that enclose between 1 and 4 lags. The output is only displayed for the first test with each command; we added `quietly` for the other tests in order to save space and we display all results more compactly in Tables 18.4 and 18.5.

The results show strong evidence in favor of Granger causality from GDP growth toward CO_2 emissions. For all groups of countries and all tests (except for high-income countries in Table 18.4), the null hypothesis of non-causality is indeed rejected at the 10% level and often with very small p-values.

The relationships from CO_2 emissions toward GDP growth are more contrasted. For the pooled sample, we obtain a significant causality with Dumitrescu and Hurlin's (2012) test, but not with Juodis et al.'s (2021) test. The results are not significant, at least for one of the two tests, for the first three income groups. For high-income countries, there is concordance between the two tests, which both reject the null hypothesis of non-causality.

Overall, Granger causality tests show that the relationships between GDP growth and CO_2 emissions differ across income groups, thereby bringing some support in

Table 18.5 Granger causality tests (Judois et al. 2021)

Y variable	*X* variable	Income group	Lags	*W*	P-value
D.co2cap	gdpcapgr	Pooled sample	2	62.003	0.000
D.co2cap	gdpcapgr	Low income	1	5.536	0.019
D.co2cap	gdpcapgr	Lower middle income	2	12.758	0.002
D.co2cap	gdpcapgr	Upper middle income	1	116.086	0.000
D.co2cap	gdpcapgr	High income	4	18.264	0.001
gdpcapgr	D.co2cap	Pooled sample	4	1.107	0.893
gdpcapgr	D.co2cap	Low income	4	5.406	0.248
gdpcapgr	D.co2cap	Lower middle income	4	3.782	0.436
gdpcapgr	D.co2cap	Upper middle income	4	8.940	0.063
gdpcapgr	D.co2cap	High income	4	7.966	0.093

favor of the EKC hypothesis. While the results are not very robust, there is evidence of a unidirectional causality from economic growth to CO_2 emissions for the three lowest income groups, while causality seems to be running in the opposite direction for the highest income group. Moreover, note that only the direction of the (Granger) causality has been determined; whether the effect of one variable on the other is positive or negative is not assessed using this simple analysis and one should implement further analyses if these aspects are to be investigated.

18.4 Summary

Granger (1969) proposed an operational definition of causality for time series that relies on fairly simple and intuitive regression analyses. With organizations such as the World Bank or OECD collecting data for wide sets of countries over long periods, Granger causality can now also be applied in the context of panel data. Given its simplicity, the concept of Granger causality is very popular and frequently used in applied research. Yet, there are a number of challenging steps that must be implemented during such an analysis and the results are not always straightforward to interpret. In particular, as with time series, stationarity problems arise in long panel data so the implementation of unit-root or stationarity tests is necessary.

This chapter shows how to implement Granger causality in panel datasets using data freely available from World Bank and Climate Watch. The emphasis is placed on the empirical exercise and on the reproducibility of the analyses. Using econometric software Stata, a dataset containing GDP growth and CO_2 emissions for 130 countries over 1981–2021 is built and investigated. All codes allowing to download the data and implement the analyses are provided and explained in intuitive terms. By reusing and adapting the codes enclosed here, practitioners of various fields should find useful elements for their own research.

References

Atukeren E (2008) Christmas cards, Easter bunnies, and Granger-causality. Qual Quant 42(6):835–844. https://doi.org/10.1007/s11135-007-9078-2

Azevedo JP (2011) Wbopendata: stata module to access World Bank databases. Statistical Software Components S457234, Boston College Department of Economics. https://ideas.repec.org/c/boc/bocode/s457234.html

Baltagi BH (2005) Econometric analysis of panel data, 5th edn. Wiley, UK

Baum CF, Hurn S, Otero J (2022) Testing for time-varying granger causality. Stata J 22(2):355–378. https://doi.org/10.1177/1536867X221106403

Breitung J (2001) The local power of some unit root tests for panel data. In: Baltagi B, Fomby T, Carter Hill R (eds) Nonstationary panels, panel cointegration, and dynamic panels, advances in econometrics, vol 15. Emerald Group Publishing Limited, Bingley, pp 161–177, https://doi.org/10.1016/S0731-9053(00)15006-6

Chang T, Cheng SC, Pan G, pao Wu T, (2013) Does globalization affect the insurance markets? bootstrap panel granger causality test. Econ Model 33:254–260. https://doi.org/10.1016/j.econmod.2013.04.008

Cox NJ (2009) Speaking stata: creating and varying box plots. Stata J 9(3):478–496. https://doi.org/10.1177/1536867X0900900309

Dumitrescu EI, Hurlin C (2012) Testing for Granger non-causality in heterogeneous panels. Econ Model 29(4):1450–1460. https://doi.org/10.1016/j.econmod.2012.02.014

Granger CW (1969) Investigating causal relations by econometric models and cross-spectral methods. Econometrica 37(3):424–438. https://doi.org/10.2307/1912791

Granger CW (1980) Testing for causality: a personal viewpoint. J Econ Dyn Control 2:329–352. https://doi.org/10.1016/0165-1889(80)90069-X

Granger CW (1988) Some recent development in a concept of causality. J Econom 39(1–2):199–211. https://doi.org/10.1016/0304-4076(88)90045-0

Grossman GM, Krueger AB (1995) Economic growth and the environment. Q J Econ 110(2):353–377. https://doi.org/10.2307/2118443

Hadri K (2000) Testing for stationarity in heterogeneous panel data. Econom J 3(2):148–161. https://doi.org/10.1111/1368-423X.00043

Harris RD, Tzavalis E (1999) Inference for unit roots in dynamic panels where the time dimension is fixed. J Econom 91(2):201–226. https://doi.org/10.1016/S0304-4076(98)00076-1

Hlouskova J, Wagner M (2006) The performance of panel unit root and stationarity tests: results from a large scale simulation study. Econom Rev 25(1):85–116. https://doi.org/10.1080/07474930500545504

Hsiao C (2005) Analysis of panel data, 2nd ed. Cambridge University Press

Im KS, Pesaran M, Shin Y (2003) Testing for unit roots in heterogeneous panels. J Econom 115(1):53–74. https://doi.org/10.1016/S0304-4076(03)00092-7

Iwata H, Okada K, Samreth S (2010) Empirical study on the environmental Kuznets curve for CO_2 in France: the role of nuclear energy. Energy Policy 38(8):4057–4063. https://doi.org/10.1016/j.enpol.2010.03.031

Jalil A, Rao NH (2019) Time series analysis (stationarity, cointegration, and causality). In: Özcan B, Öztürk I (eds) Environmental Kuznets curve (EKC). Academic Press, Chap 8, pp 85–99. https://doi.org/10.1016/B978-0-12-816797-7.00008-4

Juodis A, Karavias Y, Sarafidis V (2021) A homogeneous approach to testing for Granger non-causality in heterogeneous panels. Empir Econ 60(1):93–112. https://doi.org/10.1007/s00181-020-01970-9

Keshavarzian M, Tabatabaienasab Z (2021) Application of bootstrap panel Granger causality test in determining the relationship between renewable and non-renewable energy consumption and economic growth: a case study of OPEC countries. Technol Econ Smart Grids Sustain Energy 10(1):10. https://doi.org/10.1007/s40866-021-00106-x

Kónya L (2006) Exports and growth: granger causality analysis on OECD countries with a panel data approach. Econ Model 23(6):978–992. https://doi.org/10.1016/j.econmod.2006.04.008

Kuznets S (1955) Economic growth and income inequality. Am Econ Rev 45(1):1–28. http://www.jstor.org/stable/1811581

Levin A, Lin CF, Chu CSJ (2002) Unit root tests in panel data: asymptotic and finite-sample properties. J Econom 108(1):1–24. https://doi.org/10.1016/S0304-4076(01)00098-7

Lindsley E (2012) INSHEETJSON: stata module for importing tabular data from JSON sources on the internet. Statistical Software Components s457407, Boston College Department of Economics. https://ideas.repec.org/c/boc/bocode/s457407.html

Lopez L, Weber S (2017) Testing for Granger causality in panel data. Stata J 17(4):972–984. https://doi.org/10.1177/1536867X1801700412

Maddala G, Kim IM (2004) Unit roots, cointegration, and structural change, 6th edn. Cambridge University Press

Minlah MK, Zhang X (2021) Testing for the existence of the Environmental Kuznets Curve (EKC) for CO_2 emissions in Ghana: evidence from the bootstrap rolling window Granger causality test. Environ Sci Pollut Res 28(2):2119–2131. https://doi.org/10.1007/s11356-020-10600-x

Payne JE, Taylor JP (2010) Nuclear energy consumption and economic growth in the US: an empirical note. Energy Sour Part B: Econ Plan Policy 5(3):301–307. https://doi.org/10.1080/15567240802533955

Pesaran MH (2007) A simple panel unit root test in the presence of cross-section dependence. J Appl Econom 22(2):265–312. https://doi.org/10.1002/jae.951

Stern DI (2004) The environmental Kuznets curve. In: Cleveland CJ (ed) Encyclopedia of energy, vol 2. Elsevier, New York, pp 517–525. https://doi.org/10.1016/B0-12-176480-X/00454-X

Usman O, Iorember PT, Olanipekun IO (2019) Revisiting the Environmental Kuznets Curve (EKC) hypothesis in India: the effects of energy consumption and democracy. Environ Sci Pollut Res 26(13):13390–13400. https://doi.org/10.1007/s11356-019-04696-z

Xiao J, Karavias Y, Juodis A, Sarafidis V, Ditzen J (2023) Improved tests for granger noncausality in panel data. Stata J 23(1):230–242. https://doi.org/10.1177/1536867X231162034

Zellner A (1962) An efficient method of estimating seemingly unrelated regressions and tests for aggregation bias. J Am Stat Assoc 57(298):348–368. https://doi.org/10.1080/01621459.1962.10480664

Chapter 19
Panel Count Data Models: Examining Dengue Incidence in Malaysia

Wan Fairos Wan Yaacob, Nik Nur Fatin Fatihah Sapri, and Yap Bee Wah

Abstract Understanding the discrete non-negative nature of count data is important for econometricians to model panel count data type. Panel count data is one of the nonlinear data type where the underlying assumption of a linear model to follow normal distribution is not appropriate. The Poisson distribution and its extensions are more suitable to provide the basis for modeling count and panel count data. The generalized linear model (GLM) is widely used for count data as these models fulfilled the statistical properties of such data that is it follows the exponential family distribution. However, if the count data type is repeated over individuals and nested in time period and known as panel data, the fixed effects Poisson and Negative Binomial Generalized Linear Model (GLM) is more appropriate choice to model panel count data. When there exists unobserved heterogeneity caused by spatial and temporal variability within the individuals, the fixed effects are replaced by the random effects in the GLM model. The random effects model allows the model to vary across individuals and time within the same group. Specifically, the negative binomial random effects model can effectively manage the unobserved heterogeneity and over-dispersion in the panel data. Thus, econometricians may consider several options of the fixed effects or the random effects of generalized linear model (GLM) to model panel count data. This chapter also discusses different types of panel count

W. F. W. Yaacob (✉)
Mathematical Sciences Studies, College of Computing, Informatics and Media, Universiti Teknologi MARA Cawangan Kelantan, Kampus Kota Bharu, 15050 Kota Bharu, Kelantan, Malaysia
e-mail: wnfairos@uitm.edu.my

Institute for Big Data Analytics and Artificial Intselligence (IBDAAI), Kompleks Al-Khawarizmi, Universiti Teknologi MARA, 40450 Shah Alam, Selangor, Malaysia

N. N. F. F. Sapri
Mathematical Sciences Studies, College of Computing, Informatics and Media, Universiti Teknologi MARA 40450 Shah Alam, Shah Alam, Selangor, Malaysia
e-mail: nikfatinfatihah@uitm.edu.my

Y. B. Wah
UNITAR International University, Tierra Crest, Jalan SS6/3, Kelana Jaya, 47301 Petaling Jaya, Selangor, Malaysia
e-mail: bee.wah@unitar.my

D. Mukherjee (ed.), *Applied Econometric Analysis Using Cross Section and Panel Data*, Contributions to Economics, https://doi.org/10.1007/978-981-99-4902-1_19

data models involving fixed effects and random effects of GLM models with an application to dengue disease panel count data. Other variants of dynamic panel count model and multivariate panel count model for multiple counts are also discussed in this recent development.

19.1 Introduction

Count data encountered in almost all areas of research including, economics, medicine, management, industrial organizations, and many more. Examples of count data include the number of dengue cases, the number of road accidents on a particular highway in a specified period of time, the number of insurance claims paid by an insurance company in a year, etc. (Ahmed et al. 2015; Cameron and Trivedi 1998; Choi et al. 2016; Hausman et al. 1984; Radin et al. 1996). In the context of modeling discrete, non-negative integer nature of count data, the use of least square regression models suffers several methodological limitations and statistical properties (Miaou and Lum, 1993; Karlaftis and Tarko 1998; Shankar et al. 1995). In contrast with the classical linear regression model, the Generalized Linear Models for counts are suitable with properties for the response variable that relate to discreteness, nonlinearity and deal with non-negative values. Thus, in statistical modeling, it is important to understand the type of count data whether it is cross-sectional, time series, or panel count data type. The organization of the chapter is as follows. Section 19.2 gives an overview of count models and extensions to panel count models. This is followed by the basic count model in Sect. 19.3. The discussion on FE and RE of the GLM panel count model is in Sects. 19.4 and 19.5 respectively. Sections 19.11 and 19.12 illustrates the practical application of GLM for both fixed effects and random effects model in modeling dengue incidence data using R and Stata.

19.2 Overview of Count Model and Its Extension to Panel Count Model

In statistical modeling of cross-sectional count data, the Poisson regression model of Generalized Linear Model (McCullagh and Nelder 1981) is a good starting point as it suits well with the discrete nature properties of count data (Chin and Quddus 2003; Shankar et al. 1995; Yap et al. 2012). The Poisson regression model is often used as the benchmark model for count data that takes integer values $y = 0, 1, 2, 3$ (McCullagh and Nelder 1986; Yaacob et al. 2012; Oppong et al. 2017. Despite the advantages highlighted, the Poisson model assumes equality of mean and variance of the response variable. When this assumption is violated, and if the variance of the observed counts exceeds the mean, there is the problem of "overdispersion." Overdispersion could lead to invalid test statistics due to biased standard errors as the standard errors of estimates may be deflated or underestimated. One of the approaches to address this issue is to use the Quasi-Likelihood estimation technique proposed by Wedderburn (1974). With the Quasi-Poisson model, the standard Poisson regression model is adjusted to estimate an additional dispersion parameter. The parameter estimates of the quasi-Poisson model are the same as that of the standard Poisson model. However, the standard errors are adjusted (increased), by multiplying the covariance matrix of the parameters by the value of the over-dispersion parameter.

Alternatively, one can also use the Negative Binomial (NB) regression model which is the generalization and extension of the Poisson-gamma regression model (Ahmed et al. 2015; Agresti 2003; Cameron and Trivedi 1998, 2005; Lee et al., 2015; Lowe et al. 2011; Oppong et al. 2017; Yaacob et al. 2010; Yap et al. 2012; Zhang et al. 2016). The NB model addresses the issue of overdispersion by introducing a dispersion parameter to accommodate for unobserved heterogeneity in count data.

Unlike the Poisson distribution, the variance of negative binomial distribution exceeds its mean. Besides the problem of overdispersion, it is also common in real life count data to exhibit excess zeros. This allows for another extension of Inflated Poisson model. While the negative binomial model can deal with overdispersion, the Hurdle and Zero-inflated Poisson and Negative Binomial Regression models can be used to handle excess zeros in their own way. In almost all practical cases, the count data are skewed, non-negative, overdispersed, and have excess zeros. These features have motivated the application of various extension methods and models for count data regressions.

For a case of time series count data type, it demands one to deal with the discreteness as well as its time series properties. As pointed by Cameron and Trivedi (1998), when a count dataset exhibits time dependence the benchmark Poisson regression is not adequate. The main issues of time series data are autocorrelation and a common feature of count data is overdispersion where variance is larger than the mean. Both autocorrelation and overdispersion can be addressed simultaneously using Integer autoregressive conditional Poisson or Negative Binomial model or other alternatives of time series models for count. In this model, the count is assumed to follow Poisson distribution and their mean, conditional on the past observation is autoregressive. Thus, conditional on the past observation, the model variance is equal to the mean.

Alternatively, if we have a combination of cross section and time series count data (panel count data), the appropriate panel count model to be used are the fixed effects and random effects of Poisson or Negative Binomial model. This model can handle the assumption of independent (or at least uncorrelated) observations in the standard Poisson GLMs which may not be valid. There could be strong temporal correlation effects within some area and there could also be spatial clustering effects in neighboring microregions. Hence, the FE and RE can allow for such latent effects and correlation structures.

Most of the literatures on panel count model include the fixed and random effects model beginning with the seminal work of Hausman et al. (1984). However, currently the random effects model has been refined by introducing the combination of unstructured and spatio-temporal structured random effects model via a Bayesian framework using Markov Chain Monte Carlo which can be explored further. This offers an extension of the FE and RE of NB GLM which can be modeled using Generalized Linear Mixed Model (GLMM).

In summary, Fig. 19.1 provides a count data model framework ranging from simple count GLM models to time series count model and panel model and extensions of GLMM models. The choice of models depends on the count data types. This chapter focused on panel count data with illustration on modeling dengue incidence data using Random Effects GLMM model.

19.3 Generalized Linear Model

This chapter begins with the basic concept of generalized linear model (GLM). GLM is essentially an extension of classical general linear models. The GLM model was first introduced by Nelder and Wedderburn (1972) and later described in detail by McCullagh and Nelder (1984).

There are three important components in the GLM:

(i) the first is the *random component* which specifies the conditional distribution of $Y_i (i = 1, 2, \ldots, n)$ given the explanatory variables in the model. In the original formulation by Nelder and Wedderburn, the distribution of Y_i is from the natural exponential family distribution such as Gaussian, binomial, Poisson, gamma, or inverse-Gaussian families of distribution. The binomial distribution is used for modeling a categorical response variable with values 0 or 1. While the Poisson distribution is used for modeling count data. The gamma and inverse-Gaussian distributions are for modeling positive continuous response variable. The GLMs has been extended to multivariate families (multinomial distribution) to certain non-exponential family of distributions.

(ii) The *systematic component* which is usually a linear function of the explanatory variables such as $\beta_o + \beta_1 X_{i1} + \beta_2 X_{i2} + \cdots + \beta_k X_{ik}$

(iii) The *link function* g(.) that links both random and systematic component,

$$g(\mu_i) = \eta_i = \beta_o + \beta_1 X_{i1} + \beta_2 X_{i2} + \cdots + \beta_k X_{ik}$$

To illustrate the formulation of the GLM model, one needs to understand the standard general linear model. An example is the multiple linear regression model in matrix notation (Montgomery et al. 2001) which is given by:

$$\boldsymbol{Y} = \boldsymbol{X\beta} + \boldsymbol{\varepsilon} \tag{19.1}$$

where $\boldsymbol{Y}$ is a (n × 1) vector of responses, $\boldsymbol{X}$ is a (n x p) matrix of constant and $\boldsymbol{\varepsilon}$ is a vector of independent random error terms with expectation $\boldsymbol{E}\{\boldsymbol{\varepsilon}\} = 0$ and variance co-variance matrix of

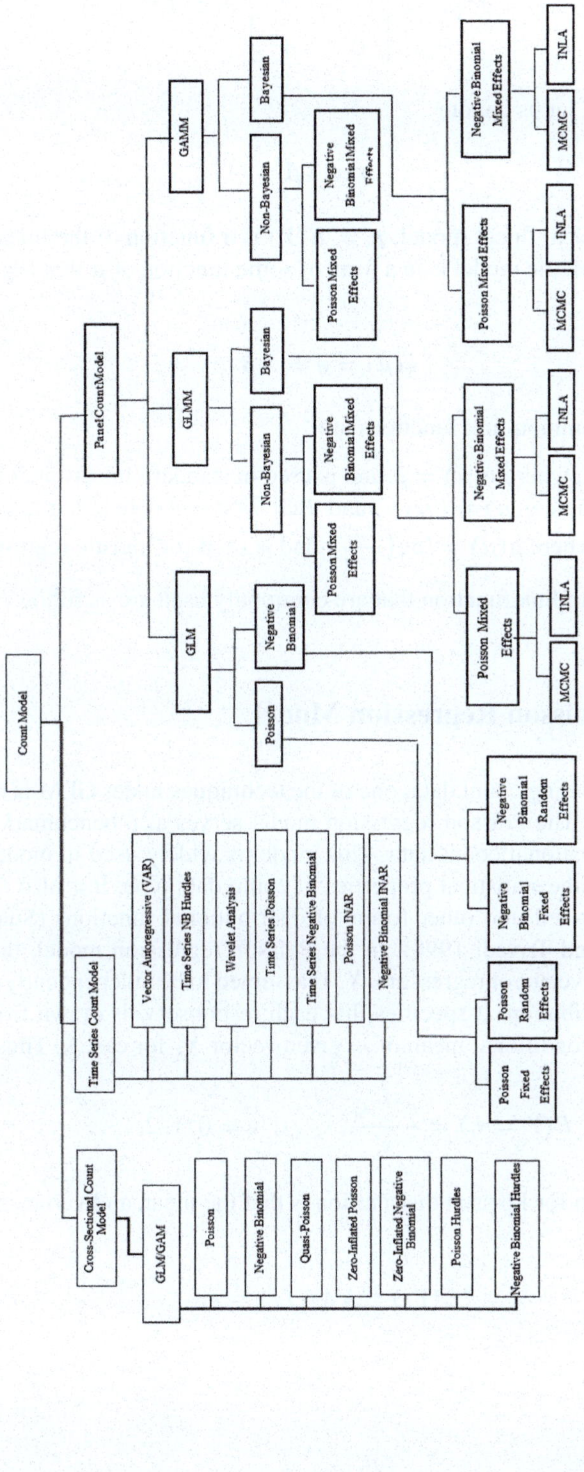

Fig. 19.1 Count data model framework and its extension

$$\sigma^2\{\varepsilon\} = \begin{bmatrix} \sigma^2 & \cdots & 0 \\ \vdots & \ddots & \vdots \\ 0 & \cdots & \sigma^2 \end{bmatrix} = \sigma^2 \boldsymbol{I}$$

From Eq. 19.1, let us denote

$$\eta = \boldsymbol{X\beta}$$

where in the classical linear model, $\boldsymbol{\mu} = \boldsymbol{E(Y)}$ is a function of the linear predictor $\boldsymbol{X\beta}$**,** while in GLM, the model is in a form of some function of $\boldsymbol{\mu}$ that is given by the link function,

$$g(\boldsymbol{\mu}) = \eta = \boldsymbol{X\beta} \tag{19.2}$$

Some of the common link functions are:

(i) Identity link, where $g(\mu) = \mu$ and is used in standard linear models.
(ii) Log link, where $g(\mu) = log(\mu)$ and used for count data in log linear models.
(iii) Logit link, where $g(\mu) = log\left(\frac{\mu}{1-\mu}\right)$ and is used for logistic regression.

The examples of link function that are commonly used are as follows:

19.4 Basic Poisson Regression Model

Focussing on modeling count data, one of the techniques under GLM is the Poisson regression model. The Poisson regression model serves as a benchmark model for modeling cross-sectional count data. This model is widely used in modeling count data as it fulfilled the statistical properties of count data type. It is also flexible and can be reparametrized into other forms of distributional functions (Shanker et al. 1995; Cameron and Trivedi 1998). In the Poisson regression model, the response variable Y given a vector of regressors, X_k is assumed to be independently distributed with Poisson distribution. It specifies that each response y_i is drawn from Poisson distribution with conditional mean of λ_i given vector X_k for case k. Thus.

$$P(Y = y_i) = \frac{e^{-\lambda_i}\lambda_i}{y_i}, \qquad y = 0, 1, 2, \ldots, \tag{19.3}$$

The assumption for Poisson distribution is that the mean and variance are equal, that is

$$E(Yi) = Var(Yi) = \lambda_i$$

To develop a Poisson model, λ_i is expressed as a function of some explanatory variables through a log link function in the following form (Green 2008);

$$ln\,\lambda_i = X'\beta$$
$$\text{or } \lambda_i = \exp(X'\beta) \tag{19.4}$$

where $\boldsymbol{X}$ is a vector of covariates and $\boldsymbol{\beta}$ is a vector of parameters.

Note that the Poisson regression model is a generalized linear model with log link function. One unique feature of the Poisson regression model is that the conditional mean and variance is assumed to be equal. The exponential form is to ensure the parameter λ_i is non-negative. The parameter can be estimated using maximum likelihood method (Cameron and Trivedi 1998).

Although the application of the Poisson regression model is widely used for count data by econometricians, it is subject to the assumption of equality of variance and mean of the response variable. When the variance of Y is found to be larger than its expected value, an overdispersion exists. Otherwise, the Poisson model implies a property of so-called "equidispersion." When overdispersion occurs, the Poisson maximum likelihood estimator obtained from the model will be inaccurate (Cameron and Trivedi 1998; Cameron and Trivedi 2005). If this assumption is violated, it also leads to biasedness in the estimation of the standard error and this will produce incorrect test statistics (Shankar et al. 1995; Miaou 1994). Several alternative models have been proposed to correct overdispersion. Among which are the Quasi-Poisson estimation and the NB regression model. Wedderburn (1948) has developed a quasi-likelihood estimation technique to estimate parameters under the GLM model. This technique corrects for overdispersion by multiplying the standard error of the model with the dispersion parameter value. McCullagh and Nelder (1989) suggested estimating the ratio of the deviance or the Pearson Chi-Square to its degree of freedom. This treatment will not give any change to parameter estimates or intercept but their standard errors will be corrected thus giving wider confidence interval and higher p-value. Various studies have employed this conventional Quasi-Poisson technique to correct for overdispersion problem (Breslow 1984; Radin et al. 1996).

Another alternative that can be used to model overdispersion is the Negative Binomial (NB) model. Several researchers (Miaou 1994; Kumara and Chin 1995; Shankar et al. 1995) have employed the NB model to relax for overdispersion. This was done by introducing a stochastic component into the relationship between observed count and covariates. A detailed explanation on this method will be discussed in the next section.

19.5 Negative Binomial Regression Model

Negative binomial (NB) model is an alternative to model overdispersion Poisson model. It is an extension of Poisson models that allow the variance of the dependent variable to differ from the mean. The combination of Gamma and Poisson distributions that form a Negative Binomial distribution is well known (Cameron and Trivedi 1998; Hilbe 2011).

The standard negative binomial model is termed as the NB2 model (Cameron and Trivedi 1998) due to quadratic nature of its variance function, $\mu + \alpha\mu^2$. While the NB1 appears to have variance function of $\mu + \alpha\mu$. Let's see the derivation of NB2 model. To show the derivation of the NB2 model as a Poisson-gamma mixture model, we begin with conditional mean of a Poisson model as below;

$$E[y_i|\boldsymbol{x}_i, \boldsymbol{\varepsilon}_i] = exp\left(\boldsymbol{\alpha} + \boldsymbol{X}'\boldsymbol{\beta} + \boldsymbol{\varepsilon}_i\right) = \mu_i\lambda_i \tag{19.5}$$

where $\mu_i = exp(\boldsymbol{\varepsilon}_i)$ is assumed to have a one parameter distribution of $\mu_i \sim Gamma(v, v)$ with mean 1 and variance $1/v$ (Cameron and Trivedi, 2011). Thus, the unconditional distribution (or marginal distribution) of Y is;

$$\begin{aligned} f(y) &= \int_0^\infty f(y_i : \lambda, \mu) \cdot g(\mu_i) d\mu_i \\ &= \int_0^\infty \frac{e^{-\lambda\mu_i}(\lambda\mu_i)^{y_i}}{y_i!} \cdot g(\mu_i) d\mu_i \end{aligned} \tag{19.6}$$

By defining $g(\mu_i)$ as gamma distribution with mean of 1, that is $\mu_i \sim Gamma(v, v)$,

$$\begin{aligned} f(y) &= \int_0^\infty \frac{e^{-\lambda_i\mu_i}(\lambda_i\mu_i)^{y_i}}{y_i!} \cdot \frac{v^v}{\Gamma(v)} \mu_i^{v-1} e^{-v\mu_i} d\mu_i \\ &= \frac{\lambda_i^{y_i}}{\Gamma(y_i+1)} \cdot \frac{v^v}{\Gamma(v)} \int_0^\infty e^{-(\lambda_i\mu_i)} \cdot e^{-v\mu_i} \mu_i^{y_i} \mu_i^{v-1} d\mu_i \\ &= \frac{\lambda_i^{y_i}}{\Gamma(y_i+1)} \cdot \frac{v^v}{\Gamma(v)} \int_0^\infty e^{-(\lambda_i+v)\mu_i} \cdot \mu_i^{(y_i+v)-1} d\mu_i \\ &= \frac{\lambda_i^{y_i}}{\Gamma(y_i+1)} \cdot \frac{v^v}{\Gamma(v)} \cdot \frac{\Gamma(y_i+v)}{(\lambda_i+v)^{y_i+v}} \underbrace{\int_0^\infty \frac{(\lambda_i+v)^{v_i+v}}{\Gamma(y_i+v)} \mu_i^{(y_i+v)-1} e^{-(\lambda_i+v)\mu_i} d\mu_i}_{1} \\ &= \frac{\lambda_i^{y_i}}{\Gamma(y_i+1)} \cdot \frac{v^v}{\Gamma(v)} \cdot \frac{\Gamma(y_i+v)}{(\lambda_i+v)^{y_i+v}} \end{aligned} \tag{19.7}$$

From Eq. 19.7, the probability density function for NB2 was obtained as follows:

$$
\begin{aligned}
f(y;\lambda,\nu) &= \frac{\lambda_i^{y_i}}{\Gamma(y_i+1)}\cdot\frac{\nu^{\nu}}{\Gamma(\nu)}\cdot\Gamma(y_i+\nu)\left(\frac{1}{(\lambda_i+\nu)^{y_i+\nu}}\right)\\
&= \frac{\lambda_i^{y_i}}{\Gamma(y_i+1)}\cdot\frac{\nu^{\nu}}{\Gamma(\nu)}\cdot\Gamma(y_i+\nu)\left(\frac{1}{(\lambda_i+\nu)^{y_i}}\right)\left(\frac{1}{(\lambda_i+\nu)^{\nu}}\right)\\
&= \frac{\Gamma(y_i+\nu)}{\Gamma(y_i+1)\Gamma(\nu)}\cdot\left(\frac{\nu^{\nu}}{(\lambda_i+\nu)^{\nu}}\right)\left(\frac{\lambda_i^{y_i}}{(\lambda_i+\nu)^{y_i}}\right)\\
&= \frac{\Gamma(y_i+\nu)}{\Gamma(y_i+1)\Gamma(\nu)}\left(\frac{\nu}{\lambda_i+\nu}\right)^{\nu}\left(\frac{\lambda_i}{\lambda_i+\nu}\right)^{y_i}\\
&= \frac{\Gamma(y_i+\nu)}{\Gamma(y_i+1)\Gamma(\nu)}\left(\frac{1}{1+{}^{\lambda_i}/_{\nu}}\right)^{\nu}\left(1-\frac{1}{1+{}^{\lambda_i}/_{\nu}}\right)^{y_i} \qquad (19.8)
\end{aligned}
$$

Equation 19.8 is a form of negative binomial distribution. By inverting ν the gamma scale parameter, gives α the negative binomial overdispersion parameter and equating $\lambda = \mu$, we will get

$$
\begin{aligned}
f(y;\mu,\alpha) &= \frac{\Gamma(y_i+\nu)}{\Gamma(y_i+1)\Gamma(\nu)}\left(\frac{1}{1+\mu_i/(1/\alpha)}\right)^{\frac{1}{\alpha}}\left(1-\frac{1}{1+\mu_i/(1/\alpha)}\right)^{y_i}\\
&= \frac{\Gamma(y_i+\nu)}{\Gamma(y_i+1)\Gamma(\nu)}\left(\frac{1}{1+\alpha\mu_i}\right)^{y_i}\left(\frac{\alpha\mu_i}{1+\alpha\mu_i}\right)^{y_i} \qquad (19.9)
\end{aligned}
$$

This model is called the NEGBIN 2 (NB2) model by Cameron and Trivedi (2011). For the NB 2 model, the mean and variance are as follows;

$$E(Y_i) = \mu_i \text{ and } Var(Y_i) = \mu_i + \mu_i^2\alpha \qquad (19.10)$$

where $\alpha > 0$ is referred to as the index or dispersion parameter. This model allows for the variance to exceed the mean. Note that when α approaches 0, this model yields the Poisson model where $(Y_i) = Var(Y_i) = \mu_i$. Another form of negative binomial model is the NB1. Cameron and Trivedi re-parameterized the model such that;

$$
\begin{aligned}
Var(Y_i) &= \mu_i + \mu_i\alpha\\
&= \mu_i(1+\alpha)
\end{aligned}
$$

This form of NB1 model is not often used by the researcher as it is less flexible in capturing the variance.

19.6 Panel Count Model

Analyzing panel data is useful because it allows the researcher to sort out effects that could not be distinguished with the use of either cross-section or time series data alone (Pindyck and Rubinfeld 1998). Properly formulated pooled time series and cross-sectional approach are more superior than individual model as it takes both the historical and contemporaneous source of variance compared to estimating the equation separately which may not produce statistically optimal results and not economical. Hence, the application of panel count data has gained much attention in recent years. The pooling procedure can control for individual-specific unobservable effects that may be correlated with explanatory variables (Hausman and Taylor 1981; Hu 2002). It also allows for differences in behavior over time for a given cross-sectional unit. In the next sub section, this chapter will introduce the fixed effects, random effects, and dynamic panel count model.

19.6.1 Fixed Effects Model

In this section, we will explore the extension of univariate Poisson Count model to multivariate setting with panel count data by assuming that the data follow Poisson distribution. To illustrate the model specification for Fixed Effects Generalized Linear Model (GLM), suppose that we have panel count data for i district, each district observed a total of T_i times. Let η_{it} be the count variable for individual i at time t. Then the expected value of η_{it} is linked to asset of regressors by

$$E(\eta_i) = \tilde{\lambda}_{it} = \exp(d_i + x'_{it}\beta) = \alpha_i \lambda_{it} \tag{19.11}$$

$$i = 1, 2, \ldots, N;$$
$$t = 1, 2, \ldots, T$$

where d_i are district-specific dummies, $\alpha_i = e^{d_i}$ are the individual specific effect, x_{it} is a vector of regressors. The Fixed Effects Poisson GLM model can be used to estimate the model parameter via conditional maximum likelihood method. However, fitting Fixed Effects Poisson GLM may also result in overdispersion. Hence to explicitly allow for overdispersion in panel count model, the negative binomial Fixed Effects GLM is utilized. In this book, the FE negative binomial GLM model was illustrated using the number of dengue cases are daily figures for individual district with defined climatic characteristics. When cross-sectional heterogeneity exists, the fixed effects model is more appropriate. Based on the fixed effects negative binomial formulation of Hausman et al. (1984) the dengue model is expressed as

$$\log \lambda_{it} = \alpha_i + \beta x_{it} \tag{19.12}$$

$$i = 1, 2, ..., N;$$
$$t = 1, 2, ..., T$$

where $\lambda_{i,t}$ is the expected number of dengue in district i in day t, α_i is the fixed effects associated with i, and β vectors of parameters to be estimated for the vector of explanatory variables x_{it}. Here, the number of dengue, y_{it} for a given time period, t is assumed to follow a negative binomial distribution with parameters $\alpha_i\lambda_{it}$ and ϕ_i, where $\lambda_{it} = \exp(x'_{it}\beta)$ giving y_{it} has a mean $\alpha_i\lambda_{it}/\phi_i$ and variance $(\alpha_i\lambda_{it}/\phi_i) \times (1 + \alpha_i/\phi_i)$. This model allows the variance to be greater than mean. The parameter α_i is the individual-specific fixed effects and the parameter ϕ_i is the negative binomial overdispersion parameter which can take on any value and varies across individuals. The negative binomial mass function is given by

$$f(y_{it}) = \frac{\Gamma(\lambda_{it} + y_{it})}{\Gamma(\lambda_{it})\Gamma(y_{it} + 1)} \left(\frac{1}{1 + \frac{\alpha_i}{\varphi_i}}\right)^{\lambda_{it}} \left(\frac{\frac{\alpha_i}{\varphi_i}}{1 + \frac{\alpha_i}{\varphi_i}}\right)^{y_{it}} \tag{19.13}$$

With conditional joint density that yields the negative hypergeometric distribution. The estimation of vector $\hat{\beta}_{NBFE}$ is done using the maximum likelihood method by maximizing the log likelihood function given by

$$L_i = \sum_{i=1}^{N} \left\{ \begin{array}{l} \log\Gamma\left(\sum_{i=1}^{T}\lambda_{it}\right) + \log\Gamma\left(\sum_{i=1}^{T} y_{it} + 1\right) - \log\Gamma\left(\sum_{i=1}^{T}\lambda_{it} + \sum_{i=1}^{T} y_{it}\right) \\ + \log\Gamma\left(\sum_{i=1}^{T}\lambda_{it} + y_{it}\right) - \log\Gamma\left(\sum_{i=1}^{T}\lambda_{it}\right) - \log\Gamma\left(\sum_{i=1}^{T} y_{it} + 1\right) \end{array} \right\}. \tag{19.14}$$

19.6.2 Random Effects Model

Usually, random effects are used in the model as to encounter for such heterogeneity due to unobserved factors. It is being applied when dispersion varies randomly across groups due to unidentified factors specific to groups. In random effects approach, the individual-specific effects are assumed to be randomly distributed across individuals and independent of x_{it}. By referring to Eqs. 3.5 and 3.6, the α_i is the individual-specific random effects which is associated with district, i specified in random effects approach. Similar to fixed effects approach, let's assume the number of dengue, y_{it} for a given time period, t is assumed to follow a negative binomial distribution with parameters $\alpha_i\lambda_{it}$ and ϕ_i, where $\lambda_{it} = \exp(x'_{it}\beta)$ gives y_{it} as mean $\alpha_i\lambda_{it}/\phi_i$ and variance $(\alpha_i\lambda_{it}/\phi_i) \times (1 + \alpha_i/\phi_i)$. Hence, in order to capture the spatial variation over time, $(1 + \alpha_i/\phi_i)^{-1}$ is assumed to follow beta distribution with parameters (a, b). Then, the random effects of Negative Binomial distribution specified by Hausman et al. (1984) are as follows:

$$f(y_{it},\ldots,y_{iT}|x_{it},\ldots,x_{iT}) = \frac{\Gamma(a+b)\Gamma\left(a+\sum_t \lambda_{it}\right)\Gamma\left(b+\sum_t y_{it}\right)}{\Gamma(a)\Gamma(b)\Gamma\left(a+b+\sum_t \lambda_{it}+\sum_t y_{it}\right)} \prod_{t=1}^{T} \frac{\Gamma(\lambda_{it}+y_{it})}{\Gamma(\lambda_{it})\Gamma(y_{it}+1)} \tag{19.15}$$

Note that standard maximum likelihood is used to estimate parameters a, b, and β.

19.6.3 Goodness of Fit GLM Model

As for this chapter, a different subset of variables for model comparison will be carried out by the use of stepwise model algorithm based on Akaike Information Criteria (AIC). It measures the penalty on the likelihood for each additional term included in the model. Hence, if the extra term does not improve the likelihood more than the penalty amount, therefore, it is not worth adding into the model. The AIC equation is given as follows;

$$AIC = -2\ \ln(L)\ + 2k \tag{19.16}$$

where L is the likelihood function and k is the number of parameters in the fitted model. The model is selected according to parsimony principle. Meanwhile, Meanwhile, BIC is computed as follows;

$$BIC = \ -2\ \ln(L) + k\ \log(n) \tag{19.17}$$

where n is the sample size.

Since the study proposes to use "linear" model, the proportion of variation in the response variable which can be explained by explanatory variables, R^2 is a typical measure used as a model adequacy. As suggested in the study by Lowe (2010), the R^2 is based on decomposition of the deviance which is termed as "pseudo- R^2."

$$D' = D\ +\ \hat{D} \tag{19.18}$$

where D' is the deviance in the intercept-only model (null model), D is the deviance of fitted model and $\hat{D}$ is explained deviance. Thus, the pseudo- $R,^2$ (R_D^2) specifies as follows:

$$R_D^2 = 1 - \frac{D'}{\hat{D}} \tag{19.19}$$

where pseudo-R^2 measures the reduction in deviance due to inclusion of explanatory variables. The interpretation of R_D^2 is similar to common R^2 at which the values closer to 1 indicate a better fit.

19.6.4 Dynamic Panel Count Model

Another panel model that introduces the dependencies over time and individual-specific effects is the dynamic panel count model. This is an alternative for panel model that specifies the distribution of y_{it} to depend directly on the lagged values of y_{it} (Cameron and Trivedi 2013).

(i) Dynamic Model Specification

Let's consider the Poisson model in the time series case, where y_t follow a Poisson distribution with mean that is a function of y_{t-1} and regressors x_t. Following Cameron and Trivedi (2013), the dynamic model specification for Poisson model is that y_t is Poisson with mean $exp(\rho y_{t-1} + x_t{\prime}\beta)$. Note that when $\rho > 0$ this model will be explosive. The researcher proposed to specify the mean to be $exp(\rho ln y_{t-1} + x_t{\prime}\beta)$ instead. However, when $y_{t-1} = 0$, then y_t will be zero. Extending this specification to panel count data, we can allow both dynamic and the presence of individual-specific effects by defining the conditional mean to be;

$$\mu_{it} = E\left[y_{it}|X_i^{(t)}, Y_i^{(t-1)}, \alpha_i\right]$$

where $X_i^{(t)} = \{x_{it}, x_{i,t-1}, \ldots\}$ and $Y_i^{(t-1)} = \{y_{i,t-1}, x_{i,t-2}, \ldots\}$.

For this chapter, we consider the simple form of specification (Cameron and Trivedi 2013) which is the linear feedback model where μ_{it} depends on just the first lag of y_{it} giving the exponential feedback model as;

$$\mu_{it} = \alpha_i \exp\left(\rho y_{i,t-1} + x_{it}{\prime}\beta\right).$$

(ii) Pooled Dynamic Model

The basic dynamic model specification is the pooled dynamic models which does not allow variation in the regression coefficient. It assumes that all regression coefficients are the same across individuals. For a weak exogenous regressors which requires no serial correlation in $(y_{it} - \mu_{it})$, several methods of estimation can be used such as GEE, method of moments or GMM based on the sample moment condition $\sum_i \sum_t z_{it}(y_{it-\mu_{it}})$ where z_{it} can include $y_{i,t-1}$ and x_{it} and even consider additional lags in these variables. This approach may lead to inconsistent estimation if fixed effects are present.

(iii) Random Effects Dynamic Model

The formulation of random effects dynamic model is just an extension of the Random Effects GLM model that incorporates the lag of y_{it} as additional regressors. In this model, the log-likelihood will depend on initial condition of y_{io} which will be correlated with the random effect of α_i. Hence, based on decomposition and controlling for the initial condition, using conditional approach on y_{io}, Wooldridge (2005) specifies the joint distribution for nonlinear dynamic Poisson panel as

$$f(y_{i1}, \ldots, y_{iT}, \alpha_i | X_i . y_{io},) = f(y_{i1}, \ldots, y_{iT} | X_i, y_{io}, \alpha_i) f(\alpha_i | X_i)$$

It requires numerical integration for the implementation which involves the specification of the functional forms of $f(y_{io}|X_i, \alpha_i)$ and $f(\alpha_i|X_i)$. Then, the standard random effects conditional ML approach can identify the significant parameters. The possible model specification for $f(y_{io}|X_i, \alpha_i)$ with y_{io} as regressor is,

$$\alpha_i = \exp(\delta_o y_{io} + \overline{x}_i{\prime}\lambda + \varepsilon_i)$$

where $\overline{x}_i$ denote the time-average of the time varying exogenous variables and ε_i is i.i.d random variable.

(iv) Fixed Effects Dynamic Model

The Poisson fixed effects dynamic panel count model allows predetermined regressors that may be correlated with past occurrence by assuming the regressors are weakly exogenous. In dynamic models, the lag of dependent variables is treated as regressors with the following assumption with the mean conditioning on the current, past regressors, and past values of y_{it}.

$$E\left[y_{it} | X_i^t, Y_i^{t-1}\right] = E\left[y_{it} | x_{it}, \ldots, x_{i1}, y_{i,t-1}, \ldots, y_{i1}\right] = \alpha_i \lambda_{it}$$

Considering the linear dynamic model, y_{it} on the case where α_i is a fixed effect, and T is small, the model cannot consistently estimate α_i. The mean difference will yield

$$\left(y_{it} - \overline{y}_i\right) = \gamma\left(y_{i,t-1} - \overline{y}_{i,-1}\right) + (x_{it} - \overline{x}_i){\prime}\beta + (\varepsilon_{it} - \overline{\varepsilon}_i)$$

The regressor $\left(y_{i,t-1} - \overline{y}_{i,-1}\right)$ will be correlated with $(\varepsilon_{it} - \overline{\varepsilon}_i)$ and lead to inconsistency called Nickell bias. Thus, extending the Arellano-Bond estimator from linear to nonlinear model, the sequential moment conditions are given by;

$$E\left[y_{it}|y_{it-1},\ldots,y_{i1,}x_{it},\ldots,x_{i1}\right] = \alpha_i\lambda_{it}$$

where $\alpha_i\lambda_{it} = \alpha_i \exp\left(\rho y_{i,t-1} + x\prime_{it}\beta\right)$.

Then, $E\left[\frac{\lambda_{it-1}}{\lambda_{it}} y_{it}|y_{it-1},\ldots,y_{i1,}x_{it},\ldots,x_{i1},\alpha_i\right] = \alpha_i\lambda_{it-1}$

And $E\left[y_{it-1}|y_{it-2},\ldots,y_{i1,}x_{it-1},\ldots,x_{i1.}\alpha_i\right] = \alpha_i\lambda_{it-1}$

Thus, subtracting the equation eliminating α_i will yield

$$E\left[\left(\frac{\lambda_{it-1}}{\lambda_{it}}\right)y_{it-1} - y_{it}|y_{it-1},\ldots,y_{i1,}x_{it},\ldots,x_{i1}\right] = 0$$

Then, the GMM estimator can be estimated based on moment conditions.

$$E\left[z_{it}\left\{y_{it} - \left(\lambda_{i,t-1}/\lambda_{it}\right)y_{it-1}\right\}\right] = 0$$

where$z_{it} = (y_{it-1}, x_{it})$.

19.7 Recent Development on Multivariate Count Model

Most of the methodologies discussed in this book focus on single count variable in regression concept. On occasion of multiple counts, previous researchers report good work using a bivariate Poisson distribution as described by Kocherlakota and Kocherlakota (1992) and Cameron and Johnson (1993). This model can capture the individual heterogeneity as one of the drawbacks of the previous single count econometrics method is lack of controlling the unobserved individual-specific heterogeneity. This is important especially when the modeler deal with analysis that involve unobserved heterogeneity from two outcomes of unobserved determinant (Greene 2007; Munkin and Trivedi 1999). It can be measured by two possible sources which are (i) source from correlation between the unobservable determinants of the two dimensions of the response variables and (ii) source from the error term control for shocks which at any period may affect both outcomes. Hence, it is plausible to formulate a model estimation which can account possible correlation between the two outcomes.

We first illustrate the multivariate count model specification for bivariate panel count model. In bivariate panel count model, we assume every individual i has g different outcome observations y in any period t. Hence, we assume

$$y_{itg} \sim Poisson(\lambda_{itg}), g = 1, 2$$

And the estimated models characterized by a dual error structure are given by;

$$ln(\lambda_{it1}) = \beta_i{}'x_{it1} + \mu_{i1} + \varepsilon_{it1}$$

$$ln(\lambda_{it2}) = \beta_2{}'x_{it2} + \mu_{i2} + \varepsilon_{it2}$$

where the random error ε follows a bivariate normal distribution with the assumption that

$$(\varepsilon_{it1}, \varepsilon_{it1}) \sim N_2(0, 0, \sigma_{\varepsilon 1}^2, \sigma_{\varepsilon 1}^2, \rho)$$

The outcome-specific error terms μ represent individual-specific unobserved heterogeneity which is constant over time and

$$\mu_{i1} \sim N(0, \sigma_{\mu 1}^2, \sigma_{\mu 2}^2)$$

and

$$E[\varepsilon_{itg}\mu_{jh}] = 0\forall i, t, tg, j, h$$

$$E[\varepsilon_{itg}\varepsilon_{jsh}] = 0 if\, t \neq s \vee i \neq j \vee g \neq h$$

$$E[\varepsilon_{it1}\mu_{jh}] = 0 if\, i \neq j \vee g \neq h$$

The likelihood function for bivariate panel estimator involves intractable integrals. The joint error of ε_{it1} and ε_{it2} for given individuals μ and ε equation was integrated numerically. Using Gaussian quadrature procedure, the distribution of individual-specific unobservable was integrated using Gauss-Hermite approximation while the cross-equation errors distribution was integrated using modified Gauss-Leguerre integration (Riphahn et al. 2003). The likelihood can be optimized using quasi-Newton procedure.

Although the above-mentioned distribution has been widely used by many researchers, the disadvantage of such distributions is that the correlation between the count variables is restricted to being positive (Riphahn et al. 2003). Hence, many other approaches have been proposed recently to analyze multivariate count data. Among the proposed methods are the semi-parametric mixture model (Alfo' and

Tovato 2018), bivariate negative binomial regression model (Famoye 2015), Poisson-lognormal distribution (Chib and Winkelmann 2021; Jeong et al. 2023), copulas-based model (Cameron et al. 2021) and log-linear Poisson (Munoz'-Pichardo 2021). These proposed methods in the recent development of multivariate panel count model have shown satisfactory performance and allow for more flexible correlation structure which can take both positive and negative correlation.

19.8 Data Description Using R

An illustration of panel count data with more than one input is shown as below by taking a sample of secondary data from the Ministry of Health (*MOH*) *Malaysia.* The dataset describes the dengue incidence occurrence at four selected states namely Selangor, Johor, Perak, and Kelantan. This dataset was collected at a daily basis which comprises from January 1, 2013 to December 31, 2017 for every district from these states. Weather data (e.g., temperature, rainfall, and relative humidity) are also included in the analysis. These data were accessed from https://power.larc.nasa.gov/data-access-viewer/. Daily lag time effect (e.g., lag of 7, 14, 21, and 28 days) on weather data were taken into consideration in the analysis part as to examine the contribution in the dengue incidence in particular areas. The dataset comprises a set of district, $i = 1,2,...I$ non-overlapping areal units which recorded for every unit for $t = 1,2,...T$ consecutive time periods. Therefore, the dataset will be in the form of I x T rectangular array with I rows (refer to spatial units) and N columns (refer to time periods). The response data are represented by the notation $Y = (Y_1, ..., Y_T)_{I \times T}$, where $Y_t = (Y_{1t}, ..., Y_{It})$ represents the $I \times 1$ column vector of observations for all I spatial units for time period t. Finally, $x_{it} = \left(x_{it1}, ..., x_{itp}\right)$ is a vector of p known covariates for areal unit i and time period t, and can comprise factors or continuous variables as well as a column of ones for the intercept term.

To display the dataset, ***head (s,12)*** command can be used as follows.

Next, ***str ()*** command displays the basic information of the variables from the above dataset.

summary () function can be used to obtain descriptive statistics like mean, standard deviation, minimum, and maximum of variables.

```
> head(s,12)
   DisCode Time Dengue DailyPop      Pop        DIR      Exp2  Temp Humid Rain Temp_7 Humid_7 Rain_7 Temp_14 Humid_14 Rain_14
1        1    1      2   722234 13.49010 0.27691856 15.531863 24.98 88.87  0.0  23.83   93.43   0.00   24.93    87.97   26.50
2        2    1      6  1221064 14.01523 0.49137474 26.232619 24.98 88.87  0.5  24.50   91.07   0.00   24.78    88.05   34.00
3        3    1      0   210466 12.25708 0.00000000  4.524170 24.20 91.87  0.0  23.23   93.83   0.00   24.15    90.19    6.50
4        4    1      7   914873 13.72654 0.76513352 19.654492 27.38 80.83  0.0  26.89   84.43   0.00   27.69    79.80   16.00
5        5    1      0   239673 12.38703 0.00000000  5.150658 26.18 85.16  2.0  25.12   91.04   6.50   26.26    84.11   30.00
6        6    1      0   221973 12.31031 0.00000000  4.774345 26.96 83.54  0.0  26.09   86.66   0.00   27.33    80.92   34.50
7        7    1     10  1924371 14.47011 0.51965032 41.339815 27.60 79.70  0.0  23.83   93.43   0.00   24.93    87.97    7.00
8        8    1      0   111734 11.62388 0.00000000  2.400838 27.02 83.15  0.0  26.77   81.98   0.00   27.46    80.12   15.00
9        9    1      1   226579 12.33085 0.44134717  4.877358 27.50 81.50  0.0  25.12   91.04  11.71   26.26    84.11   11.44
10       1    2      4   722279 13.49017 0.55380262 15.531863 25.01 89.17  0.0  24.00   90.39   0.00   24.84    87.84   14.00
11       2    2      1  1221137 14.01529 0.08189089 26.232619 25.01 89.17  0.0  23.83   93.43   0.00   24.93    87.97    2.50
12       3    2      2   210479 12.25714 0.95021356  4.524170 24.30 90.80  0.0  23.31   92.36   0.00   24.21    89.86    1.00
   Temp_21 Humid_21 Rain_21 Temp_28 Humid_28 Rain_28
1    25.32    85.13   20.00   25.11    87.06   43.00
2    25.32    85.13    0.00   25.11    87.06    5.00
3    24.77    85.97    0.00   24.45    89.33    2.00
4    26.95    82.96    0.20   27.06    80.63    5.50
5    26.35    82.36   26.50   26.46    81.49   12.00
6    26.85    82.69    0.00   26.40    84.83    4.50
7    25.32    85.13    0.00   25.11    87.06   50.00
8    27.25    80.24    0.00   26.72    83.60   51.50
9    26.35    82.36    1.23   26.46    81.49   19.48
10   25.43    85.03    1.00   25.38    84.14    0.00
11   25.43    85.03    3.50   25.38    84.14    0.00
12   24.84    86.38    1.50   24.58    87.46    1.00
```

Fig. 19.2 R Command to display dataset with output

```
> str(s)
'data.frame':   16425 obs. of  22 variables:
 $ DisCode : int  1 2 3 4 5 6 7 8 9 1 ...
 $ Time    : int  1 1 1 1 1 1 1 1 1 2 ...
 $ Dengue  : int  2 6 0 7 0 0 10 0 1 4 ...
 $ DailyPop: int  722234 1221064 210466 914873 239673 221973 1924371 111734 226579 722279 ...
 $ Pop     : num  13.5 14 12.3 13.7 12.4 ...
 $ DIR     : num  0.277 0.491 0 0.765 0 ...
 $ Exp2    : num  15.53 26.23 4.52 19.65 5.15 ...
 $ Temp    : num  25 25 24.2 27.4 26.2 ...
 $ Humid   : num  88.9 88.9 91.9 80.8 85.2 ...
 $ Rain    : num  0 0.5 0 0 2 0 0 0 0 0 ...
 $ Temp_7  : num  23.8 24.5 23.2 26.9 25.1 ...
 $ Humid_7 : num  93.4 91.1 93.8 84.4 91 ...
 $ Rain_7  : num  0 0 0 0 6.5 ...
 $ Temp_14 : num  24.9 24.8 24.1 27.7 26.3 ...
 $ Humid_14: num  88 88 90.2 79.8 84.1 ...
 $ Rain_14 : num  26.5 34 6.5 16 30 ...
 $ Temp_21 : num  25.3 25.3 24.8 26.9 26.4 ...
 $ Humid_21: num  85.1 85.1 86 83 82.4 ...
 $ Rain_21 : num  20 0 0 0.2 26.5 0 0 0 1.23 1 ...
 $ Temp_28 : num  25.1 25.1 24.4 27.1 26.5 ...
 $ Humid_28: num  87.1 87.1 89.3 80.6 81.5 ...
 $ Rain_28 : num  43 5 2 5.5 12 ...
```

Fig. 19.3 R Command to display data structure with output

19.9 Data Visualization

In order to obtain a better understanding on the situation in the specific area, it is worth to analyze the data at district level within the selected states. Using R, we can produce the line plot to observe the severity of the dengue incidence rate across district by individual state. Using ***mfrow*** and ***mfcol*** parameters, readers can create a matrix of plots in one plotting space. Both parameters will consider a vector of length two as an argument with the resulting number of rows and columns in the plotting matrix. This can help the econometrician to visualize the trend pattern of incidence. The plot can be executed using the following command:

```
par(mfrow=c(3,3)).
```

The above R commands were run for Selangor, Johor, Perak, and Kelantan data.

Figure 19.4a portrays the annual trend of DIR for nine districts in Selangor. This figure exhibits the annual DIR per 100,000 population which was plotted for nine districts of Selangor across seven years (2011–2017). Based on the plot, there are some similarities on the annual trend of DIR per 100,000 population. For example, all nine districts of Selangor experienced a peak in annual DIR per 100,000 population during 2015 which has the highest annual DIR reported across the years. Besides that, all the districts except for Sepang experienced a consistent increase between 2012 and 2015 in the annual DIR until it reached its peak in 2015. The visualization can be produced and interpreted for other states of Johor, Perak, and Kelantan based on Fig. 19.4b–d.

19.10 Fixed Effects GLM Model Illustration Using R and STATA

Fixed effects GLM model results can be obtained simply by using the ***glm ()*** (for Poisson model) and ***glm.nb ()*** (for Negative Binomial model) from MASS package in R. We now illustrate FENB results by using the same dengue dataset as displayed below. Suppose that we want to estimate the dengue incidence rates (DIR) using FENB GLM model, modeler can execute the following command:

```
snb<-glm.nb(de~temp+humid+rain+temp7+humid7+rain7+temp14
+humid14+rain14+temp21+humid21+rain21+temp28+humid28
+rain28+i+t+offset(log(dailypop)), data=s,link=log))
```

Note that, the above R command was applied to the data for Selangor, Johor, Perak, and Kelantan. In order to choose the best model, ***stepAIC(snb)***command was applied in the analysis.

Modeler can also produce the fixed effects negative binomial GLM model using ***nbreg*** command in STATA. A sample output from stata for the Selangor dataset can be seen as below:

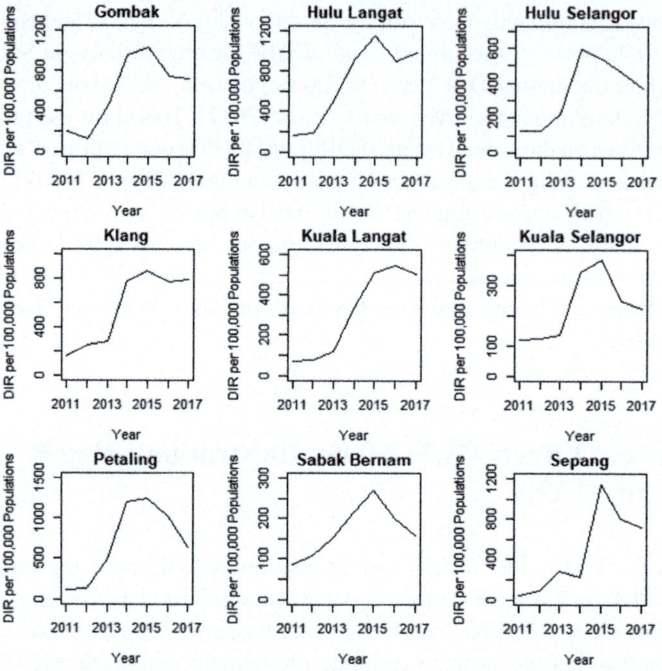

(a)

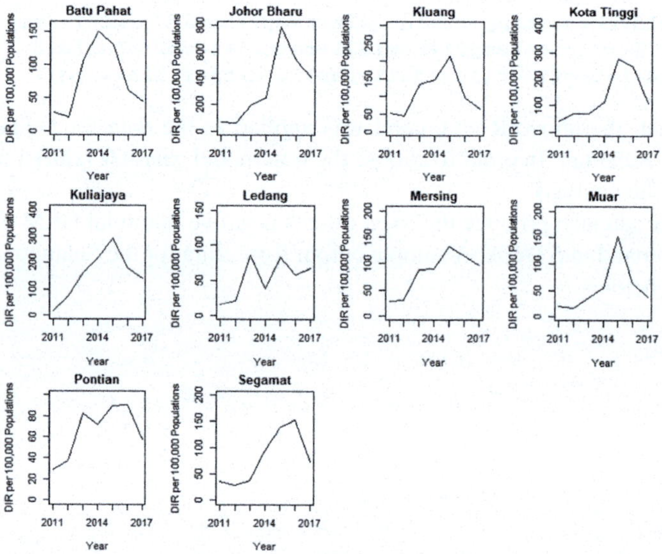

(b)

Fig. 19.4 Annual DIR for districts in Selangor (**a**), Johor (**b**), Perak (**c**) and Kelantan (**d**)

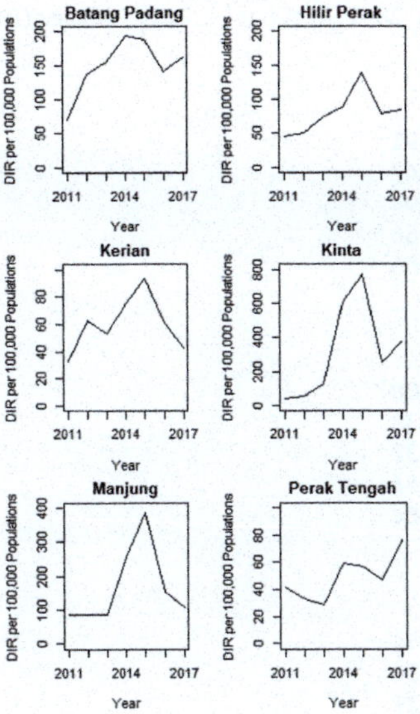

(c)

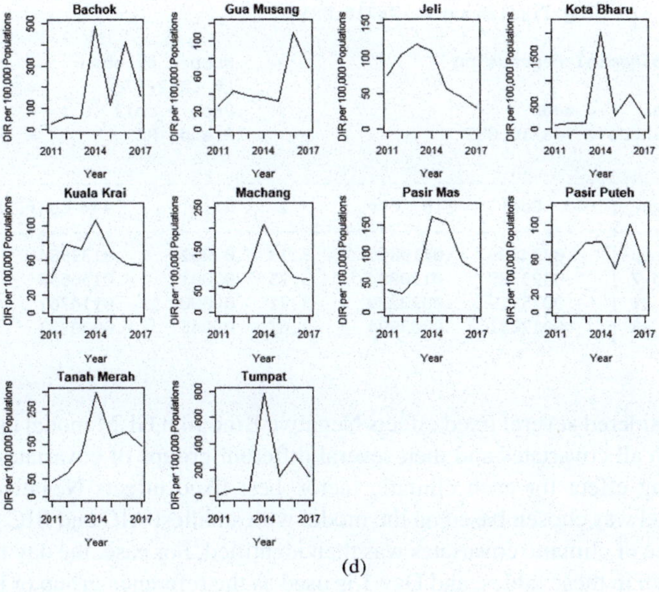

(d)

Fig. 19.4 (continued)

```
. nbreg Dengue Temp Temp_7 Humid_21 Rain_28 i.DisCode i.Day, offset(Pop)

Fitting Poisson model:

Iteration 0:   log likelihood = -95818.191
Iteration 1:   log likelihood = -87400.842
Iteration 2:   log likelihood = -87334.694
Iteration 3:   log likelihood =  -87334.66
Iteration 4:   log likelihood =  -87334.66

Fitting constant-only model:

Iteration 0:   log likelihood = -55614.608
Iteration 1:   log likelihood = -53772.638
Iteration 2:   log likelihood = -53727.437
Iteration 3:   log likelihood = -53727.164
Iteration 4:   log likelihood = -53727.164

Fitting full model:

Iteration 0:   log likelihood = -50928.934
Iteration 1:   log likelihood = -49559.714
Iteration 2:   log likelihood = -48775.581
Iteration 3:   log likelihood = -48716.127
Iteration 4:   log likelihood = -48716.085
Iteration 5:   log likelihood = -48716.085

Negative binomial regression                    Number of obs     =     16,425
                                                LR chi2(376)      =   10022.16
Dispersion     = mean                           Prob > chi2       =     0.0000
Log likelihood = -48716.085                     Pseudo R2         =     0.0933

------------------------------------------------------------------------------
      Dengue |      Coef.   Std. Err.      z    P>|z|     [95% Conf. Interval]
-------------+----------------------------------------------------------------
        Temp |   .0374399   .0119806     3.13   0.002     .0139584    .0609213
      Temp_7 |   .0393783   .0120984     3.25   0.001     .0156658    .0630907
    Humid_21 |  -.0075119   .0020229    -3.71   0.000    -.0114767   -.0035471
     Rain_28 |   .0012031   .0005994     2.01   0.045     .0000283     .002378
             |
```

We considered several fixed effects Negative Binomial GLM model using the full model with all covariates and then several different groups of covariates, including the time lag effect for each climatic factor. best fixed effects Negative Binomial GLM model was chosen based on the model with smallest AIC and BIC values. The significance of climatic covariates was then identified. For ease, the day factor effect is not shown in these tables, and Day 1 is used as the reference group or baseline for all of the states being studied.

The summary of parameter estimates for the fixed effects Negative Binomial GLM fitted to the Selangor, Johor, Perak, and Kelantan data is shown in Table 19.2. Gombak (Selangor), Batu Pahat (Johor), Batang Padang (Perak), and Bachok (Kelantan) were the reference district dummy variables for each state. Variables including temperature, temperature with a 7-day lag, humidity with a 21-day lag, and rainfall with a 28-day lag were found to be statistically significant in predicting the dengue count in

Table 19.1 Some link functions and their inverse

Distribution	Link	$\eta_i = g(\mu_i)$	Mean function $\mu_i = g^{-1}(\eta_i)$
Normal	Identity	μ_i	η_i
Bernoulli	Logit	$log\left(\frac{\mu_i}{1-\mu_i}\right)$	$\frac{1}{1+e^{-\eta_i}}$
Poisson	Log	$log(\mu_i)$	
Exponential Gamma	Inverse	$-\mu_i^{-1}$	

Selangor at the 0.05 level of significance. It was shown that there was a substantial positive link between current month temperature and lag 7 days temperature and dengue incidence. In addition, a strong negative correlation between the humidity of the lag 21 days and the incidence of dengue was discovered. Dengue incidence was correlated with rainfall lag of 28 days. The district-specific effect factors were all found to be significant except for Petaling. However, the results for Johor showed that the relative humidity lag of 7 days and the temperature lag of 7 and 14 days were statistically significant for dengue incidence in Johor. Results for Perak showed there was a negative correlation between daily dengue incidence and temperature lag of 21 days.

Additionally, the onset of the dengue outbreak was positively influenced by relative humidity lags of 7 and 28 days. A 28-day temperature lag and a 28-day relative humidity lag were also important climate variables that affected the number of cases of dengue in Kelantan. At a significance level of 0.05, these climatic factors were found to be statistically significant. Results show that all significant climatic factors in Kelantan had a positive relationship with the daily incidence of dengue. the daily current temperature and its lag had no impact on the dengue outbreak in Kelantan.

19.11 Plotting the Actual Versus Fitted FENB Model

The plot of the observed DIR (actual DIR) against the fitted DIR obtained from the selected best model for Selangor, Johor, Perak, and Kelantan illustrates how close are the fitted and observed values. To produce such plots, The ***plot ()*** command can be applied to produce the plots. The fitted DIR was first calculated where the fitted values are divided by daily population and then multiplied by 100,000 populations. Below are the R commands used to produce the output shown in Fig. 19.5. The R commands were also run for Selangor, Johor, Perak, and Kelantan data.

```
fitdir<-(snb1$fitted.values/s$dailypop)*100000
s<-cbind(s,fitdir)
str(s)
plot(log(s$fitdir),log(s$dir),xlab='Fitted log
(DIR)',ylab='Observed log (DIR)')
title(main="a",line=-0.65,adj=0.03)
```

```
plot(ts(s$dir,start=1,end=365),ylab="DIR per 100,000
Populations",xlab="Day",type="l",ylim=c(0,6))
title(main="b",line=-0.65,adj=0.03)
lines(ts(s$fitdir,start=1,end=365),type='l',col='red')
legend("topright",inset=0,c("Observed DIR","Fitted
DIR"),col=c("black","red"),lwd=2)
mtext("Selangor", outer=TRUE, cex=1.2, line=0)
```

The observed log DIR and fitted log DIR are shown in Fig. 19.5 for the districts of Selangor, Johor, Perak, and Kelantan. Between these states, there was a noticeable random scatter. Despite a significant scatter, it demonstrated that for Selangor, Johor, Perak, and Kelantan, respectively, there was a generally positive relationship between the observed log DIR and fitted log DIR. The positive relationship between observed log DIR and fitted log DIR can also be seen in several local states, such as Gombak, Hulu Langat, Klang, and Petaling (Selangor), Johor Bharu, Kinta (Perak), and Bachok, Kota Bharu, and Tumpat (Kelantan). For Selangor, Johor, Perak, and Kelantan, respectively, Fig. 19.5b shows the temporal trend of daily observed DIR

Table 19.2 Fixed effects negative binomial parameter (FENB)Estimates

Parameter	Selangor	Johor	Perak	Kelantan
	Estimates (SE)	Estimates (SE)	Estimates (SE)	Estimates (SE)
Intercept	**−0.1282*** (0.4465)**	**−18.5365*** (0.7617)**	**−12.2892*** (0.6410)**	**−16.7809*** (0.9407)**
Temp	**0.036** (0.01185)**	–	–	–
Temp_lag7	**0.0379** (0.0119)**	**0.0863*** (0.0189)**	–	–
Temp_lag14	–	**0.0632*** (0.0147)**	–	–
Temp_lag21	–	–	**−0.0794*** (0.0173)**	-
Temp_lag28	–	–	–	**0.0932*** (0.0230)**
Humid_lag7	–	**0.0119*** (0.0034)**	**0.0079** (0.0030)**	-
Humid_lag21	**−0.0079*** (0.0020)**	-	–	–
Humid_lag28	–	–	**0.0112*** (0.0031)**	**0.0132** (0.0044)**
Rain_lag28	**0.0012* (0.0006)**	–	–	–
Deviance	19,343.87	16,981.24	15,605.86	13,000.16
R_D^2	0.1768	0.2631459	0.1901355	0.363494
AIC	98,107.04	50,745.54	47,528.48	38,865.58
BIC	101,012.4	53,690.63	50,473.57	41,802.86

(black line) and fitted DIR (red line) over a study period. Based on Fig. 19.5b for Selangor, Johor, Perak, and Kelantan fixed effects Negative Binomial GLM led to an underestimate and overestimate of the DIR over a specific period of time. According to definition, an underestimation occurs when the fitted DIR is discovered to be lower than the actual (observed) DIR, and an overestimation occurs when the fitted DIR is discovered to be greater than the observed DIR. For instance, the model overstated Selangor and Kelantan's DIR in 2013. Additionally, the model that was adjusted for each state appeared to underestimate the DIR, particularly when these four states were the focus of a significant dengue outbreak.

In addition to the scatter plot of observed versus fitted and line plot, another visualization approach that can be used to describe the actual versus the predicted data is to plot the spatial map. Spatial maps are an effective and valuable visualization

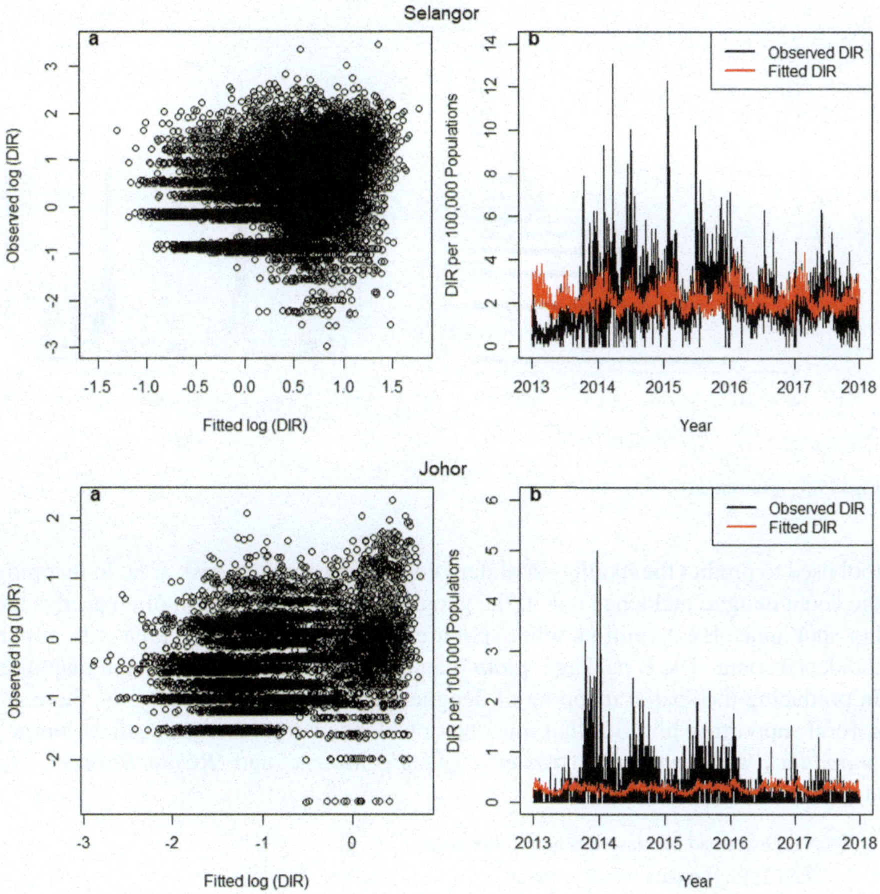

Fig. 19.5 FENB GLM of **a** Observed log and fitted log DIR for all days (1825) and districts of each state. **b** Daily observed DIR and Fitted DIR

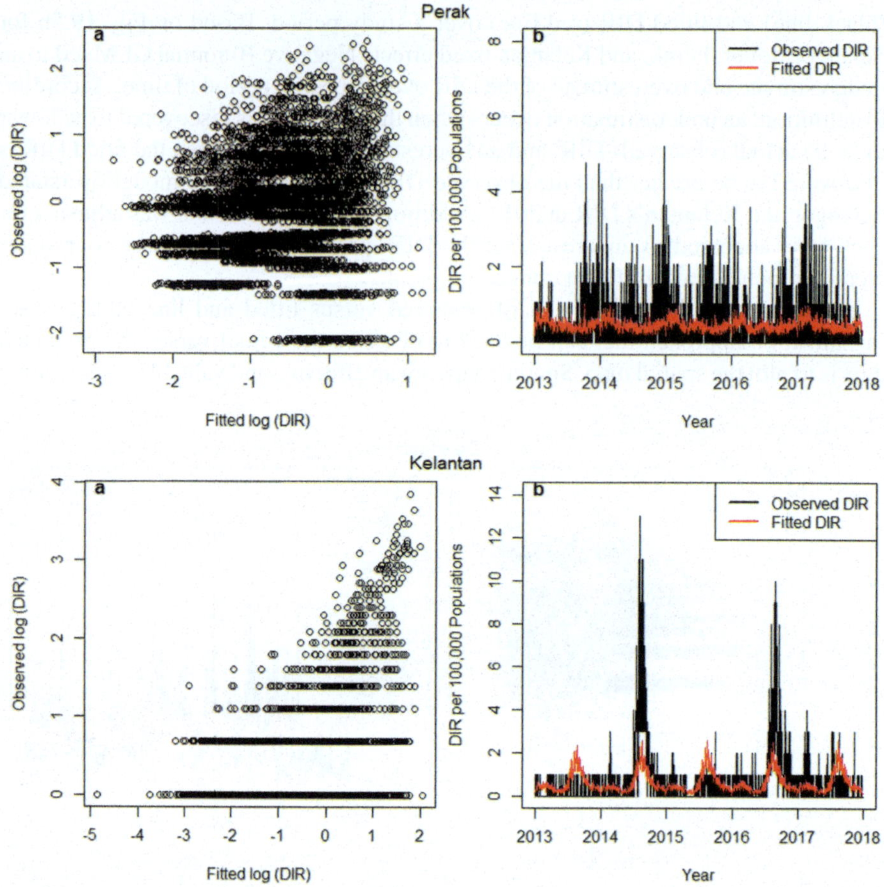

Fig. 19.5 (continued)

tool used to predict the likelihood of dengue incidence in high-risk area. In mapping the count dengue incidence risk at the geographical level, the term often used is the hot spot areas. By definition, a hot spot area can be defined as an area with a high incidence count. The R package ***'tmap'*** can be used to produce the spatial mapping. In producing the spatial mapping of dengue prediction in this case study, there are several supporting libraries that must be downloaded and installed such as ***'maps'***, ***'mapdata'***, ***'sp'***, ***'maptools'***, ***'raster'***, ***'spdep'***, ***'Matrix'*** and ***'RColorBrewer'***. The steps involved are as follows:

Step 1: Download and install required libraries

Step 2: Import data into R software

Step 3: Get the basic frame of the map of a particular individual

Step 4: Define the object into adjacency polygon and adjacency matrix

Step 5: Check the dissimilarity of the name of particular individuals between R and imported data.

Step 6: Set id of the imported data as numeric

Step 7: Merge the imported data and the map

Step 8: Map particular states/districts using ***'tmap'*** function.

Figure 19.6 presents the spatial map of the observed dengue incidence rate and fitted dengue incidence rate by year (2013–2017) across districts of Selangor. These maps aim to highlight the ability of the fixed effects Negative Binomial GLM to predict the dengue incidence rate in districts of Selangor. The spatial map helps the researcher and readers to easily identify the dengue endemic areas. These spatial maps are produced with a variety of red colors in which the lightest color represents the lowest dengue incidence rates and the darkest color represents the extremely high dengue incidence rates in specific districts. There are five categories of dengue incidence rate found which are very low incidence, low incidence, medium incidence, high incidence, and very high incidence which were set at <100, 100–200, 200–300, 300–400, and >400 incidence rates per 100,000 populations respectively.

Based on Fig. 19.6, in 2013, the FENB model overestimated DIR in Hulu Selangor, Kuala Selangor, Klang, Kuala Langat, and Sepang. When serious epidemic occurred in 2015, the model underestimated the dengue incidence rates, especially in Kuala Langat, Kuala Selangor, and Sabak Bernam. This implied that the fitted model could not fully capture the spatial variability in dengue incidence rates, particularly in these areas. However, the model managed to correctly capture the incidence rates in Gombak, Hulu Langat, and Petaling over the years. The model appeared to correctly predict dengue incidence rates in Kuala Selangor which has low dengue incidence rate. Nevertheless, the model was able to correctly capture the dengue incidence rate in 2016 in nine districts of Selangor.

Thus, the same spatial map of annual observed and fitted dengue incidence rates for districts of Johor, Perak, and Kelantan can be portrayed using the same command.

19.12 Random Effects GLM Model Illustration Using STATA

The analysis of the panel count data model using dengue count data was then expanded by taking into account the random effect approach on dengue counts for Negative Binomial model. This approach was adopted in the study as to investigate whether it is able to capture heterogeneity factors in panel data especially when the serious outbreak occurred which failed to be captured by fixed effects Negative Binomial model in the previous section. For Random Effects NB model, modeler can also use STATA to fit the model. In this chapter book, we illustrate another option for the output of Random Effects NB using STATA 16 as follows:

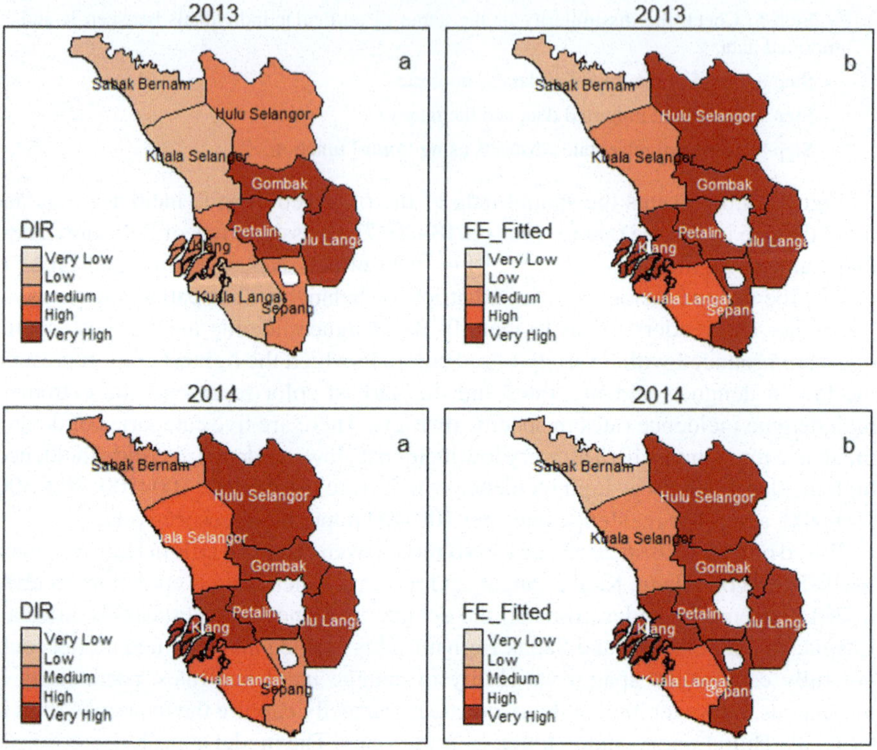

Fig. 19.6 Observed DIR (Left) and model fit (Right) of fixed effects negative binomial GLM (Selangor). Category boundaries are defined by 100, 200, 300, 400, and more than 400 cases per 100,000 population

```
. xtset DisCode Time
. quietly xtnbreg Dengue Temp Humid Rain Temp_7 Humid_7 Rain_
7 Temp_14 Humid_14 Rain_14 Temp_21 Humid_21 Rain_21 Temp_28
Humid_28 Rain_28 i.DisCode i.Day, re offset(Pop)
. est store M1
. quietly xtnbreg Dengue Temp Temp_7 Humid_21 Humid_28 Rain_28
i.DisCode i.Day, re offset(Pop)
. est store M2
. lrtest M1 M2, stats
. estimates stats
. predict fit, nu0
```

Table 19.3 tabulates the results of the Random Effects Negative Binomial model for Selangor, Johor, Perak, and Kelantan.

It can be seen that the significant climatic factors obtained by the random effects approach were found to be almost similar to results obtained by the fixed effects approach. For instance, the results on random effects Negative Binomial model of Selangor indicated that the dengue outbreak was strongly influenced by current temperature, temperature lag of 7 days, relative humidity lag of 21 and 28 days, and

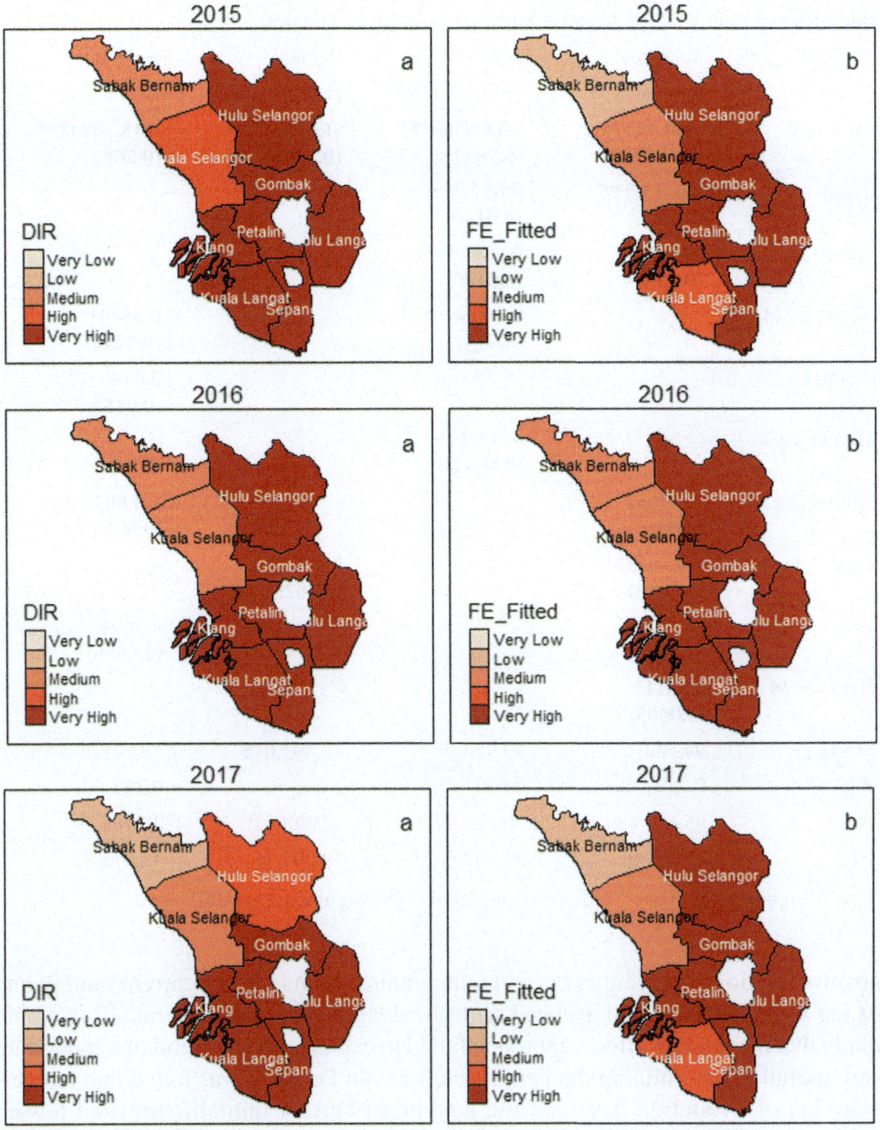

Fig. 19.6 (continued)

amount of rainfall lag of 28 days. Meanwhile, in Johor, the random effects approach showed that current temperature, temperature lag of 7 and 14 days, and relative humidity lag of 7 days were positively significant in affecting the dengue outbreak in the region of southern Malaysia. Surprisingly in Perak, out of 15 climatic factors considered in the analysis, the random effects approach was only able to indicate that relative humidity of lag 28 days significantly affected the dengue transmission with a

Table 19.3 Random effects negative binomial parameter estimates

Parameter	Selangor	Johor	Perak	Kelantan
	Estimates (SE)	Estimates (SE)	Estimates (SE)	Estimates (SE)
Intercept	**−14.4487*** (0.4149)**	**−19.6766*** (0.7937)**	**-13.5552*** (0.3395)**	**−15.9499*** (0.7682)**
Temp	**0.0415 *** (0.0096)**	**0.0577*** (0.0140)**	–	–
Temp_lag7	**0.0233* (0.0096)**	**0.0597*** (0.0185)**	–	–
Temp_lag14	–	**0.0608*** (0.0141)**	–	**0.0546** (0.0180)**
Temp_lag28	–	–	–	**0.0740*** (0.0181)**
Humid_lag7	–	**0.0093** (0.0032)**	–	–
Humid_lag21	**−0.0052*** (0.0016)**	–	–	**−0.0098** (0.0035)**
Humid_lag28	**−0.0045** (0.0016)**	–	**0.0063* (0.0025)**	–
Rain	–	–	–	**0.0014* (0.0006)**
Rain_lag28	**0.0011* (0.0005)**	–	–	–
Deviance	94,848.754	49,964.06	46,594.616	38,945.3
R_D^2	0.249	0.072	0.063	0.242
AIC	95,601.43	50,724.07	47,348.62	39,705.29
BIC	98,529.92	53,692.6	50,293.71	42,673.82

Note '*'Significant at 0.05, '**'Significant at 0.01, '***'Significant at 0.001

positive relationship. Neither current temperature and its lag nor current rainfall and its lag were found to be correlated with the dengue outbreak in Perak. This would imply that the random effects approach failed to capture any variation of temperature and rainfall in determining the dengue outbreak in Perak. It was found that temperature lag of 14 and 28 days and the amount of current rainfall correlated toward dengue outbreak in a positive effect, while there was a negative relationship between relative humidity lag of 21 days and dengue outbreak in Kelantan.

19.13 Plotting the Actual Versus Fitted RENB Model

To observe how good the RENB model is, again modeler can plot the observed DIR (actual DIR) against the fitted DIR obtained from the best model above separately for Selangor, Johor, Perak, and Kelantan. For this Random Effect NB model evaluation, using ***plot ()*** command in R we display the observed DIR against the fitted DIR. Same as in Fixed Effects NB model, the fitted DIR was first calculated such that the fitted values divided by daily population then multiplied by 100,000 populations before producing the plot. Below are the commands used to produce the output as shown in Fig. 19.7. Again, note that, this command is only shown for Selangor dataset.

```
par(mfrow=c(1,2),mar=c(4,4,0.5,2), oma=c(1.5,2,1,1))
plot(log(sre$fitdir),log(sre$DIR),xlab='Fitted log
(DIR)',ylab='Observed log (DIR)')
```

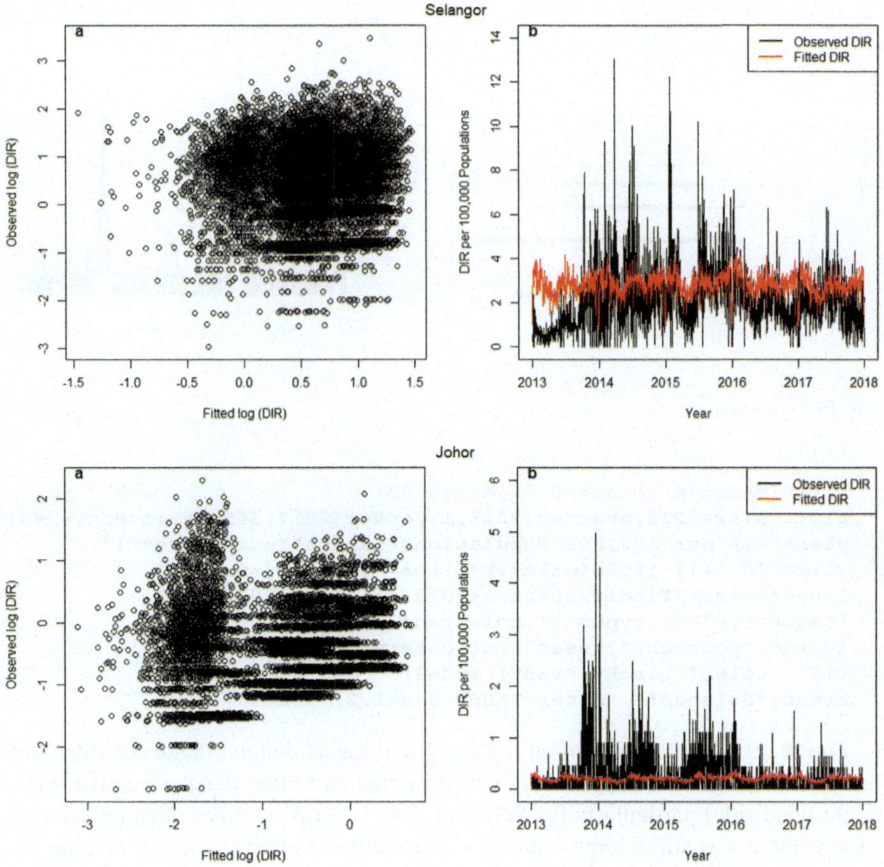

Fig. 19.7 RENB GLM of **a** Observed log and fitted log DIR for all days (1825) and districts of each state. **b** Daily observed DIR and Fitted DIR

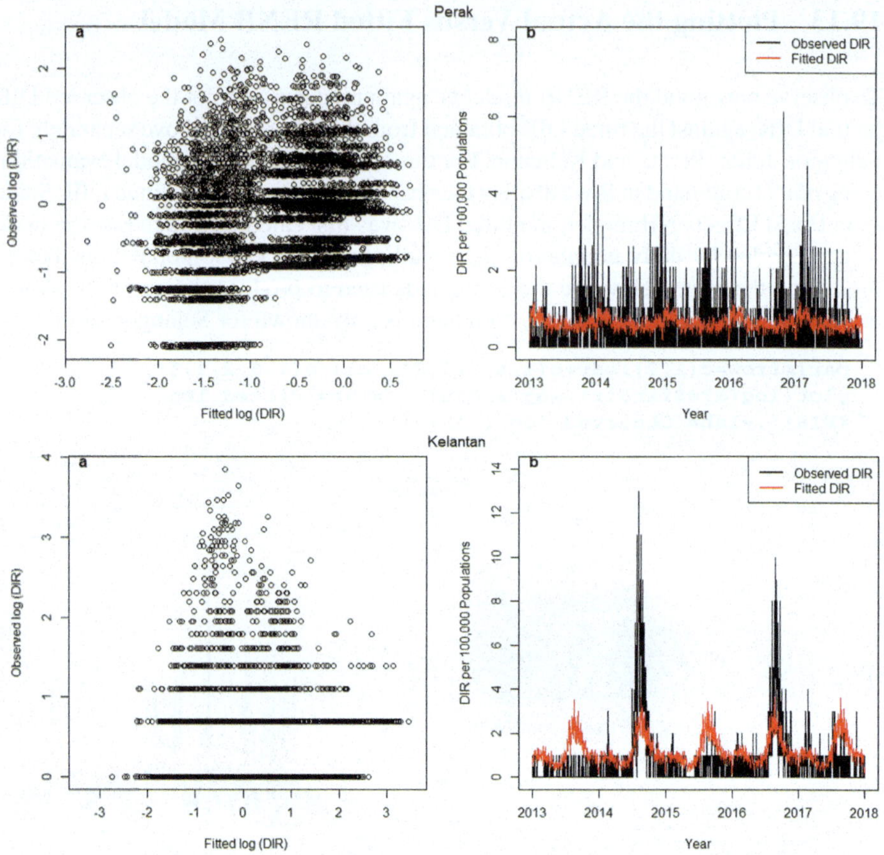

Fig. 19.7 (continued)

```
title(main="a",line=-0.65,adj=0.03)
plot(ts(sre$DIR,start=c(2013,1),end=c(2017,365),frequency=365)
ylab="DIR per 100,000 Populations",xlab="Year",type="l",
ylim=c(0,14)) title(main="b",line=-0.65,adj=0.03)
lines(ts(sre$fitdir,start=c(2013,1),end=c(2017,365),
frequency=365),type='l',col='red')
legend("topright",inset=0,c("Observed DIR","Fitted
DIR"),col=c("black","red"),lwd=2)
mtext("Selangor", outer=TRUE, cex=1.2, line=0)
```

Figure 19.7 displays observed log and fitted log of dengue incidence rates (left-hand side) and daily temporal series of observed and fitted dengue incidence rates (right-hand side) particularly for Selangor, Johor, Perak, and Kelantan respectively. Firstly, there was still a large random scatter between observed log of dengue incidence rates and fitted log of dengue incidence rates as portrayed in Fig. 19.7a. Besides that, temporal trend of daily observed DIR (black line) and fitted DIR (red line) over a period of study for Selangor, Johor, Perak, and Kelantan are presented in Fig. 19.7b.

Based on this figure, there were slightly overestimation and underestimation introduced by random effects model in predicting the daily dengue count in these four states. For example, random effects model resulted in overestimating the daily dengue count of Selangor in 2013. Moreover, fitted dengue incidence rates based on random effects approach failed to capture the trend of daily dengue count which caused an underestimation in both Johor and Perak over the period of time.

However, in Kelantan, the random effects model hardly captured the observed daily dengue count and there also existed overestimation problem especially when serious epidemic occurred in 2014 and 2016. In addition to this, a large and random scattered for the observed log DIR and fitted log DIR can also be seen in several districts of Selangor, Johor, Perak, and Kelantan. In comparison between fixed effects and random effects approach, both of these approaches failed to capture accurate daily dengue count especially when serious outbreak occurred under states level.

As in the fixed effects model section, in addition to the scatter plot of observed versus fitted and line plot, the spatial mapping visualization approach can be used to describe the actual versus the predicted data. Again, spatial maps can be used to visualize and map the incidence risk at the geographical level. Using the same R package of ***'tmap'*** and steps as in Sect. 19.12, the spatial mapping was produced for the random effects model.

The spatial map of fitted annual dengue incidence rates for each state obtained from random effects approach appeared to be different from fitted annual dengue incidence rates obtained from the fixed effects approach whereby the model produced by the random effects model for Selangor produced some systematic errors (see Fig. 19.8). For example, in Selangor, the random effects model had classified the annual dengue incidence rates of the eight districts of Selangor (except Petaling) as a very high DIR across the years (see Fig. 19.8). Meanwhile, the annual dengue incidence rates of Petaling were predicted as high DIR across the years. Thus, the random effects approach has slightly overestimated the DIR in most of the districts of Selangor. In other words, the random effects Negative Binomial GLM was not able to fully capture the spatial variability in dengue incidence rates in most of the districts in Selangor.

Spatial map of annual observed dengue incidence rates and fitted annual dengue incidence rates of random effects model across districts for Johor, Perak, and Kelantan can also be produced using the R command for Selangor.

19.14 Concluding Remarks

Count data work has gained much attention by econometrician ranging from basic count model, its extension to panel count model, and multivariate count model. This chapter guides the readers to understand the basic count model and its extension of panel count model through the development of fixed effects and random effects of Negative Binomial GLM model. A special variant of dynamic panel count model that includes lag of dependent count was discussed. Various models were tested using

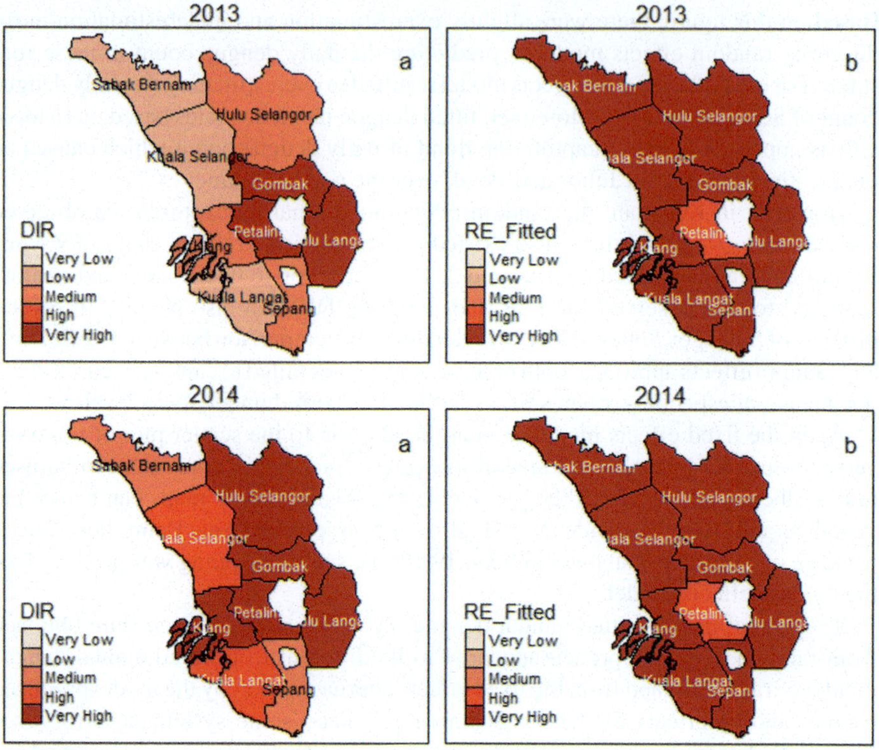

Fig. 19.8 Observed DIR (Left) and model fit (Right) of random effects negative binomial GLM (Selangor). Category boundaries are defined by 100, 200, 300, 400 and more than 400 cases

dengue count data with the maximal model based on all covariates followed by different subsets of variables including the time lag effect for each climatic variable of both models. Firstly, the fixed effects approach was applied to the dengue data of the four states. The results indicated that the fixed effects approach does not ultimately capture spatial variability within the districts of the states. Then, in order to counter heterogeneity factors that existed in the panel count data, the random effects Negative Binomial GLM was applied to the data. The results showed that the random effects model also resulted in slightly overestimation and underestimation which means it was unable to correctly predict dengue incidence rates across the districts. Although fixed effects and random effects models can handle the assumption of independent observations and temporal correlation effects within some areas by allowing such latent effects and correlation structure, the model slightly underestimates the dengue incidence rates especially when there is a large outbreak. Thus, further variant of dynamic panel count model or improving the fixed effects and random effects GLM model by considering more advance techniques of Generalized Linear Mixed model using spatial temporal random effects of INLA or CAR Bayesian method can be done for future work. The ability of the panel count model to correctly predict the

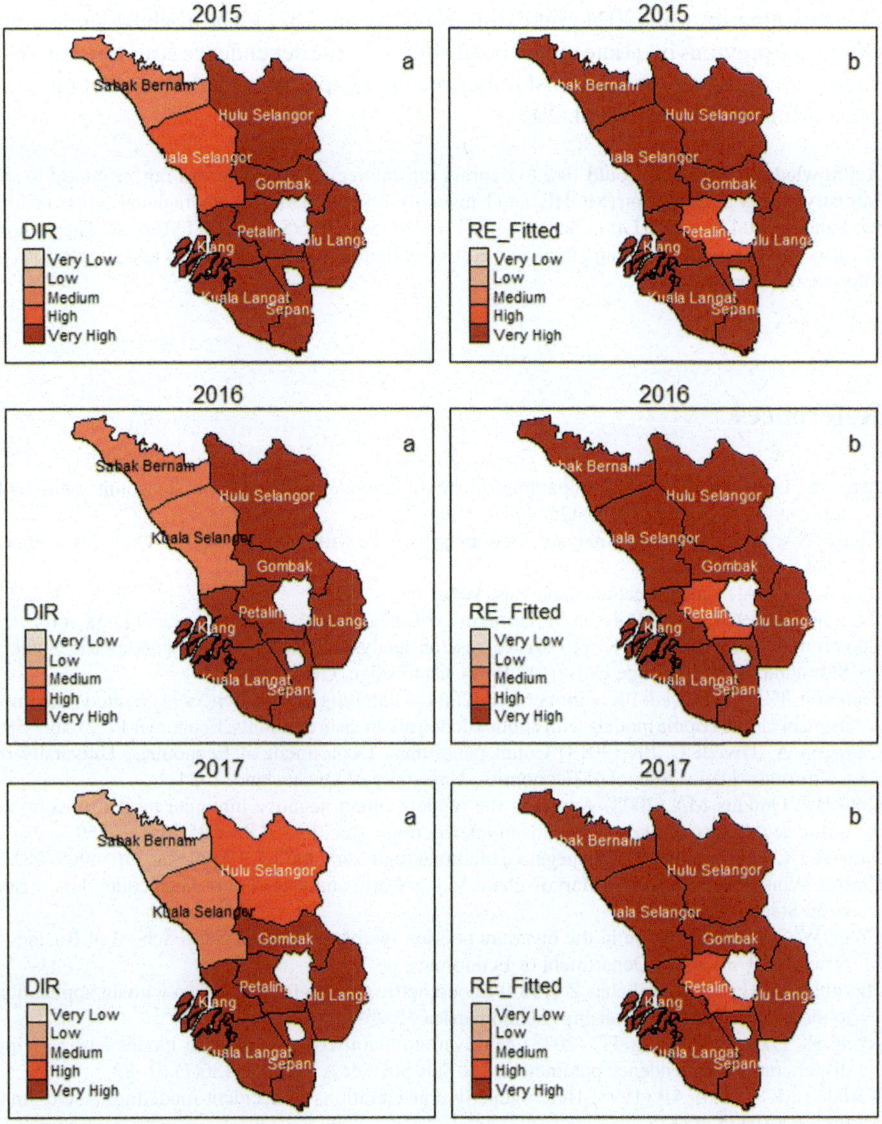

Fig. 19.8 (continued)

count response is important especially when a serious epidemic occurs in dengue disease.

In this chapter, much work has been discussed using single count data covering basic count model to variant of panel count model, but models for multivariate count data are still limited. For multiple counts, recent work on a new multivariate count regression model has been proposed by Chib and Winkelmann (2021), Jeong et al.

(2023), Cameron et al. (2021), and Munoz'-Pichardo (2021). The model does not only extend the previous bivariate model but it allows for the dependence structure between count variables and the relationship between the explanatory variables (Jeong et al. 2023; Munoz'-Pichardo et al. 2021).

Acknowledgements We would like to express our appreciation and record our gratitude to the Ministry of Higher Education (MOHE) and University Teknologi MARA for financial support under the Fundamental Research Grant Scheme(FRGS) (FRGS/1/2016/STG06/UITM/02/2). The authors are also grateful to the editor and associate editor for their insightful comments and suggestions to improve this book chapter.

References

Alfò M, Trovato G (2004) Semiparametric mixture models for multivariate count data, with application. Economet J 7(2):426–454
Ahmed SA, A, Junai (2015) Analysis of climate structure with Karachi Dengue Outbreak. J Basic Appl Sci 11:544–552
Agresti A (2002) Categorical data analysis. Wiley
Breslow NE (1984) Extra-Poisson Variation in Lo-Linear models. J R Stat Soc 33(1):38–44
Cameron A, C., Trivedi, P. K. (1998) Regression analysis of count data (Econometric Society Monographs). Cambridge University Press, Cambridge, UK
Cameron AC, Li T, Trivedi PK, Zimmer DM (2004) Modelling the differences in counted outcomes using bivariate copula models with application to mismeasured counts. Economet J 7(2):566–584
Cameron A, Trivedi C, PK (2013) Count panel data. Department of Economics, University of California—Davis. School of Economics, University of Queensland, 1–24
Chin HC, Quddus MA (2003) Applying the random effect negative binomial model to examine traffic accident occurence at signalized intersections. Accid Anal Prev 35(2):253–259
Famoye F (2010) On the bivariate negative binomial regression model. J Appl Stat 37(6):969–981.5
Chib S, Winkelmann R (2001) Markov chain Monte Carlo analysis of correlated count data. J Bus Econ Stat 19(4):428–435
Green W (2007) Correlation in the bivariate poisson regression model. Stern School of Business, New York University, Department of Economics, pp 1–18
Hausman JA, Hall BH, Griliches Z (1984) Econometric models for count data with an application to the patents-R&D relationship. Econometrica 52:909–938
Jeong H, Tzougas G, Fung TC (2023) Multivariate claim count regression model with varying dispersion and dependence parameters. J R Stat Soc Ser A Stat Soc 186(1):61–83
Karlaftis MG, Tarko AP (1998) Heterogeneity considerations in accident modeling. Accid Anal Prev 30(4):425–433
Lee JS, Mogasale V, Lim JK (2015) A multi-country study of the household willingness-to-pay for dengue vaccines: household surveys in Vietnam, Thailand and Columbia. PLOS Negelected Trop Dis 9(6):e0003810. https://doi.org/10.1371/journal.pntd.0003810
Lekdee K, Ingsrisawang L (2013) Generalized linear mixed models with spatio random effects for spatio-temporal data: an application to dengue fever mapping. J Math Stat 9(2):137–143
Lowe R (2010) Spatio-temporal modelling of climate sensitive disease risk: towards an early warning system for Dengue in Brazil (Doctoral thesis, University of Exeter). https://ore.exeter.ac.uk/repository/handle/10036/120070
Lowe R, Bailey TC, Stephenson DB, Graham RJ, Coelho CA, Carvalho MS, Barcellos C (2011) Spatio-temporal modelling of climate-sensitive disease risk: towards an early warning system for dengue in Brazil. Comput Geosci 37(3):371–381

Lowe R, Cazelles B, Paul R, Rodó X (2015) Quantifying the added value of climate information in a spatio-temporal dengue model. Stochastic Environ Res Risk Assessment 1–12

McCullagh P, Nelder JA (1983) Generalized Linear Models, 2nd Ed. Chapman and Hall

McCullagh P, Nelder JA (1989) Generalized Linear Models, 2nd edn. Chapman and Hall, London

Miaou SP, Lum H (1993) Modeling vehicle accidents and highway geometric design relationships. Accid Anal Prev 25(6):689–709

Muñoz-Pichardo JM, Pino-Mejías R, García-Heras J, Ruiz-Muñoz F, Luz González-Regalado M (2021) A multivariate Poisson regression model for count data. J Appl Stat 48(13–15):2525–2541

Montgomery DC, Peck EA, Vining GG (2021) Introduction to linear regression analysis. Wiley

Nelder JA, Wedderburn RW (1972) Generalized linear models. J R Stat Soc Ser A Stat Soc 135(3):370–384

Oppong FB, Mbukam EC, Agyapong AA (2017) Statistical model for analysing count data. Int J Sci Eng Res 8(2):454–460 (2017)

Radin URS, Mackay MG, Hills BL (1996) Modelling of conspicuity-related motorcycle accidents in Seremban and Shah Alam, Malaysia. Accident Anal Prev 28(3):325–332

Riphahn RT, Wambach A, Million A (2003) Incentive effects in the demand for health care: a bivariate panel count data estimation. J Appl Economet 18(4):387–405

Shankar V, Mannering F, Barfield W (1995) Effect of roadway geometrics and environmental factors on rural freeway accident fequencies. Accid Anal Prev 27(3):371–389

Wah YB, Nasaruddin N, Voon WS, Lazim MA (2012) Decision tree model for count data. Proc World Cong Eng

Wedderburn RWM, Quasi-Likelihood functions, generalized linear models, and the gauss-newton method. Biometrika 61(3):439–447

Yaacob WFW, Azaki WW, Lazim MA, Wah YB (2010a) Modelling Dengue Fever (DF) and Dengue Haemorrhagic Fever (DHF) outbreak using poisson and negative binomial model. World Acad Sci Eng Technol 38:903–908

Yaacob WFW, Lazim MA, Wah YB (2010b) A practical approach in modelling count data. Proc Reg Conf Stat Sci 2010:176–183

Zhang Y, Wang T, Liu K, Xia Y, Lu Y, Jing Q, Yang Z, Hu W, Lu J (2016) Developing a time series predictive model for dengue in Zhongsan, China based on weather and Guangzhou Dengue Surveillance Data. PLoS Negl Trop Dis 10(2):e0004473

Chapter 20
Estimation of Systems of Regression Equations with Unbalanced Panel Data and Random Effects: Modelling Food-Expenditure Shares in Vietnamese Households

Minh Cong Nguyen and Hoa Bao Nguyen

Abstract The paper develops an econometrics framework and describes its associated Stata command, `xtsur`, for the estimation of a system of seemingly unrelated regression equations with unbalanced panel data and random effects. The paper applies `xtsur` to estimate Vietnam's household demand system, expenditure and own-price elasticities for seven different food categories. The application analyzes Vietnam's food consumption behavior using an unbalanced panel of Vietnam's Household Living Standards Surveys (VHLSS) conducted in 2002, 2004, and 2006. Our results suggest that income elasticities are positive and own-price elasticities are negative as expected. Household characteristics such as household head's age, marital status, education, household size, household location (urban/rural), ethnicity and poverty status appear to affect food group consumption significantly. Households with a larger size or poverty status tend to consume more necessities such as rice, cereal and other starches while consuming less of meat, fruits, and dairy products. These results highlight empirical evidence for policy-makers to make useful food policy recommendations in Vietnam.

Keywords One-way random effects · Unbalanced panel data · Generalized least squares · Maximum likelihood estimation · Almost ideal demand system · SUR model · `xtsur`

Supplementary Information The online version contains supplementary material available at https://doi.org/10.1007/978-981-99-4902-1_20.

M. C. Nguyen (✉) · H. B. Nguyen
World Bank, NW Washington, USA
e-mail: mnguyen3@worldbank.org

D. Mukherjee (ed.), *Applied Econometric Analysis Using Cross Section and Panel Data*, Contributions to Economics, https://doi.org/10.1007/978-981-99-4902-1_20

20.1 Introduction

System of Seemingly Unrelated Regressions (SUR) is used in many empirical applications (Zellner 1962; Greene 2003). This system contains multiple equations with distinct dependent and independent variables, and different coefficients are linked together by some correlated error terms.

Examples include systems of factor demands by a particular firm, agricultural supply-response equations, and capital-asset pricing models. In the literature of panel data econometrics, SUR is generally considered with balanced panel data since empirical researchers are attracted by its simplicity compared to unbalanced panel data. However, an unbalanced panel is more frequently seen in empirical settings. First, the respondents may move out, decease or refuse to give answers during the subsequent waves of the survey. Second, the survey design requires a larger sample that may rotate individuals or firms out of the sample based on specific rules. In practice, balanced panel data assumption leads to dropping observations in the real dataset of an unbalanced panel. That causes loss of data information and inefficient estimation of the system. Therefore, we will have more informative and reliable data if we can use a naturally unbalanced panel. However, the more important issue is to get more efficient estimators (see Matyas et al. 1991; Baltagi and Chang 1994).

The purpose of this paper is to introduce a Stata command `-xtsur-` and an application for the SUR model with unbalanced panel data and random individual effects following the original estimation developed by Erik Biørn (2004). This new command can be applied to the model of SUR equations known with a large-N-fixed-T case (many observations but for a fixed number of periods), but not to the model of simultaneous equations. For the application of `xtsur`, we later apply this new `xtsur` command to estimate a food demand system for Vietnam using unbalanced panel data of households over three periods.

The rest of the paper is outlined as follows. Section 20.2 provides a methodology with a theoretical model specification and estimation procedure of a system of SUR equations with unbalanced panel data and random effects. Section 20.3 describes the development of the `xtsur` command to implement this model estimation in Stata. Section 20.4 presents a Monte Carlo study of a system of SUR equations with unbalanced panel data and random effects. Section 20.5 illustrates an application of SUR with unbalanced panel data and random effects on Vietnamese panel data of households' demand. This section describes summary statistics of all variables in the data set and presents estimation results with a discussion of the findings. The conclusion following from the application results is given in the last section.

20.2 Model Specification and Estimation Strategy

20.2.1 Model Specification

Consider a panel data of firms where there are N firms observed in at least one and at most P periods. If all firms are observed in different periods, we will have unbalanced panel data of firms. One may be interested in estimating a system of supply equations for these firms. The system of seemingly unrelated equations with unbalanced panel and random effects will be considered as follows.

For a system of G equations, the gth equation is expressed as:

$$y_{git} = \mathbf{x}_{git}\boldsymbol{\beta}_g + \alpha_{gi} + u_{git} \tag{20.1}$$

where G is the number of equations, indexed by $g = 1, 2, ..., G$, and N is the number of firms, indexed by $i = 1, 2, ..., N$. Equation (20.1) explains the dependent variable y_{git} of firm i, observed in time period t in the gth equation, the $1 \times H_g$ row vector of explanatory variables $\mathbf{x}_{git}$, and the unobserved effect α_{gi}. $\boldsymbol{\beta}_g$ is the $H_g \times 1$ parameter vector of interest. u_{git} is the unobservable disturbance of firm i, at period time t in the gth equation.[1]

Stacking the above G equations for each firm i at period time t, we have:

$$\begin{bmatrix} y_{1it} \\ y_{2it} \\ \vdots \\ y_{Git} \end{bmatrix} = \begin{bmatrix} \mathbf{x}_{1it} & \mathbf{0} & \cdots & \mathbf{0} \\ \mathbf{0} & \mathbf{x}_{2it} & & \mathbf{0} \\ \vdots & \mathbf{0} & & \vdots \\ \mathbf{0} & \mathbf{0} & \cdots & \mathbf{x}_{Git} \end{bmatrix} \begin{bmatrix} \boldsymbol{\beta}_1 \\ \boldsymbol{\beta}_2 \\ \vdots \\ \boldsymbol{\beta}_G \end{bmatrix} + \begin{bmatrix} \alpha_{1i} \\ \alpha_{2i} \\ \vdots \\ \alpha_{Gi} \end{bmatrix} + \begin{bmatrix} u_{1it} \\ u_{2it} \\ \vdots \\ u_{Git} \end{bmatrix} \tag{20.2}$$

and in general, we can express the above equations as the following model:

$$\begin{aligned} \mathbf{y}_{it} &= \mathbf{X}_{it}\boldsymbol{\beta} + \boldsymbol{\alpha}_i + \mathbf{u}_{it} && (20.3) \\ &= \mathbf{X}_{it}\boldsymbol{\beta} + \boldsymbol{\varepsilon}_{it} && (20.4) \end{aligned}$$

where $\mathbf{y}_{it}$, $\boldsymbol{\alpha}_i$, and $\mathbf{u}_{it}$ are $G \times 1$ vectors, $\mathbf{X}_{it}$ and $\boldsymbol{\beta}$ are $G \times H$ and $H \times 1$ matrices, respectively. We define $H = \sum_{g=1}^{G} H_g$ and $\boldsymbol{\varepsilon}_{it} = \boldsymbol{\alpha}_i + \mathbf{u}_{it}$. One important assumption is that the unobserved effects and the disturbances are mutually uncorrelated and uncorrelated with $\mathbf{X}_{it}$, given $E(\boldsymbol{\alpha}_i) = E(\mathbf{u}_{it}) = \mathbf{0}$, $Var(\boldsymbol{\alpha}_i) = \boldsymbol{\Sigma}_{\alpha}$, and $Var(\mathbf{u}_{it}) = \boldsymbol{\Sigma}_u$.

We can easily sort the firms in this example of unbalanced panel by the number of times in which firm observations are available. Let P be the maximum number of times that firms could be observed, and p is the number of times that firms are observed with the range of $p = P, P - 1, ..., 1$. For any given number of p times,

[1] We employ the same notations described in Biørn (2004).

denote N_p is the number of firms observed p times. We assume that firms that are observed in different time periods could have the same number of p times counted. For example, the same firms interviewed in year 2001, 2002, and 2004 could have the same number of times observed ($p = 3$) as the firm which was interviewed in 2003, 2005, and 2007. With this definition in mind, we could get the total number of N different firms where $N = \sum_{p=1}^{P} N_p$, and the total number of firm observations across times $n = \sum_{p=1}^{P} pN_p$.

With firm observations sorted by the number of times they were observed, firm observations in the unbalanced panel are rearranged into P balanced panels. In each balanced panel, all observations are observed with the same number of times regardless of different time periods. Following Biørn (2004), the model can be rewritten for each p where $p = P, P-1, ..., 1$ as:

$$\mathbf{y}_{i(p)} = \mathbf{X}_{i(p)}\boldsymbol{\beta} + (\mathbf{e}_p \otimes \alpha_i) + \mathbf{u}_{i(p)} \tag{20.5}$$
$$= \mathbf{X}_{i(p)}\boldsymbol{\beta} + \varepsilon_{i(p)} \tag{20.6}$$

and

$$E(\varepsilon_{i(p)}, \varepsilon'_{i(p),}) = \mathbf{I}_p \otimes \boldsymbol{\Sigma}_u + \mathbf{E}_p \otimes \boldsymbol{\Sigma}_\alpha \tag{20.7}$$
$$= \mathbf{K}_p \otimes \boldsymbol{\Sigma}_u + \mathbf{J}_p \otimes \boldsymbol{\Sigma}_{(p)} \tag{20.8}$$
$$= \boldsymbol{\Omega}_{\varepsilon(p)} \tag{20.9}$$

where $\mathbf{y}_{i(p)} = (\mathbf{y}'_{i1}, ..., \mathbf{y}'_{ip})'$, $\mathbf{X}_{i(p)} = (\mathbf{X}'_{i1}, ..., \mathbf{X}'_{ip})'$, $\varepsilon_{i(p)} = (\varepsilon'_{i1}, ..., \varepsilon'_{ip})'$, $\boldsymbol{\Sigma}_{(p)} = \boldsymbol{\Sigma}_u + p\boldsymbol{\Sigma}_\alpha$, $i \in I_p$, $p = P, P-1, ..., 1$. $\boldsymbol{I}_p$ is an identity matrix $(p \times p)$, $\mathbf{e}_p$ is the $(p \times 1)$ vectors of ones, $\mathbf{E}_p = \mathbf{e}_p\mathbf{e}'_p$, $\mathbf{J}_p = (1/p)\mathbf{E}_p$, and $\mathbf{K}_p = \mathbf{I}_p - \mathbf{J}_p$.

Using the overall within-firm and between-firm covariation matrices, Biørn (2004) derived the unbiased estimators of $\boldsymbol{\Sigma}_u$ and $\boldsymbol{\Sigma}_\alpha$ for each balanced panel. Using those estimated covariance matrices, the generalized least squares (GLS) problem is considered by minimizing $Q_{(p)} = \sum_{p=1}^{P} \sum_{i \in I_p} \varepsilon'_{i(p)} \boldsymbol{\Omega}^{-1}_{\varepsilon(p)} \varepsilon_{i(p)}$ with respect to $\boldsymbol{\beta}$. We then obtain the GLS estimator for the firms observed p times[2]:

$$\widehat{\boldsymbol{\beta}}_{GLS(p)} = \left[\sum_{i \in I_p} \mathbf{X}'_{i(p)}[\mathbf{K}_p \otimes \Sigma_u^{-1}]\mathbf{X}_{i(p)} + \sum_{i \in I_p} \mathbf{X}'_{i(p)}[\mathbf{J}_p \otimes \boldsymbol{\Sigma}^{-1}_{(p)}]\mathbf{X}_{i(p)}\right]^{-1} \times \left[\sum_{i \in I_p} \mathbf{X}'_{i(p)}[\mathbf{K}_p \otimes \boldsymbol{\Sigma}_u^{-1}]\mathbf{y}_{i(p)} + \sum_{i \in I_p} \mathbf{X}'_{i(p)}[\mathbf{J}_p \otimes \boldsymbol{\Sigma}^{-1}_{(p)}]\mathbf{y}_{i(p)}\right] \tag{20.10}$$

with the covariance matrix

[2] For more details, see Biørn (2004).

$$V(\widehat{\boldsymbol{\beta}}_{GLS(p)}) = \left[\sum_{i \in I_p} \mathbf{X}'_{i(p)}[\mathbf{K}_p \otimes \boldsymbol{\Sigma}_u^{-1}]\mathbf{X}_{i(p)} + \sum_{i \in I_p} \mathbf{X}'_{i(p)}[\mathbf{J}_p \otimes \boldsymbol{\Sigma}_{(p)}^{-1}]\mathbf{X}_{i(p)}\right]^{-1}. \tag{20.11}$$

The *one-step* overall estimator $\widehat{\boldsymbol{\beta}}_{GLS}$ can be shown to be the functions of $\widehat{\boldsymbol{\beta}}_{GLS(p)}$ and $\vee(\widehat{\boldsymbol{\beta}}_{GLS(p)})$ as follows:

$$\widehat{\boldsymbol{\beta}}_{GLS} = \left[\sum_{p=1}^{P} \vee(\widehat{\boldsymbol{\beta}}_{GLS(p)})^{-1}\right]\left[\sum_{p=1}^{P} \vee(\widehat{\boldsymbol{\beta}}_{GLS(p)})^{-1}\widehat{\boldsymbol{\beta}}_{GLS(p)}\right]. \tag{20.12}$$

In order to get more efficient estimator of the system, Biørn (2004) suggested the multi-step Maximum Likelihood (ML) estimation.[3] The important assumption is normality of random effects and disturbances, i.e., $\boldsymbol{\alpha}_i \overset{iid}{\sim} N(\mathbf{0}, \boldsymbol{\Sigma}_\alpha)$ and $\mathbf{u}_{it} \overset{iid}{\sim} N(\mathbf{0}, \boldsymbol{\Sigma}_u)$, hence the log likelihood for group p and for all firms, respectively, are:

$$\mathscr{L}_{(p)} = -\frac{GN_p p}{2}\ln(2\pi) - \frac{N_p}{2}\ln\left|\boldsymbol{\Omega}_{\varepsilon(p)}\right| - \frac{1}{2}Q_{(p)}(\boldsymbol{\beta}, \boldsymbol{\Sigma}_\alpha, \boldsymbol{\Sigma}_u) \tag{20.13}$$

$$\mathscr{L} = \sum_{p=1}^{P} \mathscr{L}_{(p)} = -\frac{Gn}{2}\ln(2\pi) - \frac{1}{2}\sum_{p=1}^{P} N_p \ln\left|\boldsymbol{\Omega}_{\varepsilon(p)}\right| - \frac{1}{2}Q(\boldsymbol{\beta}, \boldsymbol{\Sigma}_\alpha, \boldsymbol{\Sigma}_u) \tag{20.14}$$

where $Q_{(p)} = Q_{(p)}(\boldsymbol{\beta}, \boldsymbol{\Sigma}_\alpha, \boldsymbol{\Sigma}_u) = \sum_{i \in I_p} [\mathbf{y}_{i(p)} - \mathbf{X}_{i(p)}\boldsymbol{\beta}]'\boldsymbol{\Omega}_{\varepsilon(p)}^{-1}[\boldsymbol{y}_{i(p)} - \boldsymbol{X}_{i(p)}\boldsymbol{\beta}]$, $Q = Q(\boldsymbol{\beta}, \boldsymbol{\Sigma}_\alpha, \boldsymbol{\Sigma}_u) = \sum_{p=1}^{P} Q_{(p)}(\boldsymbol{\beta}, \boldsymbol{\Sigma}_\alpha, \boldsymbol{\Sigma}_u)$, and $\left|\boldsymbol{\Omega}_{\varepsilon(p)}\right| = \left|\boldsymbol{\Sigma}_{(p)}\right| \left|\boldsymbol{\Sigma}_u\right|^{p-1}$.

The ML problem for group p can be done in two steps: (A) Maximization of $\mathscr{L}_{(p)}$ with respect to $\boldsymbol{\beta}$ for given $(\boldsymbol{\Sigma}_\alpha, \boldsymbol{\Sigma}_u)$, and (B) Maximization of $\mathscr{L}_{(p)}$ with respect to $(\boldsymbol{\Sigma}_\alpha, \boldsymbol{\Sigma}_u)$ for given $\boldsymbol{\beta}$.

Since the problem (A) is identical to the GLS problem for group p, we can done this easily by using the solution given by the GLS problem in Eq. (20.10). For the problem (B), the solution for the ML for group p is given as: for $p = 1$, we get $\hat{\boldsymbol{\Sigma}}_{(1)} = \hat{\boldsymbol{\Sigma}}_{u(1)} + \hat{\boldsymbol{\Sigma}}_{\alpha(1)} = \boldsymbol{B}_{\varepsilon\varepsilon(1)}/N_1$, while for $p > 1$

$$\hat{\boldsymbol{\Sigma}}_{(p)} = \hat{\boldsymbol{\Sigma}}_{(p)}(\boldsymbol{\beta}) = \frac{\tilde{\boldsymbol{B}}_{\varepsilon\varepsilon(p)}}{N_p}, \ \hat{\boldsymbol{\Sigma}}_{u(p)} = \hat{\boldsymbol{\Sigma}}_{u(p)}(\boldsymbol{\beta}) = \frac{\tilde{\boldsymbol{W}}_{\varepsilon\varepsilon(p)}}{N_p(p-1)} \tag{20.15}$$

and

$$\hat{\boldsymbol{\Sigma}}_{\alpha(p)} = \hat{\boldsymbol{\Sigma}}_{\alpha(p)}(\boldsymbol{\beta}) = \frac{1}{N_p p}\left[\tilde{\mathbf{B}}_{\varepsilon\varepsilon(p)} - \frac{\tilde{\mathbf{W}}_{\varepsilon\varepsilon(p)}}{p-1}\right] \tag{20.16}$$

[3] We used the term "multi-step" instead of "stepwise" in Biørn (2004) in order to avoid confusion.

where $\tilde{\mathbf{B}}_{\varepsilon\varepsilon(p)} = \sum_{i \in I_p} \tilde{\mathbf{E}}_{i(p)} \mathbf{K}_p \tilde{\mathbf{E}}'_{i(p)}$, $\tilde{\mathbf{W}}_{\varepsilon\varepsilon(p)} = \sum_{i \in I_p} \tilde{\mathbf{E}}_{i(p)} \mathbf{J}_p \tilde{\mathbf{E}}'_{i(p)}$, and $\varepsilon_{i(p)}$ =vec($\tilde{\mathbf{E}}_{i(p)}$) with 'vec' is the vectorization operator, and $\mathbf{K}_p$ and $\mathbf{J}_p$ are defined earlier.

20.2.2 *Estimation Strategy*

Using the multi-step Maximum Likelihood estimation (MLE) as suggested by Biørn (2004), the estimation procedure is as follows:

(a) Obtain first *one-step* overall estimates $\hat{\beta}$ using GLS method for group p, which are equivalent to estimates using MLE method as explained in problem A, maximize the log likelihood $\mathscr{L}_{(p)}$ (see Eq. 20.13) with respect to ($\mathbf{\Sigma}_\alpha$, $\mathbf{\Sigma}_u$) for given $\hat{\beta}$. We get estimators of the covariance matrices for $\mathbf{\Sigma}_\alpha$ and $\mathbf{\Sigma}_u$.

(b) Estimate the system again by MLE method using the covariance estimators in part (a). Obtain the new *one-step* overall estimates $\hat{\beta}$ for given ($\hat{\mathbf{\Sigma}}_\alpha$, $\hat{\mathbf{\Sigma}}_u$). The multi-step algorithm will stop until convergence of the *one-step* overall estimates $\widehat{\beta}_{GLS}$ as computed in Eq. 20.10.

(c) Once the convergence is complete, we use the formula as in (Eq. 20.12) for all observations to get the overall estimates.

20.3 The `xtsur` Command

This section presents an implementation of a new Stata command, `xtsur`. The command estimates the parameters of the system of equations or the Seemingly Unrelated Regressions (SUR) model with random effects, and displays the regression outputs in the Stata format. This command runs under Stata 9 or later versions with Mata support. In order to run this command, `xtset` must be set before running the estimation.

20.3.1 *Syntax*

Basic syntax

```
  xtsur (depvar1 = varlist1) (depvar2 = varlist2) ...
(depvarN = varlistN) [if] [in] [,Level(cilevel)
TOLerance(real 1e-6) ONEstep MULTIstep]
```

Full syntax

```
  xtsur ([eqname1:]depvar1a  [depvar1b ... =] varlist1)
        ([eqname2:]depvar2a  [depvar2b ... =] varlist2)
```

```
        ...
        ([eqnameN:]depvarNa [depvarNb ... =] varlistN)
        [if] [in] [,Level(cilevel) TOLerance(real 1e-6)
ONEstep MULTIstep]
```

20.3.2 Options

`onestep` implements the one-step algorithm where overall GLS estimates is obtained.

`multistep` implements the multi-step algorithm where the estimated parameters are repeated until convergence from the multi-step ML and GLS procedures. This is the default option.

`level(#)` sets the level for confidence intervals, as a percentage. The default is `level(95)` or as set by set level.

`tolerance(#)` sets the convergence tolerance. The default tolerance is `1e-6`.

20.3.3 Display Output

The command, `xtsur`, produces standard regression outputs. A small table describes the structure of the panel data set (for both balanced and unbalanced panel data). The main table presents the estimated parameters, standard errors, degrees of freedom, *p*-values, and confidence intervals.

20.3.4 Save Results

`xtsur` saves the following in `e()`:

Scalars:
`e(N)`: the number of observations
`e(T)`: the maximum number of times observed
`e(k_eq)`: the number of equations
`e(N_g)`: number of unique units in groups
`e(g_min)`: the minimum number of panels
`e(g_max)`: the maximum number of panels
`e(tol)`: convergence tolerance
`e(cilevel)`: confidence interval level

Macros
`e(cmd)`: the name of the command
`e(cmdline)`: the full command typed

`e(method)` : display estimation method
`e(title)` : title of regression
`e(version)` : version of the command
`e(properties)` : properties of estimation
`e(eqnames)` : equation names
`e(depvar)` : dependent variables
`e(exog)` : exogenous variables
`e(endog)` : endogenous variables
`e(tvar)` : time variable
`e(ivar)` : ID variable

Matrices
`e(b)` : estimated parameters
`e(V)` : variance of estimated parameters
`e(sigma_u)` : panel level covariance of random effects
`e(sigma_e)` : variance-covariance of error terms

Functions
`e(sample)` : sample used in estimation

`xtsur` saves the following in `r()`:
Matrices
`r(xtsur)` : the structure of the unbalanced panel data set.

20.4 Monte Carlo Simulation

This section describes a Monte Carlo study of a system of seemingly unrelated regression (SUR) equations with unbalanced panel data and random effects.

Simulated data are generated from the following SUR model:

$$\begin{cases} y_{1it} = \beta_{11}x_{1it} + \beta_{12}x_{2it} + \beta_{13}x_{1it} + \alpha_{1i} + u_{1it} \\ y_{2it} = \beta_{21}x_{2it} + \beta_{22}x_{3it} + \beta_{23}x_{4it} + \alpha_{2i} + u_{2it} \\ y_{3it} = \beta_{31}x_{3it} + \beta_{32}x_{5it} + \beta_{33}x_{6it} + \beta_{34}x_{7it} + \beta_{35}x_{8it} + \alpha_{3i} + u_{3it} \end{cases} \tag{20.17}$$

All explanatory variables $x_{1i} - x_{8i}$ are generated as independent standard normal random variables. Random individual (firm or household) effects, i.e., $\alpha_{1i} - \alpha_{3i}$, are generated from a multivariate normal distribution with variance covariance matrix $\mathbf{\Sigma}_{\alpha}$. The error terms $u_{1i} - u_{3i}$ are drawn from a multivariate normal distribution with variance covariance matrix $\mathbf{\Sigma}_{u}$. In order to create a balanced panel, we also generate panel ID and year variables.

We set the parameters for the baseline model in Eq. (20.17) as follows: $\beta_{11} = 0.1$, $\beta_{12} = 0.2$, $\beta_{13} = 0.3$, $\beta_{21} = 0.1$, $\beta_{22} = 0.2$, $\beta_{23} = 0.5$, $\beta_{31} = 0.1$, $\beta_{32} = 0.5$, $\beta_{33} = 0.2$, and $\beta_{34} = \beta_{35} = 0.1$. In addition, we assume that individual effects are drawn from a multivariate normal distribution with mean **0** and covariance matrix $\sum_{\alpha}$ where

$$\sum_{\alpha} = \begin{bmatrix} 1 & 0.5 & 0.25 \\ 0.5 & 1 & 0.5 \\ 0.25 & 0.5 & 1 \end{bmatrix}$$

and disturbance terms are also drawn from a multivariate normal distribution with mean **0** and covariance matrix $\sum_{u}$ where

$$\sum_{u} = \begin{bmatrix} 1 & 0.7 & 0.49 \\ 0.7 & 1 & 0.7 \\ 0.49 & 0.7 & 1 \end{bmatrix}.$$

To construct an unbalanced panel from the above balanced panel, we introduce a series of indicators s_{it}^* for individuals across time periods such that when $s_{it}^* = 1$, we use the observation i at time period t in the model. The random variable s_{it} is generated from a uniform distribution [0, 1], and we get a indicator variable s_{it}^* from the following:

$$\begin{aligned} s_{it}^* &= 1 \text{ if } s_{it} > 0.5 \\ &= 0 \text{ otherwise} \end{aligned}$$

We assume that a firm is observed when $s_{it}^* = 1$, otherwise $s_{it}^* = 0$. Using all observations where $s_{it}^* = 1 \; \forall \, i = 1, ..., N$ and $t = 1, ..., T$, we have an unbalanced panel dataset.

We run 1,500 replications with the two choices of a maximum number of observations, 500 and 1,000, respectively, for each period. The maximum number of periods is $Tmax = 10$. We aim to investigate whether: (i) the means of the point estimates are close to their true values, (ii) the means of the estimated standard errors are close to the standard deviations of the point estimates, and (iii) the rejection rate of each test against the null hypothesis is close to the assumed size of the test for all parameters in the model.

We report results for all means and standard deviations of point estimates as well as rejection rates in Tables 20.1 and 20.2.

The result shows that our estimator performs very well in a finite sample. The means of point estimates are close to their actual values for all parameters in the model. When the sample size increases from 5,000 to 10,000 observations, the means of point estimates converge closer to their true values. This result suggests that the estimator is unbiased. In terms of the rejection rates, they are smaller than 0.05 when the sample size is larger. The 95% confidence intervals for all parameters are included, and they show that the actual values of parameters lie within their confidence intervals. On a larger sample, the ML estimates of the SUR model have smaller variances indicating a higher efficiency level. The standard deviations of the point estimates are also close to the means of the standard errors. Our estimation

Table 20.1 Point estimates from 1,500 replications

Observations	$n = 5{,}000$ ($N = 500$, $T = 10$)				n max = 5,000 ($N = 500$, T max = 10)			
Point estimates	Balanced panel				Unbalanced panel			
	Mean	s.d.	Mean std.err	Rejection	Mean	s.d.	Mean std.err	Rejection
$\beta_{11} = 0.1$	0.1001	0.0107	0.0106	0.052	0.0994	0.0537	0.0576	0.061
$\beta_{11} = 0.2$	0.2000	0.0133	0.0129	0.057	0.1993	0.0617	0.0662	0.074
$\beta_{13} = 0.3$	0.3003	0.0146	0.0148	0.043	0.3024	0659	0.0698	0.072
$\beta_{21} = 0.1$	0.0999	0.0106	0.0106	0.05	0.0986	0.0438	0.0662	0.038
$\beta_{22} = 0.2$	0.2003	0.0148	0.0148	0.056	0.2012	0.0594	0.0754	0.031
$\beta_{23} = 0.5$	0.4995	0.0084	0.0086	0.038	0.5003	0.0386	0.0568	0.016
$\beta_{31} = 0.1$	0.1003	0.0147	0.0148	0.044	0.1001	0.0609	0.0762	0.057
$\beta_{32} = 0.5$	0.5001	0.0108	0.0106	0.059	0.5026	0.0513	0.0664	0.063
$\beta_{33} = 0.2$	0.1996	0.0107	0.0106	0.056	0.2003	0.0497	0.0654	0.056
$\beta_{34} = 0.1$	0.1001	0.0109	0.0106	0.063	0.0990	0.0650	0.0667	0.064
$\beta_{35} = 0.1$	0.0998	0.0106	0.0106	0.046	0.0981	0.0431	0.0660	0.059

Table 20.2 Point estimates from 1,500 replications

Observations	$n = 10{,}000$ ($N = 1{,}000$, $T = 10$)				n max = 10,000 ($N = 1{,}000$, T max = 10)			
Point estimates	Balanced panel				Unbalanced panel			
	Mean	s.d.	Mean std.err	Rejection	Mean	s.d.	Mean std.err	Rejection
$\beta_{11} = 0.1$	0.0998	0.0076	0.0074	0.058	0.1013	0.0294	0.0543	0.037
$\beta_{11} = 0.2$	0.1995	0.0091	0.0091	0.040	0.2007	0.0335	0.0637	0.036
$\beta_{13} = 0.3$	0.3005	0.0103	0.0104	0.051	0.3008	0.0345	0.0671	0.041
$\beta_{21} = 0.1$	0.0997	0.0076	0.0075	0.059	0.0998	0.0271	0.0634	0.016
$\beta_{22} = 0.2$	0.2004	0.0104	0.0104	0.048	0.2002	0.0313	0.0732	0.014
$\beta_{23} = 0.5$	0.4998	0.0061	0.0061	0.052	0.4993	0.0241	0.0550	0.015
$\beta_{31} = 0.1$	0.1001	0.0107	0.0105	0.052	0.0998	0.0341	0.0735	0.038
$\beta_{32} = 0.5$	0.4998	0.0077	0.0075	0.058	0.0289	0.0289	0.0633	0.034
$\beta_{33} = 0.2$	0.1995	0.0076	0.0075	0.051	0.2004	0.0296	0.0627	0.035
$\beta_{34} = 0.1$	0.0998	0.0072	0.0075	0.038	0.1001	0.0277	0.0631	0.03
$\beta_{35} = 0.1$	0.0999	0.0073	0.0074	0.044	0.0994	0.0296	0.0625	0.038

procedure using in this simulation is based on a multi-step algorithm, and simulation results show that the multi-step procedure produces efficient estimates.

In addition, we find that the averages of the estimated covariance matrices of random effects and error terms are close to their actual values as defined in the model. The result suggests that our estimates are unbiased and efficient.

$$\widehat{\sum}_{\alpha} = \begin{bmatrix} 1.0193 & .5093 & 0.2539 \\ 0.5093 & 1.0212 & 0.5108 \\ 0.2539 & 0.5108 & 1.0214 \end{bmatrix} \text{ and } \widehat{\sum}_{u} = \begin{bmatrix} 1.0023 & 0.7005 & 0.4892 \\ 0.7005 & 1.0008 & 0.6992 \\ 0.4892 & 0.6992 & 1.0020 \end{bmatrix}$$

20.5 Application and Estimation Results

The almost ideal demand system (AIDS) proposed by Deaton and Muellbauer (1980) is a widely recognized model of consumer demand. It aimed to capture the complexities of consumer behavior by incorporating various factors, including prices and total expenditure. Deaton and Muellbauer (1980) applied AIDS to analyze annual British data from 1954 to 1974. Based on their empirical results, Deaton and Muellbauer (1980) concluded that including influences other than current prices and total expenditure was necessary for a more comprehensive understanding of consumer behavior. Building upon Deaton and Muellbauer (1980), Ray (1980) extended the AIDS model by including family size as an additional variable. His application of the extended model to Indian budget data provided valuable insights into consumer behavior in a different cultural and economic context.

While the AIDS model has proved to be a valuable tool for analyzing consumer behavior, one of the main criticisms is the assumption of separability between goods, which may not always hold in reality. Even though the outcomes of Deaton and Muellbauer (1980)'s analysis yielded plausible estimates for price and income elasticity, they encountered the rejection of homogeneity and symmetry restrictions as another limitation of the model. Deaton and Muellbauer (1980) suggested that their static model needed explicit incorporation of dynamic elements and other factors to enhance the original AIDS framework. This proposal opened up avenues for further research and extensions of the model. To enhance the original framework, Blanciforti and Green (1983) added habit effects to improve the dynamic structure into the AIDS.

The AIDS model, in budget share w_i form of group i, is given by

$$w_i = \alpha_i + \sum_j \gamma_{ij} \ln p_j + \beta_i \ln (x/P) \tag{20.18}$$

where P is a price index defined by

$$\ln P = \alpha_0 + \sum_k \alpha_k \ln p_k + 1/2 \sum_j \sum_k \gamma_{kj} \ln p_k \ln p_j \tag{20.19}$$

and p_j is the price of the jth food group and x is household's income or expenditure. In practice, $\ln P$ can be approximated by $\ln P^* = \sum_k w_k \ln p_k$.

The AIDS model implies that the Marshallian price elasticity for good i with respect to good j is

Table 20.3 Number of observations in unbalanced panel data

	year			
	2002	2004	2006	Total
Panel: households interviewed in these years				
2006 only			4,996	4,996
2004 only		2,908		2,908
2002 only	25,598			25,598
2004 and 2006		2,349	2,349	4,698
2002 and 2004	2,087	2,087		4,174
2002, 2004, and 2006	1,844	1,844	1,844	5,532
Total	29,529	9,188	9,189	47,906

$$\epsilon_{ij}^{M} = \frac{\gamma_{ij} - \beta_i (w_j - \beta_j \ln (x/P))}{w_i} - \delta_{ij} \tag{20.20}$$

where δ_{ij} is the Kronecker delta ($\delta_{ij} = 1$ if $i = j$, and 0 otherwise).

Income elasticity is given by

$$e_i = \frac{\beta_i}{w_i} + 1 \tag{20.21}$$

Expanding on this concept of incorporating dynamic structure, we extend the AIDS from cross-sectional data into panel data analysis in order to understand consumer behavior in an empirically robust manner. Moreover, the econometrics framework and applications developed by this paper can be used for unbalanced panel data as well.

We illustrate the `xtsur` command by estimating a system of seven food-demand equations as defined in Eq. (20.18) for an unbalanced panel of households from Vietnam's Household Living Standards Surveys (VHLSS) conducted in 2002, 2004, and 2006 by the General Statistics Office of Vietnam. The dataset consists of 47,906 households across three years. Since these are rotating panel surveys, not all households in one year are interviewed in another year, and as a result, we have an unbalanced panel of households. This unbalanced panel is split into three types of balanced panels. The first type of balanced panel consists of households interviewed once only, in either 2002, or 2004, or 2006. The second type of panel contains households interviewed twice, i.e., either in 2002 and 2004 or in 2004 and 2006, and finally, the third type of panel is a panel of households interviewed in all of the three years (Table 20.3).

The empirical unconstrained AIDS model of 7 group system, in budget share w_{kit} form of group k of household i in period t, is given by:

$$\begin{cases} w_{1it} = \sum_{j=1}^{7} \gamma_{1j} \ln p_j + \beta_{11} \ln exp2 + \boldsymbol{\beta}_{12}\mathbf{X}_{1it} + \alpha_{1i} + u_{1it} \\ w_{2it} = \sum_{j=1}^{7} \gamma_{2j} \ln p_j + \beta_{21} \ln exp2 + \boldsymbol{\beta}_{22}\mathbf{X}_{2it} + \alpha_{2i} + u_{2it} \\ w_{3it} = \sum_{j=1}^{7} \gamma_{3j} \ln p_j + \beta_{31} \ln exp2 + \boldsymbol{\beta}_{32}\mathbf{X}_{3it} + \alpha_{3i} + u_{3it} \\ w_{4it} = \sum_{j=1}^{7} \gamma_{4j} \ln p_j + \beta_{41} \ln exp2 + \boldsymbol{\beta}_{42}\mathbf{X}_{4it} + \alpha_{4i} + u_{4it} \\ w_{5it} = \sum_{j=1}^{7} \gamma_{5j} \ln p_j + \beta_{51} \ln exp2 + \boldsymbol{\beta}_{52}\mathbf{X}_{5it} + \alpha_{5i} + u_{5it} \\ w_{6it} = \sum_{j=1}^{7} \gamma_{6j} \ln p_j + \beta_{61} \ln exp2 + \boldsymbol{\beta}_{62}\mathbf{X}_{6it} + \alpha_{6i} + u_{6it} \\ w_{7it} = \sum_{j=1}^{7} \gamma_{7j} \ln p_j + \beta_{71} \ln exp2 + \boldsymbol{\beta}_{72}\mathbf{X}_{7it} + \alpha_{7i} + u_{7it} \end{cases} \tag{20.22}$$

where $\ln p_j$ is the log of the food group j, $\ln exp2$ is the log of real expenditure ($\ln (exp/P^*)$), and $\mathbf{X}_{kit}$ are the list of covariates of equation kth, such as `headmarried`, `headfemale`, `headage`, `num0to6`, `num7to14`, `num15to24`, `num25to59`, `headyrschl`, `femaleyrschl`, `urban`, `hhsize`, `ethmaj`, and `poor`. The sum of all $\sum_{k=1}^{7} w_{kit}$ is 1.

In this dataset, dependent variables are food-expenditure shares of seven food groups consumed by households in the surveys, i.e., from w_1 to w_7 as described below. Explanatory variables are log values of food groups' prices (from $\ln p1$ to $\ln p7$), log of total food expenditure over the overall price index P^* ($\ln (exp/P^*)$), household head's marriage status (`headmarried`), household head's gender (`headfemale`), household head age (`headage`), numbers of people in each age group, such as age group from 0 to 6 years old (`num0to6`), from 7 to 14 years old (`num7to14`), from 15 to 24 years old (`num15to24`), and from 25 to 59 years old (`num25to59`). We also add household head's years of schooling (`headyrschl`), average years of schooling for all female adults in the household (`femaleyrschl`), household size (`hhsize`), urban dummy (`urban`), ethnic majority (`ethmaj`), and a household poor dummy variable (`poor`).

We use the default `multistep` option of multi-step ML estimation in `xtsur` for the empirical unconstrained AIDS model in Eq. (20.22). The results show that household characteristics and household composition have distinct impacts on each food-group-expenditure share. For example, if household increases budget on food consumption, it will consume more of food group 1 (`w1`-rice and cereal) and more of food group 2 (`w2`—meat, fish and rich protein). Similarly, poor households increase consumption of "rice and cereal" group but reduce consumption of "meat, fish and rich protein" group. All other estimated parameters are reported in Table 20.6.

The budget share for each food group can be expressed as a function of log of food prices within and across food groups, and total real food expenditure. The elasticities estimated for the unbalanced panel demand system for the food groups are reported in Table 20.7. Our results suggest that income elasticities are positive

Table 20.4 Summary statistics of food budget shares and food group prices

Food groups	Budget shares			Log prices		
	2002	2004	2006	2002	2004	2006
Group 1—Rice, cereal and other starches	0.46	0.31	0.29	2.03	1.57	1.77
	(0.15)	(0.14)	(0.14)	(0.30)	(0.33)	(0.34)
Group 2—Meat, fish, tofu, rich protein	0.19	0.33	0.34	2.48	2.80	3.03
	(0.08)	(0.11)	(0.11)	(0.39)	(0.31)	(0.33)
Group 3—Fats and oils, other favors	0.06	0.05	0.04	2.28	1.84	2.01
	(0.03)	(0.02)	(0.02)	(0.23)	(0.26)	(0.35)
Group 4—Vegetables	0.06	0.06	0.06	0.66	1.17	1.38
	(0.04)	(0.03)	(0.03)	(1.02)	(0.42)	(0.45)
Group 5—Fruits	0.03	0.04	0.04	1.25	1.45	1.63
	(0.03)	(0.04)	(0.04)	(0.59)	(0.50)	(0.48)
Group 6—Dairy products	0.04	0.04	0.04	2.57	2.30	2.51
	(0.04)	(0.04)	(0.04)	(0.53)	(0.63)	(0.67)
Group 7—Other food	0.16	0.17	0.18	2.38	2.56	2.77
	(0.14)	(0.14)	(0.14)	(0.48)	(0.55)	(0.51)

Numbers in parenthesis are standard deviation

and own-price elasticities are negative as expected. Household characteristics such as household head's age, marital status, education, household size, household location (urban/rural), ethnicity and poverty status appear to affect food group consumption significantly. Households with a larger size or poverty status tend to consume more necessities such as rice, cereal and other starches while consuming less of meat, fruits and dairy products. These results highlight empirical evidence for policy-makers to make useful food policy recommendations in Vietnam (Tables 20.6 and 20.7).

20.6 Conclusion

This paper develops an econometrics framework and implements a new Stata command, `xtsur`, to estimate a system of seemingly unrelated regression (SUR) equations with unbalanced panel data and random effects. A Monte Carlo simulation study is discussed to show that our estimates are unbiased and efficient using a multi-step maximum likelihood method. Moreover, the paper applies `xtsur` to estimate Vietnam's household demand system, expenditure and own-price elasticities for seven different food categories. The application analyzes Vietnam's food consumption behavior using an unbalanced panel of Vietnam's Household Living Standards Surveys (VHLSS) conducted in 2002, 2004, and 2006. Our results suggest that income elasticities are positive and own-price elasticities are negative as expected. Household characteristics such as household head's age, marital status, education, household size, household location (urban/rural), ethnicity and poverty status appear to affect

Table 20.5 Summary statistics (N = 47,906)

	Mean	SD	Min	Max
w_1—Rice, cereal and other starches	0.40	0.17	0	0.97
w_2—Meat, fish, tofu, rich protein	0.25	0.12	0	0.81
w_3—Fats and oils, other favors	0.05	0.03	0	0.81
w_4—Vegetables	0.06	0.03	0	0.39
w_5—Fruits	0.04	0.03	0	0.78
w_6—Dairy products	0.04	0.04	0	0.74
w_7—Other food	0.17	0.14	0	1.00
ln $p1$—Log (price of cereal and other starches)	1.89	0.37	0.20	3.75
ln $p2$—Log (price of meat, fish, tofu, rich protein)	2.65	0.43	–0.22	4.70
ln $p3$—Log (price of fats and oils, other favors)	2.15	0.32	–0.69	3.71
ln $p4$—Log (price of vegetables)	0.89	0.90	–4.50	3.40
ln $p5$—Log (price of fruits)	1.36	0.58	–1.10	7.09
ln $p6$—Log (price of dairy products)	2.51	0.59	–2.53	6.03
ln $p7$—Log (price of other food)	2.49	0.52	–0.69	5.30
ln (exp/P^*)—Log(expenditure over the price index)	6.68	0.52	3.34	10.37
headmarried—HH head is married	0.98	0.15	0	1.00
headfemale—HH head is female	0.24	0.43	0	1.00
headage—HH head's age	48.19	14.13	15.00	107.00
num0to6—number of kids aged 0 to 6	0.44	0.70	0	8.00
num7to14—number of children aged 7 to 14	0.83	0.95	0	8.00
num15to24—number of individuals aged 15 to 24	0.91	1.09	0	8.00
num25to59—number of individuals aged 25 to 59	1.84	0.85	0	10.00
headyrschl—HH head's years of schooling	7.07	4.15	0	20.00
femaleyrschl—Average years of schooling of females	6.33	3.50	0	20.00
urban—Urban	1.76	0.43	1.00	2.00
hhsize—Household size	4.42	1.77	1.00	20.00
ethmaj—Ethnicity (1- Majority, 0- Minority)	0.86	0.35	0	1.00
poor—Household's poor dummy (1- poor)	0.24	0.43	0	1.00

food group consumption significantly. Households with a larger size or poverty status tend to consume more necessities such as rice, cereal and other starches while consuming less of meat, fruits, and dairy products. These results highlight empirical evidence for policy-makers to make useful food policy recommendations in Vietnam. The demand system based on SUR allowing for a dynamic unbalanced panel data structure appears to be a more viable demand system to use in modeling consumer behavior.

Table 20.6 Estimated parameters of unbalanced panel model of unconstrained AIDS

	Food shares						
	w_1	w_2	w_3	w_4	w_5	w_6	w_7
ln $p1$	0.0559*** (0.000958)	–0.0154*** (0.00104)	0.00134 (0.00177)	0.00615 (0.00362)	–0.00452 (0.00350)	0.00517*** (0.000734)	0.00676*** (0.000999)
ln $p2$	–0.0433*** (0.000829)	0.0677*** (0.000902)	–0.00509*** (0.00152)	–0.00649* (0.00308)	0.00328 (0.00299)	0.00609*** (0.000631)	0.000543 (0.000859)
ln $p3$	0.0606*** (0.000932)	–0.0415*** (0.00102)	0.0227*** (0.00169)	0.00269 (0.00343)	–0.000161 (0.00333)	0.000639 (0.000710)	–0.00531*** (0.000964)
ln $p4$	–0.00759*** (0.000234)	0.00213*** (0.000254)	–0.000360 (0.000436)	0.00370*** (0.000896)	0.00158 (0.000865)	0.00157*** (0.000179)	0.000384 (0.000244)
ln $p5$	–0.0242*** (0.000441)	0.00628*** (0.000479)	0.000398 (0.000814)	–0.00187 (0.00167)	0.00754*** (0.00162)	0.00385*** (0.000336)	0.00803*** (0.000459)
ln $p6$	0.00398*** (0.000528)	–0.00247*** (0.000574)	–0.00198* (0.000979)	–0.00167 (0.00203)	0.00155 (0.00196)	0.0104*** (0.000406)	–0.00176** (0.000553)
ln $p7$	–0.000506 (0.000571)	0.00935*** (0.000623)	0.000337 (0.00104)	0.00138 (0.00210)	0.00101 (0.00204)	–0.00148*** (0.000434)	0.0100*** (0.000589)
ln (exp/P^*)	0.0106*** (0.000543)	0.0252*** (0.000591)	–0.00255* (0.00101)	0.0143*** (0.00203)	0.00426* (0.00196)	0.000308 (0.000413)	0.0316*** (0.000562)
headmarried	0.0688*** (0.00190)	–0.0128*** (0.00208)	0.00914** (0.00342)	–0.00358 (0.00676)	–0.00385 (0.00658)	0.00475*** (0.00144)	–0.0196*** (0.00194)
headfemale	0.0110*** (0.000648)	–0.000368 (0.000708)	0.00257* (0.00117)	0.00198 (0.00233)	0.000877 (0.00227)	–0.00507*** (0.000491)	0.000147 (0.000665)
headage	0.000286*** (0.0000242)	0.000194*** (0.0000264)	0.000116** (0.0000436)	–0.0000130 (0.0000859)	0.000147 (0.0000836)	–0.000104*** (0.0000182)	0.000224*** (0.0000247)
num0to6	–0.00199** (0.000608)	0.00470*** (0.000665)	0.00300** (0.00110)	0.00167 (0.00216)	0.000478 (0.00211)	0.00612*** (0.000458)	–0.000671 (0.000620)
num7to14	0.0111*** (0.000512)	0.00114* (0.000561)	0.00244** (0.000925)	0.00105 (0.00182)	–0.00000828 (0.00177)	–0.000414 (0.000386)	–0.00575*** (0.000522)
num15to24	0.00452*** (0.000461)	–0.00139** (0.000505)	0.00124 (0.000832)	0.000567 (0.00163)	–0.000916 (0.00159)	–0.00192*** (0.000347)	0.00385*** (0.000470)
num25to59	–0.00137** (0.000501)	0.000261 (0.000549)	0.00161 (0.000904)	–0.000603 (0.00178)	–0.00170 (0.00173)	0.00139*** (0.000378)	0.00283*** (0.000511)
headyrschl	0.000226** (0.0000875)	–0.000389*** (0.0000957)	–0.000201 (0.000158)	–0.000631* (0.000313)	0.000348 (0.000305)	–0.000182** (0.0000661)	0.00158*** (0.0000895)

(continued)

Table 20.6 (continued)

	Food shares						
femaleyrschl	0.000566*** (0.000100)	–0.000957*** (0.000110)	–0.0000570 (0.000181)	–0.000632 (0.000360)	0.000245 (0.000351)	–0.000184* (0.0000760)	0.0000583 (0.000103)
urban	0.101*** (0.000725)	0.00352*** (0.000779)	0.0127*** (0.00165)	0.00106 (0.00312)	–0.00371 (0.00286)	–0.00988*** (0.000562)	–0.0572*** (0.000771)
hhsize	0.00694*** (0.000456)	–0.00943*** (0.000499)	–0.00333*** (0.000823)	–0.00461** (0.00162)	–0.00169 (0.00157)	–0.000811* (0.000344)	–0.00715*** (0.000465)
ethmaj	–0.0241*** (0.000626)	0.0101*** (0.000677)	0.0108*** (0.00122)	–0.00878*** (0.00250)	–0.00126 (0.00239)	0.00452*** (0.000482)	0.0248*** (0.000659)
poor	0.0894*** (0.000593)	–0.0264*** (0.000648)	0.00359*** (0.00107)	0.00740*** (0.00215)	–0.00500* (0.00209)	–0.00717*** (0.000450)	–0.0236*** (0.000610)

Standard errors in parentheses
* $p<0.05$, ** $p<0.01$, *** $p<0.001$

Table 20.7 Own-price and expenditure elasticities from unconstrained AIDS

Group food i	Own-price	Expenditure
w_1—Rice, cereal and other starches	–0.868	1.027
w_2—Meat, fish, tofu, rich protein	–0.733	1.103
w_3—Fats and oils, other favors	–0.573	0.952
w_4—Vegetables	–0.929	1.242
w_5—Fruits	–0.791	1.119
w_6—Dairy products	–0.760	1.007
w_7—Other food	–0.931	1.191

References

Baltagi BH, Chang Y (1994) Incomplete panels: a comparative study of alternative estimators for the unbalanced one-way error component regression model. J Econom 62:67–89

Blanciforti L, Green R (1983) An almost ideal demand system incorporating habits: an analysis of expenditures on food and aggregate commodity groups. Rev Econ Stat :511–515

Deaton A, Muellbauer J (1980) An almost ideal demand system. Am Econ Rev 70(3):312–326

Greene WH (2003) Econometric analysis, 5th edn. Prentice Hall, Upper Saddle River, NJ

Biørn Erik (2004) Regression system for unbalanced panel data: a stepwise maximum likelihood procedure. J Econom 122:281–291

Matyas L, Lovrics L (1991) Missing observations and panel data: a Monte-Carlo analysis. Econ Lett 37:39–44

Ray R (1980) Analysis of a time series of household expenditure surveys for India. Rev Econ Stat :595–602

Zellner A (1962) An efficient method of estimating seemingly unrelated regressions and tests for aggregation bias. J Am Stat Assoc 57:348–368

The manufacturer's authorised representative in the EU is Springer Nature Customer Service Centre GmbH, Europaplatz 3, 69115 Heidelberg, Germany. If you have any concerns regarding our products, please contact ProductSafety@springernature.com

Printed and bound by CPI Group (UK) Ltd, Croydon, CR0 4YY
01/10/2026
02225866-0019